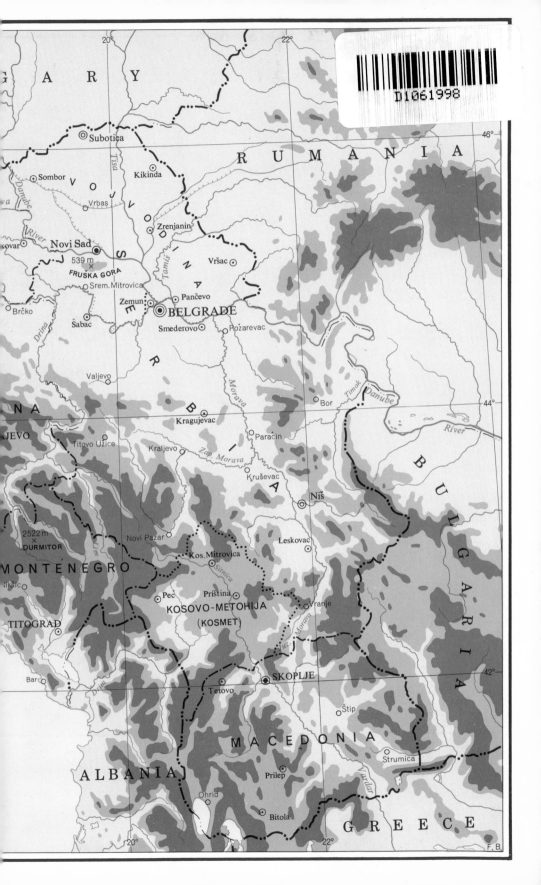

YUGOSLAVIA

AND THE

NEW COMMUNISM

YUGOSLAVIA

AND THE

NEW COMMUNISM

GEORGE W. HOFFMAN

FRED WARNER NEAL

TWENTIETH CENTURY FUND

NEW YORK · 1962

FIRST PUBLISHED MAY 1962
REPRINTED JANUARY 1963
THIRD PRINTING APRIL 1969

FOREWORD

THE Twentieth Century Fund has concerned itself at one time or another with a number of separate countries, relating them to the larger regional studies which have formed an important part of its work. In Eastern Europe, the Fund had already surveyed the economies of Turkey and of Greece, when the opportunity arose of looking somewhat closely at Yugoslavia. This seemed the more inviting as Dr. Dewhurst and his associates, in their monumental *Europe's Needs and Resources*, had not included Yugoslavia among the eighteen countries with which they dealt.

A study of Yugoslavia suggested from the start a somewhat broader approach from that which had been used in other similar cases. The nature of the Yugoslav economy, patterned as it is on Communism yet with many significant differences, called for an impartial, open-minded analysis; and the country's unique political orientation left many questions unanswered. The literature in this field, we felt, needed to be supplemented by a comprehensive up-to-date picture of what was occurring. A study for the United States public, setting the problems of economic development in relation to the country's basic social, political and economic conditions, seemed a worthwhile project.

The Fund was fortunate in being able to encourage and help support the efforts of two highly qualified scholars, both of whom had specialized in the area: George Hoffman, Professor of Geography at the University of Texas, and Fred Neal, Professor of International Relations and Government at the Claremont Graduate School, Claremont, California. Through the period the work has been under way, with both men engaged in activities at their separate universities, the tasks of collaboration, including organization, writing, revising and editing, have gone forward effectively, and in harmony with the Fund staff. With the long labor completed, the Fund expresses its thanks to them both.

AUGUST HECKSCHER, Director
The Twentieth Century Fund

41 East 70th Street, New York. March 1962

PREFACE

I N THIS study we have attempted to analyze Tito's unique Communist system in some detail, and to place it in the perspective of its historical, geographic and cultural setting. There have been good studies of certain aspects of Yugoslavia's development, and scholars have published a wealth of definitive background data in other years. Yet it seemed to us that a comprehensive treatment was needed which would look upon the new Yugoslav system objectively and with the benefit of further research.

Our aim may be overly ambitious, for Yugoslavia is one of the most complicated countries in the world, and it presents many problems on which the experts differ. Moreover, emotion runs high these days on anything involving Communism, and there is not always agreement on what is objective and what is not. There will probably be both Yugoslavs and Americans who will take exception to certain parts of this study. We can only say that we have tried to avoid biases. We have no axes to grind; our sole aim has been to contribute to an informed American public opinion and thus to the interests of the United States and its ideals.

For several reasons, the highly significant developments in Yugoslavia since World War II are inadequately known and understood in the United States. Our culture, for one thing, suffers generally from an over-orientation toward Western Europe. Those Americans who think about Eastern Europe at all tend to do so emotionally and only in terms of Cold War strategy. Another reason is that, along with some excellent books and articles, there is much writing on Yugoslavia that is hortatory and partisan rather than factual. Both admirers and critics of the Tito regime, whether on the Communist or the anti-Communist side, have been guilty of this. Nor is the intricate Yugoslav system always easy to understand. This is perhaps particularly so for Westerners who are unfamiliar with Marxist theory and practice.

The Yugoslavs themselves, in their voluminous publications, even when they do not intend to mislead, often leave the American reader more confused than enlightened. Still another factor is the inadequate reporting of the Yugoslav story in the American press. For this the Yugoslavs cannot be blamed; of all the Communist countries, Yugoslavia alone imposes virtually no restraints on foreign journalists. Yet at present the *New York Times* correspondent in Belgrade is the only full-time American reporter in this important listening post.

A persistent difficulty encountered in preparing this study has been the continual change on the Yugoslav scene. While the broad outlines of the Titoist system are fairly well fixed, many of the mechanisms by which it operates are in flux. For example, we had to alter the manuscript, as it was nearing completion, to take account of important changes in the economic system in 1961. And as this book goes to press, the Yugoslavs are readying a new constitution. Where possible, we have included information which became available during 1961.

Although this study is a joint product, there has been a rough division of responsibility between the authors. Fred Neal handled most of the historical, institutional and political material, and George Hoffman concentrated on geographic, economic and cultural aspects.

So many persons assisted us, directly or through their writings, that a complete list would be impossibly long. Among the Americans, we would like to single out for special thanks the staff of the U. S. Embassy in Belgrade; Mr. Steven Palmer, former consul in Sarajevo; Mr. Moncrieff Spear, under whose direction the Yugoslav desk in the State Department became an important instrument of U. S. foreign policy; Mr. Paul Underwood, Belgrade correspondent of the *New York Times*, one of the best of journalists; Mr. Salih Alich of Pomona, Calif., an expert in and connoisseur of things pertaining to his native Yugoslavia; the External Research staff of the State Department, which made available to us the invaluable Joint Translation Service of the Yugoslav Press; and various officials of the International Cooperation Agency and the U. S. Department of Agriculture, who helped with statistics and analyses.

Yugoslavs, from top officials to ordinary citizens, were most helpful. A list would have to include dozens of federal and republic officials, university professors, enterprise and cooperative directors, officers and staffs of workers' councils, union officials, municipal authorities, church dignitaries, and workers and peasants—people in all walks of life, including both admirers and critics of the regime. Without their courteous cooperation, our study could never have been written.

The comparative part of the study involved field work elsewhere in Eastern Europe, particularly in Poland and the Soviet Union. In both countries U. S. Embassy officials and their staffs assisted us, and many Polish and Soviet citizens, both official and non-official, went out of their way to help. In no country did we encounter anything but friendliness.

A special debt of gratitude is owed to a group of American experts on Yugoslavia who read several chapters of the manuscript and conferred with us at a meeting at the Twentieth Century Fund headquarters. The group included Mr. John Campbell of the Council on Foreign Relations; Professors Alex Dragnich of Vanderbilt University, John Hazard of Columbia University and Charles Jelavich of the University of California at Berkeley; and Messrs. Palmer and Spear of the U. S. Department of State. Certain chapters benefited from critical reading by Professors Lorne Cook of Pomona College, Chauncey D. Harris of the University of Chicago, H. Malcolm Macdonald of the University of Texas and Murray E. Polakoff of Rochester University.

Indebted though we are to all these persons, none of them bears responsibility for any part of the study. That responsibility is ours alone.

We are also grateful to the members of the Twentieth Century Fund staff. Mr. August Heckscher, Director, Mr. Ben Moore, Associate Director, and Mrs. Elizabeth Blackert and Mrs. Ruth Rocker of the editorial staff gave us encouragement and offered valuable suggestions and advice without interfering in what we sought to do.

We were fortunate in obtaining a highly skilled cartographer, Dr. Francis Barkoczy. Preparation of the manuscript was greatly expedited by the services of Mrs. Viola S. Hoffman and Mrs. Marian K. Walker in typing and editing.

We wish to express thanks to our respective institutions, the University of Texas and the Claremont Graduate School, for their leniency and understanding in the course of this work. The study also benefited from research on Polish and Soviet affairs made possible by a grant to Fred Neal from the American Philosophical Society and earlier research grants received by George Hoffman from the Social Science Research Council and the American Philosophical Society.

Finally, a word should be said about the forbearance shown by our wives and families during the arduous hours spent in research and writing over a period of more than three years.

G. W. H.

F. W. N.

EXPLANATORY NOTES

Pronunciation of Serbo-Croatian Words

Names of persons and places and certain other words used in this book have been given their Serbo-Croatian spelling in the Latin alphabet, with diacritical marks. In Serbo-Croatian the accent is usually placed on the first syllable. The letters of the alphabet are pronounced as in English with the following exceptions:

Serbo-Croatian	English	Example
c	ts	Stepinac = *Stepinats*
č	ch	peča = *pecha*
ć	ch	Ranković = *Rankovich*
dj	j	Djilas = *Jeelas*
j (see below)	y	Pijade = *Peeyade*
i	ee	Tito = *Teeto*
š	sh	Nis = *Neesh*
ž	zh	Žabljak = *Zhablyak*

N.B.: When j follows a consonant at the end of a name, as in "Kardelj," it is unpronounced but makes the consonant soft; thus "Kardelj" is adequately pronounced simply *Kardel.*

Symbols Used in Tabular Material

In statistical series the dash and marks of ellipsis have been used with the following significance:

— Nil (0 is used for a quantity less than .5)

. . . Data not available

A Note on Statistics

Official Yugoslav statistics have been relied on extensively in this book as the best available. It should be noted, however, that such statistics, while abundant, are not consistently issued on the same basis. Thus data are frequently not comparable, particularly over a period of time. Not only are series prepared on different bases from year to year, but district boundaries are continually realigned with the result that it is extremely difficult to trace economic and other developments within a district. Moreover, figures from different Yugoslav agencies frequently conflict. One reason for this is an inadequate reporting service, which, perhaps, is a concomitant of decentralization. As far as investment statistics are concerned, the Yugoslav Investment

Bank has provided the following explanation for discrepancies between its own data and data published by the National Bank and the Federal Statistical Service:[1]

1. Up to 1957, the calculation of the annual value of investments was made on the basis of the value of actually completed capital construction works; in other words, the physical volume of capital construction works carried out in a given year was assumed to represent the volume of investments in that year, no heed being taken of whether payments for these works were made in the same calendar year or in the next one. Beginning with 1958, however, the total amount actually paid for capital construction works in a given year was taken as a basis without making any distinction as to the time at which these works had actually been completed. The National Bank data go back only as far as 1952 and the Bank statisticians recalculated their figures for 1952–1957, using the new basis. The Yugoslav Investment Bank and the Federal Statistical Bureau, whose series began in 1947, decided to retain the old basis for the years prior to 1958, because it has proved impossible anyway to carry out the recalculations for the years 1947–1951.

2. Up to July 1, 1957, investment maintenance was included in the investment outlays. After that date, however, this item was included under the heading of regular expenditure of enterprises, instead of under investment outlays as before. In order to assure the comparability of the data which they published, both the National Bank and the Yugoslav Investment Bank excluded investment maintenance from the total investment outlays for all the earlier years, while the Federal Statistical Bureau, not wishing to introduce correction of already published figures, decided to leave investment maintenance in their total investment figures for the earlier years.

3. Beginning in 1952, National Bank data exclude from the category "Investment Outlays" certain federal budget expenditures which the Investment Bank continues to include in this category.

[1] In a communication to the authors dated April 5, 1960.

CONTENTS

PART V THE IMPACT OF TITOISM

PART VI PROBLEMS OF TITOISM

YUGOSLAVIA

AND THE

NEW COMMUNISM

INTRODUCTION

IN THE relations between East and West, probably no country occupies a more vital spot than Yugoslavia, strategically slung between the Danube and the Adriatic, between the Balkans and the Alps.

"Yugoslavia" means the Land of the South Slavs. Its importance, once mainly geographic, lies today most of all in its politics, in the political system developed by the people of this crossroads land after a long history of turmoil. For under Tito's leadership a peculiar form of Communism has emerged. In many ways it is like its Soviet counterpart. But in many other ways it is so different that its very existence has constituted one of the severest challenges confronting the Kremlin.

The new Yugoslavia is an enigma to both East and West. It is a Communist country but staunchly independent of Moscow, often in opposition to it and on friendly terms with the West. It is an Eastern European dictatorship but one with certain elements of democracy and personal freedom. It has a planned socialist economy but one which is decentralized, competitive and — in a peculiarly Yugoslav way — free (although not private).

We know the Communist system primarily in its Soviet totalitarian pattern. Contemporary Yugoslavia indicates that this is not the only pattern. Yugoslav Communism contains enough features in common with Soviet Communism to make it unattractive to capitalist and democratic America. But to many in Soviet-dominated Eastern Europe as well as to those socialistically inclined leaders of the new and underdeveloped countries of Asia and Africa, the Yugoslav experiment with Marxism has great attraction. Perhaps as much as any other single factor, the existence of Yugoslavia as an independent Communist state following its own "road to socialism" has been responsible for the crisis of nationalism in the Soviet-led international Communist movement. One has only to mention the humbling about-face performed in connection with Yugoslavia by Khrushchev in 1955, the Soviet stand on "independent paths to socialism," the spectacular developments of 1956 in Poland and Hungary and the question marks in Soviet-Chinese relations.

Before World War II, when the Soviet Union was the only socialist state, the problem of "national Communism" did not exist in a meaningful way. Almost from the start, the role of other Communist parties was to support the Soviet Union as the "socialist fatherland" and the home base of international Communism. Indeed, once the other parties accepted Lenin's analysis of the long-run stability of capitalism, they had little *raison d'être* except as tails on the Soviet dog. Even when the Kremlin ruthlessly exploited the foreign Communists for its own nationalist ends, there were only occasional demurrers, virtually never real dissent. With this relationship of foreign Communist parties to the USSR elevated to the status of a dogma by Stalin, the Communists were such prisoners of the pattern that they could see no other. In 1938 Bukharin told a Western questioner: "There is no possibility for a conflict [in the future] between Communist states."[1]

With the creation of other Communist states in Eastern Europe, satellites or not, the whole situation changed. Even where they were installed and kept in office by Soviet power, the satellite Communist leaders now had concerns other than the Soviet Union. But the Kremlin continued to operate on the same pattern as before and demanded that the satellite Communists continue to use their new authority primarily for Moscow's benefit. Almost from the beginning there were conflicts. They were muted and concealed at first, but they were there.

In a sense, the fundamental issue was between two views of Communism: the old, pre-1945 view of Communism primarily in the interest of the Soviet Union, and the new, post-1945 view of Communism with perforce a national interest to defend and hence loyalties not limited to but in addition to loyalty to the USSR. Only in Yugoslavia, however, were conditions such that these conflicts could come to a head. In vain, Stalin established the Cominform as an instrumentality of Soviet domination. When the Yugoslav leaders still refused to come to heel, he expelled them from the Communist community and tried to break them by subversion and an economic blockade.

The outcome was what we know today as "Titoism." If Stalin could not have foreseen it in 1948, neither could Tito. For Titoism is as different from Soviet Communism as it is from the Yugoslav Communism of 1945–1949.

From its beginnings, Titoism has puzzled the West. Although the old question whether Titoism is "simply a Soviet trick" is seldom heard any more, a host of questions still present themselves. Is Titoism merely national

[1] Hamilton Fish Armstrong, *Tito and Goliath*, Macmillan, New York, 1951, p. ix.

Communism, a dictatorship of the proletariat without the Soviet form? Or is it a new form of socialist state? Is it merely a makeshift formula for keeping a "new class" of rulers in power? Or does it really strive to bring political democracy into socialism?

Other questions are asked in regard to American policies and attitudes toward Yugoslavia in particular and Eastern European Communism in general. To what extent can Tito be "trusted"? Is Yugoslavia "going back to the Kremlin"? Is the Titoist will to independence firm and invariable? Or is it for sale to the highest bidder? More fundamental may be questions like these: How viable is Titoism as a system? What are its prospects after Tito leaves the scene? To what extent is there a conflict between Tito's adherence to Communism, with all Communism's international implications, and his insistence on national independence at home and abroad?

Tito has professed a desire to be a "bridge" between East and West. Some Westerners hope the "bridge" can be used to help break down Soviet domination where it exists and steer would-be socialist countries away from it where it does not yet exist. Others worry for fear the "bridge" will instead aid the chances of Communism and hurt the chances of democracy and freedom.

The Soviet bloc countries profess strong opposition to the Yugoslav system. Yet some of them have seemed to borrow from it. A significant question is the extent to which Titoism has actually influenced other regimes in Eastern Europe. Another is, How much of Titoism is "exportable"?

Communism and nationalism are perhaps the two strongest political forces in the world today. Ostensibly diametrically opposed, Communism — following Lenin's tactics — nevertheless has frequently been able to use nationalism to achieve its goals. The nationalist question is especially important in Yugoslavia. Not only have the ethnic groups comprising this multi-national state had a violent and tempestuous history of feuding among themselves, but Yugoslavia sits uneasily in the maelstrom of conflicting Balkan nations.

In this context, it is not always clear whether Communism is using nationalism or whether nationalism is using Communism. But, as the two forces are probably better blended there than anywhere else, Yugoslavia seems to offer an excellent opportunity to learn more about the nature of both Communism and nationalism, not only in Eastern Europe but generally. From the confused relationship between the two forces stems the difficulty the West has in distinguishing between the evils and dangers of Soviet power and — to the extent they differ — the evils and dangers of Communism generally. An examination of Yugoslav developments is inevitably addressed also to this distinction.

Implicit in all this is the high priority of a study of contemporary Yugoslavia. One of the things, indeed, that sets Yugoslavia off from other Communist countries is that it is free and open enough to be studied thoroughly. The new Yugoslav system has already had a great impact on Marxist theory and practice. What can be learned from studying it further may have an impact far broader, not excluding the question of war and peace itself.

In considering the new Yugoslavia, it is important to keep in mind that it is a land of sharp contrasts and a land decidedly in flux. Old ways of life persist alongside the new, with backwardness gradually giving way to progress. Sometimes a sense of confusion results.

Nothing illustrates this point better than an incident one of the authors witnessed on Belgrade's main street in 1958. A colorfully costumed peasant was driving his horse and wagon past one of the few traffic signals in the city. In the middle of the intersection, the horse balked, reared up and refused to go on. Just then the traffic signal changed. Automobiles ranging from Model A Fords to 1958 Cadillacs converged and were blocked. So were a rickety old trolley and a modern, streamlined bus.

In the wagon, the peasant's wife was holding two piglets. Somehow they got away. Soon everybody was rushing about madly trying to retrieve them. Horns blared. Drivers shouted. The horse neighed. The piglets squealed. The policeman began to berate the peasant.

Finally the piglets were caught, and the horse started off. As he left the scene, the peasant shouted imprecations not only at the policeman but at the government, at Communism and even at Tito. In the back of the wagon, half covered with straw, was revealed a shiny new electric refrigerator, which then sold for about 350,000 dinars.

Traffic moved, and things were peaceful once more. But the contrasts remained. Even the names of the streets at the intersection were symbolic of them. One was Prince Miloš Avenue; the other, Marshal Tito Boulevard.

PART I

THE LAND OF
THE SOUTH SLAVS

THE GEOGRAPHIC

SETTING

Few European countries are as diversified in their physical, cultural and economic make-up as Yugoslavia. Its crossroads position largely accounts for this diversity. Situated between the chain of the Eastern Alps and the mountains of the southeast European peninsula (the Balkan Peninsula, as it is often called), and between the Pannonian Basin and the Adriatic Sea or the Mediterranean region, Yugoslavia has a complex structure and relief and a varied climate. It has been subject to cultural influences stemming from Central Europe, the Mediterranean region and the Orient. The interaction of natural and social factors has complicated its relationships with neighboring regions and the relationships between the various parts of the country itself.

Trending in a northwest-southeast direction, Yugoslavia faces Albania, the Adriatic and northern Italy on the west, and Austria and Hungary on the north. Rumania and Bulgaria border it on the east, Greece on the south. The country's boundaries total 3,083 miles, of which 1,238 miles are along the Adriatic Sea. Important areas are structurally connected with or part of the neighboring regions. The Dinaric ranges, for example, are linked with the Southern Alps; the mountains of northeast Serbia connect the Carpathians in Rumania with the Stara Planina of Bulgaria; the Plain of the Vojvodina is part of the Pannonian Basin; the Adriatic littoral has all the characteristics of the Mediterranean region. Yugoslavia has access to the continental interior and to the Mediterranean Sea; the Morava-Vardar Valley provides a connection between the Aegean Sea and the Danube Valley. Yugoslavia's geographic position became even more advantageous when it obtained a railroad link through the Postojna gap to Trieste, and the ports of Rijeka and Pula after World War II.

Of all the political and economic changes Yugoslavia has undergone since its organization in 1918–1919 none had more far-reaching results than those brought about by World War II. After having been occupied and divided up by its ·neighbors during the war, a new Yugoslavia emerged as a multinational Communist state. The Federal People's Republic of Yugoslavia has a population of about 18.5 million (1961 census), an area of 98,740 square miles (roughly equal to that of Wyoming) and a population density of 188 per square mile. It is eighth in population of the countries of Europe and second among the countries of Eastern Europe.[1] Administratively, Yugoslavia is divided into six people's republics, which roughly coincide with the ethnic divisions of the population: Serbia (largest both in area and in population), Croatia (second in size), Bosnia and Herzegovina (third in size), Slovenia, Macedonia and Montenegro. (See Figure 4–5.) The people's republic of Serbia includes Serbia proper, the autonomous province of Vojvodina and the autonomous region of Kosovo-Metohija (Kosmet). Its capital, Belgrade, is also the national capital.

Regional Characteristics

It is a basic truth about Yugoslavia that an understanding of its geographical situation and physical properties is essential for an understanding of its stormy past and present problems. It has been said that "social efforts cannot do away with decisive natural factors but only restrict their negative influence."[2] Let us consider how far economic and cultural changes have restricted the negative influence of natural factors in Yugoslavia; how each of the major regional divisions — the mountainous heartland and the peripheral zone—and each of the regions within these divisions have acted upon the other and contributed to the formation of a unified state.

The mountainous heartland largely coincides with the Dinaric ranges; the peripheral zone consists of fertile plains, hill lands, and basins connected with interior valleys. (See Figure 2–1.)[3] The mountainous part of the country (over 1,500 feet) comprises 45 per cent of the total area, while 29 per cent is classified as lowlands (below 600 feet). The varied relief separates the people of one

[1] During the interwar years Yugoslavia had an area of 95,588 square miles; in 1939 it had a population of approximately 15.4 million and a population density of 161 per square mile. Preliminary figures of the March 1961 census were published in *Statistički Bilten*, No. 203, April 1961.

[2] Josip Roglić, ·"Prilog Regionalnoj Podjeli Jugoslavije" ("Contribution to the Understanding of the Regional Division of Yugoslavia"), *Geografski Glasnik*, 1954–1955, p. 13.

[3] This basic division follows Roglić's classification. (*Ibid.*, p. 13.) The terms "mountain heartland" and "mountain fortress" (*Dinarische Gebirgsfeste*) were discussed as early as 1907 by E. Richter; they were further developed by N. Krebs and made the core of a valuable study by K. Kayser.

valley from those of another, bringing about local particularism and political fragmentation.

The mountainous heartland is triangular in shape and extends in a north-west-southeast direction from the valleys of the Sava and Kupa and the Kapela and Velebit mountain ranges to the Ibar valley of Serbia and the basin of Kosovo-Metohija; the Adriatic littoral forms a sharp boundary toward the southwest. The borders of the heartland toward the peripheral zone are not always clearly defined.

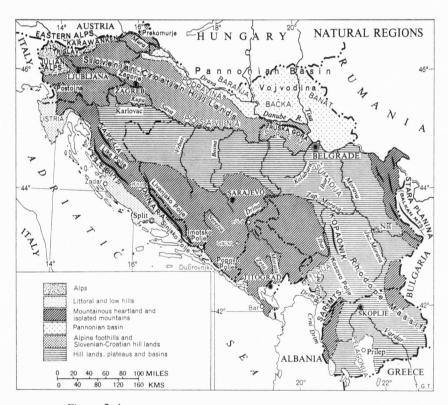

Figure 2–1

Most of the mountainous heartland is within the Dinaric Mountains. They cover about one fourth of Yugoslavia, and trend from the spurs of the Julian Alps in the northwest and the Sava-Kupa valley in the north to the Rhodope Massif in the southeast and the Beli Drim (White Drin) River in the south. The Dinaric ranges vary from 60 to 100 miles in width and their elevation averages 4,000–6,000 feet. Great diversity characterizes these ranges, from the barren dissected and waterless ranges in the west to parallel forested mountains and hill lands in the north and northeast. Physiographically the Dinaric ranges are usually divided into three zones.[1]

1. There is the narrow coastal zone, the Adriatic littoral (or *primorje*), with its many islands which broke from the coast, and depressions which have been invaded by arms of the sea. The main climatic characteristics of this zone are mild winters and hot summers, a small range between January and July temperatures, and heavy rainfall unevenly distributed, falling for the most part during autumn and winter.

2. Access to the interior is blocked by the High Karst,[2] a barren, deeply fissured limestone mountain region with many caverns and underground streams.[3] It reaches its greatest width in the Dinara Mountains. The High Karst stretches for 350 miles from northwest to southeast and has a maximum width of 50 miles. Because precipitation falling upon the exposed limestone rocks sinks quickly underground, the river valleys are very short and widely spaced. The rivers flow in deeply dissected valleys or through gorges which are difficult to transgress. Their flow is variable and they have considerable differences in elevation between source and mouth. Rivers typical in these respects are the Zrmanja, Krka, Cetina, Neretva and Morača — all of them highly suitable for hydroelectric projects. The whole region consists of a series of rocky plateaus with flat ridges; longitudinal troughs, *polja* (fields), which were formed from subsiding hollows and subsequently enlarged when rain water and rivers dissolved the calcareous rocks, and which are subject to flooding; *doline*, small round depressions also formed by the solution of calcareous rocks, or *uvale*, larger *doline*. These *polja*, *uvale* and *doline* are covered with alluvial deposits and/or red earth (*terra rosa*), a relatively fertile soil formed by the nonsoluble material in the limestone.

3. The inner part of the Dinaric ranges, northern Bosnia and western Serbia, is less barren and rugged. Sandstone and limestone are predominant in a few places and crystalline rocks of pre-Cambrian origin are visible. These rocks, unlike limestone, retain some surface water. Narrow and open valleys are interspersed, and extensive mining and logging activities are carried on.

[1] For a detailed discussion see Jovan Cvijić, *La Péninsule Balkanique*, Armand Colin, Paris, 1918, p. 73. Also George W. Hoffman, "Eastern Europe," in George W. Hoffman (ed.), *A Geography of Europe*, 2d edition, The Ronald Press, New York, 1961, Chapter 7, pp. 539–637. Some of the material in this section originally appeared in Chapter 7; it is used with the permission of The Ronald Press.

[2] The name "Karst" (from which the common noun "karst" is derived) is the Germanized form of *Kras* (Slovenian), the designation for the hinterland of Trieste.

[3] Alfred Šerko, "Kraški Pojavi u Jugoslaviji" ("The Karst Phenomena in Yugoslavia"), *Geografski Vestnik* (Ljubljana), 1947, pp. 43–66.

The Dinaric ranges slope gradually toward the north, the Posavina (Sava Basin), and northeast (Central Serbia).

While the peripheral zone is easily accessible from neighboring countries, parts of the mountainous heartland are inaccessible and have been both fortress and manpower reservoir. The heartland has offered the people from the periphery refuge in times of stress, has served as a base to mount counterattacks (this was well demonstrated during World War II), and has sent its surplus population to the peripheral lands in times of peace. The effect of this is shown in a considerable displacement of individual groups, for example, the northwest movement of the Vlachs during the period of Turkish advances and the settlement of many Christian Serbian people along the northern boundary of the heartland and far into the Pannonian Plains. In the more recent past people from the heartland took the place of the Germans in the Vojvodina who left with the retreating German Army or were forced to leave after 1944–1945.

The seclusion of certain impenetrable regions of the heartland favored stable social organizations; stockbreeders' and tribal associations, for example, flourished until very recent times.

With the exception of forestry and mining, the heartland was considered poor and backward before 1945. The region as a whole was underdeveloped, and little attention was given to it in the interwar years.

The mountainous heartland is by no means a uniform region. Certain of the border regions were the foci of a number of the early national states: Croatia in the northwest with its first capital at Knin; Bosnia with its foci around the upper and central parts of the Bosna and Vrbas rivers; Zeta on the margin of the Scutari lakes basin; and Raša (Raška) on the southeastern slopes of the heartland for the Great Serbian state of the Nemanjici dynasty during the later Middle Ages. In more recent times, Šumadija (literally, region of forests) on the northeastern slopes of the heartland was a base for the organization of modern Serbia in the early nineteenth century and received most of its population from the mountains of Montenegro and Bosnia and Herzegovina.

The least populated and most inaccessible region of the heartland is the immediate hinterland of the Adriatic littoral. Scarcity of soil and water discouraged settlement. The rugged terrain made conquest, either from the sea (Roman legions, Venetians) or from the land (Byzantines, Turks), nearly impossible. Only in recent years have some of the transverse valleys been opened to the outside world.

During the past hundred years, especially before World War I, there was much migration from this poverty-stricken region to coastal towns and emigration overseas. Since World War II many of the people have gone to industries newly established in other parts of the heartland. Summer droughts and floods at sowing and harvesting time make life extremely difficult even on the few agriculturally important *polja*. The only areas economically more advantageous are parts of the hinterland of Dubrovnik and some of the larger *polja* — Sinjsko, Livanisko, Imotsko, Popovo, etc.

The type of agriculture in the mountainous heartland changes from northeast to southwest. Barley, oats, rye and buckwheat are predominant in the northeast; vineyards, tobacco, almond trees and maize are found in the southwest. Drainage of the repeatedly flooded *polja* could greatly improve the quality and quantity of the crops, but only a few patches were drained before World War II. In the northeastern part of the High Karst, animals graze on the sides of the *polja;* during the winter they must be fed on hay. Stockbreeding declined gradually in the interwar period. As a result of recent laws prohibiting goats and of the decline of sheep breeding, many of the isolated settlements have lost their livelihood. There are coniferous forests, but lack of forest roads and railways hampers their utilization. Increased attention has been given to forestry only during the past fifteen years. The Adriatic hinterland is rich in bauxite; deposits stretch from Istria to Montenegro. Until World War II this region was culturally and economically one of the most backward areas of the country.

The southern part of the mountainous heartland, a region stretching to the Drina and Ibar rivers, consists of a series of plateaus interspersed with deeply cut river valleys. The country is easily passable and the dolomite-lime structure with impermeable bedrock in the high mountains assures a summer water supply and mountain pastures that provide the basis for a rich stockbreeding economy. Sheep were the main animals at first. Later goats were added or substituted. The nature of stockbreeding led to the formation of tribal associations, the recognition of grazing rights and land tenure, the security of major travel routes, and the need for commerce.

This commercial exchange — the sale of surplus products such as fattened animals, wool, skin and cheese, and the buying of salt and other necessities — was negotiated by the merchants of Dubrovnik and contributed to the early rise of Dubrovnik as a trading center.[1] As the trade grew in scale, trade routes and caravan traffic were organized. Heavy traffic developed between Dubrovnik and the important Byzantine cities of Skoplje, Salonika (Thessaloniki), Constantinople, Sofija and Belgrade. Crossroad and relay stations, at Trebnje, Gracko, Foča, Novi Pazar and other points, facilitated travel into the Morava-

---

[1] Josip Roglić, "The Geographical Setting of Medieval Dubrovnik," in Norman J. G. Pounds (ed.), *Geographical Essays on Eastern Europe*, Russian and East European Series, Vol. 24, Indiana University Publications, Bloomington, Indiana, 1961, pp. 141–159.

Vardar region. Returning, the traders brought metals, both precious and utilitarian, from the hinterland. The heavy caravan traffic was responsible for the rapid expansion of the state of Raša near the Adriatic littoral. Even after the rapid Turkish conquest of parts of this region, the caravan traffic retained its importance. It reached its greatest height in the fifteenth and sixteenth centuries when it had to satisfy the needs of the Turkish people.

The occupation of Dubrovnik by Napoleon's troops and the later introduction of the railroad and the steamship, which took other routes than the caravan and the galleon, interrupted this brisk trade. And with the introduction of tobacco, grapes and vegetables, stockbreeding yielded land often unsuited for plowing to these more lucrative uses. As the land was denuded of its deciduous forests, larger areas were planted to grains. In time the closely knit social organization lost heavily by migration, especially of its younger members, to the growing urban concentrations. World War II accelerated this process, and newly built industries in the Bosna, Vrbas, Neretva and other valleys (e.g., the steel plant in Nikšić and a pressed hardwood plant at Foča) and the rapidly enlarging coastal cities have been taking up the surplus population of the interior region.

The more isolated and rugged mountainous region south of the old trade routes, the Montenegrin Mountains, with their very harsh climate, restricted stockbreeding. The difficulty of life in Montenegro is evidenced by the character of its people.

The northern area of the mountainous heartland is interspersed with arable valleys. Cultural developments in Bosnia have centered in these valleys, which trend toward the north where the main rivers flow. This area, excellent in location, extends roughly from the Vrbas to the Drina rivers.

Though the mountainous heartland and the isolated mountain regions occurring in the peripheral zone are poor agriculturally, they contain many resources, some of which were exploited at an early period. Mining of nonferrous metals, including copper, gold, silver, lead and zinc, goes back long before Roman times, and in the Middle Ages smelting specialists from Bosnia and Serbia were in demand all over Europe.

Considerable development of mineral reserves and water power has enhanced the economic value of many parts of the mountainous heartland since the war. During the past fifteen years much emphasis has been given to developing a new industrial base, and this in turn has brought about a rapid change in the life of the whole area. Roads and railroads have followed the discovery of new raw materials; urban centers have grown in population; and a large section of the heartland has been integrated with the more economically advanced regions of the northern peripheral zone.

Surrounding the mountainous heartland is the economically important and culturally diverse peripheral zone, with its many clearly defined regions; the Plain of the Vojvodina; the Croatian-Slovenian Hill Lands; Central Serbia; the Kosovo-Metohija and Vardar region; and the Adriatic littoral. The peripheral lands are easily passable, though there are isolated mountain areas.

The Plain of the Vojvodina, at the confluence of the Drava, Danube, Sava and Tisa rivers, is part of the Pannonian or Carpathian Basin, a great depression which is enclosed by the arc of the Carpathian ranges and the Eastern Alps. This was an inland sea (the ancient Pannonian Sea) until rivers from the surrounding mountains filled it with alluvial deposits. The Vojvodina is a region of wide valley basins, alluvial plains, sandy dune areas and crystalline hills covered with fertile loess.

The climate of the Vojvodina is characterized by cold winters and hot summers; a January–July temperature range averaging 73° to 77° F. is typically continental. Precipitation is low; the rainfall averages 27 inches a year and comes as sudden downpours, usually heaviest in late spring and early summer. Since summer showers are often followed by high temperatures, evaporation is excessive and only a small portion of the rain is absorbed by the crops. Cold continental air masses form in the Pannonian Basin, and, especially during the glacial period, the strong cold winds have separated the fine sand and gravel from the rich alluvial soil. The landscape has undergone and is still undergoing many changes.[1] Formerly, vast level areas were flooded every spring because of the low gradient of the rivers. Irrigation, drainage, and the building of embankments and dikes are bringing the rivers under control and reclaiming the land. The areas which were regularly flooded, once usable only for pastures and meadows, are now cultivable and form the basis of large-scale maize and wheat culture.

Other areas in the Vojvodina Plain were covered by wind-blown loess and grass vegetation. The fertile loess plateaus (northern Bačka and southern Srem), generally below 300 feet, were turned into valuable arable lands; the steep slopes were planted to vineyards. The lower sections between the slopes and the alluvial plains, with easily accessible drinking water, became the preferred area for settlements.

A third region, common in the Vojvodina, includes the sandy areas once largely in bare dunes (southeastern Banat). Over a period of 150 years the dunes were planted to trees and grass, and they now support vineyards and livestock.

---

[1] Borivoje Ž. Milojević, "Die Geographischen Gebiete Serbiens" ("The Geographic Regions of Serbia"), *Mitteilungen der Geographischen Gesellschaft* (Vienna), 1957, pp. 45–51; also George W. Hoffman, "The Vojvodina (Yugoslavia), A Study in Agricultural Evolution," *Bulletin of the Geological Society of America*, Vol. 71, No. 12, Part 2, December 1960, pp. 2098–2099.

Still another area in the Vojvodina Plain is the Fruška Gora, an isolated, low mountain range stretching in an east-west direction for roughly 50 miles between the Danube and the Sava. Vineyards, on the southern slopes, and forests are made possible by higher precipitation than in the surrounding areas.

Many parts of the Vojvodina were devastated during the Turkish wars, and land was abandoned, but gradually the area was resettled and damages were repaired. A very mixed ethnic group settled in these lands: soldiers from the victorious armies and people from the areas occupied by the Turkish conqueror who had sought refuge in the northern part of the heartland and the Croatian-Slovenian Hill Lands. Population shifts in the Vojvodina continued until very recent times, owing to the many changes in the political-territorial framework and in land ownership. In 1959 about 10 per cent of Yugoslavia's population lived in the Vojvodina, which comprises 8.4 per cent of the country's total area.[1] The population of the urban centers has increased rapidly during the past forty years, especially since World War II.

A dense network of roads, navigable waterways and railroads connects all important parts of this vital region, and links the Vojvodina with the rest of the country. Agriculture is the backbone of the economy, with maize and wheat the principal cereals. Fishing in the many rivers and the raising of geese near rural settlements are also of importance. Industries, mainly those connected with the processing of agricultural products (canning, sugar refining, alcohol distilling and flour milling), were built up in the period of Hungarian control before 1918. These were enlarged and new ones were added during the interwar years and after 1945; the most recent are industries producing agricultural machines, fertilizers and building materials. Some low-grade coal on the Fruška Gora, loess for bricks and quartz sand for the glass industry are available locally. Because the Vojvodina is Yugoslavia's chief food-producing region, special emphasis has been placed on increasing agricultural productivity through a program of mechanization and land drainage. As part of this program the construction of the Danube-Tisa-Danube canal system is being pushed toward completion.

The Croatian-Slovenian Hill Lands. Adjoining the Vojvodina on the west are the Croatian-Slovenian Hill Lands, which lie between the Drava, Danube and Sava rivers and the foothills of the Alps. These are very fertile loess-covered lowlands interspersed with limestone and crystalline hills. The northern part

---

[1] For a more detailed discussion of the changes in this and other peripheral regions see George W. Hoffman, "Yugoslavia: Changing Character of Rural Life and Rural Economy," *American Slavic and East European Review*, December 1959, pp. 571–577. Some of the material contained in this section originally appeared there; it is used with permission of the *American Slavic and East European Review*.

of Slovenia shares in the southern extension of the Alps. The limestone Julian Alps, the summit of which is Triglav at 9,393 feet, continues in the Dinaric Mountains. The Karawanken chain extends eastward and fades out toward the Pannonian Basin. The climate of this region varies from extreme cold in the Alpine parts of Slovenia, with an annual average temperature of about 48° and an average January–July temperature range of 71°, to somewhat higher annual average temperatures (53-56°) in the middle Drava and Sava valleys, to typical continental conditions farther east in the Slavonian hill lands. Precipitation is heavy to ample and fairly evenly distributed throughout the year.

The fertile valleys of this area have been of importance throughout history for military, ethnic and commercial movements. Between the north and north-western part of the heartland and the spurs of the Eastern Alps, between the valleys of the Sava and Kupa and the Adriatic littoral, the Pannonian Basin and the Adriatic Sea come within 75 miles of each other. Here where the mountains are narrow, *cols* permit easy passage between the Dinarics and the Alps, the Pannonian Basin and the Adriatic. This link or gap was used by the old Amber Road, a route between the Baltic and the Mediterranean, and has been used by invaders from the sea as well as from the continental interior. It was a key region for defending the Habsburg Empire and connecting the Italian and Turkish battlefields. The thoroughfare was defended against Turkish attack by the Military Frontier, a defense zone established by Austria along its border with Turkey.[1] The importance of this gap has by no means diminished with time. It affords the shortest route between the ports of Rijeka and Trieste and the Danubian hinterland. Modern highways today run between the Adriatic ports and the cities of the interior.

The Croatian-Slovenian region is the oldest and most important industrial area of Yugoslavia. It is an area which was already inhabited in prehistoric times. In the valleys there is mining (especially of coal, zinc and lead) and industrial activity, some of which goes back to the Middle Ages. Some of the valleys, such as Hrvatsko Zagorje, are the most densely populated in all of Yugoslavia. Others have been declining in population for nearly a hundred years as peasants moved off the land.

After the military border was abolished in the latter part of the nineteenth century, large numbers of people moved from the marginal lands to better regions, or emigrated. Encouraged by the building of rail and road connections to Vienna, Budapest and the ports of the Adriatic, a number of industries — ironworks, machinery, textiles, furniture, building materials, etc. —

[1] Gunther Erich Rothenberg, *The Austrian Military Border in Croatia, 1522–1747,* Illinois Studies in the Social Sciences, Vol. 48, University of Illinois Press, Urbana, 1960.

were developed in the late nineteenth and twentieth centuries, in Ljubljana, Maribor, Celje, Jesenice,[1] Karlovac and Zagreb. Owing to the accelerated industrialization during the past ten years, internal migrations have again assumed large proportions. This is visible in the landscape, especially of northwest Hrvatsko Primorje and Istria; war damages still remain and often the only signs that the land was once cultivated are the stone walls which divided property. Elsewhere small plots are located on the periphery of industrial settlements; they are typical of a more advanced Western economy.

With the acquisition of vital territory along the Adriatic, in Istria and northwestern Slovenia after World War II, the function of this region as the country's prime communication center with Western Europe has been greatly enhanced. Increased industrial production, modernized agriculture and the key transportation position make the Croatian-Slovenian area the most important all-round region of the new Yugoslavia.

Central Serbia. South of the Vojvodina is a region generally known as Central Serbia. It is transitional to the neighboring regions of the peripheral zone. Included in it are the fertile valley of the Morava River, the rolling hills and foothills of the Dinaric Mountains toward the west, particularly the lower part between the lower Sava, the Danube and the Zapadna and Velika Morava at Čačak, called Šumadija, and the somewhat isolated mountainous areas of northeast and eastern Serbia. Central Serbia shows Pannonian characteristics in the lower Morava and Mediterranean, Macedonian characteristics in the upper Morava.

Central Serbia also has had an important historical role as a crossroad, with Belgrade serving as the focal point. Roads leading from the Aegean Sea through the Vardar and Morava valleys, from Constantinople to Niš, from Kosovo through the valley of the Ibar over Kraljevo into the Šumadija, from the Sava valley from the west and from the Pannonian Basin from the north, converge at the confluence of the Sava and the Danube (Figure 2–3). Here on a limestone crag rising 140 feet above the Danube a citadel and town have been located for centuries. At this strategic spot the Celtic fort and Roman city of Singidunum and the Turkish fortress of Kalimegdan were built, overlooking the loess plains of the Sava and the Danube and the fertile hills of Central Serbia. Only a little to the southeast, near the confluence of the Morava and the Danube, is the medieval fortress of Smederevo, today an

---

[1] The first small ironworks existed in the neighborhood of Jesenice as early as the fourteenth and fifteenth centuries. Local iron ores and timber for charcoal were used. Based on these traditions the ironworks at Jesenice were organized in 1868, but neither iron ore nor coal came from local resources. Instead the location on the newly opened railway from Jesenice to Tarvisio (now Italian) and Carinthia to Trieste via Jesenice made possible the cheap importation of iron ores from overseas via Trieste and coal from different parts of the Monarchy. Coal was imported both in the prewar and post-World War II period mostly from Poland and Czechoslovakia.

industrial and marketing center. Any invader wanting to cross the Danube had to control Central Serbia, and its valleys were home to many warriors. With the defeat of the Turks and the re-emergence of an independent Serbian state this region became the core of the unified state of Yugoslavia.

The valleys of Central Serbia are extremely important agriculturally, especially the Morava valley. Climatic differences are reflected in the distribution of crops; maize and wheat are predominant in the lower Morava valley, wheat, tobacco and, to a lesser extent, cotton in the more southern parts. The original oak and beech forests are now confined to higher altitudes in the southern and western mountains. The slopes of the lower mountains are deforested and planted to wheat; the steeper slopes still have a good cover of forests but are used also for orchards and vineyards. Fruit in great variety is grown throughout Central Serbia, especially plum trees, which are found everywhere. Some of the plums are exported, and many of the fresh prunes are made into brandy (*Šljivovica*). Stockbreeding has diminished in importance, but cattle are raised in the west, pigs (now fed on corn) in the north and central parts, and sheep in the south and east. Before industrialization was emphasized, after World War I, maize, wheat, fruit, pigs and sheep were the main products of Central Serbia.

With the unification of Yugoslavia after World War I, new rail lines and roads were built and attention was given to agriculture, to building and textile industries, and also to mining. All were carried on on a very small scale. Belgrade is the major center, but in numerous towns in the Morava valley, and in the Šumadija and Raška regions, industrial concentrations are emerging. These are evident in cities such as Pančevo, Smederevo, Palanka, Paracin, Svetozarevo, Niš, Kragujevac and Kraljevo. Industries established during the past few years are in part based on the minerals found in the basins and valleys. These rich mineral resources and the great physical diversity of the landscape, together with a strategic location, have made this region increasingly important.

The Kosovo-Metohija and Vardar region. South of Central Serbia is a most diverse region, including all the territory of southeastern Yugoslavia. This is the Kosovo-Metohija and Vardar region; it encompasses all of the Federal Republic of Macedonia and the autonomous region of Kosovo-Metohija (Kosmet). This region consists of a series of basins connected with each other by low mountain passes and isolated mountain blocks.

The relief of the eastern and southeastern part of Yugoslavia is strongly influenced by the Morava and Vardar depression. Its many basins afford a short route between the lowlands of the north and the Aegean Sea and its head port of Salonika, a distance of 300 miles. West of the depression are the spurs of the Dinaric ranges, the detached mountain blocks and basins of which are connected by narrow passages. Parallel to the Kosovo-Metohija and Vardar region and crossing the Morava and Vardar depression in an easterly direction is a mountain strip, the Rhodope Massif, which broadens southeastward into Bulgaria. The mountain tops are rounded and the slopes are very steep. The original forests having been destroyed, soil erosion on the hills and sheet erosion in the basins are widespread.

In the southeastern region, especially in the Vardar valley, wheat rather than maize, as in most of the Morava valley, is the main cereal. Irrigation has received greatly increased attention, and cotton, rice and tobacco are the chief crops. In Macedonia, only 10 per cent of the total area is cultivated; excessive soil erosion and poor drainage of the bottom lands have contributed to the great poverty and backwardness of its people. Soil erosion has been so devastating in Macedonia that special protective measures have received high priority.

Five hundred years of Turkish rule have left their mark on the people and economy of this southeastern area and much of the oriental influence is still in evidence. Many of the earlier Christian Slavic settlers departed at the time of the Turkish conquests and their places were taken mostly by Albanians who embraced the Islamic faith. Wide areas were left depopulated and others became a cultural mosaic. Local feuds and the replacement of the original settlers laid the basis for countless controversies. With the decline of the Turkish Empire, this area became the meeting ground of Serbian, Greek and Bulgarian nationalism. The new Yugoslavia has attempted to solve this problem by giving Macedonia federal status, with equal rights in the multinational state, and by giving autonomy to the people in Kosovo-Metohija. At the same time, economic aid in the form of large investments has been extended to a number of activities — irrigation schemes, mechanization of agriculture, power plants, new industries, the opening of new mines and the modernization of old ones, such as Yugoslavia's largest lead mine at Trepča. The effect of this large-scale effort is already visible in the appearance of Macedonian cities (Skoplje, Priština, Veles, Ohrid, Prilep) and in the penetration of the modern aspects of life into interior valleys and remote villages.

The Adriatic littoral. Along the full length of the Yugoslav Adriatic coast stretches a narrow coastal zone, the Adriatic littoral. The coastal fringe, including the islands and the terraced hillsides, has a limited amount of good soil. Here, in areas not affected by the strong winds, or *bura*, Mediterranean crops such as olives, vines and figs are raised; and in the southern parts, which are well protected against the *bura*, there are orange groves. There is also limited pasture land and cereal acreage (maize), together with some fishing

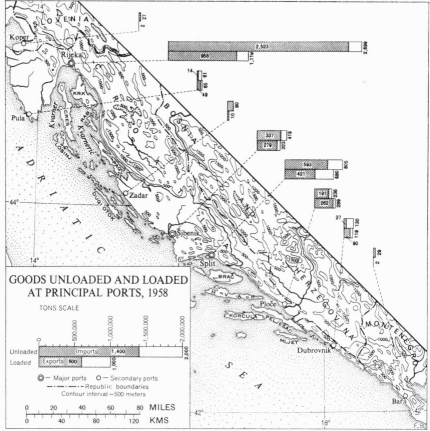

Figure 2–2

SOURCE: Based on *Statistički Bilten*, No. 149, 1959, pp. 92–93.

(sardines, mackerel, tunny and oysters). All have been important but they provide an insufficient source of income for the population.

Blocked from the interior for the most part by the steep slopes of the High Karst, the people of the coastal lands traditionally looked to the sea for their livelihood. In earlier times the harbors and towns were important, economically and politically, and Italian influence, especially in the architecture of the towns, is still in evidence, though nearly all of the people speak Serbo-Croatian. Before World War I, emigration, especially to the United States, attracted the surplus population. Today employment opportunities are provided by new industries.

The changes in the economic and political development of postwar Yugoslavia are shown in the role of the littoral. With industrialization and trade

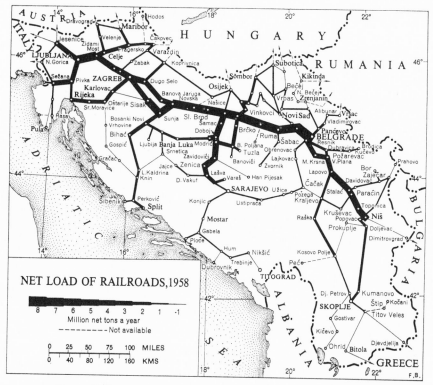

Figure 2–3

SOURCE: "Saobraćaj I Veze, 1958," *Statistički Bilten*, No. 149, Belgrade, October 1959, p. 56.

receiving greatly increased support from the government, work opportunities are now available to the ever-increasing number of people who cannot be supported by the land in the poorer mountainous areas of the Karst hinterland. The many new industries in the interior require raw materials from abroad and Yugoslavia must export its surplus products to pay for these imports. Although the harbors of most of the small towns serve coastal traffic only, many of these ports are engaged in shipbuilding and are also the site of chemical works, factories processing imported raw materials, canneries and aluminum plants, which utilize the nearby bauxite and the newly developed hydroelectric power. Split, Šibenik, the new port of Ploče, and Gruž (the port of Dubrovnik) are particularly active in the increased overseas trade. (See Figure 2–2.) Bar, in the southernmost part of the littoral, is being developed as the main port for a future Belgrade–southern littoral traffic artery. Rijeka, Yugoslavia's largest and most modern port, occupies an advantageous

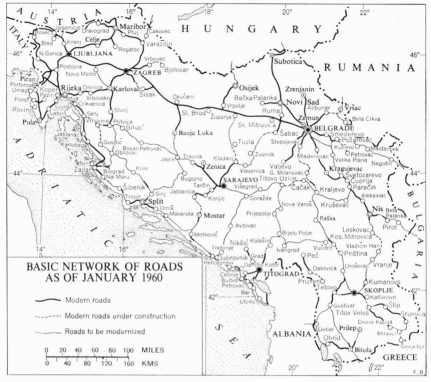

Figure 2–4

SOURCE: *Yugoslav Life*, V, No. 41, February 1960, p. 12.

position in the northern part of the littoral where the Pannonian Basin is closest to the Adriatic. It has the best rail and road connections with the peripheral zone and the Danubian countries. Trieste, at the head of the Adriatic, is much handicapped in its trade by its proximity to political boundaries.

The formidable mountain barrier and the highlands made communication with the interior extremely difficult and costly in the past. With the exception of Dubrovnik, and to a lesser extent Split, no city of the littoral succeeded in establishing contact with the hinterlands in medieval times. But the isolated position of the littoral is slowly being overcome and the importance of the "frontage facing the sea and the world" is now being realized. With the changing economic and political geography of the new Yugoslavia, dependence on world markets and the need for closer communication with the interior have greatly increased. Improved communication certainly demands priority in the future. It also will help to open up the more backward areas of the heartland, and reduce isolationism through increased economic possibilities. Yugoslavia's acquisition of Rijeka at the end of World War II greatly improved its position as a Mediterranean power.

Another significant change in the littoral is the large increase in international tourist traffic, and with it the building of modern highways and hotel accommodations. With financial assistance from the United States, a new and modern highway is being built which will eventually permit even the less-experienced driver to enjoy the beauties of the Adriatic coast. The many domestic and foreign tourists provide a welcome income to both the urban and rural population.[1]

Isolated mountain regions. All of the isolated mountain regions in the peripheral zone are located along the national frontier (Figure 2–1). These mountain regions are typically poor and their surplus population seeks employment in the neighboring plains. As Roglić points out, they are to the adjoining plains what the mountainous heartland is to the country as a whole.[2] The most developed of these regions is the Yugoslavian part of the Eastern Alps. The resources and people of this mountain area are closely connected with the whole economic development of Slovenia. A very isolated and backward mountain region is located in northeast Macedonia and southeast Serbia, along the frontier with Bulgaria. Its people emigrate to distant urban centers. Another isolated mountain region is in western Macedonia, the mountain plateaus with the Sara Planina at its center. It is located between the upper Vardar and the Drim River valleys, the basins of Tetovo and Prizren. This region is closely linked with the adjacent Albanian territory and has always served as an easy entry point for Albanians following old-established pastoral practices. The region is close to the autonomous territory of Kosmet, which has a predominantly Albanian population. Here also new economic life has penetrated; a new wool mill at Tetovo is being supplied with wool from the local sheep.

Shaping a Nation

Several things emerge from this analysis of the separate regions and their changing roles. It is apparent first that Yugoslavia is composed of a number of diverse regions and, secondly, that political, cultural and economic developments have largely broken down the barriers created by its natural features. This process has been greatly accelerated since World War II. Thirdly, the relationship between the rich agricultural and industrialized peripheral zone and the centrally located mountainous heartland, which blocks direct com-

[1] In 1959 over 800,000 foreign tourists, an all-time high, traveled in Yugoslavia. Over 60 per cent of these visitors stayed in tourist accommodations along the Adriatic coast. Opatija in the north and Dubrovnik in the south were the most popular places.

[2] "Prilog Regionalnoj Podjeli Jugoslavije," p. 17.

munication between the sea frontage and the hinterland, has serious political-geographic repercussions. The concentration of important resources in this easily accessible peripheral zone greatly weakens Yugoslavia's military potential, as was demonstrated in the last war. The peripheral zone is at the same time an area of great cultural diversity. Certainly the fact that the most valuable parts of the country are also ethnically the least homogeneous represents a great problem for the state. The mountainous heartland, on the other hand, provides the state with a strong fortress and a staging area for counterattacks and offers refuge in time of stress. In addition, it supplies the weaker peripheral regions with its surplus population and in this way strengthens the unity of the state.

In the interwar years economic advances were largely confined to the peripheral zone, although Macedonia and the present autonomous region of Kosovo-Metohija remained much as they were during the centuries of Turkish subjugation. The most advanced agricultural and industrial areas were found largely in Slovenia and Croatia, except for the south central part of the littoral, and in the Vojvodina. Central Serbia was less developed, but it received most attention during the interwar years. The areas longest under the Ottoman Empire and Montenegro, the mountainous heartland, had hardly changed by 1941 from their pre-World War I economic status. Exploration and development of the mineral resources of the heartland, modernization of agriculture, and most of all the establishment of an integrated system of transportation and replacement of the outdated rail equipment, were scarcely attempted during the two decades between the wars. In all this period of independence, the state was never able to establish close ties between its various regions, and the standard of living of most of its people remained low. Granted that such an undertaking, after generations of foreign rule, was not easy, progress was still very slow.

World War II brought untold hardship to the people, and complete collapse to the economy. A fresh beginning was made under a new and totally different economic and political system following the war. In Yugoslavia's present stage of economic development, the continuing great contrasts between the component parts of the state are a disadvantage. However, insofar as the regions supplement each other and are closely interconnected, their diversity should, in the long run, provide more elements of strength than of weakness. Yugoslavia's concentrated efforts during the past sixteen years to diminish regional contrasts, both cultural and economic, have already yielded results, the details of which will be discussed in the following chapters.

THE PEOPLE

THE Yugoslav peoples, for the most part South Slavs, are composed predominantly of Serbs, Croats, Slovenes and Macedonians. A number of migrations and settlements had come to the territory of what is now Yugoslavia long before Slavic tribes found their way into its valleys and basins in the sixth century. People speaking the Illyric tongue were numerous before the Celts invaded the southeast European peninsula in the third century B.C., but they left little as a permanent legacy. The Goths and Huns repeatedly made destructive raids through the major northern and eastern valleys. The Slavic people, coming from the Carpathians and the Pannonian Basin, occupied two distinct regions of the peninsula.[1] In the north they settled the valleys of the Sava River and its tributaries; south of it, they occupied the area of the mountainous regions.

Their neighbors, Byzantines, Magyars, Rumanians, Austro-Germans and Italians, each tried to influence and control the Slavic peoples. This often was made easier because of the greater number of these neighboring people. Political and religious pressures were exerted also from Western and Eastern sources: Roman Catholic and Latin, Orthodox and Byzantine, Ottoman and Moslem. Some of the Slavic peoples succumbed to these pressures.

The religious-political conflicts between the East and the West for dominance of the South Slavs was accelerated after the Ottoman Turks succeeded in subjugating most of southeastern Europe. The Turkish conquest and the rapid Islamization, especially of the southern and central part, was in part due to earlier conflicts between the inhabitants and their rulers.

Throughout these centuries of war and upheaval, and in spite of long periods of subjugation during which entirely different and alien cultures were at times superimposed upon them, the South Slavs succeeded in living, on the

[1] Jovan Cvijić, *La Péninsule Balkanique*, Armand Colin, Paris, 1918, p. 92.

27

whole, on the originally settled lands. The geographic diversity of this land and the many cultural-political influences are expressed in differences in the way of life of the people, their customs, speech, religion, and in the demographic structure of the population. The centuries-long conflict on the territory which makes up today's Yugoslavia resulted in many difficulties for the inhabitants which continued after they were unified into one state. The process of working together is still new and often fraught with hazards.

National Groups and Minorities

Most of the people of Yugoslavia belong to one of the five national groups officially recognized since 1945: Serbs, 41.7 per cent of the total population; Croats 23.5; Slovenes 8.8; Macedonians 5.3; and Montenegrins 2.8. (See Table 3–1 and Figure 3–1.) The 1953 census also listed close to 6.0 per cent of the population as "undeclared."[1] Most of the people in this category are Moslems in Bosnia and Herzegovina who sometimes call themselves simply Turks, even though they are in fact Slavs. The people of Bosnia and Herzegovina are mainly Serbs or Croats. In the classification of Serbs and Croats, the determining factor has been religion (that is, Orthodox or Roman Catholic) rather than strict ethnic origin, which in most cases would be impossible to determine in any event. In all, 88 per cent of the population of Yugoslavia was classified as belonging to the national groups and 12 per cent as being part of national minorities.[2]

While the relative importance of the national minorities changed very little between the 1948 and 1953 censuses — declining from 12.6 to 12.0 per cent of the total — between the censuses of 1921 and 1948 the national minorities dropped from 16.9 per cent to 12.6 per cent of the total (Table 3–1). This decline was brought about by World War II, which resulted in the voluntary or forced migration of many Germans,[3] and to a lesser degree Italians.

---

[1] The problems of the distribution of nationalities within a population for statistical purposes are discussed by Milan Babić in "Problemi Statističkog Ispitivanja Narodnosne Pripadnosti Stanovništva" ("Problems of Statistical Assessment of Nationality Groups"), *Statistička Revija*, December 1954, pp. 385–388. One of the most thorough studies published about the population of Yugoslavia in the English language is by Paul F. Myers and Arthur A. Campbell, *The Population of Yugoslavia*, International Population Statistics Reports, Series P-90, No. 5, Bureau of the Census, U. S. Government Printing Office, Washington, 1954.

[2] Minorities have cultural and linguistic freedom in the autonomous region of Kosovo-Metohija (Kosmet), and in the Vojvodina. They also have substantial administrative autonomy. For detailed information and documentation of the minorities from a Yugoslav point of view see Ljubiša Stoiković and Miloš Martić, *National Minorities in Yugoslavia*, Jugoslavija, Belgrade, 1952, and Koča Jončić, *The National Minorities in Yugoslavia*, Information Service Yugoslavia, Jugoslavija, Belgrade, 1960.

[3] Germans in 1921 numbered 506,000, and in 1948 roughly 57,000. They decreased from 4.2 to 0.4 per cent of the total population. See also Joseph B. Schechtman, "The Elimination of German Minorities in Southeastern Europe," *Journal of Central European Affairs*, July 1946, pp. 152–166.

Table 3–1

POPULATION BY NATIONALITIES, SELECTED YEARS, 1921–1953

(Number in Thousands)

	1921		1931		1948		1953	
	Number	Per Cent	Number	Per Cent	Number	Per Cent	Number	Per Cent
Total	11,952	100.0	13,934	100.0	15,763	100.0	16,937	100.0
National groups	9,931	83.1	11,866	85.2	13,791	87.4	14,887	88.0
Serbs	} 8,911	74.6	} 10,731	77.0	{ 6,547	41.5	7,066	41.7
Croats					{ 3,784	24.0	3,976	23.5
Slovenes	1,020	8.5	1,135	8.2	1,415	8.9	1,487	8.8
Macedonians	a		a		810	5.2	893	5.3
Montenegrins	a		a		426	2.7	466	2.8
Undeclared	a		a		809 b	5.1	999 b	5.9
National minorities	2,021	16.9	2,068	14.8	1,973 c	12.6	2,050 c	12.0
Albanians (Shiptars)	440	3.7	505	3.6	750	4.8	754	4.4
Magyars	468	3.9	468	3.4	496	3.2	502	3.0
Turks	150	1.2	133	0.9	98	0.6	260	1.5
Slovaks	115	1.0	76	0.5	84	0.5	85	0.5
Gypsies	d		70	0.5	73	0.5	85	0.5
Bulgars	d		d		61	0.4	62	0.4
Germans	506	4.2	500	3.6	57	0.4	61	0.4
Rumanians	231	1.9	138	1.0	64	0.4	60	0.3
Vlachs	d		d		103 e	0.7	37	0.2
Ruthenians	...	...	...	...	...	...	37	0.2
Italians	12	0.1	9	0.1	79	0.5	36	0.2
Czechs	f		53	0.4	39	0.2	35	0.2
Russians	21	0.2	36	0.3	57	0.4	12	0.1
Jews	...	...	...	...	7	0.0	...	...
Others	78	0.7	80	0.5	5	0.0	18	0.1
Unknown							6	

Source: Official Yugoslav statistics.

a Prewar Yugoslav statistics listed Serbs, Croats, Macedonians, Montenegrins, Bulgars and "undeclared" all as Serbo-Croats. The 1931 statistics were considered so unreliable that they were never officially published.

b Mainly Moslem in Bosnia and Herzegovina.

c Differences among some minority groups between the censuses of 1948 and 1953 can be traced to the changes in Yugoslavia's relations with its neighbors, e.g., Albanians, Turks, Germans and Hungarians; sometimes, to incorrect enumerations.

d Was combined with other minorities, probably Rumanians.

e 197,000 people registered as Vlachs in 1953 according to their mother tongue and only 37,000 as of "Vlach nationality." This is based on the definition of nationality in the 1953 census and may account for differences between the distribution of the population according to nationality and mother tongue.

f Probably together with Slovaks.

Note: The pre-World War I census of Austria was based on language commonly used (*Umgangssprache*) to determine nationality. The Hungarian census used mother tongue. Censuses were taken in Yugoslavia in 1921, 1931, 1948, 1953 and 1961. The 1921 census used mother tongue and religion, the 1931 census mother tongue and nationality. However, the nationality figures of the 1931 census were considered so unreliable that detailed results were never officially published. Mace-

Continued on following page

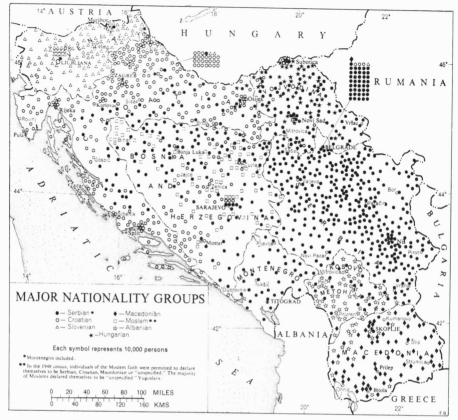

Figure 3–1

SOURCE: Based on *Stanovništvo Po Narodnosti* (*Population by Ethnic Nationality*), Volume IX, Belgrade, 1954. (Final results of the population census of March 15, 1948.)

Next to the Soviet Union, Yugoslavia has the largest population of national minorities of any of the European countries. Of a total 1953 population of 16.9 million, slightly more than 2 million (12 per cent) belonged to minority groups. The largest of these minorities were the Albanians, the Magyars and the Turks. The total number of Albanians was roughly 754,000 (as against 1.2 million in Albania), and Albanians made up 4.4 per cent of the population.

Notes to Table 3–1 continued

donians, Montenegrins and Bulgars did not figure as separate entities in the 1921 and 1931 census; they all were entered as Serbians. This obviously reflected the Greater Serbian influence prevalent during the interwar years. Nationality is the best criterion because it permits four distinct nationality groups: Serbs, Croats, Montenegrins and Macedonians. Using mother tongue as a criterion all four would be joined as "Serbs and Croats." The 1948 and 1953 censuses were based on nationality.

Magyars accounted for 3.0 per cent of the total population. The Turkish minority was roughly 260,000 (1.5 per cent) and was concentrated in Macedonia (200,000) and Serbia (60,000).

Generally speaking, each national group is concentrated in one republic; the Moslems of Serbian and Croatian origin are largely concentrated in Bosnia and Herzegovina, where they make up 31.3 per cent of the population. The national groups form a large majority in their respective political units. In the republic of Serbia, for example, Serbs account for 74.3 per cent of the total population. The autonomous region of the Vojvodina — attached to the republic of Serbia — has a population composed of only 51 per cent Serbs, however. Of the Vojvodina population, 26 per cent are Magyars (the Vojvodina has 88.1 per cent of all the Magyars in Yugoslavia), and the remainder are principally Croats, Montenegrins, Slovaks, Rumanians and Germans. In the autonomous region of Kosmet — also attached to Serbia — 24 per cent of the population are Serbs, while 68.4 per cent are Albanians (Kosmet has 66 per cent of all the Albanians in Yugoslavia). In Croatia 79.8 per cent of the population are Croats and 15.1 per cent Serbs; in Slovenia, 96.5 per cent Slovenians; in Macedonia, 66 per cent Macedonians, 12.5 per cent Albanians and 8.3 per cent Turks. In Montenegro 86.4 per cent of the inhabitants are Montenegrins and 5.5 per cent Albanians. In Bosnia and Herzegovina, 44.4 per cent of the population declared themselves as Serb in the 1953 census, 23 per cent as Croats, 31.3 per cent as Moslem (i.e., not identifying themselves with a particular national group). Of all people listed as "undeclared," 90 per cent live in Bosnia and Herzegovina.

A clear distinction in terms of national orientation should be made between the various Macedonians—Yugoslav, Bulgarian and Greek. The claim of many Yugoslav Macedonians to a separate nationality is often disputed.[1] Much has been written about the ethnic composition of the Macedonian population. There is no disagreement as to the predominance of the Slavic element, but rather as to the affinity to Bulgarians or Serbians. Macedonians were closely associated with Bulgarians until the beginning of this century.

[1] See the important work by H. N. Brailsford, *Macedonia: Its Races and Their Future*, Methuen & Co., London, 1906. Jovan Cvijić's work *Rémarques sur l'Ethographie de la Macédoine*, Rouston, Paris, 1907, became the turning point for considering Macedonians as Bulgarians. He insisted that Slavic Macedonia was of transitional character — Serb or Bulgarian — but added that there did not exist a "national consciousness." After World War I, Macedonians were officially referred to as ethnically Serbs, and Macedonia was called "South Serbia." The Communist parties of Bulgaria and Greece agreed during World War II on an independent republic within a Balkan Communist federation, but Yugoslavia insisted on Macedonia remaining within a Yugoslav federation. Macedonian nationalism, especially in the cultural field, received official Yugoslav Communist sanction after the war. For a recent Yugoslav Communist interpretation of Macedonia's struggle, see the lengthy address by Lazar Koliševski, *Macedonian National Question*, Jugoslavija, Belgrade, 1959. For a Greek view, see Nic. P. Andriotes. *The Confederate State of Skopje and Its Language*, Athens, 1957.

Since the federal republic of Macedonia was organized as part of Yugoslavia in 1945, many steps have been taken to encourage national cultural activities — Serbian and Bulgarian influences have been minimized in the Macedonian language (the Bulgarian suffix *or* and the Serbian suffix *ić* have been changed to the Macedonian *ski* and place names such as Skoplje to Skopje); the alphabet and grammar have been standardized[1] and introduced in all schools; and a university was organized in Skoplje. All these measures seem to be both successful and popular.[2]

As for the general distribution of national groups and minorities, Slovenia is the most homogeneous republic, followed by Montenegro, while Macedonia and the autonomous region of the Vojvodina are the most heterogeneous. Eighty-seven per cent of the national minorities live in Macedonia and Serbia, mainly in the two autonomous regions of the Vojvodina and Kosmet. Both republics have a substantial minority population, Serbia 20.6 per cent and Macedonia 30.7 per cent of the total. This reflects the concentration of Albanians and Turks in the Kosmet and Macedonia; and Magyars, Rumanians, Slovaks and Germans in the Vojvodina. This distribution has remained largely unchanged since the organization of Yugoslavia in 1918, except for the major changes referred to earlier — the migration and expulsion of almost the entire German population and the exodus of the Turks. In addition, the Albanians have expanded somewhat into Serbia proper.

The present-day distribution of the minorities reflects migrations and changes in boundaries which occurred over many centuries. Pressures from neighboring regions and the boundary changes following World War I account for the large groups of Magyars and Rumanians in the Vojvodina.[3] The other national minorities in the Vojvodina — Germans, Slovaks, Ukrainians, etc. — are descendants of colonists who settled there in the eighteenth century after this area was freed from Turkish subjugation. As a result of the Balkan wars and the boundary changes after World War I, Serbia received the Sanjak of Novi Pazar and parts of Macedonia with a mixed population of Macedonians, Serbs, Albanians, Turks, Bulgarians and other minorities. The Turkish invasions caused the most extensive migrations among the

[1] An American scholar did a major part of the work; cf. Horace Lunt, *A Grammar of the Macedonian Literary Languages*, Government Publishing House of the People's Republic of Macedonia, Skoplje, 1952.

[2] For a valuable brief review and assessment of the postwar situation in Macedonia, see H. R. Wilkinson, "Jugoslav Macedonia in Transition," *Geographical Journal*, December 1952, pp. 389–405. Also, two reports in the *New York Times* by Paul Underwood on November 17, 1958 conclude with an optimistic view as to the success of the new Macedonian nationalism which has been encouraged by the Yugoslav government.

[3] According to C. A. Macartney (*National States and National Minorities*, Oxford University Press, London, 1934, p. 206), in order to annex the city of Subotica with its Croat population, over 250,000 Magyars of the surrounding areas were incorporated into Yugoslavia after 1918. These Croats call themselves "Bunjevci."

Slavic people. Serbs, largely from the basins of Kosovo and Metohija, fled into Hungary. Later, when the Austrian armies were forced to retreat after advancing deep into Turkish-occupied territory at the end of the seventeenth and the beginning of the eighteenth centuries, many Serbs fled and were settled along the Military Frontier in Croatia and north of the Danube in the Vojvodina. The Islamized Albanians who took their place forced many of the remaining Serbs to take on the Moslem faith or migrate to the north.[1]

Religious Groups

Religion is as important as ethnic origin and language in Yugoslavia and is, indeed, intrinsically bound up with the complex nationality problems of the country. The religious communities include the Serbian Orthodox Church, the Roman Catholic Church, the Islamic Religious Community, the Old-Catholic Church, the Hebrew Religious Community, the Rumanian Orthodox Church, a number of Protestant churches and some minor religious organizations. The majority of the Yugoslav peoples, according to the 1953 census, are at least nominally members of either the Serbian Orthodox or Roman Catholic churches, or belong to the Moslem faith. Twelve per cent of those questioned in the census indicated no religious affiliation. (See Table 3–2.)

Table 3–2

RELIGIOUS AFFILIATION OF THE POPULATION, 1921, 1931 AND 1953

(*Number in Thousands*)

Religion	1921		1931		1953	
	Number	Per Cent	Number	Per Cent	Number	Per Cent
Total population	11,952	100.0	13,933	100.0	16,937	100.0
Orthodox	5,602	46.8	6,785	48.7	7,011	41.4
Roman Catholic	4,705	39.4	5,218	37.4	5,383	31.8
Protestant	217	1.8	231	1.7	148	0.9
Moslem	1,302	10.9	1,561	11.2	2,083	12.3
Other Christian	42	0.4	68	0.5	71	0.4
Jews	64	0.5	68	0.5	—	—
Others and undeclared	20	0.2	2	0.0	156	0.9
Without religious affiliation					2,085	12.3

Source: Official statistics for 1921 and 1953. For 1931: Werner Markert (ed.), *Jugoslawien,* Osteuropa-Handbuch Böhlau-Verlag, Köln-Graz, 1954, p. 16.

These figures should be considered, however, within the context of the Yugoslav ethnic mores. Traditionally, being a Serb meant being a member of the Orthodox faith, and being a Croat meant being a Roman Catholic; and, indeed, the identification also works the other way around. Thus many

[1] Wayne S. Vucinich, "Yugoslavs of the Moslem Faith," in Robert J. Kerner (ed.), *Yugoslavia,* University of California Press, Berkeley, 1949, pp. 262–264.

contemporary Yugoslavs (including Communists) who are not churchgoers or believers still list themselves in a census as being Orthodox or Roman Catholic, simply because their parents belonged to these confessions.

The distribution of the religious groups throughout the country is extremely complex, owing to the historical development of the various peoples of Yugoslavia. The Serbian Orthodox Church is the largest, 41.4 per cent of the total population identifying themselves with it in the 1953 census.[1] (See Table 3–3.) Like other Orthodox churches in Eastern Europe, it is based on the Greek rite, but differs in minor respects from the Greek Orthodox Church and from other national Orthodox churches such as the Russian. It is autonomous under a Patriarch, although a theoretical ecumenical relationship is maintained with all Orthodoxy under the Constantinople (Istanbul) Patriarch.

The greatest stronghold of the Serbian Orthodox Church is, of course, Serbia proper, where 82.2 per cent of the inhabitants list themselves as members. Also included in the Orthodox population are 45.2 per cent of the people in Montenegro, 35.1 per cent of those in Bosnia and Herzegovina (the Serbs), 45.5 per cent of those in the Vojvodina and 57.3 per cent of those in Macedonia. In Macedonia there is a semi-independent (autocephalous) Macedonian Orthodox Church, which has its own bishops but operates under the Serbian Patriarch in Belgrade. Abolished in the twelfth century, it was re-established in the fall of 1958. The decision by the Yugoslav government to permit the split within the Serbian Orthodox Church is closely linked to the Macedonian struggle for greater autonomy.

Nearly 32 per cent of the Yugoslav population is Roman Catholic. This includes 84.1 per cent of the population in Slovenia, 73.5 per cent in Croatia, 33.0 per cent in the Vojvodina, and 21.4 per cent in Bosnia and Herzegovina (the Croats). A small percentage of Albanians are also Roman Catholic. The Roman Catholic Church has four archbishoprics, but the church in Croatia has a special organization in which its bishops operate under a Croatian Primate.

The Moslem population amounts to 12.3 per cent of the total population, and is concentrated largely in Bosnia and Herzegovina (43.5 per cent), Kosovo-Metohija (26.4 per cent) and Macedonia (18.6 per cent). Most of the Moslems in Kosovo-Metohija and a smaller number in Macedonia are of Albanian origin (roughly 800,000), while the Turkish-Moslems (approximately 100,000) are largely in Macedonia. A substantial number of the latter have emigrated to Turkey during the past ten years. The majority of Moslems (1,183,000) are ethnically Slavic and live in Bosnia and Herzegovina, Serbia

[1] *The Church in the Federal People's Republic of Yugoslavia*, Information Service Yugoslavia, Belgrade, 1959.

Table 3–3

DISTRIBUTION OF POPULATION BY RELIGIOUS ATTITUDE AND REPUBLIC, 1953 (PRELIMINARY)*

Religion	All Republics	Serbia Proper	Vojvodina	AKM (Kosmet)	Croatia	Slovenia	Bosnia & Herzegovina	Macedonia	Montenegro
	Number (*Thousands*)								
Total	16,930	4,461	1,714	809	3,914	1,463	2,844	1,304	420
Orthodox	7,012	3,669	780	175	449	4	998	747	190
Roman Catholic	5,384	51	565	25	2,878	1,231	609	5	20
Moslem	2,083	145	5	546	7	—	918	387	75
Without religious affiliation	2,086	575	225	63	499	139	293	158	134
Others	365	21	139	—	81	89	26	7	2
	Per Cent								
Total	100.0	100.0	100.0	100.0	100.0	100.0	100.0	100.0	100.0
Orthodox	41.4	82.2	45.5	21.6	11.5	0.3	35.1	57.3	45.2
Roman Catholic	31.8	1.1	33.0	3.0	73.5	84.1	21.4	0.4	4.8
Moslem	12.3	3.3	0.3	67.5	0.2	—	32.4	29.7	17.9
Without religious affiliation	12.3	12.9	13.1	7.9	12.7	9.5	10.3	12.1	31.7
Others	2.2	0.5	8.1	—	2.1	6.1	0.8	0.5	0.4

Source: Based on *Statistički Bilten*, No. 29, pp. 60–61.

* The 1953 census inquired into religious attitude but not actual membership. Total population figure does not include inhabitants of Zone B.

and Montenegro. The Islamic religious community is governed by the Supreme Vakuf Assembly and the Supreme Islamic leadership headed by the Reis-ul-ulema with headquarters in Sarajevo.

Protestant groups are widely scattered throughout Croatia, Slovenia and the Vojvodina, and make up less than one per cent of the total Yugoslav population.

The membership in the various religious groups has undergone considerable change between censuses. Although the Moslem population increased more rapidly between 1921 and 1953 than the other religions owing to a higher rate of natural increase — roughly six times that of the total population[1] — the Serbian Orthodox Church added about twice as many members. The Roman Catholic population increased very slowly, while Protestants lost more than one-third of their members, largely through emigration.

Languages

The Yugoslav languages evolved, together with Bulgarian, from Primitive Slavic and belong to the South Slavic linguistic group.[2] Over the centuries the original Primitive Slavic broke up into a number of dialects. The differences are not expressed by a clear-cut linguistic boundary between Macedonian, Serbo-Croatian and Slovenian. As Noyes emphasizes, "Each small locality, even a single isolated village, might develop its own linguistic peculiarities."[3] Cultural, dialectic, political and religious factors influenced the growth of the language. Language differences have lessened over a period of years, but are still marked in some localities.

There is no such thing as a Yugoslav language, nor is there an official language for the country. The major languages are Serbian, Croatian, Slovenian and Macedonian. Serbian is the official language of Serbia, Croatian of Croatia, Slovenian of Slovenia, Macedonian of Macedonia, and both Serbian and Croatian of Bosnia and Herzegovina. Yugoslavia, however, is no Tower of Babel. All four languages are related closely enough to enable people from different parts of the nation to understand one another, even though not always easily. And Serbian and Croatian, although by no means identical and written in different alphabets—Cyrillic for Serbian and Latin for Croatian—can for most practical purposes be considered a single language, Serbo-Croatian. This is the lingua franca of Yugoslavia. The Army provides training for all its soldiers in Serbo-Croatian, in both alphabets.

---

[1] From this high relative increase it is clear that the Moslem population will form a steadily larger share of the population in the years to come.

[2] George R. Noyes, "The Serbo-Croatian Language," in Kerner, *op. cit.*, pp. 279–301.

[3] *Ibid.*, p. 281.

Even though it is possible to speak in a general way of Serbo-Croatian, it is necessary to distinguish between Serbian and Croatian. There are not only two alphabets, but also dialects, especially Ekavština (used in Serbia) and Jekavština (used in Croatia, Bosnia and Herzegovina, and Montenegro). Again, these two dialects are by no means strictly limited by republic boundaries. The Cyrillic alphabet (devised by two Greek missionaries, Cyril and Methodius, to help teach Christianity to the Slavs) has some letters similar to the Greek plus certain others. The Latin alphabet adds diacritical marks. Serbian is close to but differs in a few letters from the Cyrillic alphabet of Russian and Bulgarian. The differences in speech between the Serbian and Croatian regions are slight. Many words differ and many are pronounced differently, but on the whole, Croats can understand Serbs without difficulty and vice versa. Both alphabets are used in Bosnia and Herzegovina, where both Serbian and Croatian are used. *Borba*, the major Communist newspaper, is published in Cyrillic in Belgrade and in Latin in Zagreb.

Slovenian has something in common with Slovak and is more akin to Russian than to Serbo-Croatian. Most Slovenes and Serbo-Croats understand each other, but sometimes with difficulty. The Latin alphabet is used for Slovenian.

Macedonian is spoken by the Macedonians and has received much attention since the organization of the people's republic of Macedonia, in postwar Yugoslavia. Before the war Macedonian was officially considered a Serbian dialect. It has a comparatively brief literary history;[1] a grammar and dictionary was introduced only in 1945. Macedonian is close to Bulgarian and uses the Cyrillic alphabet.

The large number of national minorities speak many different languages. The largest minority, the Albanians, generally speak the Gegan dialect of the Albanian language.[2] Many Albanians also speak Macedonian or Turkish. The Magyars, the second largest minority, speak Hungarian but most are fluent in Serbo-Croatian and often in German and Rumanian as well. The mother tongue of the Turks is Turkish, but here again most are bilingual.

Peoples and Their Customs

The Yugoslav peoples throughout their history have been much influenced by their neighbors and conquerors. Societal organizations, national customs, songs and dances, apparel, dwellings, furniture, occupations and food show many traditional influences, especially in communities far from the main stream of civilization. The rich and varied folk customs have been preserved

---

[1] Radmila Ugrinova, Blaže Koneski and others, *The Macedonian Literary Language*, Jugoslavija, Belgrade, 1959.

[2] The Tosca dialect is spoken by a small minority around Lake Ohrid.

in the hamlets and villages. Only with the building of new roads, the slow and steady penetration of emigrants visiting their former homes, the increasing number of foreign tourists and the industrialization of the countryside will old-established customs undergo modifications or die out.

The South Slav peasant families lived in groups known as *zadruga*, or joint family units.[1] The origin of these peasant societies can be traced back to the early tribal organizations. Many different kinds exist, but the societal organization can be broadly described as "a household composed of two or more biological or small families closely related by blood or adoption, owning its means of production communally, producing and consuming its means of livelihood jointly, and regulating the control of its property, labor and livelihood communally."[2] The old *zadruga* was usually a self-contained social unit. It was often a large establishment, sometimes comprising as many as 200 persons, related in one way or another. Because of the change from an autarchy to a money and market economy and from a largely pastoral to a largely crop-type agriculture, this type of *zadruga* became disorganized by the end of the nineteenth century, and large-scale emigration to towns and overseas led to its gradual disappearance. Family farms, amounting to family cooperatives — also called *zadruga* — took the place of the older institution, and many of them remain, especially in the interior valleys and in parts of Serbia and Croatia.[3]

The types of villages and houses of the peasants are a dependable guide to both the past history and the geography of the countryside. Rural villages can be classified generally in two main categories: (1) scattered houses surrounded by a fruit and vegetable garden and separated from each other by small patches of woods or fields in such a way that the houses at the extremes of the village may be as much as an hour's walk apart; (2) houses separated only by a small farmyard and clustered along the main street and a few side streets. People of different religions live either in the same village but in separate quarters, each with its own type of buildings, or in separate villages. A village may have a Moslem quarter, a Serbian Orthodox quarter or, in rarer cases, a Roman Catholic quarter.[4] The town hall (*opštinski dom*) and the church or mosque are usually in the center of the village. The slender minarets

[1] For the most critical and authoritative discussion of the *zadruga* see Jozo Tomasevich, *Peasants, Politics and Economic Change in Yugoslavia*, Stanford University Press, Stanford, 1955, pp. 178–202.

[2] Philip E. Mosely, "The Peasant Family: the Zadruga, or Communal Joint-Family in the Balkans and Its Recent Evolution," in Caroline F. Ware (ed.), *The Cultural Approach to History*, Columbia University Press, New York, 1940, p. 95.

[3] The term *zadruga*, in the sense of an agricultural collective, is also applied at present to mean a cooperative farming organization.

[4] For a detailed description see Olive Lodge, "Villages and Houses in Yugoslavia," *Geography*, June 1936, pp. 94–106.

of the mosque always dominate the Moslem village scene. The inn (*kafana*) is the traditional meeting place where the men drink their coffee, wine and *rakija* (made from plums) and talk about their affairs.

Houses are built from local materials; their structure varies with the kind of material used, with climate and terrain and with the traditions of the locality. In the plains, houses are usually built of clay; in the mountains, of wood. Houses of stone are typical in the karst region and the Adriatic littoral. In the lowlands of the Sava, Danube and Tisa rivers, long narrow houses and small flat-roofed houses are found. Sometimes these have an enclosed yard. Many variations are found all over the country. The typical Serbian house has one story, and an open-sided chimney in the center of the roof. Houses consist of a kitchen and one or more rooms with a balcony running along one side. Sometimes the balcony is protected by overhanging eaves, or it may have a simple roof held by posts or arches. The kitchen may be in a separate building, and several additional houses needed for the married men in the *zadruga* are all within the fenced-in yard. Another house type is prevalent in Croatia, for example in the Zagorje. Usually this is a one-story building with an overhanging thatched roof. These houses usually have only a bedroom and kitchen, although those of wealthier peasants have a second bedroom. The attic usually provides space for storage of winter food for animals, which are kept at a separate place nearby. Thatched roofs are also common in many parts of Montenegro and Serbia proper. The relationship between the stables and the main houses varies according to the region and, often, individual preferences. Houses in the snowy mountainous regions of Bosnia and Serbia have high pitched roofs.

The Moslem population, as a rule, lives much closer together than the Christian, and the two- or three-story houses usually have a balcony jutting out beyond the lower floors — the famous women's alcoves. This type of house is found both in the countryside and in the towns. The Moslem houses, especially those of the Albanian Moslems in Kosovo-Metohija, are not unlike fortresses and are known as *kule* or towers. The house and yard are protected by a strong gate and a high brick or stone wall.

Finally, there is the Alpine type of house, common in the more hilly and mountainous parts of Slovenia. This often closely resembles the typical houses of the Alps, with a pitched roof — but less sharply pitched than those mentioned above — and with considerable storage space under the main roof and with the stable often part of the main house.

Houses often are whitewashed or painted different colors. In the Vojvodina, the color usually denotes nationality, blue, for example, being used by the Slovaks.

Western clothing is nearly universal in cities and increasingly worn in rural areas. Traditional costumes may still be seen in the countryside, but they are reserved for holiday wear. The American blue jeans, favored because they are practical, are worn by many of the younger generation. Peasant clothing is colorful and is mostly of homespun materials, with linen and woolens, and sometimes leather, most popular. Notable items of apparel include the Moslem turbans, sandals with toes turned up in Turkish fashion, embroidered linen shirts and heavy felt jackets.

Coffee is the national drink of nearly all the Yugoslav peoples. While it sometimes is served in Central European fashion, with cream and sugar, in the northern and western parts of the country, "Turkish coffee," heavily sugared and boiling hot, is served in all territory formerly under Turkish domination. "Shashlik"—meat such as mutton, goat or veal, cut into small cubes and broiled over open fire on a long skewer — is popular all over the country. It was introduced by the Turks and is also common in the Near East and North Africa. Food heavily spiced with paprika and with special sauces is especially popular in the Vojvodina.

Folk songs and dances are popular all over Yugoslavia and the visitor will often see and hear a group of young and older people dance Yugoslavia's national dance, the *kola* (danced in a large circle), on the outskirts of a village on a Sunday or holiday or during some special festivities. Only the men are active, the women mainly marking time with their feet. The *kola* is accompanied by the accordion, or a modern version of the traditional instrument, the *gusle*, a guitar-like stringed instrument. Songs and dances show much foreign influence and, with the exception of Slovenia and Croatia, folk music tends to have definite oriental overtones. Modern dances, such as rock-and-roll and American jazz, are increasingly popular all over the country, especially in the cities.

Demographic Structure

The population of Yugoslavia according to the census of March 31, 1953 amounted to 16.9 million. After the annexation of Buje and Kopar (Free Territory of Trieste, Zone B) in 1954, this figure was increased by about 63,000. There were approximately 4 million households, or an average of 4.4 persons per household.[1] (Appendix Table 3-1.) The population increase between the 1953 census and March 1961 was estimated at 1.6 million, giving a total of about 18.5 million.[2] Based on the 1953 census, 81.1 per cent was

---

[1] Preliminary figures for 1961 show an average of 4.0 persons per household.

[2] Population figures, unless otherwise stated, are taken from various issues of *Statistički Godišnjak FNRJ*, prewar official statistics, and the *Statistički Bilten*, No. 203, April 1961. Data

concentrated in three provinces: Serbia (40.6 per cent), Croatia (22.6 per cent), and Bosnia and Herzegovina (17.9 per cent).

Yugoslavia's population density in 1961 was 188 persons per square mile (170 in 1953). The regional distribution of the population is most uneven. The majority of the people live in the Sava-Danube-Morava valleys, with the highest density in Serbia and the lowest in Montenegro.

Between 1920 and 1960 the population increased by 6.6 million (57 per cent), but, as a result of World War I and II losses and the large emigration before World War I, Yugoslavia ranked relatively low among European countries in its total population increase during the interwar period.[1]

It is generally agreed that about 1.1 million people, or close to 7 per cent, lost their lives during World War II as a result of military action and persecution or "indirectly as a result of abnormal health conditions." By migration or expulsion another 700,000 to 800,000 persons who lived in Yugoslavia at the outbreak of the war were lost. Included in these figures are 445,000 *Volksdeutsche*, 100,000 out of a total of 700,000 Yugoslav prisoners or workers in German war industries who chose to remain abroad, at least another 100,000 Yugoslavs who fled since the end of the war (many to the United States), and most of the 150,000 Italians living in the Julian March who emigrated to Italy when this area was transferred to Yugoslavia after the war. There were also the 40,000 Magyars who were exchanged for an equal number of Serbs and Croats from Hungary, several hundred Poles who left in 1946, and most of the surviving Jews, roughly 8,000, who emigrated to Israel. Between 1950 and 1959 over 100,000 Turkish inhabitants, mostly from Macedonia, returned to Turkey.

Not included in the figures above is the flight across the frontiers of Austria, Italy and Greece since 1955: 26,000 in 1957, 12,000 in 1958. These refugees comprise a cross section of society — peasants, skilled and unskilled workers, a small number of students and professionals; the great majority are in the age group 18-25.[2]

---

are also taken from the 1948 and 1953 Population Censuses, all published by the Federal Statistical Institute in Belgrade.

[1] These figures and the following data on war and postwar losses have been taken from various official compilations and were summarized and evaluated by Myers and Campbell, *op. cit.*, pp. 20–23. (Their compilations deal with the period 1940–1948 and sources are listed on pages 26–27.) Official Yugoslav publications often mention 1.7 million lost as a direct result of the war, excluding emigration after the war, and are not always reliable. Cf. Vladimir Dedijer, *Tito*, Simon & Schuster, New York, 1953, p. 239. See also Dolfe Vogelnik, "Demografski Gubici Jugoslavije u Drugom Svetskom Ratu" ("Demographic Losses of Yugoslavia in Second World War"), *Statistička Revija*, May 1952, pp. 15–36.

[2] *European Refugee Problems 1959*, A Special Report by the Zellerbach Commission on the European Refugee Situation, March 1959.

World War II also brought in its wake internal migrations from the mountainous areas to the urban centers and the valleys.[1] The surplus population, especially of the mountainous heartland, was encouraged to migrate into the fertile lands of the Vojvodina, vacated by the Germans, and the areas subsequently made available by confiscation and the post-1945 land reform. Serbs and Croats from the poorer areas of their republics and members of large households also migrated to the Vojvodina in the early postwar years.[2] The 1953 census reflects these migrations, with the highest percentage coming into Serbia (6.8 per cent of the total population were recent immigrants), and the highest percentage of emigration from Montenegro (21.5 per cent) and Bosnia and Herzegovina (8.7 per cent). The 1953 census lists 62.5 per cent of the population living in place of birth as against 68.5 per cent in the 1948 census.[3]

Both the birth and death rate declined rapidly in the postwar period as compared with the prewar period. (See Fig. 3–2.) The death rate, ranging from 20.9 to 15.0 per 1,000 inhabitants between 1920 and 1940, reached its lowest point in 1958, at 9.2 deaths per 1,000. The highest rate is in Kosmet (12.9 in 1958) and the lowest in Montenegro (7.5). The birth rate ranged from 36 to 26 per 1,000 inhabitants during the prewar years and was 23.8 per 1,000 in 1958. The natural increase for the country as a whole in 1958 was 14.6 per 1,000 inhabitants, but regional differences, as shown in Figure 3–3, are great. The average for the whole postwar period amounted to 15 per 1,000 inhabitants a year, or approximately one million people for every three and a half to four years.

Of particular significance is the rapid decline of the death rate among infants (those under one year). The prewar infant death rate ranged between 132 and 165 per 1,000. The rate was 166 in 1953 and dropped to 86 in 1958. Infant deaths amounted to 26.5 per cent of all deaths in 1953. They declined to 22.2 per cent in 1958. Still this rate was larger than in most western European countries. The average life expectancy in 1952–1954 was 56.9 years for males and 59.3 years for females, a slight improvement over prewar years.

[1] See Miloš Macura, *Stanovništvo i Radna Snaga kao Činioci Privrednog Razvoja Jugoslavije* (*Population and Labour-Force as Factors of Economic Development of Yugoslavia*), Ekonomska Biblioteka 7, Belgrade, 1958, for a discussion of the postwar migrations in the period 1948–1953 and their effect on economic developments in Yugoslavia. Macura is Vice Director of the Federal Statistical Institute of Yugoslavia.

[2] In all 41,633 new families with close to 250,000 members came to the region. Vladimir Djurić, "Changements de Structure de la Population dans la Vojvodina" ("Changes in the Structure of the Population in the Vojvodina"), *Recueil de Travaux de l'Institut de Géographie* (in Serbian with French abstract), III, Belgrade, 1956, pp. 3–13, and Branislav Bukurov, "Poreklo Stanovništva Vojvodina" ("Origin of the Population of the Vojvodina"), *Matica Srpska* (Posebna Izdanja), Novi Sad, 1957.

[3] The internal migrations included 1.3 million people or an average of 250,000 a year between the census years 1948 and 1953.

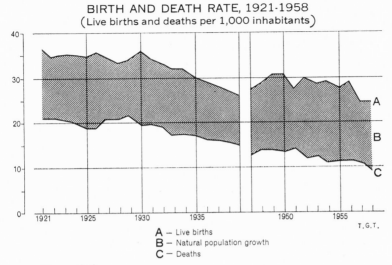

BIRTH AND DEATH RATE, 1921-1958
(Live births and deaths per 1,000 inhabitants)

A — Live births
B — Natural population growth
C — Deaths

Figure 3–2
SOURCE: Compiled by Federal Statistical Institute, Belgrade.

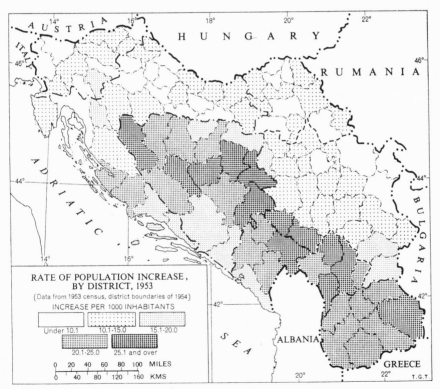

RATE OF POPULATION INCREASE,
BY DISTRICT, 1953
(Data from 1953 census, district boundaries of 1954)
INCREASE PER 1000 INHABITANTS

Under 10.1   10.1-15.0   15.1-20.0

20.1-25.0   25.1 and over

0   20   40   60   80   100   MILES
0   40   80   120   160   KMS

Figure 3–3
SOURCE: *Statistički Godišnjak FNRJ*, 1956, p. 414.

Generally speaking, the fertility rate has declined in spite of a rising number of marriages. The result has been smaller families, even though the total number of families with children increased between the prewar and postwar years. The number of children born per 1,000 women of child-bearing age in 1957 amounted to 72 as against 143 in 1921, 112 in 1939, and 106 in 1953. The average number of people per household in Yugoslavia at the last census was 4.3 members, but this average fluctuates in the different republics — from 3.7 in Slovenia to 5.3 in Macedonia. The size of the family has been decreasing for many years. In Croatia, for example, there were an average of 3.8 people per household in 1953 as compared to 8.4 in 1857. In Serbia proper the average number of people per household declined from 7.0 in 1910 to 4.5 in 1953.

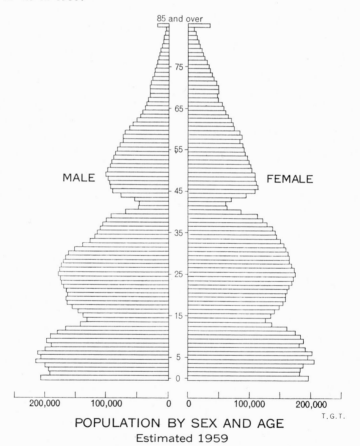

POPULATION BY SEX AND AGE
Estimated 1959

Figure 3–4

SOURCE: Federal Statistical Institute, *Statistical Pocket-Book of Yugoslavia, 1959*, Belgrade, 1959, p. 18.

The sex and age structure of the population shows the impact of World Wars I and II, as may be seen from Fig. 3–4. The disproportion between the sexes — 1,064 females to 1,000 males at the 1953 census — is the most apparent result. Females outnumber males in all age groups above 24 years, but this disproportion is slowly declining: there were 1,081 females to 1,000 males in 1948, 1,064 to 1,000 in 1953. Again, regional variations are large: at the 1953 census Kosmet had 961 females to each 1,000 males; Slovenia and Croatia, 1,115.[1]

Table 3–4
POPULATION BY AGE, 1931 AND 1953

Age Group	1931		1953	
	Number (*Thousands*)	Per Cent	Number (*Thousands*)	Per Cent
Total	13,935	100.0	16,936	100.0
Below 15 years	4,825	34.6	5,160	30.5
15–29	3,832	27.5	4,914	29.0
30–44	2,486	17.8	2,906	17.2
45–64	2,052	14.7	2,944	17.4
65 years and over	740	5.4	1,012	6.0

Source: Compiled from official statistics.

Changes in the age structure of the population are indicated in Table 3–4. The impact of both World Wars is clearly seen in the age group 30–44 years: 59.6 per cent of the total population in 1953 was below 29 years of age; for the male population alone the percentage was 61.7; for the female, 57.4. Comparing the age structure with that of other European countries, Yugoslavia ranks high in the age group below 15 years, is average in the age groups between 15 and 64 and very low in the age group 65 years and over. The regional variations found in birth and death rates obtain also for age structure. The relatively large number in the age groups below 29 years is important for the economic development of the country, since it indicates a substantial population of working age and a dependable labor supply in the future.

[1] Macura, *op. cit.*, pp. 105–107.

THE CLIMB TO

STATEHOOD

Few nations have had such a turbulent and romantic past as Yugoslavia. Although a Yugoslav state did not exist until 1918, the South Slavs comprising it have had a long, colorful history. An understanding of it is essential to an understanding of the country as it is today.

Yugoslav history has had two main motifs: national-religious conflict among the peoples occupying the land; and struggle for freedom from foreign domination. These two strands of history are intertwined. Long foreign domination led to a general economic and social backwardness and to marked unevenness of development between regions. Ethnic-religious conflict made the struggle against foreign oppression more difficult. The two factors together helped produce a fiery nationalism, and they established preconditions for the peculiar development of Yugoslav Communism.

The several South Slav tribes found their way into the area between the Danube and the Adriatic in the sixth and seventh centuries, having migrated southward and westward over the Carpathians. Those that went South — the modern Serbs and Macedonians[1] — came under the influence of Byzantium, from which they accepted Christianity. They thus became Orthodox Catholics. The tribes that went westward — primarily the modern Croats and Slovenes — early came under Germanic and Hungarian influences, and through them became Roman Catholics.

In ancient times, particularly before the schism between Rome and Constantinople, the South Slavs lived peaceably enough side by side. The major

---

[1] The modern Bulgars are also South Slavs, but at the time of the Slav entry into southeastern Europe the Bulgars were an Asiatic people; over the centuries they became completely absorbed by the Slavs.

46

conflict later concerned primarily the Orthodox Serbs and the Roman Catholic Croats, despite their near identity of language and ethnic origins. The Slovenes, Roman Catholic but differentiated by a separate — although related — language, have played a more or less passive role politically on the side of the Croats. The Orthodox Macedonians, having a still different language and lacking a separate cultural history of their own, have been apart from the main controversy among the South Slavs, although involved in another — concerning their own self-determination.

The Slovenes

The Slovenes had been engulfed by the medieval empire of Charlemagne as early as the eighth century. Remaining completely under Germanic domination until the end of World War I, they never developed into a nation in the modern sense of the term. Organized life and culture were Germanic and the religion was Roman Catholic. The masses of the people — peasants under serfdom — were, of course, Slavs, who spoke Slovenian. The distance that separated them from their masters was so great that they felt little identity with the political society. There were no elite groups to foster a feeling of Slovenian nationalism, and the Roman Catholic Church had an altogether Germanic orientation.

At the same time, the culture of the Habsburg empire spilled over into Slovenia. Literacy and health standards were higher and industrialization developed there to a greater extent than anywhere else among the South Slavs, and today Slovenia is the most advanced of the Yugoslav republics. By the eighteenth century Slovenes were beginning to make distinguished contributions to a South Slav culture. This was a force in the Yugoslav movement which ultimately moved all South Slavs toward independence and unity. However, in a positive political sense, Slovenia, as a national entity, played little part in Yugoslav history until a South Slav state was founded after World War I.

Medieval Croatia

Croatia had a different history. Between the tenth and twelfth centuries an active and independent Croat state flourished. But although they had succeeded in getting out from under the Germans, who had conquered them in the ninth century, the Croats, split among themselves over the issue of papal influence, succumbed when the Magyars pressed in from the East. After their defeat in 1102, the Croatian nobles swore allegiance to King Kolman of Hungary in return for autonomous political institutions, ultimately under a Croatian *ban*, or governor.

Thus not only did Croatia have a national past and culture of its own — however short-lived — but its national identity was preserved. Although the old Croatian aristocracy gradually lost out to first the Hungarian and then the Austrian nobility, many Croat nobles were in fact strengthened by the so-called donational type of feudalism imposed by Hungary. Thus they were able to insist on the observance — at least theoretically — of "Croat state rights," which preserved a basis for later Croat nationalism.

As the Turkish invasion of Europe progressed, both Croats and Hungarians looked increasingly to Vienna for protection. After the Turks defeated the Magyars at Mohács in 1526, the Croat nobles elected Ferdinand of Austria as their king, and the Hungarians soon thereafter went under Habsburg rule. Hungarian influence, however, continued in Croatia, despite the growing role of Austria, down to World War I.

Foreign domination both aided and inhibited the growth of a Croatian culture. As elsewhere during this period, cultural development in Croatia was connected with the Church and it thus acquired a strong Austro-Hungarian influence. It was partly for this reason that in later years, when religion and nationalism in Croatia were blended, some religious-national leaders tended to see their development better served by remaining under the protection of Roman Catholic Austria-Hungary than by independence, which might expose them to the inroads of the Orthodox Church. This attitude was augmented by the relative well-being of the Croats and their feeling of Westernness in comparison with the backwardness and more Eastern orientation of the Orthodox Serbs.

The Great Serbian Empire

A more fully developed as well as a more romantic national history is found among the Serbs. The first real Serbian state dates from about 1077. Even before this, the Serbs had received Christianity via Constantinople, and their culture was, in fact, a product of Byzantium. In 1219 the Serbs were granted an independent archbishopric under their patron saint, Sava.

Under the Nemanja dynasty, the medieval Serbian state flourished. By the time of Tsar Dušan (1331–1355), the Great Serbian Empire, as it was known, with its capital at Skoplje, embraced all of Macedonia, Bulgaria, Albania and much of Greece. It was one of the great empires of the day, with a comparatively highly developed culture. (See Figure 4–1.) Dušan had proclaimed a famous Code of Laws, setting forth legal concepts of justice comparable to codes of the West. By this time, a patriarchate had been established at Peć, and Serbia had a national church.

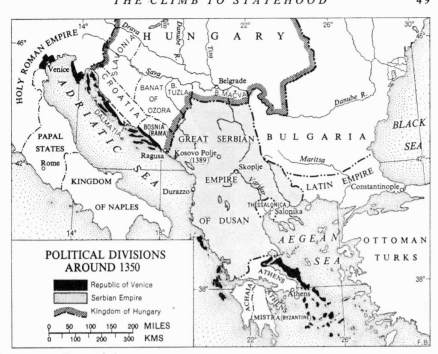

Figure 4–1

SOURCE: Base Map—*Prentice-Hall World Atlas*, pp. 70–71.

But with Dušan's death troubles began to press in on the Orthodox Serbian state. His successors were not able to hold its outer parts. Conflicts arose with the Roman Catholics, particularly the Hungarians. Gravest of all was the threat from the Ottoman Turks, who had begun their drive into Europe. Engulfing the Bulgarians, the Turks turned on the Serbs, who barred their way up into the continent.

On June 28, 1389, the Turks conquered the Serbs at the Battle of Kosovo Polje (Blackbird's Field). This was in many ways one of the great battles of history. For centuries thereafter, European affairs were in no small way concerned with the threat of the Turks. Certainly Kosovo was the decisive battle of Serbian history. The Serbian state was destroyed, its culture laid waste, the cream of its manhood put to the sword. For five hundred years thereafter, Serbia was little more than an outpost of the Turkish empire. The early period of occupation was not notably oppressive; in fact, Serbia was permitted a semi-autonomous status until 1459. From this time on, however, and especially when the janissaries began to dominate the decaying Ottoman empire, the oppression became progressively worse. All in all, during the half a millennium of Turkish domination, the Serbs were treated as probably few conquered peoples have been treated in modern times — worse, for example, than the Russians under the Mongols.[1]

A great Serbian legend — perpetuated in a folk epic — has grown up about the Battle of Kosovo Polje.[2] The date of the battle, St. Vitus Day or Vidovdan, as it is known, is still celebrated as the Serbian national holiday. According to the legend, the Serbian tsar, Lazar I, was visited on the eve of the battle by an angel in the form of a falcon. The angel offered Lazar his choice between an earthly kingdom and a heavenly kingdom: if he chose the earthly kingdom, he would defeat the Turks; if he chose the heavenly kingdom, they would defeat him. He chose the heavenly kingdom and died on the battlefield. The Serbian legend is ambiguous, however, as the defeat is also attributed to treachery on the part of Lazar's son-in-law.

Serbian Nationalism and Religion

Serbian nationalism,[3] in which the Kosovo legend has played such an important role, did not die with the medieval Serbian state. It was kept alive chiefly by the Serbian Orthodox Church.[4] A merger of religion and nationalism resulted which was perhaps more complete than any before or since, not excluding the relationship of the Russian Orthodox Church to Russian nationalism during the two hundred and fifty years under the Tartar yoke. One has only to visit the few remaining ancient Serbian monasteries, with their exquisite religious art, to see it. After the Battle of Kosovo Polje, for example, the widow of Tsar Lazar gave the Serbian Patriarch two gigantic candles, perhaps fifteen feet high and a foot in width. She told him to guard them unlit in some Serbian holy place until the day when Serbia regained its freedom. On that day, five hundred years later, the candles were lit. They can still be seen, well preserved, in the Dečani monastery, near Peć, where trappings of ancient Serbian state glory are such that it is difficult to say if the place is primarily a religious or a national monument.

The Montenegrins

But while the son of Lazar gave in to the Turks and received some sort of status, one group of Serbs refused to be conquered. They took off to the

[1] It is interesting to note the bitterness reflected in Serbian religious art after Kosovo, especially as seen in the faces of Christ and the Heavenly Host. The most developed of its time, in many ways anticipating the Renaissance, Serbian religious art went into a decline after the Turkish conquest.

[2] A contingent of Croats is believed to have fought with the Serbs at Kosovo, but is not mentioned in the legend. The Croats recognize the importance of the battle but feel that the Serbs exaggerate it.

[3] Strictly speaking, "nationalism" is a comparatively modern term growing out of the nation-state organizations of the nineteenth and twentieth centuries. It is used here broadly to connote a strong sense of ethnic-religious unity and love of homeland.

[4] The Serbian Church maintained its identity despite the fact that the Turks put it under Greek administration. The Phanariots, as the Greek administrators were called, tried but failed to shift the church away from its Serbian national orientation.

mountain fastness of Crna Gora — Black Mountain — and never surrendered. These Serbs became known as Montenegrins. Their history, at least up
until the end of the nineteenth century, was one of almost continuous war for
survival, their livelihood coming from tilling the few patches of barren soil
they could find. The Montenegrins fought the Turks to a man, individually
and collectively. Almost without exception, male Montenegrins were warriors
or guerillas. Fighting was not only an accepted occupation for a Montenegrin;
it was *the* occupation. All this was encompassed in a fiery Montenegrin nationalism rather than a Serbian nationalism. As with the Serbs, religion was
an important factor. The Montenegrins were all Orthodox, and their early
leaders were, in fact, priests. Government in Montenegro began and long
continued as a theocracy, the head of the church being also the head of the
state.

The Serbs of Serbia, although engulfed, also continued to harass the Turks.
For centuries their guerilla activities were largely unorganized. The profession
of outlaw, or *haiduk*, was a proper and respected one, and killing the Turks
and robbing their emissaries was a glorified calling, blessed by the Church and
respected by society.

Under such conditions of intense religious nationalism, oriented toward
violence, both Serbs and Montenegrins developed traits among which mod-
esty, restraint, order and respect for authority were conspicuously lacking. In
later years, when the major problem no longer involved warring against the
Turks but living in peace and cooperation with their fellow Slavs, these traits
served them to less advantage.

The warlike qualities of the Serbs and Montenegrins were exhibited not only
against the Turks but also often against each other in family feuds. This
emphasis on the family, or patriarchal, organization of society has led some
writers to distinguish between the culture of these peoples, which they refer to
as *dinaric*, and the more democratic culture of the *zadruga* society, especially
as found in the Croatian Plains.[1] However, the *zadruga*, a sort of collective
farm on which several families lived and farmed in common, was found
among all the South Slavs, even though it may have varied in its internal
organization in different sections of the country. In any event, historical
differences alone go far toward explaining the apparently greater propensity
to violence and warlike behavior of the Serbs and Montenegrins.[2]

After the Turkish conquest, the center of Serbian life gradually shifted
northward. The Macedonians, now a Slavic people by the process of absorp-

[1] See, for example, Dinko Tomasic, *Personality and Culture in Eastern European Politics*,
George W. Stewart, New York, 1948.

[2] On the other hand, the events of World War II, if nothing else, indicate that such characteristics are not the monopoly of any part of Yugoslavia, either ethnic or geographical.

tion, had long since lost their cultural identity with the empires of Philip and Alexander. Without the spur of a national church and regarded by the Porte simply as an extension of Turkey, Macedonia vegetated under Ottoman rule. Gradually the various parts of Macedonia became identified with the more vigorous border societies of Serbia, Bulgaria and Greece, among which it was finally divided in 1912. The division paved the way for some later problems.

The Ottoman successes against the South Slavs resulted not only from Turkish prowess and, as the Serbian legend has it, from heavenly intervention. The conflict between the Orthodox and Roman Catholics was also a factor. The split between the Greek and Latin churches, which erupted in open war during the thirteenth century, left a legacy of hatred. Some Orthodox Slavs preferred the Turks to the Roman Catholic Magyars, who might have assisted them. After the Battle of Kosovo, Hungary dominated Belgrade, and for a while kept the Turks out. Later the Austrians for some years also engaged the Turks. But a not untypical reaction was seen at Smederevo, where Orthodox forces surrendered the important Danubian fortress to the Turks in 1459 rather than accept Roman Catholic rule.

It was not until after the Turkish defeat of the Austrians in 1690 that there occurred a migration of a considerable number of Serbs to Hungary, led by the Patriarch Arsenije. Known as *Prečani*, meaning those on the other side of the river, these Serbs acquired fertile lands and, despite some Roman Catholic persecution, achieved a greater level of prosperity and culture than their more heavily oppressed brethren under the Turks. With their own Patriarchate, these *Prečani* Serbs helped keep Serbian nationalism alive and were to play an important role later in moves for Serbian independence.

Conflict over Bosnia and Herzegovina

The province of Bosnia and Herzegovina to the west already had been an arena of conflict between the Orthodox and Roman Catholic religions. The Serbs and Hungarians had fought over it, as the Serbs and Croats were to do later. The Bosnians themselves, principally from the same stock as the Serbs and Croats, had early accepted the Christian heresy of Bogomilism, which had come to them via Macedonia. Both Orthodox Catholics and Roman Catholics persecuted the Bogomil Bosnians, who, in turn, rejected both. When the Turks approached, many Bosnians became Moslems in an effort to get Turkish protection from both Christian sects. When the king of Bosnia embraced Roman Catholicism in the 1440's, resentment among the Bosnians, Bogomil and Moslem alike, was a factor in Bosnia's failure to resist the Turks, who conquered it in 1463. Almost at once, many Bosnian nobles and serfs accepted

Islam, the nobles thus preserving some of their property and power and the serfs acquiring land — or *čiftlik* — free of feudal obligation.

Thus a sizable proportion of the Slavic people of Bosnia and Herzegovina became Moslems and tended to identify themselves with Turkey rather than with the Slavic lands. They constituted something of an elite group compared to the remaining Bosnians — Orthodox and Roman Catholic, including emigrants from Serbia and Croatia — who remained in serf status. Although religious and political oppression of Christian Slav by Moslem Slav did not reach major proportions until much later, nevertheless the foundation for fratricide was laid.

Pan-Slavism and the Yugoslav Idea

During the main period of development in the West, all the South Slavs except those in Montenegro were thus under foreign domination. As the mighty Slav nation of Russia arose in the East and came in conflict with both Turks and Austro-Hungarians, it was not surprising that a movement for liberation and unity appeared. The first articulate exponent of Pan-Slavism was a seventeenth century Croat priest, Juraj Križanić. At first the idea was more romantic and spiritual than practical and political — a union of all the Slav peoples, north and south. This concept of Pan-Slavism encountered two serious snags. Since a part of the Slavs were under Austrian rule, liberation of all of them ran counter to Russia's alliances with Austria. Since these Slavs were generally Roman Catholic, it also encountered the opposition of the Russian Orthodox Church.

But the idea of South Slav unity — or Yugoslavism — continued. In the late eighteenth century the Serb Dositej Obradović, pioneer of the Serbian literary language, caught the vision. The concept developed especially among the Slovenes and Croats. It received great impetus when Napoleon's Illyrian Republic brought them under united political rule for the first time, although "Illyrianism" itself was to grow into a "Greater Croatia" movement. As far as Russia was concerned, however — and real liberation was possible only with Russian aid — the Slovenes and Croats, as well as the Slav peoples to the north, were excluded from any practical application of Pan-Slavism. Ironically, it was from Slovenia and Croatia that the main drive for the Yugoslav movement was to come.

Serbian Independence

The spirit of independence burned fiercest among the Serbs. In 1804, under the famous Djordje Petrović, known as Karadjordje or Black George, the Serbs of Šumadija, the Belgrade district, revolted and drove out the Turks.

They successfully resisted until 1813. Two years later, under a different leader, Miloš Obrenović, the Serbs revolted again, this time forcing the Sultan to grant them limited autonomy.

It was not, however, until the Russians decisively defeated the Turks in Eastern Europe in 1878 — five hundred years after Kosovo — that the Serbs finally regained their independence. Serbian independence sparked the Yugoslav movement. But under the fiery Serb nationalists, proud of their long suffering as well as their successes, the new state now became attached to the idea not of Pan-Slavism but of Pan-Serbianism. Its origins in dreams of Dušan's medieval empire, the goal was to wrench from the Turks the remainder of old Serbia, including Macedonia and Bosnia and Herzegovina, and also annex the Vojvodina from Hungary.

Serb-Croat cooperation had flourished briefly during the Revolution of 1848, when the Serbs supported the Croats against the Hungarians. But now it began to fall by the wayside, in part for religious reasons. The Orthodox Church, hotly anti-Roman Catholic, was able to give Pan-Serbianism a special Orthodox flavor which brought it more and more into conflict with the Roman Catholic Croats, who were convinced that Bosnia was theirs if anybody's.

As a result of the agreement of 1868 between Austria-Hungary and Croatia, the Croats became more integrated with the Habsburg empire, and the Austro-Hungarians were able to play on Croat Roman Catholic hostility to Orthodoxy to help accomplish this. The major Croat national leader at the time was the famous Bishop of Zagreb, J. J. Štrosmajer. Although Bishop Štrosmajer was an ardent exponent of the Yugoslav idea, his Church connections were enough to arouse Orthodox Serbian opposition. On the other hand, a wide segment of Croats looked askance at Serbia, not only because of religion and conflicting nationalist claims but also from a sense of superiority bred by the less advanced Serbian cultural and economic development. Envy at the wide acclaim given Serbian valor against the Turks doubtless was also a factor.

Serbia vs. Austria

The Serb-Croat conflict as it concerned Bosnia and Herzegovina worsened when that province came under Austrian rule. While the Turks had oppressed both Orthodox Serbs and Roman Catholic Croats in Bosnia, it was not unnatural, once Serbia loomed as a menace to the Turkish position, that the Serbs were treated more stringently and the Croats favored. Ill feeling between the two religionists was thereby engendered. Because of this and because they had no wish to come under Orthodox rule, the Croats of Bosnia did not look with enthusiasm on Belgrade's aims. When Roman Catholic Austria took over, the Croats were favored still more. As Vienna was inclined to see in every Bosnian Serb a potential revolutionary — and with reason — even Moslems were often accorded better treatment than Serbs. Consequently Serbian passions, both in Bosnia and in Serbia proper, burned more fiercely than ever.

The twin nationalisms of Serbia and Croatia were blended inextricably with their respective religions. What counted in determining who was a Serb and who was a Croat was more religion than place of residence or ethnic origin. This was particularly true in Bosnia, where it was virtually impossible to untangle the population on a strictly ethnic basis, and in Croatia, where several hundred thousand persons of Orthodox faith, Serbs or not, were considered Serbs. The Croatian Serbs, despite frequent persecution at the hands of Croat nationalists, became prominent in the Yugoslav movement.

In Serbia, during the latter part of the nineteenth century, the Obrenović dynasty followed a policy of subservience to Austria. In 1903, King Alexander, Queen Draga and their entourage were brutally murdered, the dynasty deposed and the heirs of Karadjordje again recalled to the throne.[1] The new King, Peter I, threw in his lot with Russia, and Serbia began to challenge not only the Turks but also the Austrian position in southeastern Europe. This in turn encouraged those anti-Austrian Croats who hoped for an independent Croatia as well as those whose ideal of Yugoslav unity rose above Roman Catholic particularism.

It became clear that the Dual Monarchy and Serbia, backed by Moscow, had conflicting aims in southeastern Europe. When, after the Balkan Wars of 1912–1913, Austria deprived the Serbs of some of the spoils of victory, tensions reached a high point. They exploded in Bosnia with the assassination of the Austrian Archduke, Franz Ferdinand, in 1914, and led to World War I.

There is no greater testimony to the intensity of Serbian nationalist passions than the reverence in which the Archduke's assassin, a Bosnian Serb named Gavrilo Princip, is still held. On the corner where Franz Ferdinand was shot in Sarajevo there is today the Gavrilo Princip Museum. It borders the Gavrilo Princip bridge. Outside, Princip's footprints are embedded in the concrete sidewalk at the spot where he stood when he fired his pistol at the Archduke.

World War I and the Yugoslav Movement

The Serbs, joined by the Montenegrins, demonstrated almost incredible valor and heroism during World War I, initially driving out the Austrian

---

[1] The *coup d'état* not only concerned the hostility of the pro-Russian Serbs to Austria but also involved the King's highly unpopular marriage.

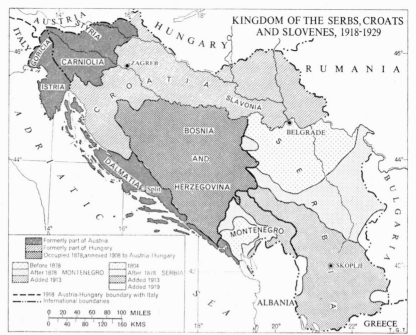

Figure 4–2

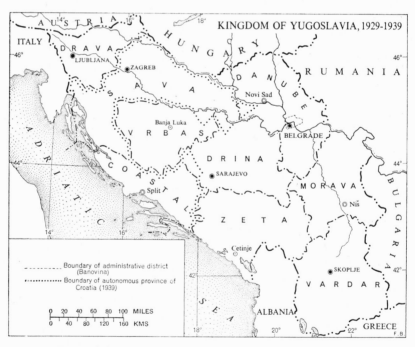

Figure 4–3

56

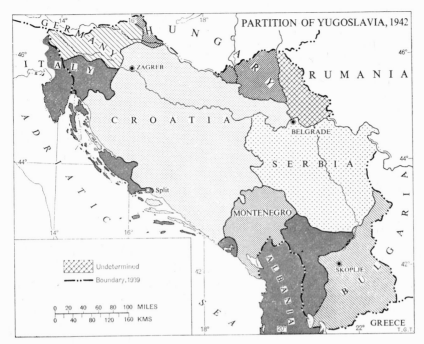

Figure 4–4

Figure 4–5

57

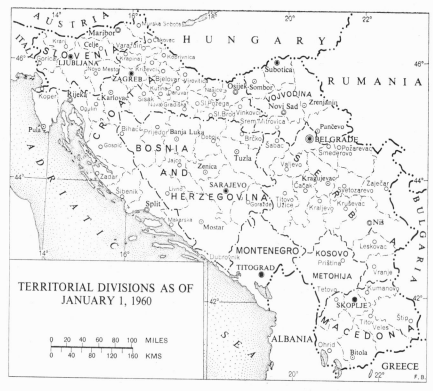

TERRITORIAL DIVISIONS AS OF
JANUARY 1, 1960

0   20   40   60   80   100   MILES

0   40   80   120   160   KMS

Figure 4–6

SOURCE: *Statistički Godišnjak FNRJ*, 1961.

invaders. Even when vastly superior German forces became involved, the Serbs refused to surrender. Led by old King Peter and his son Alexander, they retreated across Serbia, Montenegro and Albania to the Adriatic coast. The major battle of the war in Serbia took place on the historic field of Kosovo. The survivors, evacuated to the island of Corfu, later joined Allied forces in Salonika and played a leading role in eventually driving the enemy from Serbian soil. The great fight put up by the Serbs won them the acclaim of all South Slavs, irrespective of religion or nationality.

Serbian wartime propaganda espoused South Slavic unity, and an all-Yugoslav legion, including Slovenes and Croats, fought with the Serbian army. The Yugoslav idea now quickly came to the fore, the more so as the likelihood of a collapse of the Austro-Hungarian empire meant that something would have to be done about Slovenia and Croatia. As early as 1915 a Yugoslav Committee was formed under the presidency of Dr. Ante Trumbić, a Dalmatian Croat, proclaiming as its aim a new state embracing all South

Slavs. In 1918, shortly before the Armistice, a National Council of Slovenes, Croats and Serbs was organized in Zagreb, and the Croatian parliament, ending its eight-hundred-year tie with Hungary, voted to transfer its powers to the Council.

These, however, were mainly efforts of the Austro-Hungarian Slavs — those in Slovenia and Croatia. They aimed clearly at a federal-type state with carefully delineated autonomy for the three major South Slav ethnic groups.[1] The Serbian government remained cool to these overtures. If there was to be union at all, the Serb leaders desired that the Slovenes and Croats should unite into a Greater Serbia. Only reluctantly did they sign the Declaration of Corfu, embodying the principle of a new state in which all the South Slav peoples would be equal though under the Serbian monarchy. The state, created late in 1918, was called not Yugoslavia but the Kingdom of the Serbs, Croats and Slovenes. (See Figure 4–2.)

The Serb-Croat Conflict

From the beginning, the new state ran afoul of the conflict between the Serbs and Croats. The Croatian delegates to the Constituent Assembly, under the peasant leader Stjepan Radić, refused to vote for the highly centralized constitution. This constitution, proclaimed in 1921 without their vote, was more a victory for the idea of Greater Serbia than for Yugoslavia. Significantly, it was proclaimed on June 28, Vidovdan, the Serbian national holiday, and was known as the Vidovdan Constitution.

Not only were there such issues as Croatian autonomy and the Croatian claim to Bosnia, but the whole country was desperately poor. The extreme underdevelopment of much of Serbia, Montenegro, Bosnia and Macedonia imposed an additional strain. Furthermore, with the populace expecting revolutionary changes and the Orthodox population traditionally sympathetic to Russia, a vigorous Communist Party emerged to harass the government. In addition to winning municipal elections in both Belgrade and Zagreb, the Communists polled some 200,000 votes in the 1920 election and won 58 out of 419 seats in the Skupština, or parliament, becoming the third largest party. Quickly the regime denied the Communist deputies their seats and outlawed the Party. It did not appear again as a force in Yugoslavia until the eve of World War II.

The new state amounted to a Serbian hegemony, with not only king and court but also administration, army and police predominantly Serbian, and

[1] For an interesting discussion of the founding of Yugoslavia—objective though from a Croat point of view—see P. D. Ostović, *The Truth about Yugoslavia*, Roy Publishers, New York, 1952. Mr. Ostović was prominent in the Yugoslav movement.

therefore tending to be anti-Croat. Under a government dominated by Serbs, Croats had less to say about their affairs than before the war. And the Orthodox Church had certain rights denied the Roman Catholics. Croat passions, not unnaturally, began to burn.

Despite the seemingly good intentions of King Alexander, the Serbs handled the problem with a remarkable lack of finesse. By 1923–1924, Croatia was virtually in a state of insurrection. Its leading political party, the Croat Peasant Party, was outlawed, and its leading political figure, Radić, imprisoned.

The Croat Opposition

The Croat Peasant Party had been founded by Stjepan Radić and his brother Antun in 1905. It was strongly nationalistic and at first anti-clerical. In theory it was radical in somewhat the same way as the pre-1917 Social Revolutionary Party in Russia. Its concept of the peasantry was romantic and, despite the efforts of some able young economists like Rudolf Bicanić, it lacked a practical economic program. Although many of its leaders remained sincere spokesmen for peasant interests, as time went on the Party became dominated by urban middle-class elements, who in fact opposed much of what the Party stood for. Radić himself, both anti-capitalist and anti-socialist, at one time appeared to be enamored of the Bolshevik experiment in Russia, which he later rejected. Despite its confused ideology, the Croat Peasant Party was the dominant force in Croatia and the major opposition party in Yugoslavia during the interwar period.

Released from prison in 1925, Radić entered the government as minister of education, only to resign a year later. Two years thereafter, an ardent Serb patriot — in fact a Montenegrin — shot and killed him during a debate in the Skupština. Radić's successor, Vladimir Maček, now demanded Croat autonomy and a federal constitution. A rump parliament met in Zagreb. Alexander's answer was to suspend the constitution, put Maček in jail and proclaim a royal dictatorship. A few months later, in October 1929, the King changed the name of the state to the Kingdom of Yugoslavia and established administrative districts cutting across the traditional ethnic-national boundaries. (See Figure 4–3.)

Lack of Democracy

The Kingdom of the Serbs, Croats and Slovenes was never a democracy in the Western sense. Yugoslavia now became little more than a police state under Serbian direction. The term "Communist" was loosely applied to all and any critics of the regime. While there was, in fact, no real Communist danger as such, there was nevertheless a revolutionary potential throughout the land, and if it were not to be met by needed reform it had to be met by a strong hand.

For one thing, there was among the Yugoslavs little experience with political democracy as the term is understood today. The Slovenes had lacked self-government altogether, and virtually the same was true of the Croats. Although Serbia had been independent for some decades, in the early period, at least, it had "free peasant property but not a free peasantry."[1] In later years, parliamentary forms, and even the concept of representative government, were more firmly established; yet many feel that the masses achieved neither legal security nor economic freedom in any meaningful sense.[2] In the way stood not only government bureaucracy and corruption but also the extreme backwardness of the population as a whole.[3]

Yugoslav unity did not alter matters much. The *zadruga*, long the nucleus of South Slav culture, had steadily disintegrated during the nineteenth century. Taxes, always the chief peasant complaint, had increased markedly. It has been estimated that in 1931–1932 taxes on the peasant population amounted to 50 per cent of total estimated cash income.[4]

This tax burden fell at a time when the world-wide depression was crippling agricultural economies like that of Yugoslavia. Moreover, Yugoslavia, sadly underdeveloped as a result of its long foreign domination, did not possess a real capitalist system that might have relieved the peasantry through industrialization. As the outstanding economic historian of Yugoslavia, Jozo Tomasevich, has remarked, "Capitalism destroyed the social and economic system that the peasantry had developed through a centuries-old process of adaptation, without replacing it with another which would have enabled the peasantry to improve its economic lot."[5]

It is not surprising, therefore, that an astute Western observer considered that despite the absence of a strong Communist party, there was a strong revolutionary potential in Yugoslavia between the wars and, even, great sympathy with "Communism."[6]

Not only did King Alexander's dictatorship not alleviate any of the conditions of social unrest but it substantially exacerbated national disunity.

---

[1] Slobodan Jovanović, "Prince Miloš and the Peasant Problem," *Sociološki Pregled*, Vol. I, p. 26.

[2] See, for instance, Jozo Tomasevich, *Peasants, Politics, and Economic Change in Yugoslavia*, Stanford University Press, Stanford, 1955, especially pp. 41–42.

[3] According to the 1921 census, there was 51.5 per cent illiteracy in Yugoslavia as a whole. The range was from 8.8 per cent in Slovenia to 83.8 per cent in Macedonia. The figure for Serbia was 65.4 per cent and for Croatia 32.2 per cent.

[4] Tomasevich, *op. cit.*, p. 702.

[5] *Ibid.*, p. 213.

[6] Hugh Seton-Watson, *Eastern Europe Between the Wars, 1918–1941*, Cambridge University Press, Cambridge, 1946, pp. 256–265.

Croatia fared especially badly, both at the hands of Alexander's Serbian-dominated police and at the hands of an extra-legal Serbian nationalist organization, the Četnici.[1] Harsh treatment stimulated the growth of the Croatian nationalist organization, the Ustaša, which came into existence following the murder of Radić. In both organizations overtones of ultra-nationalism and religion were mixed. As a foretaste of the mutual slaughter that was to follow, roving bands of Četnici and Ustaše frequently collided in armed conflict. Croatian patriots were the favorite Četnik targets.

Assassination of Alexander

King Alexander, although authoritarian and inflexible, seems to have realized that the dictatorship was a failure practically and that it should evolve into a form which would give Croatia autonomy. But before he could do anything about it he was assassinated. Alexander went to France to discuss with French Foreign Minister Louis Barthou a possible change in Yugoslavia's firm anti-Soviet policy. Those who had an interest in blocking such a change were obvious and many. The actual assassination appears to have been arranged by a combination of Bulgarian terrorists, Croatian Ustaše and the Hungarian and Italian governments. The King was shot shortly after he landed at Marseilles on October 9, 1934. With him died M. Barthou.

Since King Alexander's son, Peter, was then only eleven years old, a regency took over. It was headed by Alexander's cousin, Prince Paul. In foreign policy, Prince Paul and his Serbian ministers pursued a course that took Yugoslavia closer and closer to the Nazis. Domestically, they maintained the dictatorship, but showed some indications of compromise on the Croatian question. Responsible Croatian leaders had been shocked by Alexander's assassination, and, even though Maček was still in jail, the Croat Peasant Party offered its cooperation with the government. Maček was then released from prison. Although the Croats continued their boycott of the Skupština, Paul directed his new prime minister, the pro-fascist Serb Stojadinović, to consider collaboration with Zagreb. Instead, Stojadinović joined forces with the anti-democratic leader of the Slovene Clerical Party, Monsignor Antun Korošec, and, if anything, oppressive measures became worse.

One of the steps taken by the new government was to announce a draft Concordat with the Vatican that had been approved by Alexander before his death as a step toward rapprochement with Croatia. The move proved to be extremely unpopular in Serbia; the Orthodox clergy led a public campaign against it, and Patriarch Barnabas even threatened excommunication of gov-

[1] This is not the same as the World War II Cetnici (Chetniks, in the anglicized version). See Chapter 5.

ernment leaders if it were adopted. After seven months of heated controversy, the Skupština ratified the Concordat. Three hours later the Patriarch died, amid rumors that he had been poisoned by Roman Catholics. A conference of Roman Catholic clergy, called by Monsignor Šarić, archbishop of Sarajevo, protested the Orthodox attacks and warned that it would "defend the rights of the Catholic Church and of the six million Catholics in the state." Nevertheless, apparently in deference to Serbian opinion, Stojadinović did not submit the Concordat to the Senate, and it was allowed to die. The step begun as a means of appeasing Croat feelings in fact aroused them anew.

Maček now formed an alliance with the Serbian opposition parties and presented a more liberal program to the Prince Regent. Paul rejected it. By this time, the regime had become unpalatable to what seems to have been a clear majority of Yugoslavs, and Maček, as its chief opponent, gained in popularity. So did the idea of Serb-Croat collaboration. A crowd of 50,000 Serbs hailed Maček when he spoke in Belgrade in August 1938, denouncing police terror.

Serb-Croat Agreement and the Axis Pact

Now the rising Nazi menace began to dominate the scene. Although there was a Fascist party in Serbia, it had no popular following. In Croatia, on the other hand, the Ustaša, led by an extremist named Ante Pavelić, had acquired definite pro-Fascist leanings and was a potential fifth column. Settlement of the Croatian question was more urgent than ever. Accordingly, Paul ordered his new prime minister, Dragiša Cvetković, to reach terms with Maček forthwith. Even so, the resulting agreement — known in Yugoslavia as the *Sporazum* — was not reached until the day before the Nazi-Soviet Pact was signed and World War II was ready to break out.

The *Sporazum* failed to halt the internal discord in Yugoslavia. Although it gave an enlarged Croatia autonomy, the Croatian extremists were not satisfied. Because it gave Croatia autonomy, the Serbs were dissatisfied. In addition, in the new province, or *Banovina*, were included some 850,000 persons identified as Serbs. Maček, apparently attempting to woo Pavelić, indulged in extravagant anti-Serb propaganda, which was answered with violent anti-Croat propaganda in Serbia. The terrorist groups of the respective nationalities swung into action.

Then the Germans began to make concrete demands on Belgrade. Prime Minister Cvetković and his foreign minister, Cincar-Marković, conferred with Hitler at Berchtesgaden, and German forces moved into Bulgaria. Despite a growing revulsion in Yugoslavia at ties with Berlin, the government, on March 25, 1940, signed the Axis Tripartite Pact.

Coup d'État

At this point there occurred a dramatic turn of events, all the nuances of which are still not clear. The Yugoslav army, with popular backing in Serbia, overthrew the Cvetković government, exiled Prince Paul and installed his young nephew on the throne as Peter II. Ostensibly, this was a move in opposition to the Axis, and it was widely interpreted as such both in Yugoslavia and abroad — including Berlin. Hitler's reactions were violent, even for him, and there is little doubt that the coup hastened the German invasion.

Yet it seems clear that other factors were involved in the *coup d'état*. Many persons, Croats in particular, are convinced that it also represented a move by the Serbs — who controlled the army — against Croatian autonomy.[1] It is interesting that on April 3, 1941, seven days after the *coup*, the new government formally assured the Nazis that Yugoslavia would adhere to the Tripartite Pact. On the same day, however, the army mobilized, with the public support of Maček.

The mobilization did little good. On April 6, 1941, the Germans began their bombardment and invasion of Yugoslavia. They were joined by Italian, Hungarian and Bulgarian forces. The fighting lasted barely fourteen days. Its army ill-equipped and ill-organized and its people disaffected and torn by dissension, Yugoslavia virtually disintegrated. After surrender, young King Peter and his government fled into exile.

The day after the Axis attack, Pavelić, leader of the Ustaša, asked Mussolini's assistance in forming a separate Croat state. On April 15, 1941, "independent" Croatia was recognized by Rome and Berlin. The new puppet state included, in addition to Croatia proper, most of Bosnia and Herzegovina, Srem, Slavonia and part of Dalmatia. (See Figure 4-4.) Puppet Croatia was formally a kingdom. The throne was offered to the Italian Duke of Spoleto, but he never came to Croatia, and the reins of government were entirely in the hands of the Ustaša leaders.[2]

Creation of a Croat state was but the first act of dismemberment. Germany directly annexed two-thirds of Slovenia. Italy got almost all of the rest of it, along with most of the Adriatic coast and all of Montenegro. Italian Albania received Kosovo-Metohija and part of Macedonia, the remainder going to Bulgaria. Hungary was awarded small segments of Slovenia and Croatia and the Bačka and Baranja regions of the Vojvodina. Serbia was permitted a separate status under German control, its internal affairs handled by a govern-

---

[1] Cf. Hugh Seton-Watson, *The East European Revolution*, Methuen & Co., London, 1950, p. 66. Additional information and opinion on this score is given by Ostović, *op. cit.*, pp. 158–167.

[2] The major ones, in addition to Pavelić, were Eugene Kvaternik, head of the police; Andrija Artuković, minister of the interior; and Mile Budak, minister of education. The Ustaša regime lacked wide popularity among the rank and file of Croats. See Chapter 5.

ment led by General Milan Nedić, a former minister of war. Nedić seems to have considered himself not a collaborator but loyal to Serbia and the King, trying to make the best of a very bad situation.

Between the two World Wars, Yugoslavia was a state but never really a nation. Now, two decades after its establishment, the state vanished. Created by one war, it was destroyed by another. The same war was soon, however, to give birth to a new Yugoslavia, very different from its predecessor, yet in many ways much the same.

PART II

YUGOSLAV COMMUNISM—
SOVIET STYLE (1945-1949)

WORLD WAR II
UPHEAVALS

Yugoslavia suffered a harsh fate during World War II. Its land was ravaged by bombing, invasion and military struggle. Its people were subjected to Fascist cruelties by the Axis occupiers. At the same time the divided Yugoslavs engaged in internal conflicts which amounted to civil wars. There were two of these — one growing out of the traditional conflict between the Serbs and the Croats, which now degenerated into an orgy of torture, murder and massacre; the other involving mainly the pro-Serbian Četnik organization and the Communist-led Partisan movement. Political and military lines were often hopelessly entangled. It was not always clear who was fighting whom or for what. But the results were invariably death, suffering and destruction on a vast scale.

Almost as soon as the Yugoslav army disintegrated, a resistance movement began. It developed first out of remnants of the army — largely Serbs and Montenegrins — who took to the woods and organized themselves under a general staff colonel named Draža Mihailović. They were called Četnici, after the Serbian guerillas of former times.[1] The name was fitting because Mihailović and his followers were first of all Serbs and only secondly Yugoslavs in the broader sense. Mihailović, who soon gained recognition from the Yugoslav government-in-exile, in which he became minister of defense, saw his task as primarily that of gathering together a force that would be ready to rise up and take over when the fortunes of war turned against the Germans. He regarded himself as a protector of Serbian interests and Serbian lives. Because

---

[1] The Serbian word *četa* means a guerilla band. The Mihailović Četnici are not to be confused with the para-military Serbian patriotic organization of the same name which sprang up between the wars. This latter now served General Nedić, chief of the government organized by the Germans for Serbia during the war.

the Germans extracted merciless reprisals for opposition, Četnik strategy was to limit action to occasional sabotage and small skirmishes here and there but mostly to play a waiting game as far as the Axis occupiers were concerned.

Četnici versus Ustaše. The Četnici were early arrayed against the Ustaše, now agents not only of extreme Croatian nationalism, with strong clerical orientation, but of the Axis as well. While Fascist Croatia had a regular army, known as the *Domobranstvo*, or Home Guard, the storm-troop-like Ustaša organization was far more in evidence. The Ustaša began at once to attack with abandon all Serbs within reach, all Jews and many democratically inclined Croats. In Četnik attacks on Croats, the Mihailović men were less than careful to distinguish which were pro-Ustaša and which not. In particular, the Četnici vented their rage in Bosnia and border regions on Moslems, traditional foes of the Orthodox Serbs and now ostensibly allied with the Croats.

The conflict now, as before, was religious as well as political. It was a shocking atavism that in the twentieth century blood was often shed in attempts at forced conversions.[1] Although Četnik atrocities were many, they did not equal those of the Ustaša, perpetrated in the name of Croatia and Roman Catholicism. The contemporary Western mind has a difficult time coming to grips with all this. While some Serbs were given the choice of abandoning their Orthodox faith for Roman Catholicism or submitting to torture or death, in some cases whole village populations were herded into Orthodox churches and burned alive. These atrocities produced a frenzy of fear and hatred on both sides which led only to greater excesses.[2]

Such savagery by no means reflected the attitude of a majority of Croats, and many members of the Roman Catholic clergy inveighed against it. Nevertheless, the Ustaša, as a Croatian nationalist movement, was by that very fact also a Roman Catholic religious movement. Certain priests participated in the tortures and massacres, and some members of the hierarchy endorsed them. Although the leading Croatian prelate, Archbishop Stepinac, was vicar general of the Croat armed forces, he protested — in vain — to the head of the Ustaša, Pavelić, against the excesses. That Monsignor Stepinac, like so many other Croats, supported the Ustaša regime had less to do with ideology than with the inextricable union between the Roman Catholic Church in Croatia and Croatian nationalism, which, by the fates of history, the Ustaša then represented.

[1] The matter of forced conversions is complicated. Threatened by Ustaše because they were Orthodox, hundreds of Yugoslavs besieged Roman Catholic priests with demands to be accepted into the Roman Catholic confession. Thus many priests were faced with the choice of accepting conversions based on fear or exposing the supplicants to torture and death.

[2] While the extent of the atrocities has been exaggerated on both sides for political purposes, they are well documented. In addition, the authors have talked with many survivors, some of them horribly mutilated.

The Partisans

Far more than the Ustaša, however, the real opponents of the Četnici became the Partisans. After the Yugoslav Communist Party was outlawed in 1921, it had operated as an underground movement, often in an atmosphere of conspiratorial unreality. The Yugoslav Communists were rent both by some of the same dissension that infected the country as a whole and also by the impact of the conflict raging in the Soviet Party during the 1920's and 1930's. Initially taking a stand for national unity, the Yugoslav Party, at Moscow's direction, by 1926 had endorsed Croat separatism. When, a few years later, Moscow was pushing the idea of the popular front against the Nazis, the Yugoslav Communists again faithfully switched back in favor of Yugoslav unity. It was during one of the purges in the Yugoslav Party over the national question that a Croat named Josip Broz came into the leadership and in 1937 was named secretary-general.

The Yugoslav Communist Party in those days numbered only a few thousand, and on the eve of the war its membership was only 12,000. However, as Tito said later, the Party's influence "should not be judged by the number of its members. It was a cadre party," well disciplined and tightly organized, in the Leninist tradition. When the Germans invaded, the Party went into action and began to organize a resistance. This resistance did not actually begin to function as such, however, until after the Soviet Union was attacked on June 21, 1941. Tito now insists that the entry of the USSR into the war only hastened but was not itself responsible for the Communist-led uprising.[1]

Be that as it may, the Partisans, as this group was called, soon struck a responsive cord throughout much of Yugoslavia. Before long, they had become more powerful than the Četnici. There were several reasons for this. One was that the Partisans from the start actively engaged the Axis enemies in military action instead of following Mihailović's cautious tactics. This appealed to the fiery Yugoslavs despite the fearful reprisals they suffered from the Germans as a result.[2]

Also, the Partisans were an all-Yugoslav organization, in contrast to the intensely Serbian orientation of the Četnici. The Partisans therefore attracted the growing number of people who hoped for national unity and had become disgusted with the violent feuding of the ethnic-religious groups. Tito

[1] While there is no doubt that the Nazi invasion of the USSR decided the timing, it is equally clear that Communist plans for action had been in preparation ever since the fall of Yugoslavia. There is some logic in Tito's plea that the intervening time was needed for completing the planning. See Vladimir Dedijer, *Tito*, Simon & Schuster, New York, 1953, p. 150.

[2] Their opponents have charged that the Partisans actually sought to provoke reprisals because in this way the people were reduced to a state of hopelessness and thus encouraged to enlist under the Partisan banner.

himself was a Croat, and other leaders came from the various parts of Yugoslavia. Particularly Croats who could not stomach Ustaša Fascist extremism but who likewise opposed anything smacking of Serbianism veered toward the Partisans.

Further, and not least important by any means, the Communist leadership played down its ideological orientation and Marxist goals. Propaganda was focused on Yugoslav nationalism, democracy and hostility to the invaders. Where, as was the case in Montenegro in the beginning, the Partisans permitted their Communist coloration to govern their policies, they lost out. At the same time, especially in Montenegro, they sought to capitalize on the traditional pro-Russian feeling of the Orthodox South Slavs. Generally speaking, however, devotion to the struggle against the Germans and Italians, not ideological conformity, was the criterion of Partisan membership. Many field commanders were non-Communists, and the Partisan armies even came to include priests from both Serbian Orthodox and Roman Catholic churches. Although the Party leaders kept a tight grip on the organization, non-Communists who had risen to prominence in the period between the wars joined with them in leading posts. In areas liberated from the enemy, the Partisans established people's committees under local rule.

Finally, the Partisans conducted themselves toward the people in general decorously and with restraint not usually found in either guerilla or more formally organized forces in the field. Looting was forbidden, and it was usually punished by death. Among the largely apolitical population, the Partisans were therefore respected for justice and fairness at the same time that they were feared for their ruthlessness.

Mihailović

Partly as a result of their early activity against the Germans and Italians, partly as a result of propaganda assiduously circulated by the Royal government-in-exile, the Četnici soon gained a reputation outside Yugoslavia of fantastic proportions. Mihailović was hailed as a great hero throughout the West and particularly in the United States. The British hastened to send him a military mission and supplies, as, later, did the Americans. Even Moscow for some time considered him to be the leader of the real Yugoslav resistance movement.

Not all of this reputation was undeserved. There is no doubt that Mihailović and his followers were brave and patriotic men. There is no doubt that their sympathies were with the Allies. Many of them risked their lives, for example, to help British and American airmen shot down over Yugoslavia. But the simple, stubborn fact is this: generally speaking, the Četnici did not fight the Germans and Italians en masse and the Partisans did. Moreover, following out his duty as he saw it — to Serbia, the King and the government-in-exile — Mihailović soon came more and more to take actions which, whether he intended so or not, served the interests of the Axis.

Despite some early cooperation, the Četnici and the Partisans were soon in conflict. Tito and Mihailović conferred amiably enough, but Mihailović would have formal cooperation only if the Partisans were put under his command. This condition clearly was unacceptable to Tito.

To Mihailović, the Partisans represented a threat almost from the start. He early saw in them a movement seeking to bring Communism to Yugoslavia. Bitterly anti-Communist, he seems to have half-believed that Tito was a Russian. Mihailović's concept of Yugoslav patriotism excluded driving out the foreign enemy only to have the country taken over by Communists. Furthermore, he feared that the reprisals exacted by the Germans for military action such as the Partisans insisted on conducting would result in extermination of the Serbs as a people.

For these reasons, Mihailović soon came to consider the Partisans a more serious menace to what he stood for than the Axis forces. This led him to decide to attack the Partisans — once with arms they had given him. It also led to collaboration with the Germans and Italians against them. While Mihailović seems to have stood aside from collaboration personally, his chief lieutenants repeatedly joined forces with the Axis in his name.

This collaboration was, of course, motivated not by a desire to aid the occupiers but by a desire to smash the Partisans, although, as time went on, motives became hopelessly entangled. Nevertheless, Četnik collaboration not only alienated still more Yugoslavs but finally resulted in the transfer of British and American assistance to the Partisans. Possibly confused by the fact that the Americans, unlike the British, continued to maintain contacts with his forces, Mihailović kept hoping for a resumption of Western support. But like the hero of a classic Greek tragedy, he served the ends he believed in by following a course that led inevitably to his downfall. Ultimately, he was jettisoned even by the Royal government-in-exile for which he fought.

Tito

Meanwhile, the Partisan movement burgeoned. From 80,000 in 1941, its army grew to 200,000 in 1942, 300,000 in 1943 and by the end of 1944 to 800,000.[1] The Partisan army was headed by Tito, now with the rank of

---

[1] Membership in the Communist Party was, of course, far smaller; even in 1945, it was only 140,000. See Report of Aleksandar Ranković, *Sixth Congress of the Communist Party of Yugoslavia*, Belgrade, 1953.

marshal, and by one of the best officers of the prewar general staff, Arso Jovanović.

The military history of the Partisans is in the best Yugoslav tradition of heroism and valor. They fought against tremendous odds, both in manpower and armament, and were often ill-clad and undernourished. Tito was wounded, as were all the top Partisan military commanders. Time after time, Tito and his chief aides only narrowly escaped capture. At one point, twenty-six German divisions were in the field against them. The Partisan forces suffered fantastic casualties, including 350,000 killed and 400,000 wounded. Of the 12,000 Yugoslav Communists in the Partisan movement at the beginning, only 3,000 survived the war. Biographies of Tito by Vladimir Dedijer and Fitzroy Maclean give something of the flavor of the Partisan struggle, and Dedijer's *Diary*, in Serbo-Croatian, gives still more,[1] but it is difficult to portray adequately in words the drama of the Partisans' blood, suffering, courage and infinite faith in their cause.

As the name of Tito became widely known, there was speculation about who this once obscure figure was. Conditioned by their cloak-and-dagger past and fully engaged in fighting a war, the Partisan leaders had not bothered about the formalities of public information. In the West, Tito was variously identified as a Soviet officer, as a glamorous and mysterious woman and as the post of leader filled from time to time by different persons. Another version had it that Tito represented the Serbo-Croatian initials of something called the Secret International Terrorist Organization or stood for Third International Terrorist Organization.

Even when it became known that Tito was Josip Broz, there remained confusion over how he happened to be called Tito. A widely circulated story said that the name came from Tito's habit of giving peremptory orders, telling his men, "You do this, you this, you that" — in Serbo-Croatian, "*Ti to, ti to.*" The fact is that "Tito" is a fairly common name in the part of Croatia where the Yugoslav leader was born, and that sometime in the thirties Josip Broz adopted it as one of several "Party names," finally using it exclusively. In Comintern circles, Tito was known as Walter, and Stalin chose to call him Walter even after the war.

Tito, 50 years old in 1942, was the unquestioned leader of the Communists who presided over the Partisan movement. With him served Communists from other parts of Yugoslavia. They included Edvard Kardelj, a former schoolteacher from Slovenia; Aleksandar Ranković, once a tailor in Serbia;

[1] Fitzroy Maclean, *The Heretic: The Life and Times of Josip Broz-Tito*, Harper, New York, 1957; and Vladimir Dedijer, *Dnevnik* (*Diary*), Vols. I, II, III, Belgrade, 1945. The Partisan struggle is also described in Maclean, *Escape to Adventure*, Little, Brown, Boston, 1950, and Stephen Clissold, *Whirlwind*, Cresset Press, London, 1949.

Milovan Djilas, a young and fiery Montenegrin; Koča Popović, poet son of a Belgrade millionaire; Vladimir Bakarić, son of a Croat judge; and Moše Pijade, the oldest of the group, a Jewish intellectual who had shared a prison cell with Tito.

Political Operations

Fighting did not occupy the full time of these men. As early as the fall of 1942, they created a political structure for the Partisan movement — the Anti-Fascist Council of National Liberation of Yugoslavia, known as AVNOJ, the initials of its Serbo-Croatian name. Including some outstanding representatives from the prewar political parties but dominated by the Communists, AVNOJ at first was not set up as a national government. However, when AVNOJ met again in 1943, at Jajce, ancient capital of the kings of Bosnia, it established a National Liberation Committee as a provisional government. Dr. Ivan Ribar, a member of the Democratic Party who had been speaker of the Constituent Assembly in 1921, was president of AVNOJ, which continued to serve as a broad front organization for the actual government. Tito was named president of the National Liberation Committee. Serving with him were Dušan Sernec, a leader of the Slovene Clerical Party and a former governor of Slovenia, and Father Vlado Šečević, an Orthodox priest who had earlier held a command under Mihailović.

Resolutions were adopted at Jajce forbidding the return of the King pending a postwar decision on the future regime of Yugoslavia. The National Liberation Committee, with AVNOJ, was the direct precursor of the Communist Federal People's Republic established in 1945.

The Partisans and the Western Allies

The tangled wartime political situation was complicated by the stands taken by the allied powers, the British and Americans on the one hand and the Soviet Union on the other. All three powers recognized the Royal government-in-exile, with its seat first in London and then in Cairo. Young King Peter, who exercised virtually no authority independently, was under the influence of conservative Serbian advisers. It was natural that the government-in-exile should name General Mihailović its official adviser in Yugoslavia and adopt an attitude of strong opposition to the Partisans. Initially, all three allies supported the Četnici, the British with material assistance. But once the British became convinced that it was the Tito group which was really fighting the Axis, they aided the Partisans also. After the Teheran Conference in 1943, when Mihailović refused specific opportunities to act against the Germans, the British stepped up their aid to the Partisans and cut off all assistance to the Četnici. The Americans also were now aiding the Tito forces.

Western aid to the Partisans was based entirely on military grounds. Neither the British nor the Americans had any illusions about Tito's Communist or even Soviet orientation. Particularly on the part of British Prime Minister Churchill was there a lack of concern that contrasts strangely with the fears he voiced both during and after the war about Soviet influence in Eastern Europe. At one point, Brigadier Fitzroy Maclean, the chief British liaison officer with the Partisans, told Churchill he was convinced that Tito was planning to institute a Communist regime in Yugoslavia strongly allied with the Soviet Union. The Prime Minister replied: "Do you intend to make Jugoslavia your home after the war?" "No sir," answered Maclean. "Neither do I," said Churchill. "And, that being so, the less you and I worry about the form of government they set up, the better."[1]

A key to Churchill's ambivalent attitude may lie in the "spheres of influence" agreement he reached with Stalin in Moscow in October 1944. According to this agreement, the Soviet Union and Great Britain were to share "preponderance" in Yugoslavia on a 50-50 basis.[2] Having recognized that the Partisans were, willy-nilly, the strongest force there, the Prime Minister may have figured that the best way to exercise the British 50 per cent influence was to establish smooth working relations with the powers-that-would-be.

Conflict with the West

If so, Churchill was soon disillusioned. The Yugoslav Communists ignored the agreement, except insofar as it may have been reflected in certain arrangements made with the government-in-exile, and they were, in fact, both nonplused and angered when they learned of it.[3] This was indicated when they came in conflict with the Western powers over the issue of the Istrian Peninsula. At the Jajce session of AVNOJ, the Yugoslav Partisans had laid claim to the Italian province of Venezia Giulia, including the city of Trieste, that is, the entire Istrian peninsula. Partisan forces did, in fact, take most of Istria from the enemy and were already in Trieste when allied forces arrived on May 2, 1945. They refused an allied request that disposition of the peninsula be left to a peace conference, and for a while it appeared that a military conflict between Yugoslav and British troops might occur. Only when the

---

[1] Maclean, *Escape to Adventure*, pp. 304–310.

[2] Winston Churchill, *The Second World War*, Vol. VI, *Triumph and Tragedy*, Houghton Mifflin, Boston, 1953, pp. 227–233. Presumably Churchill made these proposals once he realized, following the failure of his hopes for an allied invasion of the "soft underbelly of Europe," that the USSR was inevitably going to play a strong role in the Balkans.

[3] At first they refused to believe that such an agreement existed. See Dedijer, *Tito*, p. 223.

Yugoslavs were given a virtual ultimatum did they retreat to roughly what became known as Zone B, leaving Trieste in allied hands.[1]

The Partisans' Strong Position

Whatever the attitude of the Yugoslavs, the West's alternative to support of the Partisans was limited not only on military grounds. Even before the decision to render aid exclusively to Tito, the Partisans were well on their way to becoming the dominant force in the country. As Brigadier Maclean saw the situation, "nothing short of armed intervention on a larger and more effective scale than that undertaken by the Germans would dispose of the Partisans."[2] Wholly aside from this, however, one may doubt whether an organization representing the government-in-exile, with its strong Serbian orientation, could have served as a vehicle for postwar unification of Yugoslavia. The alternative may well have been not between the Partisans and the Četnici but between the Partisans and a civil war of fearful dimensions.

Already on the offensive, the Partisans were greatly strengthened when, after the collapse of Italy, large quantities of Italian matériel fell into their hands. At strong British insistence, the government-in-exile then shifted its emphasis on the concept of "Greater Serbia" to a policy which was ultimately, and with great reluctance, to accept Tito. Finally, in June 1944, a new premier, Ivan Šubašić, the last governor of Croatia, arrived in Yugoslavia to sign an agreement with Tito. This recognition of the Partisans and the King's subsequent formal abandonment of Mihailović dealt the final blow to the Četnici. It was significant particularly in Serbia, where the Partisans began to attract new adherents, including many former members of Mihailović's forces.

The Partisans and the Russians

Although no hint of it reached allied ears, the fact was that relations between the Partisans and the Soviet Union were strained almost from the beginning. The Partisans received recognition earlier from the West, at least from London, than from Moscow, and they received considerably more material support. His suspicion of foreign Communists perhaps intensified here by the old Russian disdain for other Slavs, Stalin continued to recognize Mihailović as the leader of the real Yugoslav resistance for some time after

---

[1] The Americans and British opposed Yugoslav claims to the whole of the ethnically tangled peninsula both because they wished to safeguard the Italian city of Trieste and also because they saw possession by Yugoslavia as an extension of Soviet influence. Ironically, the Yugoslav claims seem to have embarrassed Moscow. Although Foreign Minister Molotov supported the Yugoslavs at first, soon thereafter he accepted a French compromise, which in turn infuriated Belgrade.

[2] *Escape to Adventure*, p. 252.

the West began to embrace Tito. Repeated, often frantic, Partisan requests to Moscow for even token aid were of no avail.

Not only did the Russians deny aid to the Partisans — on grounds of inability to supply it — but they took a dim view of Partisan political activity. The Kremlin especially opposed anything so much as suggesting Communist influence. For example, Moscow criticized the adoption of a Partisan flag with a red star and the designation of shock military units as Proletarian Brigades. The Soviet reaction to the formation of AVNOJ was coldly negative. And when, during the Teheran Conference, the National Committee of Liberation was created as a provisional government — without advance notice to either East or West — Stalin is reported to have been furious.[1]

The Soviet government was doubtless motivated in large part simply by a desire not to disrupt allied unity in wartime. However, in the early part of the war the Russians virtually ignored the Balkan arena. Of course, they were fully occupied fighting the Nazis at home. But Stalin seems to have been not only misinformed about the military situation in Yugoslavia but also convinced that even after the war the country would not be ripe for Communism.[2] This reluctance to back Communist movements not directed by the USSR was in keeping with Stalin's theory of the "ebb and flow of the revolutionary tide" and also reflected Leninist doctrine about the necessity for "objective conditions" for revolution. Stalin manifested similar caution in regard to Greece and China.[3]

The Kremlin's attitude was a source of acute disappointment and puzzlement to the embattled Yugoslav Communists, who were so devoted to the USSR and its interests. It was also a source of embarrassment. Having rallied their comrades in the name of the socialist fatherland, it was not easy for Tito and his aides to explain continued Soviet recognition of the Četnici. Nor was it easy to explain why assistance was coming from the capitalist West but not from Moscow. Although Tito constantly turned the other cheek in replying to abrupt messages from Moscow, once in desperation he radioed: "If you cannot send us assistance, then at least do not hamper us."[4]

It was not until March 1944 that the Soviet Union finally sent a military mission to the Partisans. In the meantime, it had dawned on Stalin that Tito

---

[1] Dedijer, *Tito*, p. 209.

[2] In 1944 Stalin warned Tito: "Walter, be careful, the bourgeoisie in Serbia is very strong." He did not like it a bit when Tito replied: "Comrade Stalin, I do not agree with your view. The bourgeoisie in Serbia is very weak." *Ibid.*, p. 233.

[3] *Ibid.*, pp. 321–322.

[4] In Moscow later, Tito was told that Stalin was so angered by this telegram that "he stamped with rage." *Ibid.*, p. 232. This and similar Yugoslav revelations came during the most violent period of the Soviet-Yugoslav controversy, when Belgrade was trying to put Stalin in the worst possible light.

did represent the real fighting force in Yugoslavia and that the Western allies, far from objecting to the Partisans, were supporting them. But, although he then greeted the "heroic struggle of the brotherly Yugoslav peoples and their glorious National Liberation Army," he was still inclined to discount Tito's strength and to question Tito's tactics.[1]

Ten years afterwards, reviewing the origins of the Soviet-Yugoslav dispute, Tito declared: ". . . we can rightly say that there were elements of disagreement between us as far back as 1941, from the first day of revolution."[2] At the time, however, no such thoughts were in the minds of the Yugoslav Communist leaders. Soviet revelations that Kardelj once talked of bringing Yugoslavia into the USSR as a Soviet republic have been denied, and nowadays the Yugoslav Communists indignantly reject the notion that they fought more for the Soviet Union than for Yugoslavia. But there is no doubt about their intense wartime devotion to Moscow. To Stalin's greeting in 1944, Tito replied: "Recognition by the Soviet people and their army of our struggle against the German Fascists — that was our dearest recognition."[3]

Victory for the Partisans

With Belgrade still in German hands, the Red army bore in from the East in the fall of 1944. Under prior agreement with Tito, Soviet forces crossed the Danube into Yugoslavia, promising to withdraw to the Hungarian front as soon as German resistance was liquidated. Partisan and Red Army forces together liberated Belgrade on October 20. Tito's Committee for National Liberation now ruled all of Yugoslavia from its traditional capital city.

Soon after the liberation of Belgrade, a new Tito-Šubašić agreement provided for a provisional government with a three-man regency to act for the King until the future of the monarchy could be decided by plebescite. Partly as a result of the decisions at Yalta, Šubašić was accepted as foreign minister and Milan Grol, leader of the Serbian Democratic Party, became deputy premier. Tito was both premier and minister of defense, and twenty-three of the twenty-eight ministers were his men. Under the agreement, AVNOJ, now the provisional parliament, was broadened by the addition of 121 new members, including representatives of six non-Communist parties.

The campaign for the election of a Constituent Assembly, which began immediately, was dominated by Communist strong-arm tactics. Both Šubašić

---

[1] On the other hand, when Milovan Djilas asked Stalin in the spring of 1944 if "our line was correct," Stalin replied: "You yourself know best and you should judge." *Ibid.*, p. 215.

[2] *Ibid.*, p. 256.

[3] *Ibid.*, p. 213.

and Grol were harassed and their publications suppressed. Šubašić and two other non-Communist ministers resigned in protest, and the opposition parties, now as so often in the past unable to agree positively among themselves, boycotted the election.

Thus only the Popular Front list, sponsored by the government, was presented to the voters. The voting took place without obvious intimidation; special ballot boxes were provided for those wishing to oppose the list. Eighty-eight per cent of the eligible voters are said to have cast ballots. Under the circumstances, few were surprised when the government announced that 90 per cent of them voted for the Popular Front list.

The Constituent Assembly met on November 29, 1945, three years after the first session of AVNOJ. It promptly denounced the King and proclaimed a republic. Then it proceeded to adopt a new constitution, declaring itself the People's Assembly of the Federal People's Republic of Yugoslavia. The Communist-led resistance movement had become a constitutional regime. That it had achieved political power, as it had earlier achieved military power, largely by its own steam and not at Soviet hands, was to be an important factor in events to come.

CHAPTER 6

THE HARD-BOILED

DICTATORSHIP

THE Federal People's Republic of Yugoslavia during the years 1945–1949 was modeled on the Soviet Union. To a fine degree, it approximated the USSR both in structure and in operation. As Tito put it later, "We had too many illusions and were too uncritical in taking and replanting in Yugoslavia everything that was being done in the Soviet Union."[1] What this meant was that Yugoslavia in this period was a police state under the dictatorship of the Communist Party operating behind the thinly veiled fiction of a "popular front" embracing remnants of some of the prewar parties.

The new Yugoslavia was not technically a "satellite"; it was not *forced* by Moscow to do things against its will. Nevertheless, up to 1948 it was, no less than the satellites proper, oriented to Moscow in word and deed and thus, in effect, represented an extension of Soviet power.

Not only was it one of those states which Moscow was pleased to call "people's democracies," but it was far ahead of the others in taking great leaps and bounds toward socialism, Soviet-style. The head start of the Yugoslav regime resulted from the fact that, beginning with the wartime Partisan and AVNOJ organization, it commenced to function as a government before it was formally established as such.

Professor Seton-Watson notes three stages through which the Eastern European regimes generally progressed after the war. The first was a "genuine coalition" of Communist and other political parties. The second was "bogus coalition," characterized by increasing Communist domination of the non-Communist parties, the use of violence against opposition and the beginnings

[1] Josip Broz Tito, *Workers Manage Factories in Yugoslavia*, Jugoštampa, Belgrade, 1950, pp. 10–11.

of nationalization and planning. The third, or "monolithic," stage was complete Communist domination with a single Communist-managed front organization, elimination of all opposition and sweeping nationalization and economic planning.[1]

But Yugoslavia went through no such stages. The Communist Party was firmly in control even before the postwar government was set up. Non-Communist parties were either eliminated at the start or submerged in the National Liberation Front, now renamed the People's Front. Fifty-four per cent of Yugoslav industry had been in effect nationalized before the end of the war. And immediately all efforts were bent toward a full-fledged Five Year Plan, which was formally initiated in 1947. Most of the features of totalitarian Communism which the West finds so repugnant were therefore present in Tito's Yugoslavia sooner than elsewhere in Eastern Europe. And this advanced development was a factor in the intramural Communist difficulties which were soon to appear.

Federalism

The new constitution promulgated on January 30, 1946, charted a far different governmental organization from that which existed before the war. First of all, it was clearly federal in form. Although in fact virtually all decision making rested with the central government in Belgrade, six equal and theoretically autonomous republics were set up with governments of their own. Besides Serbia, Croatia and Slovenia, these included Bosnia and Herzegovina as a single republic (thus removing the old apple of discord between the Serbs and the Croats), Montenegro and Macedonia. In addition, the Vojvodina and Kosovo-Metohija were given the status of autonomous provinces attached to Serbia.

To many, the most significant fact about the new Yugoslavia was that the old Serbian domination was ended and that there no longer existed the clearly untenable presumption of a single Yugoslav people. If others felt that the new equality now extended to the major national groups meant only equal subjection to a regime they considered alien, still it was an equality that had not before been present. Especially many of those who had wanted unity but opposed the leading role of Serbia tended to see advances in the new state, even if they were opposed to Communism. As Ivan Mestrović, the noted sculptor, himself a Croat and an *émigré*, wrote of Tito and his comrades: "One thing must be admitted: They have at least attempted to find

---

[1] See Hugh Seton-Watson, *The Eastern European Revolution*, Methuen & Co., London, 1950, pp. 169–171.

an equitable solution for inner-relations between the various Yugoslav peoples. . . ."[1]

Ethnic-religious particularisms were far from eliminated, and the new recognition of the various nationalities fell short of pleasing all Serbs and Croats. But in the raw and violent form in which it existed before and during the war, the problem was no longer present. Its abatement was due not only to the new political divisions. The Communists were themselves an all-Yugoslav group in that they drew equally from the various national groups. Although Tito was a Croat, each of the republics had strong representation in both Party and government. The Communists, interested in other things than the old nationalisms, could best serve their ends by promoting unity. Moreover, by eliminating the old political parties and shearing the respective churches in Serbia and Croatia of political power, they eliminated some of the main sources of particularistic feeling.

While some Serbs were contending that the new state was dominated by Croats, some Croats were claiming to see undue Serbian influence — in part because Belgrade, capital of Serbia, remained the capital of Yugoslavia. But it was difficult to justify such assertions. If the new regime was unpopular it was primarily for reasons other than national favoritism.

The Government

According to the 1946 constitution, the highest legal authority was vested in a People's Assembly (Narodna Skupština), consisting of two chambers, a Federal Council (Savezno Veće) and a Council of Nationalities (Veće Naroda). The Federal Council was composed of deputies elected from the country at large, while the Council of Nationalities comprised thirty representatives from each republic plus twenty from the Vojvodina and fifteen from Kosovo-Metohija.

The People's Assembly acted like parliamentary bodies in other Communist countries; that is to say, it unanimously accepted legislation presented to it with virtually no debate. One of its functions was to elect a presidium. As the People's Assembly resembled the Supreme Soviet in the USSR, so did its presidium resemble the presidium of the Soviet body. The presidium issued the bulk of the legislation in the name of the Assembly, held supreme sovereignty while the Assembly was not in session and exercised powers of judicial review and appointment. Among the latter was the task of appointing a council of Ministers, where real governmental authority lay.

[1] P. D. Ostović, *The Truth about Yugoslavia*, Roy Publishers, New York. 1952, p. xv. Ostović's book is itself an interesting example of the grudging approval given the Tito regime by some anti-Communist Croats.

The Council of Ministers wielded control over the entire life of the country. As in the USSR, its ministries were of two kinds, federal and federal-republic. Federal ministries included foreign affairs, national defense, communication, shipping, posts and telegraph, and foreign trade. Federal-republic ministries — which had their counterparts in the governments of the republics — were for finance, interior (police), justice, commerce and supplies, labor, agriculture and forestry, public works and the various divisions of industry. As in the USSR, the republic ministries were actually no more than regional offices of the national headquarters.

In addition to the ministries proper, the Government — or Vlada, as the Council of Ministers was officially known — included a Federal Control Commission — a super-inspection agency with vast powers — and a Federal Planning Commission, which was charged not only with detailed planning of all economic life but also with enforcing its own plans. There was also a Public Prosecutor, whose office handled all prosecutions and in fact controlled the courts, and there were federal committees dealing with education, religious affairs, social welfare, culture and art.

The Council of Ministers was empowered to issue legislation of its own — called decrees and ordinances. These, along with similar enactments by the presidium, technically had to be submitted to the Assembly for approval, but, as with other powers of the Assembly, this approval was only *pro forma*.

The Party

The keystone of this structure was the Communist Party, from which all power emanated. The Party exercised its power in four ways. First, it controlled the "commanding heights" of society, its leaders holding the chief positions in government and the economy. This relationship extended throughout the country, down to towns and districts, whose local governmental bodies were invariably headed by the secretary of the Party committee. Secondly, the Party exercised control by frequent direct—and usually extra-legal — intervention of its functionaries in governmental and economic affairs. As in the Soviet Union, the responsible official in any given area was the chief of the Party organization even where he did not happen to hold a job in the government or the economy.

The third method of Party control was through the People's Front. This body theoretically consisted of the Socialist, Democratic, Republican and Agrarian parties of Serbia, the Croat Peasant Party and the Independent Serb Democrats, together with the Communist Party. Since the Communist Party alone maintained a separate organization, what the People's Front really consisted of was the Communist Party and individual non-Communists who had belonged to the prewar parties and now were willing to collaborate with the regime. By 1948 the People's Front had a membership of seven million persons, who could be counted on in one way or another to do the Party's bidding. This usually involved propaganda planned by the "agit-prop" section of the Party apparatus, headed by Milovan Djilas. The fact that the Yugoslav Party's positions were advanced in the name of the People's Front distinguished it from the Communist parties of other Eastern European countries, whose programs were advocated in their own names.

Finally, and by no means least important, the Party exercised control through OZNA (Odelenji Zašite Naroda, or Department of Defense of the People),[1] the political police headed by Aleksandar Ranković. All members of OZNA were Communists, and its "defense of the people" was in large part a defense of the Party from its opponents.

Presiding over this entire state and party structure was Josip Broz Tito. Tito was Premier of Yugoslavia, Secretary General of the Communist Party and chief of its Politburo, President of the People's Front, Marshal of Yugoslavia, Minister of National Defense, commander-in-chief of the army, a deputy in the Assembly and a member of the presidium. His top lieutenants also were officials in the party, the government and the People's Front. Chief among them were Ranković, Djilas, Edvard Kardelj, Boris Kidrić and Moše Pijade—all comrades of his Partisan days.

Public Reaction

At the end of the war, Tito and his Partisans, despite vigorous and varied opposition, were popular among a wide segment of their fellow countrymen. In addition to the readily apparent reasons — the Partisans' war record and their stand on national unity — was the perhaps even more important fact that, although the Communists had made no secret of their domination of the wartime movement, they had carefully concealed their aims for socialization. This was of significance especially among the peasants, traditionally conservative and devoted to their land. Since Yugoslavia was predominantly a peasant country, it was not unnatural that the overwhelming majority of the Partisans were peasants.

But much of whatever popularity the Tito regime enjoyed at the close of the war did not long survive the hard realities of the war's aftermath. A Communist revolution, by its very nature, begets opposition. To carry out their program, the Communists must take property away from those who have it and persuade the masses of people to alter deep-seated mores. To accom-

[1] Its name was later changed to UDBA (Uprava Državne Bezbednosti, or Administration of State Security). See Chapter 19 below.

plish either, force is invariably required. Where, as in Yugoslavia, the force is applied by ruthless men trained in the Stalinist tradition against a people reared in a milieu never characterized by gentleness or moderation, it is bound to produce not only opposition but violent opposition. Moreover, Communists newly come to power, having until recently been conspirators and warriors, lack experience in the arts of government. They may first appear to the populace as heroic liberators, but their heavy-handed efforts are quickly disillusioning.

In postwar Yugoslavia, economic chaos and extreme poverty made the task of governing especially difficult. If those who had hoped for political democracy were repelled by the hard-boiled dictatorial practices of the regime, many more were embittered by hunger and privation alone. It is difficult to exaggerate the country's economic plight. Even the most ordinary necessities of life, when not lacking entirely, were in extremely short supply.

Extent of War Devastation

The war left in its wake in Yugoslavia devastation and destruction of unprecedented magnitude. A detailed report of losses does not adequately portray the effect on the economy, and the extent of human suffering involved defies even approximation.

The economic impact was apparent in loss of manpower, destruction of productive facilities, exploitation by the occupying powers and disintegration of the country as an economic unit.

The loss of manpower included both military and civilian casualties as well as a great number of deaths resulting from wartime hardships. (For details see p. 41.) Of the countries participating in the war, Yugoslavia was second only to Poland in losses relative to population. Approximately 11 per cent of the Yugoslav people — 1.7 million out of a total estimated at the outbreak of the war at nearly 16 million — were killed, fled or were expelled, or refused repatriation.

The numerical loss alone does not tell the whole story. Among other important factors was the average age of those killed — twenty-two years. The age group playing perhaps the key role in production was thus decimated. Also, death and migration due to the war made heavy inroads in the group with better education and skills.[1]

The economic impact of the loss of manpower, great as it was, was small, however, compared with the destruction of private property and productive facilities. Roughly one-sixth of all prewar housing was either destroyed or

[1] Gerald G. Govorchin, "Reconstruction in New Yugoslavia," *Social Science*, April 1948, p. 114.

heavily damaged.[1] In Belgrade alone more than 40 per cent of the housing was rendered unusable. In all, 25 per cent of Yugoslavia's population was homeless.

Though the capacity of individual industries, especially smelting and mining, was enlarged during the war, production in December 1945 was only 30 to 40 per cent of prewar in the textile industry, 40 to 50 per cent in the food processing industries and 15 to 20 per cent in the metal industries. Mines were flooded and machinery destroyed by the retreating German army. At the end of the war not a single railroad line was in operation, and more than 50 per cent of all rails and rolling stock was either destroyed or badly damaged. The merchant marine was reduced from 410,000 gross registered tons to 55,000.

Productive capacity was further sapped by the Axis occupiers, especially Germany. Certain key mines, industries and transport facilities were put directly under the administration of German firms. While they, in turn, enlarged and modernized some facilities, this was altogether tied in to the German war effort.[2] For example, Bor copper, Trepca lead and zinc mines, and Danube shipping all came under the Hermann Göring Works. I. G. Farben took over all chemical production; Krupp, steel and chrome enterprises; and Mannesmann, engineering firms and steel production. Some estimates indicate that Yugoslav mines supplied roughly 45 per cent of German copper and 40 per cent of German chromite requirements.

The devastation was equally heavy in agriculture. Vast quantities of farm machinery and other equipment, draft animals and livestock were destroyed, damaged or looted. The total reduction amounted to between 40 and 60 per cent of total prewar holdings, e.g., 53 per cent of cattle, 67 per cent of horses, 52 per cent of hogs, 80 per cent of plows and harvesting machinery (comparatively scarce even before the war) and 40 per cent of peasant carts. Nearly 40 per cent of the area under vineyards and fruit trees was seriously damaged. It was estimated that damages in forestry, largely due to overcutting, amounted to more than 12 per cent of prewar production. The effect of all this was also long-term, in the form of reduction of available fertilizer, decreased output per acre on Yugoslav farms and a substantial reduction in the available lumber supply.

[1] UNRRA Operational Analysis Paper No. 23, *Agriculture and Food in Yugoslavia*, February 1947, p. 4.

[2] Such take-over was all the easier because so many Yugoslav industrial facilities were owned by Western business interests and were simply confiscated by the Germans. Roughly 46 per cent of all industrial production was owned by foreign companies, viz., 20.6 per cent, France; 16.3 per cent, England; 14.3 per cent, Switzerland; 7.4 per cent, the United States; and varying percentages for Germany, Belgium, Austria, Italy, Sweden, etc. Nearly all mining operations were under foreign control — 46 per cent British, 41 per cent French, 5.5 per cent Belgian. The chemical industry was completely foreign-controlled.

An additional war-engendered impediment to the economy was the loss of the small but important gold reserves. Of these, $12 million (in gold and silver) was taken by Germany. Some $60 million had been put in safekeeping in the United States, the United Kingdom and Brazil, but none of it was available for reconstruction purposes at the war's end.

UNRRA Aid

To a very considerable extent, the Tito regime was enabled to get over this hump by the receipt of food and material from the United Nations Relief and Rehabilitation Administration, much of it supplied by the United States. U. S. aid was also received through lend-lease supplies and services and emergency civilian relief from military surpluses.[1] CARE parcels, clothing from church organizations and gifts from emigrants provided direct economic assistance to individuals and families. It was UNRRA, though, that swung the balance. Without UNRRA aid in 1945 and 1946, mass starvation would likely have resulted. It has been estimated that "on an annual basis [the total value of] UNRRA aid corresponded to 138 per cent of the average tax revenue of the Yugoslav state between 1936 and 1939."[2]

Yugoslavia's relations with UNRRA were involved in political controversy from the start. When negotiations started in 1944, the Committee for National Liberation refused to accept UNRRA relief unless supplies were distributed by local Partisan authorities. UNRRA agreed to this after it had been promised that UNRRA officials could observe the distribution without restrictions. Dispute also arose over who was to head the UNRRA mission in Belgrade, and many in the West were not happy when a Soviet colonel, Mikhail Sergeichik, was appointed. Criticism of distribution by the Yugoslavs concerned sale of UNRRA supplies to the populace—proceeds of which went for rehabilitation and reconstruction—denial of food and material to those refusing political cooperation, and the use of certain supplies for the army rather than for civilians.[3]

Vast as were the accomplishments of its life-saving mission, UNRRA did little more than cover the most immediate and minimum relief needs. Having assumed power, the regime then had to secure its hold. This it sought to do by prompt political and economic action. The political action involved

[1] For a discussion of United States aid, see pp. 347–354.

[2] Jozo Tomasevich, "Postwar Foreign Economic Relations," Robert J. Kerner (ed.), *Yugoslavia*, University of California Press, Berkeley, 1949, p. 405.

[3] For a comprehensive study of the aims, goals and accomplishments of UNRRA, see George Woodbridge, *UNRRA, The History of the United Nations Relief and Rehabilitation Administration*, 3 vols., Columbia University Press, New York, 1950. Discussions on Yugoslavia specifically are in Vol. II, Pt. 5, pp. 138–170 and the tables on pp. 494–497.

rooting out all opposition, actual and potential. The economic action involved, first, recovery from the damage left by the war and then, almost simultaneously, setting in motion a plan for industrialization. The Yugoslav approach to both was exceedingly doctrinaire.

Reconstruction and Nationalization

A better argument could be made for industrialization than for embarking on it so quickly and so boldly. There was general agreement that, in the long run, industrialization was the answer to many of agricultural Yugoslavia's economic problems. The country's dependence on world agricultural prices had long put it at a disadvantage. In addition, there was great overpopulation — and underemployment — in an agriculture that was itself in many ways the most backward in Europe. As usual in Communist practice, for both economic and ideological considerations, industrialization was tied to collectivization. As usual, also, industrialization, if it were to be accomplished at all, had to be accomplished by forcing an already hungry people to tighten belts still further. Even if such a program had waited until some degree of recovery from the war was achieved, the repercussions would have been dire enough. As it was, Tito and his lieutenants plunged ahead into economic tasks so ambitious that they were foredoomed to failure. In the process, more and more political opposition was engendered, and, in a vicious circle, this opposition further complicated the economic tasks.

Reconstruction and nationalization were launched officially by the provisional government even before Croatia and Slovenia were finally liberated. The main aims during the period 1944–1945 were the organization of governmental machinery, the establishment of internal transportation, the rehabilitation of agriculture and industry, the feeding and clothing of the population, the prevention of epidemics, and the enactment of fiscal measures.

The problems of welding the different parts of the country into a whole and organizing its economic life were attacked by the promulgation of a series of laws. These laws dealt with confiscation of property, management of industry, banks and transportation, and land reforms. They sought to achieve the basic goals of Communist economic dogma — industrialization, collectivization and nationalization. A brief summary of the major laws shows the Yugoslav approach to reconstructing the economy.

The first item of attention when reconstruction started in October 1944 was the restoration of rail traffic. By the end of 1945, 75 per cent of the war damage had been repaired, and restoration was nine-tenths completed at the end of 1946. Industrial rehabilitation received the second order of attention. Based on 1939 as 100, the over-all index of production reached 79 in late 1946, but this was due at least in part to the earlier-mentioned increased productive facilities built by Germany.

A decree issued on November 24, 1944[1] provided for confiscation of the property of collaborators, former enemies and war profiteers, and those persons who had fled the country and refused to return. A basic law on "Agrarian Reform and Colonization" was enacted by the provisional parliament in August 1945. This law incorporated the November 1944 decree and provided for the acquisition, by expropriation without compensation, of land for a land pool from which government-owned farms were to be organized. More than 80 per cent of the arable land was distributed among landless peasants and veterans. This land was confiscated not only from individuals but also from banks, corporations, churches and other religious institutions. The law set a limit of from 25 to 45 hectares of arable land which individuals were permitted to own.[2] Close to 40 per cent of the confiscated land formerly belonged to the German-speaking population in the Vojvodina and Slovenia and was perhaps the best-managed land in the country. In all, 11 per cent of the land in private hands was affected by the reform; 70,000 landless families received land. In late 1945 all peasant debts were cancelled. A "Basic Law on Cooperatives" was enacted in July 1946 dealing with collective farming and the organization of state tractor stations. Under its provisions, the cooperatives were to be the main village outlets for goods manufactured in cities.[3]

Finally, in December 1946, a Nationalization Law was passed making all industries of "national importance" and all transportation, banking and wholesale trade facilities the property of the state.

At the end of the reconstruction period, during the first half of 1947, the country's productive facilities were again in operating condition, with output in some cases above the prewar level. But lack of modern equipment, especially machine tools and agricultural machinery, remained a major handicap.

Economic recovery and the early industrialization efforts were aided significantly by reparations payments from Hungary, Italy and Germany. Yugoslavia's share of Bulgarian reparations was voluntarily renounced in August 1947. Hungary was committed to pay $70 million over a period of eight years, starting in 1946, mostly in petroleum and coal, but deliveries

---

[1] "Law on State Appropriations of Enemy Property and on Sequestration of the Property of Absentee Persons," published in the official gazette, *Službeni List*, No. 2 (Feb. 1945), later amended in No. 61 (July 1946).

[2] Property consisting of more than 45 hectares in all or more than 25–30 hectares of arable land was confiscated without compensation if such land was farmed by tenant farmers or agricultural workers. Land held by banks, industries or churches was confiscated without compensation if it consisted of more than 100 hectares.

[3] Detailed discussion of the different agrarian reforms, their background and impact will be found in Chapter 15.

were stopped in 1948 after the outbreak of the dispute with the Cominform.[1] Italy paid Yugoslavia $125 million out of its total reparations bill of $360 million, mostly in raw materials and services, over a period of seven years. Also, the Inter-Allied Reparations Agency gave Yugoslavia 9.6 per cent of all capital equipment available as reparations and 6.6 per cent of German assets abroad. While this was actually only a small percentage of total reparations demands made by Belgrade, it came at an important period and contributed industrial raw materials and capital payments vital to economic recovery.

The various nationalization laws and the progress thus made in reconstructing the economy from the ravages of war laid the basis for beginning the "big leap" into industrialization, the Five Year Plan, officially proclaimed in April 1947.

The Police State

In the political arena, action was twofold. First, the regime moved against "collaborators." Second, it dealt with non-Communist politicians who had cooperated with the Communists to some extent but were now insisting on their right to dissent. In both cases there was resort to kangaroo court procedures, which may have had a certain Balkan tradition but which had little if anything to do with legality as the term is known in the west.

Action against "collaborators," natural enough at the end of a long and bloody war, had wide approval, and the Yalta Conference had placed its imprimatur on such action. But who was a collaborator? Originally a collaborator was considered to be a person who had actively helped the enemy. But in practice, in Yugoslavia and elsewhere in Eastern Europe, a collaborator was liable to be practically anybody the regime did not like and who had not actively fought with the Partisans. This included persons ranging from Mihailović and the Četniks and the Roman Catholic hierarchy of Croatia and Slovenia to pro-Western politicians and businessmen who had in fact demonstrated hostility to the Nazi-Fascists.

Communist strong-arm tactics, already tried out in the 1945 election, soon dominated the scene. The whole government and party organization was involved in the political terror, but the key agency was OZNA, or, as it was later known, UDBA. Acting much as did its Soviet counterpart, the NKVD, during the purge period, this agency was often police, prosecutor, jury and judge combined. As always with police terror, the innocent suffered along with the guilty.

[1] A new agreement was signed in May 1956, regulating all unsettled economic questions. Hungary agreed to ship goods valued at $85 million in five equal installments. See *Borba*, May 30, 1956.

There is no way of telling how many of the thousands of persons imprisoned and manhandled or shot by Ranković's police were innocent of any real offense against the state. Some idea may be gained by Ranković's later admission that in 1949 — by which time police terror was substantially lessened — 47 per cent of all UDBA arrests were "unjustified" and 23 per cent of them were for non-political crimes of "minor significance." Ranković himself is also the source of the charge that the courts, instead of offering protection, were an instrument in the terror. The whole legal machinery of the state, according to Ranković, was guilty of "converting ordinary crime into political criminal offenses" and thus indiscriminately and wrongly depriving people of their liberty.[1]

The Mihailović Trial

In particular, Tito could not rest securely as long as his defeated opponent Draža Mihailović remained at large. Mihailović, deserted by all but a handful of his once proud Četnik band, was hiding in Bosnia, and top priority was put on his capture. He was taken in March 1946,[2] charged with treason and brought to trial in Belgrade on June 10. Requests of the United States government that Americans who served with Mihailović during the war be permitted to testify were denied. The trial, in keeping with Communist mores, was not a judicial process but a political demonstration. There was, of course, ample evidence of Četnik collaboration with the Germans. In addition to attacking Mihailović's character, the prosecution tried to discredit the Western powers and charged that the defendant had collaborated with the Germans against the Partisans on British instructions. Few raised their voices in defense of Mihailović. The defeated Četnik leader, drawn and haggard, refused to confess to all the charges against him. His testimony in his own behalf had an air of bewilderment about it. "I found myself in a whirl of events and intrigues," Mihailović told the court. "Destiny was merciless toward me . . . I wanted much, I began much, but the whirlwind, the world whirlwind, carried me and my work away."[3]

The tragedy of Draža Mihailović ended with his execution on July 17. Other political trials followed. Miloš Trifunović, former leader of the Serbian

---

[1] Ranković made these admissions to the Fourth Plenum of the Central Committee of the Yugoslav Communist Party in 1950, when the tide was running strongly in favor of stricter legality. His address was published under the title "Za Dalje Jačanje Pravosudja i Zakonitosti" ("For Further Strengthening of the Judiciary and Legality"), *Komunist*, No. 2, March–May 1951. See especially p. 6.

[2] Tito, en route to Poland at the time, was informed of Mihailović's capture by Ranković in these words: "*Plan Ostvaren*" ("Plan fulfilled").

[3] *The Trial of Dragoljub-Draža Mihailović*, Belgrade, 1946, p. 499.

Radical Party and prime minister of the government-in-exile, who returned to oppose Tito in the 1945 election and had later articulately defended Mihailović, was sentenced to prison. Mihailović's attorney, Dragić Joksimović, was executed. Dr. Dragoljub Jovanović, leader of the Serbian Peasant left wing and a member of the People's Assembly, where he spoke out against regime policies, was convicted of conspiring with British agents to organize a peasant opposition. Franjo Gazi, a Croat Peasant Party radical, was tried with him. Still other trials involved Boris Furlan, a Slovene professor, and Tomo Janciković, a former Croat Peasant Party deputy. These and other "demonstration" trials had their effect. Articulate political opposition virtually ceased.

Conflict with the Church

Simultaneously the regime moved against the Church. By their very nature, religion and Communism are in conflict. In Yugoslavia this was especially so, for although the Partisans included among their supporters clergymen of all faiths, still, by and large, each of the church organizations had been arrayed against them. In addition, to the extent that Serbian and Croatian nationalistic feeling ran counter to the Yugoslav unity espoused by the Communists, the Orthodox and Roman Catholic Churches, as leading forces in those nationalisms, represented continuing opposition to the regime. The hostility of the religious groups was intensified when the regime launched land and educational reforms. The limitation of land holdings hit the Orthodox and Roman Catholic Churches especially hard, and the educational reforms were aimed in part at eliminating religious influences among young people.

The Moslem community was not involved to a comparable extent. Certain members of its clergy came in conflict with the authorities, but in general this religious group did not prove a problem, even when, later, the regime forced abandonment of certain Moslem customs, such as the veil for women.

The Serbian Orthodox Church was in a less exposed position than the Roman Catholics. In the first place, as a national church the Serbian Church was traditionally more accustomed to accommodate itself to differing political regimes. In the second place, religion among the Serbs generally tends to be less passionate than among, say, the Croats. In the third place, the Orthodox clergy had cooperated with the Partisans more than the Roman Catholic clergy had. Few if any Orthodox priests were compromised by overt support of the Germans or Italians, and Patriarch Gavrilo, who had been imprisoned and then deported to Germany during the war, returned with his skirts clear of collaboration.

A campaign was waged against the Orthodox Church nevertheless. Many churches were closed down, priests who opposed the government were terrorized, and some members of the hierarchy were imprisoned. Strenuous efforts were made to force the Holy Synod to recognize a government-sponsored association of priests.

The Stepinac Trial

But the real conflict was with the Roman Catholic Church, particularly in Croatia. Having the usual foreign ties of Roman Catholic churches and at the same time a nationalist orientation, together with a record of support of the Ustaše, the Church in Croatia was a natural target for the regime. This was the more so because the Primate of Croatia and Archbishop of Zagreb, Aloysius Stepinac, was an outspoken foe of Communism. Already in 1945 the Croatian hierarchy had issued a pastoral letter which declared: "The enemies of the Catholic Church, being also followers of materialistic Communism, which the entire Croatian nation with one assent rejects, have in our Croatia exterminated with fire and sword its priests and the more eminent of the faithful".[1]

In the fall of 1946, Monsignor Stepinac and a number of prelates were arrested and charged with crimes against the state. The Primate, in particular, was accused, among other things, of supporting the Pavelić government and the Axis powers, and of active cooperation with the Ustaše and chairmanship of the committee which directed the forced conversion of Orthodox Serbs to Roman Catholicism. Like the trial of Mihailović earlier the same year, it was a political rather than a judicial process. The prosecution produced seventy-one witnesses against Monsignor Stepinac, including the Franciscan provincial of Croatia, but the defense was permitted no more than seven. The archbishop was defended by Dr. Ivo Politeo, who eighteen years before, in the same Zagreb courtroom, had defended the secretary of the local branch of the Communist Party, one Josip Broz.

There was no doubt, of course, about Monsignor Stepinac's formal support of the Fascist regime in Croatia, although he was on occasion in conflict with the Ustaša authorities. Less clear was his connection with forced conversions or his responsibility for the actions of other prelates. If the trial was an opportunity for anti-Catholic propaganda, the Primate himself used it to lecture the regime. Stern and ascetic-looking, he stood up in court and declared: "If you think that the people of Croatia are satisfied with their present lot, then give them a chance to declare themselves freely. I, for my part, will gladly abide by their decision." His real accuser, he said, was the

[1] *New York Times*, October 27, 1945, p. 1.

Communist Party, and he charged the regime with putting to death more than 260 Roman Catholic priests and trying to force the Church out of existence.

On October 11, Archbishop Stepinac was found guilty and sentenced to sixteen years in prison. Sentenced with him to lesser terms were eight other priests and Franciscan friars. An Ustaša official, Colonel Erik Lisak, clearly guilty of atrocities, was tried at the same time — doubtless with the political effect in mind — and condemned to death. The outcome of the Stepinac trial was not unpopular in the Orthodox areas of the country, but it, even more than the Mihailović case, brought a wave of feeling against Yugoslavia in the West. Soon thereafter, the Vatican formally excommunicated all those directly or indirectly concerned with the trial.

Religious Freedom

Generally speaking, the government's attitude toward religion in this period was one of reluctant semi-toleration provided the clergy did not manifest opposition to the regime. There was freedom of worship, in the sense that the churches were open and functioning. Some efforts were made to discourage public employees from attending church, but, by and large, the faithful worshipped without discrimination. The governments of the republics contributed large sums annually to the religious groups, and monasteries and convents were maintained. But there was not freedom of religion in the sense that the clergy was free to express itself on secular affairs.

The regime and the churches treated each other warily. On the government's side, as long as the churches stayed out of politics, there was little point in trying to force a showdown and inflaming public opinion — of which even a totalitarian government must take cognizance. On the churches' side, as long as they were permitted to operate at all there was hope that their religious mission could be fulfilled. Furthermore, as impossible as it may seem to Western Christians, there were numerous cases of persons who were either Orthodox or Roman Catholic — or Moslem — and Communist at the same time. This was especially true among backward peasants, whose grasp of the philosophy in neither Christianity nor Communism was sufficient for them to see the incompatibility of the two. Thus, while there was no real *modus vivendi* between church and state, neither was there open warfare.

The Five Year Plan

Among the things the Tito regime lacked were leaders with experience and ability in administration and economic affairs. On the other hand, that there was no lack of boldness or bravado was demonstrated by the Five Year Plan of 1947. The commission which drew up the plan was presided over by Boris Kidrič, a Slovene, but the impossibly high goals caused many Yugoslavs (who like to poke fun at Montenegrin heroics) to claim it was the work of Montenegrins. The Five Year Plan had political as well as economic objectives, and if it failed in the latter it had more success with the former. For as a concomitant of the Five Year Plan came completion of nationalization, which eliminated any private business except the smallest of service enterprises.

The second nationalization law, adopted in April 1948, was held to be "imperative for successful fulfillment" of the Five Year Plan. In addition to taking over the remaining producing enterprises, it also affected retail trade, insurance organizations, and cultural and health institutions. In some ways, the new law merely formalized the status quo, especially the many confiscations carried out minus legal sanction during the first two postwar years. Nationalization had in fact proceeded so rapidly that Kidrič, chairman of the Federal Economic Council, could report to the Fifth Congress of the CPY in 1948 that the state sector of the economy in 1946–1947 "already held the whole of industry on the federal and republican levels and 70 per cent of local industries."[1]

The new economic system was patterned closely after that in operation in the Soviet Union at the time. The outstanding feature was extreme centralization, which reached its apex in the elaborate planning hierarchy. In addition to the Federal Planning Commission and planning departments in each Belgrade ministry dealing with production, there were also republic planning commissions and planning sections in each republic ministry. According to a Yugoslav economist, "some 217 federal and republican ministers gave orders to directors [of industrial groups] and those in turn [gave orders] to factory managers."[2] The Five Year Plan, along with detailed annual and quarterly plans and even shorter plans by individual enterprises, rigidly fixed not only what and how much was to be produced but also from whom to buy and to whom to sell, together with wages and profits. All investment was centrally controlled, "profits" of enterprises being funneled into a centralized investments fund. Individual enterprises were under the control of a manager, appointed by governmental authority, but the manager had virtually no autonomy.[3]

[1] Boris Kidrič, *On the Construction of Socialist Economy in FPRY*, speech delivered at the Fifth Congress of the CPY, Office of Information Yugoslav Government, Belgrade, 1948, pp. 7–8.

[2] Rudolf Bicanić, "Economic Growth under Centralized and Decentralized Planning in Yugoslavia — A Case Study," *Economic Development and Cultural Change*, October 1957, p. 64.

[3] *Ibid.*, pp. 66–67.

The Five Year Plan proposed an increase in gross output of industry five times higher than in 1939. Productivity was to be increased by 66 per cent. Electric power production was to be boosted to four times that of 1939. Total investments were to amount to 27 per cent of the total national income during the last year of the plan.[1] The plan called for production of many items not previously made in Yugoslavia — "trucks, tractors, heavy loco-motives, heavy construction machinery, cranes, water turbines, large steam boilers, heavy and medium electrical machines, transformers, bicycles, type-writers, agricultural machinery of large type, electrical cables, coke, seamless pipe, prefabricated houses, radio sets, plastics, synthetic rubber, artificial fibres, nitrogenous fertilizers, etc."

An important aim of the plan was to distribute the new industries in such a way as to lessen the economic differences among the various parts of the country. Thus it was planned to locate more new factories in the most under-developed sections, particularly Bosnia and Herzegovina, Macedonia and Mon-tenegro, than in the more highly industrialized Slovenia and Croatia. This would, as the planners realized, increase costs. Further, it meant that Slovenia and Croatia were to contribute a large share of the new investment for the other republics. In time this became a political as well as an economic problem.

Agriculture

The political and economic duality of the plan also applied to agriculture, where the goals were less spectacular but still lacking in realism. Tito assured the peasants at the time that there would be no nationalization of land. Yet it was clear that collectivization was desired by the regime, not only for ideological reasons — i.e., it was seen as necessary for socialism — but also because it was intimately, if indirectly, tied up with the Five Year Plan. The regime's reasoning was that increased agricultural output was a necessary concomitant to industrialization, that increased output could come only through mechanization, that mechanization would be useful only if land were collectivized and that one important function of the new industrial economy would be to provide the necessary agricultural machinery.

The plan emphasized an increase in the number of tractors, in the consump-tion of fertilizer, in land drainage and irrigation, and in the acreage in cotton, wheat, corn, rice, sunflowers and sugar beets. Also, great emphasis was placed on increasing the number of Peasant Work Cooperatives (Seljačka Radna Zadruga), as the kolkhoz type of collective was called. The goal was that by 1951, 50 per cent of arable land was to be plowed by such collectives.[2]

[1] See *Law on the Five Year Plan*, Jugoslovenska Knjiga, Belgrade, 1947.
[2] See pp. 270–275

Yet the regime was inhibited by two factors from general forced collectivization. The first was that it rested heavily on peasant acceptance, if not support, and forced collectivization might knock this prop out from under it. The second was that there was no large body of "kulaks," or rich peasants, against whom to move. Even before the 1945 land reform law the average size of holdings was only 5 hectares. In Yugoslavia, as Tito acknowledged later, a kulak was simply a peasant who opposed the regime. There were also practical difficulties in that many of the dwarf holdings were on terrain which made them impossible to collectivize.

The result was that, although Tito in 1945 saw collective farms as "a matter of life and death,"[1] the regime adopted a "go slow" policy in agriculture in the years 1945-1948. Nevertheless, it did harshly discriminate against the peasants, with exorbitant forced deliveries, fixed low prices, high taxes, virtually no credit, and police intimidation of those peasants who resisted. What mechanized equipment was available was given only to collectives, and private peasants were forbidden to hire help. Despite all this, only 932 Peasant Work Cooperatives existed by 1948, with holdings amounting to 2.6 per cent of the total arable land.[2] Meanwhile, peasant antagonism toward the regime mounted.

Foreign Trade

The foreign trade part of the Five Year Plan reflected the great shift of trade to the Soviet Union and other Eastern European countries. By 1948 trade with Eastern Europe exceeded 50 per cent of the total. Trade agreements, involving investment credits, were signed with the Soviet bloc countries and were given an important role in developing industrial production.[3] The trade pattern set by the plan, at least for the first period, was supposedly based on exchange of agricultural goods and metals for capital goods. Each of the trade agreements signed in 1946 and 1947 with Eastern European countries listed exports to them of important metals and ores, with imports made up of heavy machinery and mining equipment.

[1] See Sir Malcolm Darling, "Collective Farming in Yugoslavia," *Manchester Guardian Weekly*, April 24, 1952, p. 7.

[2] For a discussion of agriculture during this period, see Ranko M. Brashich, *Land Reform and Ownership in Yugoslavia, 1919-1953*, Mid-European Studies Center, New York, 1954, pp. 44–60 and pp. 67–81. See also Petko Rašić, *Agricultural Development in Yugoslavia*, Jugoslavija, Belgrade, 1955. Yugoslav agricultural policy in general is analyzed in Chapter 15.

[3] Following the cessation of UNRRA supplies, no credit from Western countries was forthcoming until after the Yugoslav-Soviet dispute. As has already been mentioned, reparations did become available and were an important source of capital investment in this period. The organization of foreign trade is briefly discussed in J. V. Mladek, E. Sturc and M. R. Wyczalkowski, "The Change in the Yugoslav Economic System," *Staff Papers*, International Monetary Fund, November 1952, p. 414. See also Werner Markert, ed., *Jugoslawien*, Osteuropa-Handbuch, Böhlau-Verlag, Köln-Graz, 1954, pp. 236–240.

Failure of the Plan

The Five Year Plan failed ignominiously. In part this was because of the economic blockade imposed by the Cominform countries in 1949. But at least as much of the responsibility must be laid to the nature of the plan itself. Czeslaw Bobrowski, an eminent Polish government economist, in his generally sympathetic account of Yugoslav developments, derided the plan as "too far removed from reality to warrant its presentation." He termed it "a conglomeration of correct and mistaken ideas . . . mistaken most often as a consequence of a lack of moderation."[1] Other criticisms centered on the low priority given to agriculture as expressed in the small amount of investment for this sector of the economy. This policy was a factor in the crisis which soon came about in agriculture.

The Yugoslavs, forced to overhaul their production goals drastically, ultimately came to see the errors of the plan. Major contemporary Yugoslav criticism of it, however, concerns mostly the evils of centralized economic administration and bureaucracy and the lack of incentive to enterprise.[2] This meant, among other things, that enterprises could not increase profits because prices of their own factors of production were fixed and the suppliers were determined in advance. There was no relation between wage bills and profits since practically the whole profit was taxed away and wages were fixed. Thus, there were no means or tools for stimulating productivity. Further, a great number of the enterprises worked at a loss because prices were set too low.

In later days, the Yugoslavs were to refer to the period 1945–1949 as their "administrative period," a euphemism for a highly centralized, hard-boiled and doctrinaire totalitarianism. Yet, even though they repudiated many of the practices of the time and the theories that led to them, they continued to insist that the "administrative period" was essential for their development. Politically, it enabled them to consolidate their hold by silencing all active political opposition. Ideologically, it prepared the way for socialism by nationalizing virtually all the means of production, except in agriculture. Economically, even though the Five Year Plan itself was a colossal failure, it did set the country on the road to industrialization. Perhaps most important, it gave the leaders hard and costly lessons about what not to do.

Foreign Policy

The self-confidence and assertiveness with which the Tito regime came out of the war also reflected itself in foreign policy. Ambitious aims in foreign

---

[1] Czeslaw Bobrowski, *La Yougoslavie Socialiste*, A. Colin, Paris, 1956, pp. 81–82.

[2] Cf. Jaša Davičo, "Economic System and Planning in Yugoslavia," lectures presented at the Institute of Social Studies, The Hague, April 1957, p. 16 (mimeographed). Davičo was the editor of the influential and authoritative Belgrade economic journal *Ekonomska Politika*.

policy produced relations with the West which were the worst of any Eastern European country; and they were a factor in the growing uneasiness of Yugoslav-Soviet relations, although this facet of affairs was long concealed behind the Iron Curtain.

Foreign policy in the period 1945–1948 was dominated by territorial disputes in Eastern Europe and ideologically prompted hostility between Yugoslavia and the capitalist West. It may be that the uncertainty with which it increasingly viewed its big Soviet brother influenced the Tito regime, at least subconsciously, to be more intransigent than it might otherwise have been.[1]

There were, however, important issues involved. The dispute over Venezia Giulia, already referred to,[2] remained as a source of friction between Yugoslavia and the West long after a *modus vivendi* had been established. The Yugoslavs were indignant at the compromise that was worked out establishing two zones, with the city of Trieste in the Western zone. Further, they felt, but did not express at the time, resentment at the Soviet failure to support to the bitter end their demands for the whole of the peninsula.

Another touchy point concerned the Austrian province of Carinthia. Partly Slavic, the population of Carinthia had voted in 1920 to stay with Austria. In the last stages of World War II, Partisan troops had occupied part of the region of Carinthia along the Drava River, and, as in Trieste, a clash with the British was narrowly averted. Now Tito revived the claim to Carinthia, which the West steadfastly denied. After the break with Belgrade, the USSR accepted the principle that Austria should lose no territory. And ultimately the 1955 Austrian peace treaty, of course, included Carinthia in Austria as nearly everybody—including, very likely, most Yugoslavs—assumed that it ultimately would.

Balkan Policy

In the Balkans, Yugoslav ambitions were of a different nature, and undoubtedly of greater significance to basic state interests. The most important issue concerned the question of a South Slav Union which would include both Yugoslavia and Bulgaria. The two peoples, both South Slavs, had repeatedly feuded over Macedonia, and a federation had long been advocated as one way out. Even before the end of the war, Edvard Kardelj, Tito's chief

---

[1] Dedijer, in his official biography of Tito, wrote that at this time "we thought it was necessary to push these disputes and disagreements with the Soviet Union into the background because during the early postwar years Western pressure against us was heavier and the greater danger threatened us from that quarter." Vladimir Dedijer, *Tito*, Simon & Schuster, New York, 1953, p. 251.

[2] See Chapter 5.

spokesman on foreign affairs, had made two propositions to the Bulgarians. One was that Bulgarian Macedonia, or Pirin Macedonia as it is sometimes called, be merged with Yugoslav Macedonia. The other was that Bulgaria itself become a republic inside Yugoslavia. The Bulgarians demurred at the latter proposition, suggesting instead a dual federation with Bulgaria and Yugoslavia as equal component parts. This suggestion was unacceptable to the Yugoslavs. The issue, which was to become a factor in the Soviet-Yugoslav dispute, was referred to Stalin, who apparently decided in favor of the Yugoslav position.[1] Meanwhile, the Bulgarians agreed — at the Party level but not governmentally — to go through with a merger of the two Macedonias. The affair, shrouded in the mysteries of Balkan politics, came to naught when Moscow later abruptly disavowed the whole matter of a Balkan Federation.[2]

The issue of a Balkan Federation, which the Yugoslavs clearly hoped to dominate, was related also to the question of Albania, where Yugoslavia had been playing a leading role since the end of the war. Albania was something of a Yugoslav satellite in the immediate postwar period: Belgrade advised Tirana on many decisions, the country was flooded with Yugoslav advisers, and Yugoslav economic assistance was administered by joint Yugoslav-Albanian companies. Albania's absorption into a powerful Balkan federation was considered most likely. This too was an irritant to Moscow, although, according to Dedijer, Stalin approved Yugoslavia's Albanian policy and in 1948 told Djilas: "Yugoslavia is free to swallow Albania any time it wishes to do so."[3]

Conflict with the West

More important to Yugoslavia's relations with the West was still another Balkan matter, that of Greece. During the war the ubiquitous Yugoslav Communists had been active in Greek Macedonia, and their efforts contributed to the strong Communist-led Greek guerilla movement against the monarchial government re-established by the British. The main support for the Greek guerillas, headed by Moscow-trained Markos Vafiades, came from Yugoslavia. The USSR may have favored the struggle in Greece at one point, but indications are that, contrary to belief in the West, by 1947, at least, had taken a stand against it. Stalin was here motivated apparently by the same

---

[1] So Dedijer reported. See *Tito*, p. 304. In Dedijer's opinion Stalin was deliberately trying to drive a wedge between the Yugoslavs and the Bulgars.

[2] See Chapter 8.

[3] Dedijer, *Tito*, p. 311. When Djilas protested that "there is no question of swallowing Albania, but of friendly relations between two countries," Molotov spoke up and, according to Dedijer, declared: "Well, that's one and the same thing."

tactical reasoning that explained his earlier coolness to the Partisans, namely, that it was unlikely to succeed. Indeed, according to Dedijer, Stalin told Foreign Minister Kardelj in February 1948: ". . . we do not agree with Yugoslav comrades that they should help further the Greek Partisans. . . . Yugoslav comrades should stop helping them. That struggle has no prospects whatsoever."[1]

By this time, however, British and American alarm at developments in Greece had been sufficient to produce the Truman Doctrine and active U. S. intervention. A United Nations commission of inquiry had been established to look into Greek matters, and Albania and Bulgaria, which also had been aiding the Greek rebels, together with Yugoslavia refused to permit its members to work inside their borders.

Relations between Yugoslavia and the United States, which still viewed Belgrade primarily as an adjunct of Soviet policy, had become strained indeed. Bad feeling toward Yugoslavia was widespread in America not only because of the Mihailović and Stepinac cases, but also because the Yugoslavs had, in August 1946, shot down two American airplanes, resulting in the death of several U. S. soldiers. The State Department, branding the Yugoslav action "outrageous," delivered a virtual ultimatum to Belgrade. If U. S. demands in connection with the attacks on the aircraft were not met within forty-eight hours, the State Department declared, the Security Council of the United Nations would be called upon "to take appropriate action." Belgrade retorted that American military aircraft continually violated Yugoslav territory despite official protests. But in the end Yugoslavia satisfied the American demands and promised that no U. S. transport planes would be fired at, even if making unauthorized flights over Yugoslav territory.

Still further disputes between Yugoslavia and the United States involved detention of the Yugoslav Danube fleet in Germany, the gold deposited in New York by the Royal government and frozen by U. S. action, and claims resulting from expropriation of American-owned property and from lend-lease accounts. Unfailing supporters of the USSR in cold war issues before the United Nations and elsewhere, Yugoslavia in 1948 was regarded as the most intransigent of all the Soviet bloc countries. The Yugoslav Communists, in turn, saw the capitalist West as an implacable enemy, hostile, imperialist and warlike. On neither side were these views destined long to continue without change.

[1] *Tito*, pp. 321-322.

PART III

THE EMERGENCE

OF TITOISM

YUGOSLAVIA'S

UNIQUE POSITION

IF observers generally in the West saw any difference at all between Yugoslavia and the rest of the Communist-dominated countries of Eastern Europe
in the spring of 1948, it was that the Yugoslav regime seemed to be the most
pro-Soviet, the most completely "communized" and the most hard-boiled
of the lot. That Yugoslavia was a model satellite of the USSR none doubted.

From the vantage point of hindsight, it is now apparent that the West
was the prisoner of a rigid prototype which did not fit the facts. The facts —
obscured by Iron Curtain secrecy — were that there were sharp differences
between the situation in Yugoslavia and that elsewhere in the Soviet bloc.
The principal difference was that, as mentioned earlier, the Yugoslav Communists, unlike their comrades elsewhere in Eastern Europe, had come to
power and were kept in power largely through their own efforts rather than
by Soviet might.

It is true that the Communist regimes in Czechoslovakia and Albania were
not installed by Soviet forces either. In both of these regimes, however, Soviet
might was an important factor, while other factors worked against their
taking an independent course. Czechoslovakia in the first postwar years was
not a Soviet satellite, in any formal sense. The Red Army did not stay in
occupation. The Communists were the largest party, but they achieved
parliamentary strength through a free election in 1946, and the country continued its earlier democratic path until the Communist *coup d'état* of February
1948. Although the Czechoslovak Communists pulled this off themselves,
without physical interference by the Soviet Union, the Red Army's occupation of two-thirds or more of the country in 1945 did, in fact, lay the groundwork for Communist strength at the local level. Furthermore, most of the

top Czech Communist leaders were creatures of Moscow from the start, having been in the USSR during the war and acting afterwards on Soviet orders, presumably even in the timing of their *coup d'état*. In contriving their *coup*, they used the threat of Soviet military intervention as a club over the heads of the opposition. Although numerically stronger than Communists elsewhere in Eastern Europe, the Czech Communists presided somewhat precariously at first, both because they were shattering traditions of political democracy in Czechoslovakia and also because some members of their own party inclined toward a nationalist stand.

In Albania — in many ways less a nation than a group of clans or tribes — Yugoslav influences had been considerable. The Communist leadership was split, apparently more over the issue of personal power than ideology. With Yugoslavia isolated after the break with the Cominform, it was not too difficult for the more Soviet-oriented faction to oust those whom Belgrade had been backing and then cling tightly to Moscow for support.

The Satellites Proper

In all of Eastern Europe except Czechoslovakia, the Communist parties had been outlawed during most of the period between the wars. For a good part of this time their leaders were in the Soviet Union. With the exception of the Yugoslav leaders, most of the top men in the Eastern European Communist parties had sat out the war in Moscow.[1] They were virtually unknown in their own countries, and they were out of touch with their own followers. While all the Communist parties in Eastern Europe participated in underground activities against the Germans during the war, except in Poland and Yugoslavia these did not amount to much. In Poland there was conflict between the Communist and non-Communist resistance forces as there was in Yugoslavia, although different and of smaller proportions. But in Poland the Communists were from the start intimately tied in with the Soviet war effort, as a result of the Soviet occupation of part of the country in 1939, and they were unable to win over the non-Communist forces, i.e., the Polish Home Army, without the support of Soviet forces.

When the Red Army came into Eastern Europe, driving the Germans before it, the refugee Communist leaders — Bierut of Poland, Rákosi of Hungary, Gheorgiu Dej of Rumania, Gottwald of Czechoslovakia, Dimitrov of Bulgaria and others — returned to their homelands with the Soviet troops. With virtually no following in their own countries, they would have had little chance of coming to power — at least without long and bloody civil wars — if the Soviet occupation forces had not installed them in power. Nor could

---

[1] An exception was Wladislaw Gomulka of Poland, who was deposed in 1948.

they then have been assured of staying in power without Soviet support. They began operations, furthermore, without any organization they could really call their own.[1] The parties had to be built up almost from scratch. While the Communists, with the backing of the Soviet Army, were the dominant forces in these countries, there were at first coalition governments rather than Communist governments as such. Communist control of the police and army was far from certain, the more so as these organizations contained many holdovers from the old regimes. The parties were organized with the assistance of Soviet advisers, who also gradually helped the Communists reorganize the police and armies and then launched them on the road to planning, industrialization and socialism. The Soviet advisers naturally saw to it that both the new organizations and the policies adopted were oriented to the USSR. In Poland, Hungary, Rumania and Bulgaria, all this was accomplished while the Red Army was still in occupation.

The Yugoslav Exception

In the case of Yugoslavia, however, regardless of how important the Red Army was in administering the *coup de grâce* in Belgrade, the Partisans had liberated most of their country themselves — and with more assistance from the West than from the Soviet Union. Thus, far from feeling beholden to the Russians, the Yugoslav Communists were trying to bury in their subconscious the resentment built up during the war when Moscow ignored their pleas for help and even gave comfort to the Četnik enemy.

Furthermore, the Partisans constituted a nationwide organization whose valiant military successes had produced a not inconsiderable *esprit de corps* and loyalty to the wartime leadership. It is true that this loyalty was given by many either out of ignorance of the ideological orientation of the Partisan movement or, in some cases, in spite of it. And it is true also that when the leadership donned its true Communist colors many backed off. By and large, however, an overwhelming majority of the 800,000 to 900,000 Yugoslavs in the Partisan movement at the end of the war remained loyal to Tito the peacetime leader as they had to Tito the wartime leader. Nor was support for the new regime initially limited to those who had been Partisans.

In addition, the Yugoslav Communists had a thoroughly tested organization. Tito and his lieutenants had never neglected Party affairs even at the height of the war, and the Party's domination was always certain. While the Partisan army provided the nucleus of the Yugoslav peacetime army, there had already been established, through AVNOJ, a government, with its own

---

[1] As indicated above, the situation in Czechoslovakia does not quite fit the pattern. The Czech Communist leader, Klement Gottwald, did return to Prague only with the Red Army, but he had waiting for him a going Party organization and some following in addition.

police and other controls. Having accomplished the liberation of Belgrade and having found things well under Communist control, the Soviet forces left almost immediately for the Hungarian front. Thus Yugoslavia was never subjected to actual Red Army occupation. Although the usual bevy of Soviet advisers remained — a great many of them at the request of the Tito regime — they were thus forced to operate within the framework of the Yugoslav setup rather than being able to take orders from and appeal to Soviet military authority on the spot.

All this is to say that the Communist regime in Yugoslavia was a going concern, with its own established ways of doing things, even before it formally and legally took over the government in Belgrade. And having ensconced themselves in power, the Yugoslav Communists were well able to stay there. The only formal opposition to them, from Šubašić, Grol and others, was never such as to jeopardize their position, and after the 1945 election, even this vanished. What's more, progress toward a socialist system, begun before the war's end with the nationalization decree of 1944, was supplemented immediately with more far-reaching measures. About the thoroughgoing Communist nature of the regime there was no doubt whatsoever.

The Yugoslav Party

The Yugoslav Communist Party itself was different from the parties elsewhere in Eastern Europe. Of the 12,000 who were members in 1941, only 3,000 survived the war. By 1945 Party membership was 140,000, and by 1948 it had increased to 448,175. The core of the party consisted, therefore, of Partisans and Partisan sympathizers who were bound together not only by the ties of Marxist devotion. They had come to Communism during and as a result of an intense national experience, when the interest of their country, rather than the interest of world Communism and the USSR, was uppermost. While their allegiance did not exclude the Soviet Union, it also very definitely included their own country and its leaders.

Also significant was the social composition of both the Party and the People's Front. In 1948 about half of the membership of the Party consisted of peasants. In the People's Front, which was formed out of the Partisan movement, the percentage of peasants was considerably greater. But in the other countries, even those with as large a proportion of peasants as Yugoslavia, the role of the peasants was noticeably weaker. The other Eastern European Communist parties in particular included considerably fewer peasants and drew their members more from workers and other city people. A Communist Party thus constituted is, obviously, much more in the Leninist mold than the Yugoslav organization was.

Other Factors

Three other factors should be mentioned in distinguishing the Yugoslav situation. One is the traditional fiery nationalism of the South Slavs and, particularly in the case of the Serbs and the Montenegrins, their propensity to indulge in romantic and heroic measures. Attribution of national characteristics is always dangerous and liable to exaggeration, especially in the case of a people so heterogeneous as the Yugoslavs. Yet in matters like intense nationalism and willingness to tackle overwhelming odds, there is no doubt that the South Slavs as a whole differ from, say, the Czechs. (On the other hand, the Poles also are more than a little touched with some of the same nationalist fervor and romanticism that characterizes the Yugoslavs.)

The second factor is Tito himself. Alone among the Communist leaders of the new regimes in Eastern Europe, Tito was a national figure and military hero commanding support and loyalty outside of and beyond the Party. Tito was, in fact, more popular than his regime. There was about him, this Croat peasant boy turned revolutionary and now head of his country, the dynamic and magnetic quality of a leader. Whereas the "strong men" of the other Eastern European parties were strong men primarily because they had been tapped by Moscow, Tito was a strong man in his own right.

The third factor is geography. Except for Albania, Yugoslavia was farther removed from Soviet frontiers than the other new Communist states of Eastern Europe. This factor has sometimes been exaggerated in the West, in part for the same reasons that made Western observers generally ignore the other differences. The firmer Soviet hold on the other people's democracies was not basically dependent on their proximity to the USSR. Furthermore, its hold on Bulgaria, Rumania and Hungary, bordering Yugoslavia on the East, surely was sufficient to give the USSR most if not all the advantages vis-à-vis Belgrade that might have ensued from a common frontier. Perhaps the importance of this geographical factor was more psychological than geopolitical. Yet it may well have influenced Soviet policy toward Yugoslavia and vice versa.[1]

What all these differences add up to is simply that Yugoslavia was never a Soviet satellite in the same sense as the other Eastern European states. At the same time, the Yugoslav Communists were bound to Moscow and to Soviet policies by ideological ties that were *almost* as binding as those circumscribing the other countries. Despite their wartime experiences with Soviet cooperation, the possibility of real conflict between their interests and

---

[1] In this connection it is interesting that an anti-Soviet orientation also developed in Albania. Again, geography may have been a factor, although it is likely that a change in Moscow's policy—plus factors involving relations with China—was more important.

the interests of the USSR never seemed to enter their minds. To Tito and his chief aides, the differences — if they thought about them at all — meant not any departure from Soviet leadership but only a consideration of themselves as being in a rather special category, subordinate to Moscow but perhaps ranking somewhat above the other Communist states.

The general failure in the West to understand the true situation was due in part to a failure to understand the nature of the international Communist movement and of those participating in it. The idea of religiouslike devotion of the Communists to Soviet leadership tended to elude the pragmatic West. Soviet domination, in the prevailing Western view, was entirely an enforced domination. A satellite was a satellite, and that was that.

Perhaps, however, the West should be excused for its inability to see the differences between Yugoslavia and the other new Communist states, because these differences were to some extent ignored by the Soviet Union also.

The Prewar Pattern

During the days when there was only one Communist nation, the USSR, the pattern of Soviet domination of foreign Communist parties was in some ways a logical one. At the time of the Bolshevik Revolution, it was not unnatural for those left-wing socialists outside Russia to defend it by all possible means as a spark from which a Marxist flame could spread throughout the world. They willingly joined in the Comintern not only as a general staff for world revolution but also as a device to aid the beleaguered Bolshevik state against its capitalist invaders. When, not long afterwards, Bolshevik expectations for world revolution were dampened and Lenin had to turn his attention to building up the Soviet state, it was again not unnatural that there developed the idea that the main function of Communists elsewhere was to safeguard the unique Communist state — precariously existing in what Stalin later described as a hostile capitalist sea — as a home base for future Marxist developments elsewhere.

Not only was this function in keeping with Lenin's cautious admonitions against "left-wing Communism," but, indeed, as the normalcy of the twenties proceeded, there was not much else for the Communists to do. There was ideological conflict, the Trotsky opposition and occasionally some personal resentment at the Kremlin's high-handed methods, but in general it was accepted that the Communists' first — and perhaps only — allegiance was to the Soviet Union.[1] As long as the Soviet Union remained the sole Communist state, there was little basis for conflict on this point.

---

[1] See, for example, the account of Comintern procedure by Ignazio Silone in Richard Crossman (ed.), *The God That Failed*, Harper, New York, 1949, especially pp. 99–114.

Stalin, however, apparently failed to recognize the change brought about by the establishment of other Communist states. He persisted in treating those Communists in power in Eastern Europe exactly as he had treated foreign Communists in the period of the single Communist state. It is hard to say whether he was merely a prisoner of his own stereotype or whether this was a deliberate policy based on considerations of security, his well-known distrust of foreign Communists, and his conviction that times were such that no revolution could succeed without Soviet direction. It is true, of course, that the new Communist leaders were inexperienced in statecraft and more expert at conspiracy than in the ideology of Marxism-Leninism-Stalinism. In any event, Soviet policy right after the war was, in brief, to dictate to the Eastern European Communist parties in all things and to use them to subordinate the interests of their countries to the interests of the USSR.

People's Democracy

To deal with the new situation in theoretical terms, the Kremlin, possibly borrowing from Mao Tse-tung,[1] devised the concept of the people's democracy. The term was never clearly defined, but in general in the years 1945–1948 a people's democracy was considered to be a regime moving toward socialism without the dictatorship of the proletariat. This meant a situation in which the Communist Party was able to play a leading role because it had the support of the Red Army, but in which the Communists collaborated with non-Communist parties; as initially put forward, a people's democracy was a regime that was not fully socialist, one where there was less than complete nationalization and, especially, no over-all collectivization of agriculture.[2]

The concept of people's democracy apparently reflected the tendency of the Soviet Union to act within a theoretical framework even if the theory had to be stretched to fit the action. Soviet Marxist-Leninist ideology excludes the "export of revolution." It holds that a Communist revolution can develop only out of what Lenin termed "objective conditions," and the Communists are seen as coming to power by two stages — first a "bourgeois revolutionary stage," in which the liberal-nationalist non-Communist forces prevail, but in which the Communists collaborate; and then a Marxist revolution, in which the Communists take over and establish a dictatorship of the prole-

---

[1] See Mao's *New Democracy*, published in 1940, and Benjamin Schwartz, "China and the Soviet Theory of People's Democracy," *Problems of Communism*, September-October 1954.

[2] Cf. Samuel L. Sharp, "The Theory of People's Democracy," in C. E. Black (ed.), *Readings on Contemporary Eastern Europe*, Mid-European Studies Center of the National Committee for a Free Europe, New York, 1953, pp. 71–76; and Doreen Warriner, *Revolution in Eastern Europe*, Turnstile Press, London, 1950. See also *Pravda*, October 17, 1946.

tariat. On the other hand, in Eastern Europe, where Soviet power was dominant, the Kremlin had already decided to install Communist governments but, because of Soviet power, the second revolution and, possibly, a dictatorship of the proletariat were unnecessary.

In any event, the idea of people's democracy, as first put forth, seems to have envisaged a situation — however temporary — where Soviet power would permit Communist direction of society — in collaboration with "bourgeois" groups — without full and formal Communist domination, that is, without a dictatorship of the proletariat.

Since the USSR would be "protecting" the position of the Communists in the people's democracy, it was implied in the theory that Moscow had not only the right but the duty to direct things, to make sure that progress toward full socialism was maintained and was in the right direction. Thus there was blended together the justification of continued Soviet direction of foreign Communist parties with the new reality of these Communist parties in positions of national power.

Alone of the countries of Eastern Europe, Yugoslavia did not fit this concept of people's democracy. In Yugoslavia there was no question about full Communist domination. There were no "bourgeois" groups collaborating with the Communist Party. There was a dictatorship of the proletariat, however "unproletarian" (because of agrarian influences) it may have been. There was, of course, no Soviet protecting power, nor was there any need for it under these circumstances. With the Five Year Plan of 1947, especially, the Tito regime had launched itself on the road to socialism.

Moscow's attitude, nevertheless, was to treat Yugoslavia simply as another people's democracy. In one sense, therein lay the essence of the historic Soviet-Yugoslav dispute soon to come. Even where the Communists operated more slowly and under "protection" of Soviet forces, conflicts arose between what Moscow wanted and what the local Communist leaders thought feasible. But these presented no serious problem for the Kremlin — nor, really, for the local Communists either, since they had no alternative but to do Moscow's bidding. For the Communist leaders in the satellites to have opposed Moscow would have undercut their own positions, since they were maintained by Moscow. In Yugoslavia the situation was almost exactly the reverse. For the Yugoslav Communist leaders to have given in to Moscow would have undercut their position, since it was maintained not by Moscow but by factors internal to Yugoslavia.

CONFLICT WITH

THE USSR

IN ITS broad outlines, the conflict that developed between Yugoslavia and the Soviet Union after the war was a conflict between the idea of Communism primarily in the interest of the USSR and the idea of Communism in the interest of an individual nation. What this amounted to in practice was a Soviet effort at political and economic domination and Yugoslav resistance to it. There were also overtones of ideological differences which ultimately were to become important.

Similar conflicts existed between the Soviet Union and the other new regimes in Eastern Europe. But because of the differences between Yugoslavia and the other countries, the conflicts with Belgrade were sharper and less easily resolved.

We have already noted the tendency of the Soviet Union to consider developments in Yugoslavia almost exclusively from its own standpoint. The Soviet view of the Partisan war effort was one example, and the Soviet attitude on Trieste was another. In both cases, the Kremlin's position was displeasing to the Yugoslav Communist leaders. In both cases, the Yugoslavs reacted sharply and critically. And in each instance, Moscow was offended by the reaction.

Early Tensions

The Yugoslavs' sense of grievance at the failure of Moscow to support them down the line on the issue of Trieste was particularly displeasing to Stalin since Tito gave vent to it in public. His speech at Ljubljana on May 28, 1945, may have also reflected pique at learning of Stalin's agreement with Churchill to share influence in Yugoslavia on a 50-50 basis. He declared:

It is claimed that this is a just war, and up to now we have considered it as such. But we also want a just end to it. We demand that everyone shall be master in his own house. We do not want to pay other peoples' bills. We do not want to get involved in any spheres of influence. . . . Never again will we be dependent on anybody.

Almost at once, Sadchikov, the Soviet ambassador in Belgrade, protested to Kardelj, Tito's foreign minister. He was obviously acting on instructions from Moscow, for on June 5 he followed this up with a formal communication from the Soviet government which read:

We regard Comrade Tito's speech as an unfriendly attack on the Soviet Union and Comrade Kardelj's explanation as unsatisfactory. The public here understood Comrade Tito's speech in the manner stated; nor can it be understood in any other. Tell Comrade Tito that, if he should once again permit such an attack on the Soviet Union, we shall be obliged to reply with open criticism in the press and disavow him.[1]

These were strong words to address to an equal and independent government, nor, as it turned out, was this the last of the matter. However, whether or not, as the Soviet government later claimed, Kardelj not only agreed with the Russians but also told Sadchikov of his hopes that Yugoslavia would become a "constituent part of the USRR,"[2] Belgrade in those days had no thought other than following Soviet leadership. The incident seems to have been interpreted in Yugoslavia not at all as a harbinger of things to come. In Moscow, however, careful note was made of it in a dossier which was soon to be filled with case after case where the Yugoslavs had incurred Soviet displeasure. Also listed were Yugoslav efforts to prevent the USSR from acquiring direction of the army and police, infiltrating the country with intelligence agents and exploiting the economy.

Already there had been a minor crisis in Soviet-Yugoslav relations involving Soviet troops during their brief stay in Yugoslavia at the time Belgrade was liberated. The Red Army was never known for undue gentleness toward the civilian populations of countries it occupied. The forces under Marshal Tolbukhin which drove the Germans from Belgrade in 1944 had, it seems, behaved in a way shocking to even the most hardened student of army depredations. According to the Yugoslavs, with their Communist penchant for statistics, the Soviet forces during their brief stay in Yugoslavia were

[1] Royal Institute of International Affairs, *The Soviet-Yugoslav Dispute*, Oxford University Press, London, 1948, p. 36.

[2] Subsequent Yugoslav denials of the accuracy of Sadchikov's report may well be valid, although, on the other hand, it would not be surprising if Kardelj, in 1945, had indeed spoken in the vein indicated.

responsible for 1,219 rapes, 329 attempted rapes, 111 rapes with murder and 1,204 robberies with violence.[1] The dangerous antics of intoxicated Russians with light trigger fingers had been legion in Belgrade at the time of liberation. One soldier had even wounded Tito's son Žarko in a night club; on another occasion, the wife of a member of the National Committee had been assaulted.[2]

Such was the political impact of these atrocities that the Yugoslav Politburo invited General Kornieyev, chief of the Soviet military mission, to attend a discussion on the matter. In the course of the meeting, Milovan Djilas remarked, according to Dedijer, that "the acts were all the more unfortunate as the bourgoisie in Belgrade was using them against the Red Army, saying that the British Officers . . . were more civil than the Soviet."[3]

At this, General Kornieyev broke up the meeting by protesting violently that such accusations were untrue. He forthwith complained to Moscow that Djilas said Soviet officers were morally inferior to British officers. Stalin reacted angrily and at once with a telegram to Tito. Both Tito and Djilas wrote Stalin explanations, and, a year later in Moscow, orally explained what had happened. Presumably Stalin was appeased, but this incident also went into the dossier on Yugoslavia for later use.

Soviet Efforts to Dominate

Now, with the Red Army gone, a horde of Soviet military advisers took its place. Initially they came at Yugoslav request, but in numbers exceeding what the Yugoslavs had expected.[4] Moreover, their advice was not limited to areas where the Yugoslavs desired it. In particular, the Soviet generals present bucked Yugoslav plans for a self-sufficient army. They refused to recommend Soviet aid for building an armaments industry and, instead, proposed that the Soviet Union supply the Yugoslav army with arms and equipment. But it was to be arms and equipment considered necessary in Moscow, not in Belgrade. What the Russians wanted, in effect, was that the Yugoslav army be remodeled so as to become subsidiary to the Red Army. Furthermore, they scorned to draw on the Partisans' experience against the Germans and Četnici and called for training based on Red Army tactics.

[1] See Vladimir Dedijer, *Tito*, Simon & Schuster, New York, 1953, p. 263. Dedijer's biography is a primary source for information concerning the Soviet-Yugoslav dispute. A comrade of Tito's and a leading journalist, as well as a Communist official, Dedijer was close enough to events to know, even though not often personally involved. Much of the material comes directly from Tito. The biography thus reflects an official Yugoslav view, and in some of its nuances and omissions it tells less than a completely objective story. The evidence indicates, however, that in general Dedijer's *Tito* can be relied on.

[2] Fitzroy Maclean, *The Heretic: The Life and Times of Josip Broz-Tito*, Harper, New York, 1957, p. 267.

[3] Dedijer, *Tito*, p. 264.

[4] So says Dedijer. Stalin, however, claimed just the opposite. See *The Soviet-Yugoslav Dispute*, p. 12.

In addition, the Soviet officers were paid salaries many times higher than those paid to Yugoslav officers of comparable rank. They demanded orderlies, which do not exist in the Yugoslav army. They were highhanded and arrogant in their relations with the Yugoslavs.

Complaints began to multiply. Conflicts between Yugoslav and Soviet army men were on occasion brought to Tito, who more often than not took the side of his own officers. The question of the army, whose army it really was to be, and what kind of an army, was undoubtedly of prime importance to both Tito and Stalin.

Similarly, the Russians tried to get the Yugoslavs to make over their civilian agencies on the Soviet pattern, and had constant advice about how to run the Communist Party. The Soviet ambassador, as was the custom of Soviet envoys in the satellites, followed the practice of asking secondary officials of both government and Party for detailed information and was piqued when, as often happened, he was rebuffed.

Soviet army and civilian advisers alike repeatedly tried to recruit Yugoslav citizens to be Soviet agents. Such efforts were aimed particularly at pene-trating the army, the economic administration, the interior and transport ministries and, even, the Party apparatus. According to Dedijer, when Colonel Ivan Stepanov thus approached a young coding clerk in the interior ministry, he spoke "about the leaders of the Communist Party of Yugoslavia in disparaging terms" and said "there was at present nothing to suspect Comrade Tito of, that he was working as he should for the present, but that this was not the case with the others." A General Soldatov, Soviet military instructor attached to the headquarters of the Fourth Yugoslav Army, similarly seeking to sign up the Yugoslavs as agents, was said to have declared: "Yugoslavia is a small country which can exist only with the Soviet Union. We Russians and no one else liberated Yugoslavia, and we are entitled to request you to do what we require and what we tell you to do."[1]

There were dozens of such instances.

As it turned out, these Soviet efforts were successful in some very high places. Among those who, one way or another, were enlisted to the Soviet cause were General Arso Jovanović, the chief of staff of the Yugoslav Army; Andrija Hebrang, a member of the Politburo; and Sretan Žujović, a member of the Central Committee.

Economic Exploitation

The case of the latter two, Hebrang and Žujović, also involved the con-troversy over economic matters. Dedijer insists "the fundamental matter on

[1] Dedijer, *Tito*, pp. 261–262.

which the conflict began," was that "the Soviet Union intended to subjugate Yugoslavia economically, to prevent Yugoslavia's industrialization and to delay the further socialist development in our country."[1]

As far as exploitation goes, it was apparent in several ways. The most obvious was the proposal for joint stock companies that worked so well elsewhere in Eastern Europe. Two were formed, Justa, for air transport, and Juspad, for Danube shipping.

In the case of Justa, both the Soviet Union and Yugoslavia put up capital of 100 million dinars. The Yugoslavs provided airports, communications and 5 million dinars cash, while the Soviet Union provided the aircraft, technical installations and an equal amount in cash. But Yugoslav assets were calculated at 1938 prices, which were comparatively low, while Soviet assets were calculated at 1946–1947 prices, which were comparatively high. When the Yugoslav government provided an airport near Belgrade, its real value, according to the Yugoslavs, was twenty times higher than that for which they were given credit. The Russian director-general of the joint company, in figuring valuation of airports, refused to count the value of labor involved, only of the land. On the other hand, he claimed for Justa all installations, buildings and other fixtures. Since profits were divided on the basis of capital invested, the Soviet return was enormously higher than the Yugoslav. On top of this, Justa demanded that the Yugoslav national airline relinquish all foreign runs and generally subordinated it to the joint company.[2]

Yugoslav interests came off still worse in connection with Juspad. In addition to gaining control of the better Yugoslav Danube vessels on extremely favorable terms, the Soviet director of Juspad discriminated against Yugoslavia in the fixing of shipping rates. For Soviet goods, the basic rate was 0.19 dinars; for goods of other Danubian countries, 0.28 dinars; and for Yugoslav goods, 0.40 dinars. Dedijer says the result was that in 1948 Yugoslavia had to pay an extra 38 million dinars for the privilege of shipping Yugoslav goods on Yugoslav vessels.

The Russians also proposed joint companies for the production of steel, iron, nonferrous metals, bauxite and oil. When, during negotiations on the matter, the Yugoslav representatives protested that they were primarily concerned about agreements to aid their industrialization plans, the chief of the Soviet delegation, Yatrov, declared, according to Dedijer: "What do you need heavy industry for? In the Urals we have everything you need." The Soviets turned down point-blank a Yugoslav request for an aluminum plant.[3]

[1] *Ibid.*, pp. 267 and 289.
[2] *Ibid.*, pp. 282–284.
[3] *Ibid.*, pp. 278 and 287.

Other than Justa and Juspad, no joint companies were ever formed, however, because the Yugoslavs balked at Soviet terms. In the case of proposals for a joint oil company, the concern would have exclusive rights of prospecting and exploitation of all oil fields in Yugoslavia but would, at the same time, be exempt from Yugoslav laws. The value of the oil fields was not to count in computing Yugoslavia's share in the undertaking, no return was to be paid for the oil extracted over and above the cost of land use, and the price of oil sold in Yugoslavia would be higher than that sold to the USSR.[1]

In addition to all this, the Russians proposed a Soviet-Yugoslav Bank for the joint companies and all Soviet-Yugoslav trade, which was constantly looming more important. The Bank itself would not be a joint undertaking but entirely a Soviet enterprise, a Soviet agency. Yet it would also engage in domestic banking operations inside Yugoslavia.[2]

Finally, it was determined that Kardelj, in Moscow on other matters in March 1947, should present the whole question to Stalin. Although Kardelj told Stalin the Yugoslavs were unable to accept Soviet proposals "for both political and economic reasons," he then declared that "we are interested in founding a joint oil extraction refining company."

To Kardelj's surprise, Stalin waved his remark aside, saying, "Of course it is not a good form of cooperation to found joint-stock companies in an allied and friendly country like Yugoslavia. . . . Such companies are suitable for satellite countries." Instead, Stalin proposed that the Soviet Union directly assist the Yugoslavs in oil production and give them an aluminum factory and a steel plant.

This conversation was followed by an agreement in 1947 under which the USSR promised to grant Yugoslavia capital goods credits in the amount of $135 million, involving a steel factory complete with coking plant, refinery and drilling equipment, a zinc electrolysis plant, a sulphuric acid factory, copper and aluminum rolling mills and machinery for producing molybdenum. Before Soviet-Yugoslav relations were ruptured a year later, the USSR had sent capital goods worth only $800,000.

Dedijer claims that Stalin promised capital goods to Yugoslavia only "to throw us off our guard," that "the agreement was a mere ruse" and that "the Soviet Union had no intention of honoring it."[3]

It was obvious that the Soviet proposals for the Yugoslav economy were in direct conflict with the Yugoslav Five Year Plan for rapid industrialization. As mentioned earlier, the plan reflected more enthusiasm than wisdom and

[1] *Ibid.*, p. 278.
[2] *Ibid.*, pp. 281–282.
[3] *Ibid.*, pp. 287–289.

was, because of the unreality of its goals, impossible of fulfillment. Of this, the Yugoslavs were accordingly advised by the Russians. They may have spoken out of their wider experience with planning, or because they saw that if the Yugoslavs tried to fulfill their plan they could not possibly provide what the Soviet Union wanted, or both. However it was, the Yugoslav plan became an issue in itself. The Russians frankly called it megalomaniac and utopian.

Hebrang and Žujović

The plan was in the hands of Andrija Hebrang as minister for industry and president of the Economic Council and the Planning Commission. Also, for a time, it partly depended on Sretan Žujović as minister of finance. Both of these men were, or soon became, spokesmen for Moscow's point of view rather than Belgrade's.

Hebrang, in particular, was an interesting figure. Not only was he one of the ablest men in the Yugoslav Communist Party, but he was the closest thing to an opponent to Tito. A long-time Communist, he had been jailed by the Royal Yugoslav police. By the time he was released, Tito had taken over the Party, and Hebrang felt that he was not treated well enough. In 1942 the Ustaše arrested him and tortured him. Soon thereafter he was exchanged for several Ustaša officials held by the Partisans and became secretary of the Croat Communist Party.

The Yugoslavs claim that Hebrang had given way under torture and agreed to work for the Ustaša and the Gestapo. When the Russians found his dossier in Berlin after the war, it is said, they pressed him into service as a Soviet agent.[1]

Tito had trouble with Hebrang from the start. Dissatisfied with his work in Croatia, Tito sent Kardelj to investigate. Kardelj reported that Hebrang was guilty of Croat separatist sentiments and was a disruptive force. Although Tito removed him as secretary of the Croat Party, Hebrang's undisputed ability was rewarded with the important post of minister for industry and with the presidencies of the Economic Council and Planning Commission. Here he immediately began to combat the romantic planning notions of his comrades. This action, too, doubtless stemmed from a recognition of the ill-conceived nature of the plan as well as Moscow's orders.

Hebrang was invariably supported by Žujović, who belonged to the Central Committee but not to the Politburo. "Crni" ("Black"), as the lean and swarthy Žujović was called, had been Tito's deputy commander-in-chief during the war. A Communist from the days before Tito's direction of the Party, Žujović was among those ordered purged by the Comintern. He had

[1] *Ibid.*, pp. 260-261. Dedijer does not say whence the information about Hebrang came.

then been taken back in the Party before the war at Tito's suggestion. As a reward for his wartime services, he was first made minister of finance, then minister of transport. There is no evidence that Žujović was ever a Soviet agent in the formal sense, although he certainly reported to the Russians. He supported Hebrang against the plan, apparently simply because he agreed with him and because his Communist faith was unable to comprehend the idea of Moscow in error.

It was typical of the Yugoslav Communists that they should decide on an impossibly over-ambitious economic plan on the one hand and on the other hand entrust it to men who were not only not economic experts but also opposed to its general outlines. When Hebrang had tried to force a showdown in the spring of 1946 by complaining formally to the Central Committee about the way Tito treated him, he was expelled from the Politburo and removed from his posts as minister for industry and president of the Economic Council. But he continued to be president of the Planning Commission.

It is true, of course, that running a revolution is not easy and that most of the Yugoslav Communist leaders were busy twenty-four hours a day. It is also true that Hebrang, and Žujović too, were men of ability. But it is also likely that those comprising the inner circle of leadership, flush with victory and eagerly planning a new Yugoslav society, simply did not themselves want to be burdened with the mundane tasks of economic and fiscal administration.

Agricultural Issues

Somewhere along the line there was injected into the growing area of dispute between Yugoslavia and the Russians the question of collectivization of agriculture and the role of the peasants. Doreen Warriner, the British socialist economic writer, holds that sometime between 1946 and 1948 the Kremlin decided the time had come to prepare a collectivization drive in Eastern Europe and change the nature of the people's democracies into out-and-out dictatorships of the proletariat. As evidence, she cites a Party speech made in April 1947 to that effect by Hilary Minc, Polish minister of industry, who was a spokesman for the Moscow line.[1] Although until June 1948 there was no public indication that the line of permitting gradualism in collectivization had changed, it is quite possible that Miss Warriner is correct.

The decision of the Yugoslav Politburo to go comparatively easy on the peasants had its basis in both the large size of the peasant population and

[1] Doreen Warriner, *Revolution in Eastern Europe*, Turnstile Press, London, 1950, p. 43 and pp. 51–54. Her argument in this connection is waved aside by Adam B. Ulam in his *Titoism and the Cominform*, Harvard University Press, Cambridge, 1952, pp. 113–115.

the backing the regime received from the many peasants in the Party and the People's Front.[1] Yet it was bitterly fought by Hebrang — supported by Žujović — who argued that collectivization was an economic necessity and was also called for by the traditional Leninist view that private ownership in the villages inevitably bred capitalism. The cornerstone of any really socialist regime should be the industrial proletariat, they insisted, not — as Tito had said and as was the fact in Yugoslavia — the peasants.

Actually, the Yugoslavs were ahead of Poland and Hungary in collectivization. However, they included as a part of their "socialist sector" not only kolkhoz-type collectives but also general cooperatives composed of private peasants who pooled their efforts for buying and selling. The arrangement for general cooperatives and the fact that in some of the kolkhoz-type collectives peasants retained ownership of their land were objectionable to the Russians. On top of this, in 1947, at the very time when Moscow may have been taking a decision for firmer measures in agriculture, the Yugoslavs relaxed their pressure on the peasants by revising the system of compulsory deliveries.[2] That Soviet representatives in Belgrade complained about this move[3] lends weight to Miss Warriner's contention that a new line was being adopted in Moscow. It is doubtful, however, if the issue of collectivization by itself was as significant in the Soviet-Yugoslav dispute as she implies it was.

Foreign Policy

Not all of the issues between Yugoslavia and the Soviet Union concerned domestic affairs. Probably more important in Moscow's eyes was the tendency of the Yugoslavs to proceed independently in foreign policy, as already indicated in connection with Trieste. There was not only the issue of Yugoslav relations with Albania and the matter of federation with Bulgaria — referred to earlier — but also the growing role of Tito throughout Eastern Europe generally.

That Tito saw himself as the foremost of the Communist leaders in Eastern Europe none could doubt. Accordingly, he took the lead in establishing close relations with the other people's democracies and in urging them also to maintain an active inter-bloc diplomacy. It was not unnatural that, since

[1] In 1948 peasants constituted about half of the Party members and a majority of the members of the Socialist Alliance.

[2] See Fred Warner Neal, *Titoism in Action: The Reforms in Yugoslavia After 1948*, University of California Press, Berkeley, 1958, pp. 187–188.

[3] That they did so was indicated to one of the authors by Milovan Djilas in 1954. See Fred Warner Neal, "Yugoslav Communist Theory," *American Universities Field Staff Reports*, FWN-5-'54.

Moscow appeared to regard Tito as a favorite son,[1] his words were carefully heeded in the Eastern European capitals. In Bucharest, for example, the Yugoslavs apparently persuaded the Rumanians that their wartime experiences provided a better basis for building a new Rumanian army than the experiences of the Red Army. Present at the discussions about this were the chief Soviet police agent in Rumania and the Yugoslav ambassador who, either then or later, also was a Soviet agent.[2]

It is certain that Tito on his visits to other capitals touched at least generally on the idea of some close political and economic cooperation among the Eastern European states. Such an idea was unpalatable to the Russians. Even if Soviet-Yugoslav relations were not souring in other respects, it is likely, therefore, that the Russians would have looked askance at Yugoslavia's numerous treaties and diplomatic talks with the other countries. Given the conflicts in other areas, the repeated spectacle of Tito in his brilliant marshal's uniform receiving the homage of street-lined thousands in Sofia, Bucharest, Budapest, Prague and Warsaw must have been displeasing to the Kremlin in the extreme. To what extent Stalin's vanity was offended by what was, in part, Tito's vanity one can only conjecture. Except for a state visit to Rumania, Tito had advised the Russians of his other comings and goings among the satellites. The omission was duly entered in the dossier in Moscow.

Balkan Affairs

Tito's immediate ambitions were centered on the Balkans. He looked forward to a federation embracing Yugoslavia, Bulgaria and Albania in which he would play the dominant role. It seems likely that he considered Rumania also as a likely candidate for the federation, and even, possibly, Hungary. Because of his close connections with the embattled Greek Com-

---

[1] For example, at the funeral of Mikhail Kalinin, chairman of the Presidium of the Supreme Soviet, Stalin invited Tito alone of the foreign guests to stand in the main reviewing stand with him and the Soviet Politburo. Dedijer, *Tito*, p. 277. Dedijer implies that this action was part of a plan to promote conflict between Tito and Dimitrov. Other commentators also have read various interpretations into Stalin's apparent regard for Tito. Robert Lee Wolff in *The Balkans in Our Time* (Harvard University Press, Cambridge, 1956, p. 316) credits to Dedijer his statement "that Stalin in Dimitrov's presence actually offered to Tito the leadership of the . . . Cominform." What Dedijer says (*Tito*, p. 292) is that Stalin suggested Tito should be the "initiator" of the Cominform, that is, should launch the idea publicly in the international Communist community. Tito in turn suggested the French, and actually the proposal publicly first came from Jacques Duclos, the French Communist leader. Dinko Tomasic in *National Communism and Soviet Strategy* (Public Affairs Press, Washington, 1957, p. 118) even indicates that Stalin may have considered Tito his "successor" as head of the international Communist movement. It is doubtful if anything could be further from the fact. Tomasic apparently bases his statement on Dedijer's report of a meeting Tito and several other Yugoslav leaders had with Stalin in 1946. Stalin, announcing that he did not expect to live much longer, declared: "Tito should take care of himself lest anything happen to him. Because I won't live long, and he will remain for Europe. Churchill told me about Tito, that Tito is a good man." (Dedijer, *Tito*, p. 275.)

[2] Dedijer, *Tito*, p. 310.

munists, they too, if victorious, would be expected to join the Balkan federation.

Relations with Albania seemed to be already well worked out. The Albanian Communist Party was under strong Yugoslav influence. As the USSR had joint companies in Yugoslavia, so the Yugoslavs had them in Albania, although apparently less economic exploitation was involved in the latter instance than in the former. Yugoslav advisers and even a regiment of Yugoslav troops were in Albania at Tirana's request. Moscow appeared to approve.

Bulgaria, however, posed more serious problems. Discussions on a federation had begun even before the war was over, and by 1947 there was strong Yugoslav influence in Pirin Macedonia, on which Belgrade had its eye in any event. But the Yugoslavs wanted simply to form the federation by adding Bulgaria as another republic, while Bulgaria wanted to come in as one of two equal parts. Stalin seems to have decided for the Yugoslavs, but when the matter was then taken up by representatives of the USSR, Bulgaria and Yugoslavia, the Russians delayed any action. Considering this in a meeting at Bled in August 1947, Tito and Dimitrov concluded a treaty, including a customs union, but decided to approach federation gradually.[1] The treaty had been cleared with the Soviet foreign office, and it was proclaimed in Sofia the following November. On that occasion, Tito declared: "We shall establish cooperation so general and so close that federation will be a mere formality."[2]

It is not known at what point in this development Stalin decided to use the iron glove. In January of 1948, Djilas went to Moscow at Stalin's request for a general discussion of issues, including Albania. He was accompanied by Koća Popović, chief of staff of the Yugoslav Army, and by a military delegation. Stalin was cordial in the extreme. Both he and Marshal Bulganin, then Soviet defense minister, promised the Yugoslavs "everything" they wanted for their military needs. "There are," said Stalin, "no secrets from a friendly and allied army like the Yugoslav." It was at this meeting that Stalin suggested that Yugoslavia was "free to swallow Albania" whenever it wished.[3]

The Yugoslavs now assert that all this was just an example of the extremely cunning and devious tactics for which Stalin had such a reputation. Dedijer is of the opinion, for example, that when Stalin urged Djilas to embody his ideas about swallowing Albania in a telegram to Tito, he was trying to compromise the Yugoslavs. In any event, the more cautious telegram composed by Djilas and passed along to Stalin was never sent. Furthermore,

---

[1] *Ibid.*, p. 304; *Borba*, August 30, 1947.
[2] See Wolff, *op. cit.*, p. 319.
[3] Dedijer, *Tito*, pp. 309–312.

nothing came of Stalin's and Bulganin's promises. After a week of waiting, when General Svetozar Vukmanović-Tempo queried Bulganin, the Soviet minister told him briefly, "complications have arisen."[1] In vain the Yugoslav delegation waited.

They were still waiting when, on January 28, *Pravda* published a statement made by Dimitrov at a press conference in Rumania. Asked about the prospects for an Eastern European federation, Dimitrov said that the question was "not on the agenda at present." But he added: "When the question matures, and it must inevitably mature, then our peoples, the nations of the people's democracy, Rumania, Bulgaria, Yugoslavia, Albania, Czechoslovakia, Poland, Hungary and Greece — mind you, and Greece — will settle it. It is they who will decide what it will be — a federation or confederation, and when and how it will be formed. I can say that what our peoples are already doing greatly facilitates solution of this question in the future. I also emphasize that when it comes to creating such a federation, our peoples will not ask the imperialists, and will not heed their opposition, but will solve the question themselves, guided by their own interests. . . ." Dimitrov also referred to plans for a Bulgarian-Rumanian customs union.

This, for Stalin, was a sort of last straw. He was furious. The next day, *Pravda* tersely explained that just because Dimitrov's statement was published it did not mean Soviet approval. "On the contrary," declared *Pravda*, "these countries need no questionable and fabricated federation or confederation, or a customs union; what they require is the consolidation and defense of their independence and sovereignty by mobilizing and organizing internally their people's democratic forces. . . ."

Without informing the Djilas group, Stalin now summoned the Bulgarian and Yugoslav leaders to Moscow. Dimitrov headed the Bulgarian delegation, and the Russians obviously expected Tito. However, Tito sent Kardelj and Vladimir Bakarić, head of the Party in Croatia, instead.

Stalin Intervenes

It was clear that the Kremlin was thoroughly aroused. Earlier, Albania had asked the Yugoslavs for two more divisions of troops, and Belgrade tentatively agreed. As Kardelj and Bakarić prepared to leave for Moscow, Molotov, in a telegram, virtually forbade the Yugoslavs to send troops. If the proposed move were not canceled, he warned, the Soviet disagreement would be made public. Dedijer says it "became clear" later that Stalin planted with the Albanians the request for extra Yugoslav troops.[2]

[1] *Ibid.*
[2] *Ibid.*, p. 319.

In Moscow, Kardelj and Bakarić, together with Djilas and the Bulgarian leaders, were arraigned before a querulous Stalin. Molotov led off. There were, he declared, serious differences between the USSR on the one hand and the Yugoslavs and Bulgars on the other which were "inadmissible either from the Party or the state point of view." In particular, Bulgaria and Yugoslavia had concluded a treaty despite Moscow's advice to wait for expiration of peace treaty limitations, and the Soviet government learned about it only from the newspapers. Then there was the affair about sending Yugoslav troops to Albania. And, further, there was Dimitrov's statement on federation and the customs union.[1]

Stalin broke in to complain that it was believed abroad that whatever Dimitrov or Tito said was said with "our knowledge." As an example, he cited the Poles: "The Poles were here. I asked them what they thought about Dimitrov's statement. They said 'A wise thing,' and I told them it was not a wise thing. Then they countered that they also thought it was not a wise thing."

Stalin was especially harsh on the old Comintern leader, Dimitrov. Finally, however, he said a federation of Bulgaria and Yugoslavia — including Albania — was all right; indeed, he insisted it should be done right away, and said there should also be federations between Rumania and Hungary and between Czechoslovakia and Poland. But no customs union between Bulgaria and Rumania.

Kardelj irritated Stalin when he explained that the Yugoslav-Bulgarian treaty had been approved in advance by the Soviet foreign office. (Interestingly enough Stalin apparently did not know about this, nor had he been aware that there had been similar clearance of the Bulgarian-Rumanian customs union.) Kardelj protested that there was no case of an important Yugoslav foreign policy move in which Belgrade did not consult with the Kremlin, and that there were no differences between Yugoslav and Soviet views on foreign policy.

"It isn't true," Stalin interrupted sharply. "You do not consult with us at all on any question. There exist differences and deep ones. What would you say about Albania? . . . There remains the fact that you didn't consult us about sending the two divisions to Albania."

Stalin then proceeded to lecture the Yugoslav and Bulgarian representatives about the Greek situation. The Yugoslavs should stop helping the Greek Communists because "that struggle has no prospect whatsoever."

Before the meeting was over, Stalin had bluntly warned the Yugoslavs that they must consult the Soviet government on foreign policy moves and

---

[1] The material on this conference, which was held February 10, 1948 in the Kremlin, is taken from *ibid.*, pp. 316–323.

virtually ordered them to sign a formal agreement to that effect. This Kardelj did, reluctantly and "boiling with rage," before he left Moscow.

It is not absolutely clear whether by the time of this conference Stalin had decided to bring the Yugoslavs to heel once and for all or whether he came to such a decision only in the following weeks. The Yugoslavs feel that Stalin told them to go ahead and promptly federate with Bulgaria and Albania only because he felt so sure of his control of these two countries that he believed that this would be a way to better control Belgrade. It seems quite likely that Stalin's vehement declaration against aid to the Greek Communists was influenced in part by the close cooperation between them and the Yugoslavs and that Dimitrov's inclusion of the Greeks in his statement on federation was one reason why the old dictator reacted so strongly against it. Despite his insulting remarks to Dimitrov, it apparently was the Yugoslavs whom Stalin wanted to curb. Still it is quite possible that Stalin had not yet at that time made up his mind on strong measures. Stalin had told Dimitrov that the issue between them was not mistakes but "conceptions different from our own." This was the closest he ever got to hinting that he saw the conflict on an ideological plane.

The Cominform

In the meantime, apparently to combat just such trouble with the satellites as had now arisen, the Kremlin had formed the Communist Information Bureau, known in Eastern Europe as the Informburo and elsewhere as the Cominform. Originally, Stalin may have thought of the new international Communist agency as broader, but, as it turned out, it included only the French and Italian Communist parties in addition to the parties of the Soviet Union and the Eastern European countries.[1] Stalin first mentioned the Cominform to Tito as early as June 1946, but it was not actually formed until the fall of 1947. This was about the time that Moscow was beginning to fret about Yugoslavia. It may have also coincided with a decision to proceed with collectivization and make the people's democracies formally dictatorships of the proletariat.

At the organization meeting, in Poland, Zhdanov emphasized the division of the world into two camps. There was also, apparently, discussion of collectivization policies, since we have Dedijer's report that Gomulka, the only Communist leader to oppose formation of the Cominform, "said above all that collectivization in Poland should be pursued cautiously." Dedijer also feels that Zhdanov's instructions to the Yugoslav delegates — Kardelj and Djilas — to criticize the French Communists were made for the purpose of

[1] Excluding Albania.

setting the French Party, most powerful of the Communist parties outside the Iron Curtain area, against them. On the other hand, Dedijer adds, "Kardelj and Djilas needed no persuading, because the Yugoslav Party had deeply critical observations to make on the work of these two parties."[1]

The purpose of the Cominform seems clearly to have been to keep the Eastern European Communist parties in line. It is not impossible that it was formed with Yugoslavia primarily in mind. The announcement of its establishment listed the Yugoslav Communist Party first among the members. The Cominform's seat was, at Stalin's specific designation, Belgrade. Actually the Cominform as such never did a great deal, except to publish a newspaper, *For a Lasting Peace, for a People's Democracy*. After its formation, it only held three meetings. One, in Belgrade, dealt exclusively with setting up the newspaper. Another expelled Yugoslavia, and the last one was devoted to combatting "Titoism." And when the rift with Belgrade appeared to be healed later, the Cominform was disbanded.

Regardless of how the Kremlin first conceived it, now that a showdown with Yugoslavia was at hand, the Cominform was readily available for formally administering the *coup de grâce*.

[1] *Op. cit.*, p. 295.

THE SHOWDOWN

THROUGHOUT the early months of 1948, Soviet-Yugoslav relations moved rapidly to a crisis. Even before the February conference with Stalin, Tito had deposed Andrija Hebrang, his chief opponent and the Kremlin's chief supporter in Yugoslavia, as president of the State Planning Commission and put him in the lesser post of minister of light industry. While the chagrined Yugoslav delegation, still dismayed by Stalin's harsh treatment, was en route home, the Rumanians ostentatiously removed all Tito's portraits, and in Albania the Soviet *chargé d'affaires* publicly questioned Tito's loyalty to the Communist bloc.

Then, several days later, the Soviet government seems abruptly to have postponed for a year negotiations on renewal of its trade agreement with Yugoslavia. It was probably this last, more than anything else — since the whole economy now depended largely on trade with the USSR — that goaded Tito into action.[1] Thus far, troubles with the Russians had remained within the Politburo. Now Tito called the Central Committee to a meeting on March 1 to take up the entire question.

At this meeting, the leadership reviewed the whole gamut of difficulties with the Soviet Union, stressing military matters, joint companies and the economic crisis bound to result from the failure to conclude a new trade pact. The issue, Tito said, was Yugoslavia's independence. He, Djilas and Ranković opposed any federation with Bulgaria then, despite Stalin's virtual order to proceed

[1] That the two sides do not agree on how the break-off of trade negotiations came about is one of several curious circumstances surrounding the outbreak of verbal hostilities between Belgrade and Moscow. According to the Yugoslavs, it was Aleksei Krutikov, Soviet deputy foreign trade minister, who notified the Yugoslav deputy foreign trade minister, Bogdan Crnobrnja, and the Yugoslav commercial attaché in Moscow of the postponement. Yet the Kremlin twice quoted Krutikov's categorical denials that he had so advised the Yugoslavs and insisted that "the Soviet Government never raised the question of suspending trade agreements and trade operations." Royal Institute of International Affairs, *The Soviet-Yugoslav Dispute*, Oxford University Press, London, 1948, pp. 12, 21 and 41.

with it immediately. Kardelj, for the first time putting matters on a broader basis, saw the issue as whether socialism should develop "by the equal co-operation" of socialist states or "by further enlargement of the Soviet Union." Yet there was also emphasis on the need to maintain close and friendly relations with Moscow.[1]

Not surprisingly, the Central Committee backed a firm stand. They also voted to expel Hebrang. Hebrang's inveterate supporter, Sreten Žujović, was noticeably silent during the meeting. Afterwards, although those present were pledged to the highest secrecy, Žujović reported the whole proceedings to the Soviet Ambassador.[2]

Soviet reprisals at this show of defiance — reported by Žujović — were prompt and vigorous. On March 18, General Barsov, chief of the Soviet Military Mission, notified the Yugoslav government that all Soviet military advisers and instructors were being withdrawn "because they were surrounded by unfriendliness and treated with hostility." The next day, the Soviet embassy in Belgrade announced the withdrawal of all Soviet civilian advisers and specialists.

Tito's Letter

Worried, perplexed and annoyed, Tito decided to take matters up directly and frankly with Molotov. His letter, dated March 20, is the first of the now-famous exchange of correspondence between the Yugoslavs and the Russians that was later published.[3] Ostensibly the communications were between the Central Committees of the two Communist parties. Actually, they were between Tito, with Kardelj participating, on one side, and Stalin, joined by Molotov, on the other.

Tito's letter expressed hurt and amazement at the Soviet action in withdrawing advisers. He denied that the Soviet advisers were surrounded by

---

[1] Vladimir Dedijer, *Tito*, Simon & Schuster, New York, 1953, pp. 326–328.

[2] See Žujović's later confession in *Borba*, November 25, 1950. Dedijer's account of the March 1 meeting omits all reference to Hebrang or his expulsion from the Central Committee, which is curious since Hebrang was clearly regarded as the chief culprit. It is not unlikely that his firm stand for a revision of the plan and in favor of collectivization measures was considered too delicate to report even in a period of considerable frankness. Ulam speculates that Hebrang must have had considerable Party backing or have been "a protégé of the Russians, or both," if he were so gingerly treated that even in January 1948 he was not ousted completely but only transferred to another post. Adam Ulam, *Titoism and the Cominform*, Harvard University Press, Cambridge, 1952, p. 110.

[3] The correspondence, made public by the Yugoslavs, is available in English in *The Soviet-Yugoslav Dispute*. But not all the correspondence has been made public. There are curious gaps and inconsistencies. The published exchange begins with Tito's letter to Molotov, dated March 20. The first Soviet communication published, dated March 27, refers to an earlier Yugoslav letter of March 18 and begins: "Your *answers* of 18 and 20 March have been received." (Italics ours.) If, as one might infer, there were an initial Soviet communication, one might conclude that it contained demands the Russians wanted kept private and accusations the Yugoslavs were not anxious to publish.

hostility and said he could not believe that this was the real reason for the action. It was true that secondary officials were forbidden to give out information, but this was for reasons of security against "our common enemies." Soviet representatives could always see either responsible officials or Tito himself and learn what they wanted without reservation. Up to now none of them had complained. Since the Russians were, apparently, receiving information from "various other people," information that was not always objective, accurate or well-intentioned, it had to be used cautiously. It was the Yugoslav desire that the USSR inform Belgrade openly what the trouble was so as to be sure of maintaining friendly relations.

Stalin's Reply

This was a restrained letter, but it was the closest any Communist had come to challenging Stalin in years. From here on, no holds were barred on the Soviet side. Tito was in Zagreb when the Soviet ambassador delivered the reply. When he scanned its opening lines, he told Dedijer, he felt as if a thunderbolt had struck him. Tito's views, said Stalin's letter, were "incorrect and therefore completely unsatisfactory."

The tone of the Soviet communication was arbitrary, harsh and peremptory, as if a very senior official were laying down the law to an incorrigible junior.

The military advisers were withdrawn, it stated, because they themselves reported that the Yugoslavs were abusing them and discrediting the Soviet army. Here the episode of Djilas' remarks about Soviet troops, made in 1945, was trotted out again. As for the civilian advisers, they were unable to function because of lack of cooperation and because they were followed by the Yugoslav secret police. So was Yudin, chief of the Cominform.

However, if Tito wanted to know about other causes of Soviet dissatisfaction, they were three in number. First, leading Communists in Yugoslavia were circulating anti-Soviet rumors, such as "The CPSU is degenerate," "Great-power chauvinism is rampant in the USSR," "The USSR is trying to dominate Yugoslavia economically" and "The Cominform is a means of controlling other Parties by the CPSU." It was "laughable to hear such statements . . . from such questionable Marxists as Djilas, Vukmanović, Kidrić, Ranković and others." What they said was not criticism but slander, made in secret because "the Yugoslav Party masses would disown it if they knew about it." Trotsky also had started with accusations of the CPSU as degenerate, and "the political career of Trotsky is quite instructive."

Secondly, the Yugoslav Communist Party was not really a "Marxist-Leninist, Bolshevik" organization because it hid behind the People's Front and lacked internal democracy. Furthermore, the CPY was not engaging actively in the class struggle. An increase of capitalist elements in both villages and cities was evidence that the CPY was "being hoodwinked by the degenerate and opportunist theory of peaceful absorption of capitalist elements by a socialist system, borrowed from Bernstein, Vollmar and Bukharin." The Yugoslavs' theory of Party organization in relation to the People's Front was borrowed from the Mensheviks, whom Lenin had described as "malicious opportunists and liquidators of the Party."

Thirdly, Vladimir Velebit, the Yugoslav deputy foreign minister, was known by the Yugoslavs to be an English spy.[1] The Soviet government could not understand why an English spy was kept in the foreign office unless, as was sometimes the practice with bourgeois governments, it was done intentionally. In any event, the Soviet government could not carry on correspondence with the Yugoslav foreign office "under the censorship of an English spy."

The more Tito read, the more he must have felt as if several thunderbolts had hit him, for this was now more serious than anybody in Belgrade had imagined. The dispute on concrete issues had become a charge of ideological deviation. The references to Trotsky and Bukharin were ominous, as was the thinly veiled threat that the rank and file of the Yugoslav Party, if the facts were known, would repudiate the leadership. Tito immediately sent for Kardelj, Djilas, Ranković and Kidrić, and they decided that a reply should be submitted to the Central Committee.

Tito Stands Firm

Again the members of the Central Committee responded favorably for a firm stand, except for Žujović. Whereas Tito had said the issue was not ideology but independence, Žujović insisted there were ideological differences and that, right or wrong, one could not oppose the Soviet Union. As he spoke, Tito paced up and down, muttering: "This is treason." Before the session ended, a commission was appointed to take up the case of Žujović and Hebrang. A few weeks later they were in jail.

The Yugoslav reply was a combination of both humbleness and firmness. It denied all the Soviet charges, blaming them again on "inaccurate and slanderous information," which it was now stated came from Hebrang and Žujović. The Yugoslavs' "only desire was to eliminate every doubt and disbelief" of their loyalty to the USSR, and they were sure this would be accomplished if only the Soviet Central Committee would send one or more of its members to Belgrade to investigate. But the essence of the reply is contained in one

---

[1] This Soviet charge against Velebit had been the subject of an earlier conversation between Molotov and Kardelj.

sentence which read: "No matter how much each of us loves the land of Socialism, the USSR, he can, in no case, love his country less."

As the letter went on, its tone became more confident. The Yugoslavs would, if asked, say openly that they were dissatisfied with a number of things on the Soviet side. Particularly, it was considered improper for the Soviet intelligence service to recruit Yugoslav citizens. Further, to oppose the masses to the leadership was wrong; the Soviet government should know that love for the USSR among the broad masses existed in Yugoslavia only because it had been "stubbornly inculcated" by the Yugoslav leaders.

With regard to the People's Front, not only did the Yugoslav Party not hide behind it, but the People's Front itself was better than some Communist parties that accepted anyone into their ranks. Moreover, in Bulgaria and Poland the Communist parties even operated under other names, but they were not told they were in danger of dissolving in the people's front.

As for the charges against Velebit, it was "surprising and insulting" to compare Yugoslavia to a bourgeois state. If the Soviet comrades had any actual evidence against Velebit, it should be produced, but in any case he could not be removed immediately.

Then, for the first time hinting at what became the real issue between the USSR and Yugoslavia, the letter went on to explain that although the Soviet system was still the prime example, socialism in Yugoslavia was developing "in somewhat different forms . . . under the specific conditions which exist in our country."

Stalin's Fury

Stalin, of course, was furious when he read this communication. He was contemptuous. He may have also been puzzled. The Yugoslav Communists were arguing with him! This, as he retorted in a letter dated May 4, did not improve matters but further complicated and sharpened the conflict. Here was no Marxist reaction to criticism, no honest admission of errors. "Comrades Tito and Kardelj, it seems, do not understand that this childish method of groundless denial of facts and documents can never be convincing, but merely laughable."

Tito and Kardelj denied that the Yugoslav police followed Soviet advisers? Why should the Soviet Central Committee believe Tito and Kardelj in preference to its own people, including Comrade Yudin? Tito and Kardelj said Velebit wasn't an English spy? Velebit *was* an English spy. Moreover, so was the present Yugoslav ambassador in London. And while this situation was tolerated, the United States ambassador in Belgrade "behaves as if he owned the place," American agents were increasing and moved about freely, and friends and relatives of "the executioner of the Yugoslav people, Nedić," easily obtained jobs in the state and Party apparatus.

About the role of the Soviet ambassador, what did the Yugoslavs mean by identifying him with "an ordinary bourgeois ambassador, a simple official of a bourgeois state, who is called to undermine the foundation" of a socialist state? How could Tito and Kardelj "sink so low"? Didn't they understand that their anti-Soviet attitude "means the negation of all friendly relations between the USSR and Yugoslavia"? Didn't they understand that the Soviet ambassador "not only had a right but is obliged to" discuss all questions of interest with Yugoslav Communists? The trouble was that the Yugoslav leaders were unable to see the difference between Soviet and Anglo-American foreign policy. Even in 1945, talking about Trieste, Tito made this error. Such an attitude was found only in Yugoslavia, not in the other people's democracies. Retaining such an attitude meant "renouncing all friendly relations with the Soviet Union, and betraying the united socialist front of the Soviet Union, and the people's democratic republics." It would also mean no assistance, material or otherwise, from Moscow.

Tito and Kardelj denied that they were not pursuing the class struggle because they did not understand that in the transition from capitalism to socialism the class struggle becomes sharper. Especially in the villages, the Yugoslavs were falling down. They did not try to exploit class differences among the peasantry but claimed that the whole peasantry, kulaks and all, were the strongest pillar in the new Yugoslavia. "This attitude is in complete contradiction to Marxism-Leninism." The working class, not the peasantry, should be the pillar of a socialist state. Until the final liquidation of the kulaks, this question had never been forgotten in the USSR. "To underestimate the experiences of the CPSU in matters relating to the development of socialism in Yugoslavia is a great danger and cannot be allowed for Marxists."

Then there was the whole matter of the "alarming situation" in the Yugoslav Communist Party. The Yugoslav fear of openly acclaiming the Party and its decisions instead of working through the People's Front was wrong in principle both because the Party should stand on its own feet before everyone and because of bourgeois elements in the Front. Tito and Kardelj were just repeating the error of the Mensheviks and passing it off as their own Party theory. Furthermore, the Party was "semi-legal and sectarian-bureaucratic" because of a lack of internal democracy and an absence of self-criticism. The Yugoslav Politburo considered the Party only a Partisan detachment, and this attitude cultivated "militarism." Trotsky similarly had tried to force on the CPSU a leadership based on militarist principles.

Finally, the "arrogance" and "conceit" of the Yugoslav Communist leaders was "deeply anti-Party." By not admitting and correcting their errors, they were "crudely destroying" the principal directive of Lenin on self-criticism.

Other Communist parties were more modest and accepted criticism. The services and successes of the Yugoslav Party were no greater than those of the other Communist parties of Eastern Europe and less than the services of the Italian and French parties. The only reason the Italian and French parties had less success was that the Soviet Army could not come to their aid as it came to the aid of the Yugoslav Communists "and in this way created the conditions which were necessary for the CPY to achieve power." In any event, past services did not exclude the possibility of serious error. "In his time, Trotsky also rendered revolutionary services."

Finally, the Soviet letter refused the Yugoslav invitation for members of the Soviet Central Committee to come to Yugoslavia. Instead, it said, the matter should be taken up at the next session of the Cominform.

A Mild Rejoinder

The strength of the ties binding Belgrade to Moscow was nowhere more clearly revealed than in the Yugoslav response to this Soviet tirade. The Yugoslav leaders were already sorely goaded by their treatment at Stalin's hands. Now Stalin was belittling the great source of their pride, the wartime achievements of the Partisans. There is no doubt that this stung Tito and his aides as nothing else had done or could do. The Yugoslav temperament under such conditions is inclined to follow the Biblical injunction to take an eye for an eye, a tooth for a tooth. But the Yugoslav leaders either were so indoctrinated with respect for the USSR or felt they had to appear to be, or both, that they turned the other cheek. They decided almost at once not to attend the Cominform meeting because, Dedijer says, "it was realized that there was no guarantee that Tito would return alive from such a meeting."[1] Instead, Tito and Kardelj drafted a rather meek letter back to Stalin. The previous Soviet communication convinced them, they wrote — with masterful understatement — that their explanations were in vain. They did not "flee from criticism," they insisted, "but in this matter we feel so unequal that it is impossible for us to agree to have this matter decided now by the Cominform." As it was, they said, naught remained for them to do except "resolutely construct socialism and remain loyal to the Soviet Union; loyal to the doctrine of Marx, Engels, Lenin and Stalin." The future would show, as did the past, "that we will realize all that we promise you."

[1] *Tito*, p. 357.

A final Soviet communication simply stated that the Yugoslav refusal to attend the Cominform meeting violated the equality of Communist parties and indicated that the Yugoslavs had nothing to say in their own defense. It was an attitude of nationalism against the international solidarity of the workers and "hostile to the cause of the working class." As far as assurances of loyalty were concerned, "the Politburo of the CPY, and especially Comrade Tito, should understand that the anti-Soviet and anti-Russian policy" they had pursued had "done all that was needed to undermine faith in them on the part of the CPSU and the Government of the USSR." Whether the Yugoslavs attended or not, the next meeting of the Cominform was going to consider the matter.

Expulsion from the Cominform

Accordingly, the Cominform met at Bucharest in late June and duly adopted a resolution condemning the Yugoslav Communists and expelling them from its ranks. By their refusal to attend the Cominform meeting, the Resolution declared, the Yugoslav Communists had placed themselves beyond the international Communist pale — "outside the family of fraternal Communist Parties, outside the united Communist front and consequently outside the ranks of the Information Bureau."

In addition to the now-familiar charges made by Moscow, the Cominform Resolution added still a new one. While the exchange of correspondence with the Soviet Union had been going on, the Tito regime had adopted an extreme nationalization measure and a new grain tax. The former especially had all the appearances of being hastily put into effect.[1] The Resolution denounced the new measures as ill-conceived, "leftist," "adventurist," "demagogic and impracticable." They were, the Resolution charged, merely an attempt of the Yugoslav leaders "to cover up their refusal to recognize mistakes and honestly correct them." Rather than prove the truly socialist character of the regime, the new legislation would reduce urban supplies and still further "compromise the banner of socialist construction in Yugoslavia."[2]

The most significant aspect of the Cominform Resolution, however, was its open invitation to the Yugoslav Communists to get rid of Tito and the other leaders. The "brutal measures" against Hebrang and Žujović, said the Resolution, were evidence of "a disgraceful, purely Turkish, terrorist regime," and it added: "The interests of the very existence and development of the Yugoslav

[1] See Robert Lee Wolff, *The Balkans in Our Time*, Harvard University Press, Cambridge, 1956, p. 329.

[2] In a final statement refuting all the Cominform allegations, the Yugoslavs denied that the measures were rushed through to cope with Soviet criticism and asserted they were prepared six months prior to the Soviet charges.

Communist Party demand that an end be put to this Regime." The Cominform did not doubt that inside the Communist Party of Yugoslavia there were "sufficient healthy elements, loyal to Marxism-Leninism," to accomplish this. Their task was to force their present leaders to rectify their mistakes, and if the present leaders wouldn't do it, then the job of the healthy elements was to "replace them and to advance a new internationalist leadership of the Party."

The Kremlin's Motives

It is easier to impugn Moscow's sincerity in making the charges and the implications drawn from them than it is to question the charges themselves. For, by and large, they were true. The Yugoslav Party had opposed the Soviet Union and thus, in Moscow's eyes, was guilty of "anti-Soviet" conduct. Its policy toward the peasants was not in accord with traditional Marxist-Leninist tenets. The Party and its program did not stand out clearly from the People's Front. There was no democracy in the Party. The Party had tried to "cover up" by rushing through "leftist" measures. It had not responded in the traditional and accepted way to criticism. In one sense, all this was "nationalism."

On the other hand, all the evidence indicates that the Kremlin saw fit to make such accusations against the Yugoslavs only because they would not knuckle under to Soviet domination. Even if, as Miss Warriner maintains,[1] behind the scenes the Yugoslavs were bucking a still-secret decision to proceed full speed with collectivization, as far as what had been *done* was concerned their agricultural policy was at least as Marxist-Leninist as that being followed elsewhere in Eastern Europe. As the Yugoslavs pointed out, theirs was not the only Communist Party whose true colors were somewhat obscured. And as for Party democracy, regardless of how many members of the Yugoslav Central Committee were co-opted,[2] there could not be less democracy in the Yugoslav Party than in the Soviet Party under Stalin, where there was none at all.

All this is not to say that the Soviet concern for these doctrinal factors was necessarily altogether insincere. It is possible, of course, that the ideologically phrased superstructure of the Soviet charges was purely and simply a façade for forcing the Yugoslavs into submission. But it is more likely that this is too simple an explanation. The Soviet Communists — and this was true of Stalin no less than others and perhaps more — tend to be ideological beings to whom

---

[1] See Chapter 8, pp. 120–121.

[2] One of the Soviet allegations — denied by the Yugoslavs — was that a majority of the members of the Yugoslav Central Committee were "co-opted," that is, appointed rather than elected.

theory is essential. Their doctrine, moreover, posits a virtual identity of theory and action. To them, a wrong action, a wrong result, is indication of a faulty ideological concept. The logical question for Stalin and the Russians to ask when the Yugoslavs balked at following their lead down the line was, "Why?" And once they asked it, they began to give the Yugoslav scene an intense scrutiny that revealed, for them, the answer.

Dedijer claims that at the Cominform meeting called to excommunicate the Yugoslavs, the Soviet representatives had difficulty getting the satellite Communists to go along with the Resolution. What did the trick, Dedijer says, was not the Soviet arguments but Zhdanov's statement that "We possess information that Tito is an imperialist spy."[1] This theme was developed in some detail later in the Soviet anti-Yugoslav campaign, and it is indeed likely that Zhdanov alluded to it at the Cominform meeting. The main "evidence" that he did was produced at the trial of László Rajk in Hungary a year later.[2] Not only was much of it obviously fabricated, but the trial itself was "revised" several years later, the evidence admitted to be false and Rajk "posthumously rehabilitated." Yet even in this case, it is not impossible that the chronically distrustful Muscovites believed the charges against Tito. One of the things that had bothered Stalin all along about Tito was his wartime relationship with Churchill, the arch-imperialist. There was also the baffling 50–50 influence agreement. Tito had had private talks with Churchill. About what? It is not difficult to picture Stalin's mind working something like this:

Tito's refusal to accept Soviet leadership was jeopardizing both socialist unity and socialism in Yugoslavia, because without Soviet leadership they wouldn't be able to do it right. Already they were off course. Tito's attitude seemed to be due to faulty ideological premises. But Tito was an old and experienced Communist, trained in Moscow. He understood these matters properly. And anybody could see that without outside economic assistance Tito's regime faced a short and unhappy future. Since Tito had, in effect, waived aid from the USSR, could he be counting on assistance from the imperialist West? But Tito knew the imperialists would not aid a socialist country. The American ambassador in Belgrade was acting "as if he owned the place." The Americans had recently indicated a willingness to discuss with the Tito government disposition of gold stored in the United States by the Royal Yugoslav regime. Why? Why? What was the real nature of Tito's discussions with Churchill, anyway? Some sort of plot must have been hatched. In any event, Tito was now consciously playing the imperialist game. Besides, to charge him with being an agent would help line up the satellite Communists more solidly against him. Tito might be confused, but the others knew that the butter on their bread could never come from the West. All right, then, Tito was an imperialist spy. There was evidence enough, and if more were needed it could be found.

[1] *Tito*, p. 361.

[2] See *László Rajk and His Accomplices before the People's Court*, Budapest, 1949.

To the Western, non-Communist mind, this kind of thinking is either non-sense or the sheerest hypocrisy. But Stalin's mind was neither Western nor non-Communist. And such pseudo-reasoning combined with self-delusion is exactly the sort of thing that does characterize the non-Western, Communist mind. It was, at any rate, the sort of thing that seemed to characterize Stalin's mind.

Having reached his decision, Stalin then had to decide what to do about it. Again, one can guess the train of thought of the ever-cautious old *Vozhd:*

Military action was out. It was too dangerous. The USSR was still weak after the war, and one could never be sure what the Americans, who had already intervened militarily in Greece, would do. Then, too, this Yugoslav affair indicated that things in the satellites might not be as well in hand as had been thought. The satellites couldn't be counted on to take care of Yugoslavia by themselves. Besides, none of this was necessary. Who was Tito anyway? Was it not Stalin and the Soviet Union to whom all Communists owed allegiance? Surely the Yugoslav Communists would not support Tito against the Kremlin and the CPSU. Had not Moscow's agents in Yugoslavia reported as much? The thing to do was get rid of Tito. This would not be difficult. Stalin would raise his little finger and there would be no more Tito.[1] The Yugoslav Communists would take care of it, and some of them had been advised just what to do. If need be, even let Yugoslavia go for the time. It was just a small country. The historical forces producing socialism had been inexorably set in motion and would inevitably right things on a true course. Meanwhile, the purity and solidarity of the movement were what counted. Better a Yugoslavia that was not really socialist outside the bloc where it could be exposed to all the faithful than inside the bloc where Tito, who was serving the imperialists, could work his machinations.

Always in the Kremlin's book public exposure of opposition was a possible ultimate weapon in case foreign Communists got out of line. Moscow had threatened Tito with such exposure during the war, again at the time of the Trieste affair and still again in 1948 in regard to Albania. Now the ultimate weapon had been used. Tito was not only disowned but excommunicated. Like Mark Anthony concluding his funeral oration, Stalin must have thought: "Now let it work: mischief, thou art afoot, take thou what course thou wilt!" As it turned out, the course was not what the wily Soviet dictator expected.

---

[1] This boast was attributed to Stalin by Khrushchev in his so-called secret speech attacking Stalin before the Twentieth Congress of the Soviet Communist Party in 1956. See the *New Leader,* July 16, 1956. Although Khrushchev has denied that the text of the speech published in the West is authentic, there seems to be no doubt that he did make a secret address attacking Stalin and the "cult of the individual" at least along these general lines.

THE YUGOSLAV

REACTION

THE Cominform Resolution was published on a date long marked in South Slav history for fateful events — June 28, St. Vitus Day or Vidovdan. It was the 559th anniversary of the Battle of Kosovo Polje. And the Resolution confronted Tito with a decision not unlike that which, according to Serbian legend, faced Tsar Lazar on the eve of the Turkish assault: a worldly kingdom or a spiritual one. Unlike Lazar, Tito chose the worldly kingdom.

It is hard for non-Communist Westerners to appreciate fully the impact of the Resolution on the Yugoslav Communist leaders. It is not unapt to liken them to high priests in a secular religion. For them, Communism is not merely a political theory or program; it is a way of life to which they have dedicated themselves completely. A basic tenet of the vows the Yugoslav Communist leaders had taken was love and obedience for Stalin and the Soviet Union. To be criticized by these objects of their adoration made them unhappy. To be denounced made them miserable. But to be excommunicated — for the Cominform Resolution can be compared only to excommunication — when they considered themselves not only faithful but the most faithful of the faithful was something that simply could not happen.

It is true that Tito and the other top leaders had realized for some months previously that they were in for a difficult time, but the cold fact of excommunication was nevertheless both terrifying and unexpected. As Tito remarked later, in spite of many doubts they "yet at heart had faith in the Soviet Union, in Stalin."[1] Nor was the crisis only one of faith. For the Yugoslav leaders it was also political, and in an intensely personal way. The very center of Communist authority had now called on their followers to throw

[1] Vladimir Dedijer, *Tito*, Simon & Schuster, New York, 1953, p. 377.

139

them out. Feeling as they did about Stalin and the USSR themselves, they must have wondered if their rank and file did not, perhaps, feel an even greater devotion to the fatherland of socialism and its mighty leader. During the war, Tito had seen Partisans dying "with Stalin's name on their lips."[1] From such as these he now had to seek support against Stalin.

Psychological Trauma

Under the circumstances, faced with that which by its nature simply could not happen and, as a result, faced also with a threat to their political existence if not their lives, the Yugoslav Communist leaders suffered a mental shock of a kind psychiatrists can understand better than laymen. A number of them suffered psychosomatic disturbances. Tito suffered his first gall bladder attack at the time. Kidrić developed ulcers and skin disease and later told how he "spent agonizing, sleepless nights" and struggled with his conscience. Djilas lost his hair. For Moše Pijade, the Resolution was "the end of the world," and for Blažo Jovanović, head of the Communist Party in Montenegro, it was "the most terrible thing that ever happened."[2]

Both the nature of the crisis and the plight of the leaders were without precedent. The excommunication of Yugoslavia has been compared to Martin Luther's defiance of Rome; but the analogy is faulty. Luther deliberately proclaimed himself a heretic when he nailed his Theses to the cathedral door. And he was backed by the might of the German princes. The Yugoslavs, on the other hand, denied heresy; they had no desire really to challenge the authority of the Kremlin. The initiative was Moscow's, not Belgrade's, and Tito was uncertain what support he would have, if any. The idea of a Yugoslavia which "escaped" from Stalin's clutches or "broke" with Moscow is less fact than imagination — Western and, as it developed a few years after the Cominform Resolution, Yugoslav.

Courage and Ambivalence

Yet if the Yugoslav leaders were frightened and confused at having the rest of the Communist world arrayed against them, they were also courageous. It does not detract from the respect to which this entitles them to note that their courage was not produced alone by their rugged South Slav characters. It was made easier by their psychological inability to face up to the fact of a complete break with Moscow and by their lack of any real choice other than sticking to their guns. What they did now reflected both of these aspects. Boldly they published the Cominform Resolution as well as their correspond-

---

[1] *Ibid.*

[2] *Ibid.*, p. 365; see also Fred Warner Neal, *Titoism in Action: The Reforms in Yugoslavia after 1948*, University of California Press, Berkeley, 1958, p. 4.

ence with Stalin and proceeded to hold a Party Congress.[1] At the same time, they acted as if the trouble did not really involve Stalin and the USSR so much as it did the Cominform as an organization and the "traitors," Hebrang and Žujović.

This stand was tactical in part. As Tito put it later:

It was necessary to pay thorough attention to illusions about the Soviet Union that existed or left their traces among practically all our people. We dared not give free reign to indignation and reply to all lies and slander coming from the Soviet Union . . . merely with sharp rejoinders. It was necessary to allow Stalin time to do such things toward Yugoslavia as would move the people themselves to say: "Down with Stalin," instead of estranging ourselves from the masses by being the first to raise such a cry in a moment of fury.[2]

Whatever the reasons, in the days immediately following their excommunication, the attitude of the Yugoslav Communist leaders appeared highly ambivalent. At the Fifth Party Congress, which convened July 21, Tito spoke for eight hours with hardly an indication of conflict involving the Soviet Union. Concentrating on the history of the Yugoslav Party, and especially its wartime contributions, he referred to the Cominform Resolution only at the very end of his remarks. He rejected the charges *in toto*. "Can we renounce everything and say it is true we are nationalists simply because it says so in the Resolution of the Information Bureau?" Tito asked. "Of course we cannot . . . admit this. . . . The signers [of the Resolution] did not take objective truth into account at all."

Yet, other remarks of Tito at the Congress amounted to a plea to be taken back into the Cominform fold. The Yugoslav Communists, he promised, would "work with all our might to mend the relations between our Party and the Soviet Union." Again he expressed the hope "that the comrades, leaders of the CPSU(B), will give us an opportunity to show them here, on the spot, everything that is inaccurate in the Resolution." And he asserted that Yugoslav foreign policy was in full accord with the foreign policy of the Soviet Union, for the Soviet policy "corresponded and corresponds to the interests of our country."

On the rostrum behind Tito as he spoke were busts of Marx, Engels and Lenin — and Stalin. He concluded his speech with the words: "Long live the Soviet Union! Long live Stalin!" And the hall responded with cries of "Hail Stalin! Hail Tito!"

---

[1] The decision to hold the Congress was announced May 25. Although Dedijer indicates the decision was taken "earlier" (*Tito*, p. 359), it was clearly taken as a result of the Soviet charges of undemocratic procedures and illegal secrecy in the Yugoslav Communist Party. The Congress was the first public appearance, as it were, of the Yugoslav Party.

[2] *Ibid.*, pp. 379–380.

Then there was the strange performance of the Yugoslav delegates to the Danube River Conference which met in Belgrade on July 30. The conference was dominated by Soviet tactics aimed at legalizing control of the Danube by the USSR, which was to result in serious discrimination against Yugoslav interests. The Yugoslav delegation not only voted down the line with the Soviet bloc and spoke in its behalf, but a top Yugoslav foreign office representative helped Andrei Vishinsky, leader of the Soviet delegation, ram through the Kremlin's program.

These actions are inexplicable except on the theory that the Yugoslavs, psychologically unable to accept their position, still hoped Moscow would forgive and forget. In January 1949 Belgrade solemnly applied for membership in the Kremlin's Council for Mutual Economic Aid, and appeared hurt and baffled when the request was sharply denied. Not, apparently, until the summer of 1949 did Tito and Kardelj finally abandon the notion that Stalin did not mean what he said and that reconciliation was still possible.[1]

The Yugoslavs Close Ranks

Neither the regime's hopes nor its disorientation, however, prevented it from taking strong action to consolidate its position at home. A general crackdown was ordered on all known opponents of Tito's leadership, Communist and otherwise. Yugoslav émigrés, both Royalist and Ustaša variety, tried in various ways to take advantage of the crisis, either on their own initiative or, sometimes, at Soviet prompting, and the Government was taking no chances. With Hebrang and Žujović in jail, the Kremlin's chief agent was General Arso Jovanović, Tito's former chief of staff. He was shot as he tried to escape across the border into Rumania. Two other high officers, including the brother of Chief of Staff Peko Dapčević, got away but were later captured and imprisoned. Ranković's ubiquitous UDBA arrested thousands of persons suspected of backing the Cominform Resolution.[2]

Although numerous underground groups of "Resolutionists" were formed, by and large Party solidarity was well maintained. This was due not only to Tito's popularity as a leader and his extremely cautious tactics but also, to some extent, to the low ideological level of many of the rank and file. The reaction of some Yugoslav Communists was naïve, to say the least — although perhaps not more so than that of their leaders. One Party unit, voting support for Tito, sent the following telegram to Stalin: "Comrade Stalin, we deeply

[1] So wrote the late Louis Adamic, who had intimate conversations with Tito and the other Yugoslav leaders in 1949. See his *The Eagle and the Roots*, Doubleday, Garden City, N. Y., 1952, pp. 76, 130, and 250.

[2] Between 1948 and 1952 nearly 14,000 persons were arrested and punished for "pro-Cominform activity." See Report of Aleksandar Ranković, *Sixth Congress of the Communist Party of Yugoslavia*, Belgrade, 1953, p. 67.

believe in you, that you will do everything you can to remove this unjust accusation thrown at our whole country, our Party, and our Central Committee."[1]

If the comparative calm which prevailed in the weeks and months following the Cominform Resolution indicated how solidly Tito controlled both Party and country, it was not all due by any means to Ranković's efficiency as a policeman or Tito's popularity as a Communist. There is no question that by and large the Yugoslav people did rally in defense of their independence against Soviet inroads. As frightened and perplexed as the leaders were at finding themselves defying the rest of the Communist world, they were at the same time, in a typically Yugoslav way, increasingly stimulated by the prospect. And their resilience met a response in the population, whose patriotism was stirred. Dedijer quotes the reaction of his mother, no Communist. "We are," she commented to her son,

a very strange people. When Hitler was at the peak of his power, when the whole continental Europe was at his feet, we tore away the pact which we had with him. When Americans were at the summit of their power in 1946, when everybody in the world was afraid of the atom bomb . . . we shot down their airplanes because they violated our national territory. And now when Stalin is bursting with strength, we reject his ultimatum. This reminds me of little Serbia rejecting the ultimatum of the Austro-Hungarian Empire in 1914. We are so strange a people, we know how to defend this land of ours.[2]

The fact is that the Cominform Resolution if anything strengthened the Tito regime among its people. While it made little impact one way or another on the traditionally apolitical peasantry, the Resolution put anti-Communist Yugoslavs generally in a difficult position. They now had to choose between the hated Tito Communists and the hated Soviet Union. Some of them hoped that the crisis would bring Tito's downfall, but many more became perforce reluctant supporters of the regime. In addition to this, the national unity thus produced tended to submerge still further the old ethnic-religious feeling. By 1951, Djilas could say with reason that "Our government is in a much stronger position among the people as a result of the firm defense of national independence against the USSR."[3]

The Soviet Blockade

The Soviet Union was far from willing to let matters rest with an exhortation, even one as solemn as the Cominform Resolution, especially when it failed to bring the results Stalin hoped for and apparently expected. Much

[1] Dedijer, *Tito*, p. 363. Such political naïveté could, of course, work both ways.
[2] *Ibid.*, p. 363.
[3] *Borba*, November 13, 1951.

more tangible evidence of his displeasure came in the form of an economic blockade launched against Yugoslavia. Economic pressure began almost immediately when Albania, on July 1, 1948, denounced all economic agreements with Belgrade. By fall, the satellites generally were reneging on promised, and often paid-for, deliveries of vitally needed manufactures, industrial goods and raw materials. By the first of the year, the Soviet Union had abrogated its capital goods agreement. The agreement was still "in existence," Moscow blandly admitted, but had "lost its validity" because "conditions have changed."[1]

Although the Yugoslav Five Year Plan could not possibly have been fulfilled in any event, the result of this economic blockade was disastrous. Yugoslavia was then dependent on the Eastern bloc for roughly 50 per cent of its imports, but for some key items dependency was much greater. All of Yugoslavia's coal and coke imports, 80 per cent of its pig iron needs, 60 per cent of its petroleum products, four-fifths of its fertilizer requirements and virtually all specialized machinery, steel tubes, railway cars and locomotives came from the Soviet Union and its satellites. Now trade from this source dried up completely.[2] Over-all industrial production slowed down and by 1952 was actually lower than in 1949. Unemployment due to curtailment of operations because of raw material shortages became a serious problem.

The disruption of the trade pattern caused by the economic blockade, incidentally, not only hurt Yugoslavia but had serious effects on satellite countries as well, since most of them had counted on economic cooperation with Yugoslavia and imports of Yugoslav raw materials.

If the doctrinaire and over-zealous Yugoslav approach to planning also contributed to the country's difficulties in the industrial sphere, the regime was even more responsible for what happened in agriculture. Stung, apparently, by Soviet charges of un-Marxist policies toward the peasants, in 1949 the Yugoslavs launched a drive to force collectivization. The drive brought a serious crisis in agricultural production which was only exacerbated by the unavailability of Soviet bloc fertilizer. By 1951 peasant resistance to the collectivization efforts amounted to what some observers considered "a nationwide slowdown strike."[3] Cereal production amounted to only 41 per cent of prewar output. A part of the difficulty was caused by a devastating drought in 1950 which seemed, mysteriously, to stop at the west bank of the Danube. A

---

[1] Economic and other pressures by the Soviet bloc against Yugoslavia are spelled out in detail in *White Book on Aggressive Activities by the Governments of the USSR, Poland, Czechoslovakia, Hungary, Rumania, Bulgaria and Albania toward Yugoslavia*, Ministry of Foreign Affairs of the Federal People's Republic of Yugoslavia, Belgrade, 1951.

[2] See Table 17–1 and p. 98.

[3] *New York Times*, October 31, 1951, p. 1.

Soviet diplomat in Belgrade commented sacrilegiously at the time to one of the authors that "God is on the side of the Cominform."

On top of all this, the regime soon decided it was necessary to expand its armed forces.[1] The result was a drastic pinch for the impoverished economy and still more belt-tightening for the people.

Other Soviet Tactics

Nor were economic pressures all that the Kremlin plotted against Yugoslavia. The Soviet Union and its satellites sponsored "Free Yugoslavia" movements composed of Yugoslav émigrés and defectors. The lives of Yugoslav diplomats in Eastern Europe were made miserable. Treaties of alliance were broken. The violence of the Soviet bloc's propaganda campaign knew no bounds. Typical were references to "traitorous scum," "running dogs of capitalism, gnawing imperialist bones," "worthy heirs of Hitler," "despicable imperialist hirelings," "Judas Tito," and "new tsar of the Pan-Serbs and the entire Yugoslav bourgeoisie." Utilizing the Yugoslav affair as an excuse to crack down on potential oppositionists throughout its satellite empire, Moscow sought by such trials as that of Rajk in Hungary and Kostov in Bulgaria to show that Tito was an agent in the employment of the Americans, the British or whomever. And there were border incidents around the periphery of Yugoslavia designed, apparently, to scare the Yugoslav leaders into submission.

These tactics had little effect on the Yugoslavs except to stir them, ultimately, to reply in kind. Indeed, the more virulent the Soviet invective waxed, the more solidly the country seemed to be unified against Soviet pressure.

Military Threats?

Why, then, when other methods failed, did the Russians not simply march in and take over Yugoslavia? Western commentators particularly have struggled unsuccessfully with this question ever since 1948. By 1951 the Yugoslavs began to charge that they had been threatened militarily from the time of the Cominform Resolution.[2] Fitzroy Maclean, whose biography of Tito gives an intimate picture of official Yugoslav attitudes, declares that "there can be little doubt that by the summer of 1949 the Russians were actively weighing" armed invasion.[3] Yet the public reaction of the Yugoslav leaders to such danger was curious. It is true that Tito moved soon after the break with the

---

[1] Defense expenditures were tripled between 1948 and 1951.

[2] The charges are detailed in the *White Book*, cited in note on p. 144. See also *Review of International Affairs*, February 1, 1953, pp. 17–18.

[3] *The Heretic: The Life and Times of Josip Broz-Tito*, Harper, New York, 1957, p. 359.

Cominform to increase his army, but he was also at pains to deny emphatically any military threats from the East that he later claimed existed. For instance, he told the Third Congress of the People's Front in 1949 that "tales . . . about a concentration of troops in the direction of Yugoslavia in the countries of the People's Democracies and the USSR, about our alleged troop movements in the frontier regions, etc.," were only a "veritable hysteria of warmongering . . . [by] the Western reactionary press and over the radio, calculated to provoke fear and alarm in our country and to prevent peaceful work on the Five Year Plan." The aim, he said, was simply "to create a psychosis of war and distrust among the peoples of our country and the People's Democracies and the USSR."[1] A year later, when one of the authors suggested to Milovan Djilas that Yugoslavia might be in danger of invasion, Djilas shrugged it off as a "typical Western point of view."

There are several possible explanations for the fact that the Yugoslavs denied the danger when others thought it was greatest and then later insisted that it had existed all the time. One is that it reflected the inability of the Yugoslav leaders for a year after the break to see their exposed position as it really was. Another is that it was a part of Tito's cautious tactics of deliberately playing down the nature of the conflict. A third is that the danger of Soviet military intervention did not exist until after 1950, when Yugoslavia had established ties with the West, and then it appeared, in retrospect, that it had always existed. Still another possibility is that no real danger of invasion existed but that later it seemed in Tito's interest to assert that there was one. It could be that all of these explanations have some validity.

Fears of the West

Whether any of them is correct, it seems likely that an important factor was the official Yugoslav attitude toward the West on the eve of the Cominform Resolution. The view of the West held by the Yugoslav leaders was no less doctrinaire than their view of the East. It is an indication of how doctrinaire this view was that at the time of the break with Moscow many in Belgrade were more afraid of Western intervention than of Soviet intervention. The United States and Great Britain, in particular, were seen as imperialist and aggressive. There is doubtless something in Dedijer's hint that fear of these countries was one reason why the Yugoslavs were anxious to placate Moscow.[2] Thus it may well be that Tito was anxious to avoid any impression in the West that he was exposed to military danger from the East.

[1] *Third Congress of the People's Front of Yugoslavia: Political Report Delivered by Marshal Tito,* Jugoslovenska Knjiga, Belgrade, 1949, p. 8.
[2] Cf. *Tito,* pp. 251, 307–309.

Certainly it is true that the Yugoslav Communists did not anticipate that the West would come to their aid. The Yugoslavs were "not loved in the East," in Tito's words, but "reaction in the West hates us." Not only was assistance from this quarter inconceivable to the Yugoslav leaders, but they felt that even indication of such an eventuality would compromise them further with their erstwhile comrades abroad as well as with their rank and file at home. Thus, in the winter of 1948, following the Cominform Resolution, Kardelj tried to outdo the Soviet representatives in attacking the West at the United Nations General Assembly meeting in Paris. And in 1949 Tito lashed out at his favorite whipping boy, "the Western reactionary press," for "lies and fabrications" to the effect "that we have no other course but toward the West." He assailed as "lies and slanders" reports that "the American government is considering the question of giving aid to Yugoslavia, that Tito met with Western representatives." Such "fabrications," he explained to the People's Front, were intended only to widen "the rift which was created by the Cominform Resolution."[1]

Tito then asked what in those less inflationary days would have been called the sixty-four dollar question: "Well, what now? Can we go on this way?" His answer — "Of course we can, because we must" — reflected more stubbornness, and possibly resignation, than analysis of his plight. Isolated internationally, internal problems piling up, its economy almost at a standstill, the Yugoslav Communist regime was already in a bad way in 1949. When this distressing situation was compounded by the crippling drought of 1950, Tito was forced to be more interested in survival than in doctrine. He hastily sought American aid. Fortunately for Tito, he was as wrong in his fears about the West as in his hopes about the East.

The Western Reaction

In truth, the Western foreign offices were at first no less befuddled by the Cominform Resolution than the Yugoslav Communists. The suspicion that the whole incident was a complex Soviet plot was widespread. Belgrade's frenzied protestations of loyalty to Moscow and its continued hostility to the West did not help to clarify matters. Yet not long after the break the West began cautiously working up to aiding Yugoslavia.

Even before the Resolution, the Yugoslavs had indicated a willingness to settle pending economic disputes with the United States, and Washington had responded favorably. Three weeks after Moscow's axe fell, an agreement was reached. The Yugoslavs undertook to pay claims involving nationalization of American property and lend-lease and other debts, and the United

---

[1] *Third Congress of the People's Front*, p. 8.

States released the $47 million in gold entrusted to its safekeeping by the Royalist regime at the outbreak of the war. In December, a £30 million trade agreement was concluded with Great Britain. Neither side, however, regarded these arrangements as primarily political.

The American "softening" was further evidenced in the decision of August 1949 to permit Yugoslav purchase of a $3 million steel finishing mill in the United States, and in September, the Export-Import Bank granted Belgrade a loan of $20 million.[1] It was still a year, however, before formal aid materialized and the U. S. government officially declared itself in favor of supporting Tito. The Yugoslav government had formally asked for drought relief, and President Truman made available $16 million of Mutual Defense Assistance funds. "The continued independence of Yugoslavia is of great importance to the security of the United States," the President advised Congress. "We can help preserve the independence of a nation which is defying the savage threats of the Soviet imperialists, and keeping Soviet power out of one of Europe's most strategic areas. This is clearly in our national interest."[2] By the end of the year, Congress had adopted the Yugoslav Emergency Relief Act, providing $50 million more. Both economic and military aid were included.

A Shift in Yugoslav Policy

Thus, reluctantly and hesitatingly on both sides, did there occur a rapprochement between Yugoslavia, which the West had seen as Moscow's arch-satellite, and the West, which Yugoslavia had regarded as imperialistic and aggressive. If American aid did not result in, it at least was accompanied by, a shift in Yugoslav foreign policy. Already, at last, outspokenly anti-Soviet, Belgrade now became "pro-Western," even if much less outspokenly so.

At the same time, in Tito's eyes the military threat from the USSR became greater. Accepting a U. S. military mission in Belgrade in November 1951, Tito declared that the Soviet Union represented "a menacing threat to our country and world peace." And asked what the United States got in return for its aid to Communist Yugoslavia, he replied: "The United States gets several years." Whereas in 1950 Belgrade still condemned the North Atlantic Treaty Organization as "a provocative force," now, in 1951, Tito saw NATO as "the logical consequence of Soviet policy" and even pledged limited cooperation with it.

The change in Yugoslav fears of Soviet military aggression may well have coincided with an increase in the actual danger. Certainly, in Stalin's eyes

---

[1] See Table 17–8 and the discussion of U. S. aid in Ch. 17.

[2] The President's letter, dated November 29, 1950, is in the *Congressional Record*, 81st Cong., 2d sess., Vol. XCVI, Pt. 12, p. 15954.

Yugoslavia's rapprochement with the West topped all its previous sins — and, of course, proved them. Furthermore, while a dissident Tito was a serious liability, a dissident Tito allied with the West may have appeared to Moscow as a real threat. Under such conditions, the Kremlin, if it had not actively considered military intervention before, may have started thinking about it then. If so, the idea was abandoned, possibly on the grounds that it was now too late. The Western defense posture had developed considerably, as had American military prowess. And the new U. S. Ambassador to Yugoslavia, George V. Allen, had pointedly quoted President Truman's view that the United States was just as opposed to aggression against Yugoslavia as against any other country.

Despite all this, it is difficult to discount entirely the possibility that the Yugoslav Communist leaders, once they saw the potentialities of American assistance, may have deliberately stressed their military danger on the theory that such aid was the more certain the more the country appeared to be threatened.

With the reorientation of Yugoslav foreign policy came a thoroughgoing reconsideration in Belgrade of Soviet theory and practice generally. The helpful attitude of the West hastened it along. The Yugoslavs were gratefully impressed by American aid, particularly since it was given with no strings attached. This in itself raised some questions about Soviet theories.

The Yugoslavs Rethink Marxism

But such aid was by no means alone responsible for the furious re-thinking about Communism that now took place. What happened is both interesting and important for an understanding of Yugoslav developments. The mounting and implacable hostility of the Soviet Union, and especially the harsh impact of the economic blockade, finally rid the Yugoslav Communists of their illusions and got them back on the path of reality. And when they thus recovered from the mental shock they had suffered, they were changed men. Their Soviet blinkers torn away, they now could — indeed, they had to — view the world in a new way. The old world, in which everything fitted foursquare within the folds of Stalinist Marxism, was gone. Communism, capitalism, the state, the Party, the individual, life generally, now had to be re-evaluated. The analogy of Plato's men emerging from the cave into the sunlight suggests itself. Few things appeared in true perspective, but it was obvious that there were new things. Something akin to pragmatism was thus forced on those who had been rigid, doctrinaire, dogmatic and impervious to reason. A comment which soon was on the lips of all Yugoslav Communists truly characterized their new situation: "We are searching for our way."

The clearest things they saw from their new vantage point were two: one, that they were good Communists, and, two, that the Soviet Communists were against them. This could only mean that the Soviets were not good Communists. And since the Yugoslavs were following Soviet practice to the best of their ability, it meant also that Soviet-type Communism was not good Communism. But if it wasn't, what, then, was good Communism?

This was the kind of thinking events had forced on the Yugoslav Communists in the spring and summer of 1949. Pijade, Kardelj and Djilas, soon joined by others, took the lead in working out an ideological basis for Yugoslavia's position as a Communist country outside the Soviet community.

Re-examination of Communist theory and practice was by no means limited to the top leaders, however. By 1950, Yugoslav Communists in all walks of life were indulging in the discussion. Much of it took the form of self-accusation for having been "duped" by the Soviet Union. Eager to explain themselves, their conversations, especially with Westerners, sometimes sounded like confessions. There was a frantic interest in new ideas. The remark of a minor Yugoslav official to one of the authors that he was "free for the first time to consider various points of view" was typical. If it was naïve, it was also honest. To those accustomed to the Soviet Communist mind, it was also amazing.

The official efforts at re-thinking Marxism, as they appeared publicly in the fall of 1949, were at first almost wholly negative, concerned primarily with what was wrong with Communism in the Soviet Union. The essence of the new ideological approach was that Communism had to be based on Marxism-Leninism and that the Soviet Union under Stalin had deviated from the theories of "true Marxism-Leninism." The proof offered was the USSR's "imperialist denial of equality between Socialist States," which was seen as a fundamental tenet of Lenin. And equality meant above all the right of any state to pursue its own path to socialism.[1] What happened in the USSR, the Yugoslav theorists contended, was that Stalin had established in his own interest an "independent bureaucracy," centered in the Soviet Politburo, which transformed the dictatorship of the proletariat into a dictatorship over the proletariat. Thus Stalin, not the Yugoslavs, was guilty of "revisionism" and "deviation."[2]

From such essentially negative positions, the Yugoslav ideologues quickly went on to a more positive idea: If Stalin's major fault was centralizing

[1] Cf. Milovan Djilas, "Lenjin o Odnosima Medju Socialističkim Državama" ("Lenin on Relations between Socialist States"), Komunist, No. 3, September 1949, pp. 1–53.

[2] Cf. Pijade's statement in Borba, November 12, 1949, and Maks Bače, "O Kritike i Samo-Kritike u SSSR" ("On Criticism and Self-Criticism in the USSR"), Komunist, No. 6, November 1949, pp. 61–143.

power, then what should be done in Yugoslavia was to decentralize it. This conclusion ultimately resulted in a whole new ideological framework for socialism, and when some of the new theories were put into practice, they resulted in a new type of socialist system — Titoism.

The essence of Titoism was its independence from and criticism of the Soviet Union. The Titoist system came to involve new socialist concepts and methods, a drastic decentralization of the whole state structure, abandonment of Soviet-type planning, worker-management of industry, a competitive (but not private) economic system and the end of collectivization in agriculture. It also involved a decided move away from totalitarianism, with drastic restrictions on arbitrary police and other state activity and, even, a delimited role for the Communist Party. Yugoslav "socialist democracy," as Belgrade called it, was no democracy as the term is known in the West, but it was a lot closer to it than the system it replaced. All in all, it constituted the most significant development in Marxism since the Bolshevik Revolution.

PART IV

TITOISM AS
A SYSTEM

THE THEORETICAL

BASE

UNDERPINNING Titoism as a system is a theoretical base as distinctive and significant as its unique political and economic institutions. Although thus far less appreciated in the West, in some ways it may be even more important.

As has been emphasized before, Communists — and Yugoslav Communists in this sense are no different from any others — are essentially theoretical beings. No greater mistake could be made than to assume that Communists do not believe their theories. This does not mean either that Communist practice always follows Communist theory or that many Communist theories have not originated as little more than rationalizations. It does mean, however, that ideology provides a binding orientation for the direction of society, a view of both tactical and strategic goals and a guide to the thinking of at least the leadership.

Although the Yugoslav Communists may have been "guilty" of many of the practices criticized by the Soviet Union and the Cominform in 1948, they were correct in denying formal theoretical deviation. But once they were repudiated by Soviet Communism, they repudiated it. There did evolve then, as a consequence, a cohesive body of ideology distinguished from Soviet theory in many important particulars. It provided, for the first time, a theoretical framework for socialism[1] independent of Soviet guidance and sharply at variance with Soviet practice. And in so doing it addressed itself more consciously than any Leninist-type Marxists have yet done to one of the vital questions of our times, namely, the question of the compatibility — or incompatibility — of socialism and political democracy.

---

[1] According to Marxist theory, Communism is a final stage of development; it does not, therefore, yet exist anywhere. The states which are known in the West as Communist, e.g., those in Eastern Europe, are technically socialist states or states on the road to socialism.

In discussing Yugoslav Communist theory as something separate and original, two important qualifications are necessary. The first is that the essential bases of Yugoslav theory, no less than Soviet theory and all other modern-day socialist theory, derive from Marxism. This is true of both historical analysis and ultimate goals, to say nothing of methods of reasoning. Thus there is an essential core of theory which is the same in both the Soviet and Yugoslav cases. This involves primarily the concepts of dialectical materialism and the class struggle, the nature of the basic contradictions in capitalism and the inevitable triumph of socialism and Communism. "As far as the final goal of the League of Communists[1] is concerned," says Edvard Kardelj, the Yugoslav Party's chief theorist, Yugoslav Communism "proceeds from the scientific premise that the final disappearance of capitalism . . . is inevitable; that it is just as inevitable for society to undergo a revolutionary transfer to socialist relationships . . . until the achievement of Communism. . . . This historical evolution of society is the final aim simultaneously of the ideological, political and economic activity of the Communists."[2]

Similarly, both Soviet and Yugoslav Communist ideologies have their roots in the theories advanced by Lenin. But whereas in the Soviet case the roots have become enmeshed with the tree itself to form the single doctrine of Marxism-Leninism, in the Yugoslav case the Leninist roots remain roots, with some of Lenin's theories incorporated into Titoist ideology and others not.

This fact has relevance for the second qualification, which is that it is useful to differentiate between tactical-operational theories and basic, strategic doctrine. Marx is detailed enough when it comes to historical analysis and bold enough — if fuzzy — when speaking of end goals. But where he is not clear at all is about the present and how to reach the future. Much of Lenin's addendum to Marxist doctrine concerns interpretations of developments since the time of Marx and ways and means of establishing socialism in Russia. This tactical side of Communist doctrine to an even greater extent characterizes those theoretical contributions which come under the opprobrious term of Stalinism.

It is primarily in the realms of interpretation of original Marxist gospel, and of operational theory, that Yugoslav ideology differs so sharply from its Soviet model. However, Yugoslav theoretical innovations are not confined to methodology and in several important instances take original positions on basic strategic doctrinal issues also.

[1] In 1952 the Yugoslav Communist Party was renamed the League of Communists of Yugoslavia. In this and the following chapters, the terms "Party" and "League" are used interchangeably.

[2] Edvard Kardelj, "Povodom Nacrta Programa Saveza Komunista Jugoslavije" ("On the Draft Program of the League of Communists of Yugoslavia"), *Sedmi Kongres SKJ*, Kultura, Belgrade, 1958, p. 147.

The doctrinal base of Titoism emerged by bits and pieces, chiefly in pronouncements of individual leaders, over the period of a decade. Beginning from a negative position — opposition to Soviet ideas — and charting unexplored territory, the various theoretical observations were sometimes so cautious as to be vague. Reflecting the emerging and changing Titoist system, they were sometimes contradictory and had a pragmatic quality not always easily distinguishable from confusion.

Prior to the Seventh Congress of the Yugoslav League of Communists in April 1958, the scattered pieces of Yugoslav theory were pulled together in a formal Program.[1] As Yugoslav theory was emerging, it was uncertain. The Yugoslavs were fond of saying, "We are searching for our way, we are not sure." Such expressions of uncertainty are lacking in the 1958 Program. It does, however, maintain the comparatively undogmatic approach which has characterized the new theory from its beginning. The Program, for example, states:

Marxism is not a doctrine established forever or a system of dogmas. Marxism is a theory of the social process which develops through successive historic phases. Marxism, therefore, implies a creative application of the theory and its further development, primarily by drawing general conclusions from the practice of socialist development and through attainments of scientific thinking of mankind.

The major theoretical positions which distinguish Yugoslav Communism, as exemplified by the 1958 Program and other authoritative pronouncements, may be roughly divided into the following categories: national forms of socialism, the nature of the transition from capitalism and the idea of proletarian internationalism; the roles of the state and Party under socialism and the nature of the dictatorship of the proletariat; ownership of property, surplus value and the idea of state capitalism; the relationship of socialism to democracy; socialism and collectivization of agriculture.

National Communism

Yugoslavia is the prime exemplar of what has come to be called "national Communism" because of the Titoists' insistence on "independent paths to socialism." But the Yugoslavs reject the term "national Communism," both because it suggests "bourgeois nationalism," which they, like other Communists, deplore, and because it tends to further their unwanted isolation from the world Communist community. Moreover, "national Communism"

[1] The Program and other materials concerning the Seventh Congress were published in a book entitled *Sedmi Kongres SKJ (Seventh Congress LCY)*, Kultura, Belgrade, 1958. The Program itself, in an excellent translation by Stoyan Pribichevich, was published in English under the title *Yugoslavia's Way: The Program of the League of Communists of Yugoslavia*, All Nations Press, New York, 1958.

is, of course, technically a misnomer, since Yugoslav theory foresees Communism ultimately as a world system, with national differences eliminated. What the Yugoslavs really have is "national socialism." Such a term would be repugnant, of course, because of its associations with Nazi Germany.

In any event, in many ways the concept of "independent paths to socialism" is the main theoretical pillar of Yugoslavia's unique position as a Communist state outside the Soviet community. The basis for it is found in Lenin's theory of the uneven development of capitalism. Since capitalism develops unevenly, with some states ripe for transition to the next stage ahead of others, so, the Yugoslavs reason, does socialism develop unevenly. Since socialism is seen as a reflection of reality and reality differs from country to country, therefore each nation must develop its own approach to and its own forms of socialism. Failure to adhere to this principle means unnecessary difficulties in developing socialism and possibly even failure, with resulting harm to the whole socialist movement.[1]

For these reasons, the Yugoslavs say, Lenin espoused the equality of socialist states, and for these reasons also one form of socialism is as good as another. The Yugoslavs, therefore, reject the Third International Communist opposition to Second International socialism and view with approval even the mildly socialist Scandinavian countries.

Although the experiences of one socialist state affect the forms in others, these experiences are held to belong to the "whole working class movement," and — most important — no one socialist state can occupy a leading position, let alone dominate the others. The Yugoslavs here distinguish between the situation today, when several socialist states exist, and the situation between the wars, when the USSR was the sole socialist state. During the earlier period, it is admitted, it may have been the duty of all Communists to work for the USSR and even follow Soviet orders. But Moscow's attempts since the war "to proclaim the path and form of [Soviet] socialist development . . . as the only correct one is nothing but dogma, obstructing the process of the socialist transformation of the world."

What Yugoslav theory on this point amounts to is to claim for Yugoslavia and all other states what Stalin and his successors have claimed for the Soviet Union, i.e., the right and ability to build socialism in a single country and go on from there to Communism. (The Yugoslavs see the world Communist community coming into existence *ipso facto* only when all nations have ultimately achieved Communism voluntarily.)

---

[1] See Josip Broz Tito, "Zadaći Saveza Komunista" ("Tasks of the League of Communists"), *Sedmi Kongres*, pp. 35–36. See also Kardelj, "Povodom Nacrta Programa Saveza Komunista Jugoslavije," *Sedmi Kongres*, p. 173.

However, Yugoslav theory, in its defense of Yugoslavia's solitary socialist position outside the world Communist community, avoids one important issue. In enunciating his theory of socialism in one country, Stalin emphasized that the Soviet Union was sufficiently large and self-contained to be able to achieve socialism alone. Yugoslavia is a small country with limited resources. What happens there is bound to be conditioned by what happens elsewhere in the world far more than is the case with the USSR.

Capitalism and the Transition to Socialism

The contradictions inherent in capitalism have weakened it, according to Yugoslav theory, but not necessarily in the manner Marx anticipated. The trend, as studied in Belgrade, has been for capitalism to cope with its contradictions through greater state intervention in the economy. Such "interventions" as social security, government controls of business and labor, even income taxes, are seen as socialist tendencies, even though not so intended. This, to the Yugoslavs, means that the nature of capitalism has changed. "Pure capitalism" no longer exists, they reason, because all contemporary capitalism has within it not only socialist tendencies but some socialist forms.

Nor is there "pure socialism," in Belgrade's view, because "vestiges of old systems intermingle and laws of commodity production operate. . . . Certain contradictions and antagonisms of the last phase of capitalism are carried over into the first phase of construction of socialist society." Thus, contrary to Khrushchev's opinion, it follows that there are contradictions in socialism as well as in capitalism. These center around conflicts "between the state and labor, between the state and social self-government, between communal and central administrations, between coercion and freedom and between general policies and personal self-determination of man."

From these views, the Yugoslavs derive several important and interesting theoretical positions concerning the transition from capitalism to socialism and the relations of socialist and capitalist states.

First of all, they assert, in contemporary conditions the forces of socialism in the world are much stronger than they were during the periods on which Marx and Lenin based their observations. Secondly, the socialist forces are diverse. "The conception that Communist parties have a monopoly on every aspect of the movement toward socialism and that socialism is expressed only in them and through them is theoretically incorrect and very harmful in practice." Therefore, Belgrade believes that Communist parties, instead of opposing, should cooperate with Social Democratic parties, with the labor movement as a whole and even, in certain cases, with those capitalist forces which, consciously or unconsciously, are held to be furthering socialist tendencies.

Thirdly, the prospects of a peaceful transition from capitalism to socialism are not only present but are greater than in previous periods. There is, in fact, posited a unity of revolution and evolution, which are two aspects of a single process. Evolution, to the Yugoslavs, represents a quantitative piling up of factors in social development which at a certain stage "cause an indispensable leap from quantity to quality." While a sharp revolutionary conflict may be necessary to achieve the "leap," in Yugoslav eyes it is preferable, to the extent possible, to achieve the transfer by evolution because in this way socialism will be better able to develop once it takes hold. "Socialist thinking" — at least in Yugoslavia — "no longer concentrates on the mere overthrow of the capitalist system."

But the Yugoslavs at the same time are careful to reject the theory of "automatism," according to which capitalism, because of its internal contradictions, will inevitably and of its own accord be transformed into socialism and Communism. The tendency is there, according to the Yugoslav thinkers, but the very adaptation of "socialist forms by the capitalist state" tends to bolster the capitalist system. Quoting Lenin to the effect that there is "no absolutely hopeless situation" which would drive capitalism to automatic transition to socialism, Kardelj has asserted that results depend "not only on objective conditions but also on the conscious action of socialist forces."[1]

Probably, warn the Yugoslavs, this means that a dictatorship of the proletariat is necessary, but they hasten to add that, as they see it, dictatorship of the proletariat means no special "form of state or method of organization of the political system." Rather it signifies only a situation in which the working class will be strong enough to determine the direction of society. In the past this has in practice meant the Leninist form, but in contemporary conditions it can and inevitably will take other forms, among which parliamentary government is included as a possibility.

Coexistence

The fourth conclusion the Yugoslav Communists draw from their view that neither pure capitalism nor pure socialism exists is that the conflict between the two systems, at the level of states, is not fundamental. Therefore, the Soviet conception of the inevitability of capitalist hostility is considered invalid, as, indeed, is the Marxist idea that capitalism inevitably breeds war. Prior to the Twentieth Congress of the Soviet Communist Party, in 1956, the

[1] *Sedmi Kongres*, pp. 156–158.

principal reason for this conclusion of the Yugoslavs was their view that neither pure capitalism nor pure socialism exists. Now they bulwark their position with Khrushchev's reasoning that war is not inevitable because of the strength of socialist forces in the world. Further, they are influenced explicitly, as Khrushchev certainly was implicitly, by the hard facts of nuclear weaponry.

Thus, for the Yugoslavs, coexistence is not only possible but necessary because socialism, as the inevitable development in the world, is now inextricably tied to peace, without which it — as all else — is likely to be destroyed. Whereas for Lenin, Kardelj says, coexistence was primarily a defensive tactic, today it must be a continuing, permanent policy both because socialism is no longer on the defensive and because the alternative is against the interest of socialism.

From this position stems the well-known and controversial Yugoslav opposition to "division of the world into military blocs." In the first place, the real division of the forces of capitalism and socialism, as the Yugoslavs see it, is not geographic but is present inside both capitalist areas and socialist areas. Thus blocs based on geographic distribution cannot affect either the progress of socialism or the defense of capitalism against it. But blocs, whether socialist or capitalist, are held to jeopardize coexistence and thus increase the risk of war, which is in the interest of neither side.

For these reasons, the Yugoslavs argue, there is little to choose between capitalist bloc and socialist bloc, between NATO and the Warsaw Pact. They see NATO as arising from "Stalinist aggression." But because it is anti-Communist in character, they say, it gave rise to the Warsaw Pact. Belgrade insists that it is in the interest of socialist forces to work for the elimination of both.

In the preliminary Draft Program, published before the 1958 Congress, NATO and the Warsaw Pact bloc were simply equated.[1] The Soviet Union attacked the Draft Program more strongly on this point than on any other.[2] In an effort to meet Soviet criticism, the Yugoslavs altered the language so that the final Program sees the Warsaw Pact as now more defensive than NATO and as comprising states striving more actively than the NATO states for relaxation of international tensions. Nonetheless, the final Program retains the view that the continued existence of the blocs is a manifestation of "reactionary forces" in both camps, in that of the socialists as well as that of the capitalists.

[1] *Nacrt Programa Saveza Komunista Jugoslavije (Draft Program of the League of Communists of Yugoslavia)*, Kultura, Belgrade, 1958.

[2] Soviet criticism of the Draft Program is spelled out in detail in an article in *Kommunist*, No. 6, April 1958, pp. 16–39.

In this connection arises the peculiar Yugoslav view of "proletarian internationalism." This phrase, to the Kremlin, means primarily recognizing the Soviet Union as the center of the Communist movement and as the leading socialist nation and following the Soviet position in international affairs, come what may. Practically, it means active affiliation with the Soviet bloc. Conversely, it means abstaining from criticism of the USSR and its policies. Neither Yugoslav theory nor practice fits this conception. Nevertheless, the Yugoslavs do espouse a doctrine of proletarian internationalism of their own. In fact, the 1958 Program maintains: "In all its contacts with other Communist, Socialist, Progressive and anti-imperialist movements and in all its international relations in general, the League of Communists of Yugoslavia has upheld and will continue to uphold the great idea of proletarian socialist internationalism as its guiding principle."

It is easier to say what proletarian internationalism does not mean to the Yugoslavs than what it does mean. Apparently the Yugoslav concept involves little more than a feeling of ideological solidarity among "socialist forces" including but by no means limited to Communist parties. There should also be cooperation, but only on a basis of equality and without a formal organization. Kardelj admits Yugoslav caution here is dictated by its experiences with the Cominform. He recognizes that conditions have changed but warns that in relationships between socialist countries there is still a danger "of diverse mistakes and negative tendencies."[1]

One final position derives from Yugoslav views about the nature of capitalism and socialism. This is rejection of the Leninist theory of just and unjust wars. "Socialism cannot be exported or imposed by force on other peoples," Kardelj holds, and "no one can prescribe the socialist forms any one country shall apply." It follows, he says, that "we consider as aggressive every attempt at interference in the internal life of a socialist country for the purpose of restoring the old order or of encouraging the vestiges of reactionary forces."[2]

Kardelj's formulation here appears as an interesting, although not overly successful, attempt to harmonize the Yugoslav stand on just and unjust wars, first set forth as early as 1951, with Belgrade's ambivalent stand on Soviet intervention in Hungary in 1956. Although Tito both criticized and deplored the intervention at the time, he also contended that it was justified if it was necessary "to save socialism" in Hungary. In 1951 Kardelj said the only just wars were those for defense, and he specifically excluded from this category

---

[1] *Sedmi Kongres*, pp. 159–160. The stress placed on the concept is, however, indicative of the strong Yugoslav yen for camaraderie with other Communists. See Chapter 20.

[2] *Ibid.*, p. 126.

attempts of "the Soviet Union . . . to bring happiness to other peoples by forcing its political system and hegemony on them."[1] The 1958 view obliquely maintains this position by reference to "encouraging the vestiges of reactionary forces," which to the Yugoslavs means Cominform or Stalinist influence. But it is now implied that at least an equal danger is intervention "aimed at restoration of the capitalist order."

Role of the State

The Yugoslav Communists' concept of the state under socialism is one of the most significant points of theoretical difference between them and Moscow. The Yugoslavs see the state as an indispensable force in the beginning of the transition from capitalism to socialism. But once the "initial transition period" has been accomplished — as manifested by nationalization of the means of production and "isolation of exploiting elements" — then, in order for progress toward socialism to continue, the state must begin to "wither away." This means, in effect, that the dictatorship of the proletariat, with its ownership and management of the means of production, its large state apparatus and its arbitrary use of what Lenin called the "organs of suppression," must not be a continuing thing. Although the withering-away process does not have to be completed within any concrete time period, it must begin. Indeed, to the Yugoslavs a state is not really socialist unless it is in the process of withering away, and the withering away "arises as the fundamental and decisive question of the socialist system."[2]

Soviet theory, of course, also embraces the Marxist concept of the withering away of the state. But whereas Yugoslav doctrine insists that the process must get under way at once in order for a state to be truly launched on the road to socialism, Soviet theory skirts the question of when the process should start and holds only that the state will wither away when Communism is reached. In the meantime, as Stalin put it, the state must grow stronger in order to create the conditions under which it can ultimately wither away.

The withering-away process, as explained by Kardelj, begins in practice in the fields of state economic functions, education, cultural activities and social

[1] *Medjunarodna Scena i Jugoslovenski Položaj* (*The International Scene and the Yugoslav Position*), Belgrade, 1951, pp. 6–8.

[2] The Program reflects a considerable Yugoslav literature on this point. See, for instance, Tito's speech to the Skupština, *Borba*, June 27, 1950; Kardelj, *Socijalistička Demokratija* (*Socialist Democracy*), Belgrade, 1952; Kardelj's 1954 address to the Norwegian Labor Party, *Borba*, January 1, 1955 (published in English in 1956 by the Yugoslav Embassy in New Delhi as *Socialist Democracy in Yugoslav Practice*); Jovan Djordjević, "Some Principles of Socialist Democracy in Yugoslavia," *New Yugoslav Law*, July–December 1952; and Milovan Djilas, *Is Stalin Turning in a Circle?* reprinted from *Borba*, October 11 12 and 13, 1952, by the National Committee for a Free Europe, New York, 1952.

services, that is, in those areas where the Yugoslav state has in fact divested itself of direct control and management. However, Kardelj warns that the role of the state "as an instrument of power . . . against anti-socialist forces and activities or as regards protection of the country's independence" — principally police and army — will diminish more slowly. The process, he explains, will depend on how long "in international relations the influence of antagonistic social contradictions dominates and reactionary social forces are still to be reckoned with as a factor capable of jeopardizing the existence of the free development of socialism."[1] (Since the Yugoslavs interpret these words to refer to safeguards against not only anti-Communist activity but "Cominform-type" activity as well, the comparison here suggested with the justification once advanced by Stalin for maintenance of strong state power — capitalist encirclement — is inexact.)

The tendency of the state, once reconstituted as the dictatorship of the proletariat, not to wither away is seen by the Yugoslavs as a major contradiction in the socialist process. This tendency — manifested by "state bureaucratism" — is held to be nurtured by remnants of capitalist elements, and unless it is promptly removed, the dictatorship of the proletariat, instead of moving toward socialism, degenerates into what the Yugoslavs call state capitalism.

In referring to state capitalism, the Yugoslavs obviously have in mind the Soviet Union, and earlier pronouncements of this theme flatly asserted that the Soviet system was not socialist but state capitalist. The 1958 Program repeats the earlier analysis of the Soviet system as it existed prior to the Twentieth Congress of the Soviet Communist Party, asserting that it demonstrated state capitalist tendencies and attempted to bulwark them with "a pragmatic revision of . . . Marxism-Leninism." But it also adds that following the Twentieth Congress "various deformities in the USSR born under the influence of the above-mentioned tendencies gradually began to be removed." This apparently gave Belgrade hope that conditions now exist in the Soviet Union to "make possible the further successful development of this process, furnishing a new incentive in the advance of socialism."

Yet even this bringing up to date of the Yugoslav analysis of Soviet development falls short of an appraisal which fits the Yugoslav requirement of the beginning of the withering away of the state as a prerequisite for socialism. . The contradiction is all the greater since the Soviet Union claims not only to have socialism but now to be advanced on the road to Communism itself.[2]

[1] *Sedmi Kongres*, p. 176.

[2] The extreme irritation with which Moscow reacted to that part of the 1958 Program dealing with the withering away of the state is a good indication that this point is apparent to Soviet Communists also. See *Kommunist*, April 1958, pp. 25–39.

The main danger in state capitalist tendencies, as seen by the Yugoslavs, is that "state bureaucratism" may develop into an independent system of its own, with power wielded by a "bureaucratic caste" for its own ends. This is held to be particularly true in the case of state ownership and management of industry, as exists in the USSR.

Socialist Ownership

In Yugoslav theory, state ownership of the means of production is a vital beginning for socialism, but what really counts is not only ownership but also control.

To the Yugoslavs, ownership without control is meaningless. Thus nationalization is "only the first, and the lowest, step" in the transition. As long as it does not progress beyond this, the idea that "the workers own the means of production" is only a fiction. The workers have no actual control because control is lodged in the state bureaucracy which tends to administer the means of production in such a way as to perpetuate its own control. In such cases the state bureaucracy is held to be a form of state capitalism, where surplus value — the kingbolt of the Marxist analysis of capitalist economics — is appropriated by the state and party bureaucrats much as under capitalism it is appropriated by private owners. Indeed, under capitalism, the Yugoslavs say, the interests of workers may be better protected by an independent labor movement than under a dictatorship of the proletariat turned state capitalism. Under the latter, surplus value acts as a contradiction, according to the Belgrade ideologues, in the same way it does under capitalism. Surplus value — that is, the difference between costs and price, which comprises profit — is held always to exist short of actual Communism. The question is, who gets it? To avoid the contradiction, according to the Yugoslavs, surplus value must accrue to the workers.

This formula — first enunciated by Kardelj, Kidrić and Tito — was spelled out in detail by Milovan Djilas, who later incorporated some of it in his book, *The New Class*.[1] The 1958 Program does not emphasize it, but the essence of the theory is retained.

Recognizing indirectly some of the criticism in these Yugoslav concepts, the present Soviet leadership, under Khrushchev, has placed the blame on Stalin and "the cult of the individual." Belgrade is also inclined to blame Stalin, but Yugoslav theory holds that it was not Stalin or "the cult of the individual" that caused the "statist deformations" in the Soviet Union but rather that

[1] Frederick A. Praeger, New York, 1957. Djilas' analysis, specifically aimed at Stalin's theory that surplus value is applicable only under capitalism, first appeared in *Borba*, October 11, 12 and 13, 1952, and was reprinted that year by the National Committee for a Free Europe under the title *Is Stalin Turning in a Circle?*

"the cult of the individual is caused by the political and economic system, of which it is a characteristic."[1]

"Withering away" is by all odds the vaguest of Marxist concepts, save, perhaps, only Communism itself, and the attempts to make it less vague constitute one of the unique facets of Titoism. Since mere nationalization was only the first step, and since its concomitant, state control, constituted a grave danger, the Yugoslavs had to devise "a higher form of socialism in which the state would begin to wither away." First they invoked the concept of "social property." This meant national ownership but not state ownership, "social but not state control." The mechanism for its implementation was found in worker-management. Under this arrangement, factories are run by councils elected by the workers, who organize production and by and large dispose of the proceeds of their work as they wish. They do not "own" the factories, but they manage them and control them whereas under the Soviet system practiced in Yugoslavia up until 1950 the state both owned and managed them.

"From now on," Tito declared in 1950, "the state ownership of the means of production — factories, mines, railways — is passing on to a higher form of socialist ownership. . . . Therein lies our road to socialism and that is the only right road as regards the withering away of state functions in the economy."[2]

But in order for "social property" and worker-management to be meaningful, there had to be a new theory of economic and governmental organization. "The contradictory nature of the dialectical elements" in the Soviet-type political and economic system, the late Boris Kidrić, one of the originators of new Yugoslav economic policies, explained, "inevitably becomes more obvious and more acute, and either the process of transformation of state ownership into common ownership of the nation under the management of the direct producers must commence and gain way, or else an all-powerful and all-embracing state industrial monopoly ceases to become the foundation for socialism and becomes increasingly the economic basis for the class-caste rule of a bureaucracy."[3]

The key to the new Yugoslav theories of governmental and economic organization is decentralization, particularly of state economic functions, which "lose their former character of a government of men to acquire the socialist character of a government of things." The rigid, Soviet-type state

---

[1] Kardelj, *Sedmi Kongres*, p. 161. Speaking even more frankly, the organ of the Yugoslav Communist youth organization declared that it was "social conditions themselves and the government system which made possible the appearance of Stalin and Stalinism." *Mladost*, March 6, 1957.

[2] *Borba*, June 27, 1950.

[3] Boris Kidrić, "From State Socialism to Economic Democracy," *Yugoslav Review*, February 1952, p. 5.

plan was therefore replaced by a system in which the government became merely "the social regulator" of the nation's industry by indirect controls drawn up by "the representative bodies of the country," including workers' councils. Such a system maintains "the essence of socialism," prevents bureaucratic control and promotes production by "freeing the initiative of the producers to develop according to basic economic laws."[1]

An essential part of this whole idea is emphasis on initiative of workers, not only by freeing them from bureaucratic controls but also by making it clear to them that the harder they work the more they receive directly. Such initiative, the 1958 Program proclaims, represents "a greater economic power than capitalist initiative" and guarantees that "socialism must come out a victor in economic competition with capitalism."

Theory of the Party

While the state is withering away, what becomes of the Communist Party? According to Yugoslav theory, the Party is also slated for withering away, but, although its role must be different from that of the Soviet Communist Party, the withering away of the Party cannot begin until some time later.

It was Tito's declaration in 1952 that the Party would wither away along with the state that set in motion a chain of ideas culminating in Djilas' proposal that it do so forthwith. Abruptly, then, Tito pulled back, declaring that "there can be no withering away or winding up of the League of Communists until the last class enemy has been immobilized, until the broadest body of our citizens are socialist in outlook." Rather, said Tito, the Party in the interim must become stronger, while its withering away would be "a lengthy process," developing only "through trials and difficulties."[2]

Nevertheless, the 1958 Program promises that the Communist Party in Yugoslavia "will gradually disappear in the long run . . . as the forms of direct socialist democracy become stronger, develop and expand. This disappearance will proceed parallel to the objective process of the withering away of social antagonisms."

Interpreting this, Kardelj explains that the method of the withering away of the Party will be a gradual merger of its power "into the direct power of the working masses themselves."[3]

Yugoslav theory holds that the Communist Party of the Soviet Union is a source of much of the evil in that country because there is no distinction between the Party and the state. Stalin, Tito charged, reduced "the role of the

[1] *Ibid.*, pp. 6 and 14. For a discussion of the Yugoslav governmental and economic system, see Chapters 13 and 14.

[2] *Borba*, January 18, 1954.

[3] *Sedmi Kongres*, p. 178.

party to administration of a state apparatus that still bears the stamp of a class society. . . . This stereotyped concept was beginning to take hold here, too."[1] Kardelj phrased it this way:

For Soviet Stalinist theory and practice, the "dictatorship of the proletariat" means the complete subordination of the working class and the masses to the monopolistic authority of the "wisest" and absolutely identifying the merging of the instruments of the "elite" — that is, of the party — with the state executive and administrative apparatus, the maximum centralization within that system — that is, the concentration of all authority in the hands of a central few — and the subjection of the whole field of science and ideas to the interests of the system's survival.[2]

Yugoslav theory sees "bureaucratic statism" as a danger not only in the state but also in the Party, especially where government decision making is concentrated in Party hands. Instead of being the spokesman for the working class, the Party in Yugoslavia is supposed to speak through the working class. The Party, it is held, cannot have *the* leading role in a socialist society like Yugoslavia, but only *a* leading role, in cooperation with other organizations. The doctrine bars direct Party intervention in government affairs. The task of the Communists is seen as one not of ordering and directing but of leading by education and propaganda.

To symbolize this new theory of the Party, the Yugoslav Party in 1952 transformed itself into a League of Communists, and underwent some decentralization, although continuing to be based on the principle of democratic centralism.

The League now "considers it untenable dogma . . . that absolute monopoly of political power by the Communist Party is a universal and 'eternal' principle." For the time being, nevertheless, it in fact retains what is very nearly an "absolute monopoly of political power." Kardelj admits that he "would be guilty of hypocrisy" if he did not state "that at present the Communists do exert, as they should, a direct influence on the key positions of power."[3] According to Yugoslav theory, the influence is exercised by members of the Party as individuals rather than the Party as an organization. In practice the difference is not always easy to see.

Socialist Democracy

The Belgrade theorists call their new system *Socialist Democracy*. Political democracy of some kind is posited as necessary to socialism. As Aleksandar Ranković declared in 1952, a society "reaching the socialist path of withering away of the state" must inevitably be concerned with freedom and human

[1] Josip Broz Tito, *Workers Manage Factories in Yugoslavia*, Jugoštampa, Belgrade, 1950, p. 30.
[2] *Socijalistička Demokratija*, p. 23.
[3] *Sedmi Kongres*, p. 178.

rights.[1] Moše Pijade emphasized that "decentralization is the first and most vital step to democracy."[2]

The Yugoslavs are careful to point out what their kind of democracy does not mean. Above all, it does not mean Western-type democracy. According to Yugoslav theory, "there is no such thing as a universal form of democracy . . . a democracy without qualification, which would have the same meaning for everybody and could remain unchanged." For example, "bourgeois democracy always remains a democracy of a minority, of a ruling class," because the "majority has not the necessary economic, social, intellectual and cultural resources to allow it to manifest itself fully and make decisions freely." This does not mean that a political system "grown on capitalist soil cannot be called democratic." But socialism must develop its own type of democracy as "a new social phenomenon," not merely "transplanting or modifying the political democracy of capitalism." Abraham Lincoln's concept of government of, by and for the people is accepted as "a postulate for any real democracy." But when this postulate is applied under a socialist system it results in "a more real form of democracy" than under capitalism.[3]

Adaptation of certain forms of "bourgeois democracy" is possible for Yugoslavia, but not all of them, even if socialist forces "should obtain complete mastery of them," for Western democratic forms "contain seeds of capitalism." What really troubles the Yugoslavs about such forms is that they would open the way for anti-socialist criticism. Such criticism is permissible, according to Yugoslav concepts of democracy, only when it is voiced by individuals, without organization, and is not considered by the government to endanger the socialist system. Kardelj, who earlier had asserted "not only the right but the duty" of a socialist state to "resist anti-socialist criticism by administrative means,"[4] told the 1958 Congress: "Only those forms of democracy can be a suitable instrument of social advance which allow . . . socialist economic and social relationships to 'rest' comfortably."[5]

Within these limits, there not only can but must be free expression and "a struggle of opinion." "Conditions are being created," boasts the 1958 Program, "for considerate hearing of everybody's opinion."

There must also be a rule of law. "The working class and socialist society" should "feel safe not only from remnants of the bourgeoisie, but also, as

[1] See his report to the Fourth Plenum of the Central Committee, *New Yugoslav Law*, October–December 1951, p. 3.

[2] *Borba*, November 1, 1952; see also Fred Warner Neal, "Certain Aspects of the New Reforms in Yugoslavia," *University of Colorado Studies*, Series in Political Science, No. 1, June 1953, p. 53.

[3] Cf. Djordjević, "Some Principles of Socialist Democracy in Yugoslavia," p. 19, and "O Socijalističkoj Demokratiji" ("On Socialist Democracy"), *Mejunarodna Politika*, January 1, 1953, p. 1.

[4] *Socijalistička Demokratija*, p. 23.

[5] *Sedmi Kongres*, p. 172.

Marx says, from their own officials." Accordingly, the 1958 Program stresses the right of citizens to secure protection from state action through the courts. Such emphasis on individual rights is referred to as "socialist humanism."

None of this, however, permits of a multi-party system. In principle, a multi-party system may be possible "in certain phases of the transitional period," according to Kardelj, "but . . . in a comparatively backward country like Yugoslavia . . . such a system would inevitably destroy not only the socialist foundation of such a country but even its independence." Advocates of such a system for Yugoslavia, Kardelj asserted, are either enemies "of the independence and freedom of our peoples" or else they understand "nothing of what is happening in the world today."[1]

Furthermore, according to Yugoslav theory, political parties are unnecessary because they are "either a reflection of clashing economic interests or they are meaningless as far as real issues are concerned." Since, according to Kardelj, "in Yugoslavia there is no clash of economic interests in the Marxist sense . . . to have meaningless parties in a country with our level of cultural and ideological development would only mean confusion."[2]

Instead of political parties, Yugoslav socialist democracy is "direct and mass democracy." This, the 1958 Program contrasts with "bourgeois democracy which, both in theory and practice, is indirect democracy through intermediaries." Direct democracy is seen as coming about when, as a result of the withering away of state functions, masses of citizens themselves make political decisions affecting their lives. It is carried on, as the Yugoslavs see it, through the Socialist Alliance, workers' councils and a variety of political instrumentalities ranging from voters' meetings to citizen-action committees in local government and direct citizen management of such institutions as schools and hospitals. Especially is direct democracy seen in the commune, a new form of local government with wide economic functions.[3] The commune, says the 1958 Program, "represents the outstanding institution of direct socialist democracy. . . . The commune is not only primarily a school of democracy but democracy itself — the basic cell of self-management of citizens in common affairs."

From Marxism-Leninism to Titoism

Having seen their system in the beginning primarily as rescuing Leninism from Stalinist deviation,[4] the Yugoslav Communists are still often wont to

---

[1] *Socijalistička Demokratija*, pp. 28–29.

[2] Cf. Fred Warner Neal, "Yugoslav Communist Theory," *American Universities Field Staff Reports*, FWN-5-'54, p. 11.

[3] For a description of this and other Yugoslav governmental organizations and practice, see Chapter 13.

[4] See Tito's remarks in *Borba*, June 27, 1950.

think of themselves as "Marxists-Leninists." Although Stalinism is openly repudiated, Leninism is not quite repudiated as such. Where the Yugoslav Communists still pay prime attention to Lenin, other than verbally, is in his basic approach to Marxism, certain aspects of which had a pragmatic quality now highly esteemed in Belgrade. The 1958 Program, for example, quotes Lenin approvingly as follows: "We do not at all look on Marx's theory as something finished and inviolable. . . . We do not pretend that Marx or Marxists know the road to socialism in all its concrete aspects. This is nonsense. We know the direction of the road and we know which class forces lead the way, but concretely, practically, only the experience of millions will tell when they get down to work." Yet Leninism, insofar as the term means a cohesive body of theoretical and operational principles, has also been abandoned by the Yugoslav theorists. As Kardelj told one of the authors: "Leninism is simply a series of ideas and methods that grew out of the Russian experience. Our experience is different."

In addition to Yugoslav theories on the state and Party, the most obvious departure from what is generally considered Leninist doctrine concerns the approach to agriculture. This is also a prime example of the comparatively pragmatic quality of Yugoslav Communism.

Prior to the Cominform Resolution, the Yugoslavs may not have acted on the basis of the Leninist dogma that socialism in the villages is necessary for socialism in the country, but their stepped-up collectivization drive in 1949 shows that they really never questioned it. By 1954, however, even the most rigid Yugoslav Communist had to admit that collectivization was a failure. Accordingly, it was abandoned, although the Party remained committed to the concept of collectivization as a goal.

It was to cope with this situation theoretically that the Yugoslavs formally cast aside the Leninist doctrine about the priority of collectivization and adopted a theory of what might be called "socialism by osmosis." The gist of this idea is that instead of proceeding with socialism in the villages first, the Yugoslavs would let the private peasants alone — except to limit capitalist influences by limiting the size of land holdings — and proceed with completion of socialism elsewhere through industrialization. The theory is that as this process develops, a generally socialist *zeitgeist* will be created in the country as a whole which ultimately will alter the individualist outlook of the peasant. When it does, the Yugoslavs feel, the peasants will be in a mood for acceptance of cooperatives "of some sort." The Soviet-type *kolkhozi* are definitely ruled out as an acceptable form, even for the future. The whole process is seen as taking a long time, according to Kardelj "maybe 25 or 50 years." In the meantime, the Yugoslavs anticipate that agricultural production will be increased and the individualism of the peasants softened up through the development of voluntary cooperatives of other types.[1]

Importance of Yugoslav Theory

What the Yugoslavs do is more important than what they say, and it is not always the same thing. But leaving aside this aspect, a number of conclusions suggest themselves concerning this half-original, half-fundamentalist framework which the Yugoslav Communists have erected to explain and justify their position and bulwark their views.

First of all, here is a fresh approach to contemporary Marxism that maintains most of what is appealing to those interested in the theory generally and omits or alters much of what is most distasteful to those who, although attracted to Marxism, have been repelled by Soviet dogmatism and brutality. In one sense, it offers a bridge between the positions of the Second and Third Internationals, although certainly closer to the latter. There are, as Soviet spokesmen have charged, some elements of both "right and left deviation" in Yugoslav theory, some elements of both Trotsky and Bukharin, although there is much more of Lenin than of either of them. Certain aspects of the doctrine approach the position of Eduard Bernstein and other German revisionists, but the Yugoslavs make it clear that they reject Bernstein's view that the aim of a proletarian movement is only political democracy rather than Communism, and they emphasize that the inevitability of Communism is meaningful only if consciously fought for by Communists.

Secondly, Yugoslav theory subjects Soviet development and policies and Soviet theories to a devastating criticism that is the more meaningful because of the wide area of agreement between Yugoslav and Soviet Communism.

Thirdly, Yugoslav theory offers an ideological basis, well within the confines of Marxism and even Marxism-Leninism, for an independent and less totalitarian Marxist development in which more attention can be paid to human values and individual rights. The significance of this not only for areas already Communist but for underdeveloped nations groping their way into some sort of socialism may be considerable.[2]

Finally, but by no means least, is the importance of Titoist theory for the Yugoslav Communists themselves. "Theory," observed Stalin, ". . . gives practical people strength and orientation, a clarity of perspective, confidence at work, faith. . . ."[3] It is noteworthy that even during the period of their

---

[1] Cf. Neal, "Yugoslav Communist Theory," pp. 12–13, and *Yugoslavia's Way*, pp. 141–142, and 210–216. For a discussion of Yugoslav agriculture, see Chapter 15.

[2] For a discussion of this point, see Chapter 21.

[3] J. V. Stalin, *Voprosy Leninizma* (*Problems of Leninism*), Gosizdat, Moscow, 1934, pp. 299–300.

closest rapprochement with the Soviet Union — 1956–1958 — the Yugoslav Communists departed hardly at all from their basic tenets, no matter how distasteful these were to Moscow. The existence of a cohesive body of theory underpinning the unique Yugoslav approach to Communism does not prove that the Titoists will never abandon their new directions for the mirage of socialist unity under Soviet tutelage, or slip back into Stalinist ways, but it does make such possibilities far less likely than would otherwise be the case. This theoretical framework is also one of the most important factors setting off Yugoslav developments from the "October reforms" in Poland after 1956. Gomulka's reforms have far more of an "NEP" tactical quality about them because of the virtually complete absence of a new theoretical orientation.[1]

[1] The Polish reforms are analyzed in Chapter 21.

THE LEAGUE OF

COMMUNISTS

T HE Yugoslav Communist Party has been able to adapt to the new directions of Titoism by altering its methods of operation, and even delimiting its authority, without thus far fundamentally weakening its domination of the country. The Party is the single most important institution in Yugoslavia, and the story of its trials and tribulations and how it meets them is in one sense the essence of the story of Titoism.

Although the Cominform Resolution did not succeed in shaking the allegiance of the great bulk of Yugoslav Communists to Tito, it did cause the Party untold woes. Tito's complaint that the Resolution produced "a certain spiritual demoralization" is a masterpiece of understatement. Not only the elimination of the Soviet Union as an inspiration and a model but also the new theories that soon arose in Yugoslavia contributed to the "spiritual demoralization" of the Yugoslav Communists. For the Soviet Communist Party was now being denounced for a role that was little different from that of the Yugoslav Party. On top of this came the bold program of economic decentralization on which the regime embarked in 1950.

Despite all this, the leadership considered that it had the Party situation well in hand. Of the 448,175 members of the Yugoslav Communist Party in 1948, only 3,000 had been Communists before the war. In the six months following the Cominform Resolution, Party membership increased to 530,812. By the end of 1950, it had grown to 607,443; by December 1951, to 704,617; and by June 1952, to 779,382.[1] Thus, virtually the entire membership had come to the Party under conditions fostering solidarity with the Yugoslav

[1] See Tito's report to the Sixth Party Congress, *Borba*, November 4, 1952.

rather than the Soviet leadership, and nearly half had joined since the break with Moscow.

What was immediately needed, therefore, was more firm support from a broader section of the population. Even though the Party had been operating to a considerable extent behind the façade of the People's Front, its strong-arm methods and the privileged position of its members were a constant irritant. Not only this fact but also the difficult economic situation already manifesting itself threatened to undercut the new popularity Tito was acquiring as a result of his defiance of Moscow.

Privileges Eliminated

In the fall of 1950, the regime moved to strengthen its position with the general populace by calling for the elimination of special privileges for Party members. Declaring that the legal position of Communists was exactly the same as that of non-Communists, the Central Committee ruled that "henceforth" no one could have special treatment just because of membership in the Party. In particular, the Committee decreed a halt to those practices that caused most popular irritation — the issuing to Communists of special rations and housing rights denied the rest of the population.[1]

Both inside and outside Yugoslavia, this action was received with surprised approval. "For the first time," wrote the Belgrade correspondent of the *New York Times*, "a Communist state has abolished the line of demarcation separating the rulers from the people and has adopted as a fundamental principle a modicum of equalitarianism."[2]

The favorable response to this action was encouraging. Yet the traditional role of the Party seemed clearly out of keeping with the changing conditions in Yugoslavia. As the new theories of "socialist democracy" developed, along with the sweeping decentralization of state functions, the monopolistic and highly centralized Communist Party, with its large and highhanded bureaucracy, presented an ever-sharper contrast. In addition, many Communists, misunderstanding the new line and reluctant to give up their accustomed authority, were bucking the decentralization program. People were asking, "Since the Party runs everything, what is the difference really between our system and that of the Soviet Union?"

The answer was, as far as the Party itself was concerned, not much. Party units dominated government at all levels. Almost without exception, the heads of local Party committees were also the heads of local government bodies and often acted like little dictators. Local government was, as a result, little more

[1] See *Yugoslav Newsletter*, October 23, 1950, pp. 1–2.
[2] M. S. Handler in the *New York Times*, October 30, 1950, p. 1.

than an extension of the Party organization. In the factories, what Party spokesmen said was law. And the Party units themselves repeated only what they were told from Belgrade. Up until 1952, according to Tito, "the entire ideological-educational work [of the Party] was run predominately from the center. The subject matter and even the forms were determined and initiated by the agitation-propaganda department of the Central Committee."[1] The Party statute adopted by the Fifth Party Congress was, despite the Cominform Resolution which preceded it, only "a copy of the Statute of the Soviet Communist Party . . . weighed down by Soviet practices and requirements."[2]

Changes in the Party

The year 1952 brought important changes in the nature of the Yugoslav Party. First, in June the Fourth Plenum of the Central Committee issued a series of directives applying the principle of decentralization to the Party and limiting its direct role in local government and in economic matters. Secondly, in November the Sixth Party Congress spelled out a whole new theory for the Party which, if it did not change its role, altered its methods of operation considerably.

The June 1952 directives of the Central Committee ordered local Party secretaries to give up forthwith their positions as heads of local government bodies. This situation typified the "bureaucratic caste system" of the Soviet Union, the Committee held, and it had to be changed. For the same persons to hold both jobs was found to be incompatible with the new autonomy being extended to local government. Moreover, it tended to interfere with the Party's ideological work, on the one hand, and obstructed proper criticism of local officials on the other. The same was true of economic affairs, the Committee said; Party officials must stop interfering with worker-management and let workers' councils make decisions in the factories.

The June directives also extended more autonomy to local Party units, with the aim of expanding "intra-Party democracy and eliminating bureaucracy." Under the new rules, although propaganda activities were to follow the general Party line, local Party units, in the absence of specific orders, were to decide for themselves what to do and how to do it.[3]

Liberalization was now in the air, and, despite the fact that these changes produced considerable confusion among the rank and file, five months later the Sixth Congress went much further in decentralizing the Party organization and delimiting its role in active direction of affairs. The measures adopted by

---

[1] Tito's report to the Sixth Party Congress.
[2] Ranković's report to the Sixth Party Congress, *Politika*, November 9, 1952.
[3] *Komunist*, No. 4, June 1952.

the Congress, along with explanatory statements by Tito, Ranković, Kardelj and Djilas, amounted to a new theory of the Party.[1]

According to the new theory, the Party was to cease governing directly and confine itself to "political and ideological education." No longer were Party units to impose their will on government and other bodies, nor were Party members to use their position as such to give orders. Instead, Communists were to exert their influence by functioning as individual members of various governmental and other organizations.

All this meant, according to Kardelj, the end of the Party's monopoly in political affairs. "No longer," he declared, did the Party "consider the determination of the political line of struggle for construction of socialist relationships as its monopoly alone." The Party was thus abandoning its "leading role" in society. Henceforth, it would play only "a conscious role" and must win a leading role for its policies "on the basis of good work and knowledge of the laws of society and not by a decree determining for itself that it is the leading political force."

The Resolution adopted by the Sixth Congress proclaimed: "The League of Communists cannot be and is not the direct operational leader and director of economic, government or social life. It is rather, by its political and ideological activities, primarily by discussion, to work in all organizations, agencies and institutions for the adoption of its line and standpoint, through the activities of individual members."

The Sixth Congress, Ranković said, was casting aside Soviet-type "bureaucratic obstructions" and adopting a statute embracing "the fundamental principles for . . . the Party at the present stage of development and socialist democracy." The new statute, embracing the directives of the June 1952 Plenum of the Central Committee, reformed Party practice in these important areas:

1. Party meetings. These henceforth were to be public, and non-Communists should be especially urged to attend meetings of the basic, or lowest, Party units. "This is no propaganda slogan," warned Ranković.

2. Organization. Party units in government administration branches and in nongovernmental organizations were abolished, and Party members were to work in such bodies only as individuals. Henceforth, Party organizations were to be based only on production and territorial divisions, i.e., factories, *opština* or ward, village, district, etc. Further, permanent bureaus of Party officials in these units were to be abolished, although local Party organizations might retain a secretariat of no more than five members, headed by a secretary.

[1] See *Sixth Congress of the Communist Party of Yugoslavia*, Belgrade, 1953, for the Resolution and Statute adopted by the Congress as well as major statements of the leaders. See also material on the Fourth Congress of the People's Front, *Borba*, February 21, 1953, and *Yugoslav Review*, March–April 1953, especially p. 17.

3. Decentralization. Higher Party organs would no longer have authority to assign specific operational tasks to lower units but only to lay down broad lines of policy and make general suggestions for implementation. Republic Party Congresses, which under the 1948 Statute could only determine "the tactical line," now had the right to "determine the political line of the Party in their areas, based on the general political line of the CPY."

4. Autonomy for lower organs. The Central Committee was no longer empowered to appoint Party organizers to take over affairs in certain areas. Such authority, "literally copied from the Soviet Party's statute, was again simply an undemocratic measure to justify the existence of commissars wherever they were thought necessary." Also, basic Party units were now to have the right to expel any of their members or to take in new members without reference to higher Party authority. And the requirement for an eighteen-month period of candidature prior to full membership was abolished.

To symbolize these reforms in Party structure and operations, the Party changed its name to the League of Communists of Yugoslavia. There were now new "conditions in which the revolution is in the main consummated," Tito declared. Hence it was necessary to change the role of the Party "and the word Party is no longer adequate."[1] At the same time, as if to remove even the terminology of Stalinism, the name of the Politburo was changed to Executive Committee. (See Figure 12–1, pp. 192–193.)

The leadership was careful to tell Communists not to be too liberal in interpreting the new Party theory and emphasized that, above all, no change in the one-party system was implied. A multi-party system, Tito declared, would only "permit the organized destruction of revolutionary achievements for which blood has already been shed." Milovan Djilas warned that any trend toward "bourgeois democracy" would be "but a mask for turning back" to the "semi-feudal" conditions which existed before World War II.

Already the liberalizing effects of the June directives had produced some undesirable results. The "ideological and educational level of the membership" was lagging, Tito reported, because many local Party units were not able to work properly by themselves. As a result, he said, "various conceptions . . . alien to the Party began to penetrate in the ranks of the membership . . . various elements . . . began to conceive our expansion of democracy wrongly and to raise their heads. Various theories began appearing on the freedom of this or that."

---

[1] Tito's report to the Sixth Party Congress. The new name of the Party in Serbo-Croatian is *Savez Komunista Jugoslavije*. The word *savez* may also be translated as association or union. The terms "League" and "Party" are used interchangeably in Yugoslavia except in official references.

Aleksandar Ranković, the chief Party functionary below Tito, added that some Party members had gone too far in interpreting Party democracy while others had not gone far enough. Some of them, he said, were not even attending meetings and paying dues. Ranković also attacked those who thought the Party should be a mass organization or should lose its identity or cohesiveness. What counted, he said, was not numbers "but internal unity, purity and intense political activity." But at the same time the Communists had to be "responsible for their work and behavior not only to the Party organization and leadership but to the people, to the whole of society."[1]

The Socialist Alliance

Tito then explained that what was called for were "new forms of organized mass political forces" with "an indispensable uniform program." This meant doing something about the People's Front. The Front, which in 1952 had more than 7 million members, was concerned in nearly everything but did very little. Its chief function was simply as a front for Party activity. Its members were apathetic, and even the Communists conceived of the Front, Tito complained, only in terms of "voluntary work drives," i.e., as a vehicle for coercing people to do various things the Party wanted to do. The People's Front now had to be reorganized and adapted to the new conditions.

In keeping with Tito's suggestions at the Sixth Party Congress, the People's Front, when its Fourth Congress convened in February 1953, changed its name and its structure. It became the Socialist Alliance of Working People of Yugoslavia. As such, it embraced just about everybody and everything: all organizations and groups, from sports societies to veterans' associations, and all individuals who were willing to go along with the regime even part of the way. The Socialist Alliance, explained Kardelj, should have a broad enough political platform "so as to enable the participation in it of every citizen who comports himself honorably toward the social community and accepts the general aims of socialism — regardless of ideological and other differences of opinion."

The League of Communists as an organization did not belong to the Alliance, but all members of the Party belonged as individuals. The Socialist Alliance, in fact, was to be the main mechanism for putting Communist ideas into action and for transmitting them back to the Party. Whereas the League of Communists would provide "general ideological leadership" and "political and educational work," Kardelj explained, the Socialist Alliance would deal with "concrete, political and other social questions."[2]

[1] Ranković's report to the Sixth Party Congress.

[2] Kardelj's address to the Fourth Congress of the People's Front, *Yugoslav Review*, March–April 1953.

What this meant, in effect, was that the Communists, sitting as a Party, would make broad, general policy, and then, sitting as individuals, would apply it to specific situations in the name of the Socialist Alliance. At first sight, this seemed much the same as previous practice, according to which, Kardelj explained, "party organizations at their meetings decided all political and other questions and then simply forwarded these decisions to the People's Front organizations for approval." Yet Kardelj demanded that this practice now stop, and he exhorted the non-Communist members of the Socialist Alliance to be independent. The difference now was, apparently, that individual Communists themselves had to propose action to the Alliance, instead of simply transmitting a Party decision, and then the Alliance could approve or not, depending on whether Communist members had convinced the others.

Following the Sixth Party Congress, the decentralization and curtailment of Party functions proceeded at all levels, particularly in connection with propaganda. The agitation-propaganda department of the Central Committee's secretariat in Belgrade was eliminated, as were the cultural and military departments and the Party schools for training professional Party workers. As reconstituted, the apparatus consisted of a personnel or cadre department, an organization department, a financial department and a record-historical department. The Party Control Commission, charged with seeing to it that Communists did not get too far out of line, was also attached to the Secretariat.

The administrative organization of the republic central committees was even further reduced. By 1954 the total number of professional party functionaries had been more than halved. Much of the work went on, however, only under different auspices. At the higher levels, government officials did it on government time. At lower levels, local secretaries assigned it to groups of their Party members, especially work on cadres and so-called ideological-educational work. All agitation-propaganda functions and cultural activities involving such organizations as women's and youth groups were turned over to the Socialist Alliance, and many functionaries formerly employed by the Party now simply went to work for the new Alliance organizations.

In 1954 the Socialist Alliance had a membership of about 8 million. It comprised both organizations and individuals. While organizations as such could affiliate with the Alliance, their members, in order to be members of the Alliance, had to enroll personally. The Socialist Alliance was organized at federal, republic, district, local and "bloc" levels, as Figure 12–1 shows.

Trade Unions and the Army

Aside from the Party, the only organizations in Yugoslavia that formally remained outside the Socialist Alliance were the trade union Sindikat and the

Army. They maintained this position not only because of the nature of their functions but because they were so important that direct Party control was considered essential.

With the extensive decentralization of government and economy that was taking place, the trade unions acting as the voice of the Party in the factory provided virtually the only means of enforcing the Party's will in many enterprises. About 40 per cent of the members of the Sindikat were members of the Party, and its officials held high posts in the Party. The important role of the trade unions is discussed in detail later.

The Army was especially important. It was important not only for external defense, but also, of course, represented a bulwark of strength of the regime internally. Furthermore, it was a focus of Soviet efforts at subversion. It is not surprising, therefore, that unusual attention was paid by the Party to the armed forces. Practically the entire officer corps belonged to the Party, and there were more Communists in the Army in 1954 than in any republic except Serbia and Croatia. Tito reported to the Sixth Congress that some 650 Party courses had been organized in the Army during the preceding year as well as nearly one million separate lectures and 700,000 political discussion groups.

Party Dominance

It quickly became apparent that the Socialist Alliance was, as it was supposed to be, completely dominated by the League of Communists. Of the twenty-seven-man presidium, the Alliance's highest body, twenty-one were members of the Central Committee of the League, and these included all but two members of the Party's Executive Committee. Tito was president of the Socialist Alliance, and Kardelj was its secretary-general up until 1960, when he was replaced by Ranković. Each of the Socialist Alliance republic organizations was headed by a member of the Party Central Committee of the corresponding republic.

The Socialist Alliance operated primarily in three areas. The most important was the coordination of the approximately 300 organizations affiliated with it. The second was the carrying on of general propaganda activities aimed at instilling popular support for the regime and its policies, that is, at "raising the cultural and political level of the population." The third was the specific area of government, especially at the local level, where the Socialist Alliance was supposed to supervise elections and serve as a watchdog over activities of various governmental and semi-governmental bodies. A typical example was the people's committee of Kragujevac in Serbia, which reported in 1954 that it did not "deal with a single important question without its having been discussed in the Socialist Alliance."[1] The Socialist Alliance was thus seen as a key pillar in the Yugoslav concepts of "direct democracy" and "social self-government."[2]

A part of the concept of the Socialist Alliance was that it should embrace people who disagreed with the Communist Party but generally supported the socialist system. Religious people, of whom the Party took a dim view, were especially invited to join. It was true that most members of the Alliance fell into the non-Communist category, but there was a definite limit as to how far disagreement with the Party would be tolerated. There were numerous cases of expulsions from the Socialist Alliance of members who indulged in undue criticism. Not only Milovan Djilas but many of those who expressed agreement with him were peremptorily ousted. On many questions there was debate in Alliance organizations, and some of it spirited, but decisions were usually taken unanimously.

One trouble was that the work of the League of Communists and the Socialist Alliance was so intermingled that it was difficult and often impossible to tell where the functions of one body left off and the other began. League and Alliance organizations often met together. Particularly, "ideological-educational" activities of both bodies tended to be identical. *Borba*, the organ of the League, became the organ of the Socialist Alliance. Not infrequently Party committees made decisions outlining work for the Socialist Alliance. It was not surprising that many people regarded the Alliance simply as an arm of the Party and concluded that there was no difference between it and the People's Front. A frequent complaint of Communists themselves was that they could not see where the activities of one organization ended and those of the other began.[3]

The fact was that the Socialist Alliance functioned significantly only through its Communist members. In the words of Blažo Jovanović, head man in Montenegro and a member of the Federal Executive Committee of the Party: "In those quarters where the Communists are active, the Socialist Alliance of Working People is active. In those quarters where the Communists are inactive, and where they do not attend meetings of the Socialist Alliance, the other working men do not assign any importance to the work."[4]

---

[1] *Politika*, January 12, 1954.

[2] See Josip Broz Tito, *The Building of Socialism and the Role and Tasks of the Socialist Alliance of the Working People of Yugoslavia*, Belgrade, April 18, 1960, p. 88. This is Tito's report to the Fifth Congress of the Socialist Alliance.

[3] See Fred Warner Neal, *Titoism in Action: The Reforms in Yugoslavia after 1948*, University of California Press, Berkeley, 1958, pp. 56–57 and 59–64.

[4] *Pobjeda*, Titograd, October 24, 1954.

Confusion in the Ranks

In spite of everything, the situation might have worked out all right had there not been confusion in the ranks of the Communists. The difficulty was that the confusion already evident at the time of the Sixth Party Congress was only exacerbated by the deliberations of that body. Suddenly, as it were, the Communists — long used to being told what to do and say and accustomed to running things by *diktat* — were told to change, almost to reverse, their ways. They were told to work only as individuals and not impose their views, to tolerate different opinions, to give up their political monopoly. And in the same breath they were told they were responsible for what went on, that they must fight anti-socialist ideas, that they had to struggle for a leading role and maintain the purity and monolithic position of the Party.

On top of this now there came a new concept which still further added to the befuddlement of the average Communist. This was the concept of the "withering away of the Party." Actually, like certain other Yugoslav theories it was not really new. It had been discussed in Moscow during the early days of the Soviet Union.[1] But whereas the Soviet Communists had continued to refer to the withering away of the state as a goal, for a long time nothing at all had been said in this connection about the Communist Party. The Party, it was generally assumed, like death and taxes would go on forever.

Now Tito dusted off this concept. Since in Yugoslavia the withering away of the state had actually begun, he declared, then the Party "cannot go on in the same old way. If the State does not wither away, then the Party becomes . . . an instrument of the State, a force outside of society. If the state really withers away, the Party necessarily withers away with it."[2]

Perhaps because the idea was so startling, Tito was rather casual about "the withering away of the Party." Although he first mentioned it, in passing as it were, prior to the Sixth Congress, the concept was not referred to at the Congress. But with the publication of his biography by Vladimir Dedijer soon afterwards, everybody was talking about it, and its meaning was a topic for discussion among both leadership and rank and file. "Many of our own people do not realize the fact that the Party necessarily withers away with the state," Tito was quoted as saying. "We have to explain to them gradually of what this withering away consists, and we have begun to do so."[3]

The ideological level of the League of Communists of Yugoslavia was generally low. A great majority of the Communists had had only partial

---

[1] See, for example, a 1920 resolution of the Comintern, *Kommunisticheskii Internatsional v Dokumentakh* (*Communist International in Documents*), Gosizdat, Moscow, 1953, pp. 100–109, and V. I. Lenin, *Works*, Vol. XXIV, International Publishers, New York, 1936, p. 53.

[2] Vladimir Dedijer, *Tito*, Simon & Schuster, New York, 1953, p. 428.

[3] *Ibid.*

schooling, and many were, in fact, illiterate. In Montenegro, one of the most backward parts of Yugoslavia, the Party leader had declared that for "a considerable number of Communists . . . their prime task and obligation [is] to learn to read."[1]

Even without such conditions, the sudden proliferation of new and conflicting ideas and reforms would have been perplexing. As it was, when there was now added to these the idea that the Party, to which the Communists were expected to devote their lives, was to wither away, perplexity gave way not only to confusion but to resignation.

Some — particularly among the middle-level functionaries — met the new situation by ignoring it, continuing to act as before and to buck both Party and government reforms. Some read into the new line more than was there and actually came out against Party positions. Others just threw up their hands.

The Brioni Plenum

By June 1953 it was already apparent to the leadership that a dangerous situation was developing. The Central Committee, called to deal with the matter at Tito's summer residence on the Adriatic, found that relaxed discipline had permitted "ideological and political confusion to grow" to the point where broad areas of the Party were "ceasing to be revolutionary."[2]

The Brioni Plenum, as this Central Committee meeting became known, charged that "all kinds of uncertainty and anti-Marxist theories are starting to appear," and that "the struggle for ideological and political unity is very weak." Party discipline must be tightened at once, the Committee decreed, and democratic centralism must be construed as applying not only to Party but also to government action. "It is not a rare occurrence," the Committee observed, "that members of the Communist League believe that they have the right to protest against decrees and other measures that have been adopted in our Socialist state in a democratic manner."

It was true, the Committee said, that some Communists still believed "the party line had not changed at all" and considered the new state and party concepts merely "an agitation-propaganda tactic." But more important and more numerous were other Communists who became passive, ignored Party discipline and thought the "process of democracy meant they could contribute nothing to the Party but lectures." These Communists were adopting "petty-bourgeois-anarchist ideas of freedom and democracy" and failing to fight against "foreign and anti-Socialist manifestations."

---

[1] Blažo Jovanović in *Pobjeda*, October 24, 1954.

[2] See *Komunist*, No. 4, July 1953. Since the Central Committee began numbering its plenums anew after the Sixth Party Congress, this is officially the Second Plenum.

The concept of the withering away of the Party, the Plenum announced, had been generally misunderstood. It was important to realize that this idea concerned only the distant future, when Communism was achieved and there was no longer a need for ideological leadership. What was needed now, and for the foreseeable future, the Plenum decided, was leadership by the League of Communists as a highly disciplined and monolithic force. The Party had changed to meet new conditions, it was true, but it remained an indispensable force for the development of socialism and Communism in Yugoslavia.

The immediate result of the Brioni Plenum was a general tightening up of discipline within the Party and a rash of expulsions of members considered unreliable. By the end of 1953, the year's total of expulsions reached 72,067, reducing over-all Party membership to 732,011 as compared with 779,382 in June 1952.[1] The real impact of the Plenum, however, was much more far-reaching.

Differences in the Leadership

There is no reason to think that Tito and other Party leaders were necessarily insincere in putting forth their new ideas about democracy inside and outside the Party. But in the same way that democracy means one thing to Communists and another thing to non-Communists, so did the new Yugoslav concepts mean one thing to one group of Communist leaders, something else to another. For most of the top echelon of leaders, including Tito, the new line reflected their objection to the hard and dogmatic Moscow way of doing things and their faith that an increasing number of Yugoslavs were coming to favor the regime in its post-Cominform guise. They had no idea of any really sharp change in the role of the Communist Party but apparently expected that, with time, it could gradually step aside and permit a population already committed to their general goals to continue the direction of society along the lines they had set. The decentralization of government and economy was being accomplished, and it was felt these devices would help instill a "socialist consciousness in the masses," as Tito phrased it. The new concept of the Party was also aimed at building this socialist consciousness, but it was for the time more formal than actual. For Tito and most of the leadership, full political democracy simply meant permitting anti-Communists to overthrow the system, which they saw as still so weak as to be highly vulnerable. As they looked around them, they also saw the low cultural level of their own comrades as well as the masses generally, the muted but still smoldering fires of national and religious hatred, the hostility to the regime of large sections of the populace. Even if they had not been impressed with their own wisdom and

[1] *Komunist*, No. 4, April 1954, p. 267.

indispensability, these Communists would have no more entrusted their socialist future to an uncontrolled Yugoslav population as then constituted than they would have to, say, Winston Churchill.

For another, much smaller group of Communist leaders, however, the new directions of Titoism meant something else. They meant that the revolution had in the main been accomplished; that the masses were already overwhelmingly sold on socialism, Yugoslav-style, and no longer needed political tutelage; that the time was now at hand for a bold leap into the Good Society. Under such conditions, these Communists considered that the Party should, like the state, actually turn the direction of affairs over to others. They came to envisage the Party as little more than a forum of Marxists where new socialist ideas could be discussed before being offered to a receptive people to accept or reject. For them, democratic centralism was a device that had been useful when the Party was really at the helm of society but today simply interfered with the processes of democracy. If the country were not really turned over to the people now, in fact as well as in theory, they feared, the laws of bureaucracy would reassert themselves and both democracy and "real socialism" might be lost. Caution now could spell disaster. If they saw the difficulties that so perturbed their colleagues, at least these difficulties did not seem so serious. And, in any event, they had no doubt that they themselves, if not the other leaders, knew how to lead a socialist democracy successfully.

In one sense, what really separated the two groups was principally timing, but timing in this case was the essence of the matter. Supporting the first group was that hard core of Party functionaries and militants who in no case wanted to give up their power. It would be too much to say that the second group represented the views of the rank and file of the Party. A large section of the rank and file had no independent views. But the second group did certainly represent a wide section of the more intellectually active supporters of the regime, both in and out of the Party. Many of these were a part of the more than one-third of the Party membership that joined after 1949. It is true, of course, that many supported this position who really felt neither support nor understanding of any form of Communism.

Milovan Djilas

The leading spokesman of the second group was Milovan Djilas. Djilas and many who agreed with him came only slowly to their new enthusiasm for democracy. In the days before the Cominform Resolution, for example, Djilas was conspicuous among those advocating the most stringent dictatorial methods. Few voiced more obeisance to the Soviet Union than he. There is no question that the shock of the Cominform Resolution changed his whole outlook. After 1948 he led the attack on Stalin. But even at the time of the Sixth Party Congress he was one of those who expressed the most caution about the liberalizing trend.

To understand Djilas, one must understand first of all the Montenegrin temperament, with its tendency to bravado, extremism and fearlessness. Restraint and caution are no part of the Montenegrin make-up, and Djilas was soon to show by his fervor and by the limits to which he pushed his new faith that he was a Montenegrin to the core. Already at the Sixth Congress, he was mounting a wave of enthusiasm for democratic concepts — which were quite new to him, in any institutional sense — which was to take him ultimately to prison.

The Central Committee at Brioni, in conformity with Communist mores, took action unanimously. But Djilas and others who agreed with him did not like it. The more Djilas, especially, thought about it, the more he felt that it was "one-sided" and had "forgotten the struggle against bureaucratism." He felt, further, "that the Brioni Plenum had somehow to be corrected."[1] If anybody could correct it, Milovan Djilas was the man. A Partisan hero, a member of the Executive Committee, perhaps the Party's leading theorist and propagandist, vice president of the Federal Executive Council, he had wide popularity in the Party at all levels and was considered by many to be the number two man, second only to Tito, in the Yugoslav Communist hierarchy.

Soon after the Brioni meeting, Djilas wrote a number of articles stressing the need to fight for democracy and against bureaucratism. They were well received, and he decided to step up his campaign. Before starting, he consulted Tito about it. The project looked innocent enough. Tito considered that what Djilas had written thus far expressed much of "what many of us had already said or written about the matter." So he told him: "I'll tell you what. There are some things I do not agree with, but in the main there are good things in them [the articles that had already appeared], and I don't think the others are any reason for you not to write. Go on with it."[2]

Djilas Attacks

Thus, in the fall of 1953, Djilas began his now famous series of articles, first in *Borba* and then in the theoretical magazine *Nova Misao* (*New Thought*). In the beginning, the articles — written in Djilas' extremely vague, philosophical, rambling style — attracted little attention. His statements that the revolu-

[1] See Djilas' second statement at the Third Plenum, *Komunist*, No. 1, January–February 1954, p. 157.
[2] Tito's first speech to the Third Plenum, *ibid.*, p. 4.

tion in Yugoslavia had to be defended by more democracy, his attacks on Stalinism, his warnings against the dangers of bureaucracy, dogmatism and opportunism — all these things had been said before by him and others. But gradually the articles took a sharper turn. It was almost as though Djilas were convincing himself at each step of the way that he must go still further, almost as though, scenting the conflict, he became more eager for it. Suddenly he began to train his fire on sacred concepts.

Communism as a goal should be abandoned, he wrote in *Borba* on December 6, 1953. In the fight against bureaucracy, the goal of "complete Communism" was too distant to be meaningful and only "distracts from bureaucratic reality." In any event, Communism as a conscious goal was superfluous "because in the end it will come anyhow" once socialism and democracy have taken hold. Instead of Communism, Djilas argued, the goal "must be concrete measures, realizable from stage to stage." The goal now, he insisted, had to be "quick progress of socialism and democracy through concrete and feasible forms — not Communism."

This was too much for Kardelj and Ranković, and they expressed strong disagreement. In the course of a discussion about the articles, according to Kardelj, Djilas admitted that he knew he was bucking his fellow leaders. Kardelj reported later that Djilas told him "that Comrade Tito was defending bureaucracy and that he, Djilas, would sooner or later have to fight it out with him."[1]

Angered, apparently, by this intervention, Djilas now publicly turned his fire on his critics, without naming them. Referring to "the closed party circle," he admitted that his articles had been criticized. The criticism, Djilas wrote, was "unprincipled, Stalinist, bureaucratic, pseudo-democratic" and was simply an example of "Yugoslav Stalinism." But his critics, he proclaimed, "whether . . . justified or not . . . cannot suppress the democratic struggle against bureaucratism. . . . This struggle can be hindered and delayed, but it cannot be stopped."[2]

Three days later, Djilas returned to the fray, this time aiming his verbal blows specifically at the Yugoslav Communist Party. One could no longer speak meaningfully of a class struggle in Yugoslavia, he asserted, because all effective enemies of socialism had been liquidated in one way or another. But there was a new enemy, bureaucracy. And, Djilas contended, "the new enemy is even more dangerous than the previous one, capitalism." But the Yugoslav Communist Party was continuing to operate just as before, as if it were still fighting capitalism.

[1] Kardelj's speech to the Third Plenum, *ibid.*, p. 28.
[2] *Borba*, December 24, 1954.

The result was, Djilas charged, that "the basic organizations of the Communist League . . . have reached an impasse. From above they are requested to do something, and they do not know what to do. Indeed, they have nothing to do in the old manner. The themes for so-called educational-ideological work . . . are obsolete and tedious." Nor did party functionaries now have any purpose. In the opinion of Djilas, "professional party, youth and other workers are superfluous." Indeed, because they constituted a bureaucracy they were a positive menace to socialism.[1]

Now, swept along by his own fervor, Djilas carried these ideas to their grand and logical conclusion. He called for an end to the Communist Party. "The Leninist type of both party and state dictatorship by means of the party has become obsolete," he wrote on January 4. The League of Communists, having nothing real to do and representing a positive danger to democratic socialism, should "wither away" at once by merging with the Socialist Alliance, and individual Communists should merge "with the ordinary citizen." The Communists would thus constitute an association of dedicated citizens, he was sure, because without power it would not attract opportunists.

Under such conditions, Communists could devote their time to discussion of how to advance socialist democracy without dictation by an apparatus, without a party line, without police controls and without censorship.[2]

At last it had been said in a Communist state: get rid of the Communist Party. Up to this point, although Kardelj and Ranković had grumbled and the upper professional party cadres had fretted, there had been no attempt to stop Djilas. On the contrary, toward the end of the year he had been named president of the Skupština. But now he had gone too far. In addition, his extreme views were having, from the point of view of the Party leadership, a dangerous popularity in the country. As Djilas' views became more extreme, they electrified the murky ideological air. They were greeted by a wave of public enthusiasm. Even some members of the Central Committee hailed them. Letters to newspapers all over Yugoslavia expressed agreement. Some editors themselves took courage and echoed Djilas' opinions. A Zagreb weekly, for example, declared that the bureaucracy had created illusions of the Party as "a sacrosanct and often almost mystical power, about the leader who is full only of virtues and magnanimity as the Mother of God is full of graces." Djilas' articles, the periodical said, "are the best reflection of the feeling and thinking of each true socialist-humanist, are a tremendous impetus to all of us."[3]

[1] *Borba*, December 27, 1953.
[2] *Borba*, January 4, 1954.
[3] *Vjesnik u Srijedu*, January 6, 1954, p. 6.

Djilas Defies the Leadership

Some of these expressions of approval only meant that many, not unnaturally, on seeing the ideas of one of the very top Party leaders in the Party's leading newspaper looked upon them as a new Party line. But over and above this there can be no doubt that Djilas' ideas caught the public imagination, both in and out of the Party. It was this fact as much as the final heresy itself that moved the rest of the leadership to demand Tito's intervention. Tito, by now thoroughly aroused himself, needed no urging. He promptly sent word to Djilas to lay off.[1]

By this time, still another article had appeared in *Borba*. It was of a milder tone, defining a "true revolutionary" under present conditions as one who fights for democracy and democratic forms and asserting that the revolution could be safeguarded only through more freedom.[2] It is an indication of the state of ideological ferment and confusion in Yugoslavia at the time that if Djilas had then desisted, it is quite possible, despite the heretical nature of what he had written, that he would have experienced little more than private criticism by his comrades.

But Djilas did not desist. There was no stopping him now. Previously, he had written a long, half-satirical, half-philosophical essay for the Party journal *Nova Misao*. Whether or not he had word of Tito's disapproval, Djilas realized that he had overstepped the bounds. He could have easily stopped the *Nova Misao* article from appearing, but he did not. He was then in that wild sort of Montenegrin mood which scorns prudence. He deliberately sought a showdown that he almost certainly knew was likely to ruin him.

The article, entitled "An Anatomy of Morals,"[3] was, from a theoretical point of view, an anticlimax. But in personal and political terms, it was the *coup de grâce*. The article was a bitter and violent attack on the very top level of the Party high command — "that inner circle of Party bureaucrats . . . who own automobiles, travel in sleeping cars, buy their goods and clothes at special stores and have become convinced that their exclusive right to these rare privileges is so natural and logical that only fools or the most hardened enemies could possibly question it." They lived, he wrote, in a world closed from reality, passing their time in "their own exclusive summer resorts, in their own exclusive clubs, in their own exclusive villas, in their own exclusive loges in theatres and stadiums."

[1] So Tito advised the Central Committee later. Djilas, however, told one of the authors that Tito at no time expressed objections to his articles.

[2] January 7, 1954.

[3] The Serbo-Croatian title, "Anatomija jednog Morala," may also be translated "Anatomy of a Morality."

Djilas assailed not only his comrades in the Party hierarchy but their wives as well. In doing so, he pulled out the stops of invective. "The whole logic of the hierarchy," he declared, "is to claw your way to the top and then kick down the 'undeserving.' " He described its form as "a beastly greediness and struggle to safeguard social positions which is wilder and more cruel than any fight among beasts." This, he said, was what had "made selfish monsters out of those who were once heroic men and women." As for the women, almost all of them

come from semi-peasant surroundings and are semi-educated. . . . Imperceptibly most of them have started to assume, not only externally, but internally, an elaborate pseudo-aristocratic style and elaborately meticulous manners. . . . But the most grotesque thing of all is that some of them, with no taste whatever, have started collecting luxurious furniture and pictures, displaying not only their primitive greed and new-found pomposity, but also the pretentious omniscience of the crassly ignorant.

With a mixture of pathos and satire, Djilas described the unhappiness of the young and beautiful actress-bride of "a famous wartime commander" who had become "a high Party functionary and important state official." The young woman was snubbed by the wives of other officials because, although she was only eight years old when the war began, she had not been a Partisan and because, being an actress, it was assumed she was immoral.

Everybody in Belgrade recognized the young woman as the wife of Colonel General Peko Dapčević, chief of staff of the Yugoslav Army, and Djilas' descriptions of her chief tormentors were such that everybody knew exactly whom he had in mind. To add piquancy to the situation, Belgrade rumor had it that Djilas himself had been enamored of Mrs. Dapčević.[1]

Djilas Condemned

Once the *Nova Misao* article appeared, it did not take the urging of irate wives to convince the Party leaders that they had to act at once. The whole leadership was now angrily arrayed against Djilas, not only because the shoe fit all too well but also because of the fact that among the willing possessors of fine automobiles, exclusive villas and the like was Milovan Djilas. The next day, January 10, *Borba* tersely announced that Djilas' articles were "contrary to the opinions of all other members of the Executive Committee" and would be the subject of a Central Committee Plenum the following week.

The Third Plenum, which convened January 16, was open to the public and its proceedings were broadcast to the nation. It had been called, as Moša

---

[1] Fred Warner Neal, "Yugoslav Communist Theory," *American Universities Field Staff Reports*, FWN–5–'54, p. 7.

LEAGUE OF COMMUNISTS

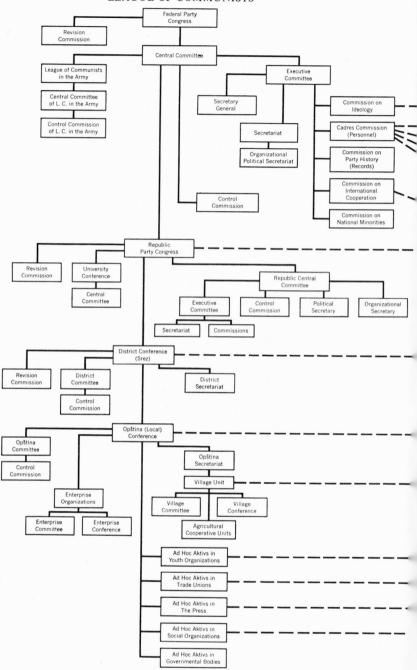

Figure 12–1

The chart is based on information as of 1960. Relationships between organizations of the League of Communists and bodies of the Socialist Alliance (indicated by the broken lines) are informal but important. Technically the League has no authority and exercises no supervision over the Socialist Alliance, and they per-

SOCIALIST ALLIANCE OF WORKING PEOPLE

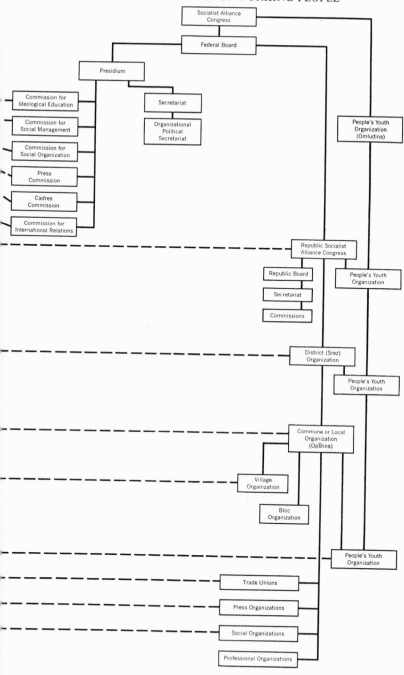

form different tasks. In fact, the Socialist Alliance works according to general policies laid down by the League of Communists and for all practical purposes is dominated by it. This is because League members invariably play the leading roles in Socialist Alliance organizations.

Pijade put it, not to argue with Djilas but to condemn him for deviationism. Tito led off, at first reluctantly it seemed, referring to Djilas as a comrade and using his old Partisan nickname, "Djido." Kardelj, in measured, schoolmasterly tones, disposed of Djilas' arguments as a mélange of Bernsteinism, mysticism, existentialism, liberalism, and bourgeois anarchy. Pijade heaped bitter invective on Djilas and termed his writings "political pornography." One by one the others joined in. Among them was Mitra Mitrović, Djilas' former wife, who expressed sympathy but not support.[1]

Only Vladimir Dedijer spoke up for his friend. "A week ago," Dedijer recalled, "Milovan Djilas' postulates in *Borba* were more or less adopted by the majority of us sitting here. . . . All of us, if we put our hands on our hearts, would admit it. . . . All at once the very same people who approved these articles are attacking Djilas fiercely. . . . How can we think one thing today and all of a sudden change our opinions overnight?"

The answer to this question, Tito said in effect, in his remarks to the Plenum, was that the leadership suddenly became aware that the popular chord struck by Djilas' articles put the position of not only the leaders but the whole Party — as they conceived it — in peril. And for them peril to the Party meant peril to the regime. "The thing that worries me most," Tito declared, "is the incredibly low ideological and political standard of the members of our Party who thought they saw in all this some sort of new theory concerning the further development of our socialist system. No wonder there was such confusion."

The fact was, Tito declared, that Djilas' ideas would lead "to anarchy, to a terrible uncertainty. If we permitted this, in a year's time our socialist reality would not exist. It would not exist, I tell you, without a bloody battle." He would never have called the Plenum, he said, if he "had not clearly seen the deplorable consequences which could arise from this state of affairs, consequences which were already increasing as fast as a snowball on a sloping roof."

Then Tito firmly disposed of the concept of the withering away of the Party. He had never said it was to take place in six months or a year or two years, he explained, but "rather that it was to be a lengthy process . . . which would only develop through trials and difficulties." Everybody should understand, he emphasized, that there could be no "withering away or winding up of the League of Communists until the last class enemy has been immobilized, until the broadest body of our citizens are socialist in outlook." Until that time, the League was "responsible for the achievements of the revolution,"

[1] The proceedings of the Djilas Plenum are recorded in *Komunist*, No. 1, January–February 1954.

and it must not only exist but "be ideologically stronger . . . conscious of the tremendous role it plays."

Tito had never imagined that anybody, "least of all Comrade Djilas, . . . thought the class enemy was already liquidated." One good thing that came out of "all this business," he said, was that "it has done a lot to open our eyes and thoroughly wake us up."

Djilas' own reactions at the Plenum were, typically, complex. First he said that, although he considered his ideas correct, he would renounce anything "the leaders of the Party considered politically dangerous." Speaking a second time, he said he accepted most of Kardelj's criticisms, but he insisted that the Party was "the main obstacle in the way of democratic and socialist development." Finally, near the end of the two-day meeting, he said he now saw that he was wrong in opposing Tito and making ammunition for the anti-Communists and that he had regained his faith in the Party.

In keeping with the new concepts of Yugoslav Communism, Tito advised the Central Committee that it was not necessary to take the action that "would have been necessary in the days of sharp revolutionary struggle." In Yugoslavia, he said, "we do not destroy those who err but rather help them understand their errors and mend their ways."

Accordingly, the Committee's punishment, in addition to expulsion from the Central Committee, was only to give Djilas "a final warning" but not expel him from the Party or consider action against his person. Given the traditional Communist treatment of heretics, such punishment was fantastically light and was, of course, in striking contrast to Soviet practice. Djilas himself, commenting on it afterwards, told one of the authors that his survival was "a monument to the Cominform Resolution." He resigned his position as president of the Federal Assembly. The constituency in Montenegro, which a few months before had elected him with an announced 98.8 per cent of the ballots, voted his recall. Ostracized by his former comrades, in April 1954 he quietly resigned from the Party.

Heresy Continued

This was not, however, the end of Milovan Djilas. In some ways it was only the beginning. Now he confided to his rare visitors that he had come to the conclusion that, if freedom of action were not to be permitted within the Party, Yugoslavia needed a two-party system. When Dedijer, heckled by the Control Commission for his support of Djilas, complained through the *Times* of London in December 1954, Djilas followed suit by giving an interview to the Belgrade correspondent of the *New York Times*, advocating a "new democratic Socialist Party" to compete with the League of Communists.

For their pains, both he and Dedijer were convicted of violating a law against "hostile propaganda" and given prison sentences. They were, however, placed on probation. Meanwhile, Djilas, especially, was going further and further away from Communism and even Marxism. Denied means of expression at home, he continued to utilize the foreign press to harass the regime. Finally, in December 1956, he was made to start serving his term. Before he did so, he somehow got out of the country the manuscript of a new book, *The New Class*,[1] which was a slashing attack on all Communism, Yugoslav as well as Soviet, from start to finish. For this, his sentence was increased to ten years.[2]

Impact on the Party

The impact of the Djilas affair on Yugoslavia was in one way small, in another enormous. There were, as Djilas himself admitted, "no Djilasites, in any formal sense," but there was, as he claimed, "lots of Djilasism."[3] That is to say, there was no organized opposition based on Djilas' ideas. There never was even the remote likelihood of a challenge to Tito's leadership. What acknowledged "Djilasites" there were, were quickly taken care of by Party discipline, although one, a Zagreb editor, was reported to have been a suicide. But it is clear that the whole affair shook the Party far more seriously than any of the leaders admitted.

What affected the Party, however, was not only the Djilas episode but also the action which initiated it, that is, the Brioni Plenum of June 1953, calling a halt to liberalization and reinforcing Party discipline. In the period right after the 1953 Plenum it became apparent that the Party was beset by confusion in its organization and apathy in its ranks.

First, membership dropped off alarmingly, both as a result of expulsions of purge proportions and also as a result of resignations and slackening recruitment. The purge of Party ranks began right after the Brioni Plenum. During 1953 a total of 72,067 members were expelled, most of them in the second half of the year, and more than 32,000 left the Party of their own accord.[4] In the next two years, expulsions amounted to 273,464, while only 136,887 new members were added.[5] By the end of 1955, as indicated in Table 12–1, membership had dropped to 642,805 from the high of 779,382 in 1952.

---

[1] Published by Frederick A. Praeger, New York, 1957. See Chapter 23.

[2] See Neal, *Titoism in Action*, especially pp. 74–75. The treatment of Djilas and Dedijer is also discussed in Chapter 19.

[3] Neal, "Yugoslav Communist Theory," p. 9.

[4] Ranković reported to the Fourth Plenum of the Central Committee in 1954 that 25,096 persons had joined during this period and that membership had decreased by 47,371. But total membership as of January 1954 was officially put at 700,030, making the total decrease 79,352. Cf. *Komunist*, No. 4, April 1954, p. 267.

[5] Cf. report by Ranković in *Borba*, March 15, 1956.

Table 12-1

MEMBERSHIP IN THE YUGOSLAV COMMUNIST PARTY, 1945-1959

Date	Number of Members
June 1945	140,000
June 1948	448,175
December 1949	530,000
December 1950	607,443
December 1951	704,617
June 1952	779,382
January 1954	700,030
December 1955	642,805
June 1956	635,984
December 1957	755,066
December 1958	823,460
March 1959	857,537

Sources: For 1945-1952 period, reports of Tito and Ranković, *Sixth Congress of the Communist Party of Yugoslavia*, Belgrade, 1953. Figure for 1954 is from *Komunist*, No. 4, April 1954, p. 267; for 1955, Ranković's report to Fourth Plenum, *Borba*, March 15, 1956; for 1956, *Komunist*, Nos. 11-12, 1956, p. 14; for December 1957, *Komunist*, April 16, 1959; for December 1958 and March 1959, *Komunist*, June 18, 1959.

By mid-year of 1956, it was down to 635,984. Some party units were reduced by almost half.

As serious as the declining membership, if not more so, was the obvious lack of enthusiasm in the ranks. Party leaders noted that intellectuals were avoiding writing about the Party and Marxist theory. Others complained that "there does not seem to be an intensive life in the League of Communists." Djilas was blamed for much of it. One Montenegrin Party official, warning of "anarchistic manifestations which Djilas fanned," declared that the situation was "acute . . . not only in Montenegro but in general."[1]

One of the most serious aspects of this malaise was the growing disinterest in Party and civic matters among young people. After the Fifth Party Congress, the official Party youth organization had been disbanded — according to Tito, at the urging of Djilas — and merged with the young people's group affiliated with the People's Front to form a separate People's Youth Organization. The new body soon began to suffer from the ideological and organizational confusion which gripped the Party. On top of this, there was evidence at every hand that the enthusiasm with which Yugoslav youth greeted the 1950-1952 liberalizations had waned markedly, certainly in part, at least, as a result of the Brioni Plenum and the Djilas affair. Some leaders referred openly to "the estrangement between the country's youth and the Communist Party," and Tito later remarked that there was "a certain crisis" in regard to

[1] *Borba*, November 1, 1954. See also Neal, *Titoism in Action*, pp. 73-74, and *Pobjeda*, October 24, 1954.

youth activities. Marked concern was shown about the fact that in the spring of 1954, for example, only about 35 per cent of Yugoslavs between the ages of 14 and 25 were members of the People's Youth Organization and about the drop in the percentage of young people among new Party members.[1]

Nor was the social composition of the Party reassuring to the leadership. The percentage of workers, especially, was considered inadequate. Prior to 1954, the number of worker members was exaggerated by Party statistics; members were listed according to social origin instead of occupation. With party statistics based on actual occupation, the figure for worker members decreased by 45,000 and that for peasant members decreased by 93,000, while the number of white-collar employees and professional army men increased correspondingly.[2] Thus was the Yugoslav revolution reflected in changes in social status and occupation of Party members.

Of those purged after the Brioni Plenum, nearly 25 per cent were workers, 54 per cent peasants and 18 per cent white-collar workers. The resulting proportion of workers in the Party, 27 per cent (see Table 12–2), was held to be "quite unsatisfactory."[3] At the same time, the continuing drop in the number of peasants in the Party was also a source of concern, especially as agriculture continued to be the major headache of the regime. The problem was especially acute because, since the abandonment of collectivization, there existed no Party organization designed for the villages.

On top of all these factors, and in part because of them, the reorganization of the Party decreed by the Sixth Congress was not working out well. The main trouble was the elimination of Party organizations in governmental and other organizations and the basing of all Party work — other than that in economic enterprises — on the local *opštine*, or wards. The result was that Communists were letting much activity in the country get out of their grasp. This, the leadership concluded, accounted for the fact that so many Party units concentrated "only on lectures" instead of dealing with "concrete problems." Some local leaders complained that there were too many organizations to keep track of and that there was no way of seeing to it that their followers played a positive role in them.

In addition, some Communists felt that since Party work in the basic units was ordinarily assigned to groups arranged according to place of residence, there was too much diversity in ability, background and interests of those thus

[1] Cf. Ranković's report to Fourth Plenum, *Komunist*, No. 4, April 1954.

[2] See *Condensed Report of the Central Committee on the Work of the League of Communists of Yugoslavia Between the Sixth and Seventh Congress*, Service d'information Yougoslavie, Belgrade, April 1958, pp. 19–21.

[3] *Komunist*, No. 4, April 1954, p. 268.

Table 12–2

MEMBERSHIP OF THE LEAGUE OF COMMUNISTS,
BY OCCUPATIONAL CATEGORY, 1954, 1958 AND 1959

Occupational Category	January 1954	January 1958	March 1959
Total	700,030	755,066	857,537
Workers	191,655	243,819	271,100
Peasants	189,392	130,783	121,684
White-collar employees	189,231	244,592	264,629
Students	a	27,455	a
Unclassified	129,752[b]	108,417[c]	200,124[b]

Sources: *Komunist*, No. 4, April 1954; *Condensed Report of the Central Committee on the Work of the League of Communists of Yugoslavia between the Sixth and Seventh Congress*, Service d'Information Yougoslavie, Belgrade, April 1958, p. 20; and *Komunist*, April 16, 1959.

[a] Included in "Unclassified."

[b] Includes students, Army officers and members of professions.

[c] Includes 18,000 teachers and 25,000 engineers, technicians, economists, physicians and lawyers.

banded together.[1] With a lesser rather than a greater number of professional Party workers now available, the higher Party organizations were simply not able to cope with things.

The Tightening Up

By the spring of 1956, Tito, concluding that the Party's position was one of "stagnation," called a Plenum of the Central Committee to take drastic action.[2] Five concrete steps were taken.

1. There were established *aktivs* — small groups of active Communists — in all the organizations where basic "cells" existed prior to the Sixth Congress reorganization. Already in 1954, the Central Committee had moved to reintroduce this form into publishing activities, theatres, health associations and a few other important bodies. Now it was decided to make this a general organizational plan. The new-type cells quickly were formed in all government departments and bodies, at all levels, in commercial offices, professional groups and even organizations with an already existing Socialist Alliance organization. In addition, the Party organizations in economic enterprises were now buttressed by the formation of *aktiv* groups in various factory units. The larger inner Party bodies had their own organization, or secretariat, and invariably soon began to play the "leading role" demanded by the Party. In this way, Ranković declared, they were able to overcome "political and

[1] See, as an example, report of Olga Marasović, secretary of the Second Ward Committee of the Sarajevo Party organization, *Oslobodjenje*, Sarajevo, December 24, 1954.

[2] The work of the Plenum is dealt with in reports of Tito and Ranković, *Borba*, March 14 and 15, 1956.

ideological alienation, lack of understanding or wrong interpretation in carrying out the line and attitude of the League of Communists."

2. It was decided to increase substantially the professional cadres and reopen the Party schools for training them. Cadre commissions were formed in each of the republic Party organizations.

3. A special Party organization was set up to "lead the million-member organization of People's Youth," concentrate on propaganda and other activities among young people and direct youth work projects, which now were to be reinstituted. In addition, Party units were now re-formed in institutions of higher learning and even in secondary schools.

4. A major campaign for new Party members was begun, with increased emphasis on recruiting workers and young people.

5. Communists in the Army were ordered henceforth to be represented increasingly in organs of local government, housing councils, the Socialist Alliance and other political organizations. The move was taken, apparently, both to cement further Party primacy in the Army and to take advantage of the "devoted, disciplined and ideologically strong Communists" in the Army to strengthen the Party position elsewhere.[1]

Party Abuses

The Central Committee's decisions did not contravene the letter of the Sixth Party Congress, but they did alter its spirit. Indeed, too much so, as it turned out, for the strong measures taken by the leadership to correct the Sixth Congress liberalizations had decidedly mixed results. One result of the reassertion of across-the-board Party control was a series of abuses by intermediate and lower-level Party officials that by 1958 reached serious proportions.

Many local Party bodies and functionaries had resumed the old practice of arbitrarily intervening in government and economic affairs. *Komunist* pointed out frankly that "suggestions" of Party bodies and officials were rarely refused, and complained that the Communists initiating such action often had little familiarity with the matters in which they were intervening.[2] Also there was in some areas a trend toward "monopoly of responsibilities" and "usurpation of power by a narrow circle." It was "by no means an isolated curiosity" for "the one same comrade" in a town to hold, for example, chairmanships of the economic council of the district people's committee, the council for planning and finances of the local people's committee, the administrative

---

[1] The following year, the Central Committee again addressed itself to Party organizations within the Army, this time merging officer and non-officer groups of Communists. *Komunist*, August 2, 1957.

[2] January 24, 1958.

board of the radio station and the theatre council.[1] Worst of all were the privileges such functionaries and others were arrogating to themselves as a result of their Party rank. Some of them were not far from the kind of thing Milovan Djilas referred to in *The New Class*.

Such situations were common enough in the days before 1950, but the increased freedom resulting from the general government and economic reforms had produced a climate in which disregard of public opinion — if it went far enough — could no longer occur without repercussions. There were growing signs that trouble was at hand when, in January 1958, a strike erupted in the Trbovlje mine in Slovenia. A strike in capitalist countries is nothing unusual, but if this was not the first strike in a Communist country it was at least the first one officially acknowledged. The strikers were not punished; in fact they won some of their demands.[2] It was the Communist leaders in the mine and district who got into trouble. The worried leadership in Belgrade decided to act.

The Circular Letter

In February, the Executive Committee issued a Circular Letter to all Party organizations sharply denouncing what had been going on. The Circular Letter declared that many Communist leaders were guilty of dictatorial methods, arrogating to themselves special privileges, favoritism and corruption, discrimination and irregularities in payment of wages, and "local selfishness and chauvinist tendencies." The situation had gotten so bad, the Executive Committee declared, that if not corrected "in good time and with due firmness . . . [it] might weaken and hold up further successes in our internal political development, and . . . harm the international prestige of Yugoslavia . . . as a Socialist country."[3]

In the factories, according to the Circular Letter, Communists were undermining the principle of worker-management, "suppressing criticism, firing those who raised their voices and generally ignoring the needs of the workers." Many officials were "lightly" authorizing foreign travel for themselves, purchasing automobiles for private use out of company funds and spending public money on gifts, celebrations and high living. Others were making use of rest homes at the expense of workers, taking over housing built for workers and changing apartments with irresponsible frequency.

Serious irregularities in awarding pay to employees, the Circular Letter charged, was "having extremely harmful political consequences." Officials of

[1] *Komunist*, May 24, 1957.
[2] See Chapter 19.
[3] *Komunist*, February 28, 1958.

economic and government organizations were raising their own salaries unjustifiably, and certain managers had received extra wages equal to the total wages paid to their workers. Through a system of premiums and over-time pay, Communists were receiving more than non-Communists working at the same job in the same place. The Letter stressed the political harm of unfair wage payments, which, it said, have "become an increasingly delicate and serious problem."

As regards favoritism, the Executive Committee declared that "the concep-tion has been spread that through 'connections' " Communists could get jobs, pensions, allowances, housing and scholarships. "Some competitive examina-tions," it added, "have become almost formalities." Communist intervention in the work of government organs, "undermining legality," was held to be responsible for most such cases.

But the Executive Committee did not limit its complaints to dictatorial, corrupt and unfair practices by Communists. It continued along the now-familiar theme to complain against "petit-bourgeois and anarchistic concep-tions of democracy" and against those who, "under the guise of a struggle against bureaucracy attack even the fundamental achievements of our Socialist development." Further, "individual Communists" were sometimes "irre-sponsible in their behavior, yielding to negative, non-constructive and criticizing gestures which are fashionable. Very often Communists, cultural workers in particular, hold discussions which are not based on principles and thus form groups and make intrigues."

The Circular Letter also criticized government officials who failed to inter-vene directly in the economy with administrative measures when necessary, the trade union organization for insufficient attention to economic and political affairs, and the Communists for failing to pay enough attention to the importance of trade unions in worker-management.

The Circular Letter also brought to light another serious problem troubling the leadership — the fact that the League of Communists was not as mono-lithic as officially claimed and that the differences dividing the republics were reflected in the Party also. Especially in matters like investment, the Executive Committee declared, "strong localistic selfish tendencies" were sometimes acquiring the form of ethnic particularism. "Very often members on the leading bodies of the League of Communists," the Letter said, "fall under the influence of the petit-bourgeois nationalistic intelligentsia and . . . are guilty of nationalist and chauvinist influences. The lack of understanding and . . . difficulties among republics represent our common problem. Commu-nists . . . must show a far greater amount of persistence in . . . further strengthening brotherhood and unity."

That this problem was indeed a serious one was indicated when two years later Tito was forced to return to it in even stronger language.[1]

Unlike the Brioni Plenum of 1953, which concentrated its fire on liberalization and lack of Party discipline, the Executive Committee now left no doubt that it was most in earnest about bureaucratic excesses. Some noted that the practices criticized were limited to the middle echelons and below, and that the privileges of the upper level of the Party officialdom were ignored.[2] Nevertheless, the impact of the Circular Letter was electric.

The Executive Committee's action, declared *Ekonomska Politika*, the Party's leading economic publication, had come "in the nick of time." The Letter was the subject for discussion — and action — in all Party units. It would be going too far to say that all the abuses mentioned were corrected, but there were immediate disclosures in the press of countless examples of what the Executive Committee had been talking about — examples which, of course, the journalists had known about all the time. A rash of expulsions from the Party was accompanied by much public confessing of error, ostentatious giving up of automobiles, removals from swank apartments, reconsideration of pay schedules and unhoarding of funds stashed away for questionable purposes. The Federal Executive Council issued additional regulations strictly defining who could use automobiles and for what, and the Federal Wage Scale Commission began an inquiry preliminary to issuing a uniform criterion for wages.[3]

The Seventh Congress

That disposed of, the Party leadership went ahead finally to hold the long-delayed Seventh Congress. The Congress, originally scheduled to meet in the fall of 1956, had been repeatedly postponed, apparently because of both the internal Party situation and the ups and downs of relations with the Soviet Union. By the time it finally convened, in Ljubljana on April 22, 1958, many difficulties remained but some, especially those concerned with Party membership, had been largely overcome.

[1] See Tito's remarks to the Second Plenum of the Central Committee, *Yugoslav Facts and Views*, No. 115, March 21, 1960. Although it had to do primarily with economic questions, national particularism also had political implications, particularly in regard to the old conflict between Serbs and Croats. The matter is treated more fully in the last chapter. The fact that the role of Serbs in the Party organizations of both Bosnia and Herzegovina and Croatia had increased was sometimes cited among the rank and file in Croatia as an indication of undue Serbian influence. An exhaustive study by an American scholar of national influences in the League of Communists led to the conclusion that the Party was "not under the influence of national prejudices," a conclusion with which the present authors agree. See Paul Shoup, *Communism and the National Question in Yugoslavia*, doctoral dissertation, Columbia University, 1960.

[2] Cf. *New York Times*, March 16, 1958, p. 31.

[3] *Politika*, May 28, 1958, and *Borba*, April 9, 1958. See also *Ekonomska Politika*, March 6; *Komunist*, February 28 and May 16; *Mladost*, February 12; *Vjesnik*, March 15; *Somborske Novine*, Sombor, April 4; and *Front Slobode*, Tuzla, February 27, 1958.

Total membership in the League of Communists, although still short of the 1952 figure, was up to 755,066; the percentage of workers had increased to 32. The number of young people in the Party had increased markedly. Of the 119,082 members who joined the Party during 1957, 63 per cent were classified as "young people." Of the total membership, 40 per cent were now under thirty years of age and about 15 per cent were under twenty-five. The number of women in the Party still amounted to only 16.4 per cent, however — down 2 per cent from 1954 — and, as at the two preceding Congresses, the Communists were taken to task for not devoting more effort to the distaff side.[1]

As shown in Table 12–2, the character of the Party changed not only because of the increases in the proportion of workers and youth. Especially significant was the drop in the proportion of peasants, a trend which continued in the year after the Seventh Congress and in part reflected the increasing urbanization of the country. No longer could the League of Communists be characterized as primarily a peasant party. From about 50 per cent of the total in 1948, peasant membership dropped steadily to 17 per cent in 1958. It was down to 14 per cent in 1959. Yet of the 33,162 basic organizations in 1959, 15,097 were in the villages as against only 9,467 in industrial enterprises.[2]

The new system of *aktivs* was found to be successful, and the Central Committee referred approvingly to the practice of district and municipal Party Committees of holding meetings of groups of *aktivs*. The situation regarding professional cadres had also shown marked improvement, and by the end of 1956, the Committee reported, 21,637 Party members had taken courses at the reactivated Party schools.

These Party successes, the Committee advised the Seventh Congress, had resulted in the Socialist Alliance overcoming the difficulties it also had encountered after the Sixth Congress. Socialist Alliance membership had dropped precipitously, to 5 million from about 8 million in 1954. But with the Communists using new methods of work, Tito saw the Socialist Alliance now playing "an immense role in the socialist construction of our country, in the development and expansion of our socialist awareness and in the strengthening and developing of our socialist democracy." There was passing criticism of Socialist Alliance work, but the keynote was enthusiasm. By the end of 1959, Socialist Alliance membership was up to more than 6 million, or about 58 per cent of the total number of voters. (See Table 12–3.)

One further outstanding success claimed by the Party was the increased role its members were playing in local government bodies, workers' councils, house

[1] See *Condensed Report of the Central Committee*, and Tito's report, *VII Kongres Saveza Komunista Jugoslavije*, Kultura, Belgrade, 1958, pp. 74–76.

[2] *Komunist*, April 16, 1959.

Table 12–3

MEMBERSHIP OF THE SOCIALIST ALLIANCE, BY OCCUPATIONAL CATEGORY,
SEX AND AGE GROUP, DECEMBER 31, 1959

Category	Number of Members
Total	6,398,915
Women	2,643,377
Men	3,755,538
Under 25	836,382
25 and over	5,562,533
Occupational category:	
Workers	1,420,737
Peasants	2,844,086
White-collar employees	794,138
Students	100,935
Unclassified[a]	1,239,019

Source: Report of the Federal Board on the Work of the Socialist Alliance of the Working People of Yugoslavia from the Fourth to the Fifth Congress, Belgrade, 1960, p. 53.

[a] Includes Army officers and members of professions.

and neighborhood committees and other "organs of social self-management." The stress in contemporary Yugoslav development is on these bodies, and the extent to which Party members participate actively in them is shown by Table 12–4. Of course, the role of the Communists is much greater than indicated by membership figures alone.

Not all the discussion at the Congress was concerned with successes. There was constant repetition of the old theme about the two negative influences "bureaucracy and petit-bourgeois democratic tendencies." A good deal of this part of the reports was almost identical with what was said at the Sixth Congress and in most of the Party documents issued since 1952, and some were reminded of Djilas' comment about "obsolete and tedious themes."

Djilas, of course, was in Mitrovica Prison rather than at the Party conclave, but the Congress could not escape him. There was a tendency on the part of those addressing the Congress to blame Djilas for many of the troubles the Party had encountered since his heresy. Tito, ordinarily restrained, used violent language. He referred to "the revisionistic and anarchistic ravings of this lunatic," and said Djilas' idea "to reestablish the multi-Party system and restore capitalism" could have come only from "the head of a corrupt person or a lunatic." Djilas, he charged, acted on "orders from abroad and for Judas' money," and he called him "a traitor . . . a renegade spitting at the finest achievement of the revolution — Socialism."

Yet, aside from its emphasis on the Party, the Program adopted by the Party — its major achievement — reflected many of Djilas' ideas, and, indeed, some of them had originated with him. Despite all that had gone before, the Program, except for a few comparatively minor changes of emphasis, did not seriously depart from the ideas put forward at the Sixth Congress. (Its major ideological implications have been treated in Chapter 11, and its major international implications are discussed in Part V.)

Table 12–4

COMMUNISTS IN LOCAL GOVERNMENT AND SOCIAL SELF-MANAGEMENT IN 1958

	Total Members	Party Members
Total	953,823	356,577
Local government		
Opštine committees[a]	68,933	41,223
District committees	11,966	10,058
Opštine councils	65,994	41,343
District councils	10,424	7,980
Economy and housing		
Workers councils	220,656	60,012
Management boards	68,836	25,569
Agricultural collective councils	147,867	36,966
Agricultural collective management boards	49,281	19,457[b]
Economic chambers and associations	5,690	3,629
Housing councils	140,385	28,514[b]
Neighborhood councils	7,365[c]	3,235[b,c]
Education		
School boards	128,996	52,433
Higher school councils	1,738	1,145
Health and social insurance		
Management boards, health insurance	15,802	8,344
Management boards, social insurance	9,090	4,649

Source: Komunist, April 16, 1959.

[a] The committees (two houses) are the elected governing bodies. The councils are citizen administrative advisory bodies. (These and other bodies listed in the table are discussed in Chapter 13.)

[b] Data at end of 1956.

[c] The real drive for establishment of neighborhood councils began only in 1958.

All in all, the Party leadership seemed more sure of itself at the Seventh Congress, particularly organizationally, than at any time since 1952. The assurance could be seen in the rather satisfied report of the Central Committee that "the League of Communists as a whole became capable of exercising and did, indeed, successfully exercise its leading role under the new conditions, and in spite of all difficulties, inadequate resourcefulness and shortcomings which accompanied its work, it successfully solved the tasks laid down by the Sixth Congress."

The Party at Work

The leadership still was not satisfied with either organizational or propaganda matters, however, and soon after the Seventh Congress decided that these matters could not be left to local leaders to carry on as they saw fit. For one thing, especially in the villages, many Communists still did not connect theory and practice. The local functionaries tended to shun successful peasants, instead of enticing them into the Party, on the ground that they were "rich men of property," a fact which, it was explained by *Komunist*, was only "relative under our conditions . . . and not very important either." On the other hand, Communist peasants often scorned new agricultural methods, "making fun of people who are milking their cows on the farm and such."[1]

To correct these and other practices and to insure all-round better work, Party members were being increasingly advised from the center how to function as Communists. By 1959 the League of Communists had a total of 110,357 functionaries, including full-time employees, secretaries, members of secretariats and committees and persons generally considered members of Party cadres. This included 30,000 Communists whose major Party responsibility was to give lectures on Party themes.[2]

An important factor in the work of these functionaries and quite typical of the trend was the change of *Komunist*, the League's chief publication, from a rather heavy, mostly theoretical periodical into a weekly newspaper dealing with specific, practical tasks and charged with whipping up enthusiasm in the Party. It was still far from *Bloknot Agitatora*, the USSR's periodical instructions for Party agitators, but it performed some of the same functions.

Komunist now advised local Communist workers, for example, that they could no longer ignore the fact that Yugoslavs read newspapers and listened to the radio. "That local political worker will be more convincing," said *Komunist*, who neither simply limits his propaganda to recital of events people already know about nor on the other hand says things people know aren't true.[3] It offered suggestions for group meetings of *aktivs* and saw their role as that of securing "harmony between the interests of governmental and economic organizations and the Community as a whole."[4] Following the Seventh Congress, *Komunist* gave specific instructions as to how the Congress' work should be used by Party workers.

[1] *Vjesnik*, February 6, 1958.
[2] *Komunist*, April 16, 1959.
[3] October 25, 1958.
[4] *Komunist*, July 1, 1958.

The emphasis on publicity for Party activities changed, too. Basic units and Party organizations at the *opština* level continued to be public as a rule, but one of the authors, who in 1954 had attended several local Party meetings, was unable over a period of several months in 1958 to find a meeting that would admit him. District meetings, which at one time were also public, were so no longer. The point was that "Party members must function publicly, particularly in the Socialist Alliance," a district Party secretary explained. The practice of holding Party meetings in conjunction with those of the Socialist Alliance had generally been discontinued.

To further tighten the organizational structure of the Party and its direction of propaganda, the Central Committee made important changes in the structure of the federal secretariat after the Seventh Congress. Particularly, it established special secretariats to handle organizational-political work, ideological activities and cadres, each with several members. The organizational-political secretariat, headed by Aleksandar Ranković, was obviously the most important and was given the assignment of "coordinating the whole work of the League of Communists." To direct its ideological program, the Committee picked Petar Stambolić, president of the Skupština, and Veljko Zeković, a powerful figure in the inner circles of the Party, was named to head the cadres commission.

Indicative of the concern the Party feels about the question of national unity was the creation also of a commission for national minorities. Two other commissions were also established as a part of the secretariat — one for "international cooperation," headed by the Party's expert on relations with foreign Communist parties, Veljko Vlahović, and the other, dealing with the history of the Party, headed by Radoljub Čolaković, a vice president of the Federal Executive Council.[1]

Soon thereafter, the Socialist Alliance also reorganized its secretariat so as to better coordinate with the new Party structure. It also created an organizational-political secretariat and an ideological commission. Interestingly enough, the presidium of the Socialist Alliance eliminated an existing commission on work in the villages on the grounds that "one commission is not capable of solving all the problems arising in the villages," and turned its work over to the organizational-political secretariat.

Other new commissions set up by the Socialist Alliance reflected the emphases of its interests. One was a commission on social management, concerned with local government, housing and other bodies, and another was a commission for social organizations to coordinate work in all the organizations affiliated with the Alliance. A third commission was to deal with the

[1] *Komunist*, June 5, 1958.

press, most of which was supervised by the Socialist Alliance. A fourth was for international relations, an important question for the Socialist Alliance, which is able to establish contact with Second International socialist groups outside Yugoslavia in a way which would be embarrassing for the Party itself, with its Third International background. The chairman of the commission on international relations was Veljko Vlahović, who was also chairman of the Party international affairs commission.

None of this helped clarify the muddy relationship between the League of Communists and the Socialist Alliance. With the assumption of the secretary generalship of the Alliance by Aleksandar Ranković in 1960, operational direction of both bodies was in the same hands. Cvijetin Mijatović, editor of *Komunist*, told members attending the Fifth Congress of the Socialist Alliance in April 1960 that they would soon take over more functions of the League. When there was official hesitation at releasing the text of his speech, some observers speculated as to whether Djilas' old idea that the League should merge with the Alliance was being dusted off.[1] While this seemed unlikely, it was possible that Socialist Alliance activities were to receive more public emphasis and those of the League of Communists less.

The period following the Seventh Party Congress, however, was one of intense and widely publicized organizational and propaganda activity in the Party. *Komunist* printed the text of the Program and distributed it widely. In addition, some 400,000 copies of the book on the Congress were sold.[2] Some 30,000 lecturers went about the countryside spreading the word, and in Serbia alone by the spring of 1959 some 54,000 persons were organized into seminars for the purpose of studying the Program.[3]

During 1958 more than 105,000 new members had been recruited for the Party, and the first quarter of 1959 saw the admission of an additional 34,077. As of March 31, 1959, Ranković advised the organizational-political secretariat of the Central Committee, total membership stood at 857,537, an all-time high. During the January–March period, 14,058 of the new members came from the ranks of workers. But this was still not considered enough, and the leadership instructed local Party organizations to lower their standards of admission for workers.

Where was the Party going from here? The role of the League of Communists was still formally what had been decreed in 1952, and, it is true, it remained a unique type of Communist Party, different from what it had been

---

[1] See *The Times* of London, April 22, 1960, p. 13. Although the official text of the speech was toned down as regards identity of the League of Communists and the Socialist Alliance, Mijatović's remarks were published as originally given. See *Komunist*, April 21, 1960.

[2] *VII Kongres Saveza Komunista Jugoslavije.*

[3] *Komunist*, February 26, 1959.

prior to 1951. It seemingly had recovered from the malaise of confusion and disorganization that infected it and had reasserted its effective control over the direction of society. The leadership appeared no longer to worry over the contradiction of a Party dictatorship in a Yugoslavia which emphasized democracy and decentralized government and economic functions. But the contradiction remained nonetheless, and others, both in and out of the Party, worried about it if the leadership did not. The future of the League of Communists still remained one of the big question marks of Titoism.

THE INSTITUTIONAL

FRAMEWORK *

P<small>ERHAPS</small> never before, other than as a result of war or violent revolution, has the political and economic organization of a nation been changed as radically as in Yugoslavia during the decade 1950–1960. One may dispute the extent to which the sweeping institutional reforms of Titoism altered the basic nature of Yugoslav society but not the extent of the reforms themselves.

The new institutions reflect the new theories which the Yugoslav Communists, perforce freed from the necessity of copying the Soviet Union, developed in the years immediately following the Cominform Resolution. These institutions launched what the Yugoslavs call "socialist democracy" and what they believe constitutes "a new and different type of socialism." Two main themes are central to the changes: decentralization and popular participation in public affairs at all levels. Decentralization and popular participation provide, as the Yugoslavs see it, the mechanism for the "withering away of the state," and they must be present in one form or another before a society is really socialist.

The period before 1950, characterized by a "Stalinist-type" state and economic system, is euphemistically referred to in Yugoslavia as "our administrative period." Although the Yugoslavs have repudiated in theory and practice the harsh dictatorial and bureaucratic methods employed in this period, they steadfastly insist that these methods were necessary to launch socialism, "develop working class consciousness and root out enemies." But the break with Moscow opened their eyes to what Edvard Kardelj termed "the danger

---

* There is discussed here only what might be characterized as "official" institutions, omitting treatment of the League of Communists and the Socialist Alliance. These are discussed in Chapter 12.

of bureaucratic centralism . . . of state capitalist despotism . . . of suppression and restriction of socialist initiative of the working masses."[1]

There resulted, in Yugoslav Marxist eyes, a crisis which could "only be resolved either by the victory of the revolutionary forces of the broad masses or by that of the bureaucracy," falsely pretending to act for the masses.[2] To insure the "victory of the revolutionary forces," the Yugoslavs dipped into not only the experience of the French Revolution and the early days of the Bolshevik Revolution but also American theory and practice. They came up with a system that as a whole was new and original, including certain institutions held to be "unique in the annals of political and economic organization."[3]

By no means all the institutional innovations of the new Yugoslav system are governmental. In fact, the Titoist system is perhaps best known for new departures in the economic sphere, especially worker-management of enterprises, decentralized planning and control of an economic system that is relatively competitive and free (although not private) and socialist at the same time, and decollectivized, privately owned agriculture. These developments, as well as those concerned with the legal system, are treated in ensuing chapters, and emphasis here is placed on the structure and administration of governmental and what might be called semi-governmental institutions. The major ones include:

1. A federal system under a constitution of delegated and enumerated powers, with a novel executive-legislative arrangement.

2. Direct worker representation in legislative bodies.

3. Wide autonomy for local government, with the basic unit an *opština*, or commune, whose chief function is to supervise and coordinate all economic activity and social services in its territory.

4. Forms of "direct democracy" and "social management," ranging from nomination of candidates by voters' meetings to management of public but non-governmental activities by groups of private citizens.

The main outlines of the new system evolved during the period 1950–1954, a period of extreme decentralization in all respects. In the economy, the elimination of direct federal controls, plus wide autonomy for local governments, went so far as to produce almost an atomization of autonomous economic units and extreme forms of "localism." The years since 1954 have

[1] Edvard Kardelj, "The New Social and Political System of the Federal People's Republic of Yugoslavia," *New Fundamental Law of Yugoslavia*, Union of Jurists Associations of Yugoslavia, Belgrade, 1953, pp. 7–10.

[2] Jovan Djordjević, "Status and Role of the Executive Organs during the First Stage of Yugoslavia's Political and Constitutional Development," *International Social Science Bulletin*, 1958, p. 262.

[3] *Ibid.*, pp. 32–35. See also Jovan Djordjević, *Novi Ustav Federativne Narodne Republike Jugoslavije (New Constitution of the Federal People's Republic of Yugoslavia)*, Službenog Lista FNRJ, 1953, pp. 125–127.

witnessed some tightening up, partly through reimposition of certain direct controls, but even more so, especially in economic matters, through the introduction of organizational controls formally outside the government. At the same time the general pattern has been maintained and, in connection with "social management," considerably extended.

THE FEDERAL SYSTEM

The governmental forms of Titoism were apparent in the Constitutional Law of 1953. Although this law officially only modified the 1946 constitution — which was the legal basis of the Stalinist-type state — it created constitutional changes of such magnitude that it amounted to a new constitution, and it has been generally considered as such. Its aim was to create a "socialist democracy" combining socialism with elements of democracy, although by no means purporting to establish a political democracy in the Western sense. The 1953 constitution — or Fundamental Law, as it is officially called — did not set forth specific individual rights which could not be invaded by any political power, although it did guarantee "free association of working people," "personal freedom and other rights of man" and "the right to work." It was a more honest and realistic document than its predecessor or, say, the Soviet Constitution, in the sense that it promised less but resulted in more.

A new constitution was drafted beginning in 1959—this time a full-fledged constitution—and scheduled for adoption sometime in 1962. Although important changes were involved, no basic departures from the structure of the governmental system were envisaged. The new constitution was motivated in part by a desire to remove technical ambiguities resulting from formal retention of the 1946 document and to pull together the multitude of new laws and practices which appeared after 1953. In Belgrade, the new constitution was seen as legal recognition of the continued process of the "withering away of the state" in Yugoslavia.

The nature of Yugoslav federalism — a delicate issue because it involves the touchy nationalities question — was a subject of sharp differences while the 1953 Fundamental Law was being drawn up. The differences were largely of a formal nature — as to whether the republics were "sovereign" or not, and if so whether this meant they had the right of secession. In the end both the concept of sovereignty for the republics and the theoretical right of secession contained in the 1946 constitution lost out. Yet the multi-state structure was retained, and the system continued to be regarded as federal.[1] In fact, the six constituent republics in some ways acquired more autonomy and greater admin-

[1] See definition in Jovan Djordjević, *Ustavno Pravo Federativne Narodne Republike Jugoslavije* (*Constitutional Law of the Federal People's Republic of Yugoslavia*), Arhiva za Pravne i Društvene Nauke, Belgrade, 1953, p. 24.

istrative powers than they had previously. Nevertheless, many were unhappy with this resolution of the question of federalism. The new constitution planned for 1962 was likely to broaden it, without basically altering its substance.

It was the local governmental units, more than the republics, which gained power and authority under the 1953 constitution. This document provided for a government of enumerated and delegated powers. Both federal and republic governments had only those rights and powers specifically delegated to them. All other power was held to reside in "the working people" as a whole, expressed through local people's committees, workers' councils and certain forms of "direct democracy." While theoretically this made Yugoslavia more of a unitary state than it had been, the identity and equality of the republics was carefully preserved, and care was taken to avoid any indication of ignoring ethnic differences, an attitude which had caused so much trouble under the monarchy.

An important innovation for Yugoslav federalism was to be included in the 1962 constitution. This was a Constitutional Court, with authority to pass on the constitutionality of laws of both the Federal Assembly and republic parliaments as well as on constitutional questions raised in connection with government administration. It was to replace a Constitutional Commission of the Federal Assembly which ruled on conflicts between republic law and the federal constitution and whose actions were a source of some bickering between federal and republic governments. The new judicial body was to have both original and appellate jurisdiction and was to act either on the basis of actual cases or on request of social organizations and accused persons claiming violation of constitutional rights. It was to have ten members, each elected by the Federal Assembly for ten-year terms and half of them subject to re-election. The Constitutional Court was modelled in part after the Supreme Court of the United States, but since its members would not have the absolute tenure of American judges it was unlikely to play the same role.[1]

The Federal Assembly

One of the major innovations of the 1953 system was a new and unique institution of worker representation in government, the Council of Producers. This body and the Federal Council make up the bicameral Skupština, or Federal Assembly. (See Fig. 13–1.)

Under the 1953 Law the two chambers established by the 1946 constitution — the Federal Council, representing all citizens, and the Council of Nationalities, representing the republics — were merged into one chamber,

[1] In 1959 Yugoslav legal experts discussed plans for the new court with justices of the Supreme Court of the United States.

GOVERNMENT BODIES

MAJOR ECONOMIC INSTITUTIONS

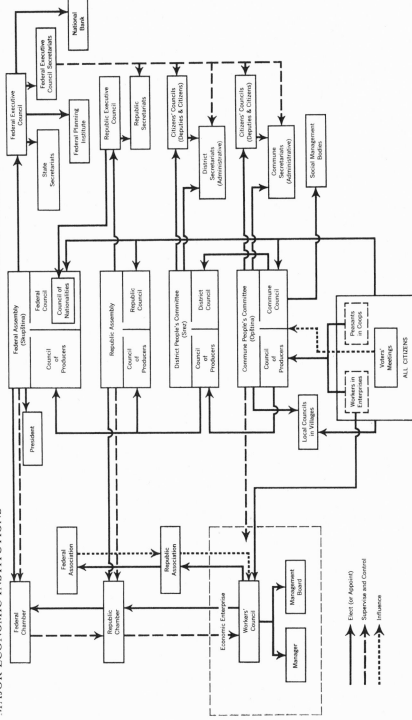

Figure 13–1   The chart shows agencies and relationships as of 1960.

the Federal Council. All citizens vote for members of this body, on the basis of one deputy for each 60,000 inhabitants. But the Federal Council includes, in addition, a set of deputies elected by the executive bodies of the republics and the autonomous areas; there were 70 in 1958 — ten from each republic, six from the autonomous province of Vojvodina and four from the autonomous region of Kosovo-Metohija. These deputies ordinarily vote as a regular part of the Federal Council. Matters involving constitutional changes must be considered by these deputies sitting as a Council of Nationalities, however, and the same group may sit separately to consider the economic plan and questions affecting the status of the republics. When in this guise the deputies comprising the Council of Nationalities disagree with the whole Federal Council, according to the 1953 constitution the Federal Council is dissolved. In practice, the Council of Nationalities has rarely functioned in a significant way except on constitutional amendments, and there have been no instances of disagreement resulting in dissolution.[1]

The second chamber of the Skupština is the Council of Producers. It consists of deputies elected by two groups — one, workers in industry, commerce and the crafts, and the other, peasants who are members of agricultural cooperatives. The number of deputies elected from each group, under the 1953 constitution, depended on the contribution of each of the two sectors of the economy to the "total social product," i.e., the value of their production, on an over-all basis of one deputy to every 70,000 of "producer population." The 1962 constitution envisaged eliminating this relationship between production and election and basing the number of deputies solely on "producer population." The Council of Producers is in some ways a full-fledged chamber of the parliament, in some ways not. On economic matters, including the annual plan, the budget, investment, wages, taxation and social security, it is co-equal with the Federal Council, and it has exclusive authority to render certain types of decisions affecting economic enterprises, labor and social insurance. But the Council of Producers does not participate in much non-economic legislation, although in all cases it can propose amendments. In matters where both chambers participate equally, the 1953 constitution provided that an unresolved disagreement must result in dissolution of the entire Assembly and the calling of new elections.[2]

[1] The dissolution provision seemed likely to be removed in the constitutional revision.

[2] Under the constitution, there are three types of legislation handled by the Federal Assembly: exclusive, basic and general. Exclusive legislation concerns areas entirely within federal and outside republic jurisdiction, e.g., national defense. Basic legislation involves areas in which republics enact their own complementary laws or act in the absence of federal law. General legislation concerns matters of national interest where the republics have not acted. The Council of Producers has no competence in this field. Cf. Articles 16 and 40 of the Constitution, *New Fundamental Law of Yugoslavia*, Union of Jurists' Associations of Yugoslavia, Belgrade, 1953, pp. 62–63 and pp. 71–72.

Although the essence of this structure of the Skupština was to be retained in the 1962 constitution, some changes were slated, especially as regards the concept of the Council of Producers. The new constitution envisaged the addition to the Skupština of other, smaller "councils of producers" representing those engaged in education, scientific and cultural work. Technically this appeared to change the bicameral nature of the Skupština, but since the jurisdiction of the new bodies was to be narrowly limited to legislation concerning their own activities, the bulk of parliamentary work would continue to be the concern of the Federal Council and the Council of Producers.

Prior to the 1962 constitution, the bicameral organization of the Federal Assembly was repeated at all levels of government—the republic assemblies and the people's committees of the districts (*srez*) and communes (*opština*)—that is, in each case there was a chamber of general representation and a council of producers. This organization seemed likely to be maintained, although probably with additional bodies, following the federal pattern.

As originally adopted, the 1953 constitution provided for direct election of deputies in all cases. After 1954, however, members of councils of producers at federal, republic and district levels were elected indirectly, and in 1957 the indirect system of elections applied to all except the Federal Council and both houses of the commune people's committees.[1] Under this system, members of the commune people's committees—elected directly—elected members of the district chambers, each chamber electing members to the respective houses. The district producers' councils elected members of both the republic councils of producers and the Federal Council of Producers. A change in this system was to be provided in the 1962 constitution. Under the proposed method, the commune people's committees were to select candidates for houses of federal and republic assemblies, as well as for the district people's committees, from lists nominated by voters' meetings.[2]

Usually the various local deputies chose from among their own number in selecting legislators for higher levels. Thus there has been a high degree of overlapping of membership of elective governmental bodies, even in the case of the Federal Council, membership on which is considered a full-time occupation.

Under the system as it operated up until 1962, the councils of producers, although representing workers in both industry and agriculture, were an instrument for rather frank discrimination against peasants in favor of industrial employees. This discrimination, deeply rooted in Marxist philosophy, also reflected the regime's recognition that socialism finds less understanding

[1] For discussion of communes, see below, pp. 225–228.
[2] For further discussion of elections, see pp. 230–232 and Chapter 19.

and favor with peasants than with certain other segments of society. The discrimination stemmed from two factors. One was that the "total social product," based on somewhat arbitrary official price lists, tended to undervalue agriculture's contribution and thus to reduce the number of deputies from agriculture on councils of producers. In the 1958 elections, the industry-commerce-trade contribution to the "total social product" was set at 2,293 billion dinars, or 77.9 per cent, and agriculture's contribution at 650 billion dinars, or 22.1 per cent; 168 deputies were named to the Federal Council of Producers from industry, commerce and trade and only 48 from agriculture. In 1954 there were 135 from industry and 67 from agriculture. In the republic councils of producers in 1958 the proportion was as follows: Serbia, 57 industry, 22 agriculture; Croatia, 45 industry, 10 agriculture; Slovenia, 23 industry, 2 agriculture; Bosnia and Herzegovina, 30 industry, 9 agriculture; Macedonia, 11 industry, 4 agriculture; and Montenegro, 4 industry and 1 agriculture.

It appeared that this discrimination against peasants in councils of producers would be removed by a provision of the 1962 constitution abolishing contributions to "total social product" as the basis for determining the number of deputies from industry and agriculture respectively. Henceforth, it was anticipated—according to plans for the new constitution—that members of councils of producers would be elected from industry, and elections for councils of producers would be based only on the number of persons engaged in the two major sectors of the economy. The envisaged removal of this discrimination against peasants appeared to reflect the fact that, with the development of industry, peasants no longer represented a clear majority of the population.

Some discrimination remains, however, in that only those peasants who are members of cooperatives are eligible to vote. The many peasants who still do not belong to cooperatives of any type do not vote at all in elections for councils of producers. As for the majority who are members of general cooperatives, it is by and large the administrators and technicians, rather than the real "dirt peasants," who represent these cooperatives in political matters.

The Executive

With age rapidly overtaking Tito, the organization of the executive branch of the Yugoslav government could best be described as in a state of "incipient change." Some important new departures were planned in the 1962 constitution, but they were likely to have little effect on either organization or practice as long as Tito remained as Chief of State.

In establishing new federal executive organs, the 1953 constitution sought to "combine the best aspects of both separation and unity of executive powers and also separate executive power from administrative power."[1] To do this, it created the office of the President of the Republic and a Federal Executive Council, both named by the Assembly. The President acted as head of state in proclaiming laws, signing treaties and receiving ambassadors, etc. He had authority to suspend acts of the Federal Executive Council, referring these for ultimate decision to the Assembly. He was also supreme commander of the armed forces.

The most important government organ by all odds is the Federal Executive Council, consisting of about thirty members of the Assembly plus the heads of republic executive councils as ex-officio members, which in fact runs the government. Under the 1953 constitutional law, the President of the Republic was also chairman of the Federal Executive Council. In fact, however, Tito, who has no flair for administration, was usually occupied elsewhere and the Council was presided over by Edvard Kardelj, one of its vice chairmen. The proposed 1962 constitution would create the post of President of the Federal Executive Council as a separate position. Under this provision, the President of the Republic—whose other powers would remain intact—could still convoke the Council and would, in all probability, be a member of it although not its head. As President, Tito has wielded influence and authority considerably beyond the constitutional powers of the office. He would continue to do so even under the arrangement envisaged in the 1962 constitution, although the constitutional powers of the Presidency would be reduced. Those concerned with drafting the 1962 constitution described the new office of President as being "one part that of the Presidency in the United States and one part that of a president under a parliamentary form of government." Since the President of the Federal Executive Council, along with members of the Council itself, would be members of the Federal Assembly, some argued that the change pointed the way toward a parliamentary system in the future.

The 1962 constitution heralded an important change in tenure of public officials. The terms of office of the President of the Republic and of members of the Assembly (and thus also of members of the Federal Executive Council) are four years. Under the 1953 Basic Law, they could be—and were—re-elected. The 1962 constitution would limit all elected public officials to one term, although re-election after an interval was envisaged. This was seen in Belgrade as an important move against bureaucracy and "the new class"

---

[1] Radomir D. Lukić, "Načelo Jedinstva Vlasti u Saveznom Ustavnom Zakonu" ("The Principle of Unity of Powers in the Federal Constitutional Law"), *Arhiv za Pravne i Društvene Nauke*, Nos. 1–2, 1953.

(although officially this term was not used), but the limitation on tenure was not to apply to "the first president." This meant that Tito could hold office as long as he wanted. Presumably, however, the four-year limitation would apply to Kardelj and other members of the Federal Executive Council in office at the time of adoption of the 1962 constitution, as well as to members of the Federal Assembly and heads of the Secretariats (although not to the Federal Executive Council's administrative secretariats). In such cases, however, staggered terms were provided for in order to give continuity. The one-term limit was to be applicable in both republic and local governments also.

Members of the Federal Executive Council are invariably also important Party officials. They preside over the whole gamut of governmental activity. Charged with enforcing the Assembly's laws and with general supervision of the state, the Federal Executive Council is also empowered to issue decrees, regulations and rules with the force of law, although these are subject to ultimate approval by the Assembly except in certain technical administrative matters provided for by statute. In addition, the Federal Executive Council has wide powers to override such actions of republic and local governments — other than acts of republic assemblies — as it considers contrary to law, although these may be appealed to the Federal Assembly. Such intervention, however, is not often utilized, as republic and local officials are in constant touch with Belgrade and tend to clear dubious matters in advance.

A part of the Federal Executive Council's exceptional position stems from the fact that, at least up until 1962, in practice it has originated all federal legislation. The Assembly, according to Professor Djordjević, had "in one sense abandoned the practice of drafting laws, but without renouncing its right to initiate legislation." The undemocratic aspects of this practice are mitigated somewhat by two factors: one, the Assembly often adopts resolutions laying down the principles which the Council should observe in drafting laws; and, two, more important legislation is usually worked out by joint commissions consisting of both Council and regular Assembly members. Moreover, there is invariably wide and earnest public discussion of major legislation before it is enacted into law.[1] The 1962 constitution envisaged changes in the Assembly's inner structure according to which it would draft its own laws. Whether or not this change would be more than one of form depended more on the course of events than on the change itself.

The Assembly also has a regular period during which members may question government officials. During the first five years of the 1953 constitution,

---

[1] Jovan Djordjević, "Status and Role of the Executive Organs during the First Stage of Yugoslavia's Political and Constitutional Development," *International Social Science Bulletin*, 1958, pp. 259–269.

few questions were raised, and those were usually of a non-specific nature. The question period has in recent years been utilized to a greater extent, but thus far its resemblance to the similar institution in the British House of Commons is more formal than real. A legislative proposal of the Federal Executive Council (*predlog,* or proposition) is rarely amended except in minor ways and is assured of favorable Assembly action.

In 1954 the late Moše Pijade, then president of the Skupština, said it would take "four years if not more" for the Federal Assembly to work as it should. In the years that followed, a real effort was made to build up the ability and prestige of the Assembly. Certain prominent and able men were encouraged to "take up politics," as the Yugoslav saying has it, as a career and become full-time deputies.[1] But the increase in the Assembly's ability and prestige was more pronounced than the increase in its authority and independence. Some hoped that the establishment in 1958 of a joint Skupština Committee on Social Control, with broad powers to investigate expenditures and general policies at all levels, might enhance the Assembly's independence. Further, the 1962 constitution proposed to give to standing committees of the Assembly certain authority in administration, including the power to make "binding directives" on administrative agencies. It also might well be that leaders of the regime would see in the forthcoming Constitutional Court an instrumentality that would make it possible "safely" to permit the Federal Assembly to act on its own more independently. Even with all this, however, it was clear that if the Skupština were to operate like a Western legislative body, more time was necessary than Pijade seems to have thought.

The Administration

Originally under the 1953 set-up the Federal Executive Council was supposed in the main to set broad policies and not to be charged with direct administration of them. An effort was made to separate the executive organs — the Presidency and the Federal Executive Council — from the "federal organs of administration," or state secretariats and other agencies. Under the 1946 constitution, government policy had been formulated in a council of ministers, and then executed by the ministries. The federal apparatus in 1948 numbered 47,310 employees, exclusive of those in the ministry of internal affairs. The 1953 Fundamental Law eliminated the council of ministers and abolished the ministries, along with many of their functions. A sweeping

---

[1] For example, Aleš Bebler, former undersecretary for foreign affairs and a top diplomat, was elected a deputy from Slovenia and became chairman of the Federal Council's committee on foreign relations.

reduction of federal employees — down to 10,328 in all by 1956 — resulted.[1] In place of the ministries there were established only five state secretariats, dealing with foreign affairs, national defense, internal affairs (including police), finance and commodity trade. A federal committee for foreign trade occupies a position like that of a state secretariat. These secretariats were considered administrative organs only; political functions and powers were to be wielded by the Federal Executive Council. This separation between administrative and political functions was supposed to spare Yugoslavia the kind of "independent bureaucracy" which Kardelj asserted was responsible for creating "a state capitalist despotism and imperialist hegemony" in the Soviet Union.[2]

This concept of separation of political and administrative organs was one of the vaguer flights of Yugoslav theoretical fancy, and it never worked in practice. For one thing, while the state secretariats were authorized by the constitution to "independently exercise authority granted to them," the secretaries were appointed and removed by the Federal Executive Council, worked under its supervision and could be required to submit actions to the Council for "preliminary approval." Especially since the Council had an administrative apparatus of its own, it was never clear where the jurisdiction of one stopped and the other began. In fact, the Council was usually as occupied with administrative matters as with policy, and there was much overlapping.

Accordingly, a 1956 reorganization of the executive side of the government, while still paying some lip service to the theory of separation, all but abandoned trying to practice it. The administrative apparatus of the Federal Executive Council, which formerly was supposed only to operate as an adjunct to the Council's work, was now given a separate legal status and formally included within the "state administration." It had twelve secretariats of its own — for legislation, economic affairs, industry, agriculture and forestry, transport and communications, social relations and labor, culture and education, public health, social insurance, justice, information and general administration. In addition, there was established as an arm of the Federal Executive Council a Council for Legal Affairs, charged with preparing new legislation, advising the Federal Executive Council on the legality of its prescriptions and rendering opinions on government legal policies at all

[1] Cf. Edvard Kardelj, "Our State Administration Under New Conditions," *New Yugoslav Law*, April–June 1956, p. 3. The year 1956, however, saw a gradual rise in the number of federal employees. Complaints about this trend resulted in a Federal Executive Council decree in 1959 flatly prohibiting any further increase. See *New York Times*, January 5, 1959, p. 7.

[2] Edvard Kardelj, "The New Social and Political System of the Federal People's Republic of Yugoslavia," *New Fundamental Law of Yugoslavia*, Union of Jurists' Associations of Yugoslavia, Belgrade, 1953, especially pp. 39–40. See also M. Vučković, "Uredjenje Saveznog Isvršnog Veća" ("Organization of the Federal Executive Council"), *Nova Administracija*, July–August 1954, pp. 1–18.

levels.[1] The function of the Federal Executive Council secretariats, as thus organized, was to supervise the whole administrative system, at local and republic as well as at federal levels, to make sure that policies of the Federal Executive Council were carried out.[2]

Federal administrative supervisory authority was still further enlarged with the creation, in the fall of 1959, of a Department of Social Accounting, attached to the Federal Bank, which itself operates under the aegis of the Federal Executive Council. The new department has the status of a controller, passing on the legality of concrete acts involving expenditures of both government and publicly financed nongovernmental bodies. Some saw in it a potential wedge into such autonomy as exists in units below the federal level. It is still true, however, that the Federal Executive Council secretariats operate only within the confines of powers extended to them by the Council itself, while the state secretariats are full-fledged ministries, dealing with continuing tasks and having a more elaborate administrative structure. Originally, the law on administrative disputes permitted the filing of suits by citizens against the state secretariats and their employees for damages resulting from "unlawful activity." No such suits originally could be taken against formal acts of the Federal Executive Council, but the 1956 law permitted legal action against the Federal Executive Council secretariats as well. Suits of this kind are frequent in Yugoslav courts.

Surveying these developments, Professor Djordjević concluded that "the Yugoslav experiment shows how difficult it is to make a functional separation between the two aspects — politico-executive and administrative — of the executive function."[3]

In organizational structure, the governments of the republics are patterned closely after the government in Belgrade, except that they have no independent chief executive, like the president of the federal government. As indicated above, the republic parliaments are bicameral, one chamber, the republic council, elected by all voters and the other, a council of producers, elected by producers' councils of the district units within the republic.[4] Executive power in the republics is lodged in executive councils. The chairmen of the republic executive councils have no independent status and, in fact, are usually not the most powerful figures. In each republic, the top leader is president of the assembly. Similar governmental organizations are found in the autonomous

---

[1] There was discussion of making the Legal Council an organ of the Federal Assembly under the 1962 constitution.

[2] Cf. discussions in *Borba*, March 24, 1956, and in *New Yugoslav Law*, April–June 1956.

[3] "Status and Role of the Executive Organs during the First Stage of Yugoslavia's Political and Constitutional Development," p. 269.

[4] Following the federal pattern to be set up under the 1962 constitution, other chambers were likely to be added to the republic parliaments.

province of Vojvodina and the autonomous region of Kosovo-Metohija, both attached to the republic of Serbia.

Local Government

The decentralization of both economic and political power which is the basis of Yugoslavia's unique approach to socialism is nowhere better illustrated than in local government. The wide administrative authority, the considerable autonomy and the extent of citizen participation in local government are major factors in the Yugoslav claim to have blended political democracy with socialism. And the basic local unit, the *opština* or commune, is held to be a genuinely new form of government, "that basic cell of the socialist organization which Marx, Engels and all the great socialist thinkers called 'the free association of free producers.' "[1]

In Cominform days, local governments were no more than administrative arms of the central government and Party organs. The local governmental bodies — known as people's committees from Partisan days — were the lowest rungs in a hierarchal system, having only those powers granted them by the federal government and the constitution. They functioned almost entirely through their executive committees, which in turn were completely dominated by the local Party apparatus and often composed of the same people. When, after the break with the USSR, Yugoslav theories on "socialist democracy" and "withering away of the state" began to appear, Belgrade increasingly felt the need to alter this situation "by broadening and strengthening the people's right to self-government."[2]

The first indication of a change was a 1949 law giving the people's committees more authority and defining as "local" certain areas in which they had autonomy. In 1951, the Party itself decreed abolition of the executive committees and ordered its local minions to keep hands off the people's committees themselves. A year later, the General Law on People's Committees[3] changed the whole nature of local government, establishing the people's committees as the chief governmental units in the country, in both political and economic spheres, and enormously broadening their base. This was followed by the 1953 Constitutional Law, which gave to the people's committees all authority other than that specifically delegated to the federal and republic governments. Now, it was held, "the whole system of government rests on the people's committees and derives therefrom."[4]

[1] Jovan Djordjević, "From Local Self-Government to Communes," *Review of International Affairs*, November 1, 1954, p. 13.

[2] Cf. Jovan Djordjević, "Local Self-Government in Yugoslavia," *American Slavic and East European Review*, April 1953, pp. 188–200.

[3] *Opšti Zakon o Narodnim Odborima*, Službenog Lista FNRJ, Belgrade, 1952.

[4] Jovan Djordjević, "Some Principles of Socialist Democracy in Yugoslavia," *Yugoslav Review*, September 1953, p. 21.

Under the system launched by the 1952 act and the new constitution, people's committees existed at the level of the *srez*, or district; the *opština*, or subdivisions of districts; and the *grad*, or city. The city and the district people's committees were bicameral, with one chamber elected by all the voters in a given area and the other named by workers and those peasants in collectives, as explained above. The *opština* committees, functioning mostly in rural villages or subdivisions of cities, had only a single chamber.

The people's committees were full-fledged local governments. Their most important functions, however, were economic. Under the decentralized economic system, the people's committees were the major organs of control and regulation of economic enterprises. They were the basic units in formulation of the economic plan and the chief initiators of new enterprises. Since there were no limits on the authority of the people's committee to tax enterprises, once federal and republic obligations were met, the local units were financially autonomous. In fact, their independence in this regard caused serious economic problems, since they tended to drain enterprise funds by taxation, often for uneconomic investment.[1]

The Commune

Local government as thus organized was only transitional to the present system of communes, initiated in 1955. The Yugoslav commune has nothing in common with the Chinese institution of the same name. Although in theory a Yugoslav commune is more than a unit of local government, it can best be envisaged as such. As now set up, there are but two major levels of local government, the commune (*opština*) and the district (*srez*), which is a collection of communes. (An exception is the small republic of Montenegro, where the district has been eliminated.) Larger cities have the status of districts, and smaller cities have special town councils, operating under district or communal authorities.[2] The transformation was accomplished territorially by enormously expanding the size and contracting the number of local government units through mergers. The districts were reduced from 357 to 95, and the 4,000 *opštine* were changed into 1,193 communes, as of 1958, with still

---

[1] See Fred Warner Neal, *Titoism in Action: the Reforms in Yugoslavia after 1948*, University of California Press, Berkeley, 1958, pp. 144–151.

[2] The terminology of local government in Yugoslavia is confusing in the extreme, especially in English translation. In various works, district, commune, city and village units are all referred to as "municipalities." In the case of cities, *opština* is sometimes translated as "ward." At times, the concept of the commune is rendered in Serbo-Croatian by the unofficial term *komuna* instead of *opština*, and it is then said that the commune is not a division of government at all. See, for instance, Živorad Kovačević, *Communal System in Yugoslavia*, Jugoslavija, Belgrade, 1958. The key to understanding the system is to keep in mind that *opština* and "commune" refer to the same territorial unit.

further consolidations contemplated. Of these communes, 245 had a population of more than 20,000, 824 a population of 5,000 to 20,000, and only 124 less than 5,000.[1]

At present, the districts retain jurisdiction over the more strictly governmental, i.e., political, matters like law enforcement and elections, and are responsible for coordinating activity generally within their jurisdiction. But the communes have become the key local units. They have three primary concerns. One is economic, in connection with planning, investment, internal trade, and supervision of economic enterprises. Another is municipal services, such as water supply, sewerage, streets and public utilities. A third is the whole area of "social management," which means nongovernmental citizen-management of public activities.

The communes are in a sense financially autonomous, although under the present financial system local governments no longer may impose unlimited taxes on the income of economic enterprises. Communes are allocated a share (determined by federal law) of federal taxes on enterprise profits and wages, and they may supplement some other federal taxes up to a rate of 5 per cent. The communes are also entitled to levy taxes up to 2 per cent on retail consumption and up to 20 per cent on "collective consumption" of enterprises, a term applied to their expenditures on workers' housing, nurseries, etc. In addition, communes may tax as they see fit their own communal enterprises, i.e., local public utilities, private trade and catering services, and land within their jurisdiction used for economic purposes. Such financial resources make the communes an important source of investment. Together with individual enterprises, communal expenditure accounts for about two-thirds of total investment. How such funds are spent is legally entirely up to the communal people's committees, although other government levels—district, republic and federal—are able to exert strong influence on their decisions.

Although this system of financing was generally considered an improvement over the earlier system of uncontrolled local taxes, both commune and republic officials felt they did not have enough financial autonomy. In response to this sentiment, a new law was adopted in 1959 which was something of a compromise between unrestricted local and republic taxing authority and the system of federal distribution of all tax revenues. Under this measure, units below the federal level are supposed to have taxing authority to raise funds to meet at least their basic operating costs.

[1] "Worker Management and Labour Relations in Yugoslavia," *International Labour Organization*, Labour-Management Relations Series, No. 5, 1958, p. 11. According to Djordjević, in 1959 the number of districts was further reduced to 91 and the number of communes to 1,100. See his *Društveno-Političko i Državno Uredjenje Jugoslavije*, Savez Udruzenja Pravnika Jugoslavije, Belgrade, 1959, p. 221.

The commune people's committees are the key governmental administrative agencies for regulation and control of economic activity, especially as regards the operation of workers' councils.[1] The commune participates with workers' councils in setting pay scales and in hiring and firing directors. In most cases, enterprises may not borrow from the banks unless the commune agrees to underwrite part of the loan. The communal authorities are directly responsible for the proper operation of enterprises, and may, in cases of mismanagement, insist on election of a new workers' council, temporarily suspend worker-management and, under certain circumstances, liquidate an enterprise. Furthermore, the commune is in many ways the basic unit in planning. It coordinates the plans of workers' councils under its jurisdiction, and the communal plans are major factors in the annual Federal Plan. Although production plans are not legally binding at any level, in the Soviet sense, a workers' council that consistently fails to meet its own plan is liable to discipline or even liquidation by communal authorities.

The existence of a council of producers as one chamber of the commune people's committee makes for an especially intimate relationship between the local government organs and the workers' councils. Most members of councils of producers are members of workers' councils, the remainder coming from the local trade union Sindikat organizations. As a result, many producers' councils tend to be, from a broader point of view, too lenient in their treatment of individual enterprises. Logrolling and back-scratching — to utilize the American political vernacular — not infrequently have stood in the way of adequate regulation of workers' councils. On the other hand, since people's committee deputies were thus in responsible positions in the enterprises, they were often able to limit the propensity of workers' councils to better their own positions at the expense of the community.

Whether the commune will live up to its advance publicity it is still too early to say. Some communes, notably in Slovenia, have been operating with a high degree of effectiveness. The performance of many others has been disappointing to Belgrade. Localist tendencies are a constant problem. Formal consent was obtained from all full-fledged people's committees whose status was changed in the reorganization, but it was not infrequently given unwillingly. Sometimes the reconstituting of local government units bordered on gerrymandering, as the government sought to make sure that worker rather than peasant influence would predominate in the new councils of producers. In the process, damage was done in many cases to local pride and, on occasion, to local well-being.

[1] The authority slated to be given to commune people's committees in the 1962 constitution to elect members of both chambers of district people's committees and republic and federal assemblies would also greatly enhance the political power of these local bodies.

Another factor has been the inadequacy of local officials generally. In 1952 more than half of all local officials had had only primary schooling and only 11 per cent had completed high school. This aspect of the picture was more favorable by the end of the decade, but poorly educated personnel continued to handicap the communes in discharging the complicated tasks with which they were entrusted. Many people's committees, especially in the more backward areas, have been dominated by their administrative apparatus, particularly by the secretary, who usually has high standing in the local Party machine. Often, however, the administrative officials possess no more competence or training than the deputies, and sometimes less. Both commune and district governments are influenced strongly by the Socialist Alliance, whose main focus is the local people's committees, and by the Sindikat, which pays special attention to the work of councils of producers. Such influence is weaker in areas with high cultural standards but is always present in one way or another to some degree.

At the same time, the development of local autonomy produced a sharp increase in the number of employees, out of all proportion to the increase in the work load of the people's committees. From a total of 272,259 paid public employees at all levels in Yugoslavia in 1956, the number had increased to 303,951 by mid-1957. A year later *Borba* complained that there had been a steady increase in the "systemization of new posts" in communes, and that people's committees were trying to solve the problems mainly by adding personnel, most of whom were unskilled and incompetent. The *New York Times* correspondent in Belgrade remarked that "Parkinson's Law operates in Communist as well as capitalist lands."[1]

SOCIAL MANAGEMENT

In addition to their economic role and their strictly local governmental functions, the communes preside over and coordinate the whole gamut of public activity within their territories. This is characterized by some type of participation in public affairs of a wide variety of citizens and is generally referred to as "social management." Social management, say the Yugoslavs, is a type of "direct democracy." It is in the concept of the commune as a unit embracing all such activity that it is seen as the end result of decentralization and constituting more than simply a state instrumentality. An official commentary refers to the commune as "that basic social-economic and juridical-political organization in which the numerous and various threads of initiative of the citizens meet, intertwine and unravel in all their multitude."[2]

[1] Paul Underwood, *New York Times*, January 5, 1959, p. 7.
[2] Kovačević, *Communal System in Yugoslavia*, p. 3.

Forms of social management or "direct democracy" include participation of private citizens in affairs of the people's committees, the general meetings of voters, and management by boards of private citizens of schools, hospitals and clinics, apartment houses, neighborhoods, social insurance, radio stations and other activities which previously were operated directly by formal government bodies. Through such mechanisms, the base of local government is broadened and a wide variety of citizens are drawn into governmental or semi-governmental relationships. If the organs of worker-management and the people's committees and their advisory citizens' councils are included, there were about one million persons engaged in some form of local economic or political activity in 1958, or one out of every ten adults. In some cases, for example in Belgrade, every fifth citizen participated in some way.[1]

Citizens' Councils

Each people's committee, both at commune and at district levels, works in conjunction with several citizens' councils. At least two members of each council must be members of the people's committee; and the others are private citizens elected by the committee. These councils, under a 1956 law, are formed for planning and finance, general economic affairs, communal affairs, housing, education, culture, public health, labor, agriculture and forestry, internal affairs and general administration. Some people's committees also have formed councils for other purposes, such as town planning and tourism. The citizens' councils carry out the laws of the people's committees and have administrative-executive functions. They may also issue orders and instructions, which must be signed by the president of the people's committee, although a veto may be appealed to the full people's committee.

The citizens' councils have played an increasing role in communal matters. When the councils were first formed, their participation tended to be mostly formal, consisting mainly of reports to the people's committees, the individual members sitting silently except when called on. The trend has unquestionably been for council members to be more articulate in people's committee proceedings. One of the council's major functions is to keep a supervisory eye on the administrative organs of the people's committees. Although their chief role is advisory, this is not insignificant. Members of the councils are usually leading citizens active in one or another aspect of public affairs; often they are technical experts. Thus their opinions are of value to the people's committees, and in their day-to-day non-governmental work they are also able to give valuable advice to enterprises with which they are associated. As might be expected, the councils play a larger role in more technical activities, such as

[1] *Ibid.*, p. 28. See Table 12-4.

public health, than in political matters. There have been few indications, for example, that councils for internal affairs — or people's committees themselves, for that matter — exercise meaningful influence in matters relating to the political police, known as UDBA (Uprava Državne Bezbednosti, or Administration of State Security), although they are concerned with disposition of the militia.

As of the end of 1958, there were 65,994 persons serving as members of commune citizens' councils, of whom 41,343 were members of the League of Communists, and 10,424 persons serving on similar district bodies, of whom 7,980 belonged to the Party.[1] (See Table 12-4.) In one sense, the citizens' councils play the role of "transmission belts" for the people's committees, relaying to them public opinion and taking back the "official line" to their own groups. But their activity is broader than this, and it would be an oversimplification to think of the councils only in such light.

Voters' Meetings

The most "direct" of the various forms of "direct democracy" is the periodic general meeting of voters. Such meetings of voters — organized on the basis of special subdivisions of the commune — must be held at least once every two months, according to law, to hear reports of the people's committees and their citizens' councils. In some areas, monthly meetings are the rule.

The voters' meetings have three main functions. One is to serve as a public forum for discussion of the work of the people's committees and communal activity in general and to approve the annual social plan. The second is to make recommendations to the people's committees concerning policy and to suggest candidates for membership on citizens' councils. The third is to nominate candidates for election not only to communal people's committees but also to republic and federal assemblies.

The role of the voters' meeting varies greatly in different sections of the country and even from commune to commune in the same area. Previously these meetings were almost altogether formal (except, possibly, in regard to nomination of candidates). People's committee officials read reports, there were obviously arranged remarks from Party and other politically active people, and that was all. Although an effort is made by the Party, through the Socialist Alliance, to dominate the voters' meetings in one way or another, the trend has been toward more discussion by ordinary citizens. Especially since the League Executive Committee "cracked down" on local Party "bureaucratism" early in 1958, some voters' gatherings have taken on the aspect of

[1] *Komunist*, April 16, 1959.

regular town meetings, especially in the cities. In the more backward parts of the country, less progress has been made, and in rural areas there is sometimes little interest, indicated by sparse attendance.

Up to 1957, each voters' meeting named a nominating commission, which then submitted names back to the meeting, and every candidate receiving approval of at least one-fourth of the voters present was considered nominated and placed on the ballot. Since 1957 every voters' meeting has named from one to three persons to a nominating assembly for the whole territory of the constituency involved. Any five members of the nominating assembly can propose a name for nomination, and those obtaining the approval of more than 40 per cent of the assembly are put on a candidates' list for submission back to a general voters' meeting. The voters' meeting then can approve the list or reject it wholly or in part. In case of rejection, the voters' meeting names its own nominating commission to come up with new names. This procedure is followed for nominating candidates both for the general representation bodies and for the councils of producers, but in the case of producers' councils only "active producers" are eligible to participate in the voters' meetings. Two meetings are held, one for the industry-trade-commerce workers and the other for the agricultural workers. In addition, candidates for election to both types of bodies may be nominated by petition. This is not an infrequent procedure, especially in connection with local elections. Under the proposed 1962 constitutional changes, voters' meeting nominations for federal, republic and district offices would go to commune people's committees for election.

Party and Socialist Alliance units make a great effort to organize these nominating meetings, and they are more often than not — but not invariably — successful. The 1957 change seems to have been in part an effort to further Party and Socialist Alliance influence in the nominating procedure. Candidates bear no formal political label, however, either of the Party or of the Socialist Alliance. In elections for the Federal Assembly there are rarely more candidates nominated than posts to be filled. In the 1958 elections, for example, in all but six of 301 districts, candidates were unopposed. The number of contests is higher in the case of elections for the republic assemblies. For communal people's committees, the rule is for twice as many candidates to be nominated as there are posts to fill, and in some cases several candidates have contested for a seat. Where only one candidate is nominated for election, he must receive at least half of the eligible votes in order to be elected; if he does not, then, according to the law, a second election is held with at least two candidates running. Under the 1962 constitutional changes—making all elections except those for commune people's committees indirect—there would be no popular election of candidates for federal, republic and district offices. However, if only one candidate for a post were selected by the commune people's committee, his name would be submitted to a popular referendum in which he would have to receive a majority of votes cast.

Public Boards

A major emphasis in Yugoslav socialism, in its organizational aspects, is on participation of private citizens in the management of public but non-governmental enterprises. These activities are of several types. One embraces hospitals, clinics, libraries and schools at all levels, including universities. Such enterprises have their own worker-management organs, but superimposed on them is a board consisting of the representatives of employees and private citizens, elected by people's committees, whose main occupation is in other fields. A second category consists of such enterprises as radio stations, certain newspapers, publishing houses, etc., which also have both worker-management and boards composed of both private citizens and employee representatives. A third concerns the social insurance system, which is decentralized and managed entirely by public boards. Still another area of social management is housing. Apartment houses are managed by a house council (*kučni savet*), and urban areas are organized into housing neighborhoods (*stanbena zajednica*) under popularly elected neighborhood councils.[1] The housing neighborhoods have responsibility for problems involving residents in their territories, including the house councils.

In addition, consumers' councils are being established for certain enterprises, mostly retail concerns. These must be consulted by workers' councils on price increases and quality of goods and services and they may make recommendations to workers' councils and communal authorities. The role of consumers' councils has not been thoroughly worked out and up until 1960, at least, was not very important. The aim of these councils is to provide for an element of consumer responsibility in non-production economic enterprises, and it seemed likely that more attention would be paid to them. About 1,850 consumers' councils were in existence in 1958 — the same number as in 1957 — and there was no general pattern either for their establishment or for their operations.

All social management bodies operate under the people's committees, which set them up and supervise their work. Their activities are carried on according to federal and republic laws.

---

[1] The term *stanbena zajednica* is used both for the housing neighborhood and for its council. It is sometimes translated "dwelling community" and "neighborhood center."

House and Neighborhood Councils

Since 1958 increasing stress has been laid on house councils and neighborhood councils, especially the latter. Under a 1959 law, the scope of the neighborhood councils was substantially broadened, giving them certain functions previously handled directly by people's committees and local government administrative organs. These include in some cases management of water and sewerage systems. Supervision of hotels and restaurants also comes under the housing neighborhood, and it is envisaged that they will establish various retail enterprises of their own, in addition to public kitchens, laundries and the like. The neighborhood council also handles assignment of apartments, a highly important function since housing is so scarce.

The 1959 law provided for an element of financial independence for the housing neighborhoods, with funds coming from profits of their own enterprises, a percentage of the rent paid by apartment dwellers and loans from the General Investment Fund, as well as from contributions from people's committees. The housing neighborhoods were also authorized, "with the agreement of the citizens concerned," to levy certain taxes on individuals. About 200 urban housing neighborhoods existed at the beginning of 1959, half of them in Belgrade.

The house councils themselves, prior to the new emphasis on the housing neighborhood, played a role considerably less important than one would expect from official pronouncements. Their main function was to collect rent and authorize certain repairs. There was a tendency on the part of even many politically minded apartment dwellers — other than owners — to regard them either as a joke or a nuisance.

The emphasis placed by the government and the Party on social management in the field of housing and services reflected a major drive to improve conditions in these areas. That these social management organs would be of increasing importance was indicated particularly by two governmental actions. In December 1958 the Federal Assembly passed a law decreeing the nationalization of all apartment houses with more than three dwelling units, and in 1960 rents were increased to a point where they would pay for adequate maintenance. The nationalization law had more immediate ideological than economic significance. Apartment owners were permitted only 10 per cent of rents prior to this law, and had virtually no rights to their property other than to live in two units of it. Under the new statute, they were to continue to receive 10 per cent of the rents for a fifty-year period as compensation for their property. The establishment of "economic rents," however, which was decreed for January 1, 1960, involved doubling rent payments in most cases.

Aside from its direct impact on tenants, this measure meant a substantial increase in funds available to the house councils and the neighborhood councils.

Educational System

The educational system provides an especially significant illustration of
social management in Yugoslavia, both because of the importance of education in a country with a traditionally high rate of illiteracy and because of the
problems posed by the tremendous increase in the number of pupils and
students at all levels in recent years.

The chief characteristic of Yugoslav educational administration is its decentralization. The former system of central direction and control under a
federal ministry of education has been abolished. Although the federal government is able to retain an adequate degree of supervision, all schools, from
kindergartens to universities, operate under various forms of social management. Central policies are coordinated by a Federal Executive Council
Secretariat for Education and Culture, which acts jointly with a Federal
Board of Education. The Board consists of three members of the Federal
Executive Council[1] and the presidents of the councils of education of the
republics. The Federal Board has no legal authority in regard to schools,
other than the giving of advice, since, technically, the federal government
itself has no such authority. There is in fact little federal interference with
administration of individual institutions. With regard to policy, however, the
Federal Board is usually able to gain adherence to its ideas.

More authority is wielded by republic secretaries for education and their
councils, consisting of citizens nominated by district educational councils. The
republic and district councils — members of the latter are elected at district
voters' meetings — do exercise administrative authority and also pass ultimately on general curriculum requirements.

Each of the six universities — one for each republic — operates under a
University Council, on which serve representatives of the different faculties
as well as members elected by the respective republic parliament.[2] There is also
a representative of the student body. This Council approves broad policies,
not primarily of instructional matters but of administration. The actual administration is carried out by a University Board consisting of the rector,
pro-rector and the deans of the various faculties. In addition, each university

[1] In 1960, the Board was headed by Krste Crvenkovski, a member of the Executive Committee
of the League of Communists and of the Federal Executive Council, who also held the post of
secretary for education and culture.

[2] The Croatian parliament, for example, elected to the Council of the University of Zagreb its
vice president, six of its members, two members of the federal Skupština, a writer, the manager
of an industrial enterprise, the manager of a state farm, an architect and the director of Radio
Zagreb.

has a general assembly, consisting of representatives of the faculties, which elects the rector and pro-rector for two-year terms; it also has faculty councils, consisting of members elected by the professors on any one faculty plus representatives of professions — for example, supreme court judges are invariably represented on the law faculty councils — and government officials. Purely educational matters are dealt with in the first instance by the faculty members themselves, who elect deans and draw up the program of instruction. A student representative is an ex-officio member.[1] The program of instruction worked out by the faculties must ultimately be passed on by the university council and the republic educational council.[2]

The non-academic members of both university and faculty councils outnumber the university people, and, among them, Communists predominate. The majority of university professors, however, are non-Communists. Although political discrimination at times intrudes into educational matters, this is not a major cause of complaint among most university faculty members. There is occasional grumbling, however, about interference by non-academic personnel under the social management system.

Although funds for the universities are provided by the respective republic parliaments — supplemented in some instances from the federal treasury, the universities — with their boards and councils — have a high degree of autonomy as far as internal administration is concerned. Where national questions are concerned — as, for example, exchanges with foreign universities — there is usually reluctance to act without approval from Belgrade.

The administration of elementary and secondary schools is in some respects not unlike that in the United States. These institutions operate generally under school boards consisting of citizens named by local voters' meetings and confirmed by people's committees and of representatives elected by the teachers of the particular school. Although the board acts in conjunction with the educational council of the local people's committee, it has a measure of financial autonomy in that certain taxes are paid directly to it, and it can exact limited levies for certain purposes.

The day-to-day administration of elementary and secondary schools is carried on by a teachers' council, consisting of teachers' representatives plus the director, who is chosen by the school board.

Although Party influence, directly and through the Socialist Alliance, is sufficient to prevent the schools from becoming anti-regime instruments, education has in general remained remarkably free from ideological distor-

[1] The student members, of both the faculty and the university councils, as a rule play comparatively silent roles.

[2] Other institutions of higher learning, such as institutes and technical schools, are similarly organized.

tion. The close relationship of school administration to the people in local areas is certainly one explanation for this. Courses in Marxism are required at the university level and are taught in some secondary schools. The Communist bias of many teachers shows in their instruction. But only a small percentage of teachers are Communists. All except the most unreconstructed anti-Communists among prewar teachers were retained — partly because of the enormous teacher shortage but also as a matter of policy.

Indeed, some school officials feel there is too little ideology in Yugoslav teaching. Illustrative of the point was an incident witnessed by one of the authors in a geography class which he visited in the main secondary school of Dubrovnik. In a discussion on China, a student was trying to give the name of Chiang Kai-shek's party, the Kuomintang. Prompted by the teacher with the first syllable, the student hesitated and then ventured: "Cominform?" The only reaction was laughter.

Yugoslav educators generally, regardless of political orientation, speak highly of the extension of social management to education. When the system was just beginning, in 1954, one sometimes had the impression that the Yugoslavs thought they had invented the idea of a local public school board. A school director told one of the authors: "This is a new concept. The people whom the school serves will have some say in the direction of its affairs."

In addition to the regular schools, there is a wide variety of educational institutions for workers. The larger ones are known as "workers' universities," although they offer courses in everything from elementary reading and writing to higher mathematics and have no systematized curricula. Except where factories organize their own schools — as has occurred in many instances — schools for workers are operated by the trade union Sindikat, under rules prescribed by the Secretariat for Education and Culture. The ideological content of "social science" instruction in workers' universities tends to be higher than in the general schools, although less sophisticated. In Skoplje, for instance, one of the authors sat in on a course in the "History of Socialism." One worker-student became hopelessly confused in trying to trace the political intricacies of wartime Yugoslavia. Finally the instructor threw up his hands, and declared: "It's simple. Just remember, Partisan means progress, and socialism and nationalism. Četnik means reaction, imperialism and bourgeoisie." The following lesson, on reading, consisted merely of going through an elementary school text on the geography of Macedonia.

Social Management and Democracy

Despite the fact that some aspects of Yugoslav social management have parallels in the West — e.g., hospital and school boards — the whole concept has obvious implications for the country's socialist development. Social management is, of course, in line with the Yugoslav emphasis on "withering away of the state" and does carry decentralization of much government authority to what appears to be its ultimate limits. Moreover, it provides a school in which citizens learn about cooperative handling of public affairs and become "civic-minded" in a socialist sense. This is of no small significance in a country like Yugoslavia, with its cultural backwardness and lack of a tradition of wide citizen participation in government.

On the negative side, social management thus far has made for a certain amount of inefficiency and red tape, and, if it eliminated one kind of bureaucracy, this was often replaced with another. For one thing, in some cases decisions inevitably depended on persons with inadequate ability to make them. For another, there have been countless cases of overlapping jurisdiction, with resulting conflicts and delays. Not infrequently there has simply been disinterest on the part of citizens tapped to serve. One of the most able and enthusiastic advocates of the Yugoslav system has referred to "criticism that collective responsibility is apt to turn into collective irresponsibility" and reported that in a major city, one meeting in twelve had to be postponed because of lack of a quorum.[1]

Although the Yugoslavs insist that their social management is "real democracy," it is also a substitute for political democracy as is it understood in the West. How adequate a substitute depends, even in Yugoslav terms, on the extent to which citizens serving on boards and councils act freely or merely provide a front for political controls through the Party and the Socialist Alliance. Virtually all members of the social management bodies belong to the latter organization. Party influence is considerably greater than indicated by the fact that only about a third of the members of social management bodies are also members of the League of Communists. This is not only because Party members can usually count on support for their positions from non-Party Socialist Alliance members, but also because the practice is for many of them to serve on several social management boards at the same time. Although it is these members who usually exercise leadership, the burdens on their time — since they also have regular employment in government or an enterprise — is such that they are often inadequately briefed on problems that arise.

In practice, the authors have found that at the local level generally, including the people's committees themselves, there is ordinarily a freedom of expression not often manifested at republic and federal levels of government.

[1] Eugen Pusić, "Citizens Management of the Social Services in Yugoslavia," *Saertryk of Nordisk Administrativt Tidsskrift*, Reykjavik, Spring 1957, pp. 143 and 145.

The area of "political policy making" in the social management organs is, of course, limited, as they are concerned primarily with administration and technical matters. There are not infrequent examples of social management bodies taking decisions counter to Party positions, but these seldom involve important issues. Where they do, people's committees and the republic and federal officials are usually able to step in. However, it was reported that as of 1957 only 1.2 per cent of all decisions taken by social management organs had been overruled by state authority.[1]

Looking broadly at the Yugoslav system, it is apparent that it is characterized by new political and social institutions in which there is wide popular participation. They add up, even in their formal aspects, to a different type of socialism than has emerged in countries to the east of Yugoslavia. Some observers feel that these institutions are only a façade for Party rule. While this is unquestionably true in some cases, the investigations of the present authors have failed to bear out such a sweeping conclusion for the system as a whole. At the same time, this observation must be understood within the context of Yugoslav Communism. At no point are the fundamentals of the system, as defined by the League of Communists hierarchy, exposed to public challenge; at no point is Party dominance formally contested. The way the Yugoslav Communist leaders interpret their own roles, however, makes this less of a restraint than it might otherwise appear to be.[2]

Thus Westerners who challenge the Yugoslav insistence that the new system injects democracy into socialism are correct as far as the concept of political democracy is understood, say, in the United States. Not only do the Yugoslavs not claim such democracy, but they vehemently reject it. The new Yugoslav institutions are designed for a system that lies somewhere between Soviet-type totalitarianism and Western political democracy, although closer to the former than to the latter. While the form and theory of institutions are not as important as how they work, still institutions themselves invariably have a powerful effect on a system. This has been the case in Yugoslavia. If it is possible to have such an in-between system, the institutions of Titoism would seem well fitted to provide it. These institutions are still in the process of being worked out, but the basic pattern appears to be set. In the first five or six years after their expulsion from the Cominform, the Yugoslavs used to say, almost as a ritual, "We are searching for our way." Most of them now think that, by and large, they have found it.

[1] *Ibid.*, p. 140.
[2] For further discussion of this point, see Chapter 19.

THE DECENTRALIZED

ECONOMIC SYSTEM

THE Yugoslav economic system is unique and complex. It is socialist: in industry and commerce there is no private ownership except for occasional small service establishments and some retail food stores, yet there is not state ownership; and agriculture is carried on mainly by private peasants.[1] The Yugoslav economy is planned; at the same time it is decentralized, and economic enterprises are not administered by the state. The bevy of government ministries and councils for running industries singly or in groups has been abolished. Operating under management of their workers, enterprises are legally independent and function in a competitive and comparatively free market. Within limits and with some exceptions, they autonomously decide what to produce and how much, what prices to sell their products for and to whom, and what to do with the proceeds. The one general requirement for all of them, as for business under capitalism, is that they operate profitably.[2]

There is a Plan, but in hardly any respect is it like the plan in the Soviet Union and other Communist countries. The Yugoslav Plan is not binding on the enterprises. It does not "decree" the production of specific quantities of this and that, at such and such prices, either for the nation as a whole or for individual producing units. Instead, the government relies on indirect controls — as well as on a series of potent social pressures — to channel economic activity in desired directions and on the initiative of workers and managers, stimulated by the incentive of personal gain, to foster the desired amounts of production.

[1] For a discussion of the agricultural system, see Chapter 15.

[2] A relatively few enterprises operate "profitably" only because of indirect subsidies. Most of these are enterprises producing for export, where the subsidy is in the form of foreign exchange benefits. See pp. 258–261.

239

In the decade that this decentralized socialism has existed, constant changes in the system of controls and incentives have whittled away at the freedom of action of individual enterprises in many spheres of activity. Nevertheless, the economics of Titoism—at least in regard to its mechanics—still includes almost as many characteristics of Keynesianism as of Marxism. The ideas of competition and freedom from government intervention have at times seemed to be nearly as central to Yugoslav Communism as to Eisenhower Republicanism, only, of course, with somewhat different ends in view.

The Yugoslav system, in the judgment of an eminent Swedish scholar, has "succeeded in blending the principles of free enterprise and collective ownership."[1] The question of ownership, however, is complex. If enterprises are neither privately owned nor state owned, who does own them? Yugoslav lawyers themselves are perplexed by the question. The theory is that there is "social ownership" by the nation as a whole but not formal ownership by the state. Although in practice most of the usual attributes of ownership fall to the organs of worker-management and the local governments to which they are responsible, neither of these bodies "own" enterprises.

Worker-Management

Perhaps the key institution of the Yugoslav economic system is the workers' council. Each individual economic enterprise operates under a workers' council and is, at least in theory, a free and autonomous unit. The extent to which the theory is also fact, however much less than some Yugoslavs are wont to claim, is nevertheless considerable.

Workers' councils were first established by a law enacted on July 2, 1950.[2] Under this law, the basic features of which have been maintained intact, all the workers in an enterprise elect a council which has general responsibility for operations, including determination of how and what to produce, prices, wages, investment, and distribution of surpluses. The workers' council (*radnički savet*) actually functions, as far as day-to-day decisions are concerned, through a management board (*upravni odbor*) which it elects from among its members. In some respects, a workers' council can be thought of as a board of directors of a corporation and the management board as its executive committee.

A workers' council consists of from 15 to 200 members, depending on the size of the enterprise, and where fewer than 30 persons are employed the

---

[1] Prof. Elis Hästad, "Types of Nationalized Industry," paper delivered at the International Political Science Association, Rome, September 17, 1958.

[2] "General Law on Management of Economic Enterprises and Higher Economic Associations by Workers' Collectives." See *Službeni List*, No. 43, July 5, 1950.

workers' council is composed of all employees. Up until 1958, members of workers' councils and management boards were elected for one year. Now, as a result of an overwhelming demand from worker-management bodies, the term is two years.

Three-quarters of the membership of a management board — which ranges from three to seventeen in size — must be actual workers "directly engaged in production or otherwise in the basic productive activity of the enterprise." Only one-third of the members may be re-elected for successive terms. The management board is charged with overseeing day-to-day operations, working out proposals for the enterprise's production plan, setting wages, hours, etc. All of its decisions are subject to reversal by the workers' council, and most of them are formally submitted to the council for approval.

Decentralization and worker-management in larger enterprises has now been carried a step further than a workers' council representing an entire firm. "Little workers' councils" — *radnički savet pogona* — have been established for various divisions within an enterprise, both on a functional basis as well as where a firm has separate branches. The "little workers' councils" are subordinate to the general workers' councils of an enterprise, able to make recommendations to it but having only such powers as the general council permits. Under this system, election to the general workers' councils is in a sense indirect, members being elected by the smaller bodies — where they exist — and there is duplication of membership.[1]

The director or manager of an enterprise, who is an ex-officio member of the management board, is appointed by a commission consisting of members of the workers' council, the people's committee (local government) and the industry-wide chamber representing all workers' councils in a given economic field. Appointment is usually made on the basis of a competitive examination. The workers' council may petition the people's committee for dismissal of a director. In this case, a commission is again established. If the commission decides against firing the director but the workers' council still insists on it, then a new workers' council must be elected. If the new council again demands dismissal, then this must be ordered by the people's committee. Although Party and trade union influences are often arrayed against the workers' council in these matters, charges against a director stand more often than not. The commissions are now composed half of workers' council members, and the local government representatives are from that chamber elected by workers. The proportion of removals of enterprise managers directly by the local governments has also been increasing.

[1] *Službeni List*, No. 8, February 22, 1956. See also discussion of *radnički savet pogona* by Ivan Božečević, secretary-general of the trade union Sindikat in *Medjunarodna Politika*, July 1958.

The manager of a factory or other enterprise, however, still has consider-able powers, and some ambiguity about his position is a frequent cause of conflict. The director is the "highest employee," according to the statute, and while he "independently settles current problems" he must do so "in conformity with decisions" of the worker-management organs. However, the manager may, in certain cases, appeal decisions of the worker-manage-ment bodies to the local government. While some managers of enterprises unquestionably dominate their workers' councils and management boards, the reverse is also often true.

During the first years of the workers' councils, they had less restricted authority to fire directors, and, initially, a wave of dismissals took place. There is still much higher turnover than in the pre-workers' council period, but the situation has stabilized itself comparatively. In 1956, for instance, out of a total of 6,079 managers of enterprises, only 502 were dismissed. Causes for dismissal included laxity in the case of 82 dismissals, economic crimes in the case of 59 and "other reasons" for 422. The workers' bodies initiated 168 firings, governmental bodies (in most cases local governments) 314 and the Party 20.[1]

When the workers' councils were first established, a good measure of direct state control was maintained. In place of the abolished federal and republic ministries dealing with industry was created a complex series of government councils, boards and committees, empowered to designate directors for groups of industries and generally supervise operations of various branches of the economy. The worker-management law itself provided for all factories in a given industry to be organized in a "higher economic associa-tion." These higher economic associations were to operate under the govern-ment bodies, but they themselves were to have workers' councils elected by the workers' councils in the factories comprising an entire industry.

This arrangement, however, was only a sort of transition to more complete decentralization and increased worker-management. The interim system was cumbersome, and the precise relationships between the several government bodies and the industry-wide managers on the one hand and the individual enterprises and the higher economic associations on the other were never clearly spelled out.[2]

---

[1] *Congress of Workers' Councils of Yugoslavia*, Central Council of the Confederation of Trade Unions of Yugoslavia, Belgrade, 1957, p. 57.

[2] For a discussion of this interim system, see Fred Warner Neal, "Certain Aspects of the New Reforms in Yugoslavia," *University of Colorado Studies*, Series in Political Science, No. 1, June 1953, especially pp. 58–60. See also Alexander Adamovitch, "Yugoslavia: Industrial Manage-ment," *Highlights of Current Activities in Mid-Europe*, Library of Congress Mid-European Law Project, March–April 1957.

Consequently, by 1953, both the government control bodies and the directors they appointed, as well as the higher economic associations, were eliminated. Each enterprise was now a self-governing unit, subject only to supervision by local governments and to indirect federal and republic controls.[1]

This extreme form of decentralization produced near-chaos in some sectors of the economy. As might have been expected, the first thing workers' councils did was to raise wages, and to pay them they had to raise prices. Increases in production were by no means commensurate with the price increases, especially since there was a wave of highly uneconomic investment. A serious inflationary trend was started, and in 1954 Svetozar Vukmanović-Tempo, then the government's top overseer of economic affairs, complained that "the entire system has entered a blind alley."[2]

The Chambers

To get the system running more smoothly, the Yugoslavs were forced to go in for various forms of "recentralization," although the principle of decentralization was maintained. More direct controls were imposed, and something like the former higher economic associations was established, but now formally outside the governmental framework. Under the system as it operated after 1954, firms were grouped in self-governing associations and *komora* or chambers, according to their type of economic activity. Membership at first was voluntary, except for foreign trade firms. The associations of a given type of economic activity were grouped under a chamber, although individual enterprises also were members of chambers. Thus, for example, the most important chamber, that for industry, was composed both of industrial firms and of associations representing various industrial categories. Whereas the chambers were seen as laying down broad policies, the associations' function was to make recommendations — not legally binding — on promotion of production and sales and on business practices generally, to represent their members before government bodies and in obtaining bank credit, and to combat the tendencies of individual workers' councils to follow their own interests at the expense of the national interest.

The associations are forbidden to engage in any economic activity as such. However, certain groupings of enterprises engaged in the same type of activities are permitted to join together for making credit applications for purchases, construction and even use of facilities. Despite strict laws against monopolistic practices, such practices are not infrequent and are sometimes

---

[1] For a list of enactments accomplishing this transformation and their specific provisions, see Jovan Djordjević, *Ustavno Pravo (Constitutional Law)*, Arhiva za Pravne i Društvene Nauke, Belgrade, 1953, pp. 102–115.

[2] *Borba*, October 23, 1954.

facilitated by relationships afforded not only by the groupings but also by associations and chambers.

In 1958 membership in chambers was made obligatory for all enterprises, and representatives of governmental bodies became members of the chambers' governing organs, along with representatives of the member-enterprises. Although not all decisions of the chambers were legally binding, they were increasingly assigned semi-governmental functions in connection with preparing and enforcing government regulations. In addition, government administrative organs were empowered to hold up such action of the chambers as they considered illegal, subject to review by the Supreme Economic Court. Regulation of some sort, in fact, became virtually the sole function of the chambers, while industrial and other associations of enterprises engaged in the same general type of activity were now exclusively concerned with production methods, markets and the like. Affiliation with these associations remained voluntary, although few enterprises did not belong to one or another. The associations operated under the supervisory aegis of the chambers.[1]

This giving of the chambers a "social character" — that is, making them representative not only of enterprises but also of government — and assigning them regulatory powers is illustrative of the Yugoslav concept of having what would otherwise be governmental functions performed outside the formal framework of government. Thus it was possible to cite the new position of the chambers as a continuation of decentralization, while, in fact, insofar as it further delimited the power of individual workers' councils, it was really a form of greater centralization.

Party – Union Control

In addition to direct and indirect government controls, the chambers and the role of the manager, the workers' councils have also been subjected to the powerful influences of the League of Communists and the Sindikat, the trade union organization. Although Party units exist in all larger enterprises, there seemed to be few cases of *direct* Party intervention in management. These were formally ruled out by the Party itself after 1952. Following the Party's "tightening up" in 1956, instances of conflict between Party units and directors and worker-management bodies began to appear, but in 1958 such interference was again frowned upon.

Generally speaking, the Party has tried to work through the workers' councils and the Sindikat, particularly the latter, because, while the Party clearly controlled the trade unions, it did not control the workers' councils. As of 1958, there were 220,656 members of workers' councils, of whom only

[1] Law on Economic Organization, *Službeni List*, No. 1, January 2, 1958.

60,012, or 27.1 per cent, were also members of the League of Communists. In individual workers' councils, the extent of Party membership was spotty, running as high as 85 per cent in some cases and as low as 10 per cent in others. Of the 68,836 members of management boards in 1958, 25,569, or more than 38 per cent, were in the Party.[1] Of course, Party influence was usually greater than the percentage of Party members would indicate.

Party control via the trade union Sindikat has been a more significant factor. Nearly all Communists employed in economic enterprises belong to the Sindikat, and its president, Vukmanović-Tempo, is a member of the Executive Committee of the Party. The Sindikat has played an increasingly important role, more in protecting the "national interest" than in protecting the interests of workers as such. This, of course, is the traditional role of trade unions in a Communist country, which leads unionists in the West to deny that they are trade unions at all.

In all Communist countries, the theoretical justification for such a trade union function is that, since the workers run the state, there is no "capitalist exploitation" from which workers must be protected. What this theory has meant in practice, as in the USSR, is that the unions are primarily an instrumentality of state control over workers. In Yugoslavia, where the workers in fact do run their factories to a considerable extent, the theory that unions are not needed to protect workers against management can perhaps be argued with more validity, despite the fact that workers' councils have shown themselves capable of a certain degree of exploitation, bureaucracy and abuse of privilege.[2]

In any event, the Yugoslav government and Party do depend to a large extent on the Sindikat to curb excesses of workers' councils, and union officials see their task as representing the broad, national interest as well as individual groups of workers. Nearly all the members of workers' councils belong to the union organization.[3] The law originally gave the Sindikat a privileged position in drawing up lists of candidates for workers' council elections. This provision was eliminated in 1958, but it did not appear to have resulted in any diminution of union influence. Indeed, the advent of the dynamic Vukmanović-Tempo to the presidency of the Sindikat in the spring of 1958 meant that the union organization was to play an even greater role. Its role was the stronger because the local union officials were often in a position to provide valuable advice on technical and other matters. In addition, the

[1] *Komunist*, April 16, 1959. See also Table 12–4.

[2] See report of Djuro Salaj, president of the Sindikat, *Congress of Workers' Councils of Yugoslavia*, pp. 13–37.

[3] In 1956, of 121,648 members of workers' councils, 121,204 were members of the Sindikat. *Ibid.*, p. 55.

Sindikat handles recruitment and training of new workers and runs the workers' universities — both of which are important in Yugoslavia, where there has been a continuing influx of peasants into industry and where the educational level is generally low.

At the beginning of the workers' council system, Tito declared that its real implementation depended "on the pace of cultural development" and that "for poor peasants who have for centuries been vegetating at the lowest possible cultural level and standard of living . . . this will not be an easy or a rapid task." It has not been easy, but in some ways it has been more rapid than Tito anticipated. After a decade of workers' councils, more than two-thirds of all persons employed in the economy had served on them. (See Table 12–4.) Many, both in Yugoslavia and abroad, continue to question the extent to which these workers really run their own enterprises. That the extent, however much less than claimed, is considerable is indicated by the questions of others as to whether they are running them well or not. These questions will be answered in part by the performance of the Yugoslav economy, in part by how far the regime considers it necessary to restrict workers' council autonomy. After a decade of the system, one can only report that, despite many unresolved problems, the economy is going forward and that, despite many restrictions, the area of workers' council autonomy still is wide.

Planning

How autonomous, worker-managed enterprises fit into a planned socialist system is indicated by an examination of how planning is carried out. Planning proceeds at several levels simultaneously. For while the federal government's annual Social Plan is the basic instrument, republics, districts, communes, individual enterprises and economic chambers representing groups of enterprises all have their own plans, more or less independent of each other legally. The Federal Plan itself is in part a plan for other plans — since lesser planning units are expected to coordinate their efforts with it — and in part a summary of other plans, since it is based to a considerable extent on estimates made by the smaller units.

The Federal Planning Institute, operating under the economic secretariat of the Federal Executive Council, sets the planning ball in motion by making estimates of national income broken down into use categories.[1] There follows a decision on broad, general goals — the production of capital goods, build-

---

[1] National income, as figured by Yugoslav planners, is based on goods and productive services. These include wages, profits and taxes but exclude government salaries, income of the liberal professions, and income from personal services.

ing, consumer goods, etc. Then general investment funds are worked out. These are divided into economic investment, leading directly to production, and noneconomic investment, for public services such as hospitals and schools. Finally there is a determination of production targets, not for specific commodities but only for basic materials and certain key items.

All these computations are based in part on estimates made in the plans of individual enterprises, chambers and lower governmental units. The enterprise plans are coordinated both by the chambers and the communes in their respective plans. The commune plans are coordinated into a district plan, the district plans into a republic plan, and the republic plans into the Federal Plan.[1] Thus the Federal Plan assumes certain levels of economic activity by individual enterprises and republic and local governments. It also involves estimates of wages, prices, and domestic and foreign trade. It is able to influence considerably but by no means control absolutely.

When the Federal Plan is finally drawn up, the planners at other governmental levels and in the enterprises reconsider their own plans. In the whole process there is endless conferring among Federal Plan officials and the planners at lower levels, including, especially, those of the chambers.

Although the Federal Plan is adopted as law by the Skupština, its production and other figures are not legally binding, nor are they assigned either to individual units of government or to individual enterprises. Therefore the figures in the non-Federal plans do not necessarily add up to those of the Federal Plan since the former may be — and usually are — smaller or larger. In general, however, the total divergence is not great.

There is also a Five Year Plan,[2] and it seemed likely that an even longer range prospective plan would be worked out. The Five Year Plan is neither functional nor detailed, and its chief use is to furnish guidance to enterprises and local governments in drawing up their annual plans. The 1957 Five Year Plan, for example, foresaw development of resources as shown in Table 14–1, and this program, in turn, was elaborated each year in the annual plans.

To influence the economy in such a way that the appropriate allocation is generally achieved, along with the desired production, the Annual Social

[1] Republic plans involve comparatively smaller investments and tend to concentrate primarily on coordinating functions. Some Yugoslav economists feel that republic plans are less important than others. There has been discussion of eliminating republic plans as such and including their investment provisions in republic budgets. On the other hand, others — especially economists in Croatia and Slovenia — oppose such a move and insist that republic plans are important for both economic and political reasons.

[2] Five Year Plans under the present system were initiated in 1957, although an earlier Five Year Plan was abandoned following the break with the Cominform. The 1957 Plan was completed in four years. A new Five Year Plan was promulgated in December 1960 and is scheduled to run between 1961–1965. Certain industries operate under broad general plans with a time span of as much as fifteen years.

Table 14–1

ALLOCATION AND RATE OF INCREASE OF RESOURCES UNDER
FIVE YEAR PLAN, 1956–1961

	Million Dinars at 1956 Prices		Percentage Increase, 1956–61	
	1956	1961	Total	Average Annual
Consumption of raw materials	1,677	2,701	61.1	10.0
Total economic investments	522	701	34.3	6.1
Personal consumption and social standard	979	1,429	46.0	7.9
State organs and national defense	196	216	10.2	2.0
Social reserves and unallocated resources	—	125	—	—

Source: Branko Kubović, Jakov Širotković and Berislav Šefer, *Economic Planning in Yugoslavia*, Jugoslavija, Belgrade, 1959, p. 19.

Plan relies on a series of "basic proportions" aimed at stimulating and controlling the various economic components. These involve direct federal investment, federally determined taxes and interest rates, and wage, price and foreign trade regulations. The "basic proportions" are spelled out in specific laws and decrees known as the "instruments" of the Plan.

Investment

Possibly the most important factor in the Yugoslav economy, rapidly expanding as it is, is capital investment. The rate of capital investment for the whole of the postwar period has been more than 24 per cent of gross national product.[1] (See Table 14–2.) Total investment comprises federal, republic and local government funds as well as funds of individual enterprises. The trend has increasingly been for more investment to come from local (especially enterprise) rather than federal sources. (See Table 14–3.) Government units originally provided investment capital directly out of budgets, but now the bulk of it comes from specially financed, continuing investment funds. The most important of these is the Federal Central Investment Fund, administered by the Investment Bank. This fund is financed for the most part by fixed charges on capital installations and interest paid on loans, and into it also are fed a large part of foreign credits. The theory of the capital charges is that the capital legally belongs to the community, rather than to an individual enterprise, and therefore its use must be paid for.

[1] Augustin Papić, "Investments in Economic Development of Yugoslavia," *Vesnik*, Jugoslovenske Investicione Banke (Special English Supplement), Belgrade, March 1958. The gross investment figure includes private investment amounting to about 11 per cent of the total during the period 1952–1956.

Table 14–2

GROSS NATIONAL PRODUCT AND CAPITAL INVESTMENT, 1952–1958

(*Billions of Dinars*)

Year	Gross National Product		Capital Investment	
	Amount	Percentage Increase Over Preceding Year	Amount	As Per Cent of Gross National Product
1952	949	—	245	25.8
1953	1,134	—	295	26.0
1954	1,299	19.5	365	28.1
1955	1,552	19.5	394	25.4
1956	1,612	3.9	403	25.0
1957	1,990	23.4	480	24.1
1958	2,017	1.4	564	28.0

Source: Statistički Godišnjak FNRJ, 1959, p. 100, and information received from Investment Bank.

Note: Yugoslavs speak of Social Product (Društveni Proizvod), which denotes what we call GNP, although it is based on a less comprehensive definition than GNP, i.e., it excludes certain services like government, professional services, etc.

National income in Yugoslav statistical terminology is the amount of social product less depreciation.

The annual Social Plan determines the total amount of money available from the Central Investment Fund as well as amounts available for different segments of industry and for general borrowing without respect to end use. Sometimes, but increasingly rarely, the Plan provides for direct allocations from the Fund to specific enterprises. For example, the big reclamation and irrigation projects in the Vojvodina are financed in this way. For the most part, however, enterprises have borrowed from the Central Investment Fund.

The role of republic and local governments, especially the commune, in the acquisition and allocation of investment funds was substantially increased by regulations adopted in 1961. These funds are financed by taxes, in part federally determined, and in some cases by federal allocations, although the expenditure is solely in the hands of the local governments. Plans called for establishment of "investment institutes," operating under commune banks, which would both grant original credit and distribute credit from federal and republic sources. The new system was designed also to increase the amount of investment made by enterprises out of their own funds, since the distinction between fixed and working assets was abolished and the decision as to how much of the common fund to use for investment was left up to the workers' council.[1] Thus an enterprise may add to its capital equipment through its own funds, by borrowing from the Central Investment Fund or by receiving credits or allocations from republic and local investment funds. Direct federal budget grants to an enterprise are rare. (See Tables 14–3 and 14–4.)

[1] *Politika*, February 23, 1961.

Table 14–3

SOURCES OF INVESTMENT CAPITAL, 1954 AND 1957

Source	Billions of Dinars		Per Cent of Total	
	1954	1957	1954	1957
Total	365	481	100.0	100.0
Federal government	185	165	50.4	34.5
From Central Investment Fund	124	130	34.0	27.1
Republic governments	44	38	12.0	7.7
Local governments	42	101	11.5	20.8
Enterprises	95	151	26.1	31.5
From funds at free disposal	62	62	17.1	12.9
From depreciation funds	33	89	9.0	18.6
Others[a]	—	26	—	5.5

Source: Yugoslav Investment Bank, prepared from *Investicije 1947–1958*, Belgrade, 1959.
[a] Includes investment funds of government bodies, institutions and social organizations.

Table 14–4

THE FORMATION AND SPENDING
OF INVESTMENT FUNDS IN 1954 AND 1957

(*Billions of Dinars*)

	1954		1957	
	Receipts	Outlays	Receipts	Outlays[a]
Total	431.0	401.1	615.6	568.9
Federation	128.7	153.7	167.0	171.1
Central Investment Fund	109.0	127.4	156.4	158.0
Budget	19.7	26.3	5.3	7.8
Special social funds	—	—	5.3	5.3
People's republics	49.1	63.2	56.5	42.6
Investment funds	25.1	38.2	27.9	17.9
Housing funds	—	—	7.6	3.4
Budget	24.0	25.0	6.3	6.6
Special social funds	—	—	14.7	14.7
People's committees	47.9	40.1	111.4	116.9
Investment funds	22.9	16.1	44.0	49.5
Housing funds	—	—	45.4	45.4
Budget	25.0	24.0	7.4	7.4
Special social funds	—	—	14.6	14.6
Government organs and institutions	21.9	18.1	30.2	25.9
Economic organizations	183.4	126.0	250.5	212.4
Resources at the free disposal of the organizations	45.1	39.8	70.7	73.2
Depreciation funds	138.3	86.2	179.8	139.2

Source: Statistički Bilten (Narodna Banke FNRJ), No. 2, 1959.
[a] Outlays for working assets (27.3 billion dinars) included.

Much attention has been focused on Yugoslav utilization of competitive interest rates as a method of parceling out investment funds. Between 1954 and 1957, so-called investment auctions were the main method of allocating almost half of the funds available, those enterprises offering the highest interest rates getting the credit.[1] Although competitive interest bidding is still a factor, it is now less important and only one of a number of criteria. In allocating funds, the Investment Bank considers also how much an enterprise puts up out of its own resources, the terms for repayment, the time involved in construction, the profitability of the project, the ratio of investment per unit of output and the foreign exchange effect.[2] In its decisions, the Bank relies on special *ad hoc* technical commissions set up to consider applications from enterprises and, increasingly, on opinions of chambers and trade associations.

Whereas formerly competitive interest bidding was also the method for allocating short-term credit, now it plays hardly any role at all in this connection. Interest rates on short-term loans are fixed by the Bank and the funds parceled out among applicants which qualify.

One reason why the interest rate is no longer so significant as a control mechanism is that enterprises had a tendency to bid recklessly, without respect to their ability to repay. Thus there existed the anomalous condition — especially apparent in regard to short-term borrowing — that the higher the interest rate, the greater the amount of borrowing.

For long-term capital borrowing, enterprises are now invariably required to finance from their own resources part of the project for which funds are sought. In addition, a percentage of the loan must be underwritten by a commune people's committee or deposited with the bank by the enterprise itself. Similar guarantees are usually required also for short-term borrowing.

Since individual enterprises and local governments have their own funds for investment purposes, actual total investment invariably exceeds the estimate in the Federal Plan. A recurring problem has been — in one sense — not too little investment but too much, resulting in inflationary pressure and in unwise spending from the point of view of over-all national economic goals.

In 1959 more than two-thirds of all investment was financed by funds expended by republic and local governments and by enterprises. The Yugoslavs, properly, cite this as evidence of the extent of their decentralization. It is obvious, though, that the federal government exerts an influence upon much more than the one-third of investment financed directly by Belgrade.

[1] For a description, see Egon Neuberger, "The Yugoslav Investment Auctions," *Quarterly Journal of Economics*, February 1959, pp. 88–115.

[2] See Filip Vasić, "The Yugoslav System of Investment Financing and the Application of Criteria in the Selection of Investment Projects," *Engineering Economist*, Fall 1960, pp. 1–8.

It does this through budget allocations to republic and local governments and by the fact that a large part of the funds available to these units from their own sources is determined by tax rates fixed in federal laws. Even though such funds often must be used for certain specific areas of investment, there is no federal control over actual expenditure. Indirect pressure is exerted through the League of Communists and the trade unions, however, and, increasingly, as far as enterprises are concerned, through the chambers and trade associations. Furthermore, the federal government at times has stepped in to prevent use of certain investment funds by temporary sequestration. Nevertheless, it remains true that direct federal controls over investment have diminished considerably.[1]

Prices: Free, Controlled and Influenced

With investment provided for, from its own or other funds, the individual enterprise must then turn its attention to the prices it will charge for the goods produced. A major, but by no means the only, factor in determining prices in Yugoslavia is competition according to the law of supply and demand. The result is that similar products are sold by one enterprise for one price, by another for a different price,[2] and that prices vary from place to place. At the same time, Yugoslavia's free enterprise economy is not free of such capitalistic vices as monopoly and price collusion, although these are rigorously combated by the government.

As might be expected, once worker-management of enterprises really got underway, a general increase in wages quickly followed. The money for the increases had to be obtained by raising prices, so up went the price level, and a round of inflation began. During the first half of 1954, retail prices rose by 9 per cent, wholesale prices by 8 per cent. Under Yugoslav neo-classical economic theory, some high prices should be corrected by the law of supply and demand rather than by government intervention. But the law of supply and demand worked ineffectively because of generally short supplies and the practically insatiable demand for everything. Constant new investment requiring expansion of the money supply inhibited control by fiscal measures. The limited number of producers and the inability to import because of foreign exchange shortages placed many enterprises in near-monopolistic positions. And monopolies in Yugoslavia's laissez-faire Communism acted just like monopolies everywhere; they influenced the market rather than vice versa.

[1] See discussion of this matter in United Nations, Economic Commission for Europe, "Economic Planning and Management in Yugoslavia," *Economic Bulletin for Europe*, Vol. X, No. 3, 1958, p. 50.

[2] Although the law of supply and demand theoretically should produce uniform prices for similar products in a given area, as in the United States goods more attractively displayed or better advertised can sometimes command higher prices than warranted by their quality or usefulness.

As a result, beginning in 1955, price and wage control measures were instituted. These measures, in their various forms, have helped curb the galloping inflation which threatened the country. The wage controls are discussed below. Of the price controls it should be said that the government adopted them reluctantly,[1] has used them sparingly and still relies more on indirect than on direct means to influence prices. Where price fixing was resorted to, the government at first justified the departure from its laissez-faire position on the grounds that "monopolistic" prices were not "a purely economic matter but become a question of politics and ethics."[2] But gradually price control of some sort came to be applied to a wide variety of items.

Major federal controls affect mainly industrial and wholesale prices. The federal government in 1958 set specific prices only for tobacco, sugar and gasoline, and, in effect, coal.[3] Generally fixed but permitted slight fluctuations were the prices of steel, refined lead, aluminum and drugs. Transportation prices are also fixed at the federal level, with some ensuing republic authority. For electric power, there is a federal maximum price; below this, local people's committees may act. Such price fixing is contained in the Annual Social Plan, although changes may be made by Federal Executive Council decree.

Federal price stabilization authority by no means ends there, however. A Federal Price Office (Ured za Cene), even though it acts formally only through the Federal Executive Council, has sweeping authority to curb price increases. Any industrial producer or wholesaler (foodstuffs excepted) who wants to increase prices must notify the Federal Price Office one month in advance. In many instances advance notice of price increases also must be given to trade associations.

Upon receipt of such notice, the Federal Price Office may, after investigation, publicly declare a price increase unjustified. The Price Office cannot itself prevent the increase. What it may do is advise the Federal Executive Council to take action in regard to amounts or prices of materials believed responsible for the price pressure and, in some cases, even to fix the price in question temporarily.

In addition, a 1958 law — applicable to all prices at all levels — prohibited any income found to be due to "unjustified" price increases from being used to increase wages. Such increased income could be used for investment,

---

[1] In the late fall of 1954, *Borba*, responding to complaints about high prices, declared: "The market prices are primarily an economic question. That is why it is impossible to find a legal solution. . . ." (November 21, 1954.)

[2] See statement of Federal Executive Council, *ibid.*

[3] The price of coal was officially considered "frozen," that is, the existing price was not permitted to change without permission. The ceiling was lifted in 1961.

however, subject to the permission of the commune people's committee. Every enterprise must report semi-annually to the commune producers' council the amount of income resulting from price increases. The producers' council may order all or part of this sum sequestered for six months. Local governments have further price powers, especially at the retail level and in regard to foodstuffs. They may fix the price of bread and may require advance notice of all retail price increases and of increases in the price of food at both wholesale and retail levels.

One indirect price control was the turnover tax, applied on finished goods at the producers' level in two ways. When utilized to help balance supply and demand — chiefly of consumer goods — it was directly reflected in wholesale and retail prices. Where it was assessed as a penalty in case of "unjustified" price increases, the amount of the tax was not permitted to be passed on.

Generally speaking, wholesale prices have been more stable than retail. Taking 1958 as 100, wholesale prices varied from 96 in 1953 to 99 in 1959.[1] Retail prices have fluctuated but have maintained a steady advance since 1952. The general index of retail prices for the first eight months of 1960 was up 5.9 per cent over the comparable period for 1959,[2] and further increases were apparent in 1961.

How indirect government controls sometimes amount to price fixing is illustrated by the pricing of black bread.[3] Theoretically, the price of wheat is not fixed. However, cooperatives — subject to the jurisdiction of their chamber as well as to government laws and decrees — are the chief buyers of wheat. The cooperatives agree on the price they will offer, and the government backs them up by selling to them at these prices wheat from reserve stocks should farmers be reluctant to sell. Rail and other transportation is offered to the buying cooperatives at special rates, lower than to other commercial users. The cooperatives do not get all the wheat, and some of it is sold at prices higher than they offer. Nevertheless, there is always a "mean price" for wheat sold for coarse flour. In 1958, for example, this was 36 dinars per kilo. The price of coarse flour, therefore, averaged 44.5 dinars per kilo that year and the price of black bread 46 dinars per kilo.[4] (This was the Belgrade price. The price of bread, like other items, varies from place to place.)

Flour for white bread, on the other hand, comes from wheat not subject to this kind of government operation, and the price for white bread — higher

[1] *Statistički Godišnjak FNRJ*, 1960, p. 244.

[2] *Borba*, October 3, 1960.

[3] Black bread is a coarse, dark, whole wheat bread, often containing other cereals.

[4] Effective February 20 1961 the price was set at 56 dinars per kilo.

in any event — generally fluctuates according to supply and demand, without administrative interference. The price of white bread, of course, is not as important as that of black bread, which is known in Yugoslavia as "people's bread" and is a staple of the diet.

The cooperative buying organization price agreements on wheat and other agricultural commodities tend to be as much in the nature of price guarantees to peasants as otherwise. Retail prices of most farm products, however, are neither as stable nor as uniform as is the price of bread. This is true because farm products are often sold directly by peasants to consumers and because retail outlets themselves often buy directly from the countryside.

Price subsidies are another form of indirect price control in agriculture. They are applied to a small number of items, such as tractors, tractor fuels, purebred animals and certain types of fertilizers, the purpose being chiefly to encourage modernization of agriculture.

Officials have viewed price control as only temporary. Vice President Mijalko Todorović declared in early 1961 that the plan was "to pass on gradually to a system of free prices, to abolish ceiling and fixed prices on a wider area." However, he added that for a time there would be "firmer control of prices than ever because attempts can be made to speculate in this important transitional period."[1]

Wages, Profits[2] and Taxes

The central problem in regard to wages and profits has been how to allow workers' councils freedom and autonomy and at the same time make sure that increases result from greater production and not merely from price increases and unwise distribution of income. The price controls described above are one method of getting at the problem. Wage regulations and taxes comprise another, and one where the Yugoslavs have had much difficulty finding the right formula.

When the decentralized economy was launched, workers' councils had wide latitude in fixing wages above "average minimum" levels set for categories of producers. At first, excessive increases were combated by sliding scale penalty taxes above an "average maximum," and in 1955 local taxing power was relied on. Neither method worked adequately, however, especially in relating wage increases to productivity. In 1957, the authority of workers'

[1] *Borba*, February 25, 1961.

[2] The term "profit" has a somewhat different connotation in socialist Yugoslavia than in capitalist countries, since in the socialist sector it does not accrue as such to private individuals. Since it does, however, signify a return to the collective on capital investment and is distributed, in part, to those who comprise the collective, we are using the term here without regard to the difference.

councils to fix wages was sharply restricted by an extremely complicated set of regulations. Workers' councils were required to set aside certain portions of the earnings into various enterprise funds, including a minimum wage fund. Then they fixed their own wage schedules, based on industry-wide norms and subject to approval of both commune producers' councils and commune trade union committees. Before actual wage payments were made, however, an enterprise had to determine its income for federal profits tax purposes by deducting charges on fixed and turnover capital, depreciation, land rent, material costs, and, in the case of producers of consumer goods, a turnover tax. The profits tax was then figured on the basis of relationship of the "income," as thus determined, to the minimum wage fund.[1] Having paid its profits tax, the enterprise was not yet free to dispose of what it had left. Another progressive tax was first levied, before wage payments, on the actual monthly wages paid out.[2] Nor was that all.

That part of the total wage bill exceeding the minimum level by more than 60 per cent was subject to a 25 per cent federal tax and to a communal tax up to 2.5 per cent. What was left could be utilized by the workers' council as premiums to supplement formal wage payments, although actual monthly wage payments — wages fixed in the schedule plus 75 per cent of the premium due — were still limited to 20 per cent of the scheduled amount for any worker.[3]

The wage system, and price controls and taxes, were primarily intended to restrict enterprise income and wages to returns from efficient and increased production, that is, to curb "profiteering" and guard against further inflation. To a considerable extent they succeeded. In 1954, for example, enterprises often carried out less than planned production but had income far in excess of planned profit. In addition, it was not uncommon for an enterprise producing a non-essential commodity to pay wages far above the industry minimum — as happened in the distillery industry, for example — while adjacent enterprises making more important contributions to the economy paid below the minimum. After 1957 there were few if any such cases. On the other hand, in another sense the controls worked too well. The legal inroads on enterprise income kept wages at levels that, compared with consumer prices, were so low as often to inhibit the very productivity that was sought. A not incon-

[1] Where the income of an enterprise did not exceed its minimum wage fund by more than 25 per cent there was no profits tax. On income above this, rates ranged from 9.4 per cent to 72 per cent.

[2] The rates, levied on the basis of wages paid to each employee, ranged from 10 per cent on 20,000 dinars a month to 40 per cent on 100,000 dinars and over.

[3] This system was confusing to workers, administrators and government officials alike, and the bookkeeping involved was prodigious. For a discussion of its details, see "Economic Planning and Management in Yugoslavia," especially p. 49.

siderable number of workers held two jobs — one in the socialist sector, under a workers' council, and a second working for himself or in a private establishment.[1] The result was that energy and incentive on the socialist job were often sharply reduced.

The regime also sought to increase productivity by encouraging employment of piecework methods. Despite extensive Party and trade union efforts, however, by mid-1960 only one-fourth of all enterprises used some form of piecework. Sharply scolding both workers and managers, *Rad*, organ of the trade union Sindikat, complained that enterprises had responded to a trade union inquiry on the subject with "excuses and nothing else but excuses."[2] But before the end of the year the regime came to the conclusion that a new wage system was called for, again granting more freedom to enterprises.

The new system adopted in 1961 wiped out the wage regulations altogether and provided for determination of wages virtually at the discretion of workers' councils.[3] Enterprises could now themselves determine what portions of income they would allocate to various "funds" for wages, general operations, reserve and consumption. Wage schedules were worked out in two parts: minimum wages available to all workers, based on industry-wide minima determined in the federal plan;[4] and wages dependent on production, that is, piecework. Wage schedules had to be submitted to local producers' councils for comment but not for approval.

To encourage incentive, progressive taxation of enterprise income was eliminated and replaced with proportional rates. Total income was taxed a flat 15 per cent, and aggregate assets 6 per cent. A wide category of enterprises whose output the regime desired to stimulate — consumer goods producers, agricultural organizations, high cost–low profit industries — were exempted from these levies or assessed lower rates.[5]

An additional 15 per cent tax was levied on the amount actually paid out to workers, the proceeds going to local budgets.[6] The amount of the wage

[1] The usual Yugoslav working hours — 7 A.M. to 2 P.M., without a break for lunch — catered to the two-job system.

[2] *Rad*, July 2, 1960.

[3] For detailed discussion of the changes, see report on decisions of the Federal Executive Council in *Politika*, February 23, 1961.

[4] The commune people's committee could, within limits, raise or lower the actual minimum wage fixed by a given workers' council. Where enterprise income was insufficient to meet the minimum, the people's committee contributed to the deficit, and the enterprise made up any difference from its "funds" ordinarily reserved for other purposes.

[5] There were so many of these special cases that the Party's leading economic journal referred to "a system of exceptions." *Ekonomska Politika*, February 18, 1961.

[6] These taxes were levied on and paid by the enterprise. Individuals paid no income tax until 1959, when a progressive levy was adopted affecting the higher income brackets and aimed particularly at members of professions. As amended in 1960, rates were 5 per cent on the first 250,000 dinars above 700,000 net personal income — allowing for dependents' deductions — and increasing 5 per cent for each additional 250,000 dinars.

bill was also subjected to a 24 per cent social security tax and a 4 per cent tax for housing funds. That part of income the enterprise allocated for general business purposes — reserve, investment, etc. — was taxed 20 per cent for local investment purposes. Surplus profits — defined as income above total wage payments in excess of 6 per cent of total capital assets and revolving capital — were taxed at a rate of 25 per cent.[1]

These "radical and important measures," as a high trade union official called them, were designed to better the economic position of consumer goods producers and stimulate productivity generally. They indicated a return to greater reliance on the free market economy and sought to stimulate workers' councils "to a still better running of their businesses."[2] *Borba* compared the significance of the new wage-tax system with that of the original law on worker-management.[3] In any event, the new measures appeared to be a recognition of the difficulties in arriving at a meaningful relationship among prices, costs and profits by non-market mechanisms.

Foreign Trade

The advent of the decentralized economy meant abolition of state trading and gave individual enterprises the right to engage in foreign trade, although limited by certain government restrictions. Considering how short of foreign exchange Yugoslavia was at the time, the restrictions were remarkably few and narrow. In addition to quotas on export of certain items, the major controls involved an incredibly complicated set of "coefficients" for exchanging foreign currency for dinars at varying rates. Enterprises engaging in foreign trade had to transfer half of the foreign exchange earned from any export transaction at the then official rate of 300 dinars to the dollar, but could exchange the remainder at the "free" rate, which fluctuated around 900 dinars to the dollar. Foreign trade concerns could keep accounts in foreign banks and could — within a limited period — use earned foreign currency to make such purchases abroad as desired.

When this system started, many kinds of production and distribution firms tried to carry on their own foreign trade operations. Even though the bulk of foreign trading soon came to be carried on by about thirty big export-import enterprises, exports were inadequately controlled, especially as to quality. Needed foreign exchange was utilized for importing non-essentials. Moreover, since enterprises were mainly interested — ultimately — in their

[1] An innovation adopted at the same time was a special tax on mining enterprises calculated to raise as much as 15 billion dinars in 1961. The revenue was divided among federal, republic and local investment funds on a 70-15-15 basis.

[2] Dragi Stamenković, vice president of the Sindikat, in *Rad*, February 2, 1961.

[3] March 7, 1961.

dinar position, they frequently engaged in deals with both domestic and foreign firms which resulted in depriving the country of "hard" foreign exchange. This situation contributed to the growing balance of payments difficulties.

Although foreign trade is still within the province of individual enterprises, in 1955 foreign exchange transactions were subjected to more controls. These involved the establishment of a federal Chamber of Foreign Trade and a "foreign trade register" under the government's Foreign Trade Committee, and the creation of a Foreign Trade Bank as an adjunct of the National Bank. All enterprises whose major business is exporting and importing must belong to the Foreign Trade Chamber, which lays down rules for operations. In addition, the Chamber maintains the foreign trade register, on which all firms desiring to export must be listed. Before permitting registration, the Chamber looks into their financial and production position, and requires deposits of varying size with the National Bank so as to guarantee their credit. It sets standards of quality, and makes periodic inspections. Firms that fall below standard are subject to removal from the register, in which case they lose their right to participate in foreign trade.

The method for allocating available foreign exchange was in flux as a result of the sweeping 1961 fiscal reform, which abolished the coefficient system altogether and provided for partial foreign currency convertibility.[1] Under the system then adopted, the multiple exchange rates gave way to a uniform rate of 750 dinars to one U. S. dollar for foreign trade purposes.[2] Prior to 1961, the total foreign exchange available, as determined in the social plan, was allocated to various types of users. One portion of it was then sold at varying rates set by the Foreign Trade Bank. Theoretically, any enterprise entitled to engage in foreign trade could buy as long as the supply lasted. Actually, most of this fund was assigned to individual enterprises by the respective trade associations, which resorted to auction in case agreement was not arrived at among the member firms. Another portion of the total foreign exchange available was loaned by the Foreign Trade Bank for repayment later. Legally, this was loaned on the basis of competitive interest rate bidding, but, again, the associations in fact usually worked out distribution in advance. In addition, there was a small "free" fund of foreign currency[3]

---

[1] See *Borba*, December 27, 1960, and Nenad Popović, "Foreign Exchange Reform," *Review of International Affairs*, February 5, 1961.

[2] The "official" rate of 300 dinars to one dollar, set in 1952, technically remained unchanged but it was nowhere applicable. Even prior to 1961, this official rate had little significance. For foreign trade purposes, the base rate was 632 dinars to the dollar. Tourists received 400 dinars and diplomats 600. Under the 1961 change, the tourist rate was 600, with the expectation that it, too, would be increased to 750.

[3] In 1957, for example, the total was only 600 million dinars. This fund was always quickly used up despite the fact that the dinar price for hard currency, especially dollars, was exorbitant.

sold, as long as it lasted, to the highest bidder, without allocation to industrial branches or prior determination of individual users.

Under the coefficient system in force after 1956, the price for foreign currency fixed by the Bank varied — generally between 632 and 900 dinars to a dollar but in some cases as high as 30,000 dinars — depending on the particular currency and the purchases involved. Foreign currency proceeds from exports were sold at once to the National Bank at a rate of 632 dinars to a dollar, less discounts depending on what currency was involved. Although the number of these coefficients was reduced in 1959 from 36 to 11 for exports and from 24 to 9 for imports, the system was confusing to government officials and enterprise foreign trade men alike.[1] The main difficulty, however, was that the system made it virtually impossible for both planners and enterprises to know what the dinar was really worth in terms of either export or import items.

Under the 1961 reform, some foreign trade was permitted with full currency convertibility, some with part convertibility and some with continued full controls. Where the rate involved under the coefficient system was below the new standard rate of 750 dinars to a dollar, the 1961 fiscal-trade reforms represented a devaluation and opened the door for increased exports. Where the rate had been above 750 dinars — as it was in most cases — the new system meant re-evaluation, forcing Yugoslav enterprises to lower costs if they wanted to continue to sell abroad. Subsidies, which in 1961 amounted to 50,000 million dinars, were provided to ease the immediate burden on export-producing industries, but these were to be gradually reduced and eliminated altogether in 1965. Then Yugoslav industry would have to meet world prices or abandon the field.[2]

Under the 1961 changes, imports are controlled by a general system of import duties, now introduced for the first time.[3] The import license system, abandoned in 1959, was reintroduced, but only for some items. About 28 per cent of normal imports were freed of license requirements altogether, with the expectation that this percentage would gradually increase. For such imports, there are no foreign currency restrictions. Another portion of imports was permitted to enter the country only when licenses were obtained, although no foreign exchange controls were involved. Imports in the third category were subject both to licenses and to much of the pre-1961 mechanism for allocating foreign exchange, only now minus coefficients. Even here,

---

[1] In 1958 one of the authors took a hypothetical foreign currency transaction problem to two government economists and two export-import officials. He received four different answers.

[2] See discussion in *Yugoslav Life*, Vol. VI, No. 52, January 1961, pp. 3–4.

[3] Ironically, as a part of the process of becoming a full member of the General Agreement on Tariffs and Trade (GATT), which is devoted to reduction of trade barriers. The general system of import duties, however, meant in fact freer trade than the system of coefficients and other controls which it replaced.

however, indications were that strictly economic, i.e., market, criteria, would become increasingly important.

To help the Yugoslav economy adjust to the freer trading system, the International Monetary Fund and a group of Western countries pledged credits of more than $275 million.[1] The funds were to be used to finance conversion of industries going out of export production, to pay for increased imports and to protect the domestic price and wage level against inflationary pressures.

Problems and Trends

The extent of the relatively free and competitive market character of Yugoslavia's decentralized socialist economy has oscillated back and forth. Although the new foreign exchange system and the renewal of enterprise wage autonomy seemed to indicate a trend toward fewer controls, the economy is doubtless less decentralized and less free now than it was during the first three or four years of its operation. Analyzing this fact, some American economists have expressed concern that the concept of market freedom was being abandoned. Especially the restrictions put on price competition, they felt, were likely to damage the economy by tending to divorce prices from costs, and, in turn, requiring still more administrative measures.[2] Noting the decreasing emphasis on competitive interest bidding in allocation of capital, Professor Egon Neuberger, for instance, believes this unique experiment was never given "a full chance to prove its worth." For the curtailment of the market method of allocating funds, he blames a faulty price system and the lack of "full confidence in the judgment and integrity of managers of enterprises."[3]

In one sense, these are natural and perceptive observations. In another, they are both overdrawn and out of focus. They are overdrawn because, despite the advent of more controls, the essential nature of the Yugoslav economy, as reorganized after 1950, has not only not changed basically but has in some ways been strengthened. They are out of focus because they appear to stem from a Western and capitalist point of view, which is not an adequate basis for judging socialist Yugoslavia.

The fact is that, judged strictly by the criterion of economic efficiency, the Yugoslavs probably decentralized too far and too fast in the 1950–1954 period. It is true that supply and demand, left to themselves, balance ulti-

[1] The U. S. share was $100 million. Other countries involved in the transaction were Austria, Italy, France, Switzerland and the Netherlands, plus a group of West German banks.

[2] See, for example, John Michael Montias, "Economic Reform and Retreat in Yugoslavia," *Foreign Affairs*, January 1959, pp. 293–305.

[3] Neuberger, "The Yugoslav Investment Auctions," p. 114.

mately, one way or another. But the law of supply and demand as a device to serve an economic society presupposes some reasonable point of balance. The economic backwardness of Yugoslavia meant that until production was increased substantially it was difficult to meet even subsistence demands. Under conditions of extremely short supply and extremely heavy demand, the area in which competition works its economic magic is strictly limited. What happened at first was an increase in prices instead of an increase in production, with the former inhibiting the latter.

Yet at the same time the advantages of competition and the law of supply and demand have seldom been better illustrated than in the first four or five years of decentralization in Yugoslavia. If prices were, as Professor Neuberger suggests, unrealistic after 1955, they were far less so than in 1950. For the reliance on free market mechanisms — brutal in many instances — ultimately brought prices generally closer to costs than they had been under the pre-1950 administrative economy.[1] On the whole, the efficient enterprises weathered the storm and profited, and the most inefficient ones were shown up for what they were and in many cases closed down. The 1961 fiscal reform, with its implicit reliance on free market economics, seemed certain to bring a still greater correlation between prices and production costs. Many Yugoslav economists insist that their steadily increasing production means they are meeting the real test of any economic system. Many others feel that until the economic system gives more evidence that it can cope with fiscal problems, it is still too early to make a judgment.[2]

In an economic sense, what the Yugoslavs sought from decentralization and free competition was a correlation between prices and costs, rewards for efficiency and exposure of inefficiency and, above all, increased production. It may well be that, had the regime not imposed any more controls than existed in, say, 1954, there would have been further improvements on all three counts. On the other hand, the initial objectives had been achieved, and, meanwhile, there were some acute problems which themselves grew out of the new economic system. The major one was a serious price inflation. The inflation resulted not only from the tendency of workers' councils generally to raise wages above levels justified by their output, and to boost prices accordingly, but also from uneconomic investment and "economic chauvinism" on the part of local authorities. Moreover, the limited number

---

[1] Kiro Gligorov, Federal Executive Council secretary for economic affairs, told one of the authors in 1958 that domestic prices "generally very nearly" reflected the cost of production and that this was true "to a considerable extent even" of export prices. This latter assessment would probably have been more accurate if made after the 1961 fiscal reform.

[2] The sharp and continuing increase in the cost of living in 1961, although in large part attributable to foreign trade reforms, indicated that this point of view was not without basis.

of producers gave many enterprises a monopoly position, no matter what they did or did not do. In addition, managerial inefficiency — of both workers' councils and directors — was often found in essential industries and could not be eliminated by competition without causing serious harm to the society as a whole.[1]

Such problems would, of course, tempt even a capitalist society to resort to government controls. And when one considers that, in certain respects, the Yugoslav economy in the 1950–1954 period relied in fact on free market mechanisms more than some capitalist countries, the surprising thing is not that government controls increased but that more of them were not instituted.

It must also be remembered that although the concept of free and competitive enterprise is to some extent the same in Yugoslav socialism as in, say, American capitalism, there is an important difference. Both the Yugoslavs and the Americans see in government controls a threat to both economic efficiency and democracy. But in the United States a further major objection to government controls rests in the concept of private ownership. Since, by and large, private ownership of business does not exist in Yugoslavia, government intervention in the economy is considered less of a threat to the system as a whole than in the United States, despite the fact that Yugoslav theory — no less than American theory — regards it as an evil.

Whereas it may be that, having reinstituted certain controls, the Yugoslavs may not be able to avoid going still further along that path, official declarations hold to the contrary. The official view is that as the economy reaches higher levels, there will be less, rather than more, government interference and that, for example, the so-called instruments of the plan will diminish in importance.[2] The 1961 fiscal reform, the new wage system and promises of fewer price controls seemed to point in this direction. It was significant that when a rash of price increases occurred in early 1961, the government permitted them to stand, at least temporarily, on the theory the market would bring them into line.[3]

Furthermore, several important government economic measures have had mixed effects on freedom and autonomy of enterprises. The trend from local to federal taxes, for instance, freed many enterprises from the excessive local taxation that some observers saw as imposing a serious limitation on production.[4] Also, while enterprises were no longer as free to obtain outside capital,

[1] See Fred Warner Neal, *Titoism in Action*, University of California Press, Berkeley, 1958, pp. 143–153.

[2] See the editorial in *Ekonomska Politika*, January 24, 1959, and the statement of Kiro Gligorov in *Borba*, December 15, 1958.

[3] See, for example, discussion in *Rad*, February 25, 1961. The 1961 domestic price increases considerably exceeded official predictions.

[4] See Neal, *Titoism in Action*, p. 148.

in another sense there were fewer federal controls over investment than formerly. Over-all, Yugoslav enterprises had more of their own funds than ever before. As a result, some Yugoslav economists, including those devoted to the concept of "laissez-faire socialism," argued that, at least temporarily, more rather than fewer restrictions were needed on enterprise spending.

It is more difficult to judge the exact extent of "recentralization" and curtailment of enterprise freedom resulting from the development of chambers and trade associations. To the degree that the enterprises themselves, through representatives of their worker-management organs, comprise the chambers and associations, the resulting controls are theoretically self-imposed. Nevertheless, since these organizations are so clearly dominated in one way or another by the "government point of view," the effect is to limit the area of free decision by the individual enterprise. Although the official Yugoslav position is that the chambers and associations should not control enterprise policies, such coordination is considered desirable while formal government intervention is held to be undesirable though often necessary. To the extent that further inroads are made on enterprise autonomy, it is likely that they will come through the chambers and associations rather than through direct government controls. Carried to extremes, such a development could leave the Yugoslav economy free and competitive in name but not in fact. There is no indication, however, that the regime has such intentions.

AGRICULTURE

IN ALL countries where Communists have come to power, the regime has been at war with the peasants. In most instances, the regime has won, and by force, threat and economic penalty agriculture has been largely collectivized. Yugoslavia is unique in that the peasant has won — at least provisionally. After setting out on the same path as their erstwhile comrades elsewhere in Eastern Europe, the Titoists abandoned collectivization. More than 90 per cent of the total farm area, comprising more than 98 per cent of all agricultural holdings, is privately owned, with the peasants free to raise what they wish and to sell their produce for what they can get. But in one sense the peasants' victory does not necessarily represent an ultimate defeat for the regime. Titoism continues to try to build socialism in the villages, but by collaborating with the peasants rather than fighting them, and, in the process, devising new forms and methods.

The new Yugoslav approach to agriculture is concerned not only with questions of socialism but, perhaps even more, with increasing production. As it evolved by 1956, it was focused on expanding the non-private sector in cooperation with private peasants, with greatly increased investment funds available to both. The non-private sector involves Peasant Work Cooperatives, state-owned farms and General Cooperatives.

The Peasant Work Cooperatives — collective farms — are remnants of the Soviet-type *kolkhozi* which the regime tried and failed to foist on the countryside. Today, however, these are organized much like nonagricultural enterprises, under worker-management. Membership is voluntary, although the land is owned and farmed in common, and, indeed, these cooperatives must be profitable or they are likely to be disbanded. Except that they receive certain economic advantages from the government, the Peasant Work Cooperatives operate within the free and competitive market, subject to the same sort of direct and indirect controls as other enterprises. One innovation has been the cooperation between these Peasant Work Cooperatives and nearby private peasants; in some instances private peasants join their land to the cooperatives for production purposes while maintaining ownership. Each member of the Peasant Work Cooperative has, as is the case with the Soviet *kolkhozniki*, a small private plot of his own. In 1959, there were 229 of these Peasant Work Cooperatives, with 24,580 members working an area equal to only 1.2 per cent of the total agricultural area.

State-owned farms and holdings of state agricultural institutes, which operate under direct government supervision and control, are also of importance. They comprised 4.6 per cent of the total agricultural area in 1959.

The most important institution in the Yugoslav effort to build socialism in the villages under conditions of widespread private ownership of land is the General Cooperative. Originally, general cooperatives for the most part operated as cooperative village stores, collectively buying all manner of things for their members. They have now, however, enormously broadened their activities, with the main objective of encouraging private peasants in order to increase production. In 1959, there were 4,803 General Cooperatives, with 1,502,000 members. The General Cooperatives owned a total of only 428,027 hectares, comprising some 2.8 per cent of the farming area.

Perhaps the biggest problem regarding the private peasants — production-wise, at least — is the small size of their holdings. Almost 30 per cent of private holdings are less than two hectares in area, and 40 per cent are between two and five hectares. A majority of private peasant-owners are members of General Cooperatives, and these institutions seek to circumvent the disadvantages of dwarf farms while maintaining private ownership of land.

Importance of Agriculture

The importance of agriculture in the Yugoslav economy and the persistent problem it has presented to the regime is indicated by a few figures. More than 58 per cent of the total land area is classified as agricultural, although only 30 per cent is arable. (See Table 15-1.) In 1939, about 75 per cent of the population drew its income mainly from agriculture; in 1959, 52 per cent. Only about 29 per cent of the national income was derived from agriculture in 1959, as compared with more than 44 per cent in the interwar years.

Low agricultural production — insufficient to meet the country's needs — has been a continuing problem. By far the greatest part of the agricultural land is in small private farms which provide insufficient employment and income for the operators and their families and little surplus production.

Table 15–1

LAND UTILIZATION, SELECTED YEARS, 1921–1958

(*Thousands of Hectares*)

	1921		1939		1953		1958	
	Area	Per Cent	Area	Per Cent	Area	Per Cent	Area	Per Cent
All Land								
Total	24,755	100.0	24,753	100.0	25,527	100.0	25,580	100.0
Agricultural land	10,904	44.0	14,453	58.0	14,363	56.0	14,967	58.5
Marshes, reeds, etc.	196	1	121	0.5	75	0.5	66	0.3
Forests	7,040	28.0	8,180	33.0	7,880	31.0	8,831	34.5
Unproductive land	6,615	27.0	1,999	8.5	3,209	12.5	1,716	6.7
Agricultural Land								
Total	10,904	100.0	14,453	100.0	14,363	100.0	14,967	100.0
Arable land and gardens	6,420	59.0	7,765	54.0	7,301	51.0	7,650	51.1
Meadows	1,529	14.0	1,869	13.0	1,894	13.5	1,920	12.8
Vineyards	172	1.5	223	1.0	267	2.0	275	1.8
Orchards	237	2.0	303	2.0	376	2.5	402	2.7
Pastures	2,546	23.5	4,293	30.0	4,450	31.0	4,720	31.6

Sources: Statistički Godišnjak, 1929 (for 1921); *Statistički Bilten*, Nos. 11 and 12; and *Statistički Godišnjak FNRJ*, 1959.

The areas of agricultural production are widely scattered, as Figure 15–1 shows. The most important grain regions are located in the Pannonian Plains,[1] which contain approximately 18 per cent of the country's total area and 30 per cent of its arable land. Crops, vegetable gardens, orchards and vineyards cover more than 75 per cent of this region. It accounts for approximately 50 per cent of all bread cereals, 85 per cent of all sugar beets, and 74 per cent of all hemp produced in Yugoslavia. Abnormal weather conditions in the Pannonian Plains cause major fluctuations in Yugoslav agriculture.[2]

Grains are the principal item of agricultural production. The chief grain crops are corn, wheat, barley and rye; their combined acreage occupied 72 per cent of all cultivated land in 1958. A great variety of industrial crops is grown: hemp, flax, cotton, sugar beets, tobacco, hops, poppies, etc. Important oil-bearing plants include sunflowers, olives, linseed and rapeseed. Vegetables are produced the year round in some regions, especially along the Adriatic coast and in parts of Macedonia. Grapes and other fruits — plums, apples, pears, peaches, etc. — are widely produced.

[1] This region includes the river valleys of the Danube, Tisa, Drava and parts of the Sava.

[2] For a detailed discussion of the agricultural geography of Yugoslavia, see George W. Hoffman, "Changes in the Agricultural Geography of Yugoslavia," in Norman G. Pounds (ed.), *Geographical Essays on Eastern Europe* Russian and East European Series, Vol. 24, Indiana University Publications, Bloomington, 1961, pp. 101–140

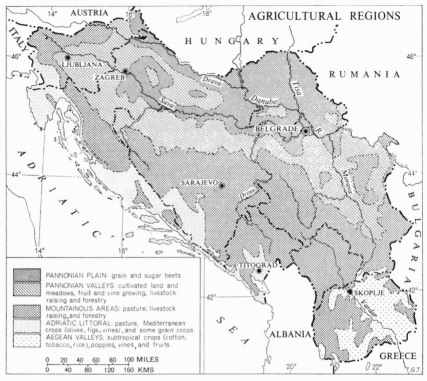

Figure 15–1

Next to grains in importance is the breeding of livestock. The extensive pasture lands and meadows in the country encourage animal husbandry, but in general the quality of the livestock is poor.

Conditions are favorable for the growth of forests in almost all regions of the country.[1] Close to 35 per cent of the total area is covered by forests. The greatest part of the forests (71 per cent of the reserves) consists of deciduous trees, with beech and oak predominant. An important export activity is carried on in such products as pulpwood, sawn timber and furniture. For several years, however, the cutting of trees has surpassed the new growth, and this trend will continue until unexploited regions become more accessible.

The Prewar Years

Before World War II, agriculture held the predominant position in the Yugoslav economy. The per cent of the population dependent upon agriculture for their principal income ranged from 78.9 in 1921 to 74.9 in 1939.

[1] United Nations Food and Agriculture Organization, *Mediterranean Development Project: The Integrated Development of Mediterranean Agriculture and Forestry in Relation to Economic Growth*, Rome, 1959, pp. 181–191.

Agriculture's contribution to the national income during the interwar years ranged between 44.3 per cent and 51.5 per cent. More than three-fourths of the population lived in rural areas at the outbreak of the war, and agricultural overpopulation was a serious problem. It was estimated that surplus population in some villages ran as high as 50 per cent.[1] This overpopulation held down the standard of living and impeded economic progress in the country as a whole. The annual per capita income of the peasants in 1936 amounted to 1,900 dinars; that of city employees 3,900 dinars. At the prewar exchange rate, this was equivalent to $38 as against $78.[2]

In spite of the importance of agriculture, farming methods were backward. Only a small amount of fertilizer was used, the number of tractors and combines was small in relation to the acreage farmed, crop specialization was rare and labor productivity low. Agriculture was beset by a "primitively organized market for agricultural products, an unsolved problem of agricultural credit, and a heavy taxation burden."[3] The economic crisis of the early 1930's left an impoverished peasantry that was forced to resort to short-term loans at high interest rates. The Agrarian Bank of Yugoslavia reported in 1932 that 35 per cent of the total Yugoslav agrarian population was in debt. Special state action later reduced this debt by 50 per cent.[4]

Holdings were extremely small; the average size was 5.3 hectares (13¼ acres) in 1931 — less than one hectare per capita. About 80,000 peasant families were without land, and 34 per cent (700,000 peasants) had holdings of less than two hectares; these holdings comprised 6 per cent of the total arable land of Yugoslavia. On the other hand, 2.5 per cent of the peasants held 27 per cent of the arable land. Although the average holding was hardly sufficient to support a family, the traditional peasant feeling for land ownership was very strong. In some regions, as for example in parts of Serbia proper, the land had been owned by peasants for more than a hundred years. Agrarian cooperatives assisted the peasants, especially those with small holdings, in various ways, e.g., by granting of credits, buying of seeds, sale of surplus goods. There were 10,628 agrarian cooperatives in 1939 with a peasant membership of over 1.3 million.[5]

[1] This overpopulation is also indicated by the population density figures for the country as a whole. In 1939 there were 114 persons per 100 hectares of agricultural land (in Europe only Bulgaria ranked higher); in 1948 there were 110, and in 1953 the figure had fallen to 102.

[2] Dušan Lopandić, "Die Agrarpolitik Jugoslawiens" ("Yugoslav Agrarian Politics"), *Südost-europa-Jahrbuch* (Munich), Vol. I, 1956, p. 179.

[3] Jozo Tomasevich, "Collectivization of Agriculture in Yugoslavia," in Irwin T. Sanders (ed.), *Collectivization of Agriculture in Eastern Europe*, University of Kentucky Press, Lexington, 1958, p. 166.

[4] Ranko M. Brashich, "Agriculture," in Robert F. Byrnes (ed.), *Yugoslavia*, Mid-European Studies Center, Frederick A. Praeger, New York, 1957, pp. 234–235.

[5] *Ibid.*, p. 235.

The devastation caused by World War II has been referred to elsewhere. In addition to population losses, roughly 80 per cent of the farm equipment, 60 per cent of the draft animals and 40 per cent of the farmhouses were considered a total loss. Agricultural reconstruction and rehabilitation were therefore of special importance if the national economy was to be restored to proper functioning.

Early Attempts at Collectivization

Nationalization measures and a large-scale agrarian reform were instituted in the immediate postwar years. The Law on Agrarian Reform and Colonization of 1945[1] nationalized more than 1.5 million hectares and restricted the size of private holdings to 35-45 hectares of agricultural land. Nearly half of the land thus made available was given to landless peasants, many of them from the less arable regions of the country. The remainder was distributed to the "socialist sector."[2]

It was at this time that the Peasant Work Cooperatives (*Seljačka Radova Zadruga or SRZ*) were organized. These collective farms were formed by joining together peasant holdings, plus nationalized land. The members, including many landless peasants, worked according to the group-brigade system and were paid on a basis of labor-days. There were several types of Peasant Work Cooperatives, differing in regard to rights which members retained to their holdings, but only one type was modeled after the Soviet *kolkhozi*. Their number increased from 31 at the end of 1945 to 779 in 1947 and 1,318 in 1948.[3]

Marketing and consumer cooperatives had existed in Yugoslavia even before World War I. These were now reorganized as General Cooperatives, and new ones were formed. Although some General Cooperatives owned land — farmed by private peasants paid in cash — their main efforts involved running village stores and marketing operations for their private peasant members rather than agricultural production.[4]

Meanwhile, private peasants, whether or not they belonged to General Cooperatives, were harassed and discriminated against in favor of the

---

[1] *Službeni List*, No. 64, August 23, 1945.

[2] This was considered to include agricultural enterprises, agricultural institutions and schools, the different types of peasant work cooperatives, cooperative business federations and general agricultural cooperatives, even though most general agricultural cooperatives could only remotely be called socialist.

[3] Tomasevich, *op. cit.*, p. 168. The 1948 figure is from *Statistički Bilten*, but authorities do not always agree on the exact number of Peasant Work Cooperatives, partly because of differences in the types included.

[4] Commercial turnover amounted to 70 per cent of the General Cooperatives' total business, and the value of their non-agricultural output was triple that of their agricultural products. For details see M. Vučković, "Recent Trends in Yugoslav Cooperative Movement," *International Labor Review*, November 1957, pp. 467–478.

collective farms. Agricultural prices were held down, credit was not obtainable, all mechanized equipment was confiscated and given to the newly created machine tractor stations,[1] discriminatory income taxes were instituted. Delivery quotas to state purchasing agencies were fixed in relation to the total agricultural area of the holding, rather than to the area of arable land or the actual sown area. The procedure, according to Brashich, was "designed to exert heavier pressure on the individual household to enter the peasant work cooperatives."[2]

Renewed Collectivization Efforts

The early collectivization drive was inhibited not only by the tenacity with which the peasants clung to their land but also by the fact that an important segment of the Tito regime's popular support came from the peasantry.[3] By the end of 1948, the private sector of agriculture still accounted for 93.8 per cent of the arable land, state farms for 3.6 per cent and Peasant Work Cooperatives for only 2.6 per cent.

This situation, plus the Yugoslav insistence on including the General Cooperatives as a part of the "socialist sector," accounted in part for Soviet charges in 1948 that "correct Marxist policies" were not being followed in Yugoslavia. And right after the break with the Cominform and publication of the Soviet accusations, a new drive for collectivization began.[4] The Fifth Congress of the Yugoslav Communist Party, July 21–29, 1948 — elaborated by the Second Plenary Meeting of the Central Committee of the CPY the following January[5] — laid the legal basis for the new drive. The directives for increased collectivization stressed the special role of the Peasant Work Co-

[1] Ranko M. Brashich, *Land Reform and Ownership in Yugoslavia, 1919–1953*, Mid-European Studies Center, Free Europe Committee, New York, 1954, p. 56. For credit regulations see *Službeni List*, No. 75, September 25, 1945, and No. 6, January 1, 1947; for the law organizing the machine tractor stations, *Službeni List*, No. 19, April 3, 1945.

[2] Brashich, *Land Reform and Ownership in Yugoslavia, 1919–1953*, p. 56. There was compulsory delivery of twenty-two of the most important agricultural products, amounting to 80 per cent of the total products. These accounted for 50 per cent of the peasant cash income. The remaining 20 per cent of the products were sold on the free market, providing the other 50 per cent of the peasant cash income.

[3] On this point see Doreen Warriner, *Revolution in Eastern Europe*, Turnstile Press, London, 1950, p. 51.

[4] See Royal Institute of International Affairs, *The Soviet-Yugoslav Dispute*, Oxford University Press, London, 1948, pp. 62–63, and "A False Understanding of Marxist Principles," *For a Lasting Peace, for a People's Democracy* (*The Cominform Journal*), Bucharest, August 10, 1949, p. 1.

[5] This resolution is published in *Komunist*, March 1949, pp. 2–10, and is called "Basic Tasks of the Communist Party Regarding the Socialist Transformation of the Village and the Advancement of Agricultural Production." For details see various statements in *Komunist* by responsible Yugoslav leaders, e.g., Vlajko Begović, January 1949, pp. 76–101; Edvard Kardelj, March 1949, pp. 39–68; Moma Marković, May 1949, pp. 97–118 and Mijalko Todorović, May 1949, pp. 119–130.

operatives in organizing farmers. Private peasants were threatened, and a vigorous propaganda campaign was carried on to bring them into the collective farms.

Legislation spelled out four types of Peasant Work Cooperatives, the fourth type, patterned after the *kolkhoz*, receiving special attention.[1] They were:

Type 1. Members would receive rent for the land they contributed to the collective, but would retain ownership and in addition keep a plot, up to one hectare.

Type 2. Members would retain ownership of the land which they brought into the collective and receive interest on a sum equivalent to the land value.

Type 3. Members would retain ownership of the land but not receive rent or interest.

Type 4. Land title would be transferred to the collective ownership, the members retaining only a small plot for personal use.

In Type 4 title to the land was transferred permanently, while membership in the other three types was only for a three-year period.

Every pressure available to the government was now used to encourage the fourth type of Peasant Work Cooperative, including a decrease in certain advantages available to the other three types in regard to machinery, credits, etc. A United Nations report published in 1954 came to the conclusion that in general the agricultural legislation enacted before 1953 "did not differ, except in detail, from that of the other eastern European governments."[2] A major weapon of the government was compulsory delivery at low prices to insure food supplies for the town and food deposit areas — in reality a tax on peasant income. The campaign for a rapid increase in large-scale collective farming was accelerated: in 1947 Peasant Work Cooperatives numbered 779; in 1948, 1,318; in 1949, 6,626; and by the end of 1950, 6,964.[3] By 1951 the drive had spent itself. At its height, close to one-fifth of the agricultural land was held by the Peasant Work Cooperatives. (See Table 15–2 for distribution of land by type of holding.) In 1951, 23 per cent of the wheat, 20 per cent of the maize, 25 per cent of the sugar beets, 31 per cent of the tobacco and 15 per cent of the potatoes were produced by the socialist sector

[1] See *Službeni List*, No. 48, June 9, 1949.

[2] United Nations, *Economic Survey of Europe in 1953*, Geneva, 1954, p. 116.

[3] Tomasevich (*op. cit.*, p. 170) quotes the following breakdown for 1950 by type of cooperative: Type I, 1,021; II, 2,212; III, 3,400 and IV, 328, from Mihailo Vučković, "About Some Elements of the Withering Away of the State in Yugoslavia," *Socijalistička Poljoprivreda* (Belgrade), June 1951, p. 5.

Table 15-2

PERCENTAGE DISTRIBUTION OF AGRICULTURAL AREA
BY PROPERTY SECTORS, 1949, 1952 AND 1957

	1949		1952		1957	
	Area	Holdings	Area	Holdings	Area	Holdings
Total	100 0	100.0	100.0	100.0	100.0	100.0
State sector[a]	5.8	0.3	5.7	0.2	5.9	0.1
Cooperative holdings	5.1	3.3	21.0	17.7	3.5	1.8
General Agricultural Cooperatives	} 4.7	} 0.4	0.3	} 0.6	1.5	} 0.3
Peasant Work Cooperatives			18.5		1.8	
Homesteads of Peasant Work Cooperative members[b]	0.4	2.9	2.2	17.1	0.2	1.5
Private holdings	89.1	96.4	73.3	82.1	90.6	98.1
Under 2 hectares	6.4	28.3	5.3	24.9	7.7	29.8
2–5 hectares	24.1	37.4	20.7	32.1	30.3	40.1
5–8 hectates	19.3	16.1	16.1	13.3	23.1	16.6
Over 8 hectares	39.3	14.6	31.2	11.8	38.9	13.5

Sources: Statistički Godišnjak FNRJ, 1958, p. 111; *Statistički Bilten*, No. 95, November 1957, p. 6; *Statistički Bilten*, No. 129, September 1958, p. 8.

[a] Includes state agricultural farms and agricultural institutes.

[b] Members of Peasant Work Cooperatives each own and work a small plot.

of agriculture. Seventy-five per cent of the agricultural land remained in the private sector even at the height of the drive.

Peasant resistance increased sharply and was expressed through decreased production, reduction of the numbers of livestock, an increase in uncultivated land and other actions, all with the ultimate goal of decreasing marketable surpluses. The output of these Peasant Work Cooperatives, which, for the most part, were forcefully imposed, continued to be extremely low.

The droughts of 1949 and 1950 concealed, to some extent, the resistance of the peasants — both those holding private property and those forced into the collectives — but this resistance had become powerful enough during 1951 to force the Yugoslav leadership into a slow and painful reappraisal of policies.[1] The same year also brought to an end the three-year term of commitments for many peasants who had been forced into collectives in 1949. A widespread withdrawal from collectives, in both advanced and underdeveloped regions, was stopped only by arrests and threats of arrest. But the damage had already been done. The harvest of 1951 again did not meet

[1] The late Boris Kidrić told one of the authors in the fall of 1950 that "there can be no question that collectivization is the right approach to our agricultural problem" but "perhaps over-enthusiastic measures" were pushing it too rapidly in certain areas. A little later a particularly critical report about the collectives was written by Slavko Komar, an influential party member from Croatia, later in charge of agriculture for the Federal Executive Council.

Table 15-3

WHEAT PRODUCTION AND IMPORTS, 1952–1959

(Amount in Thousand Tons)

Year	Production	Total Imports	Total Supply	Imports as Per Cent of Total Supply	Imports from U. S.	
					Amount	Per Cent
1952	1,684	435	2,119	20.5	56	13
1953	2,513	758	3,271	23.1	548	72
1954	1,381	832	2,213	37.6	634	76
1955	2,430	975	3,405	28.6	975	100
1956	1,600	1,322	2,922	45.2	858	65
1957	3,100	1,096	4,196	26.1	998	91
1958	2,450	739	3,189	23.1	642	87
1959	4,130	1,007	5,137	19.6	850	84

Source: Statistički Godišnjak FNRJ, 1958 and 1959

the needs, in spite of favorable weather, and the economy was saved largely by $93 million worth of wheat, fat and lard imported from the United States.[1]

Recognizing the agricultural crisis, the Yugoslav leaders initiated a series of "easing off" steps. A directive of November 24, 1951, regarding further ways of socialist transformation of the village, stated specifically that Peasant Work Cooperatives were in need of reorganization and that those operating at a loss were to be disbanded.[2] It further decreed that workers' councils were to be organized in Peasant Work Cooperatives and charged with their management and that General Agricultural Cooperatives were to be encouraged and their work closely tied to district Cooperative Associations — a completely new emphasis after years of secondary importance.[3] The directive also increased taxes on all privately held cultivated land above 10 hectares — a step generally considered as exerting pressure on those medium and larger-sized peasant land holders who thus far had successfully withstood pressure to join one of the types of collectives.[4] Hand in hand with this new emphasis in agricultural policies, the required deliveries of meat, milk and dairy products, potatoes, hay and fat were discontinued in 1951, grain in 1952 and

[1] United States aid is discussed in Chapter 17 and detailed figures are given in Table 17–8.

[2] Changes in agriculture were foreshadowed by the Fundamental Law on the Management of State Owned Economic Enterprises and Higher Economic Associations by the Workers and Employees of July 2, 1950, which introduced workers' councils. At the same time machine tractor stations were abolished as being contrary to the socialist principle "that the means of production belong to the producers themselves." According to Petko Rašić (*Agricultural Development in Yugoslavia*, Jugoslavija, Belgrade, 1955, p. 45), 2,096, or 25 per cent of the total number, were disbanded in 1952.

[3] "Farm Cooperatives Enter a New Phase," *Yugoslav Review*, January 1952, p. 9.

[4] Tomasevich, *op. cit.*, pp. 177–178, and Brashich, *Land Reform and Ownership in Yugoslavia, 1919–1953*, p. 69.

wool in 1953;[1] limited credits for agricultural machinery were granted to individual peasants;[2] and a modified tax system, based on fertility of land, crops planted and size of holdings, was set up.

That these changes did not signify a basic change of policy was clear from Tito's speech at the Sixth Congress of the Communist Party in Zagreb in 1952 when he stated that "without the victory of the socialist sector in our villages, there can be no ultimate victory of socialism in our country."[3] Continued peasant resistance, another poor harvest in 1952 — grain yields dropping to 37 per cent below the prewar average — and as a result increased dependence upon United States food shipments[4] forced the leadership to make a more thorough reappraisal of their agricultural policies.

Abandonment of Collectivization

This reappraisal, and the recognition by the government of the failure of its policy, led to the announcement on March 30, 1953, of a new government decree on Property Relations and Reorganization of the Peasant Work Co-operatives.[5] It represented a major change of policy on collectivization. Kardelj explained it as follows:

It cannot be denied that agricultural cooperation, and in the first place that of the peasant work cooperative type, is experiencing very serious internal difficulties, which are manifesting themselves in the wavering of a considerable proportion of the membership of the peasant work cooperatives. . . . It is therefore primarily necessary to secure, really and consistently, complete voluntariness in connection with the joining or leaving of cooperatives.[6]

Under the new directive peasants were allowed to leave the collectives and have restored to them all equipment and land which they had brought in with them.[7] By vote of their members, collectives could disband, but if they

---

[1] Rašić, *Agricultural Development in Yugoslavia*, p. 66. Compulsory delivery of grain accounted for 31 per cent of the total wheat production and 22 per cent of the total corn production. As a result of abolishing compulsory sales, the sale of grains declined sharply: for wheat in 1954–1955 it was only 16 per cent of the total production, 18 per cent in 1955–1956; for corn it amounted to 12 per cent in 1954, 7 per cent in 1955 and only 2 per cent in 1956. This reduction in deliveries was balanced by a rise in consumption and grain feeding on the farms.

[2] "Osnovni Zakon o Društvenom Doprinosu i Porezima" ("Basic Law on Social Contributions and Taxes"), *Službeni List*, No. 1, January 2, 1952.

[3] Tito's report to the *Sixth Congress of the Communist Party of Yugoslavia*, Belgrade, 1953, p. 36.

[4] The 1952 aid shipments from the United States amounted to $81.4 million. The deficit in the supply of wheat in 1952 amounted to 20.5 per cent of the total needs; 13 per cent of this deficit was supplied by the United States, as shown in Table 15–3. Canada supplied 43.8 per cent, Turkey 39.6 per cent and other countries 3.7 per cent.

[5] *Službeni List*, No. 14, March 30, 1953. C. De Fellner, "The Fate of Collective Agriculture in Yugoslavia," *World Crops*, February 1954, pp. 51–54.

[6] *Borba*, March 29, 1953.

[7] According to a conversation which one of the authors had in July 1953 with a Serbian peasant near Stara Pazova who had just left a Peasant Work Cooperative, the peasant's land was returned, but only one of his two horses; he received a five-year certificate for the other one. There were occasional reports of similar situations elsewhere.

did, the property they had acquired other than that brought in by the peasants themselves became the property of district cooperative unions or General Agricultural Cooperatives. Collectives which operated in the red were required to disband. The process of liquidation was put into the hands of special district commissions. New collectives and those continuing in existence had to sign contracts with their members, who received wages for work performed. The effect of this law on the number of collectives was as might have been expected: by the end of 1953 only 1,152 Peasant Work Cooperatives, with 192,582 members, were left. In Yugoslavia's breadbasket, the Vojvodina, which had the largest number of peasant households in collectives, two-thirds of the peasants left in 1953.[1]

But the mass exodus from collectives and their abandonment also had unexpected repercussions. New land was needed for those peasants remaining in collectives which now no longer had sufficient farmland — for it was the landed peasants who tended to leave and those with little or no land who tended to remain. This need for land was used by the government to express opposition to the so-called larger landowners,[2] whom it blamed, at least in part, for the disruption and breakdown of its cherished program of collectivization.[3] To solve the problem of supplying additional farmland and at the same time reduce so-called "capitalistic tendencies in the villages"[4] the law on the Agricultural Land Fund of May 27, 1953[5] was promulgated, providing for a maximum private holding of cultivable land of 10 hectares. Certain exceptions permitted family holdings up to 15 hectares, and in the case of *zadrugas* with four married families, up to 30 hectares. Indemnity payable in government bonds over a period of twenty years, amounting on the average to 59,437 dinars, was promised.[6]

The total land available for distribution to Peasant Work Cooperatives, General Agricultural Cooperatives and state-owned farms was small. It amounted to 268,000 hectares from 66,248 households, or an average of 3.3 hectares per household; the average was highest (5 hectares) in the Vojvodina. Most of this land was from disbanded collectives and not from private holdings, because so few of them exceeded the maximum. The over-all effect

[1] "Četvrtina Vojvodjanske Zemlje Opštenarodna Imovina" ("A Quarter of Vojvodina Land People's Property"), *Ekonomska Politika*, No. 89, December 10, 1953, p. 989.

[2] Those owning between 10 and 20 hectares, generally classed by European standards as small or medium-sized landowners.

[3] *Borba*, March 29, 1953, p. 1.

[4] *Ibid.*, p. 1.

[5] *Službeni List*, No. 22, May 27, 1953.

[6] According to Tomasevich, this "makes the indemnity quite nominal." (*Op. cit.*, p. 181.)

of the new land distribution was small compared with that of 1945. Only 3.7 per cent of the total arable land and 2 per cent of the total peasant population was affected.[1]

The land reforms did not solve the main problems. There still was not enough for all those dependent on agriculture for a living. They ate up much of what they produced, and price policies and taxes prevented any accumulation for productive investment. Nor was peasant confidence in the regime really restored. Fears were widespread that the 10 hectare maximum might only be the prelude to further limitations on land holdings. They were not eased by official statements indicating that the government was thinking in terms of adjustments only rather than a basic change in policy. Kardelj, for example, spoke of "adjusting the weapons to changed conditions."[2] The adjusted weapons were those portions of the social plan governing investment, credit, taxation, and the amount of machinery, fertilizer, etc., necessary for agriculture. Price policies were also important weapons. Collectivization by force may have been abandoned, but the government still had sufficient power over the peasants to enforce whatever policies it desired by indirect measures.

The agricultural policies thus initiated first appeared as temporary measures — to correct errors and appease the peasants. Agricultural production continued to lag behind.[3] In a series of public statements, the leaders tried to blame the peasants for the low productivity and the failure of collectivization in general.[4] Public statements also emphasized the search for a new policy, best characterized by Kardelj's statement: "We are searching for our way . . . We are keeping our eyes always on socialist goals and we think we have the basic organization to achieve socialism."[5] The impact of this indecision or "do-nothing" policy was eased by the large amount of Western aid, mainly American food shipments. This aid was an important factor in relaxing pressures on the peasantry, in maintaining or increasing the con-

---

[1] Report of the *Federal Executive Council for 1954*, Joint Translation Service, Supplement, April 25, 1955, p. 42.

[2] Edvard Kardelj, "Svaki Napredak u Poljoprivredi Značice Spontano Jačanje Socialističkih Snaga na Selu" ("Every Advance in Agriculture Means Strengthening of Socialist Power in the Village"), *Komunist*, June 1953, p. 336.

[3] The insecurity of the private peasants, the low priority given to agriculture generally, and catastrophic droughts in 1950 and 1952 and a less severe one in 1953 were among the main reasons why 300,000 fewer hectares of arable land were farmed in 1953 than during the prewar years. Cf. *Statistički Godišnjak*, 1959, p. 108.

[4] Apologists also explained that "the leaders had never meant collectivization to be the ruthless affair it had turned out to be." Charles P. McVicker, *Titoism, Pattern for International Communism*, St. Martin's Press, New York, 1957, p. 119.

[5] Fred Warner Neal, "Yugoslav Communist Theory," *American Universities Field Staff Reports*, FWN 5–'54, p. 13.

sumption of food, and in making it possible for Yugoslavia to continue its high rate of capital investment.[1]

The various government actions and pronouncements resulted in a series of contradictions. The regime was no longer trying to develop collectives, yet there was no real farm policy for the non-collectivized agricultural sector, which, after all, included over 90 per cent of the land holdings in the country. This hiatus may have been caused in part by the fact that the peasants were discriminated against politically in elections to the Council of Producers, which consisted overwhelmingly of nonagricultural workers and functionaries. Thus peasant participation in the development of agricultural policies was limited in extent.

The year 1953 closed with agriculture having undergone one of the most revolutionary changes since the end of World War II: peasants no longer were kept in cooperatives against their will; agriculture was freed from direct federal control; the importance of collectives was greatly de-emphasized and their operations much liberalized; and greater opportunities for development were given to the General Agricultural Cooperatives.[2] There was an announcement by Tito of a new ten-year plan for increasing agricultural production,[3] but like the previous general plan for economics development (1947–1951), it was an ambiguous one and never implemented.

Transition, 1954–1956

Yugoslavia's agricultural policy between 1954 and 1956 aimed at increasing production and at the same time laying the basis for a new type of socialism in the rural areas. To reach these goals stress was laid on voluntary participation in cooperatives and on education.[4] While the broad outline of this new policy was agreed to, the steps to be undertaken to implement it were by no

[1] George W. Hoffman, "The Geography of U. S. Foreign Aid: Yugoslavia, A Case Study," *Annals, Association of American Geographers*, September 1960, p. 326.

[2] In January 1954 a new law was passed on Regulation of Agricultural Cooperatives which allowed members of collectives to reorganize in any way they desired under workers' councils and management boards. Cf. *Službeni List*, No. 5, January 29, 1954. In spite of this, many people agreed with Brashich (*Land Reform and Ownership in Yugoslavia 1919–1953*, p. 122) that "No substantial changes have taken place since the individual peasant still is, and apparently will continue to be, regarded as the 'class enemy.' "

[3] "New Deal for Jugoslav Farmers," *The Economist* (London), October 10, 1953, pp. 109–110. Plans called for the investment of more than 600 billion dinars over a ten-year period (116 billion had been invested in industry during the preceding five years).

[4] McVicker, *Titoism, Pattern for International Communism*, pp. 128–134, summarizes his observations of the disagreements in ideology and the discussions which went on in Yugoslavia prior to the appointment of Slavko Komar as head of the Federal Executive Council's agricultural department in the fall of 1954. This appointment, according to McVicker, was considered a victory for those forces which opposed forceful collectivization and preferred to reach the ultimate goal of socializing the village through the creation of proper market conditions and peasant education. Dr. Vladimir Bakarić, President of Croatia, spoke of "raising the socialist consciousness of the village."

means consistent or simple. Peasant distrust of the regime was still widespread and, at least at the beginning, any relaxation of pressure was viewed as a weakness of those in power, and considered as temporary only. The catastrophic results of the 1954 harvest are sometimes ascribed to peasant resistance, although the drought was nearly as bad as it had been in 1950 or 1952. Peasant resistance and adverse weather conditions may have been equally responsible. The fact was that over 830,000 tons of wheat had to be imported in 1954, 79 per cent from the United States (Table 15–3).[1] Tito was forced to ask his people to change their basic diet and eat less bread.[2]

Recognition of the Private Peasant

The seriousness of the agricultural situation finally forced the government to take drastic measures, at last recognizing that the private peasant was the mainstay of agriculture and as such of the economy. Everything was now done to encourage increased production, regardless of any theories. "The private sector of our agriculture is the important sector now," a leading Communist declared. "The task of the League of Communists in agrarian policy is to see that our peasants, no matter to which sector they belong, become modern agriculturists."[3]

To implement these views, four important measures were taken between 1954 and 1956, greatly expanding the operations of the General Cooperatives[4] and making significant concessions to private peasants in regard to credit, taxes and prices.

The General Cooperative now appeared as the kingbolt of the new approach to agriculture. Although some General Cooperatives considered economically unsound were abandoned,[5] the role of the General Cooperative still further increased in the years after 1956. General Cooperatives operate in these ways:

1. They are virtually the exclusive buyers of grain from peasants for distribution to milling concerns.

[1] United States aid, mostly food shipments, amounted to $66.5 million. For a good summary of the problems faced by agriculture in 1954, see C. de Fellner, "Yugoslav Agriculture 1954," *World Crops*, December 1955, pp. 469–472 and 499.

[2] "President Tito Speaks," *Yugoslav Review*, October 1954, pp. 3–4. Among the arguments advanced in support of changing the basic diet was the high consumption of bread in Yugoslavia compared with more highly developed countries. Nothing was said about the fact that the Yugoslav people had much less choice in their basic staple food than the more advanced countries and therefore traditionally had to depend more on bread.

[3] Slavko Komar, quoted in *Vjesnik* (Zagreb), August 1, 1954, p. 1.

[4] "The Operations of General Agricultural Cooperatives in the Federal People's Republic of Yugoslavia," *Bulletin of Information and Documentation*, Glavni Zadružni Savez FNRJ, No. 3, 1957, pp. 2–11. See also United Nations, Economic Commission for Europe, "Economic Planning and Management in Yugoslavia," *Economic Bulletin for Europe* (Geneva), 1958, p. 56.

[5] There were 6,660 General Cooperatives with 2 million members at the end of 1954, compared with 5,664 with 1,286,000 members at the end of 1956. Cf. "Agricultural Cooperatives in a New Role," *Jugopres* (Weekly Features), July 21, 1957, pp. 1–6.

2. They arrange with private peasant members to cooperate in farming their respective land holdings together, either by advising and supervising or, for, say, the duration of a crop year, administering and farming directly, on a share-crop and cash basis, with the approval of the private owners.

3. They acquire land in their own name — in some cases through compulsory sales under the 10-hectare limit — which they farm as a unit together with privately owned land under the above arrangement or through direct leasing.

4. They are the chief distributors of investment funds and loans to private peasants.

5. They act as sort of "machine tractor stations" for their private owner-members, buying machines and supervising their use where possible on the small plots.

6. In some cases, in addition to their other activities, they also operate dairies, mills, wineries and a variety of consumer services.

The importance of the new role of the General Cooperatives was indicated by the fact that at the beginning of 1957 only 42 per cent of the private peasants were equipped to till their own land and 45 per cent had to borrow the necessary farm equipment. Only 13 per cent of the private peasants had sufficient equipment to till their own land and assist others in addition.[1] Between 1953 and 1956, the number of tractors owned by General Cooperatives increased from 2,000 to 4,000.

General Cooperative membership fees range from 1,000 to 3,000 dinars per holding, and the number of members varies from district to district and according to type of cooperative. Between 1953 and 1956, fixed capital of the General Cooperatives increased from 10.2 billion dinars to 17 billion dinars. Their turnover rose from 27.8 billion dinars to 56 billion dinars in the same period.

The General Cooperatives are coordinated in a Cooperative Union (Glavni Zadružni Savez) and are also members of the Agricultural Chamber. While there is no question that in this way, in addition to numerous laws affecting them, they operate under considerable government and Party influence, their main task is to increase agricultural production by aiding and cooperating with private peasants and thus, hopefully, serve to build a "socialist consciousness" in the villages.[2]

[1] "Agricultural Cooperatives in a New Role," p. 3.

[2] Cf. "Prospective Development of Agriculture and Cooperation in Yugoslavia," and "The Forms of Cooperation in the Village," *Bulletin of Information and Documentation*, Glavni Zadružni Savez FNRJ, No. 2, 1957, pp. 1–11.

In addition to expanding the role of General Cooperatives, the regime sought to encourage production by providing special credits for private peasants as a part of the 1954 Social Plan.

Credits, mostly on a short-term basis, could be used for the purchase of fertilizers, seeds, agricultural machinery, livestock and consumer goods. The interest rates varied, but basically amounted to 6 per cent.[1]

Although tax discrimination against private peasants was not entirely eliminated, rates were reduced and a new method of taxing farm income was introduced.[2] This tax was now based on cadastral assessments,[3] a method which eliminated individual harassment and discrimination and enabled the peasant to know in advance the basis on which his income tax would be calculated. The average tax rate was greatly reduced and staggered, and arrangements could be made by the peasant to pay in installments. The cadastral tax is not the only tax the peasants pay. Indirect taxes increase the price of industrial and consumer goods needed by the peasant for his daily use.[4]

Price measures beneficial to private peasants included price supports, partially paid in advance, for wheat and corn and later for meat. There were also subsidized prices on fertilizers, gasoline, heavy machinery, certain seeds, pedigreed stock and other requisites.

Many of these measures were highly successful. Average cash income of peasant households increased, by 75 per cent between 1953–1954 and 1956–1957, or slightly faster than the total cash income of the urban population, while the general price level increased less for farmers than for the general population.[5] At the same time prices of agricultural products rose from the earlier artificially low level, although most of these increases were due to the role of the middlemen (including cooperatives and state purchasing agencies).[6] The large differential between the actual price at the producers' level and the price at the retail trade outlet became a serious problem for the whole economy. This was one reason that the General Agricultural Cooperatives were assigned

---

[1] *Position of Individual Peasants in Yugoslavia,* Jugopres, Belgrade, 1954, p. 4; also, "Agricultural Credits in the Federal People's Republic of Yugoslavia," *Bulletin of Information and Documentation,* Glavni Zadružni Savez FNRJ, No. 3, 1954, pp. 1–3.

[2] C. de Fellner, "Yugoslav Agriculture 1954," pp. 471–472.

[3] A cadastre is a register of property for tax purposes. Cadastral taxation was originally introduced in 1852 in those parts under the Austro-Hungarian Monarchy. This form of taxation is supposed to be objective; it is based on the total proceeds from an average harvest calculated over several years at normal average prices, from which average usual costs to achieve this production are deducted. See also the discussion in Rašić, *Agricultural Developments in Yugoslavia,* pp. 69–70.

[4] In 1956 local people's committees were charged with collection of a special surtax of 3 per cent. *Službeni List,* No. 14, March 30, 1956. A main purpose of this tax was to siphon off the increased income of private peasants. It was abolished in 1958.

[5] "Economic Planning and Management in Yugoslavia," p. 58.

[6] Rudolf Bićanić, "Die Agrarpolitik in Jugoslawien 1953–1958" ("Agrarian Politics in Yugoslavia, 1953–1958"), unpublished manuscript, Spring 1959, p. 9.

the exclusive purchase of agricultural produce. When this measure failed to control inflationary tendencies, direct intervention of the state in the area of price policies was undertaken during 1957.

All production policies after 1954 had as their major goal increased production of both crops and livestock, but investments assigned to agriculture still were relatively small. They amounted to 4.1 per cent of the total investments in 1952, and rose to 8.5 per cent by 1956 (Appendix Table 16–1); in 1954 they were 5.2 per cent. No long-term plans were in operation in this period. The average value of investments in agriculture was only 90,000 dinars ($300) per hectare. And the private sector at the end of 1956 still included more than 98 per cent of the total holdings in agriculture and 90 per cent of all agricultural land (Table 15–2). The main reason for emphasis on increased agricultural production was the heavy importation of foodstuffs, wheat, lard, oil and sugar — running as high as $100 million a year — necessitated by the low domestic production. The high agricultural imports had, of course, a depressing effect on the whole national economy.

Production increases between 1947 and 1956 in industrial crops[1] were higher than in cereals; tobacco production increased close to two and a half times, sugar beet production doubled, and cotton production increased five times. But the production of industrial crops encompassed only a small percentage of the total agricultural production and in addition had the advantage of stable and guaranteed prices. Vine culture, on the average, produced only as much as in prewar years.

Livestock production increased slightly over prewar years — in part because of a much more liberal price policy and a greatly enlarged veterinary service[2] — but major advances did not take place until the investments added after 1956 had filtered down to the individual peasants and cereal production had substantially increased.

By mid-1956 a sufficient basis had been laid for improvements in general agricultural production. It was clear by now that forced collectivization was a thing of the past. The leadership was convinced that it would not work, and, as Kardelj stated, it was considered contrary to principles of democratic socialism. In agricultural policies the gradual approach, with heavy emphasis on specialized cooperatives which were charged to establish a close working relationship with the peasant by educating him to the value of increased

---

[1] For an excellent comprehensive summary see Vladimir Stipetić, "Poljoprivredna Proizvodnja na Današnjem Prodručju FNR Jugoslavije 1929–1955" ("Agricultural Output on the Present Territory of the Federal People's Republic of Yugoslavia"), *Ekonomski Problemi* (Zbornik Radova, Belgrade), 1957, pp. 89–138.

[2] According to *Statistički Godišnjak FNRJ*, 1958, p. 127, veterinary personnel actually employed in rural areas increased from 1,704 in 1954 to 2,537 in 1957; veterinary institutions, stations and infirmaries increased during the same period from 602 to 1,070.

production, was now official Communist policy. The ultimate goal of socialism in the villages "was 25 to 50 years off and could only come by voluntary association."

The Five Year Plan, 1957–1961

Long-range agricultural planning had been tried in the early postwar years, but the Five Year Plan of 1947–1951 was abandoned and a ten-year plan announced in 1953 was never implemented. After much debate, the Federal People's Assembly in 1956 enacted guidelines for a new plan of economic development.[1] In this plan agriculture finally was put on an equal footing with industry and other branches of the economy, and received greatly increased funds; it was no longer the stepchild of the economy. The basic principles of agricultural development are contained in the annex to the Social Plan.[2]

The Five Year Plan called for an over-all increase in agricultural production of 7.1 per cent annually and an increase by 1961 of 51 per cent over the 1951–1955 average in crop production per hectare. It was hoped that increases in crop production would permit an increase in the volume of livestock production of 53 per cent above the 1951–1955 level. The fulfillment of these goals would satisfy domestic food requirements and thus ease the burden placed on the balance of payments by high food imports.

The plan proposed massive boosts in investment in all sectors of agriculture, complete modernization and mechanization of cooperatives.[3] It also called for large-scale use of trained agronomists,[4] widespread use of higher-yield American hybrid corn and high-grade Italian wheat, and greatly increased cooperation between private peasants and cooperatives of all types.

One of the major factors that had long inhibited development of agriculture in Yugoslavia was the uneconomic size of land holdings. The further fragmentation of larger holdings after the war made this situation still more serious. One aim of collectivization had been to overcome this problem. With forced collectivization ruled out, the regime now actively sought to achieve this benefit of collectivization without disturbing the system of private land ownership but at the same time demonstrating the attractiveness

[1] *Društveni Plan Privrednog Razvoja Jugoslavije 1957–1961* (*The Social Plan of Economic Development of Yugoslavia 1957–1961*), *Službeni List*, No. 53, December 25, 1957.

[2] Chapter XIII of the Plan (pp. 62–66) deals with the basic goals in agriculture. A detailed annex containing discussions of projects, goals and methods was published separately: *Stanje Poljoprivrede i Zadrugarstva i Perspektive Njihovog Razvoja* (*The Condition of Agriculture and Cooperation and the Perspectives of Their Development*), Kultura, Belgrade, 1957.

[3] See "The Investment Policy in Agriculture," *Vesnik*, Jugoslovenske Investicione Banke, February 1958.

[4] The number of agronomists with higher and intermediate education by the end of 1959 was approximately 4,000 as against only 2,250 in early 1957.

of socialized agriculture. This meant simultaneously building up the co-operatives and providing for more cooperation between them and private peasants.

Again the General Cooperatives were emphasized, although now the idea of cooperation with private peasants was applied to Peasant Work Coopera-tives as well. The state farms and agricultural institutes, while they were to remain largely experimental units, also were to provide assistance to coopera-tives and private peasants alike. Three broad types of cooperation were envisaged:[1]

(1) Services and technical assistance may be supplied by cooperatives to individual farmers at special prices, usually on credit and with contracts for produce. If the cooperative buys the whole crop, the farmer must follow the cooperative's instructions on how to till his land, for ex-ample, deep plowing in case of high-yielding wheat varieties. Coopera-tive services include the supplying of fertilizers, selected seeds and pedigreed livestock, plowing and harvesting, and sometimes the sale of the crop at guaranteed prices.

(2) The cooperative may participate in part or fully in various production processes and in return receive a fixed share in kind of the individual peasant's profit. The size of the profit for the cooperative depends on the type of farming operations, investments, materials supplied, etc., which, of course, vary according to local conditions.

(3) Cooperatives may produce jointly with the private peasant, with profits shared in proportion to the contribution made by each partner. In such a case the peasant receives a certain amount as rental for the use of his land. Cooperatives usually are assigned certain specific tasks, such as providing heavy machinery, spreading fertilizer, insecticides, weed killers, specific seeds, etc. The private farmer usually provides manual labor and draft animals where tractors are not profitable. Costs are calculated for each individual operation and/or supply of materials provided by either partner. Often such contracts are con-cluded for a long-term period so that the cooperative and the farmer may receive larger compensation from the investments.

Cooperation is carried on in many different ways: for example, the supply-ing of pedigreed stock by cooperatives to the peasants for breeding, with payment in money or kind, including payment in young animals; the joint

[1] See United Nations, *Economic Survey of Europe in 1959*, Geneva, 1960, Chapter VII, p. 50, and Dušan Lopandić, "System of Co-operation in Yugoslav Agriculture," *Review of Interna-tional Affairs*, February 16, 1960, pp. 17–20.

Table 15–4

COLLABORATION BETWEEN GENERAL AGRICULTURAL COOPERATIVES AND THE PRIVATE
SECTORS IN AGRICULTURE, 1956–1959

	1956	1957	1958	1959
General Agricultural Cooperatives (OZZ):				
Total number	5,576	5,472	5,242	4,803
Farms only	2,350	2,600	2,989	3,304
Total membership (*millions*)	1,286	1,405	1,371	1,502
Total area (*hectares*)	181,240	202,643	289,643	428,027
Area under lease (*hectares*)			29,330	49,835
Collaboration with private farm holdings:[a]				
In crop farming				
Number of farm holdings		24,770[b]	207,849[b]	548,147[c]
Area (*hectares*)		20,861	146,300	414,016
In stock breeding				
Number of farm holdings		27,103	70,210	266,737
In plantation of permanent crops				
Number of farm holdings		2,230	4,909	
Area (*hectares*)		1,673	2,216	
Services in the cultivation of private peasant holdings:[d]				
Plowing				
Number of holdings	108,281	212,853	270,000	
Area (*hectares*)	131,286	259,858	396,187	700,824
Sowing				
Number of holdings	20,188	25,896	50,635	
Area (*hectares*)	23,563	28,752	51,339	167,135
Harvesting				
Number of holdings	15,165	49,757	54,191	
Area (*hectares*)	20,445	63,512	67,789	213,037
Threshing				
Number of holdings	389,265	524,846	692,904	
Number of tons	383,714	1,011,072	874,168	1,452,323

Sources: Compiled from *Statistički Godišnjak FNRJ*, 1958, 1959, 1960, and *Indeks*, No. 6, 1960 and No. 7, 1960.

[a] Joint production and cooperation based on advance contracting.

[b] Included are only works performed by cooperatives to individual households in the form of usual service according to price table (so-called service).

[c] Total amount of work is expressed in all forms of cooperation.

[d] For additional details of socialist cooperation of the OZZ with individual households, see *Statistički Godišnjak FNRJ*, 1960, p. 140, Tables 123, 124 and 125.

utilization of mountain pastures; soil reclamation and flood control work, plowing, sowing, harvesting and threshing.

Table 15–4 illustrates the increased collaboration between the General Agricultural Cooperatives and the private sector. In 1959 all the socially owned holdings (5,810) worked 1.3 million hectares of agricultural land or 8.7 per cent of the total agricultural area, and 722,000 hectares or 9.4 per cent of the total arable surface. Of this, the General Agricultural Cooperatives (4,803) owned 428,027 hectares of agricultural land or 2.8 per cent of the

Table 15–5

Use of Fertilizers and Tractors, 1955–1959

	1955–56	1957	1958	1959
Gross Fertilizer Consumption (*Kilograms per Hectare of Arable Land*)				
National average	48	100	128	183
Vojvodina	59	189	278	362
Other regions	45	76	89	132
Arable Area per Tractor (*Hectares*)				
National average	686	373	318	255
Vojvodina	365	178	167	133
Other regions	868	725	523	325

Source: United Nations, *Economic Survey of Europe in 1959*, Geneva, 1960, Chapter VII, p. 17.

total agricultural area. General Agricultural Cooperatives performed services (excluding threshing and transport) on 17.9 per cent of the private holdings in 1959–1960 according to the preliminary data of the 1960 census; 8.6 per cent of the private holdings were plowed with cooperative machinery and 41 per cent received seeds and fertilizers. The number of private holdings whose crops were cultivated in collaboration with the General Agricultural Cooperatives rose steadily: 24,770 holdings with an area of 20,861 hectares cooperated in 1957, 548,147 holdings with an area of 414,016 hectares in 1959. Cooperation in stock breeding and in viniculture and horticulture, and services such as plowing and sowing, also increased rapidly after 1957.

At the same time, many cooperatives, both the general and the peasant work varieties, increased in size by leasing and buying land. As more peasants moved into urban areas, increasing amounts of land were put on the market, and the cooperatives have priority in buying. In Croatia during 1959, for example, the cooperatives purchased 15,000 hectares, and 35,000 hectares more were up for sale at the beginning of 1960.[1] Some land was also taken over by cooperatives under a 1959 law which compels private peasants to sell land not cultivated in accordance with good agricultural practices, such as minimum use of fertilizers, selected seeds, etc.[2] Indications were that this law would become an increasingly important mechanism for control of private peasant farming practices.

The increased use of fertilizers and tractors, once available only to Peasant Work Cooperatives and state farms, were supplied to both General Coopera-

[1] The trend was evident in the Vinkovci district of Croatia, where during 1958 and 1959, 5,748 hectares were sold by private peasants but only 4 hectares were bought by them. *Borba* (Zagreb), February 13, 1960.

[2] *Gospodarški List*, October 2, 1959.

tives and private peasants as a part of the new approach to agriculture.[1] The increased use of fertilizers and tractors is shown in Table 15–5.

Financial Policies

Financial policies — investment-credits, prices and taxes — have played an important part in the development of Yugoslav agriculture, in both the private and socialized sectors.

The major part of agricultural investment is financed by the Central Investment Fund and special agricultural funds. Private investments were estimated at 27 billion dinars both in 1955 and in 1956 and 36 billion dinars in 1957. Investment funds available generally have been higher than those estimated in the original Five Year Plan.

In January 1959 the Yugoslav Agricultural Bank was set up to dispense government credits for agricultural developments, both for planting and for soil reclamation projects — activities previously carried on by the Yugoslav Investment Bank and the National Bank.[2] Two important innovations in granting loans for investments were initiated during 1960: (1) Only the most profitable and economically sound projects, with all agricultural organizations treated equally, were considered. The criteria used in reviewing applications included: profitability of the projects submitted, investment per unit of product, access to raw material supplies, and time for repayment of the loan. (2) The time allotted for repayment of loans was shortened — e.g., for the purchase of pigs, from five years to three, and for light farm machinery, from twelve years to eight.[3]

Applications amounting to 700 billion dinars for various purposes poured in, seven times more than the amount estimated in the Federal Social Plan for 1960. Inasmuch as every agricultural organization had the right to apply for loans, they included duplicate and unsound proposals. Only key agricultural projects received approval — supplies for livestock production, transportation, farm mechanization, purchases of high-quality seeds, primary processing plants, and farm storage and land reclamation projects which had been started in previous years. All other agricultural projects were encouraged to seek financing from local investment funds and from the resources of the

---

[1] Since 1956, the Yugoslav government has sought to finance the building of several large fertilizer plants. The financing was promised by the Soviet Union and East Germany in 1956, but did not come through because of changed political relations. During 1957 it was decided to construct several new fertilizer plants with a 1962 target production of 2 million tons. In January 1959 the United States Development Loan Fund advanced Yugoslavia $22.5 million for the construction of a nitrogen fertilizer plant at Pancevo with an annual capacity of 360,000 tons. The loan was repayable in twenty years with 5 per cent interest — 75 per cent in dinars and 25 per cent in dollars. For Yugoslavia, importing this amount of fertilizer would mean an annual expenditure of $13.6 million.

[2] *Borba*, December 17, 1958.

[3] *Ibid.*, February 13, 1960.

respective agricultural organizations, with the share from the Central Investment Fund limited to 35 per cent of the total loan. In addition, the government encouraged the agricultural organizations to coordinate their demands for the limited investment funds available. The Federation of Agriculture and Forestry Chambers of Yugoslavia serves as coordinating agency.

Another important measure to further agricultural production was the enlarged fund set aside for both long-term and short-term credits.[1] Credits were made available to private farmers through the General Agricultural Cooperatives though they could also be obtained from a bank. Most of the credits to private farmers are short-term (repayable within one year), for the advancement of agricultural production. Money also was available on a long-term basis (up to ten years) for building repairs and certain new construction and for the purchase of additional land, building materials, stock breeding, etc. For a long time the private peasant was unwilling to risk entanglement with the government, but there are indications that the government is slowly succeeding in this aspect of its plan to strengthen cooperative-peasant relationships and stimulate production. Credits to private peasants from the central banking institutions are still insignificant, however. In 1958, 738 million dinars of short-term credits and 2,100 million dinars of long-term credits were granted to private peasants. In the same year agricultural enterprises and Peasant Work Cooperatives had short-term credits of 63 billion dinars and long-term credits of 42 billion dinars outstanding.[2]

Interest rates for short-term credits granted to agricultural cooperatives were 3 per cent; the credits must be guaranteed by local people's committees in a written statement to the bank. Short-term credits to the General Agricultural Cooperatives were greatly increased between 1953 and 1959 — from 12.4 billion dinars in 1953 to 78.0 billion dinars for January–October 1959.[3] Fixed capital assets required for the necessary operation of organizations are exempt from payment of interest. General Agricultural Cooperatives pay a rate fixed by the local commune and the amount goes into the investment fund of the same cooperative. This procedure permits the organization to finance small and medium-sized investment projects.

For price stabilization, main reliance is first on agreements among the General Agricultural Cooperatives, the chief purchasers of farm products,

[1] For details see "The Forms of Co-operation in the Village," *Bulletin of Information and Documentation,* Glavni Zadružni Savez FNRJ, No. 2, 1957, pp. 8–11, and "Measures for Quicker Development of Agricultural Organizations," *Jugopres* (Weekly Features), February 23, 1958, pp. 5–8.

[2] The figures quoted for agricultural enterprises include credits from all sources. The cooperatives have their own funds and also distribute credits received by the big banks, in particular the Agricultural Bank.

[3] Figures supplied by the Federal Statistical Institute, as of February 1, 1960. Long-term figures are not available.

and second on agreements among the wholesale trade organizations. The Cooperative Union and the Agricultural Chamber of Commerce exert a strong influence on these agreements. The agreements are often violated, however. In addition, the government guarantees prices in some cases, e.g., meat production, and exacts in return minimum price agreements. Prices are fixed only on a few commodities directly affecting the cost of living — sugar, tobacco, bread and lard. Agricultural prices are also affected by government subsidies designed to keep down the cost of tractors, diesel oil and artificial fertilizers. Despite all these arrangements, agricultural prices fluctuate and have manifested a general upward trend. The index of general agricultural prices was 78 in 1953 and 103 in 1959.[1]

Besides general taxes on income, those engaged in agriculture also pay specific taxes.[2] The private peasant pays the cadastral tax mentioned previously, which is levied at a flat rate, and an additional income tax with a progressive rate is levied by communes. The commune tax is rather high and has been increasing steadily. Taxes amounted to 6.2 per cent of personal income in 1953, 9.4 per cent in 1956 and 11.0 per cent in 1958. (See Table 15-6.) Taxes paid by agricultural organizations usually are rebated in part or in whole for investment purposes. The proceeds of the cadastral assessments go to the federal budget or the social investment funds of the commune, or may be rebated in the case of economic organizations (collectives or cooperatives), in which case they become part of the investment fund.

The different agricultural organizations receive preferred treatment in the receipt of investment funds, in the payment of interest, in obtaining certain credits and in taxation. They benefit from guaranteed prices (for grains, livestock, industrial crops, etc.), lower interest rates on permanent working capital, exemption from payment of interest on basic resources, part-reimbursement of contributions from income and the land tax. Agricultural organizations also pay lower rates as their contribution to the social security fund and they enjoy considerable freedom in the formation and utilization of the amortization fund. Finally, they can obtain credits to be used to increase production by simplified procedures and without the necessity of bidding.

Production Trends, Hopes and Problems

By and large, the regime's new approach to agriculture has been remarkably successful. Agricultural production had on the whole increased slowly

---

[1] For a detailed discussion of the price system, see Chapter 14.

[2] "The System of Revenue for the Budgets and Fund in the Federal People's Republic of Yugoslavia," *Information Service Yugoslavia*, RN 106/1–59–3.

Table 15-6

INCOME FROM AGRICULTURE AND TAXATION, PRIVATE SECTOR, 1952–1959

(Billions of Dinars)

Year	Total Income	Personal Consumption	Savings	Income Tax[a]	Communal Tax[a]	Income and Communal Tax	Taxes as Per Cent of Total Income	Accumulation after Deduction of Taxes
1952[b]	193	187	6	16.2	—	—	8.4	— 10.2
1953	292	248	44	18.0	—	—	6.2	26.0
1954	291	246	45	23.6	—	—	8.1	21.4
1955	394	332	62	26.7	1.5	28.2	7.2	34.8
1956	393	333	60	27.8	9.2	37.0	9.4	23.0
1957[c]	558[d]	402	151[d]	29.6	12.1	41.7	7.5	107.3[d]
1958	456	394	61	32.9	17.4	50.3	11.0	10.7
1959[e]				28.5[f]	31.0[f]	59.5		

Source: Compiled from national statistics.

[a] *Statistički Bilten,* Narodne Banke No. 3, 1960, p. 56.

[b] *Statistički Bilten,* No. 115, pp. 11–12.

[c] *Statistički Godišnjak FNRJ,* 1958, p. 105; 1959, p. 100.

[d] Included are contributed reserves of 1957.

[e] 1959 figures not yet available.

[f] Refers to aggregate income.

Note: Figures for 1957 must be read with caution. They are not comparable with 1956 or 1958 because inventory carry-over is included in accumulation.

before 1957, but from 1957 to 1959 it averaged 41 per cent above the 1951–1959 average.

The Yugoslav planners had estimated that even if modernization of agriculture in the eight to ten years after 1956 were only to cover about 30 per cent of the cultivated area, it would be possible to realize about 75 per cent of expected agricultural needs. The rest could be met from the remaining areas, which would be extensively cultivated.[1] The government hoped that by pursuing the policy initiated in late 1956 total agricultural production at the end of the Five Year Plan would increase roughly one-third — 100 per cent on the state-owned farms and Peasant Work Cooperatives and 50 per cent on the General Agricultural Cooperatives and private farms.

As a result of the harvests of 1959, it was evident that the increases planned for 1961 had already been met by 1959 in most branches of agriculture. Moreover, the socialist sector had lived up to expectations. In the three-year period 1957–1959, total agricultural production on socially owned farms doubled. Between 1956 and 1959, the share of these farms in total production increased from 6.5 per cent to 11.6 per cent, and their share in wheat production rose from 7.5 per cent to 15.7 per cent. According to the Federal Secretariat of Agriculture, in 1958 the socialist sector accounted for 76 per cent of the marketable surplus of wheat, although it produced only 14 per cent of the total output, while private farms, which produced 86 per cent of the total, accounted for only 24 per cent of the marketable surplus.[2] In 1959, the socialist sector accounted for 53 per cent of the marketable surplus of wheat, 50 per cent of corn, 47 per cent of sugar beets, 18.5 per cent of meat and 15.5 per cent of milk.[3]

Animal husbandry, which lagged behind in the general improvement, received a big boost from the successful corn crop of 1959 and was steadily benefiting from imports of pedigreed stock.

The effort to raise crop production on grain-feed farms and in animal husbandry which started in 1956 showed its first success in 1957, when average yields of wheat rose to 16 quintals per hectare from the pre-1956 yields of 11 and 12. (See Table 15–7.) The yields of corn and sugar beets climbed correspondingly. Many felt that the exceptionally favorable weather

[1] Slavko Komar, "Agricultural Production Today and Prospects for Its Further Increase," *Review of International Affairs*, June 1, 1959, p. 18.

[2] See also later study by P. Marković, "Proizvodnja i Potrošnja Pšenice 1959" ("Production and Consumption of Wheat 1959"), *Jugoslovenski Pregled*, 1959, p. 17.

[3] *Development of Agriculture in Yugoslavia*, Information Service Yugoslavia, Jugoslavija, Belgrade, August 1960, p. 12; and "Agricultural Production in Yugoslavia in 1957–59," *Yugoslav Survey*, Vol. 1, No. 2 (1960), p. 196.

Table 15–7

AREA, PRODUCTION AND YIELDS FOR SELECTED CROPS, PREWAR AND POSTWAR PERIODS

Crop	Area (*Thousands of Hectares*)	Production (*Thousands of Metric Tons*)	Yield (*Quintals per Hectare*)
Wheat			
Prewar (1930–39)	2,140	2,400	11
Postwar (1948–56)	1,830	2,190	12
1957	1,970	3,100	16
1958	1,990	2,490	12
1959	2,130	4,130	19
Maize			
Prewar (1930–39)	2,600	4,300	16
Postwar (1948–56)	2,400	3,520	15
1957	2,590	5,660	22
1958	2,390	3,950	17
1959	2,580	6,670	26
Rye			
Prewar (1930–39)	250	212	9
Postwar (1948–56)	271	249	9
1957	256	280	11
1958	248	241	10
1959	236	265	11
Barley			
Prewar (1930–39)	423	410	10
Postwar (1948–56)	339	367	11
1957	408	604	15
1958	390	470	12
1959	378	575	15
Tobacco			
Prewar (1930–39)	15	15	10
Postwar (1948–56)	38	31	8
1957	57	63	11
1958	53	39	7
1959	49	46	9
Cotton			
Prewar (1930–39)	2	1	6
Postwar (1948–56)	17	6	4
1957	13	10	8
1958	13	7	5
1959	13	9	7
Sugarbeets			
Prewar (1930–39)	35	616	176
Postwar (1948–56)	83	1,320	159
1957	83	2,030	246
1958	71	1,480	207
1959	81	2,420	297
Potatoes			
Prewar (1930–39)	275	1,650	60
Postwar (1948–56)	245	1,920	77
1957	285	3,310	115
1958	277	2,620	94
1959	290	2,760	94

Table 15–7 (*Continued*)

Crop	Area (*Thousands of Hectares*)	Production (*Thousands of Metric Tons*)	Yield (*Quintals per Hectare*)
Hemp			
Prewar (1930–39)	42	250	59
Postwar (1948–56)	62	271	44
1957	52	312	60
1958	52	262	51
1959	39	241	62
Meadows (hay)			
Prewar (1930–39)	1,930	3,370	18
Postwar (1948–56)	1,850	3,340	18
1957	1,910	3,590	19
1958	1,900	3,030	16
1959	1,900	4,130	22

Source: Statistički Godišnjak FNRJ, 1957, 1958, 1959, 1960.

during 1957 was a major factor in these increases, and indeed there were decreases during the following year when the weather was unfavorable. But in 1959, in spite of mediocre weather, yields of wheat were even higher (19 quintals per hectare), yields of corn and sugar beets were also up, and total crop production was at its highest point in postwar years — wheat at 4.1 million tons and maize at 6.7 million tons. The 1959 production was 18 per cent above the previous record in 1957 and 20 per cent above production estimates for 1961, the completion date of the Five Year Plan.[1] Vice President Todorović was able to announce that "the government has decided that wheat will not be imported in the coming year. Available quantities will be sufficient to meet the requirements of the population." The 1960 production of cereals was below the record-breaking production of 1959 on account of erratic weather conditions. The harvest of 1961 was disappointing, especially as far as corn was concerned. Production of corn reached only about 4.5 million tons instead of the 7 million planned. This was due to droughts occurring during most of the summer and a still unsolved storage problem. The Yugoslav government again was forced to seek United States assistance and to import cereals on a large scale.

The use of Italian wheat varieties and American hybrid corn has been greatly accelerated and singularly successful. Yields were thus increased not only in the Vojvodina but also in less favorable parts of the country. The average yields of all wheat varieties in the Vojvodina increased from 18.9

[1] The plan recommended 16.9 quintals per hectare of wheat as a national average in 1961 (1959 yield, 18.9), 22 quintals per hectare for maize (1959 yield, 26.2), and 260 quintals for sugar beets (1959 yield, 297 quintals).

quintals per hectare in 1957 to 25.6 in 1959 and in other regions from 10.7 quintals to 16.8; the average for Italian wheat varieties in the Vojvodina increased from 30.0 quintals in 1957 to 43.7 in 1959 and in other regions from 27.0 quintals to 33.7. A similar increase occurred in the yields of maize with the introduction of American hybrid corn. There were marked differences in yields between the various types of farms: yields of special varieties of wheat in 1959 ranged from 44 quintals per hectare for state farms, 42 for cooperative farms, 28 for individual farmers collaborating with cooperatives and 16 for non-collaborating farmers; the comparable figures for special varieties of maize were 55, 52, 45 and 22.[1] By 1959 over one-third of the area under wheat cultivation was sown to high-yielding wheat varieties.[2]

Yields of the most important crops increased as follows: maize from 12 to 26 quintals per hectare between 1954 and 1959, wheat from 7 to 19, sugar beets from 159 to 297.[3] Wheat production in the bumper year 1959 was 68 per cent above the 1951–1955 average.

The United Nations in a recent study compiled figures on the two-year moving averages of the gross value of agricultural output for the past decade which show a steady improvement in over-all production. (See Table 15–8.)

Table 15–8

INDEX OF THE GROSS VALUE OF AGRICULTURAL OUTPUT, 1951–1959

(Moving Averages of Two Calendar Years: 1955–56 = 100;
Derived from Values at 1956 [Constant] Prices)

	1951–52	1952–53	1953–54	1954–55	1955–56	1956–57	1957–58	1959
Crops	87	85	96	97	110	123	135	157
Livestock	80	85	98	104	106	115	132	146
Total	85	85	97	110	109	121	134	154

Source: United Nations, *Economic Survey of Europe in 1959*, Geneva, 1960, Chapter VII, p. 46.

The real improvements did not come until 1957; and increased output has been due to changed governmental policies which also were reflected in the improved climate of cooperation between the socialist and private sectors. Certainly foreign assistance — mainly from the United States in the form of massive food shipments to bridge over periods of insufficient domestic production and technical assistance — has greatly aided Yugoslav planners in furthering their long-term aims.

[1] See United Nations, *Economic Survey of Europe in 1959*, Geneva, 1960, Chapter VII, pp. 17 and 49.

[2] According to *Indeks*, No. 3, 1960, 33 per cent of the total wheat acreage of the socialist sector was sown to high-yielding wheat varieties in the fall of 1959, 23 per cent of the acreage of the private sector and 44 per cent of that under joint cultivation, a total of 750,000 hectares out of 2.04 million hectares sown to all wheat varieties.

[3] United Nations, *Economic Survey of Europe in 1959* Geneva, 1960, Ch. VII, p. 47.

Neither the praise nor the blame for the production record can be placed entirely on governmental policies and collaboration. Weather conditions — droughts and floods, particularly in the most fertile regions of the country — have greatly influenced production. While the trend has been upward since 1956–1957, fluctuations in output over the past decade clearly indicate the influence of natural forces beyond the immediate control of the government.[1]

Year	Weather Conditions	Agricultural Production Index (1947–56 = 100)
1950	exceptionally unfavorable	78
1951	favorable	110
1952	exceptionally unfavorable	78
1953	mediocre	110
1954	unfavorable	97
1955	favorable	120
1956	unfavorable	100
1957	exceptionally favorable	145
1958	unfavorable	128
1959	satisfactory (poor during harvesting)	154
1960	less satisfactory than 1959	150

One ultimate goal of the Yugoslav planners is of course to make Yugoslav agriculture "weather proof," or at least to minimize the impact of unfavorable weather conditions. That this is an extremely difficult task can be seen by the developments during the period 1956–1961.

What then is the outlook for the years to come? Despite recent improvements, average production of crops and livestock still does not provide food reserves large enough for Yugoslavia's rapidly growing population. Per capita consumption of foodstuffs, while increasing, is very low when compared with the averages in the more advanced countries of Western Europe. While the average daily calorie intake of 2,800 to 3,000 per capita compares well with the rates in those countries, the biochemical composition of foodstuffs consumed has remained stable and continues to be that more typical of underdeveloped countries.[2]

Future production goals will have to take into account changes in demand due to movement of people from agriculture into industry, increased incomes and a rapid increase in population.[3] Not only will this mean a continuing

[1] Information derived from official statistics and reports.

[2] Carbohydrates make up roughly 60 per cent, fats close to 30 per cent, and albumens a little more than 10 per cent of the average worker's diet. *Statistički Godnišnjak FNRJ*, 1959, p. 243.

[3] Between 1953 and 1960 the total population increased approximately 1.7 million and the nonagricultural population 2.9 million.

shift from corn to wheat consumption, but the more expensive foods of animal origin will be in greater demand. In spite of a decreasing agricultural population and a subsequent decrease in the consumption of cereals, the task of providing sufficient food is likely to become more serious in the future.[1] In addition, greatly increased quantities of fodder are needed in order to increase the supply of meat and fats.

Increased production of a large number of crops is essential — sugar beets, fruits, vegetables and others — to meet prospective demands. Methods of increasing production in the future must include still greater emphasis on increasing yields and a more intensive use of certain arable land; for example, some land under cereals could much more profitably be put under industrial crops, orchards or vineyards, or might be reserved for grazing. The success of these efforts will in large measure determine not only how well the average Yugoslav is fed, but the whole future economic development of Yugoslavia.

The Changing Peasant Population

The social and economic revolution that has come to Yugoslavia since the war is having a profound effect on the structure of the peasant population. This in turn has considerable influence on agricultural production. According to the 1953 census, 2.8 million rural households owned land; of these 641,000 were not engaged in agriculture. In 1957, at the beginning of the new Five Year Plan, 56.1 per cent of the population depended upon agriculture for their income, compared with 74.9 per cent in 1939. This shift indicated a considerable change in rural life and economy within a relatively short time. Slovenia, Croatia, Serbia proper and the Vojvodina were most affected, but a continuing industrialization, improvements in agricultural technology and land reforms have had their effect on the rural population throughout the country.

The most important rural changes have been those involving land ownership. As a result of three land reforms in forty years — in 1919, 1945 and 1953 — Yugoslavia has become a land of small family holdings with a legal limit of 10 hectares of cultivable land. In 1957 only about 9 per cent of the agricultural area was part of the socialist sector, and there have been no important changes since that time.

A serious situation, from the point of view of efficiency, is the fact that the Yugoslav peasant by 1957 had an average of only 4.4 hectares of land; 40 per cent of the holdings covering 30 per cent of the land area were between two and five hectares, 30 per cent of the holdings with an area of 7.7 per

---

[1] Cf. Nikola Dragičević, "Perspektiva Razvoja Potencijalnih Izvora FNRJ" ("Prospective Development of Yugoslav Resources"), *Ekonomski Pregled* (Zagreb), April 1957, p. 213.

cent were below two hectares (Table 15–2). The redistribution of property by the various land reforms helped the peasant who owned no land, but was of little help to the two-thirds of the landholders who had up to five hectares of land. In part as a result of this fragmentation 19.3 per cent of the total labor force (1.3 million) lived on farms in 1960 but were permanently employed in nonagricultural jobs, and an additional 9.3 per cent (513,000) had occasional outside employment.[1]

The custom of continuing to live on the land while holding a factory job was encouraged by the serious housing situation, especially in the older industrial centers. The highest percentage of so-called peasant-workers is found in the economically more advanced regions: in Slovenia, 28.0 per cent of those living on farms are permanently employed outside and 9.2 per cent have occasional outside employment; in Kosmet, 15.5 per cent and 4.8 per cent. Naturally, the peasants with the least land are those who seek outside employment. But it is customary for households of more than one family to send at least one member to a nearby industry, as a way of supplementing the family budget.[2] This off-farm income enables those who own little land to improve their standard of living, and gives peasants with larger holdings (above 5 hectares) a chance to improve their property. Figures available from sample surveys show that the income of peasant holdings from nonagricultural activities amounted to roughly 44 per cent of the total receipts between 1953/54 and 1958/59.[3]

The Outlook for Socialization

What is the future of the private peasant in socialist Yugoslavia? What, indeed, is the future of socialism if, as Lenin once said, "socialism in the villages is necessary for socialism in the country"?

In Yugoslavia, the regime is still committed to socialism in the villages. But at the same time some 90 per cent of the total agricultural area is held by private peasants, and the regime is also committed against forced collectivization. Would not this breed capitalism, as Lenin further remarked, "every hour, every day"?

[1] Preliminary results of the Census of 1960, *Indeks*, No. 8, 1960. Total population living on farms was 12.5 million in 1960 (12.8 million in 1953); the labor force (including women performing field work) totaled 6.8 million. The number living on farms with permanent outside employment increased 65 per cent between 1953 and 1960.

[2] Rudolf Bicanić, "Neopoljoprivredna Zanimanja u Seljačkom Gospodarstvu" ("Nonagricultural Occupations in Peasant Families"), *Statistička Revija*, August 1956, pp. 97–119, and Doreen Warriner, "Changes in European Peasant Farming," *International Labour Review*, November 1957, pp. 446–466.

[3] *Statistički Godišnjak FNRJ*, 1960, p. 141. The surveys are based on an income level above the average and therefore are not to be considered as representative.

The agricultural theorists of Titoism do not think so. They have felt sure that capitalism could be prevented by limitation on private holdings, by the general socialist orientation of the country as a whole and by the favorable position of the socialist sector, which, although it comprises a relatively small part of the total area, holds a relatively high percentage of arable land and receives large-scale government assistance. "Our private peasants will not be capitalist peasants," Vladimir Bakarić told one of the authors, "even if we permit them to increase their holdings above the 10-hectare limit."

The policy of Titoism in agriculture has seemed to be to seek the benefits of collectivization without having collectivization. To achieve this, the regime worked out what amounted to a new method of socialism in agriculture. It consisted essentially in encouraging close cooperation between the private and socialist sectors and so strengthening the latter as to make such cooperation highly attractive to the traditionally individualistic Yugoslav peasants.

Both sectors, the government feels, have a mutual interest in enlarging farm output, increasing labor productivity and reducing costs of production. The optimum goal is increased output and an increased "socialist consciousness" on the part of the private peasants that will attract them to collectivist forms; the minimum goal is increased output and the prevention of private landholding "breeding capitalism." At any rate, it is felt, as Kardelj has expressed it, that boosting production through modernization and the "socialist transformation of the countryside" are a single process.

Kardelj may well be right. According to the neo-Fabian ideas of Titoism, the regime could be patient and wait. But patience and waiting are traditionally peasant traits. Whether Yugoslav agriculture ultimately will become completely socialized may depend on who can outwait whom.

INDUSTRIAL GROWTH

AND RESOURCE BASE

IN CONTRAST to the slow postwar development in agriculture, industrial growth received immediate and continuous attention in the new Yugoslavia. Government policy was basically different from that of the prewar years. All the means of production were completely nationalized, and transportation, banking and trading enterprises also became the property of the state. Large industrial investment had a slow but increasingly important impact on the whole structure of the economy. In the early 1950's, for example, industrial investment represented close to 18 per cent of national output. This policy was in part based on the Marxist dogma of the Titoist government, but priority for industrialization was also a logical development, for Yugoslavia has ample reserves of minerals, certain mineral fuels, unused water resources, and an abundance of manpower. Facilities to exploit raw materials have been modernized and enlarged during the past fifteen years, and plans call for continuing high investment.

Background to Industrial Growth

Yugoslavia's industrial development before 1941 was limited largely to the exploitation of domestic raw materials with a considerable mining and smelting industry, an insignificant iron and steel industry,[1] and a slowly growing chemical and wood processing industry. Two-thirds of the industrial enterprises were concentrated in a few places, such as Ljubljana, Zagreb, Maribor, Novi Sad and Belgrade.[2] The foreign trade structure reflected this

[1] Only 41 kilograms of iron ore and 15 kilograms of steel were produced annually per inhabitant, which is way below the European prewar average.

[2] The center of mining was in certain sections of Serbia and northern Bosnia, but for the most part mining served for export and not to attract industries requiring metals.

limited development; exports were largely confined to ores, concentrates, timber and foodstuffs, and close to 80 per cent of the total imports consisted of semi-finished and finished products.

Manufacturing's share of the national income in 1939 amounted to 26.8 per cent, an increase of 6.2 per cent over 1923. (See Table 16–1.) The government encouraged a limited program of industrialization by providing favorable freight rates, high import tariffs, tax concessions and special inducements to foreign capital. During the depression certain basic industries and their raw materials — notably iron mines, iron and steel works, and coal mines — were taken over by the government, which also built armament factories, sugar refineries, silk-weaving mills and an oil refinery. Foreign capital contributed to the large increase in the mining and smelting industry, but at the same time increased dependence on foreign economies.

Industrial production was brought to a complete standstill by World War II. All efforts were concentrated on reconstruction immediately after libera-

Table 16–1

CONTRIBUTIONS TO THE NATIONAL INCOME
BY VARIOUS INDUSTRIES, 1923–1959

(*Per Cent*)

	1923	1939	1949	1952	1956	1958	1959
Manufacturing and mining	20.6	26.8	35.6	47.0	43.5	43.0	42.0
Agriculture	51.5	44.3	34.3	25.2	29.3	27.0	29.2
Forestry	—	4.6	6.2	0.4	2.0	1.6	2.0
Construction	—	2.5	8.4	7.5	4.6	5.3	5.2
Transport	27.9	6.6	5.2	5.1	5.7	6.4	5.9
Commerce	—	8.1	6.7	6.6	9.4	11.1	10.8
Handicrafts	—	7.1	3.6	4.9	5.5	5.6	4.9
Others	—	—	—	3.3	—	—	—

Sources: Statistički Godišnjak FNRJ, 1955, 1959; Savezna Narodna Skupština, *Društveni Plan Privrednog Razvoja Jugoslavije 1957–1961* (*The Social Plan of Economic Development of Yugoslavia 1957–1961*), Kultura, Belgrade, 1957; 1959 data from Federal Economic Planning Institute.

Table 16–2

INDEX OF INDUSTRIAL PRODUCTION, 1950–1959

(*1939 = 100*)

	1950	1951	1952	1953	1954	1955	1956	1957	1958	1959
Industry total	172	166	164	183	208	242	266	311	345	391
Capital goods: equipment	510	534	582	757	785	917	971	1,127	1,275	1,491
Raw materials	160	153	156	169	193	228	255	292	323	360
Consumer goods	165	162	142	160	184	207	230	279	306	351

Source: Indeks, No. 3 (1956), p. 5; No. 10 (1959), p. 5; No. 8 (1960), p. 5.

tion, and by 1947 the prewar level had been reached. This achievement was due to a number of factors. First, Yugoslavia avoided postwar occupation by foreign troops as well as the dismantling of factories and claims on war booty or ex-German property by the Soviet Union. Secondly, Yugoslavia lost no territory; it actually gained valuable land and resources in Istria and Dalmatia (Zadar and its hinterland) from Italy. Because it did not lose territory, it avoided the difficult problem of repatriation of its nationals, other than those working in German-controlled territory at the end of the war. Thirdly, Yugoslavia was the beneficiary of sizable relief and rehabilitation aid from such international organizations as UNRRA and the World Council of Churches, and of reparations from former enemy countries.[1]

Once reconstruction had progressed, plans were made to develop new mining and industrial establishments. These plans covered the years 1947–1951 and in many ways resembled the Soviet five-year plans. Large investments were started in industries producing capital goods, transportation, power production — the so-called "basic or key projects" — and in mining and smelting facilities supplying those basic projects.[2] Over-all industrial production started to increase: based on an index of 100 for 1939, it was 121 in 1947 and 172 in 1950. But while the production index of capital equipment rose to 510 by 1950, production of raw materials increased only to 160 and consumer goods to 165. (See Table 16–2.) Besides increasing industrial production in general, and reducing the large surplus agricultural population through industrial employment, the government hoped to bring about ultimately a more even distribution of income among the different republics and regions. This was no easy task; in 1958 per capita income still was approximately ten times larger in the more advanced regions than in backward areas.[3] The correction of such an imbalance meant a large transfer of capital between different parts of the country. Furthermore, it was planned to locate

---

[1] German reparations between 1946 and 1951 consisted largely of equipment for close to 300 plants. This equipment was mainly used for modernization and rebuilding of existing plants and to a lesser degree for the expansion of their present facilities, mostly in the basic industries—iron and steel, miscellaneous metal fabricating and nonferrous plants. Ivan Avsenek ("Basic Industries," in Robert F. Byrnes, ed., *Yugoslavia*, Mid-European Studies Center, Frederick A. Praeger, New York, 1957, p. 287) estimates total German reparations at about $101 million. Reparations from Hungary before the Cominform break amounted to approximately $11 million and were largely used in electrical engineering, metal fabricating, and oil processing establishments.

[2] For example, transportation received 24.6 per cent of the total investments during 1947, with 35.4 per cent allocated to manufacturing and mining. (See Appendix Table 16–1.) In the period 1947–1956 the power industry received 30.7 per cent of the total industrial investment, basic industries 51.4 per cent and the manufacturing industry 17.9 per cent. Jaša Davičo and M. Bogosavljević, *The Economy of Yugoslavia*, Jugoslavija, Belgrade, 1960, p. 13.

[3] Mijalko Todorović, *Current Problems of Economic Policy*, Jugoslavija, Belgrade, 1959, p. 28. This statement was part of a report by Vice-President Todorović to the second plenary meeting of the Central Committee of the League of Communists on November 18–19, 1959.

many of the new heavy industrial enterprises close to the source of raw materials, including power reserves, which would benefit backward regions such as Bosnia and Herzegovina.[1] (For distribution of postwar investments, see Appendix Table 16–1.)

According to the Yugoslav planners, the successful completion of the first Five Year Plan was dependent upon large imports of capital goods, especially mining and industrial equipment from the Soviet Union and from the Eastern European countries.[2] Yugoslavia relied on the countries of the Eastern bloc, including the Soviet Union, for roughly 50 per cent of its imports (Table 17–1), and in some vital products this dependency was even greater (see Chapter 10, p. 144). The break with Moscow was immediately followed by economic pressure from the USSR and the satellite countries, and by the beginning of 1949 an economic blockade against Yugoslavia had produced a slowdown in industrial production and the building of new plants.

The Five Year Plan was first extended for an additional year and then was abandoned, with the exception of the "key projects," which received continued attention and were ultimately completed. Capital expenditures were curtailed except for national defense, which more than tripled between 1947 and 1952.[3] Consumer production stagnated and, in certain lines heavily dependent upon foreign exchange, even retrogressed until 1954. As a result of the low production level in the economy as a whole, demand for some items (coal, for example) declined as did production. This decline or stagnation in production, especially in 1951 and 1952, was also the result of extremely serious droughts in both 1950 and 1952 which made Yugoslavia dependent upon large imports of agricultural products and in turn affected production in the food processing industry. The decline in food processing output was 8 per cent in 1950 and 20 per cent in 1952 from the 1949 level. Textile industry production declined up to 26 per cent, and production of leather and shoes up to 42 per cent, between 1950 and 1953.[4] Even though capacity, especially of the basic industries, continued to expand, shortages of raw materials had

---

[1] For details, especially in regard to the relationship between the resource base and the location of new industries, see George W. Hoffman, "Yugoslavia in Transition: Industrial Expansion and Resource Bases," *Economic Geography*, October 1956, pp. 294–315.

[2] Some were extremely doubtful that the "production targets" set by the Five Year Plan ever could be reached. See United Nations, *Economic Survey of Europe in 1953*, Geneva, 1954, pp. 111 and 113, and Czeslaw Bobrowski, *La Yugoslavie Socialiste*, A. Colin, Paris, 1956, pp. 80–87. The break with the Soviet bloc and the economic blockade against Yugoslavia settled this question. In addition, the drought in 1950 in any case would have had a serious impact on the goals set.

[3] United Nations, *Economic Survey of Europe in 1953*, p. 112, Table 49, lists defense expenditures as 8 per cent of the gross national product in 1947, 7 per cent in 1948, 11 per cent in 1949, 14 per cent in 1950, and 24 per cent in 1952, the highest figure.

[4] *Privreda F.N.R.J. u Periodu Od 1947–1956 Godine* (*The Economy of the Federal People's Republic of Yugoslavia in the Period 1947–1956*), Ekonomski Institut, FNRJ, Belgrade, 1957, p. 385. See also general production statistics.

become a serious bottleneck curtailing production, and large capacities remained unutilized.[1] Unemployment made its first entrance on the scene in 1951.

To avoid a complete breakdown of the country's economy, Yugoslavia was assisted by the West with large shipments of agricultural products, especially wheat, essential raw materials and some industrial equipment. Western aid in the years 1950–1952 not only made it possible to keep most of the industries running, even though on a much reduced level, but was decisive in bringing about the adjustments made necessary by the complete standstill of Yugoslavia's trade with the Soviet Union and other Eastern European countries. United States military aid contributed to the modernization of Yugoslavia's armament industries and lessened the strain placed on the economy by defense expenditures. These new ties with the West in turn laid the basis for the revival of Yugoslavia's economic growth and increased production. The material and human resource base on which this depended is discussed later in this chapter.

Industrial Growth, 1953–1956

Starting in 1953 industrial production went through a period of renewed expansion. The basic industries proceeded to grow at a rapid rate. However, the imbalance between heavy industries and light industries continued for some years. All efforts were directed toward increased production of energy, equipment and raw materials, and toward the creation of key projects, particularly in iron and steel, machine building, tool manufacturing, hydroelectric equipment, etc. In the light industries, emphasis was mainly on adjustment of disproportions in existing capacity and reconstruction and modernization of a selected group of plants. This policy with regard to industrial growth was a continuation, with certain modifications, of plans developed in preparation for the first Five Year Plan.

With Western aid assured as far as the basic food and raw material requirements of the economy were concerned, the government could continue to pursue a policy of one-sided investment and completion of previously contemplated big central projects. In all, close to 100 key projects had been started during the period 1947–1950 and, while only a small percentage were completed by 1953, more and more were brought into full production between 1953 and 1956.[2] Thus industrial production continued to expand

---

[1] Otto Matter, "On Yugoslavia's Industrialization," *Swiss Review of World Affairs*, Vol. I, February 1952, pp. 11–13.

[2] Egon Neuberger, "General Survey of the Yugoslav Economy," in Robert F. Byrnes (ed.), *Yugoslavia*, Mid-European Studies Center, Frederick A. Praeger, New York, 1957, p. 196. Neuberger estimated that "nearly 60 per cent of postwar industrial investments were still frozen in uncompleted projects in 1955." While this figure seems too high, there is no question that most key projects were not completed until after 1955.

during this period, though the expansion was concentrated largely in so-called slow-yielding projects in electricity, mining and heavy manufacturing industries.[1]

The first signs of de-emphasizing the one-sidedness in the industrial development program came toward the end of 1954. Several reasons have been given for this change, the impact of which actually was not felt much before 1956. First of all, it came during a period of severely low agricultural production when the urgency of increasing food output had become apparent (see p. 278). Secondly, capacity available and unused in the newly completed and nearly completed plants was considered sufficient to take care of expected needs during the next few years.[2] Thirdly, by deliberately forcing progress in basic industrial production — even after poor harvests — and relying heavily on imports, especially of consumer goods, the Yugoslav government found itself with a large and growing deficit in the balance of payments that was adversely affecting the future economic development of the country. These imports of consumer goods were needed to raise the extremely low standard of living and satisfy the basic needs of the people, but the use of limited foreign exchange for this purpose curtailed imports of essential raw materials, which in turn showed itself in low plant output. In addition, this one-sided development threatened even the slowly rising standard of living, especially of the urban population. It had become obvious during 1954–1955 that the lagging production of consumer goods and the low level of agricultural production would act as a brake on the entire future economic development.

Makeshift changes were inaugurated during 1954–1956, such as the allocation of increased investments to certain consumer industries, including textiles and clothing, food processing, leather and footwear. Encouragement was given to production of goods for which a favorable foreign market was assured, e.g., the shipbuilding, woodworking and tobacco industries. The production of artificial fertilizers and other chemical products, and the expansion of the engineering industry, mainly by adding and modernizing existing plants for the production of tractors, trucks, durable goods, etc., were stressed. Industrial production, which had increased by 26 per cent between 1952 and 1954, was raised an additional 28 per cent between 1954

[1] Capital goods production showed an index of 757 in 1953 based on 1939 = 100, while that of consumer goods was only 160 (Table 16–2). Generally speaking, per capita production of consumer goods reached the 1939 level only in 1954–1955. During the period 1954–1956 Yugoslavia imported large quantities of consumer goods. These imports contributed heavily to the adverse trade balance.

[2] In 1954 there were 114 plants employing over 1,000 workers. In 1938 there were only 38. Utilization of plant capacities in 1955, as a result of various modifications in economic policies, amounted to 50 per cent. (Neuberger, *op. cit.*, p. 292.)

and 1956 by these measures. The increase in the number of those employed in manufacturing and mining during the period 1952–1956 amounted to 36 per cent.

In spite of the modifications of existing plans, however, the basic structure of industrial production had not materially changed by 1956. In fact, the constant modifications and improvisations had adversely affected certain long-term plans, and industrial production had lost much of its coordinated flow.[1] This was shown by the low capacity utilization caused by lack of machinery, insufficiently trained workers and supervisory personnel, and bottlenecks in the supply of raw materials. The shortcomings in certain branches of industrial production, in spite of a considerable increase in the over-all production, were becoming increasingly apparent.

As previously noted, the year 1956 marked a definite turning point in the government's over-all economic thinking. This was the year when detailed preparations were started in connection with the forthcoming Social Plan for the Economic Development of Yugoslavia 1957–1961. It was also the year when emphasis on industrial production was officially changed from priority for basic industries — even though this emphasis had already been watered down considerably — to all-round industrial development. The imbalance in the total industrial production, the low labor productivity — close to 50 per cent below that of neighboring Italy — and an insufficient linking of the Yugoslav economy with that of foreign markets[2] received considerable attention in the form of a re-allocation of investments, a strong drive for increased labor productivity and encouragement to those branches of the economy which could reduce imports and increase exports. A long-term plan, officially announced at the end of 1957, with 1957 included in the new production goals,[3] was the basic instrument promulgating the new policy.

The Five Year Plan, 1957–1961

The Five Year Plan for industrial development was based on an existing high rate of industrial growth — a near doubling of the industrial output between

---

[1] Report presented by Svetozar Vukmanović-Tempo on January 10, 1958 before the Federal Board of the Socialist Alliance of the Working People of Yugoslavia (*Information Service Yugoslavia*, RN. 45/58 E, p. 14).

[2] Vukmanović-Tempo in his address of January 10, 1958 made it a special point to criticize some newly built enterprises, depending on high tariffs for the protection of their domestic market, which had poorly organized and outdated working methods as well as extremely low labor productivity. He cited the need for close foreign ties to make domestic production competitive internationally and for the use of the most up-to-date production methods.

[3] Savezna Narodna Skupština, *Društveni Plan Privrednog Razvoja Jugoslavije 1957–1961* (*The Social Plan of Economic Development of Yugoslavia, 1957–1961*), Kultura, Belgrade, 1957. The plan itself was made official by publication in *Službeni List*, No. 53, December 25, 1957. Details with regard to industrial development are analyzed in pp. 58–62, 152–170 of the plan and in background material published in June 1957, Savezna Narodna Skupština, *Industriski Razvitak Jugoslavije* (*Industrial Development of Yugoslavia*), Kultura, Belgrade, 1957.

1952 and 1957. The earlier one-sidedness in production had slowly undergone changes, especially in 1956 and 1957, with an emphasis on all-round industrial growth and greater attention to branches of industry previously neglected. The plan itself in its long-range aspects called for increasing investments in light industry as well as strengthening of the power industry and the raw material base. But basically, reconstruction and modernization of existing works had first priority.

The Five Year Plan anticipated an average annual increase in industrial production of 11 per cent: raw materials, 12 per cent; power and consumer goods, 12 per cent; building materials, over 10 per cent; and equipment, over 10 per cent.[1] Special attention was given to the full utilization of plant capacities as well as an increase in productivity planned at 6-7 per cent a year.[2] The all-round production increases anticipated were to be based on increases in production of consumer goods and producer goods, an intensive exploitation of natural resources, a better utilization as well as modernization of existing equipment and plant capacities, and changes in the allocation of investment.

Special priority in investment was to be given to electric light and power systems; coal, oil, steel and nonferrous metallurgy; chemical, metal manufacturing, building and consumer goods industries; and electronic technology and prospecting to insure an ample power and mineral raw material base.[3] Stress was laid on turning out the implements needed for agricultural production (tractors, trucks, fertilizers, etc.), and on the encouragement of those consumer goods industries which would replace imports and raise foreign sales. With plant capacities sufficient for a number of years, the plan was to leave the building of additional key projects to the later stages of the Five Year Plan. The general policy on investments laid increasing emphasis on the social sector (education, health, housing) — roughly 23 per cent of the total investments in 1959 as against 11 per cent in 1952 (Appendix Table 16-1). Yugoslavia also hoped to attack the imbalance in the per capita income between the underdeveloped and the advanced regions of the country. As a first step in the gradual correction of this imbalance, investment in the underdeveloped regions was to increase.

Industrial Production: Trends and Problems

Between 1952 and 1959 Yugoslavia's industrial production increased nearly two and a half times, and between 1939 and 1959 it more than tripled.

---

[1] *Društveni Plan Privrednog Razvoja Jugoslavije 1957–1961*, p. 59.

[2] Roughly 30 per cent of the increases anticipated were to come from a more intensive utilization of plant capacities.

[3] *Ibid.*, pp. 60–61.

Production increased 42 per cent in the first three years of the 1957–1961 Five Year Plan. The increase between 1957 and 1959 was somewhat faster than the estimated 39 per cent in the original Five Year Plan. The average annual rate of growth of the GNP between 1953 and 1959 was 10.4 per cent as against 2.4 per cent between 1948 and 1952. A recent United Nations report concludes that the 1950–1958 average annual rate of growth in industrial production of 9.1 per cent (Table 16–3 and 16–4) is much higher than

Table 16–3

INDUSTRIAL OUTPUT BY TYPE OF PRODUCT, SELECTED PERIODS, 1938–1958

(*Per Cent*)

	Share of Total Output			Increase in Output		Average Annual Rate of Growth	
	1938	1950	1958	1938–58	1950–58	1938–58	1950–58
Total	100	100	100	244	101	6.4	9.1
Consumer goods[a]	34	30	25	135	56	4.6	5.7
Intermediate goods[b]	58	57	58	225	97	6.4	8.8
Capital goods[c]	8	13	17	610	152	10.9	12.3

Source: United Nations, *Economic Survey of Europe in 1959*, Geneva, 1960, Chapter VII, p. 27.
[a] Food, beverages, tobacco, textiles, clothing, shoes, printing, some chemicals, etc.
[b] Rubber, metals, nonmetallic mineral products (building materials, some chemicals, etc.)
[c] Machinery, transport equipment, electric equipment.
Note: The percentage shares of total output make no allowance for changes in relative prices. They have been derived by applying index numbers of output at a given year's prices to the percentage distribution in 1953.

Table 16–4

INDUSTRIAL OUTPUT, BY SELECTED INDUSTRIES, 1938, 1950 AND 1958

(*Per Cent*)

	Share of Total Output[a]			Increase in Output		Average Annual Rate of Growth	
	1938	1950	1958	1938–58	1950–58	1938–58	1950–58
Total	100	100	100	244	101	6,4	9.1
Mining	16	16	13	171	64	5.1	6.4
Metal-making	13	11	14	271	165	6.8	13.0
Metal-using	8	14	17	615	161	10.3	12.5
Chemicals	3	3	5	421	224	8.6	15.8
Textiles	18	16	12	118	42	4.0	4.5
Food, drink, tobacco	13	10	9	157	94	4.8	8.6
Electricity	4	5	8	531	204	10.2	14.9

Source: United Nations, *Economic Survey of Europe in 1959*, Geneva, 1960, Chapter VII, p. 25.
[a] The percentage shares of total output make no allowance for changes in relative prices. They have been derived by applying index numbers of output at a given year's prices to the percentage distribution in 1953.

Table 16–5

OUTPUT OF SELECTED INDUSTRIAL GOODS, 1939, 1948 AND 1959

Product	Unit	1939	1948	1959
Iron & steel industry				
Crude steel	1,000 Tons	235	368	1,299
Rolled steel	1,000 Tons	151	250	861
Pig iron	1,000 Tons	101	162	863
Chemical industry				
Sulphuric acid	Tons	23,233	43,630	127,720
Caustic soda	Tons	13,673	18,560	47,907
Fertilizers manufactured	Tons	72,770	79,631	300,000
Electric industry				
Rotating machines	MW	4	8	384
High voltage bulbs	1,000 units	2,522	4,348	12,184[a]
Transformers	1,000 KVA	0	302[b]	1,624
Metals				
Aluminum in blocks	Tons	1,795	1,884	19,245
Blister copper	Tons	41,643	36,870	35,251
Electrolytic copper	Tons	12,463	14,441	52,000
Refined lead	Tons	10,651	49,214	85,000
Non-metals				
Asbestos fibre	Tons	—	749	4,307
Electro-porcelain	Tons	188	492	4,902
Food & tobacco				
Edible vegetable oils	Tons	21,285	41,053	45,565
Canned fish	Tons	3,223	2,072	12,497
Sugar, refined	Tons	107,599	162,355	246,000
Canned meat	Tons	1,328	2,285[a]	43,827
Fermented tobacco	Tons	16,525	31,932	37,260
Manufactured cigarettes	Tons	6,373	8,822[c]	18,506
Rubber				
Footwear, leather	1,000 pairs	5,154	5,386	9,007
Footwear, rubber	1,000 pairs	4,208	6,277[b]	10,670
Tires for motorcars	1,000	8	36	191
Tires for bicycles	1,000	276	580	702
Textiles				
Fabrics:	1,000 sq. meter			
Cotton	1,000 sq. meter	110,617	160,606	229,000
Woolens	1,000 sq. meter	12,443	28,686	38,003
Yarn:	Tons			
Cotton	Tons	18,947	27,776	46,963
Wool	Tons	6,216	13,032	17,343
Rayon and acetate filament yarn	1,000 sq. meter	14,012	3,375[b]	16,528
Timber & paper				
Mechanical wood pulp	Tons	9,853	16,701	52,132
Cellulose	Tons	28,324	22,134	108,615
Paper & cardboard	Tons	42,438	56,810	138,000

Table 16–5 (*Continued*)

Product	Unit	1939	1948	1959
Transport equipment				
Passenger cars	Units			4,431
Tractors	Units		3	5,919
Trucks	Units		535	3,716
Buses	Units			511
Motorcycles	Units			24,530
Bicycles	Units		11,000ᵈ	134,921
Miscellaneous				
Radio sets	Units		37,880	250,153
Stoves, kitchen ranges	Units	6,305	7,231ᵉ	26,033

Source: Compiled from official data.
ᵃ 1958.　　ᵇ 1947.　　ᶜ 1946.　　ᵈ 1950.　　ᵉ 1951.

the average rate of growth in the rest of Western Europe, though industrial output per capita is only one-fourth that of the industrial countries of Western Europe.[1]

The absolute volume of consumer goods increased between 1938 and 1958, but its share in the total industrial production decreased (Table 16–3 and 16–4). The annual rate of growth of the intermediate and capital goods sector combined was nearly twice that of the consumer goods industries. While the production of consumer goods increased rather slowly in recent years compared with intermediate and capital goods, a start was made in establishing new durable and light-goods industries, such as the manufacture of household appliances, radios, vehicles, etc. (See Table 16–5.)

The increased average annual rate of growth in the production of electricity (14.9 per cent in 1950–1958 as against 10.2 per cent in 1938–1958) was reflected in the greater consumption of energy per unit of output in the new industries such as chemicals, steel, etc. (For data on the production and consumption of electric energy in 1951 and 1959, see Table 16–6.) While the increase in energy consumption between 1950 and 1958 in Yugoslavia was 7.4 per cent a year compared with 1.5 per cent in the United Kingdom, 6.3 per cent in Western Germany, and 2.8 per cent in Belgium, per capita consumption of energy was still only one-third to one-fourth that of the Western European countries.[2]

Finally, it should be noted that the production of most capital goods, especially transport equipment and electrical machinery, is of relatively recent origin (Table 16–5). In 1958 the share of capital goods in total indus-

[1] United Nations, *Economic Survey of Europe in 1959*, Geneva, 1960, Chap. VII, p. 24.
[2] *Ibid.*, Chap. VII, pp. 29–30.

Table 16–6

PRODUCTION AND CONSUMPTION OF ELECTRIC ENERGY, 1951 AND 1959[a]

(Million Kilowatt-Hours)

	FNRJ		Serbia		Croatia		Slovenia		Bosnia and Herzegovina		Macedonia		Montenegro	
	1951	1959	1951	1959	1951	1959	1951	1959	1951	1959	1951	1959	1951	1959
Gross production	2,558	8,106	637	2,009	601	1,396	1,003	2,430	255	1,849	53	377	9	45
Feeding point output of power plants	2,455	7,752	601	1,882	575	1,326	978	2,353	245	1,784	47	364	9	43
Imports	—	20	—		—	9	—	11	—		—		—	—
Power from other republics			7	137	247	870		20	1	95	20	7	—	73
Power transmitted to other republics			20	26	1	97	247	360	5	711	3	50	—	16
Transmission and switching losses	244	1,072	66	306	81	276	77	236	14	186	4	50	1	16
Available for consumption	2,211	6,700	523	1,687	741	1,832	653	1,786	227	982	60	319	7	94
Exports	34	118	—		5	66	29	52	—		—		—	
Household appliances	259	1,347	69	416	92	426	73	309	12	112	12	69	2	15
Business and social premises	83	232	32	83	24	60	13	42	10	32	4	10	0.8	5
Motor and apparatus of other consumers	100	221	32	81	37	69	18	42	9	15	3	11	1	3
Public lighting	19	68	7	20	0.6	24	2	11	3	8	0.7	4	0.4	1
Waterworks	67	114	25	43	35	48	6	13	1	5	0.3	2	—	3
Tramways and trolleys	26	50	15	28	8	17	2	3	1	2	—		—	
Electric railways	13	27	—		—	13	12	14	0.5		—		—	
Industry	1,598	4,521	341	1,013	530	1,110	493	1,300	191	809	40	223	3	66
Electrical metallurgy and chemistry	430	1,381	8	79	260	384	113	530	49	264	—	124	—	

Source: Statistički Godišnjak FNRJ, 1954 p. 155; 1960, p. 387.   [a] All figures have been rounded.

trial output in Yugoslavia was 17 per cent (Table 16-3); the share for the OEEC countries combined was estimated at 30 per cent in 1953.[1]

Industrial production at the end of the third year of the Five Year Plan (1957–1959) had not only met the goals set originally, but in certain branches had gone far beyond them. A better balance between various branches of industry also was achieved during that period. The over-all production increase was so successful that the government was able to complete the original Five Year Plan in four years, at the end of 1960.

The original priorities for the Plan called for: (1) increased production of raw materials and semi-finished products for industry; (2) increased consumer goods, fuel and power; (3) increased investment goods and building materials. The first priority has been met successfully. By the end of 1959 industrial production depended to a large degree on domestic raw materials and semi-finished goods for two-thirds of its needs.[2] Industries relying mostly on domestic supplies include oil refining, ferrous and nonferrous metallurgy, and paper.

Certain inconsistencies and weak spots in the otherwise highly successful over-all production have been evident, however. During 1958, for example, a lack of key raw materials and semi-finished products in the metal industry, especially in the production of appliances and agricultural machinery, as well as in the automotive industry, resulted in slowdowns and serious production bottlenecks.[3] The production of steel, cement and certain consumer goods has been lagging most. Production of electric power is insufficient for household, office and industrial demands at peak loads during the day and during winter months, and use must be curtailed. In spite of greatly increased production — 147 per cent between 1953 and 1958 — the power supply is still insufficient for the constantly increasing demands. During 1958 changing demand resulted in increased stocks of some goods — for example, textiles (cotton, silk and man-made fabrics) and certain minerals which are largely exported and have limited storing possibilities, especially coal.

On the other hand, 1959 was a year of high demand and consumption with the result that existing stocks rapidly declined, and shortages occurred in both investment and consumer goods. Household furniture, electrical household appliances, paper and high-quality textiles were scarce at certain times of the year. Probably the largest deficiency in production was in housing. Bricks, structural steel, flat glass and cut timber have been in short supply

[1] Etienne S. Kirschen, *The Structure of the European Economy in 1953*, OEEC, Paris, 1958.

[2] "Industry Can Rely on More Domestic Resources of Raw Materials and Semi-finished Goods," *Privredni Pregled*, April 3, 1960 (*Joint Translation Service*, April 12, 1960, pp. 45–48).

[3] *Annual Report 1958*, Narodna Banka, Belgrade, 1959, pp. 11–13.

for some years, and the low priority given to housing before 1960 did not provide the incentives necessary for encouraging production.

The rapid rise in industrial production was greatly facilitated by the successful agricultural production of 1957 and 1959 which made it possible for the food processing industries finally to reach the anticipated levels of the Five Year Plan. Since fluctuations in agricultural production are to be expected, food processing industries — fruit and sugar beets in particular — will always depend to some degree on the unpredictable weather conditions causing variations in production in related categories.

Plans for 1960 and thereafter emphasized a continuing growth of the successfully producing industrial branches, especially those making investment goods (metal-using industries). Output of electric machinery and equipment was expected to increase by one-third, because of the anticipated increase in exports and the greater use of durables in private consumption, plus a greater domestic investment in machinery and equipment.[1] At the same time those industrial branches which lagged behind received special attention. Investment in manufacturing and mining, which had declined from a high of 70.5 per cent of total investment in fixed assets in 1952 to a low of 31.4 per cent in 1958,[2] amounted to about 34 per cent in 1960. Emphasis for the most part was on modernization and automatization, completing work in progress and increasing capacity in such industries as food, building materials, nonferrous metals, chemicals, timber and wood pulp.

The 1961–1965 Five Year Plan

The year 1960 was important as the one in which the 1957–1961 Five Year Plan was completed, a year in advance, and also important for planning a new Five Year Plan for the years 1961–1965.[3] Increases of investment in manufacturing and mining amounting to between 36 and 40 per cent for each year of the new plan were proposed. Priorities worked out by government planners emphasized new factories for building materials, glass, synthetic fibre and plastics, as well as plants for coal, coke, cement and steel. Special stress was on construction of new power stations to combat the long-term bottleneck in electricity. Raw materials and semi-finished goods which have been in short supply — coke, steel, ores, metals, rolled products and others — also were to receive special attention in the years to come.

[1] United Nations, *Economic Survey of Europe in 1959*, Chapter I, p. 22.

[2] Figures based on Jugoslovenska Investiciona Banka, *Investicije 1947–1958*, Dokumentacioni Materijali No. 2, Belgrade, 1959, and special communications from Jugoslovenska Investiciona Banka dated April 5, 1960.

[3] The new Plan was officially approved on December 29, 1960 (*Službeni List* No. 53, December 31, 1960).

One of the largest projects to be realized in the new Five Year Plan was the further expansion of the iron and steel industries. The new plan called for raising production of crude steel from 1.3 million tons in 1959 to 3.5 million tons. Yugoslavia's largest iron and steel works, located in Zenica, Bosnia, was to be further expanded. In 1958 Zenica produced 50 per cent of the total Yugoslav raw steel output and 60 per cent of the pig iron and coke. It is one of Europe's most up-to-date ferrous metallurgical combines. A new iron and steel mill was planned for Skoplie, using local raw materials.[1] The iron and steel mill at Nikšić was to have a second rolling mill, the capacity of the rolling mill at Smederevo was to be increased greatly, Jesenice was to be further modernized, a plant producing thin sheets and plates was planned, and a welded tube mill and skelp mill, financed in part by the U. S. Development Loan Fund, was to be added to the Sisak Iron and Steel Works.[2]

Other projects included a new automobile factory in Kragujevac, producing the Fiat 600, the enlarging of refinery facilities owing to greatly increased petroleum production, a new coke plant, a plant for prefabricated house sections and light construction material, several textile plants, a group of wood pulp and paper factories to be built at Mostar, Livno, Belgrade and Prijedor. A number of existing plants were to be enlarged and modernized — the aluminum plant at Kidričevo, a chemical plant at Šabac, and the truck factory at Privoj, among others. Additional funds were provided in the social plan for continued development of the facilities at the ports of Bar, Ploče and Koper on the Adriatic and Prahova on the Danube. Future industrial projects also called for several new food processing and fertilizer plants. Credit for equipment for three sugar mills was obtained from Italy, and the United States Development Loan Fund provided Yugoslavia with a credit of $22.5 million for a large fertilizer plant in Pančevo, Vojvodina. The much-discussed aluminum plant in Montenegro still depended upon obtaining the necessary financing from foreign countries.

Generally speaking, production efforts called for greater diversification and closer contacts between domestic and foreign firms. For some time Yugoslavia had purchased licenses from foreign firms to manufacture new metals, electric and machine-building products, electronic equipment, trucks and automobiles, etc. It was now proposed that this practice be continued wherever it would contribute to improving and broadening the basis for

[1] According to a report published in *Information Bulletin About Yugoslavia*, June 1959, p. 4, tests have been carried out with iron ore from Macedonia and domestic semi-coke (made from lignite excavated in the Velenje and Obilić mines) with satisfactory results. This project has been discussed for a number of years and the authors have heard much criticism of the economics of an iron and steel plant in Skoplje; the lack of dependability of raw materials and the distance from centers of consumption have been given as reasons for opposing the project.

[2] The loan amounted to $8.5 million.

domestic production. Finally, production efforts directed toward a greater variety of goods would benefit foreign trade. No part of Yugoslavia's productive effort calls for self-sufficiency; indeed, government policy was to encourage an even closer link with foreign countries. Such a policy of increasing present production and opening Yugoslav industrial efforts to foreign competition and know-how, Belgrade hoped, would raise the level of production, stimulate productivity, and thus increase the standard of living.

Raw Material Resources

Fortunately for Yugoslavia's ambitious plans for industrial growth, the country has considerable reserves of some important raw materials. Yugoslavia ranks high among the countries of the world in metal reserves but has only a limited supply of certain mineral fuels. United States and United Nations technical aid has been of great assistance in bringing modern production techniques to Yugoslav mines. In 1958 about 4 per cent of gross national product was generated by the mining industries; mineral exports were 17.4 per cent of the total value of exports and the mineral industries employed 19.4 per cent of the industrial labor force, according to official statistics.

Mineral Fuels

Coal, petroleum, natural gas and oil shale are among the mineral fuels available in Yugoslavia.[1] Of the proven coal reserves, 90 per cent are in lignite, 8.9 per cent in brown coal and only 1.1 per cent in bituminous coal.[2] Figures for total reserves vary considerably. They are as low as 13.4 billion metric tons and as high as 21.6 billion metric tons.[3] Total 1959 production of coal amounted to over 21 million tons, as contrasted with 7 million tons in 1939. (See Table 16–7.) The bituminous coal mines have been modernized and greatly enlarged since 1945, but their 1959 output of 1.3 million tons does not suffice for the expanding industrial production. Lignite and brown coal are widely distributed throughout the country, as can be seen in Figure 16–1.

[1] For details see Anton Melik, *Yugoslavia's Natural Resources*, Facts About Yugoslavia, Jugoslavija, Belgrade, 1951; Karl Guenzel, "Die Industrielle Produktion," in Werner Markert (ed.), *Jugoslawien*, Osteuropa-Handbuch, Böhlau-Verlag, Köln-Graz, 1954, pp. 254–279; Victor H. Winston, "Mineral Resources," in Norman J. G. Pounds and Nicolas Spulber (eds.), *Resources and Planning in Eastern Europe*, Slavic and East European Series, Vol. 4, Indiana University Publications, Bloomington, 1957, pp. 36–86; Melrad Mellon and Victor H. Winston, *The Coal Resources of Yugoslavia*, Mid-European Studies Center, New York, 1956; and Nikola Dragičević, "Perspektiva Razvoja Potencijalnih Izvora FNRJ" ("Prospective Development of Yugoslav Resources"), *Ekonomski Pregled* (Zagreb), April 1957, pp. 217–225. For production figures see the various issues of *Statistički Godišnjak* and *Statistički Bilten*.

[2] Basing this division on probable reserves, the distribution changes as follows: lignite 89 per cent, brown coal 10.7 per cent and bituminous coal 0.3 per cent.

[3] Dragičević, *op. cit.*, p. 224, uses the higher figure. Mellon and Winston, *op. cit.*, p. 135, mentions both.

Table 16-7

PRODUCTION OF SELECTED MINERALS AND ELECTRIC ENERGY,
SELECTED YEARS, 1939–1959

(*Thousand Tons If Not Otherwise Stated*)

Mineral	1939	1946	1954	1959
Antimony ore	19	31	75	96
Asbestos ore	—	32ª	132	191
Bauxite	719ᵇ	71	681	815
Chrome ore	45	77	125	107
Coal and coke				
Brown coal	4,312	3,823	7,100	9,122
Lignite	1,320	2,072	5,565	10,687
Bituminous coa	1,410	757	980	1,298
Copper ore	984	646	1,299	2,228
Crude magnesite ore	33	13	139	245
Crude petroleum	1	29	216	592
Iron ore	667	399	1,111	2,095
Lead and zinc ore	775	617	1,485	1,831
Manganese ore	6	8	9	8
Mercury (*tons*)	378ᵇ	306	498	460
Natural gas (*thousand cubic meters*)	2,628	8,501	27,944	49,993
Pyrite concentrates	78	94	160	290
Salt, evaporated	54	70	96	115
Electric energy				
Total (*million kwh*)	1,173	1,150	3,440	8,106
Hydro (*million kwh*)	566	478	1,810	4,708
Thermo (*million kwh*)	607	672	1,630	3,398

Sources: Indeks, March 1955; *Statistički Godišnjak FNRJ, 1960*, p. 154.
ª 1947.　　ᵇ Including output of Istrian mines.

Intensive surveying and drilling for petroleum and natural gas have been pursued only during the past five years. Reserves and production figures are constantly being revised upwards.[1] The 1959 production of crude petroleum for all Yugoslavia was 592,000 tons, an increase of 174 per cent over 1954. Productive fields are concentrated in the Vojvodina (one-sixth of the total 1953 production), and in the central part of the Sava Valley of Croatia (close to five-sixths). A small amount comes from northeastern Slovenia. With only 41 per cent of petroleum needs covered in 1958, the newly discovered fields are essential sources of supply.[2] Even with increased consumption (1961 goal of 1.2 million tons) there may well be exportable surpluses in the

[1] Successful petroleum drillings were reported in 1959 from several areas in the Vojvodina — the expected production increase by 1961 was close to 100,000 tons (doubling present production) — and from Croatia. The latter wells are especially productive, with an annual production of over one million tons expected by 1960. The new fields are north and south of Sisak near Stružec (35 successful drillings were made within an area of 20 km) and have been connected by pipeline with existing refinery facilities at Sisak. Successful explorations also have been reported during the past year from Istria (Rovinj, Kućani), Dalmatia (near Zadar), Boka (Serbia) and numerous places.

[2] It is significant that according to observations by one of the authors numerous oil workers and petroleum engineers received their training in the Texas and Oklahoma fields. United States drilling equipment is now produced under license in Yugoslavia.

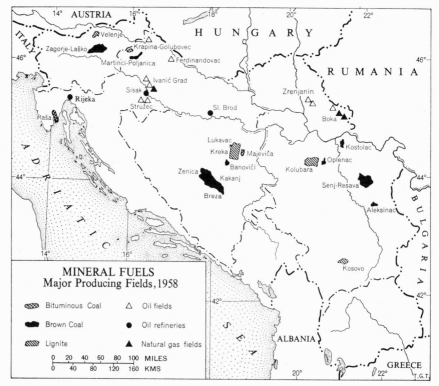

Figure 16–1

SOURCE: Miscellaneous official data, and Melrad Mellen and Victor H. Winston, *The Coal Resources of Yugoslavia*, Mid-European Studies Center, Free Europe Committee, New York, 1956.

not too distant future. Production of natural gas also has increased, and fields in the Vojvodina are expected to dispatch gas to Belgrade in the near future. The vast reserves of oil shale, estimated at over 550 million tons with an average of 10 per cent crude petroleum content, have not been exploited.

Water Power

Potential water power resources could yield about 66.5 billion kwh of electric power yearly.[1] Actual production amounted to 4.7 billion kwh in 1959 or 7.0 per cent of its potential. Yugoslavia ranks high in water power reserves,

[1] Milos Brelith, *Yugoslav Water Resources as a Power Reserve*, Jugoslavija, Belgrade, 1958, and G. P., "The Production and Consumption of Electric Power," *Yugoslav Survey*, Vol. I, No. 3, 1960, pp. 335–338. Total electric energy production in 1959 amounted to 8.1 billion kwh (1966 estimate, 19 billion kwh). For a comprehensive study of the power resources available, see Yugoslav National Committee of the World Power Conference, *Energetski Izvori Jugoslavije* (*Power Resources of Yugoslavia*), Vol. I, Belgrade, 1956.

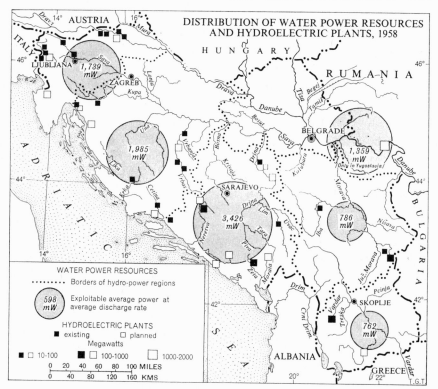

Figure 16–2

SOURCE: Base Map: Milos Brelith, *Yugoslav Water Resources as a Power Reserve*, Jugoslavija, Belgrade, 1958.

as Figure 16–2 shows, and even with plant expansions provided in the Five Year Plan in 1961, only 10.6 per cent of the capacity was utilized. Most industrially developed countries utilize between 25 and 40 per cent.

Yugoslavia is in an unusually favorable position to exploit its water reserves further. Its Alpine rivers have maximum water during the summer, while the Adriatic watershed has its maximum during spring and late fall (Figure 2–1). As a result of this evenness in the water regime and the highly dependable runoff, Yugoslavia should ultimately be able to satisfy its domestic needs and export some hydroelectric energy, even with household consumption rapidly increasing. This household consumption (44.3 per cent of the total) in 1960 was increasing much faster than new power plants could be completed, with resulting periodic power shortages. Over-all consumption of electric power between 1950 and 1955 increased 12 per cent; between 1955 and 1959, 17 per cent. According to a recent United Nations study, apparent consumption of hydroelectricity increased from 0.5 million tons of hard-coal equivalent in 1950 to 1.7 million tons in 1958.[1]

A project of great importance to power-hungry Yugoslavia, which has been studied by the United Nations and other international organizations and about which much has been written, is "Jugoexport."[2] This foresees the building of a series of hydro-power plants along the Adriatic at costs considerably lower than those for similar projects elsewhere in Yugoslavia or in other parts of Europe, owing to favorable hydrological and geomorphological conditions. It was originally hoped that the construction of several plants would be jointly financed by Yugoslav and foreign users, and that part of the power would be exported to Italy and other neighboring countries and Germany. But because of delays in the international financing of the project and because of urgent domestic needs, the Yugoslav government decided to proceed with the building of three projects: Trebišnica, Split and Senj.[3] The United States Development Loan Fund and the World Bank also agreed during 1960 to assist in the financing of the Trebišnica power project (near Dubrovnik) with a credit of $15 million, and the Senj power project (at the Velebit mountains on the Adriatic coast) including the installation of 790 miles of high voltage transmission lines, with a credit of $30 million.

Another project, under study for many years, would harness the waters of the Danube at the Iron Gate. When completed it would produce between 10 and 12 billion kwh of electricity a year, and would be the largest undertaking of its kind in Europe.[4] With hydroelectric power increasingly available and a slower increase in thermal power production (52 per cent of the total in 1939 as against 41 per cent in 1958), coal will become less important in power production but more significant as a chemical raw material base. This distribution may be further modified by the introduction of oil, natural gas or, later, nuclear energy.[5]

[1] United Nations, *Economic Survey of Europe in 1959*, Geneva, 1960, Chapter VII, Table 16.

[2] A series of memos and reports were published by the Economic Commission for Europe (Committee on Electric Power) during 1953–1955. For a full report, see United Nations, *Prospects of Exporting Electric Power from Yugoslavia*, 2 vols., EP/79 and E/ECE/EP/ 154, Geneva, April 1955.

[3] For a study of the general problem of the international exchange of electric power see George W. Hoffman, "Toward Greater Integration in Europe: Transfer of Electric Power Across International Boundaries," *Journal of Geography*, April 1956, pp. 165–176.

[4] This project — under discussion for the past thirty years — is part of a plan for better utilization of the Danube River both for power and for navigation purposes. The joint Rumanian-Yugoslav project plans to incorporate a system of locks that will make it possible for seagoing ships to ply between Belgrade and the Black Sea. A new commission, appointed in 1957, was studying the huge finances needed and the manifold technical problems of such a large project.

[5] The Boris Kidrič Institute for Nuclear Sciences at Vinča near Belgrade and the Institutes for Nuclear Sciences at Zagreb and Ljubljana have invested in modern machinery and laboratories for experimental purposes. The Institute at Vinča is a small, self-contained town which has been built since 1950. A second atomic reactor of 6.5 megawatts was put into operation in early 1960. This was a Soviet-made heavy water research reactor and produces isotopes for Yugoslavia's industries and medicine.

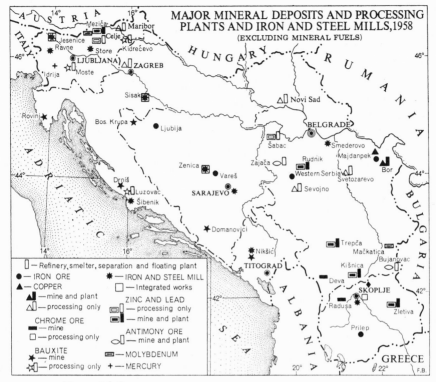

Figure 16-3

SOURCE: Official publications.

Metals and Nonmetallic Minerals

Ore mining has always played an important role in Yugoslavia. Both metals and nonmetallic minerals other than fuels are well distributed, particularly in the mountain heartland (Figure 16-3). Copper accounts for 25 per cent, lead for about 26 per cent, zinc for about 8 per cent, bauxite for about 24 per cent, antimony for about 36 per cent and mercury for roughly 6 per cent of Europe's metal reserves in 1954. Yugoslavia also has small reserves of chromium, mercury, molybdenum and manganese.

Extensive explorations have added to the reserves of nearly every ore, and new fields have been opened and old ones modernized or enlarged during the past few years. Iron ore deposits are concentrated at Vareš and Ljubija[1] in Bosnia. New deposits have been opened west of Prilep in Mace-

---

[1] Iron ore at Vareš consists mostly of siderites and contains 35 per cent iron and manganese. The deposits at Ljubija consist of siderites with 48 per cent iron and manganese, of limonites with 52 per cent iron and manganese, and of hematites with 69 per cent iron. For details see George Markon and Melrad Mellon, "Mining," in Robert F. Byrnes (ed.), *Yugoslavia*, Mid-European Studies Center, Frederick A. Praeger, New York, 1957, pp. 270-271.

donia with 35 to 42 per cent ore content, and they, together with newly opened coal fields nearby, are laying the basis for the contemplated iron and steel works in Skoplje. Iron ore reserves with an iron content of 40 to 50 per cent are estimated at 400–500 million tons. The 1959 production was over 2 million tons, more than triple that of 1939. Reserves are ample to meet the increased capacity of the iron and steel industry and still leave a small export surplus.

Yugoslavia is Europe's most important producer of copper, accounting for about 33 per cent of the European production. Important copper reserves at Bor and Majdanpek in northeastern Serbia enabled Yugoslavia to mine 2.2 million tons of copper ore in 1959 and produce 35,251 tons of copper.[1] Other minor reserves are known to exist in parts of Serbia, Macedonia and central Bosnia. The Bor mines have produced about 98 per cent of the copper output since mining started in 1905.[2] Following the enlargement of refining facilities after World War II there was a shift from export of concentrates to refined metal exports. Total copper exports accounted for 2.2 per cent of the value of Yugoslav exports in 1959. With Western financial aid, facilities were being modernized both at Bor and at Majdanpek to reach a capacity of 55,000 tons of blister copper a year.

Yugoslavia accounts for 26.7 per cent of Europe's lead production and 4.4 per cent of the world production. Lead exports amounted to 2.6 per cent of the total value of Yugoslav exports in 1959. The utilization of the lead-zinc ores has been common since the fifteenth century. The most important mines are at Trepča, Mezniča and Kišnica in Serbia, and the capacity has been greatly expanded since the war. New deposits have recently been found in eastern Bosnia, Montenegro, Macedonia and various areas of central Serbia.[3] The lead-zinc ores contain much silver, bismuth, antimony, iron, sulphur and manganese. Zinc production accounts for 13.3 per cent of the European and 2.2 per cent of the world production. Production increased with the opening of new mines and the enlargement of the zinc refinery and smelter at Celje (Slovenia) and Šabac (Serbia), and a new electrolytic plant at Šabac.[4]

Almost all of the mercury comes from the Idrija mine[5] in Slovenia (before 1945 part of Italy). Yugoslavia ranks third in Europe and exports about 85

---

[1] Estimated copper reserves are 2.3 million tons according to Bogdan Djaković, *Yugoslavia's Non-Ferrous Metals*, Jugoslavija, Belgrade, 1958, p. 12.

[2] Markon and Mellon, *op. cit.*, p. 272.

[3] Proven lead-zinc ore reserves are equivalent to 1.2 million tons, which is 20 per cent of Europe's and 2.6 per cent of the world's reserves.

[4] Djaković, *op. cit.*, pp. 16–17.

[5] The position Idrija holds in the production of mercury and its value to Yugoslavia is best seen in comparable production figures: 1944 production within boundaries of Yugoslavia at that time — 780 tons; production in same period at Idrija — 88,081 tons.

per cent of its mercury production. Antimony ore has been mined since 1880, mostly in Serbia, and reserves of high-grade ores are limited — a total of 44,000 tons. The main deposit is at Zajača (western Serbia) with a production of 2,281 tons in 1959 of antimony regulus, making Yugoslavia the largest producer in Europe.

Aluminum ore — bauxite — is mined largely in Dalmatia and Istria with smaller mines in Bosnia and Herzegovina and Montenegro.[1] At the middle of 1956 estimated reserves amounted to 23.9 per cent of the European and 5.5 per cent of the world reserves. Production is increasing; it amounted to 733,000 tons in 1958. This production is equal to about 20 per cent of European and 6 per cent of the world output. Yugoslavia has exported considerable quantities of bauxite (mainly to Germany and Italy) in the postwar years — about 16 per cent of European production and 4.7 per cent of world production. On the other hand, increasing amounts are now being used for the production of aluminum within the country. Owing to the excellent location of a large part of the reserves in Dalmatia, close to the large hydroelectric potential and to coal (lignite), plans for a greatly enlarged production of aluminum in that area have been made. (See also p. 318.) Thus far production of aluminum at Moste and Zožovac in Slovenia and at Lozovac near Šibenik has been modernized and enlarged. In addition electrolytic smelters and rolling mills of small capacities have been built.[2]

Chromite ore reserves are estimated at 1.5 million tons, with the main deposits in Macedonia.[3] Yugoslavia is Europe's second largest producer, Albania ranking first. Manganese ore is available in poor quality and is mined only in very small quantities at Čevljanovići near Sarajevo. Molybdenum is mined at Mačkatica, Serbia, and is also extracted in conjunction with lead-zinc smelting.

The maximum production can easily be increased in the metallurgy industries by an increased activity in ore prospecting. Processing plants are being expanded constantly; for many minerals, plant capacities exceed present ore extraction.

Nonmetallic minerals, too, are found in large amounts and are well distributed in Yugoslavia. Reserves are ample for a considerable expansion of the nonmetallic mineral industry. Only the most important minerals are

[1] *Ibid.*, pp. 18–20.

[2] The Yugoslav Information Service reported 1958 capacities of 62,000 tons of alumina (leached bauxite ore), 22,520 of aluminum and 26,500 tons of rolled goods annually.

[3] Djaković, *op. cit.* The Skoplje basin has supplied nearly two-thirds of the chromite and a new mine was opened in the postwar period at Deva near Dakovica, Macedonia, and a separation plant erected. Together with a separation plant at Gorče Petrov near Skoplje, their annual capacity is 116,500 tons. The main export is of chrome concentrates, but increased quantities are required for the domestic production of ferrochrome, etc.

mentioned here.[1] Pyrites are important for their sulphur content, and reserves are considerable. Today pyrites are recovered exclusively from flotation of lead-zinc ores. The prerequisites for the production of cement — almost unlimited natural limestone, cheap coal and easily accessible routes — are available along the Adriatic coast where numerous small and medium-sized cement factories have been established. Limestone is plentiful in many areas of Yugoslavia, and cement is produced in various parts of the country. Export of cement in 1958 amounted to 27 per cent of the production. Magnesite production comes mainly from mines in Serbia. Both sinter and calcined magnesite are now produced, in sufficient quantity for domestic and foreign customers. Asbestos of mediocre quality is found mainly in Serbia, with reserves amounting to over 42 million tons. Reserves of raw materials for the building industry — stone and clay — are practically inexhaustible. Other nonmetallic minerals such as rock-salt, gypsum and mica are available in significant quantities.

Manpower

Yugoslavia possesses a dependable supply of labor for its constantly expanding industrial needs. The additional manpower is available chiefly from agricultural population and new additions to the labor force. In addition, there is a "floating reserve" comprised of those forced to change jobs as a result of industrial and technological changes.

The largest group available for industrial jobs is the surplus agricultural population.[2] It has been estimated that between the early 1950's and 1957 or 1958 Yugoslavia's industries absorbed three-fifths of the increase in the labor force.[3]

The nonagricultural population increased rapidly in the postwar years — 18.8 per cent between 1945 and 1957 (an average of 1.5 per cent a year) as against 3.9 per cent between 1921 and 1938[4] — as industrialization progressed.

[1] For details, see *Yugoslavia, Economic Guide*, Privredni Pregled, pp. 109–114, and "Development of Yugoslav Economy," *Revue des Exportateurs et Importateurs*, No. 3 (Foire Internationale de Zagreb), 1958.

[2] The overpopulation is actually disguised unemployment and amounted to 35 per cent of the total agricultural population of the country before 1945. This figure was taken from a study made available to one of the authors by the Royal Institute of International Affairs (Chatham House), London, prepared by a special group chaired by Dr. P. N. Rosenstein-Rodan, dealing with problems of reconstruction, agricultural surplus population, and the economic development of eastern and southeastern Europe for the Royal Institute, 1943–1945. Doreen Warriner, *Revolution in Eastern Europe*, Turnstile Press, London, 1950, p. 176, published a table summarizing some of the findings of this study group. See also Rudolf Bićanić, *Agrarna Prenapučenost (Agricultural Overpopulation)*, Zavod Za Proučavanje Seljačkog i Narodnog Gospodarstva 'Gospodarska Sloga,' Zagreb, 1941.

[3] United Nations, *Economic Survey of Europe in 1959*, Geneva, 1960, Chapter VII, p. 33.

[4] Miloš Macura, *Stanovništvo i Radna Snaga kao Činioci Privrednog Razvoja Jugoslavije (Population and Labour-Force as Factors of Economic Development of Yugoslavia)*, Ekonomska Biblioteka 7, Belgrade, 1958, p. 238.

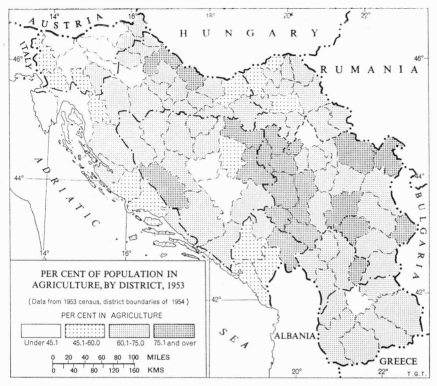

Figure 16-4

SOURCE: *Statistički Godišnjak FNRJ*, 1956, p. 415.

While the agricultural population (those deriving their major income from agriculture) still constitutes a high percentage of the total, the proportion has been steadily decreasing, and at an accelerated rate, in recent years. (See Figure 16-4 and Table 16-8.) The population occupied in agricultural and nonagricultural pursuits in 1953 and 1958 was as follows (in thousands):[1]

	1953	1958
Total population	16,936	18,220
Total labor force	7,849	8,437
Agriculture	5,183	5,189
Nonagricultural pursuits	2,666	3,248*

* Explaining the base for compiling the 1958 figure, Miloš Macura in a letter dated February 1960 stated that the total is an estimate based on the 1953 population census. This total includes craftsmen, assistant craftsmen and the nonagricultural population on military service.

As may be seen from this listing, the population of Yugoslavia increased by 7.4 per cent between 1953 and 1958. The number active in agriculture

[1] 1953 census data and United Nations Food and Agriculture Organization *Yougoslavie*, Project FAO de Développement Méditerranéen, rapport national, Rome, 1959, p. 136.

remained nearly stable while the number employed in nonagricultural occupations increased 21.5 per cent. The agricultural population declined from 66.0 per cent of the actively employed in 1953 to 61.5 per cent in 1958. Those in manufacturing and mining increased from 8 per cent of the total active population in 1953 (see Table 16–9) to 11 per cent in 1958.

Table 16–8

AGRICULTURAL POPULATION,ᵃ SELECTED YEARS, 1921–1960

Date of Census or Estimate	Total Population (*Thousands*)	Agricultural Population	
		Number (*Thousands*)	Per Cent of Total Population
March 31, 1921	11,685	9,216	78.9
March 31, 1931	13,934	10,671	76.6
March 31, 1953	16,936	10,306	60.9
June 30, 1957 (est.)	18,005	10,106	56.1
June 30, 1960 (est.)	18,667	9,124	49.8

Sources: 1957 estimate from Miloš Macura, *Stanovništvo i Radna Snaga kao Cinioci Privrednog Razvoja Jugoslavije*, Ekonomska Biblioteka 7, Belgrade, 1958; 1960 estimate from *Borba*, January 27, 1960.

ᵃ Persons deriving the major part of their income from agriculture.

Table 16–9

ECONOMICALLY ACTIVE POPULATION, BY ACTIVITY GROUP, 1953

Activity Group	Number (*Thousands*)	Percentage Distribution
Total	7,849	100.0
Agriculture	5,183	66.0
Forestry	58	0.7
Manufacturing	513	6.5
Mining and quarrying	112	1.4
Construction	202	2.6
Transportation	168	2.1
Commerce	240	3.0
Arts and crafts	366	4.8
Administration and other activities	479	6.1
Services	70	0.9
Inactive and unknown	458	5.9

Source: Statistical Pocket-Book of Yugoslavia 1959, p. 20.
Note: The only available figures are for 1953.

Manpower also is available from those seeking employment for the first time. The labor force grew on an average of 125,000 a year between 1956 and 1959.[1] The proportion of actively employed varies greatly, however,

[1] The Federal Statistical Institute estimates an average annual increase of the active population for the period 1953–1961 of 113,000. Communication received August 12, 1960.

among the different republics. Estimated at 46.3 per cent of the population in the country as a whole in 1953, the active population amounted to 52.3 per cent of the total in Serbia proper, while in Montenegro it was only 36.4 per cent and in Kosmet 33.2 per cent. The underdeveloped areas thus provide a reservoir for future manpower needs. An extremely favorable age structure of the population has helped to offset the heavy population losses during the first and second World Wars. As shown in Table 3–4, 46.2 per cent of the population were in the economically most important age groups between 15 and 44, 30.5 per cent were under 15, and 17.4 per cent were between 45 and 64 years of age.

Table 16–10
EMPLOYMENT TRENDS, SELECTED YEARS, 1953–1959

	1953	1958	1959
Total employment	1,891,425	2,569,431	2,724,618
Private sector	64,000	96,172	92,696
Socialist sector: total[a]	1,827,425	2,473,259	2,631,922
Excluding apprentices	1,777,425	2,405,919	2,558,032
Excluding apprentices and employees in noneconomic activities	1,497,198	2,023,449	2,160,000
Nonagricultural employment[b]	1,614,190	2,170,309	2,376,146

Source: Miloš Macura, communication dated February 1, 1960.

[a] Including apprentices and employees in noneconomic activities, i.e., cultural-educational, social welfare and state administrative organs.

[b] Employment in socialist sector excluding agriculture, forestry and government.

Yugoslavia's labor needs have been estimated at 110,000 to 130,000 new workers a year, for expansion of economic activities, and an additional 40,000 workers for replacements.[1] The total increase in employment in the socialist sector between 1958 and 1959 amounted to 158,663 or an increase of 6.4 per cent. (See Table 16–10.) The increase between 1953 and 1959 amounted to 804,497 or 44.0 per cent; between 1956 and 1959, a period of accelerated economic progress, approximately 449,000 or 18.2 per cent. Total nonagricultural employment in the socialist sector of the economy increased from 416,000 in 1945 to 2.4 million in 1959 or roughly six times.[2]

[1] Estimates of newly employed vary greatly as can be seen from the following: The 1957–1961 Five Year Plan spoke of 130,000 newly employed a year. Miloš Macura, "Projekcija Ekonomskog Sastva Radne Snage i Stanovništva Jugoslavije 1953–1959" ("Economic Structure Projection of Yugoslav Labor Force and Population 1953–1959"), *Ekonomist*, Vol. VIII, No. 1, 1955, pp. 16–44, estimated 150,000; the Plan for 1960 expects an increase of 160,000, and Tito in his report to the Socialist Alliance of the Working People of Yugoslavia on April 18, 1960 spoke of a rise of 190,000 in the total number of employed in 1959.

[2] Statistics in official publications differ according to inclusion or exclusion of apprentices, personnel of state institutions, part-time workers, professional soldiers, etc. Figures also vary according to the period covered (yearly averages, March or September figures).

Table 16–11

EMPLOYMENT IN ECONOMIC ACTIVITIES IN THE SOCIALIST SECTOR,
BY ACTIVITY, 1952 AND 1959

	1952		1959[a]	
Economic Activity	Number (*Thousands*)	Per Cent	Number (*Thousands*)	Per Cent
Total	1,351	100.0	2,453	100.0
Manufacturing, mining and quarrying	582	43.1	1,076	43.9
Agriculture	139	10.3	269	11.0
Forestry	22	1.6	38	1.5
Construction	168	12.4	300	12.2
Transport	159	11.8	180	7.3
Trade and catering	156	11.5	255	10.4
Arts & crafts including others	125	9.3	335	13.7

Source: Statistički Godišnjak FNRJ, 1954, p. 100; 1960, p. 344.
[a] As of September 30.

Table 16–12

EMPLOYMENT IN ECONOMIC ACTIVITIES IN THE SOCIALIST SECTOR,
BY REPUBLIC, 1952 AND 1959

	1952		1959[a]	
Republic	Number (*Thousands*)	Per Cent	Number (*Thousands*)	Per Cent
Total	1,351	100.0	2,453	100.0
Serbia	460	34.0	890	36.3
Croatia	367	27.2	659	26.9
Slovenia	217	16.1	371	15.1
Bosnia-Herzegovina	217	16.1	337	13.7
Macedonia	73	5.4	150	6.1
Montenegro	21	1.2	46	1.9

Source: Statistički Godišnjak FNRJ, 1954, p. 100; 1960, p. 344.
[a] As of September 30.

In 1959, manufacturing and mining accounted for 43.9 per cent of the total employment in the socialist sector or over 1 million people as against 43.1 per cent or 582,000 in 1952. (See Table 16–11.) The republics of Serbia, Croatia and Slovenia accounted for 77 per cent of the total employment in socialist activities in 1952, and for 78.3 per cent in 1959, indicating a continuing concentration, and even a slight increase, of economic activities in the more advanced republics. (See Table 16–12.)

The average number of unemployed during 1959 was 161,633 or 6.1 per cent of the total labor force, as compared with 3.6 per cent in 1955. Of these, 55,457 or 34.3 per cent were seeking employment for the first time; 106,176 or 65.7 per cent had been employed previously. This increase in the number of people seeking employment, 81 per cent of whom were unskilled laborers, clearly shows the problem of agricultural surplus labor. As a matter of fact, the economic expansion, in spite of its rapid increase, cannot use all the manpower available for nonagricultural employment. The result is an unusual phenomenon for a socialist state, unemployment.

The figures available indicate that a large percentage of those seeking employment come directly from small villages or scattered rural farms. Inasmuch as many still keep ties with family holdings and others seek only seasonal employment, the straight unemployment figures are not very expressive. According to the preliminary figures of the 1960 census, 19.3 per cent of the labor force living on private agricultural holdings are permanently employed outside of the holding and 9.3 per cent have occasional outside employment.

While there is enough manpower for Yugoslavia's industrial expansion for years to come, a problem requiring immediate attention is the large number of unskilled among the agricultural surplus population seeking employment in the economy.

Geographic Imbalance

Differences between the more advanced and the underdeveloped regions have posed special problems for Yugoslavia's industrial development.[1] Macedonia, Montenegro, the areas of Croatia (Lika, Banjija, Kordun) and the mountainous interior parts of Bosnia and Herzegovina are considered underdeveloped areas.[2] The per capita income in these areas in 1960 was between 30 and 50 per cent lower than the Yugoslav average. Nevertheless, most of these areas are considered well endowed with water, minerals, forests and other resources. Bosnia and Herzegovina, for example, has 28 per cent of Yugoslavia's reserves of water power, 90 per cent of the iron ore, 50 per cent of the lignite, and 33 per cent of the timber.[3] Because of the great possibilities for developing natural resources, the government gave considerable attention to industrial growth in the underdeveloped regions from the start of the first Five Year Plan. The proportion of investments allocated to

[1] For a more detailed discussion of these problems, including their political implications, see Chapters 22 and 23.

[2] Underdeveloped regions in need of special federal assistance in 1960 included only the republics of Macedonia and Montenegro and the autonomous region of Kosmet. Special economic measures were no longer needed for Bosnia and Herzegovina, and the underdeveloped regions in Croatia or other republics were generally considered the responsibility of the respective republics. Cf. "Development of Economically Underdeveloped Areas of Yugoslavia," *Information Service Yugoslavia*, RN 64–58 E.

[3] *Ibid.*, p. 34.

Table 16-13

PERCENTAGE DISTRIBUTION OF INDUSTRIAL INVESTMENTS BETWEEN
THE UNDERDEVELOPED AND ADVANCED REPUBLICS, SELECTED YEARS, 1947–1960

	1947	1949	1953	1958	1960 planned
Total	100.0	100.0	100.0	100.0	100.0
Underdeveloped republics	19.3	21.0	38.5	21.2	25.0
Serbia, Croatia, Slovenia	80.7	79.0	61.5	78.8	75.0

Source: Jugoslovenska Investiciona Banka, *Investicije 1947–1958*, Belgrade, 1959.

Table 16-14

NUMBER OF ENTERPRISES, EMPLOYMENT AND INDEX OF INDUSTRIAL PRODUCTION,
BY REPUBLIC, END OF 1958

	Number of Enterprises	Number of Employed	Index of Industrial Production ($1939 = 100$)
Total	2,500	975,730	345
Serbia	883	311,655	346
Serbia proper	417	217,192	297
Vojvodina	417	78,626	245
Kosmet	49	15,837	215
Croatia	583	267,698	306
Slovenia	505	171,587	319
Bosnia & Herzegovina	276	166,530	434
Macedonia	193	46,088	686
Montenegro	60	12,172	879

Sources: Statistički Godišnjak FNRJ, 1959, p. 358, and miscellaneous *Indeks* figures.

the advanced and the underdeveloped republics over the years can be seen in Table 16–13.

Although the most rapid development has occurred in the least developed republics (Table 16–14) industrial production was still concentrated in a few centers and in a relatively small number of enterprises in the more advanced regions. Seven cities had 44 per cent of all industrial enterprises in 1958, and the total number of enterprises increased only 16 per cent between 1954 and 1958. Zagreb, with 118 industrial enterprises, and Belgrade with 117, employing 53,289 and 58,714 persons respectively (as of March 1958) had the heaviest concentrations. They were followed by Ljubljana, Novi Sad, Sarajevo, Skoplje and Maribor.

A majority of enterprises employed between 125 and 250 persons. In 1958, there were 212 enterprises with 1,000 or more employees and 300 with 500 to 1,000 employees. Belgrade had 17 enterprises employing more than 1,000 persons, Zagreb 14 such enterprises and Maribor 8. Indicative of the trend, however, was that Macedonia, which before World War II had only two enterprises with more than 250 employees, had more than 30 such enterprises in 1958.

In spite of all the efforts during the past fifteen years to bring about a better balance in economic development of the advanced and underdeveloped regions of the country, much still needed to be done. With the less developed regions having a more rapid increase in population and a larger agricultural surplus population than the rest of the country, and large reserves of natural resources, it was clear why the government considered regional differences in the standard of living among its people the number one problem. During 1960, investment funds from the federal budget for the underdeveloped regions were to be increased to one-fourth of all federal investment funds. The location of new industrial enterprises was part of the program of correcting the imbalance between the republics.

FOREIGN ECONOMIC
RELATIONS

THAT international economics is tied up inextricably with international politics is nowhere illustrated as well as in the case of Yugoslavia's foreign economic relations. For a small and comparatively backward but developing country like Yugoslavia, politically belonging to neither East nor West, and regarded with some suspicion by both, foreign economic relations are a matter of life and death.

In addition to international developments, however, history, geography and the changing structure of Titoist society all combine to determine the shape of Yugoslav foreign economic relations. The divided past of the Yugoslav peoples has meant not only great differences in their respective levels of economic development but also traditionally different centers of gravitation. Following unification of the country in 1918, Yugoslavia had its closest economic ties with the more advanced countries of Central Europe and with Italy. In the first years after World War II, Belgrade was tied in economically as well as politically with the bordering Soviet bloc. After 1948, when Yugoslavia was cast out from Moscow's Communist community, it had perforce to seek friends and trading partners some distance from its borders.

In the meantime, the structure of the Yugoslav economy was undergoing great changes. The interwar period was characterized by agricultural export surpluses due to a low level of industrial development. Up until 1932, however, exports and imports were usually kept in balance. But with the deepening world economic crisis, exports declined in both volume and value, while imports increased. The resulting trade deficit forced the government into a moderate expansion of certain industries, as, for example, textiles, chiefly to save foreign currency. This policy fostered protectionism.[1]

In the postwar period, the pattern of economic development underwent a sharp shift. Industrialization on a large scale has been the basic policy since 1945. This necessitated large capital investments aimed predominantly at building heavy industries and boosting power production. Agriculture was first assigned a low priority, and this resulted in lagging farm production. Accordingly, it became necessary to import foodstuffs, especially wheat, flour, fats and oils.

Although some of Yugoslavia's early needs were eased by reparations and UNRRA supplies, a serious balance of payments deficit developed which continued to be one of the most important problems facing the Tito regime. It has, in fact, been bailed out only by sizable amounts of economic aid from the West, particularly the United States. Experimentation with a return to closer economic ties with the Soviet bloc boomeranged, and the early 1960's saw Yugoslavia striving not only to keep but to expand its economic ties with the West. The 1961 fiscal reform, freeing nearly a third of imports from controls, providing for partial convertibility of the dinar and presaging full membership in GATT, would seem to insure a Western trade orientation.[2]

Nevertheless, trade with the capitalist countries has its hazards, too, as the Yugoslavs found out when, as a result of the 1957–1958 recession in the United States, sales of their single biggest export item, lead, dropped by about $3 million annually.[3] Also, the Yugoslavs view with concern efforts at Western European economic integration. With the Soviet bloc already integrated, they are anxious not to fall between the two and be left out economically. As a result, one of Belgrade's major drives has been to increase its economic ties with areas outside Europe.

General Pattern, 1950–1956

The drastic change brought about by political developments in 1948–1949 necessitated a rapid geographic reorientation in Yugoslavia's foreign economic relations. Trade with the Soviet Union was insignificant before World

[1] For a discussion of this period, see Jozo Tomasevich, "Foreign Economic Relations, 1918–1941," in Robert J. Kerner (ed.), *Yugoslavia*, University of California Press, Berkeley, 1949, p. 169.

[2] See, for example, "Changes in the Yugoslav Foreign Trade and Currency System," *Yugoslav Life*, Vol. VI, No. 52, January 1961, pp. 3–4. See also Chap. 14, pp. 258–261.

[3] Other raw materials exported by Yugoslavia also are affected by world-wide price fluctuations — magnesite, bauxite, mercury, etc. A price decline in certain imported raw materials — natural rubber, crude cotton (from Egypt only), coal, crude oil (from the USSR only), etc. — benefits Yugoslavia itself. Looking at a longer time span, Vasić feels that "prices of articles which Yugoslavia has exported "have risen less sharply than the prices of imported articles." See Velimir Vasić, "Present-Day Conditions of Yugoslav Foreign Trade," *Review of International Affairs*, October 16, 1958, p. 8.

War II; after the war it played a short-lived but decisive role in the Yugo-slav economy. Before the break with the Cominform, Yugoslavia depended upon the countries of the Soviet bloc for over 50 per cent of its imports and exported about the same proportion to the East. In 1948 finished products accounted for 15.7 per cent of Yugoslavia's imports from the Soviet bloc, and raw materials 84.3 per cent; exports to the Soviet bloc consisted of raw materials (88.5 per cent), foodstuffs (9.7 per cent) and finished products (1.8 per cent). In 1950 trade with the Soviet Union and the other bloc countries was zero. (See Table 17–1.)

Fortunately for Yugoslavia, its location and its apparent insistence upon its independence were key factors in determining the national policy of the Western countries. Starting with November 1950 assistance to help Yugo-slavia preserve its independence became the accepted policy of the United States Congress and government. From then on foreign aid — economic and, for some years, military — was of increasing importance in the whole eco-nomic development of Yugoslavia. Trade with the Western countries in-creased rapidly, and United States financial aid, in the form of grants and loans, made it possible for Yugoslavia to increase its dollar purchases, particularly of materials and foodstuffs, to overcome the difficulties of this period.

When trade relations with Eastern Europe were re-established in 1954,[1] Yugoslavia's over-all volume of trade had increased sufficiently that exports and imports with other regions did not have to be reduced materially. In addition, Yugoslavia put much effort into opening new trading channels, especially with overseas regions. Its trade orientation still depends upon shifting political developments, over many of which it has no direct influence. While the general structure and volume of trade are determined by economic plans, all Yugoslavia can do about future regional orientation, according to a Yugoslav expert, "is to state the principles this country will abide by irrespective of the attitude others might take."[2]

Emphasis on continued industrialization, with special attention focused on key projects begun during the first Five Year Plan, and slowly increasing attention to agriculture, were the main characteristics of Yugoslavia's

[1] Economic relations with the USSR were resumed with a small barter deal amounting to $5 million each way concluded in October 1954. A new agreement in January 1955 provided for a $10 million exchange of goods, which was increased twice during the year. Exports to the Soviet bloc countries in 1956 reached 22.8 per cent of total exports and imports 22 per cent of the total. Cf. A. Z., "Soviet Yugoslav Economic Relations 1945–1955," *The World Today*, January 1956,· p. 41, and Helmut Roesler, "Jugoslawien zwischen Rubel und Dollar (1950–1957)" ("Yugoslavia between Ruble and Dollar"), *Osteuropa*, September 1957, pp. 630–636 and also November 1957, pp. 812–818.

[2] Vladimir Pertot, *Yugoslav Foreign Trade*, Jugoslavija, Belgrade, 1960, p. 22. Dr. Pertot was director of the Foreign Trade Research Institute, a semi-official organization, until late 1958.

Table 17-1

PERCENTAGE DISTRIBUTION OF YUGOSLAV FOREIGN TRADE, BY AREA,
SELECTED YEARS, 1939–1958

	1939	1948	1950	1953	1958
Exports by Destination					
Total	100.0	100.0	100.0	100.0	100.0
Europe	89.1	92.6	74.5	78.7	78.9
Western Europe	33.7	41.2	74.5	78.6	51.1
Western Germany	22.5[a]	.2	12.4	16.8	9.5
Italy and Trieste	10.6	10.8	13.8	15.7	12.2
Eastern Europe (incl. USSR)	19.7	51.2	—	—	27.8
USSR	0.0	15.0	—	—	8.2
Others	2.5	0.2	0.1	0.1	—
North America	5.2	2.7	13.5	14.0	7.6
United States	5.1	2.6	13.5	14.0	7.4
Asia	1.4	0.7	1.4	2.6	5.9
India	0.3	0.1	0.1	0.1	2.4
Africa	2.8	3.8	4.3	3.1	6.6
United Arab Republic[b]	1.3	3.3	4.2	1.9	4.2
Oceania	0.0	0.0	0.3	0.0	0.0
South America	1.5	0.5	6.0	1.6	1.0
Imports by Origin					
Total	100.0	100.0	100.0	100.0	100.0
Europe	87.2	90.8	66.6	57.7	70.7
Western Europe	22.4	44.8	66.6	57.7	42.4
Western Germany	38.2[a]	1.6	16.5	17.4	11.7
Italy and Trieste	11.7	12.2	11.1	7.2	9.9
Eastern Europe (incl. USSR)	10.2	45.9	—	—	28.3
USSR	0.0	10.7	—	—	8.4
Others	4.5	0.0	—	—	—
North America	5.3	3.4	21.8	36.7	19.8
United States	5.2	3.4	21.7	34.4	19.6
Asia	2.3	1.2	0.6	3.0	3.8
India	1.7	1.0	0.1	0.0	0.3
Africa	1.4	1.9	4.5	1.1	2.8
United Arab Republic[b]		1.8	4.4	0.7	1.7
Oceania	0.5	0.2	—	0.4	1.3
South America	3.3	2.6	6.5	1.1	1.6

Sources: *Statistička Spolne Trgovine FNRJ*, Belgrade.

[a] All of Germany.

[b] 1958 is for United Arab Republic; otherwise for Egypt only.

economic development which also determined the nature of its foreign economic relations between 1950 and 1956. Exports of agricultural products and raw materials and semi-finished products declined, while the share of finished products rose rapidly. Imports of raw materials generally increased to 1956 and rapidly declined thereafter; the share of semi-finished products fluctuated only little, while that of finished products rose sharply during the 1957–1961 Plan after a decline between 1952 and 1956. (See Table 17–2.)

Table 17–2

PERCENTAGE DISTRIBUTION OF YUGOSLAV FOREIGN TRADE,
BY TYPE OF GOODS AND INDUSTRY, 1939–1959

	1939	1948	1952	1953	1954	1955	1956	1958	1959*
Imports[a]									
Raw materials[b]	19.8	21.7	28.3	38.4	38.7	41.3	45.0	26.1	25.2
Semi-finished	26.3	33.1	25.3	17.8	20.5	22.3	18.9	24.6	25.1
Finished	53.9	45.2	46.4	43.8	40.8	36.4	36.1	49.3	49.7
Exports									
Raw materials	55.4	49.6	50.5	33.4	37.6	37.9	36.7	34.6	25.6
Semi-finished	39.2	35.0	42.8	50.0	45.7	46.2	42.8	35.8	37.1
Finished	5.4	15.4	6.7	16.6	16.7	15.9	20.5	29.6	37.3
Imports[a]									
Manufacturing		94.9	76.4	69.7	71.7	71.1	67.7	83.2	81.4
Agriculture[c]		5.1	23.5	30.2	28.3	26.8	32.2[c]	16.7[c]	18.5
Forestry		—	0.1	0.1	—	0.1	0.1	0.1	0.1
Exports									
Manufacturing		54.2	53.5	73.1	64.8	69.9	67.6	68.3	75.7
Agriculture		38.8	42.2	22.7	30.2	24.2	26.7	28.3	21.5
Forestry		7.0	4.3	4.2	5.0	5.9	5.7	3.4	2.8

Sources: Compiled from *Statistički Godišnjak FNRJ*, *Statistički Bilten*, and *Statistička Spoljne Trgovine FNRJ*.

[a] Imports include tripartite aid since 1951 and since 1956 imports of agricultural surpluses from the United States.

[b] Raw materials include agricultural products—food, drinks, tobacco and fuels.

[c] Cereals comprised the following percentages of agricultural imports: 77 per cent in 1956, 70 per cent in 1957 and 59 per cent in 1958.

* Preliminary data.

This whole period 1950–1956 was characterized by an extreme shortage of foreign exchange and a growing trade deficit. (See Tables 17–3 and 17–4.) The deficit was due to a number of factors, such as a long period of agricultural stagnation and the unfavorable structure of industrial production. Exports declined in both value and volume and reached the 1948 level (allowing for inflation) only in 1956. This was generally connected with the agricultural crisis. Imports of foodstuffs averaged 85 per cent of the total balance of payments deficit during 1953–1956.[1]

Cereals averaged 71 per cent of all food imports in 1955–1957. Agricultural surplus aid, beginning in 1955, relieved Yugoslavia of the necessity of paying for all food imports in foreign currencies. Since foreign exchange to pay for necessary food imports plus capital items required for industrial expansion

[1] Food imports averaged 32.5 billion dinars and the total annual balance of payments deficit averaged 37.3 billion dinars during 1953–1956. Cf. "Credit Potential of Yugoslav Economy," *Vesnik*, Jugoslovenske Investicione Banke, April–June, 1959, p. 11. Food imports amounted to 27.5 per cent of all imports in 1955, 31.8 per cent in 1956, 22.2 per cent in 1957 and 16.7 per cent in 1958.

Table 17-3

BALANCE OF TRADE, 1924–1959

(Amounts in Million Dinars at Current Prices)

		Imports		Balance of Trade		Ratio of Exports to Imports	
Year	Exports	Without Foreign Aid[a]	With Foreign Aid[b]	Without Foreign Aid[a]	With Foreign Aid[b]	Without Foreign Aid[a]	With Foreign Aid[b]
1924	9,536	8,222		+ 1,314		116	
1926	7,818	7,632		+ 186		102	
1928	6,445	7,835		− 1,390		82	
1930	6,780	6,960		− 180		97	
1932	3,056	2,860		+ 196		107	
1934	3,878	3,573		+ 305		109	
1936	4,376	4,077		+ 299		107	
1939	5,521	4,757		+ 764		116	
1946	16,231	12,205		+ 4,027		133	
1947	49,107	49,822		− 715		99	
1948	89,084	91,945		− 2,864		97	
1949	59,609	88,446		−28,837		67	
1950	46,307	69,202		−22,895		67	
1951	53,618	70,535	77,965	−16,917	−24,347	76	
1952	73,958	81,432	111,924	− 7,474	−37,966	91	60
1953	55,794	77,419	118,591	−21,625	−62,797	72	47
1954	72,113	74,743	101,819	− 2,630	−29,706	97	71
1955	76,976	98,092	132,288	−21,116	−55,312	78	58
1956	97,011	110,195	142,243	−13,184	−45,232	88	68
1957	118,533	162,536	198,394	−44,003	−78,861	73	59
1958	132,419	180,403	205,504	−47,984	−73,085	73	64
1959[c]	142,995	174,883	206,115	−31,889	−63,120	82	69

Source: Statistički Godišnjak FNRJ, 1960, p. 186.

[a] Excluding imports under tripartite economic aid (starting in 1951) and U. S. agricultural surplus aid (starting in 1956).

[b] Including tripartite aid and U. S. agricultural surplus aid.

[c] 1959 data subject to change.

simply was not available, without the aid program the whole economic development of the country would have been stymied, with possible political repercussions.

Neither the devaluation of the dinar in 1952[1] nor tighter control of imports brought a halt to the constantly increasing trade deficit. The emphasis on key, large-scale industrial projects without regard to immediate export needs required imports of capital goods and raw materials, while returns in the form of export surpluses from these major investments were far in the future. Only in 1954 did investments in export-oriented industries increase. In

[1] The dinar was devalued on January 1, 1952, from its official rate of 50 to one U.S. dollar to a rate of 300 to the dollar. But this rate was not meaningful for foreign trade, where the base rate was 632 dinars to a dollar, ranging upward to 900 and higher in many cases. See discussion in Chapter 14.

Table 17–4

BALANCE OF PAYMENTS, 1948–1958

(Millions of Dollars at Current Exchange Rates)

	1948	1950	1952	1954	1956	1957	1958
Exports of goods, f.o.b.	$322	$163	$252	$245	$327	$401	$462
Imports of goods, f.o.b.	378	289	394	367	495	674	699
Trade balance	− 56	− 126	− 142	− 122	− 168	− 273	− 237
Invisibles, net	+ 6	+ 6	+ 13	+ 11	+ 46	+ 51	+ 47
including nonmonetary gold of which							
Investment income, net		− 3	− 6	− 9	− 8	− 6	− 8
Government, n.i.e., net	− 3	− 4	− 6	− 4	+ 5		
Balance of goods and services	− 50	− 120	− 129	− 111	− 122	− 222	− 190
Private donations, net	+17	+ 13	+ 21	+ 24	+ 34	+ 50	+ 52
Official donations, net	+55	+ 24	+102	+ 91	+ 92	+ 59	+ 44
Private long-term capital, net	−36	+ 47	+ 23	+ 6	+ 48	+ 3	+ 5
Short-term capital, monetary gold and							
balancing item	+14	+ 36	+ 41	− 10	− 52	+110	+ 89

Sources: United Nations, *Economic Survey of Europe in 1958*, Geneva, 1959 and International Monetary Fund, *International Financial Statistics*, XIII, April 1960, p. 271.

n.i.e.: not included elsewhere.

addition, government policies toward agriculture were liberalized, and slowly increasing investments in agriculture reversed the earlier policy of transferring capital from agriculture to industry which had resulted in a further absolute decline of food production. Import restrictions on consumer goods were eased, starting in 1955, in the hope of encouraging higher labor productivity and at the same time forcing a decline in the costs of domestic production in order to improve the competitive position of Yugoslav products abroad.

Policies initiated between 1950 and 1955 showed their first tangible results in 1956 when exports rapidly increased as a result of the production of newly established industrial enterprises. The over-all increase in exports in 1956 over the preceding year was 26 per cent, while imports increased only 12 per cent (excluding United States outright aid), thereby reducing the trade deficit. But the improvement was only of short duration. While exports continued to increase, imports increased at a faster rate (Table 17–3).

Rising Foreign Trade: 1956 and After

The year 1956 was significant for several reasons and marked a definite turning point in Yugoslavia's foreign economic relations. The major developments between 1956 and 1959 can be summarized as follows:

(1) The volume of trade expanded each year, but the ratio of exports to imports fluctuated widely, leaving a sizable trade deficit. The deficit was

reduced between 1958 and 1959 when exports rose faster than imports; exports increased by 8 per cent, while imports (including U. S. agricultural aid) increased by only 0.3 per cent. Both exports and imports increased slightly their ratio to GNP — from 5 per cent and 7 per cent respectively in 1953 to 7 per cent and 9 per cent in 1958 — but they were still comparatively small in relation to the total GNP.

(2) Economic relations with the countries of the Soviet bloc again were normalized, enabling Yugoslavia to increase its volume of trade with neighboring regions.[1] Owing to greatly expanded foreign trade, however, increased trade with the East did not diminish trade with other regions, and, what is more important from the Yugoslav point of view, it did not bring about a dependence on any one region even slightly resembling that of the years 1946–1948.[2]

(3) International assistance in its varied forms had assumed an important role in the whole economic development of Yugoslavia. United States aid — more than $100 million annually, excluding military aid, after 1954 — made important contributions to safeguarding basic food needs and thus to the expansion of the economy. Additional aid shipments, especially food, were authorized in the fiscal year 1955–1956, putting U. S. aid on a more dependable basis.

The 1957 Five Year Plan called for a 49 per cent expansion in the total volume of foreign trade as well as for structural changes. Emphasis was on a rise especially in industrial and agricultural exports, with a somewhat slower increase in imports. Exports of finished products were to be increased and exports of raw materials and semi-finished goods decreased. (See Table 17–5.) A general improvement in agricultural production was planned to cut imports of essential foodstuffs and free foreign exchange for purchase of capital items needed for future industrial expansion.

As it worked out, exports rose in value by 47 per cent for the 1956–1959 period, while imports, including U. S. agricultural surplus shipments, increased by 46 per cent. The ratio of the total value of exports to the total value of imports, including U. S. agricultural surplus shipments, was 68 per cent in 1956, 59 per cent in 1957, 64 per cent in 1958 and 69 per cent in 1959 (Table 17–3). In 1958 the trade deficit was reduced for the second successive year. Thanks to non-commercial shipments like gift parcels (CARE) and certain U. S. aid, which do not affect the trade balance, the

---

[1] Trade with the Soviet bloc started slowly in late 1954, but 1956 was the first year of regular trade and payment agreements between Yugoslavia and every one of the bloc countries.

[2] "Trade with East European Countries," *Slovenski Poročevalec* (Ljubljana), September 18, 1959 (*Joint Translation Service*, September 26, 1959, pp. 33–35).

Table 17–5

FIVE YEAR PLAN: CHANGES IN THE STRUCTURE OF EXPORTS AND IMPORTS, 1956 AND 1961

(Per Cent)

	1956	1961
Exports		
Total	100.0	100.0
Raw materials and agricultural products	20.2	15.0
Semi-finished and finished goods of medium quality	50.3	43.0
Finished and semi-finished goods of high quality	29.5	43.0
Imports		
Total	100.0	100.0
Equipment	12.4	20.3
Raw materials and semi-finished goods	51.0	60.4
Foodstuffs	29.1	8.5
Consumer goods	5.8	7.7
Miscellaneous	1.7	3.1

Source: Savezna Narodna Skupština, *Društveni Plan Privrednog Razvoja Jugoslavije 1957–1961* (*The Social Plan of Economic Development of Yugoslavia 1957–1961*), Kultura, Belgrade, 1957 pp. 50–51.

deficit in over-all current payments was cut from 35 billion dinars in 1957 to 21 billion dinars in 1958.[1]

Transactions other than commodity shipments have assumed a greater significance in the balance of payments (Table 17–4). Included in these transactions are income from the merchant marine, transit transport, tourism, remittances by emigrants, etc. Income from the merchant marine amounted to 8 per cent of the total income flowing into the balance of payments in 1957, and has been increasing steadily. Income from remittances by emigrants amounted to at least $277 million in money orders, pensions collected and gift packages in the postwar period to 1957.[2] Income from foreign tourists during 1959 amounted to roughly $9.5 million, more than double the 1954 amount,[3] but this was only 2 per cent of the revenue from commodity exports.

In spite of important income transactions other than commodity shipments and in spite of a rapid rise in exports, the trade deficit remained uncomfort-

[1] *Yugoslavia*, The Economist Intelligence Unit Ltd., July 1959, p. 6.

[2] *New York Times*, January 30, 1959. Money orders alone amounted to $88 million. Roughly 82 per cent was in dollars, the rest in other convertible foreign currency. Of the parcels received, about 60 per cent contained textiles, 30 per cent foodstuffs and 10 per cent industrial products. Such a large amount of gifts — in 1956 it was estimated that the textiles alone were comparable to 10 per cent of Yugoslavia's textile production at that time — increased purchasing power at home, and greatly helped the country's foreign exchange position. A report published by *Borba*, March 2, 1960, gives the sum of 4,547 million dinars as total emigrant remittances in 1959, of which 3,385 million dinars was actually paid to individuals. Altogether, roughly 1.3 million people of Yugoslav origin now live abroad, 60 per cent in the United States, and a large percentage regularly send aid parcels.

[3] *Ibid.*, and United Nations, *Economic Survey of Europe in 1959*, Geneva, 1960, Chapter VIII, p. 3.

ably large. Moreover, the foreign exchange holdings in relation to imports had improved little at the end of 1958 — only one month of imports (1958 annual rate) was covered by gold and dollar holdings (about $50 million). This deficit has been covered regularly through foreign loans and grants from many different sources.

According to Yugoslav economists, the attainment of a high level of trade indicated the growing economic potential of the country. They were confident that an "equilibrium at a higher level of development" would ultimately be found. [1] Government policies were strongly set against any radical import restrictions, aiming "not to restrict imports more than is absolutely necessary."[2] As one official has said: "We have not solved [the problem of balance of payments] by reducing the volume of trade with foreign countries but on the reverse, by enlarging exports and imports because only such a policy makes possible high economic activity and further and speedier development of our economy."[3]

The far-reaching changes in the economy since the war have had a great impact on the whole structure of foreign trade. (See Table 17-6.) Of particular significance is the increase in exports of manufactured goods, which accounted for 24 per cent of the total exports in 1954–1956 and 31 per cent in 1958. Food exports lagged behind by approximately 10 per cent, largely because of the poor harvest of 1958. Based on preliminary data, imports of capital goods in 1959 dropped more than 15 per cent with the completion of contracted deliveries and greatly increased domestic production. The increasing volume of imports in 1959 was largely due to higher imports of fertilizers, industrial raw materials and investment goods.

As far as the individual commodities are concerned, besides the traditional exports of zinc, lead, chromium ore, bauxite, magnesite and certain consumer goods, Yugoslavia now exports many finished products, including diesel engines, farm machinery, ocean and river vessels,[4] office machines, electric cables, turbines and metal goods. Indicative of the structural changes in exports are the figures for the metal, electric and shipbuilding industries, which contributed 8 per cent of the total industrial exports in 1956 and 30

---

[1] Pertot, *Yugoslav Foreign Trade*, p. 29.

[2] *Ibid.*

[3] From a statement by Ljubo Babić, President of the Foreign Trade Committee, before a joint meeting of the Foreign Relations Committee and the Committee for National Economy of the Federal People's Assembly as quoted in *Borba*, June 10, 1959 (*Joint Translation Service*, June 10, 1959, p. 29).

[4] Yugoslavia reported in the spring of 1959 orders on hand from sixteen countries for the construction of 63 vessels with 575,000 GRT, amounting to $150 million; 194,000 GRT were under actual construction in Yugoslavia's shipyards. The construction of vessels for export has developed during the past three years and has been one of the most successful enterprises in Yugoslavia's newly export-oriented industries. Among the ships are tankers of 32,000–50,000 GRT.

Table 17–6

PERCENTAGE DISTRIBUTION OF IMPORTS AND EXPORTS, BY TYPE OF COMMODITY,
PREWAR AND POSTWAR

(Based on Current Values; c.i.f. for Imports, f.o.b. for Exports)

	1928		1938		1954–56		1957–58	
	Im-ports	Ex-ports	Im-ports	Ex-ports	Im-ports	Ex-ports	Im-ports	Ex-ports
Total	100	100	100	100	100	100	100	100
Food products	14	45	6	49	29	34	23	35
Food	12	43	5	46	28	28	21	29
Drink and tobacco		2		3		6		
Animal and vegetable oils and fats	2	—	1	—	1	—	2	6
Other agricultural products, mineral products and metals	30	43	38	41	31	42	29	18
Agricultural raw materials	—	30	—	24	16	23	12	16
Fuel and lubricants	—	—	—	—	9	—	10	—
Other	—	—	—	—	6	—	7	—
Manufactured goods	56	14	56	8	40	24	48	31
Consumer goods	35	...	36	...	16	21	20	22
Capital goods	21	...	20	...	24	3	28	9

Source: United Nations, *Economic Survey of Europe 1959*, Geneva, 1960, Chapter VIII, pp. 6, 9.

per cent in 1959. The initial figures for 1959 for distribution of exports by stage of production substantiate this trend. Finished goods contributed over 37 per cent of all exports in 1959, an increase from 20.5 per cent in 1956. The increased production in agriculture was marked by slowly increasing exports of the food processing industry and declining agricultural imports, releasing important funds originally earmarked for financing other essential imports.[1]

Exports of the surplus crops of the 1959 harvest lagged behind plans since no markets could be found at such short notice for early vegetables and maize, but in the long run surplus crop production should improve Yugoslavia's balance of trade. Foodstuffs were not expected to exceed 5 per cent of all imports in 1960 as against the high of 32 per cent in 1956 and 17 per cent in 1957. The improvements in agricultural output, assuming that this is more than a temporary stage, should bring about a reduction in the current balance of payments deficit as foreseen by the Five Year Plan.

Normalization of Trade with the Soviet Bloc

The economic blockade of Yugoslavia by the Cominform countries, and the disruption of the trading pattern established in the first postwar years, not only upset Yugoslavia's economy but also deeply affected the economy

[1] More than $100 million was earmarked in 1959 for essential food imports. Most of it became available for the financing of other imports.

of all the other Eastern European countries. This was especially true of those countries that were heavily dependent upon Yugoslavia for raw materials, namely Albania and Hungary. The iron and steel plant being built at Mohacs, Hungary, which depended upon the nearby Bosnian ores, was abandoned, and Soviet ores had to be imported for the new plant at Sztalinvaros, south of Budapest. The plan for a joint aluminum plant at Strnisce in Slovenia, using nearby bauxite from Hungary and water power and caustic soda from Yugoslavia, was also discarded. Albania became isolated and had to be supplied by air and sea. Planning for a power plant at the Iron Gate on the Danube, important to both Rumania and Yugoslavia, was discontinued temporarily. Direct transportation between Bulgaria and Hungary was disrupted. The important transportation artery, the Danube, became hopelessly divided, and through traffic was discontinued at various periods.[1]

It was obvious by 1954 that the boycott of Yugoslavia by the Soviet bloc had lost whatever political value it may have had. Yugoslavia had gained by broadening the geographic base of its foreign trade and by receiving valuable United States aid in the meantime. With the changing leadership in the Soviet Union, the first overtures toward re-establishing economic relations with Yugoslavia were made in the fall of 1954.[2] A small barter deal was signed in the amount of $5 million each way. An enlarged agreement was concluded in January 1955 and increased twice during that year. At the same time some moderate bilateral agreements were signed with several of the bloc countries. These new agreements all raised the question of debts outstanding at the onset of the break in 1948–1949, and a number of compensatory agreements were thus concluded.[3] After the Khrushchev-Bulganin visit to Yugoslavia in 1955, Soviet-Yugoslav trade assumed a greatly enlarged role. Normalization of economic relations with the East produced a series of credit, investment and currency agreements, all concluded between September 1955 and August 1956. Five important individual agreements were concluded with the Soviet Union alone.[4] Several of these agreements were not carried out as a result of

[1] For a good summary of the problem see Istvan Orban, "Die Kontroverse zwischen Jugoslawien und dem Ostblock" ("The Controversy between Yugoslavia and the Eastern Bloc"), *Berichte und Informationen*, July 11, 1958, pp. 1–4.

[2] A. Z., "Soviet Yugoslav Economic Relations 1945–1955," p. 41.

[3] Hungary owed $25 million for goods received before the break and still owed Yugoslavia close to $100 million of its $140 million reparation debt. A final agreement to settle both claims was signed for $85 million. Bulgaria's export surplus was used to pay an outstanding debt for transportation services.

[4] Information about these various agreements has been taken from: Andreja Partonić, "Ein einseitiger Akt der sowjetischer Regierung" ("A One-Sided Act of the Soviet Government"), *Internationale Politik*, June 16, 1958, pp. 7–9; A. Z., *op. cit.*, pp. 38–46; Vl. Saičić, "Yugoslav-Soviet Economic Relations," *Review of International Affairs*, October 1, 1955, p. 10; "Yugoslav-Soviet Talks in Moscow on Execution of Investment Agreements," *Ekonomska Politika*, 277, July 20, 1959 (*Joint Translation Service*, July 21–22, 1959, pp. 47–48); Roesler, "Jugoslawien zwischen Rubel und Dollar (1950–1957)."

one-sided action of the Soviet Union or certain of the bloc countries. A brief summary of these agreements with their 1960 status is given below. (For a general picture of Yugoslavia's trade with the countries of Eastern Europe see Table 17-7.)

(1) A $54 million credit for the purchase of coal, petroleum, cotton and and other raw materials over a three-year period was concluded with the Soviet Union in September 1955. The trade was completed.

(2) At the same time a $30 million loan in gold from the Soviet Union was agreed upon for the purpose of bolstering the dinar. Repayment was due in ten years with 2 per cent interest.

(3) Yugoslavia's debt to the Soviet Union in the amount of $90 million was written off by the Soviet Union. Nothing was said, however, about several loans promised before 1948, deliveries of which were incomplete or never started,[1] or commodities delivered by Yugoslavia in 1948 and not properly compensated for.

(4) An agreement was signed on January 12, 1956 by which the Soviet Union undertook to give Yugoslavia immediately a credit of $110 million, repayable in ten years at 2 per cent interest. This credit was to be used to buy equipment for two artificial fertilizer plants, a thermo-power plant and the modernization of mines. The equipment was to be made available within a three-year period.

(5) An agreement was signed on August 2, 1956 with the Soviet Union and the German Democratic Republic (East Germany) under which a credit was granted to Yugoslavia in the amount of $175 million at 2 per cent interest a year, repayable in twenty years. This credit was to be used to finance the first stage of a 50,000-ton aluminum producing plant as part of a large combine to be located in Montenegro. Ultimate production was planned at 100,000 tons of aluminum annually. Included in the financing of this project were necessary power plants, an open-cast coal mine, a plant for the processing of the nearby bauxite, a plant for the production of soda, cathodes, etc.[2]

---

[1] Aid of $24 million from Cominform countries was received before the break in 1948. It constituted only 6.3 per cent of the total amount of aid promised. This was used largely for the building of the so-called "key projects." Cf. Ivan Avsenek, "Basic Industries," in Robert F. Byrnes (ed.), *Yugoslavia*, Mid-European Studies Center, Frederick A. Praeger, New York, 1957, p. 288. G. J. Conrad, *Die Wirtschaft Jugoslawiens* (*The Economy of Yugoslavia*), Deutsches Institut für Wirtschaftsforschung, Sonderheft, Neue Folge No. 17, Reihe A: Forschung, Duncker & Humbolt, Berlin, 1953, p. 94, speaks of a total Soviet credit of $135 million promised but not received by Yugoslavia.

[2] From a purely locational point of view, the selecting of the site near Titograd leaves much to be desired.

Table 17–7

TRADE PATTERN OF YUGOSLAVIA AND EASTERN EUROPEAN COUNTRIES, 1948 AND 1958

(Per Cent of Total Trade)

	1948						1958					
				Western Europe						Western Europe		
	Total	USSR	People's Democracies	Total	Of Which Yugoslavia	Rest of World	Total	USSR	People's Democracies	Total	Of Which Yugoslavia	Rest of World
Yugoslavia	100	13	34	42	—	11	100	8	20	46	—	26
East Germany	100	38	37	24	...	1	100	43	29	23	2	5
Poland	100	22	19	48	5	11	100	26	29	31	2	14
Czechoslovakia	100	16	16	49	7	19	100	33	36	19	1	12
Hungary	100	16	19	58	12	7	100	27	41	26	4	6
Rumania[a]	100	50	20	23	3	7	100	46	29	20	1	5
Bulgaria	100	55	22	21	5	2	100	53	31	13	1	3
Albania[b]	100	43	57	—	—	—	100	54	42	4	1	—
USSR	100	—	56	39	5	5	100	—	73	16	1	11
Total of countries listed (excl. USSR)	100	23	22	43	5	12	100	34	31	25	2	10
Total of countries listed (incl. USSR)	100	15	34	42	5	9	100	20	48	20	1	11

Sources: United Nations, *Economic Survey of Europe in 1957*, Geneva, 1958; *Economic Bulletin for Europe*, Vol. XI, No. 1, Geneva, 1959. For Albania, *Anuari Statistikor*, 1959. Drejtoria e Statistikes. For USSR: *Spravochnik po vneshnei torgovle USSR*, Moscow, 1958; *Vneshnaia torgovlia SSSR za 1958 god*, Moscow, 1959. The table was prepared by the Research and Planning Division, Economic Commission for Europe, European Office of the United Nations.

[a] Figures partly estimated from partner countries' data.

[b] 1950 in place of 1948.

Both large credit agreements signed in 1956 were unilaterally postponed by the Soviet Union in a note delivered in February 1957. There is no doubt now that this postponement was closely connected with Yugoslavia's stand on the uprisings in Hungary and Poland and the catastrophic economic impact of the uprisings on the whole Soviet bloc. New talks were held in July 1957 about the realization of these large credits[1] and it was agreed to implement the earlier arrangements, starting in 1958, with the completion of the aluminum combine planned for 1964.

In May 1958, at the height of the renewed polemics between the Soviet bloc and Yugoslavia, the Soviet Union again postponed the 1956 credit agreements, this time to 1962–1969 for the $110 million credit and to 1963–1969 for the $175 million credit. Changes in the financial agreements were also proposed, such as shifts of initial deliveries from credit to regular trade exchanges.[2] By June 1958, actual credit agreements were signed for only $49 million of the original $110 million credit and for $670,000 of the $175 million credit. No actual deliveries had been made by mid-1960. The Yugoslav government made several protests against the unilateral postponement of an international agreement, but up to mid-1960 no new discussions regarding the implementation of these credits had been started. As a matter of fact, some of the plants included in these agreements have been financed in the meantime by the United States, including a fertilizer plant at Pančevo, the modernization of some mines and a new hydroelectric power station on the Trebišnica River near Dubrovnik.

During the period of improved foreign economic and political relations, Yugoslavia also signed a series of credit agreements with other Eastern European countries. The most significant one for Yugoslavia's economic development was a $50 million agreement signed with Czechoslovakia on February 11, 1956.[3] This accord specifically stated that all commercial agreements had to be concluded by the end of 1958 and that the investment credit had to be fully used by the end of 1960. The implementation of this agreement, too, was slowed down by the Czech government, though this was not publicly stated. By the end of 1958, only 31.5 per cent of the funds were committed in spite of several protests launched by the Yugoslav government. Agreements signed with Hungary and Poland have been implemented with greater

---

[1] "Yugoslav-Soviet Talks in Moscow on Execution of Investment Agreements."

[2] For details see Partonić, *op. cit.*, p. 8.

[3] "Problems in Connection with Utilization of Investment Credit of $50 Million with the People's Republic of Czechoslovakia," *Vesnik,* Jugoslovenske Investicione Banke, January 1959 (*Joint Translation Service,* March 3, 1959, pp. 4–13). Another credit agreement for $25 million was due to expire in 1958 and at expiration time only $3 million was actually utilized. "Why Are Credit Agreements with Czechoslovakia Not Implemented?" *Borba,* January 10, 1959 (*Joint Translation Service,* January 10, 1959, pp. 16–19).

success. Yugoslavia's trade with Poland, in fact, increased from $7 million in 1955 to $58 million in 1958, and plans called for a further increase of 20 per cent.[1] Trade with Hungary was expected to increase by 15 to 20 per cent during 1959, chiefly through normal trade exchanges without any large-scale credit agreements. Trade with Bulgaria and Rumania as well as with the Soviet Union has been continuing on a reduced level since 1958, showing the impact of the new deterioration of political relations. Rumania, for example, refused to ship oil in the 1959 list of goods to be exchanged. Trade is strictly on commercial terms with no special favors extended.[2]

Yugoslavia exports semi-finished goods, foodstuffs, raw materials, tobacco, chemical products, machines and vehicles to the countries of Eastern Europe and imports mainly fuel and lubricants, pig iron, chemical and pharmaceutical raw materials, industrial equipment and sugar. By 1957 trade with the Soviet Union and several Eastern European countries had again reached the 1948 level, but slowdowns during the latter part of 1958 resulted in some decrease in trade for that year as compared with 1957. Roughly 28 per cent of Yugoslavia's total trade in 1958 was with the countries of Eastern Europe (Table 17–7).[3] Little change in the volume of trade occurred in 1959.

Trade arrangements with the Soviet bloc are not always satisfactory to the Yugoslavs. Distant delivery dates, fluctuating prices and poor quality are factors working against an increased volume of trade. Despite closer economic ties between the countries of Eastern Europe and the Soviet Union, sponsored by the Council for Mutual Economic Aid (CMEA), foreign trade with outsiders is highly useful to the Soviet bloc countries. Yugoslavia, though an observer at some of the meetings of the CMEA during 1956 and 1957, was refused an invitation in 1959.[4]

Role in World Trade

The expansion of Yugoslavia's foreign trade in the postwar years, and especially since 1956,[5] is apparent both in absolute volume and value, and in

---

[1] Report by the Polish-Yugoslav Chamber of Commerce, November 24, 1958.

[2] A trade agreement for 1959 was signed with the USSR providing reduced trade between the two countries by 18 per cent of the planned (but never actually implemented) level of 1958. Cf. "After the Signing of the Trade Agreement with the USSR," *Privredni Pregled* (Belgrade), February 9, 1959 (*Joint Translation Service*, February 21, 1959, pp. 9–10).

[3] "Foreign Trade in 1959," *Ekonomska Politika*, February 13, 1960 (*Joint Translation Service*, February 23, 1960, pp. 11–14).

[4] Yugoslavia based its claim as an observer on the original charter of organization of the Council, inviting all nations to work together and again on an invitation extended by the Council to the countries of OEEC during 1958 for broader economic cooperation. "Trends towards the Economic Isolation of Yugoslavia," *Vjesnik*, April 27, 1959 (*Joint Translation Service*, May 6, 1959, pp. 12–13).

[5] For detailed figures see D. Č., "Foreign Trade in the Postwar Period," *Yugoslav Survey*, Vol. I, September 1960, pp. 227–236.

the actual number of trading partners (23 in 1928 and 63 in 1959). Before the war, Yugoslavia's economy was generally complementary with that of the industrial parts of Europe, exporting largely food and raw materials and importing industrial products. The structure of the economy changed so completely in the postwar period that Europe's share, exclusive of the USSR (Yugoslavia's most important trading partner), both of imports and of exports, greatly decreased. Overseas markets play an ever-increasing role because of Yugoslavia's greater needs for certain raw materials for its growing industry and a wider market for its expanding exports.

With the total volume of trade on the increase, the share of Yugoslav imports and exports in the value of world trade has risen, but it is still extremely small. Yugoslavia's share of world imports moved from 0.11 per cent in 1913 to 0.43 per cent in 1928 to 0.65 per cent in 1957–1958; that of world exports from 0.09 per cent in 1913 to 0.38 per cent in 1928 to 0.44 per cent in 1957–1958.[1] There is no doubt that the Yugoslav economy will in the future be more and more integrated within the international commodity exchange and also participate in its financial transactions.

In addition to regular trade and other transactions foreign economic relations include foreign aid in the form of credits, grants, technical assistance and cooperation, relief and rehabilitation, gift parcels through the Red Cross or CARE, etc.[2] Yugoslavia, as noted, has been a recipient of all forms of aid, but during the past few years has begun some "reverse aid" itself, in the form of both technical cooperation and assistance and credits to increase the volume of trade.

The international cooperation has taken numerous and varied forms. Besides UNRRA, other United Nations organizations concerned with technical assistance[3] and international agencies such as the International Bank for Reconstruction and Development have been involved in aiding Yugoslavia. Aid has also been extended through joint cooperation among several governments (tripartite aid — the United Kingdom, France and the United States). And bilateral agreements between Yugoslavia and a number of countries, largely dealing with technical assistance, have been concluded.

---

[1] United Nations, *Economic Survey of Europe in 1959*, Chapter VIII, pp. 5 and 7.

[2] Aid in the form of reparations or military aid while also a form of foreign economic relations is not detailed here.

[3] Among the most important that have operated at one or another time in Yugoslavia are the Technical Assistance Administration (TAA), International Labor Organization (ILO), International Food and Agriculture Organization (FAO), International Civil Aviation Organization (ICAO), United Nations Scientific and Cultural Organization (UNESCO), World Health Organization (WHO), World Meteorological Organization (WMO), International Telecommunication Union (ITU).

Relations with the U.S.A.

One of the most important aspects of Yugoslavia's foreign economic relations has been the special aid agreements concluded between Yugoslavia and the United States. The impact of these agreements has been pointed out, first in rehabilitation and relief of the country after World War II and since 1950–1951 in the form of food and raw material grants. (See Table 17-8.) Assistance was given under various names, and has been continuous since the emergency food shipments of $65 million in 1950–1951. In all, $1,157.6 million of economic aid and $724 million of military aid was granted by the United States to Yugoslavia between 1950 and June 30, 1959.

There were four types of United States aid to Yugoslavia: (1) UNRRA aid between 1945 and 1948, of which the United States share was $365 million, (2) general economic assistance between 1950 and 1959 totaling $1,066.1 million, (3) economic assistance for specific projects amounting to $91.5 million, and (4) military assistance between 1950 and 1958 totaling $724.2 million.[1] (See Figure 17–1.) Yugoslavia, in addition, secured the equivalent of $219 million in long-term credits and grants from other Western governments.

Economic aid from the United States and, to a smaller degree, from the United Kingdom and France was closely tied to Yugoslavia's economic geography. Basically it consisted of (1) emergency food and raw material shipments, and (2) long-term assistance to many different agricultural activities with the ultimate goal of self-sufficiency and the production of agricultural export surpluses, which in turn should provide sufficient foreign exchange for needed imports of raw materials and capital equipment for new industries. For a short time the United States also aided Yugoslavia with capital equipment for a number of unfinished key industrial projects. In detail, United States aid can be broken down into several categories (Figure 17–1),

(1) Foodstuffs, especially bread grains, fats and oils, accounted for 56 per cent of all economic aid received from the United States during the period 1950–1959. (See Table 17–9.)

(2) Commodities such as feed and fertilizers and fuel and raw materials totaled 24.7 per cent of all economic assistance between 1950 and 1959. Cotton, coal (Yugoslavia is short of bituminous coal), petroleum products, iron and steel products, and hides and skins were the main commodities supplied.

(3) Capital equipment — machinery and specific projects financed by long-term, low-interest credits — accounted for 8.6 per cent of all economic aid. Two loans totaling $40 million came from the Export-Import Bank in

[1] International Cooperation Administration, Office of Statistics and Reports, 1959–60.

Table 17–8

U. S. Economic Assistance to Yugoslavia, 1950–1959*

(Millions)

	Total	1950	1951	1952	1953	1954	1955	1956	1957	1958	1959
Total	$1,157.6[a]	$44.8	$127.9	$81.4	$122.6	$67.6	$157.5	$108.8	$147.4	$113.2	$162.4
Emergency Relief Legislation	50.0	—	50.0	—	—	—	—	—	—	—	—
Mutual Security Program	423.5	—	42.9	81.4	122.4	66.5	42.7	29.7	14.8	11.5	11.6
Technical Exchange	3.3	—	—	0.1	0.6	1.7	-0.8[b]	0.7	1.3	—	-0.3
Technical Cooperation	3.7	—	—	—	—	—	—	—	—	1.8	1.9
Defense Support	396.5	—	42.9[c]	81.3	121.8	64.8[d]	43.5[e]	29.0	13.5	-0.3	—
Special Assistance	20.0	—	—	—	—	—	—	—	—	10.0	10.0
PL 480	577.6	4.8	20.0	—	.2	1.1	114.8	79.1	132.6	101.7	123.3
Title I[f]	392.4	—	—	—	—	—	52.0	71.3	99.9	72.9	96.3
Title II[g]	47.1	—	—	—	—	—	46.7	-0.9	1.3	—	—
Title III[g,h]	138.1	4.8	20.0	—	.2	1.1	16.1	8.7	31.4	28.8	27.0
Export-Import Bank	55.0	40.0[c]	15.0[i]	—	—	—	—	—	—	—	—
Development Loan Fund	51.5[j]	—	—	—	—	—	—	—	—	—	51.5
Pancevo fertilizer plant	22.5	—	—	—	—	—	—	—	—	—	22.5
Trebisnica River hydroelectric plant	15.0	—	—	—	—	—	—	—	—	—	15.0
Thermal power plant, Kosovo	9.0	—	—	—	—	—	—	—	—	—	9.0
Diesel locomotives	5.0	—	—	—	—	—	—	—	—	—	5.0

Source: International Cooperation Administration, Office of Statistics and Reports, 1960.

* Obligations as of June 30, 1959. "Obligations" may be defined as amounts of orders placed, contracts awarded and services transacted during a given period requiring disbursement of money.

[a] There is usually a considerable shipping lag depending on the commodity shipped. If the obligation is late in the fiscal year, even short-lead-time commodities like cotton may well be shipped in the next fiscal year. Commodities which are manufactured to order, like some types of machinery, may be

shipped eighteen months to two years later. The pipeline of unexpended ICA obligations as of June 30, 1959 was $8.4 million. This will be shipped together with fiscal 1960 aid, which came as of January 31, 1960 to $51.9 million for ICA, DLF and PL 480 added together.

ᵇ Negative figures occur when the value of all decreases in a particular fiscal year is greater than the value of all increases. This means that during the particular period of time identified the de-obligation of prior year's programs was greater than any new obligations. This happens occasionally when earlier programs are canceled or turn out to cost less than was anticipated originally.

ᶜ Includes $15.0 million allotted by Department of Defense to Department of Agriculture for economic assistance (flour) and $27.9 million used as follows: $1.5 million for fats and oils; $23.4 million for machinery and equipment; $0.4 million for fuels and raw materials; $1.5 million for ocean freight; and $1.1 million miscellaneous.

ᵈ Includes fiscal 1954 obligations totaling $5 million originally earmarked for military OSP which is no longer programmed and therefore reflected as Economic Aid-Defense Support.

ᵉ Amount includes $29.7 million Defense Support, $3.2 million Danube flood assistance and $10.6 million Direct Forces Support.

ᶠ Purchase Authorization issued against Sales Agreement. These data represent gross aid. Sales proceeds to be used for economic development loans and grants.

ᵍ Data represent Commodity Credit Corporation cost. Export market value is about 25 per cent less.

ʰ Figures under Title III in fiscal 1954 and prior years were actually under Section 416 of the Agricultural Act of 1949 prior to enactment of PL 480 in fiscal 1955.

ⁱ Credits authorized in fiscal 1950 were consolidated with the loan authorized on August 10, 1950 for repayment purposes.

ʲ Figures include all loan agreements signed during 1959.

Note: P.L. 480, Title I, does not generate "counterpart," but results in U. S.-owned foreign currency.

P.L. 480, Title II, may generate "counterpart" if the emergency relief commodities are disposed of within Yugoslavia on a sales basis, i.e., not given to the individual recipients.

P. L. 480, Title III, are donations of surplus agricultural commodities for voluntary relief agencies.

Regular grant aid under the Mutual Security Program (MSP) also generates "counterpart."

Defense support is economic aid to Yugoslavia related to military programs.

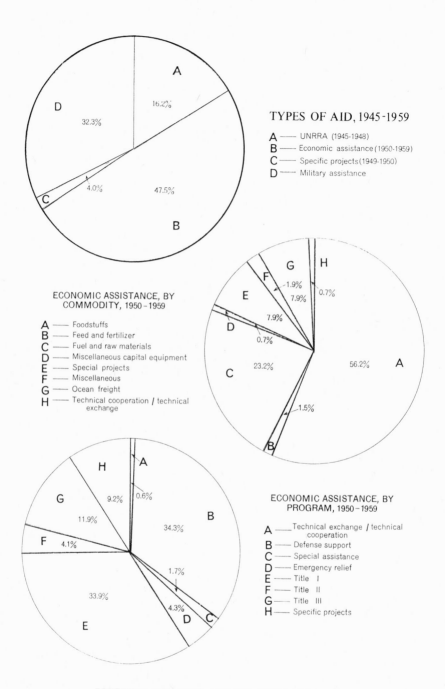

TYPES OF AID, 1945-1959

A ── UNRRA (1945-1948)
B ── Economic assistance (1950-1959)
C ── Specific projects (1949-1950)
D ── Military assistance

ECONOMIC ASSISTANCE, BY
COMMODITY, 1950-1959

A ── Foodstuffs
B ── Feed and fertilizer
C ── Fuel and raw materials
D ── Miscellaneous capital equipment
E ── Special projects
F ── Miscellaneous
G ── Ocean freight
H ── Technical cooperation / technical
       exchange

ECONOMIC ASSISTANCE, BY
PROGRAM, 1950-1959

A ── Technical exchange / technical
       cooperation
B ── Defense support
C ── Special assistance
D ── Emergency relief
E ── Title I
F ── Title II
G ── Title III
H ── Specific projects

UNITED STATES AID TO YUGOSLAVIA

F.B.

Figure 17–1

SOURCE: International Cooperation Administration, Office of Statistics
and Reports.

350

Table 17–9

UNITED STATES ECONOMIC ASSISTANCE TO YUGOSLAVIA,
BY TYPE OF AID, 1950–1959

(*Amounts in Millions*)

	Amount	Per Cent
Total	1,153.4[a]	100.0
Foodstuffs	648.7	56.2
Feeds and fertilizer	17.2	1.5
Fuels and raw materials	268.1	23.2
Capital equipment[b]	99.4	8.6
Ocean freight	91.3	7.9
Technical cooperation and technical assistance (including special assistance)	22.3	2.0
Miscellaneous	6.4	0.6

Source: International Cooperation Administration, Office of Statistics and Reports, 1959–60.

[a] The discrepancy between this total and the total of $1,157.6 (Table 17–8) arises because the commodity distribution is based on sales agreement amounts and the planned use data reflect adjustments when actual commodity purchases and currency allocations are made at a later date.

[b] Consisting of machinery amounting to $7.9 million, or 0.7 per cent, and specific projects amounting to $91.5 million, or 7.9 per cent.

1949–1953, one for rehabilitation of the nonferrous metals industry and one for the purchase of capital goods; four loans in 1959 came from the United States Development Loan Fund for a fertilizer plant in the Vojvodina, the purchase of twenty diesel locomotives, a thermal power plant in southern Serbia and a hydroelectric power plant near Dubrovnik. (In addition, there were loans of over $60 million from the International Bank for Reconstruction and Development between 1949 and 1953, mostly for capital equipment for twenty-seven specific projects.)

(4) The actual dollar outlay for "Technical Exchange and Cooperation" was minimal. This assistance, referred to by the International Cooperation Administration as "Project Assistance," amounted to only 2 per cent of the total economic aid in 1950–1959 (Table 17–9), but the list of projects and of individuals trained reads like a gazetteer of technical projects and a Who's Who of technical specialists; the projects included seed improvement institutes, irrigation training courses, maintenance of agricultural machinery, poultry management, home economics extension courses, etc. Between 1954 and 1959, 855 Yugoslavs spent periods of time in the United States studying in specialized fields. Of this number, 46 per cent were in food and agriculture, 38 per cent in industry and mining, and 5 per cent in transport. (See Table 17–10.) The remainder were in the fields of health and sanitation, community planning, public administration, education and other areas. In addition, there are many Yugoslavs studying in Western European countries. The United

Table 17–10
ARRIVALS OF YUGOSLAVS FOR TRAINING IN THE UNITED STATES,
BY FIELD OF INTEREST, 1954–1959

Field of Interest	Number	Per Cent
Total	855	100.0
Food and agriculture	395	46.2
Industry and mining	330	38.6
Transportation	40	4.7
Health and sanitation	25	2.9
Education	18	2.1
Public administration	29	3.4
Community development	13	1.5
Miscellaneous	5	0.6

Source: International Cooperation Administration, Office of Statistics and Reports, 1959–1960.

Nations and several foreign countries also have large programs of Technical Exchange and Cooperation with Yugoslavia. Technical assistance reaches thousands of people and brings together specialists from Yugoslavia and the Western countries. Major industrial projects as well as numerous small enterprises distributed all over the country have benefited from these programs.

Most of the United States aid before 1956 was in the form of outright grants. Since 1956, some form of repayment has been agreed upon, either in foreign currencies, dinars or dollars. Certain types of aid result in "counterpart funds," which are dinars, technically country-owned as opposed to United States-owned, but withdrawals by Yugoslavia are subject to United States approval.[1] The annual agreements about the use of counterpart funds are an indication of the scope and spread of United States aid, which reaches into the smallest hamlet and the most remote regions of the country. Total deposits in the Mutual Security Program counterpart fund as of June 30, 1959 came to 75,655 million dinars and total withdrawals to 67,438 million dinars, of which 60,956 million was for country use only. Of the total country withdrawals, not quite 63 per cent was used for military purposes, 16 per cent for agriculture, 11 per cent for industry and mining, 8 per cent for transportation, 2 per cent for community development and a small amount for tourism.[2] (See Table 17–11.)

Agricultural projects financed through counterpart funds include refrigeration plants, dairy plants, slaughterhouses, storage facilities, farm-to-market roads, miscellaneous agricultural developments such as livestock breeding

[1] In the counterpart program a certain exchange between dollars and the respective foreign currency is agreed upon, with the amount of local currency to be used specified by the United States and the recipient of the aid.

[2] Data received from International Cooperation Administration, Office of Statistics and Reports, April 1960.

Table 17–11
COUNTERPART WITHDRAWALS FOR YUGOSLAV USE,
AS OF JUNE 30, 1959

	Amount (*Million Dinars*)	Per Cent
Total	60,956	100.0
Military purposes	38,257[a]	62.8
Agriculture	9,604	15.8
Industry and mining	6,628	10.9
Transportation	4,818	7.9
Community development	1,219	2.0
Tourism	400	0.6
Health and sanitation	30	

Source: International Cooperation Administration, Office of Statistics and Reports, communication dated April 1960.

[a] Used for the following purposes (million dinars): airfield construction—2,300; other defense construction—14,250; operations and maintenance supplies—20,517; military personnel costs—1,190.

and the use of hybrid corn and Italian wheat varieties, flood control, and drainage and irrigation works. Examples of the latter are the Danube-Tisa-Danube Canal and irrigation works, the Neretva scheme near the coast, and several flood control and irrigation projects in Macedonia and the interior *polja.* In industry and mining counterpart funds have been used to build hydro-power stations and transmission lines, and for rehabilitation and modernization of mines. In the area of transportation, these funds have been applied to the building of bridges, freight cars, and highways such as the road from Ljubljana to Zagreb and the Adriatic highway between Senj and Dubrovnik (still incomplete). Community developments such as the Belgrade housing project, the port development at Kopar, and new hospitals and dispensaries have also been financed by counterpart funds.

The criticism that has been made of United States aid in some foreign countries has generally been absent in Yugoslavia. United States assistance to Yugoslavia, in the opinion of the authors, has accomplished the aims originally set forth in President Truman's letter to Congress requesting passage of the first emergency food aid bill. It helped Yugoslavia become independent of the USSR and contributed to a higher standard of living for the Yugoslav people by helping them to develop and utilize their natural resources. At the same time, this aid has served United States foreign policy well, inasmuch as it offers to the uncommitted nations of the world an example of U. S. aid with no "political strings" attached.

Regular trade between the United States and Yugoslavia is carried on pursuant to an Agreement on Trade and Navigation concluded on October

14, 1881 between the governments of Serbia and the United States, which is still in effect today.[1] Trade relations, in spite of the old treaty, were not substantial until 1950–1951. Exports to the United States in the period 1935–1939 averaged only 2.3 per cent of Yugoslavia's total exports. Imports averaged 4.8 per cent.[2] The postwar high was reached in 1952 when exports to the United States accounted for 14.7 per cent of total Yugoslav exports and 21.5 per cent of total imports. Since 1953 exports to the United States have declined; in 1958 the United States ranked fifth, with 7.5 per cent of Yugoslavia's total exports. The rise of exports to the United States in the early 1950's was closely connected with the Korean War when Yugoslavia exported particularly large amounts of minerals and metals, especially lead and copper. The importance of the United States as a customer of Yugoslavia's goods is indicated by the high percentage of Yugoslavia's total exports of the following three products shipped to the United States: lead, 67 per cent; tobacco, 28 per cent; hops, 27 per cent.[3] Among the important imports from the United States, besides foodstuffs, are raw cotton, coal, aircraft, technical equipment (radio transmitters, TV, instruments), hides, etc. (See Table 17–12.) Major exports to the United States include, in addition to minerals and metals, tobacco, hops, nails, finished wood products, etc. (See Table 17–13.)

Relations with Western Europe

Aid received from other Western countries totaled roughly $219 million between 1950 and 1959. When emergency food and relief aid first started in 1950–1951, France and the United Kingdom also extended grants. Between 1951 and 1955 France gave special aid valued at $32.1 million (11,240 million francs). In addition, an agreement signed on July 27, 1955 provided for economic cooperation and technical assistance and placed at Yugoslavia's disposal a revolving fund of 215 billion francs for the purchase of capital goods and a Technical Assistance Fund of 250 million francs to be used for the organization of training projects for Yugoslav technicians in France and French specialists in Yugoslavia. Only the revolving fund is repayable.[4]

The United Kingdom granted to Yugoslavia in 1951 an amount valued at $69.4 million for purchase of raw materials, consumer goods and other essential

---

[1] M. K., "Trade with the U.S.A.," *Slovenski Poročevalac* (Ljubljana), March 2, 1959 (*Joint Translation Service*, Supplement, March 14, 1959, pp. 3–5).

[2] Yugoslavia, Ministry of Finance, *Statistique du commerce extérieur 1921–1939* (Section des Dovanes).

[3] Data compiled from *Statistička Spoljne Trgovine FNRJ*, 1958 and 1959.

[4] Communication dated February 19, 1960 from the director of the Service de Presse et d'Information, New York.

Table 17–12
IMPORTS FROM THE UNITED STATES, 1958

	Amount (*Thousand Dinars*)	Per Cent
Total	40,197,506	100.0
Wheat	14,186,577	35.3
Raw cotton	4,826,215	12.0
Powdered milk	3,830,420	9.5
Soya oil	2,755,642	6.8
Wheat flour	2,303,925	5.7
Pit coal	1,792,767	4.4
Cheese (hard)	1,258,957	3.1
Aircraft, incl. parts	970,530	2.4
Melted tallow	901,678	2.2
Pig fat	711,794	1.8
Edible fats (other)	659,156	1.6
Cattle hides	643,955	1.6
Cleaned feathers	661,874	1.6
Electrolytic copper	604,550	1.5
Transmitters	369,750	0.9
Postal packages not classified as to kind	265,329	0.7
Excavating machinery	264,511	0.7
Other	3,189,876	8.2

Source: Statistička Spoljne Trgovine FNRJ, 1959.

Table 17–13
EXPORTS TO THE UNITED STATES, 1958

	Amount (*Thousand Dinars*)	Per Cent
Total	9,888,558	100.0
Refined lead	2,242,277	22.7
Fermented tobacco	2,193,566	22.2
Hops	551,295	5.6
Wooden chairs	380,441	3.8
Baskets and boxes (wicker work)	374,287	3.8
Wooden household utensils	314,564	3.2
Nails	307,110	3.1
Ferro manganese	291,050	2.9
Sinter magnesite	258,572	2.6
Other wooden furniture	228,026	2.3
Antimony regulus	167,707	1.7
Ferro chromium	164,949	1.7
Tubes, plates and sheets of copper alloys	162,140	1.6
Aluminum unwrought	157,210	1.6
Sage leaves	118,730	1.2
Barytes	101,730	1.0
Cheese	76,343	0.8
Other	1,798,561	18.2

Source: Statistička Spoljne Trgovine FNRJ, 1959.

supplies.[1] This assistance, while much smaller in amount than United States aid, has been important to Yugoslavia's economic progress. During the past few years numerous agreements in the form of commercial credits and technical assistance have been concluded with the United Kingdom.

Another form of indirect aid was extended by the Federal German Republic (Western Germany).[2] It started out in the form of reparations and commercial credits. Later it was extended to include a credit, investment, reparation and technical assistance agreement. This major understanding, reached in March 1956, provided payments of $20 million and credits for roughly $70 million payable in ninety-nine years. In addition, postwar commercial debts due in 1960 were extended until 1968 with interest lowered from 7 per cent to 3 per cent. Other credits and loans were received from Austria, the Netherlands, Switzerland, Belgium and Italy. These are bilateral agreements.

Economic Relations with the Underdeveloped Countries

A relatively recent development is the so-called "reverse aid," extended by Yugoslavia to the underdeveloped countries of Asia and Africa. Bilateral agreements on technical assistance include a large number of countries. Credit and loan agreements have been concluded with the United Arab Republic, Ethiopia, Indonesia, Sudan and Ceylon. By January 1960 total credits and loans extended by Yugoslavia amounted to $61 million. These figures do not include loan and credit arrangements between individual enterprises. For example, during 1959 agreements between Yugoslav and foreign enterprises included one with Argentina for $24 million for ships and another with Brazil for $1.5 million for tractors.[3] With increased exports of industrial products to underdeveloped countries, credit arrangements and loans will become more common. They are needed to assist Yugoslavia in opening up new markets. Yugoslav trade delegations were especially active during 1959 in Latin America, West Africa (especially Ghana) and various parts of Asia. With Yugoslavia's need for raw materials increasing, the export of industrial products becomes a natural trade activity.[4]

Another form of reverse aid is technical assistance to countries in Asia and Africa. Bilateral agreements made it possible to send 94 experts to nine countries during 1959, while 83 were being trained in Yugoslavia. In addition,

[1] Letters from the British Information Services, March 18, 1955 and October 16, 1959. Total grants amounted to £19,407,000 between 1950 and 1959.

[2] "Fragen der Deutsch-Jugoslawischen Wirtschaftsbeziehungen seit 1947" ("Questions about the German-Yugoslav Economic Relations since 1947"), *Wissenschaftlicher Dienst Suedosteuropas*, March 1958, pp. 25–31.

[3] Communication received January 1960 from Informativna Služba Jugoslavija, Belgrade.

[4] "Development of Trade between Yugoslavia and the South Eastern Asian Countries," *Privredni Pregled*, September 13, 1959 (*Joint Translation Service*, September 18, 1959, pp. 5–6).

17 Yugoslavs have been assigned to Asian and African countries via the United Nations since 1957. A total of 1,228 students from abroad studied in Yugoslavia between 1953 and 1959 on a United Nations student exchange program.[1]

Problems and Outlook

The major problem of Yugoslavia's foreign economic relations in the decade 1950–1960 was a recurring foreign exchange crisis, produced by the necessity of importing both capital items to build up an industrial base and food for the population. The Yugoslavs saw the problem as temporary, since they were convinced that both industrial and agricultural production would increase to a point where the trade deficit would be eliminated. They wanted not to cut imports but to increase both exports and imports. Large amounts of foreign aid saw them through the most difficult years.

By and large, these expectations appear to have been valid. The country's foreign economic situation has improved markedly. But Yugoslavia is still faced with the problem of expanding its export market and, in the meantime, acquiring additional foreign credit, both to help pay for expanding imports and to meet other foreign financial commitments.

How much additional credit can be obtained depends largely on Yugoslavia's "credit potential." Factors making for a good credit potential include the improved current balance of payments situation, a constantly increasing GNP and good prospects for eliminating the balance of payments deficit. Thus far, according to a 1959 report of the Yugoslav Investment Bank, this credit potential "has not been adequately utilized, as shown by our actual debts during the past few years."[2] The Bank report put actual Yugoslav foreign debts in 1958 (not including agricultural surplus aid) at $407 million as against $367 million as an average between 1953 and 1957. While the debt in 1955, amounting to $377 million, came to 88 per cent of the total export income, the Bank report pointed out, the 1957 debt of $407 million represented only 69 per cent of total export income.

Furthermore, the Yugoslavs have hopes of reducing annual payments. Debt payments, including interest, in 1957 and 1958 took 8.5 per cent of total export earnings in those years. The debt payments of $53 million in 1958 included $8 million interest. The high payments indicate rather unfavorable loan and credit arrangements, most of them short- or medium-term. Investment loans and credits arranged during 1958 and 1959 amounted to about

---

[1] The figures are taken from a special report prepared on request by Information Service Yugoslavia, Rn-5/15, January 1960.

[2] "Credit Potential of Yugoslav Economy," p. 11.

$110 million, with interest between 3.4 and 6 per cent. Long-term loans amounted to $37 million or 33.7 per cent of the total; medium-term loans (6–7 years) to $15.5 million or 14 per cent; and short-term loans (4–5 years) to $57.5 million or 52.3 per cent.[1] The Yugoslavs have been able to renegotiate some loans and hope for further successes in this direction.

The following countries extended loans and credits in 1958 and 1959 (in millions of dollars):

United States	$36	Switzerland	$7
West Germany	21	Italy	7
France	21	Austria	5.5
Great Britain	9	Other West European Countries	3

Part of the large debt payment is on obligations assumed by the present Yugoslav government but contracted by prewar governments, such as payments for outstanding bonds.[2] Others have to do with claims for nationalized property after World War II. The total amount of the various settlements was in excess of $75 million. Generally these debts are interest-free.[3] The agreement with the United States was the first one to be signed. The Yugoslav government agreed in 1948 to pay a lump sum of $17 million. Interest payments to bondholders of prewar Yugoslav obligations were resumed in April 1960.[4]

Another problem related to Yugoslavia's foreign economic relations is the possible impact of the common market and the free trade area of the Western countries and the ever-closer economic integration of the countries in the East under the Council for Mutual Economic Aid. With 28.3 per cent of Yugoslavia's exports and 27.4 per cent of its imports in 1958 going or coming from the six Common Market countries, it is obvious that any proposed change in present arrangements will have an important effect on Yugoslavia's position.[5]

One of the most serious aspects of these arrangements for Yugoslavia is the "common farm policy," the proposed continuation or strengthening of

[1] *Ibid.*, p. 12.

[2] "Balkan Debt Talks," *The Economist*, September 5, 1959. An agreement with the United Kingdom is now under discussion. France and Yugoslavia signed an agreement on outstanding debts on August 2, 1958. For details see "The Regulations of Pre-War Debts of France," *Politika*, August 28, 1958 (*Joint Translation Service*, August 29, 1958, pp. 8–10).

[3] "Economic and Financial Relations with Foreign Countries," *Information Service Yugoslavia*, RN–137, p. 3, and also "Final U. S. Awards Due in Yugoslavia," *New York Times*, October 10, 1954.

[4] *Službeni List*, No. 14, April 6, 1960; also "Yugoslavia Formally Offers to Pay Interest on Old Bonds," *New York Times*, April 7, 1960.

[5] For both negative and positive conclusions, see M. Valnišanin, "The European Economic Union and the Question of a Wider International Cooperation," *Review of International Affairs*, January 1, 1959, pp. 15–16, and "West European Integration and Yugoslav Exports," *Review of International Affairs*, January 18, 1959, pp. 7–9.

the present agrarian protection and expansion of the Common Market to include overseas territories. For Yugoslavia, which exports agricultural products to the industrial countries of the West, this posed a real problem. Of the total exports to the Common Market countries in 1958, 42 per cent consisted of food products, 9 per cent of beverages and tobacco, 28 per cent of crude materials, 14 per cent of manufactured goods, and 7 per cent of miscellaneous items. The Common Market Treaty went into effect on January 1, 1959, but steps toward real integration were slow, and their impact on Yugoslavia remained uncertain. With industrial exports increasing, Yugoslavia obviously was interested in the terms of trade of those countries which are considered, for geographical reasons, its traditional export outlets. West Germany and Italy, for example, were providing the largest markets for Yugoslav products. Belgrade sought to safeguard its interests through bilateral agreements. One such with Italy called for greatly increased exports of livestock, meat and maize and guaranteed a more liberal treatment for Yugoslav industrial exports. It also provided for increased border trade with Trieste.

Over-all, Yugoslavia's greatest strength in dealing with the possible effects of economic integration, either East or West, seemed to lie in its own importance to the respective common markets, in its imports from the West, largely industrial equipment, and its exports to Eastern Europe. Yet the danger of being left out of two integrated parts of Europe was a real one. The summary compilation in Table 17–14 shows the geographic distribution of Yugoslav trade, both prewar and postwar, in the light of various economic and political groupings.

One other problem about which there is already serious concern is the opening up of new markets for Yugoslavia's expanding industrial production. This is closely tied to the country's credit potential. Markets in Asia, Africa and Latin America are the logical sales areas for Yugoslavia's newer export-oriented industries, for competition is perhaps less strong there than in the industrial countries of Western Europe and North America. In addition, there is a political consideration. Many of the newly independent countries of Africa and Asia are seeking a greater amount of freedom from their former mother countries. Inasmuch as Yugoslavia is no longer tied to any bloc, it becomes a very desirable and natural trading partner for them. And since Yugoslavia depends upon a number of raw materials from these areas, they could provide new markets for some of Yugoslavia's exports. However, most of these underdeveloped countries are financially weak, as is Yugoslavia, and often are unable to pay immediately. Hence the importance of credit arrangements.

Table 17–14

PERCENTAGE DISTRIBUTION OF EXPORTS, BY DESTINATION,
SELECTED PERIODS, 1937–1958

	1937–38	1954–56	1957–58
Total	100	100	100
European Economic Community	52	36	30
European Free Trade Area, excluding Portugal	20	17	17
North America	5	10	8
Japan	1	3	1
Total	78	66	56
Eastern Europe and USSR	14	14	27
Southern Europe[a]	3	8	4
Other primary producing countries[b]	5	12	13
Total	22	34	44
Total exports in millions of current dollars, f.o.b.[c]	$130	$273	$418

Source: United Nations, *Economic Survey of Europe in 1959*, Geneva, 1960, Chapter VIII, p. 8.
[a] Exclusive of Italy.

[b] Including exports not allocated by country.

[c] Annual rates.

The future problem is one of finding markets for the increasing output of agricultural and industrial goods and in this way constantly expanding the total volume of Yugoslavia's trade. Policies pursued during the past few years in increasing agricultural production and building export-oriented industries, and making a consistent drive for new markets, have shown initial success. Belgrade hopes that the time when limited foreign exchange resources must be used to satisfy the most pressing national demands has passed forever. In the endeavor to expand agricultural production in the years ahead, a large part of the foreign exchange available could be spent on equipment directly promoting the economic growth of the country. The success of these measures will be an indication of Yugoslavia's level of economic activity, the extent of its foreign economic relations and, ultimately, the viability of the state.

STANDARD OF LIVING

O NE of the most dramatic aspects of the new Yugoslavia is the advance in the standard of living of most people as compared with the early postwar years. Compared with prewar standards, the situation is more complex. Here the most impressive factor is the impact of the revolution: many of those who before the war had a comfortable standard of living fare far worse now, while many of those who had been on the lower rungs of the economic ladder are better off. Yet even by prewar standards, if one considers the improvement in conditions in the more backward areas of the country, the over-all standard of living has risen.

One visible indication of improved conditions at the end of the decade was the increased supply of goods displayed in stores as contrasted with the empty shop windows of the early 1950's and before. Both quality and variety of goods had improved markedly, and included not only food and clothing but consumer durables like stoves, refrigerators and even television sets. Even in the backward areas peasants with shoes, stockings and woolen or leather clothing were the rule, and new wooden beds could be found in even the most isolated peasant houses. Construction of dwellings, both in the cities and rural areas, had begun. There was an increasing use of bicycles and motorcycles, and many people had even come to hope that one day they would own an automobile.

Most of these things were still considered luxuries, and they were by no means available to all the people. But that any sizable proportion of the population at all could enjoy them represented a remarkable change from the harsher conditions of an earlier period.[1] The change reflected higher real

[1] For a discussion of the difficulties of analyzing improvements in the standard of living, see Egon Neuberger, "General Survey of the Yugoslav Economy," in Robert F. Byrnes (ed.), *Yugoslavia*, Mid-European Studies Center, Frederick A. Praeger, New York, 1957, p. 196, and United Nations, Economic Commission for Europe, "Economic Planning and Management in Yugoslavia," *Economic Bulletin for Europe* (Geneva), No. 3, 1958, p. 59.

wages and salaries, increased purchasing power of the peasantry and a larger percentage of employed.

Progress has been slow, however, for a number of reasons. The critical situation in agriculture in the period 1945–1957 — reflected so clearly in the fluctuations in individual consumption — and the need to spend limited foreign exchange for essential food imports made it necessary to contain demand for consumer goods by artificial means. Government policies also stressed investment in heavy industries, which resulted in a high percentage of gross national product devoted to capital goods, averaging 26 per cent between 1952 and 1959, and a relatively slow return in terms of final output. Agricultural production in this period was below prewar levels. Increased food supplies apparent after 1953 consisted largely of foreign food imports, with a comparatively small amount of farm products brought to the market by peasants. Not until after 1957 did increased investment in agriculture show tangible results in foodstuffs.

The life of the individual, especially white collar workers and professionals, was difficult. It was often next to impossible in a period of rising prices to manage on wages and supplementals like children's allowances (which averaged one-third of the total income of wage earners). Although food, utilities and rent costs were fixed by the government, a whole range of necessities, especially clothing, were hard to come by. The average monthly take-home pay of a clerk in 1954 was between 5,000 and 15,000 dinars; of a teacher, between 8,000 and 15,000; a bus driver, 8,000; a bank manager, around 22,000. At the same time a pair of socks cost 480 dinars, a pair of trousers 10,000 dinars and an overcoat up to 25,000 dinars. Often items like soap, cooking stoves and hot water were unobtainable. And, with living space at a high premium, overcrowding in city apartments was severe.

Life since then has improved steadily and markedly. Real wages have increased. Production of consumer goods nearly doubled between 1952 and 1958, and imports of such goods also mounted sharply. During 1955–1957, for example, imports were deliberately encouraged in the hope of stimulating domestic production and lowering prices. By 1957 the long lines around retail stores, especially after pay day, had nearly disappeared. Larger supplies of textiles and other consumer goods began to exert a noticeable pressure on prices. Finally, twelve years after the end of the war, life had become more bearable, especially following the successful harvest of 1957, and most Yugoslavs agreed that it was easier to make ends meet. The improvement was only comparative, however. For the Yugoslavs, Yugoslavia remained a high-cost country. Differences between the living standard in Yugoslavia as a whole and, say, Austria, were still marked. But they were even more marked between Yugoslavia and Bulgaria, and visitors from the Soviet bloc were envious of successes achieved by Titoism. Factory workers and employees in various enterprises — together with upper-level bureaucrats — benefited most. For much of the urban population self-employed or dependent on the private sector of the economy — a group that included many of those well-to-do in prewar Yugoslavia — the amelioration was less noticeable.

Personal Consumption

Personal consumption is one reliable indicator of changes in living standards. Shifts in the Yugoslav economy following the break with the Soviet bloc ultimately provided for a reduction in over-all capital investment in relation to gross national product, thus making more resources available for production of consumer goods.

Production began to grow steadily after 1952, and the standard of living rose slowly. During the years 1952–1956, the rise in the standard of living averaged 6 per cent annually, with the average annual income increasing 8.4 per cent.[1] This rise was most uneven and showed a number of weak spots. In addition, personal consumption at various times was purposely kept at a low level by high prices and low production of consumer goods. The food supply was precarious until after the harvest of 1954, and even then foreign food imports were essential to keep the economy expanding. The priority given to production of capital goods made it impossible to satisfy consumer demands. Investment directed toward increasing the output of capital goods also led to deterioration of essential services and nonproductive investments, especially housing. The shortage of housing was indeed one of the most serious lacks, next in importance to the shortage of essential consumer goods. With the number of people per dwelling unit,[2] especially in the urban areas, among the highest in Europe, there was little incentive for buying consumer durables such as electrical household equipment. During the postwar years up to 1956 people were concerned only with essential needs. Because of the low incomes it was necessary also for several members of the family to contribute to the household income. Many wage earners had to perform two jobs in order to make ends meet.

[1] "The Standard of Living in the Plan of Yugoslav Economic Development, 1957–1961," *Information Service Yugoslavia*, RN 65–58 E, p. 1. The standard of living is measured by the changes in personal consumption and the social standard (housing, utilities, schooling and education), for which the median yearly rise is figured.

[2] According to Yugoslav interpretation there are variations as to the exact meaning of a separate dwelling unit. Eugen Pusić ("The Emerging System of Neighborhood Centers in Yugoslavia," *Community Development*, Belgrade, 1958) describes it as a flat (room) or combined rooms (bathroom, toilet, kitchenette) or separate rooms.

With the enactment of the Five Year Plan of 1957–1961 much greater attention was given to raising the standard of living. The Plan[1] specifically mentioned the importance of increasing real wages and personal consumption, and discussed governmental expenditures for raising the social standard (housing, public utilities, education, health, social insurance). One of the important objectives of the Plan was the establishment of a proper relationship between wages and actual labor productivity. Many laws enacted during the Five Year Plan were in line with these objectives — greater freedom regarding the use of income by economic enterprises after they have met their community obligations, the extension of piece work, the new regulation setting average minimum personal incomes of workers with increased earning differentials based on skills,[2] the law regarding taxes on personal income,[3] etc.

As for the quantitative provisions of the Plan, it was proposed that the annual increase in personal consumption should amount to 6–7 per cent and the annual increase in real wages and salaries also to 6–7 per cent, or 35 to 40 per cent for the years 1957–1961. This increase was to be tied closely to the growth in labor productivity. Actually the plan expressed the hope for a 7–8 per cent annual rise, thus assuring a safe margin for implementing the principle of earnings based on work performed. It was contemplated, for example, that real salaries of highly skilled and skilled workers and employees would rise more than 50 per cent between 1957 and 1961.

Increased personal consumption, according to the Plan, was to be based upon a rapid increase in production. Consumption of goods and services was expected to rise faster than consumption of foodstuffs — a 50 per cent increase as against a 30 per cent increase between 1957 and 1961. As personal incomes and consumption increased, it was expected that the composition of the goods and foodstuffs required would gradually change: clothing and household merchandise would be in greater demand; consumption of cereals was expected to remain fairly stable, while animal products and sugar would assume a more important part in the diet of the people — as they typically do in countries climbing the ladder of economic development.

Improvements in housing, public utilities, schooling, health and social protection were also envisaged. These services, which before 1957 had received a relatively low priority, were expected to play an increasingly important role in raising the over-all standard of living.

[1] Savezna Narodna Skupština, *Društveni Plan Privrednog Razvoja Jugoslavije 1957–1961* (*The Social Plan of Economic Development of Yugoslavia 1957–1961*), Kultura, Belgrade, 1957, p. 135; personal consumption and the standard of living are discussed on pp. 134–144.

[2] "The Standard of Living in the Plan of Yugoslav Economic Development, 1957–1961."

[3] *Službeni List*, No. 52, December 31, 1958.

The general objectives of the Five Year Plan were largely accomplished by the end of 1960. After a long period of stagnation and even regression in living standards, by the end of 1958 per capita personal consumption exceeded the level of the prewar years 1938–1939; taking account of social services, the level of consumption was perhaps 5 to 10 per cent higher at the end of 1958 than before the war. The year 1959 brought further increases in the real wages of workers and employees,[1] and with the cost of living relatively stable and an increase in labor productivity, per capita personal consumption continued its upward course. Productivity grew at an annual average rate of 8.8 per cent between 1952 and 1960. It is estimated[2] that about 4.8 per cent of the increase was due to structural changes in the economy and population transfers from agricultural to nonagricultural activities and an average of 4 per cent to output per man-hour within individual industries.

Industrial production increased faster than planned (13.6 instead of 11 per cent annually), and in 1959 it was 46 per cent above the 1956 level. Agricultural production in 1959 was 14 per cent higher than planned in the Five Year Plan for 1961.[3] Production increases were especially marked in consumer goods (Table 16–5), so long neglected. The variety of goods available as well as the quality has shown constant improvement.

Real Wages

Real wages, which reflect purchasing power, advanced sharply when the decentralized economic system, introduced in 1950, began to function, but after 1952 they were a victim of inflation and fell.[4] In 1957 they rose again, with a particularly sharp increase in 1959. Official figures indicated a 21 per cent increase in real wages between 1954 and 1958. The abrupt increase in prices halted if it did not reverse the increase. The trend in real wages and the cost of living since introduction of the 1957–1961 Five Year Plan can be seen in Table 18–2.

As to actual earnings, government figures indicated that personal money income of workers (based on a family of four) increased by 26 per cent be-

[1] In Yugoslav official usage, persons working in factories are considered "workers," while those working in offices, that is, "white collar" employees, are considered "employees."

[2] Josip Broz Tito, *The Building of Socialism and the Role and Tasks of the Socialist Alliance of the Working People of Yugoslavia*, Report to the Fifth Congress of the Socialist Alliance of the Working People of Yugoslavia, Belgrade, April 18, 1960, p. 64.

[3] The income of the peasant rose between 1952 and 1957 in spite of low production, because of the rise in agricultural prices; but since 1957–1958 the income of peasants, while still increasing, has been based more and more on productivity increases.

[4] Rationing, multiple prices and other devices used in the early postwar period make it virtually impossible to give more than the roughest of estimates for real wages between 1945 and 1950. The introduction of the decentralized economic system, including a new method of compensation, makes it difficult to draw an index for the early and middle 1950's. See Table 18–1.

Table 18–1

INDEXES OF REAL WAGES, 1939 AND SELECTED YEARS, 1951–1959

1953 = 100		*1958 = 100*	
Year	Index	Year	Index
1939	68	1956	89
1951	92	1957	96
1952	105	1958	100
1953	100	1959	111

Sources: Compiled from *Statistički Godišnjak FNRJ*, 1954, p. 308; *Statistički Godišnjak FNRJ*, 1960, p. 254; and other published statistics.

Table 18–2

INDEXES OF EARNINGS PER WORKER AND COST OF LIVING, 1957–1959

	Preceding Year = 100			
	1957	1958	1959	1959/1956
Earnings per worker	116.4	110.9	116.8	149.5
Cost of living	103.2	103.1	101.0	108.5
Real earnings per worker	112.8	107.6	115.6	137.8

Sources: Yugoslav Survey, April 1960, p. 57; *Borba,* October 3, 1960.

tween 1954 and 1958; income of employees, by 41 per cent. As Table 18–3 shows, the income of a Yugoslav wage earner is made up of regular and extra income. A large allowance for children, amounting to roughly one-fourth to one-fifth of regular income in 1958, is an important part of the total income. It is significant that as regular income (primarily wages) increased, extra income decreased — for workers from 13.6 per cent of total income in 1954 to 7.3 per cent in 1958; for employees, from 15.6 per cent to 9.3 per cent. Both wages and allowances for children were considerably increased for a large part of the working population early in 1959. One exception was the so-called peasant-worker (the worker who derives part of his income from agriculture), who under a provision of the social security regulations is not eligible for the full family allowance.

According to a report published in late 1958, the average basic wage for the four highest-skill categories of workers was approximately 280 per cent of the average for the unskilled; for the most highly skilled workers, it was 400 per cent.[1] Allowances for children have reduced these disparities, but according to a United Nations report: "If distributed profits and premia

[1] *Ekonomska Politika,* No. 345, November 8, 1958.

Table 18-3

Average Monthly Income and Expenditures of Four-Member Worker's and Employee's Families, 1954 and 1958

(Amounts in Dinars)

	Workers					Employees				
	1954		1958		Percentage Increase 1954–58	1954		1958		Percentage Increase 1954–58
	Amount	Per Cent	Amount	Per Cent		Amount	Per Cent	Amount	Per Cent	
Total income	18,076	100.0	22,728	100.0	25.7	19,952	100.0	28,138	100.0	41.0
Regular	15,623	86.4	21,077	92.7	34.9	16,830	84.4	25,509	90.7	39.7
Wages	10,228	56.6	13,425	59.1	31.3	11,353	56.9	17,264	61.4	52.1
Child allowance	5,293	29.3	5,820	25.6	10.0	5,285	26.5	5,872	20.9	11.1
Other[a]	102	0.5	1,832	8.0	1,696.1	192	1.0	2,373	8.4	1,135.9
Extra income	2,453	13.6	1,651	7.3	−32.7	312	15.6	2,629	9.3	742.6
From work[b]	1,195	6.6	495	2.2	−58.6	1,389	6.9	783	2.7	−43.6
Outside work	458	2.6	498	2.2	8.7	636	3.2	839	3.0	31.9
Other	800	4.4	658	2.9	−17.8	1,097	5.5	1,007	3.6	−8.2
Total expenditures	17,268	100.0	22,028	100.0	21.6	19,273	100.0	27,577	100.0	43.1
Food	9,102	52.7	12,054	54.7	32.4	9,706	50.4	13,827	50.1	42.5
Tobacco and beverages	1,093	6.3	1,204	5.5	10.2	1,010	5.2	1,303	4.7	29.0
Clothing and footwear	2,730	15.8	3,212	14.6	17.7	3,128	16.2	4,381	15.9	40.1
Rent	456	2.6	529	2.4	16.0	618	3.2	797	2.9	29.0
Fuel and lighting	1,231	7.1	1,223	5.5	−0.7	1,389	7.2	1,406	5.1	1.2
Furnishings	773	4.5	1,181	5.4	52.8	868	4.5	1,674	6.1	92.9
Hygiene	509	3.0	690	3.1	35.6	589	3.1	932	3.4	58.2
Cultural and social life	828	4.8	1,074	4.9	29.7	1,178	6.1	1,638	5.9	39.1
Other	546	3.2	861	3.9	57.7	787	4.1	1,619	5.9	105.7

Source: Statistički Godišnjak FNRJ, 1958, p. 244; 1959, p. 241.   [b] Includes special pay for executive position.

[a] Profit from enterprise (bonuses, etc.).

could also be taken into account, it is certain that the contrasts between the rates of increase in the different categories would be greater."[1]

All these increases have resulted in a rapid growth of money income for the urban population,[2] and a somewhat smaller growth for the rural population. It was estimated that the total monetary resources at the disposal of workers and employees were about 27 per cent higher in 1959 than in 1958.[3] The total income of workers and employees in the social sector of the economy increased by 18.3 per cent between 1958 and 1959 as against 12.3 per cent between 1957 and 1958.[4] Contributing to the growth of personal income were the increased employment, changes in the wage policies of enterprises, and wage legislation enacted at the end of 1958 and the beginning of 1959. Farmers' cash receipts were higher because of the successful 1959 harvest, although their share of the total cash receipts of the population dropped from 16.7 per cent in 1958 to 15.6 per cent in 1959. All these increased cash receipts increased the total purchasing funds available, including newly opened consumer credits, by 21.1 per cent between 1958 and 1959.[5] Total cash expenditures for the same period increased by 17 per cent, with a somewhat greater increase in non-commodity items (services and taxes).

Consumer Credit

Another factor contributing to increased personal consumption was the continuing expansion of consumer credit, introduced in 1952. Credit terms were tightened in 1957 and 1958 as an anti-inflation measure; the consumer debt was smaller in 1958 than in 1957, but it expanded greatly during 1959 — from 66.8 billion dinars in 1958 to 90.5 in 1959 (68.6 billion dinars of this was repaid). Over 2.2 million people engaged in installment buying in 1958, an increase of 147 per cent over 1953. As of March 31, 1959, 13.6 per cent of the consumer credit was for a period up to one year, 34.6 per cent from one to two years, 50.6 per cent from two to three years and 1.2 per cent from three to five years. One-half of all three-year credits were for household goods. In the poorer areas of the country fewer persons could meet the credit terms, and in the more advanced sections fewer persons needed to use them. Thus

[1] "Economic Planning and Management in Yugoslavia," p. 54.

[2] According to *Borba*, August 30, 1959, salaries and other revenues of workers and employees were 24.7 per cent higher and social assistance grants 16.6 per cent higher during the first seven months of 1959 than during the same period in 1958.

[3] For a discussion of the trend from 1952 to 1958, see Narodna Banka, *Annual Report 1958*, Belgrade, 1959, pp. 38–42. During the late summer and early fall of 1959, several reports appeared in the press discussing the dangers of such large and rapid increases in the monetary resources of the working population.

[4] "Cash Incomes of Population and Structure of Expenditures," *Ekonomska Politika*, No. 414, March 5, 1960 (*Joint Translation Service*, March 25, 1960, p. 14).

[5] *Ibid.*, p. 15.

installment buying in Macedonia was 14 per cent below the average for the country and in Slovenia 13 per cent below the average. In Slovenia, however, more money was borrowed for automobile purchases than in any other republic.

The total receipts for households continued to increase, though irregularly. The 1957 increase over 1956 amounted to 27 per cent; 1958 receipts increased only 11 per cent over 1957; and the increase for the first seven months of 1959 again was accelerated. This uneven increase in household receipts reflected the rise in urban consumer income and the fluctuations in the income of peasants. Household expenditures also increased less in 1958 — 10 per cent as against 24 per cent in 1957. The distribution of expenditures underwent some slight modification during 1958. Payments for goods decreased (by 1.4 per cent) and taxes increased slightly (by 0.6 per cent).

Table 18– 4

INDEX OF COST OF LIVING, SELECTED YEARS, 1939–1959

(1958 = 100)

Year	Index
1939	8
1951	100
1952	76
1953	81
1954	80
1955	89
1956	94
1957	97
1958	100
1959	102

Source: Combination of tables published in *Statistički Godišnjak FNRJ*, 1954, p. 308, and *Statistički Godišnjak FNRJ*, 1960, p. 252. Cost of living data are "based on a hypothetical list of consumers goods and services of a 4-member worker's family."

The National Bank pointed out that "the real increase in consumption of households was in fact smaller than is shown by the increase in monetary expenditure, in view of the rise of the general level of retail prices by 3 per cent on the average."[1] Price increases were felt much more by the urban population (especially in the large cities), since agricultural retail prices rose 7 per cent, while retail prices for industrial products rose only 1 per cent. For trends in the cost of living from 1951 to 1959, see Table 18–4.

The impact of this increased purchasing power was manifested in a greater demand for goods, especially consumer products such as household equipment and appliances, furniture and automobiles, and in certain modifications

[1] Narodna Banka, *Annual Report 1958*, p. 64.

in the structure of consumption. These changes can be seen in the volume of retail trade, inasmuch as retail trade supplies roughly 80 per cent of the people's needs,[1] and in the distribution of family expenditures.

Retail trade increased 57 per cent between 1952 and 1958 (an average annual rate of 9.5 per cent in the six-year period); it increased 6 per cent between 1957 and 1958. Among the products which had greatly increased sales between 1952 and 1958 were textiles (10 per cent), leather and rubber goods (40 per cent), metal products (60 per cent), chemical products (30 per cent) and electrical appliances (300 per cent).

Sales of other industrial goods increased from 1957 to 1958 as follows: motor vehicles, 7 per cent (16,309 sold in 1958); bicycles, 27 per cent (140,919 sold in 1958); radio sets, 14 per cent (206,122 sold in 1958); footwear, 8 per cent (21.5 million pair sold in 1958). While textile sales increased up to the end of 1957, they declined in 1958 and there was a big surge in demand for household appliances. The demand for motor vehicles, too, greatly increased during 1958, and imports were accelerated.

Cost of Food

While incomes increased considerably between 1954 and 1958, the distribution of expenditures changed only slightly (Table 18–3). Food expenditures for both income groups still amounted to more than 50 per cent. The proportion spent for tobacco and beverages decreased in both income groups, as did that for clothing and footwear. The relative expenditures for public utilities (fuel and lighting) decreased considerably; while the expenditures for household furnishings increased. The increase shown under "other" indicates added expenditures or additional time spent on vacation. Interestingly enough, cultural and social expenditures in both 1954 and 1958 were considerably higher than expenditures for rent. The low expenditures for rent, as well as for public utilities, point to the artificial pricing of these items something which experienced substantial changes in 1960.

These figures clearly show that in comparison with the economically more advanced countries many Yugoslavs still spend an abnormally large proportion of their income for food and therefore have insufficient funds available for clothing, furnishings and other essentials.

Some selected 1960 Belgrade food prices,[2] figured at the official dinar rate of 300 to a dollar, were: eggs, $1 to $1.12 a dozen; milk, 12 cents a quart;

[1] Yugoslav economists consider statistics indicating changes in the composition of retail sales a reliable indicator of changes in the standard of living.

[2] *Vecernje Novosti*, in a survey reported on October 19, 1961, found Belgrade prices the highest in Serbia; prices of some food staples were as much as four times as high in Belgrade as in some smaller Serbian communities. Belgrade prices compare favorably with those in Zagreb and Ljubljana.

beef, 86 cents a pound; potatoes, 4 to 7 cents a pound; bread, 8 to 10 cents a pound. Coffee, which all but the poorest Yugoslavs drink when they can afford it, was ⟨˅⟩ a pound and higher. A Belgrade housewife who could feed a family of four at these prices at less than $70 a month, even assuming a most modest diet and careful buying, was unusual. And an average worker's income, for a family of four, was around 24,892 dinars, or $81.97 at the official exchange rate.

Since necessities other than food had to be bought, more families than not had at least two wage earners, and many Yugoslavs held more than one job. In Belgrade in 1960, it was estimated that nearly 40 per cent of wives worked outside the home and more than 40 per cent of the men had an extra job — usually one in a socialist enterprise and the other in some private employment like handicraft, repair work, or housepainting. In other cities, the situation was much the same, although in smaller communities a higher percentage of workers lived in rural areas and could raise some foodstuffs themselves.

Per capita consumption of food increased. So did the quality of the diet, but it was still below the levels of most more advanced countries. Per capita daily consumption in 1959 was between 2,800 and 3,000 calories, an increase of 11 per cent over 1956. Foodstuffs of animal origin comprised 25 per cent of the total daily calorie consumption, as against 17 per cent in the 1951–1953 period.

Consumption of white bread has risen phenomenally. Sales increased 40 per cent in 1958 over 1957, while the sale of dark bread made from coarse flour and maize decreased 30 per cent. This trend doubtless contributed to the inadequacy of the wheat supply. There has also been an increase in the consumption of fats (11 per cent in 1958 over 1957), sugar (16 per cent), milk (26 per cent), dairy products generally (12 per cent), coffee (24 per cent) and cocoa (12 per cent).[1] The pattern of consumption in Serbia is illustrative, although it varies greatly from region to region. Consumption of foodstuffs per household in Serbia in 1955 and 1959 was as follows (in kilograms):

	1955	1959
Maize	530	413
Beans	65	44
Sugar	28	31 (to 43 in the Vojvodina)*
Fruit	100	120

* Sugar consumption rose from 5.5 kg per inhabitant in Yugoslavia in 1955 to 15 kg in 1958.

[1] "Increases in Consumption of All Products," *Information Bulletin about Yugoslavia*, June 1959, p. 4.

Housing

When the question of a higher standard of living comes up in Yugoslavia, the problem of housing usually takes first place. More than 20 per cent of all living space was destroyed in World War II, and in 1945 roughly 3.5 million people were without adequate housing.[1] The high birth rate and the migration of the rural population to the cities, together with the small amount of investment allocated to housing, made for a continuing shortage.

The first steps to stimulate housing construction were taken in 1955. Special funds for housing were established in that year, with the employed contributing 10 per cent of their income. The following compilation shows the contribution to these funds:[2]

Year	Contributions to Housing Funds (Billion Dinars)	Dwelling Units Built	
		Total	In Towns
1955	9.7	30,000	15,000
1956	37.9	37,000	17,000
1957	53.0	45,000	22,000
1958	64.4	61,000	31,000
1959*	75.0	69,000	39,000

* Provisional figures.

Funds for construction of housing units increased substantially for the first time in 1957, when 14.9 per cent of total investment was allotted to housing and communal services, compared with 7.5 per cent in 1952 and 11.5 per cent in 1956. The proportion rose to 17.9 per cent in 1958 and the estimated expenditure for housing construction in 1960 was 21.5 per cent of all investments.[3]

Excessively low rents, based on a rate of 15 per cent of the last prewar rent, posed one difficulty. Many apartments were privately owned, and even where they were not the income was insufficient to permit repairs, modernization or addition of new units. At the end of 1958 the larger apartments were nationalized, and a year later "economic rent," some 2.5 times higher than the existing rent, was decreed.[4] With rents now based on a figure allowing

[1] According to an article in *Yugoslav Life* (formerly *Information Bulletin about Yugoslavia*) in April 1960, at a recent referendum among workers of the "Rade Končar" plant in Zagreb, priority in expenditures to raise the standard of living was indicated as follows: (1) housing, (2) rest centers, and (3) recreation facilities.

[2] Vladimir Nenadović, "Housing Construction in Yugoslavia," *Review of International Affairs*, March 16, 1960, pp. 18–20.

[3] Jugoslovenska Investiciona Banka, *Investicije 1947–1958*, Dokumentacioni Materijali No. 2, Belgrade, 1959, and a communication from the Bank, April 5, 1960.

[4] For a discussion of these laws, see Chapter 13, pp. 233–234.

for upkeep, repair and amortization, owners, including enterprises, and local governments were expected to improve the housing situation. Credit for private home building was provided. A new property tax was enacted, but it was not to be levied for the first twenty-five years after construction. Building cooperatives were also established, offering an opportunity for individuals and groups to invest their own funds. New local taxes on enterprises were assessed, specifically for the purpose of creating municipal housing funds. According to government estimates, by 1959 between 20 and 25 billion dinars in private enterprise and local government funds was available for housing construction. Tito called for an estimated annual production of 100,000 flats between 1961 and 1965.[1]

The higher rents were certain to be reflected in a changed distribution of family expenditures. To avoid an adverse effect on the standard of living, the government abolished the tax on house construction and authorized a 6.5 per cent increase in wages and salaries. Pensions were increased between 6.4 per cent and 10 per cent, and unemployment compensation was raised 6.5 per cent. Nevertheless, the increased housing cost bore hard on some groups of the population, and, indeed, it was intended to do so. *Borba* had complained earlier that the low rents meant that "utilization of an apartment is often not in proportion to the incomes of individual persons nor is it in proportion to their contribution to the community."[2] Some of the pressures for housing reform came from the "new class" of engineers, technicians and administrators who could afford better housing but could not find it.

Whether the new measures would be adequate was unclear, but it was certain that the regime had decided to tackle the housing problem and, in one way or another, provide better living conditions.

Education

The Yugoslavs have achieved one of their most spectacular advances in the field of education, an area especially important in a country with a traditionally high rate of illiteracy. In 1950, a general school law made eight-year education compulsory through the country for the first time. Prior to enactment of this law, only four years were required. Now all children from 7 to 15 years of age were required to attend the eight-year primary school. Later, the concept of the four-year secondary school was broadened from the former gymnasium-type institution, considered primarily as preparation for entering the university, to a school designed to train not only for higher education but also for practical skills. A part of the curriculum now consists

[1] The housing situation is discussed in *Borba*, July 11, 1959.
[2] *Ibid.*

in spending time on jobs in enterprises.[1] Adult education of various kinds has also expanded enormously. (For types of schools and enrollments, see Table 18–5.)

Education is free at all levels, and in addition government stipends and scholarships are available to a large number of students. During 1958–1959, 57,263 scholarships, costing 294 million dinars a month, were awarded. In the preceding year, 28 per cent of all students above the compulsory primary grades received scholarships, while 27 per cent were beneficiaries of allowances for children. The rush to take advantage of the expanded educational opportunities raised severe problems for educators as well as for the community as a whole.[2] All schools are overcrowded, especially elementary schools, where in many cases three shifts of pupils use the same classrooms each day. The acute shortage of qualified teachers all along the line has made it difficult to maintain educational standards. More than 60,000 teachers with various specializations were said to be needed during 1961–1965.

Meanwhile the educational needs are constantly increasing. The number of eight-year schools was insufficient. Some 130,000 students completed secondary education between 1953 and 1957, but many had no opportunity for further schooling after completing the first four years. In rural areas the schools are often inaccessible, and small, scattered settlements, especially in mountainous areas, lack school bus service. An average of 83 per cent of the 7–15 age group actually attended the full eight-year primary school during 1957–1958. Of the same age group, 94 per cent completed a four-year elementary school in 1957–1958, while only 66 per cent completed grades five to eight.[3]

Basic education on a large scale for the working population is a pressing need. In 1953, more than a quarter of the economically active population and more than a third of those employed in agriculture lacked even the basic four-year elementary schooling.[4] A 1958 compilation showed that only 20.7 per cent of the total labor force had completed any type of schooling. Of this group, 10.9 per cent finished eight years of primary school, 7.3 per cent various types of secondary school and 2.5 per cent institutions of higher

---

[1] A similar provision, reflecting Marxist psychology as well as practical needs, is part of Khrushchev's school reforms in the USSR, although the provisions of the laws generally are quite different.

[2] For data showing impact of the new school law, see *Statistički Godišnjak FNRJ*, 1959 and 1960, "Enrollment in Schools of Higher Education," *Information Service Yugoslavia*, R No. 96/60 E and various articles in *Yugoslav Survey*, Vol. I, No. 3, December 1960, pp. 363–384.

[3] *Report of the Federal Committees* on the work of the Socialist Alliance of Working People of Yugoslavia from the Fourth to Fifth Congress, Belgrade, April 1960 (abridged text).

[4] Miloš Macura, *Stanovništvo i Radna Snaga kao Činioci Privrednog Razvoja Jugoslavije (Population and Labour-Force as Factors of Economic Development of Yugoslavia)*, Ekonomska Biblioteka 7, Belgrade, 1958, p. 280.

Table 18–5
SCHOOLS, ENROLLMENTS AND TEACHERS,
1938–1939 AND 1958–1959

Type of School	1938–39			1958–59		
	Schools	Students (Thousands)	Teachers	Schools	Students (Thousands)	Teachers
Compulsory primary	9,190	1,471	34,663	14,342	2,427	79,686
Secondary (general education—gymnasium[a])	205	125	5,607	234	77	4,894
Secondary—teacher-training[b]	37	4	555	77	24	1,698
Secondary—vocational[c]	53	11	879	257	76	6,262
Secondary—art	5	1	136	40	4	1,100
Technical schools for apprentices and for training of skilled workers[d]	766	70	6,174	741	124	9,463
Other lower vocational schools[e]	4	0	23	49	3	678
Special schools[f]	21	3	232	185	8	996
Adult education centers[g]	—	—	—	718	47	5,941
Schools for advanced specialized training[h]	45	6	452	186	19	1,517
Higher education[i] (universities, colleges with university rank and art academies)	26	17	1,204	122	97	7,916
Minority schools[j]						
Primary	266	42	734	1,432	202	6,435
Secondary	4	1	107	23	3	231
Teacher training	1	82[k]	2	18	1,659[k]	134

Source: Statistički Godišnjak FNRJ, 1960, pp. 266–271.

[a] This is a four-year general education school in which pupils graduated from compulsory primary school (8 years).

[b] Includes teacher training colleges, vocational schools, home economics training colleges, schools for educators.

[c] Includes technical schools, transportation schools, agricultural schools, veterinary schools, hydrometeorological schools, schools for librarians, etc.

[d] Includes special schools for apprentices and schools for skilled workers.

[e] Training of medical assistants and administrative positions.

[f] Schools for physically and mentally handicapped children and youth.

[g] These include nearly all types of secondary schools, e.g., secondary teacher training, vocational, schools for skilled workers, master craftsmen, social workers.

[h] Special evening schools.

[i] Yugoslavia had 3 universities before 1944 with 20 faculties and 4 art academies, and 6 universities in 1960: Belgrade (1863), Zagreb (1874), Ljubljana (1813), Sarajevo (1949), Skoplje (1946) and Novi Sad (1958). The number of faculties in 1961 will reach 200, distributed in 46 cities.

[j] Includes compulsory primary schools, secondary schools and secondary teacher training schools.

[k] Actual number of students.

learning. The remaining 79.3 per cent had no schooling at all or had not completed the compulsory eight years.[1] Between 1953 and 1957, 412,000 workers completed regular elementary education.

The state of vocational training is indicated by the fact that of 654,000 persons who entered employment during the period 1953–1957, 284,000 or 43 per cent had minimum technical training or had learned a trade, while 370,000 or 57 per cent had no occupational training. More than two thirds of the unemployed were unskilled during the same period.[2] More adult education and vocational training centers were needed to cope with this situation. Adults could obtain secondary education at the regular four-year gymnasia and at secondary vocational schools. Higher vocational schools have special branches for adults. And many factories have organized their own schools.

The so-called workers' universities are an important aspect of adult education. They are not, in fact, universities, however. The main purpose of these more or less informal institutions is job proficiency, although they do impart literacy and elementary general information as well as offering systematic courses leading toward secondary and university education. More than 125,000 persons were enrolled in workers' universities in 1958.

With government stipends provided for higher learning, university education offered special problems. Compared with the 30,000 students who were graduated from Yugoslav universities between 1919 and 1941, there were 67,000 university graduates between 1946 and 1958. During the 1955–1956 academic year, more than 30,000 scholarships, amounting to 120.2 million dinars, were made available, and this amount increased annually in ensuing years.

Prior to 1958, students who were graduated from secondary schools could go directly to the universities without entrance examinations. Indeed, the attraction of university life was such that it posed questions not only of money but also of space, professors and calibre of students. New regulations admitted to higher educational institutions workers who had not had regular schooling, provided they passed special entrance examinations. During the 1959–1960 academic year, 3,867 persons took these examinations, but only 744 were finally enrolled. Workers attending universities continue to be paid by their enterprises.

The 1958 law, while it promoted virtually unlimited expansion of primary and secondary education, sought to slow the precipitous rise in the number of students at the universities. Secondary school graduates were now required

---

[1] "Social Requirements for a Reform of Higher Education," *Borba*, November 1 and 2, 1959 (*Joint Translation Service*, Belgrade, November 12, 1959).

[2] Macura, *op. cit.*, pp. 337–338.

to pass formal entrance examinations, and, once in the university, finish their work within a specified time, depending on the faculty involved.

Facilities continued to be overcrowded, however. Roughly 24 per cent of the total student body lived in special hostels, of which there were 785 in 1957–1958. That living conditions, and scholarships also, were not considered altogether satisfactory could be inferred from riotous students demonstrations in Zagreb and Skoplje in the spring of 1959.

Generally speaking, more attention is given to technical and scientific training than to other areas of learning, but there is little pressure by public authorities to force students into particular courses or schools. The greater number of scholarships available in technical fields is the main indication of official policy. The relatively large enrollment increases in art schools and humanities courses illustrate the freedom of choice. In any event, the urge to acquire knowledge is evidenced by the constant expansion of all educational institutions at all levels as well as by the extent of patronage of libraries and cultural centers established by foreign governments and attendance at artistic and other types of exhibitions.

One persistent worry to the regime is the tendency of trained personnel to concentrate in the major cities. While the League of Communists constantly seeks to overcome this by propaganda, the government has urged higher salaries, better housing and more rapid advancement as incentives to settlement in the interior and work in newly built enterprises in underdeveloped regions. These factors, plus the emphasis on schooling in all parts of the country, were gradually easing the problem.

Social Security

Social security has come to be considered basic to all modern societies, regardless of system, and the socialist countries have stressed it especially. In Yugoslavia, with its low standard of living and wide regional variations in health, 17 per cent of the population were covered by comprehensive social security benefits even before World War II. By 1960, the Tito regime had extended some form of social security protection to 97 per cent of the population, and nearly 46 per cent were covered by full social insurance — health, disability, retirement and allowances for children.[1]

The costs of this broad system of social security are enormous. Total expenditures increased from about 103 billion dinars in 1953 to nearly 226 billion dinars in 1959, and on the whole costs have been climbing faster than income. Social security payments amounted to 9.6 per cent of national

[1] For a discussion of social security in Yugoslavia, see *Yugoslav Survey*, Vol. I, No. 1 (April 1960), pp. 65–72.

income in 1958 and 34.6 per cent of wages and salaries.[1] These payments are financed by a uniform tax rate adopted by the Federal Assembly and levied against enterprises and other employers on the basis of their wage payments. The rate of contribution is high. In 1959, for all forms of social security it amounted to 36.7 per cent of wages and salaries. The administration of the various social insurance funds thus established is decentralized and operates under social management bodies[2] according to rules established by the republics and districts. There are also special-purpose funds providing for preventive medicine work and employment service. The district funds are protected by obligatory reinsurance with republic institutes.

The social security system, as it was organized in 1960, included the following major branches:

(1) Health insurance: medical care, compensation during absence from work because of illness, and preventive health service.

(2) Mother and child welfare: compensation for loss of pay to employees during maternity leave, compensation for shorter working hours for nursing mothers, financial assistance toward the care of the new-born child, and a permanent monetary allowance for children. Allowances for children in 1958 comprised roughly 21 to 25 per cent of the total income of wage earners. (Table 18–3.)[3] In 1959, 1,025,000 families with a total of 2,096,000 children were included in the system. The full child allowance in 1959 was 3,240 dinars a month for one child and 6,040 dinars for two children, and the funds allocated for children's allowances comprised 3 per cent of the national income.

(3) Pension insurance: old-age pensions for all workers and benefits to dependents of deceased insured workers. The pension received is dependent upon the average wage of the insured over a given period, with a minimum guaranteed. Total expenditures amounted to about 1.8 per cent of the national income in 1959.

(4) Disability insurance and allowances: disability benefit or pension, old-age and family pension, and provision for rehabilitation. Disability pensions and allowances are determined by the degree of diminished working ability.[4] The total number of beneficiaries amounted to 207,000 at the

---

[1] The disparity between the percentage of national income and the percentage of wages and salaries reflected in social security payments is in part explained by the fact that many peasants and others outside the socialist sector did not receive full coverage.

[2] See Chapter 13, pp. 228–238.

[3] According to the law, "The amount of children's allowance depends on the number of children, as well as whether the family depends exclusively on the wages and salaries earned." The allowance is paid "for all children up to fifteen years of age." If the children are at school the allowance is continued until they finish school. *Službeni List*, No. 36, August 10, 1955.

[4] Disability insurance is paid according to three categories of disability. Old-age pensions are paid on completion of a specified employment period or attainment of a certain age, regardless of working ability.

end of 1959, total expenditures to approximately 1.0 per cent of the national income.

(5) Compensation for funeral expenses and death benefits: monetary compensation to the family of a deceased insured person for funeral expenses. The amount of compensation is determined by the district assemblies.

(6) Special groups of insurance beneficiaries: artists; clergymen (those priests belonging to a professional organization or whose supreme administrative body concludes a contract); lawyers; and railroad porters. Unemployment insurance is also included for this group.

Until 1955 private peasants were wholly excluded from health insurance[1] with the exception of free medical care for contagious diseases and maternity services, including medical assistance for children up to three years of age, which have been available to the entire population since 1946.[2] These free medical services are not part of the health insurance scheme but, according to the Yugoslav point of view, are based simply on the social needs of the community for treatment and control of diseases or on special needs. In the same way, for certain basic sicknesses, catastrophic in nature — forty altogether — the whole population is automatically covered.

In 1960 a new law extended health insurance to private peasants[3] providing coverage for roughly 10.5 million additional persons (farmers and their families). With the passing of this law only about 3 per cent of the population were left without basic health insurance. The private craftsman was the only actively employed person not included in health insurance schemes.[4] Part of the expanded health insurance costs are paid by the insured themselves and part by the health insurance fund. A special fund for agricultural producers was established within the district institute for social insurance and "through the joint funds, or the funds for re-insurance of local funds for the territory of the republic."[5] The amount of the contribution is determined by the republic assembly. The people's committee of the commune has the right to delay contributions from individuals in case of need. In such a case the contributions are paid through the budget of the commune. As in other branches of the social security system, the insured themselves participate in the governing of the health insurance funds. The plan is ultimately to extend other types of

---

[1] "Health Insurance of Agricultural Producers," *Yugoslav Survey*, I, September 1960, pp. 237–240.

[2] Even before the new law on peasant health insurance, 11–15 per cent of the peasantry was already included in the social security system as a result of being affiliated with cooperatives and state farms.

[3] Law on the Health Insurance of Agricultural Producers, *Službeni List*, No. 27, June 30, 1959.

[4] According to a statement by Moma Marković before the Yugoslav Parliament on June 29, 1959, this group also will ultimately be covered.

"Health Insurance of Agricultural Producers," p. 239.

social security to the peasantry — old-age and disability insurance, allowances for children, etc.

Health

The improvement in health standards was clear. The death rate for the country as a whole fell from 12.7 per 1,000 inhabitants in 1947 to 9.2 in 1958, and the infant death rate declined sharply from 166 per 1,000 in 1953 to 86 per 1,000 in 1958 (for additional figures see p. 42). More significant may be death rates for the insured and non-insured for 1958: 7 per 1,000 as against 14.6. The number of births with medical assistance increased to 50 per cent by 1957 as against 37 per cent in 1955. Slovenia had a rate of 98 per cent, the autonomous region of Kosmet a rate of only 10 per cent. To overcome regional differences of this sort, efforts were being made by social security officials to induce recent graduates of medical schools (including dentists, nurses and pharmacists) to go to backward areas. The Yugoslav government and the social security officials were also anxious to expand their services because of the great number of absentees in enterprises. In 1958, 41 million working days were lost by absence due to sickness. The government hoped that with an increasing number of doctors, this high figure could be cut down considerably.

There has been outstanding success also in combating several types of endemic diseases which had plagued various regions, especially parts of Bosnia and Herzegovina, since the Turkish occupation. For several years after the war, a team of scientists from Harvard University worked with medical authorities in Sarajevo toward this end. Tuberculosis remained the major health problem, but new sanitoriums and utilization of new methods of treatment have made great inroads on this traditional killer of the South Slavs. These and other public health developments added twelve years to life expectancy during the 1950's, bringing it to 58 years (as against 71 in the United States and 29 in Burma).[1]

There are eight medical schools in Yugoslavia, two of them established in 1960. About a thousand physicians a year are graduated. In 1958, there were 12,346 doctors, compared with some 4,000 at the end of World War II and 8,964 in 1955. The 1958 figure meant one doctor for every 1,475 people. The ratio, according to the 1955 census, was highest in Slovenia (one doctor for 1,270 inhabitants) and lowest in Bosnia and Herzegovina (one for 4,970). In the period 1953–1959 over 6,000 doctors, 1,100 pharmacists and 7,500 general health workers were trained. The proportion of doctors in 1958 compared favorably with the more advanced countries of Western Europe.

[1] Howard A. Rusk, "Health in Yugoslavia," *New York Times*, November 27, 1960, p. 79.

Medical services were not generally socialized until 1958, when private practice was sharply restricted by legislation.[1] Taking account of regional differences in the supply of doctors and the availability of medical facilities, considerable leeway was allowed republics as to when the law had to be put into force, and exemptions were permitted. The law generally exempts older doctors, those close to retirement and "Those physicians, dentists, and stomatologists who are not in the employ of health institutions." Exemptions were provided, differing in various republics, for those areas where there were insufficient doctors. One of the reasons given for the restriction of private practice was the poor equipment in private offices and the doctors' lack of concern for preventive health. This criticism appeared valid to many who had experience with private physicians in Yugoslavia. By 1960, nearly all doctors were fully occupied in hospitals and public health clinics, and only a few older or retired men kept on with their private practice.

This arrangement was not wholly satisfactory to the clientele. Although the principle of free selection of doctors and services was a part of the social insurance law, it was largely academic both because of inadequate facilities and bureaucratic arbitrariness. Rigid pay scales for doctors also contributed to bad service. In April 1961 the clinics and hospitals became independent "social management" enterprises, free to regulate their own pay scales, make their own arrangements with the social insurance bodies and arrange services as they see fit. The new arrangement permitted patients to choose their own physician or surgeon as well as hospital. The government hoped that medical services would thus be made competitive with a resulting improvement in medical care.[2]

There were also discussions on how to improve other phases of social security, particularly on questions of increasing income of the various social insurance bodies and giving insured persons greater benefits and eliminating abuses by insured persons. These matters were under review in 1960 by a commission composed of officials of the trade union organization and the Federal Executive Council.

The Yugoslav government points with pride to the accomplishments of its social security system in raising the level of health for a considerable portion of its population. Figures available from both Yugoslav and international sources give reason for being proud. There can, of course, be debate as to ways of bringing greater efficiency to such a huge and largely decentralized system; but the basic philosophy and organization, especially the large active participation of the insured themselves in determining certain basic policies, has proved its worth.

[1] *Službeni List*, No. 53, 1958.

[2] See *Borba*, March 17, 1961, for a discussion of the new system.

TOTALITARIANISM

AND DEMOCRACY

ONE notable aspect of Yugoslav Communism is a relaxation of the totalitarianism that is usually considered part and parcel of a Communist system. The relaxation began while the tyranny of Stalinism still held sway unrelieved in the USSR and its satellites. It was of a definitely limited nature, and there have been retrogressions. With the liberalizations that have occurred in the Soviet Union since 1955, the contrast between Belgrade and Moscow in this respect is no longer as great as it once was. Yet the relaxation of totalitarianism is still one factor that distinguishes the Yugoslavia of 1948 from that of 1960 and from other Communist countries.[1]

The extent to which Yugoslavia has moved away from totalitarianism is difficult to document. Neither statistics nor statutes nor public statement can tell the whole story. Rather, it is something that has to be experienced, through observations on the spot both in Yugoslavia and in the Soviet bloc countries, to be appreciated. In part, the difficulty is one of semantics. Totalitarianism may mean merely the absence of political opposition or it may mean the presence of cruel oppression; more significantly, it may mean a denigration of individuals and their complete subordination to ideas, actions or associations approved by an all-powerful state. Democracy may mean, as in the West, principally the existence of two or more political parties, free and contested elections, and a free press. On the other hand, the typical Marxist view of democracy emphasizes economic rather than political freedom and often, even, merely equates it with the absence of private property..

---

[1] The comparison with other countries is dealt with in Chapter 21. In certain areas, at least on the surface, there appeared to be in the period 1956–1958 an even greater relaxation of totalitarianism in Poland than in Yugoslavia. Whether the same could be said after 1958, however, was extremely doubtful.

To this concept of democracy, the Yugoslav Communists add certain Western ingredients plus some of their own, primarily the participation of masses of people in administering their own affairs.

Certainly by Western standards, Yugoslavia has more of the trappings of totalitarianism than of democracy. No political parties are permitted, other than the League of Communists.[1] The League itself retains a tight rein on policy making, and its major decisions are taken by a small ruling group. Its use of the Socialist Alliance, the trade unions and a variety of other organizations as "fronts" or "transmission belts" for getting its own way is often nearly as effective as if the Party itself directly ran things. Public criticism of the regime as such is discouraged, and any real and persistent opposition on major issues risks reprisals.

Yet the relaxation of totalitarianism in Yugoslavia cannot be adequately judged by Western standards. It must, rather, be judged by standards prevalent in other Communist countries and by those in Yugoslavia between 1945 and 1950. It must also be judged in the context of the backwardness of the population and the heritage of extreme poverty, savage violence and religious-national hatreds that resulted from long subjection to foreign rule.

In addition to all this, it must be remembered that, as Tito has often reminded the West, the Yugoslav leaders are Communists. Their highest values are the maintenance of socialism and progress toward Communism, not individual political freedom, particularly when it may be used in opposition to socialism. This is not to say that there has not been an increase in freedom of expression in Yugoslavia; there has been. It is not even to say that citizens may not publicly oppose policies of the regime; they may and do. But such relaxations of totalitarianism as have occurred operate only within the confines of a Communist system. As comparatively liberal and "humanized" as this may be in its Yugoslav form, it has nothing to do with Western-type political democracy as a system, which envisages the right of political opposition to the system itself. Although in the West this right is often abrogated, in Yugoslavia it does not exist.

Still, that the ends thus justify the means in Yugoslavia, reprehensible though this may be to Western political moralists, should not obscure the important limitations the Yugoslav Communists have imposed on themselves as to the means which they will use. Titoism has adopted some features of Western political democracy. Perhaps more important to the Yugoslav's claim to democracy, however, is the operation of their legal system, based on due

[1] Since the League, technically, is not a political Party, the official view is that there are no political parties in Yugoslavia, although, in fact, at all levels the terms "League" and "Party" are used interchangeably.

process of law, the great decentralization of governmental functions and the participation of a broad section of the population in administering public affairs, i.e., social management. All in all, these things add up to a real relaxation of totalitarianism in the form of curbs on the police, restrictions on Party activity, a widened area of permissible expression of opinion, a new emphasis on legality and increasing recognition of individual rights. They have also produced a more humanistic approach to politics generally.

This situation came about primarily as a result of the new, liberalized psychology — and ideology — of the Titoist leaders as well as their necessary search for non-Soviet Marxist forms. In part, it was the inevitable result of the decentralization that so characterizes the Titoist system. In part, also, it resulted from the conscious efforts of at least some Yugoslav Communists to infuse some — however few — elements of real political democracy into their brand of socialism.

There is no doubt that the Yugoslav Communists, with their new reforms, consciously sought increased public support, which they saw as necessary following their rift with the Cominform. There is no doubt, either, that they were successful in this gambit. At the same time, the areas in which harsh measures were considered necessary narrowed after 1948. The break with Moscow cut the ground out from under many anti-Communist Yugoslavs. No matter how much they hated the new regime, they hated the Russians more. Now, if they were not actual supporters of the regime on the grounds that it was defending national independence, at least their opposition lost much of its steam.

In addition, there was the new factor of the necessity for Western, particularly American, support. Many Westerners — and some Soviet observers — interpret the relaxation of totalitarianism in Yugoslavia primarily as an effort to "appease" the West. No doubt a relationship between the liberalizations and Western aid does exist, and it is true that the trend away from totalitarianism was drastically slowed down during the period of the later rapprochement with Moscow. Of course the Yugoslavs were not oblivious of the advantages that their lessened totalitarianism brought to their foreign policy. Yet it is easy to overestimate the extent of outside influences. The reforms clearly bolstered Tito's domestic position. Moreover, the theories on which they were based were being devised *before* Belgrade had much hope of Western support, and the main reforms themselves came only *after* aid to Yugoslavia seemed to be an established policy of the West in its own interest. If Tito were trying to "appease" the West by pretending to be democratic, his repeated explicit rejections of Western political democracy were a strange way to go about it.

Socialist Legality and the Police

The concept of socialist legality is not original with the Yugoslavs but was evolved at an early date in the Soviet Union. The idea is simply that a socialist system, like capitalism, must have a body of laws, but whereas under capitalism the laws are designed to strengthen the capitalist system, under socialism the laws are designed to strengthen the socialist system. The laws themselves may be rankly discriminatory, and enforcing them may result in untold hardships, but as long as the state authorities operate within their confines, "socialist legality" is being observed. Observance of socialist legality thus means primarily a minimum of capriciousness and arbitrariness in *law enforcement*. While there is an element of democracy in this concept, socialist legality in itself does not insure democracy. The Yugoslav emphasis on socialist legality goes beyond this and involves procedural guarantees for individual rights that in many ways are not too different from the legal systems of the West. In addition, although the socialist nature of Yugoslav law is clear, the Yugoslavs have made an effort — not always successfully — to restrict the scope of the laws themselves to limits which reflect democratic concepts.

Legality of any type, and personal freedom and human rights generally, invariably suffer most where the power of the police is greatest. In the years before 1949 Yugoslavia was in many ways a police state *par excellence*. None other than Aleksandar Ranković, head of the secret political police,[1] has testified to the extent of ruthlessness and unrestrained activity during this period.[2]

The UDBA[3] had a reputation in the period right after the war for being virtually a law unto itself, arresting and imprisoning whomever it wished, with or without cause, and often with great brutality. During this time, these political police frequently interpreted minor offenses as political crimes, interfered in government and economic affairs at will and intimidated officials and ordinary citizens alike. In addition, the whole legal machinery, including the courts and public prosecutors, was a part of the police terror and functioned without the thought of protecting individual rights, which, in fact, existed neither in theory nor practice. Widespread use of informers was an integral part of the system.

[1] Ranković, now a vice president of the Federal Executive Council, no longer runs the police directly as he did while minister for internal affairs, but he still has responsibility for major policies in this area.

[2] See Chapter 6.

[3] Uprava Državne Bezbednosti (Administration of State Security), formerly known as OZNA (Odelenje Zaštite Naroda or Department of Defense of the People).

Now this was just the kind of situation which by 1950 the Yugoslav Communists were beginning to criticize in the Soviet Union. Furthermore, the unrestricted power of the UDBA made a mockery of Yugoslav claims to have a more democratic socialism than that of the USSR and interfered with the workings of the decentralized system then beginning to evolve. It was not surprising, therefore, that the Yugoslavs noticed the mote in their own eye, and that in 1951 the leadership took significant moves toward modification of the police state.

In a society "reaching the socialist path of the withering away of the state," Ranković told the Fourth Plenum of the Central Committee of the Communist Party, in February 1951, "it is inevitable that citizens should become increasingly cognizant of the value of their personal freedom and human rights." Citing damning evidence of police abuses, Ranković promised that henceforth UDBA would mend its ways. The Central Committee then adopted a resolution demanding a strengthening of "socialist legality" and independence of the courts and legal system generally.[1]

The Party's will was enacted into law in the form of two criminal codes, one following the other, which transformed the procedural basis of the Yugoslav legal system, curbed arbitrary police powers and went a long way toward providing Western-type guarantees of due process of law.

The 1951 code[2] forbade any punishment except in violation of a specific statute, and all administrative penalties by UDBA or other officials were banned. The police were forbidden to hold a person for more than twenty-four hours without appearance before a court, although judges were authorized to impose "pre-trial imprisonment" up to six months in cases involving treason or espionage. Strict penalties were provided for violations.

A still more liberal criminal code was adopted in 1953.[3] According to Professor Djordjević, its principal drafter, this code included Western democratic legal practices and was based on the United Nations' Universal Declaration of Human Rights.[4] The right of habeas corpus, in its strict Anglo-Saxon sense, was still not guaranteed, but the right to counsel during pre-trial (as well as trial) proceedings was provided for. The right to appeal decisions to incarcerate for investigation was stipulated, with release on bail provided for at the discretion of the judge. Criminal proceedings could now be brought only after legal indictment, and criminal investigations were put under the

---

[1] Cf. "Za Dalje Jačanje Provosudja i Zakonitosti" ("For Further Strengthening of the Judiciary and Legality"), *Komunist*, March–May 1951.

[2] *Službeni List*, No. 13, March 9, 1951.

[3] *Službeni List*, No. 40, September 30, 1953.

[4] Jovan Djordjević, "The New Code of Criminal Procedure," *Yugoslav Review*, January–February 1954, pp. 10–12.

control of the courts, rather than the police or the public prosecutor. Any person in custody was entitled to at least eight hours of "uninterrupted rest in each twenty-four hour period." The law forbade what Djordjević admitted was "the still frequent practice of physical and psychological exhaustion of the accused, extorting his confession by means of extensive and uninterrupted cross examinations."[1] The right of an accused person not to testify against himself was proclaimed, and confessions had to be corroborated by evidence produced in court. Rights of defense attorneys were spelled out, and protection was provided for defense witnesses.

One major factor in the police state system had been the broad powers of the public prosecutor, a political grand inquisitor authorized to order arrests, criminal investigations and temporary imprisonment. Public prosecutors operated at all governmental levels, responsible to the federal public prosecutor and independent of the courts. Indeed, the federal public prosecutor could decide what cases were to be tried and where and could reopen a case after a court had once decided it.

The power of public prosecutors was substantially curbed, first by the 1953 criminal code and then by a 1954 law dealing specifically with that office.[2] This law, in effect, put the public prosecutors under the jurisdiction of the courts and made them technically simply one of the contending parties in a trial. The public prosecutors were denuded of their power either to order arrests or make criminal investigations, unless authorized to do so by a court. Their power to reopen cases was restricted to civil proceedings. Legal qualifications prescribed for the office made it less political in character and eliminated some of the more extreme Communist functionaries among the public prosecutors. Also, special courts were provided to try cases of violations of law by the public prosecutors themselves. The federal public prosecutor retains considerable jurisdiction over prosecutors at lower levels, and the post is still an important one. However, even after a 1957 law restored some of the functions of public prosecutors in civil cases, the office bore little resemblance to what it had been prior to 1953.

As a part of its strengthening of legality, the regime also moved in 1954 to increase the independence of the courts, which exist at federal, republic, district and regional levels. Each court, under its president, was made responsible for its own work, ending the hierarchical administrative arrangement, although appeals could be made from one judicial level to another. Rather strict professional legal qualifications for judges were established. Judges have "permanent appointments," but still hold office at the pleasure

[1] *Ibid.*, p. 12.
[2] *Službeni List*, No. 51, December 8, 1954.

of the federal and republic assemblies and district people's committees. But the court laws, considered as amendments to the constitution, carefully stipulated reasons for which judges could be removed, and thus made their tenure more secure.

The court system was now divided into three parts: regular courts, economic courts and military courts, with the Federal Supreme Court — a regular tribunal — the final court of appeal for all, including the military courts.[1] The economic courts do not consider criminal cases and act mostly as courts of arbitration in disputes involving economic enterprises.

There is no jury trial as such in Yugoslavia. Economic and regular courts of first instance — district and regional courts — are composed of panels of both professional, full-time judges and "lay judges" or "judge jurors," who are non-lawyer citizens named by people's committees for limited periods. The regular federal and republic courts consist only of professional judges.

Although in Yugoslav theory the courts are supposed to protect the socialist system, they are also supposed to protect citizens against arbitrary state action. For this purpose, the regime in 1952 adopted an Administrative Disputes Act giving citizens the right to contest any administrative action and to sue for damages resulting from the action of state officials. Legislative enactments may not be challenged in this way on constitutional or any other grounds, and members of the Federal Executive Council themselves are not liable for their acts, but citizens may bring suit before republic supreme courts — appealable to the Federal Supreme Court — against most other government actions, including those of the federal secretariats.

Socialist Legality in Practice

What does the new emphasis on legality mean in practice to the Yugoslav citizen? While Yugoslavia after the reforms was in many ways no longer a police state, the question must be considered from the viewpoint of the whole complex of Yugoslav life rather than merely in terms of statutory provisions. What was made clear right off was that none of these procedural guarantees meant toleration of active hostility to the regime. Ranković, while calling for greater protection for "personal freedom and human rights," was explicit about this. It would be a "great mistake," he warned, to think that there would result any "appeasement in the struggle against enemies of socialism." Rather, he said, the courts had to be "merciless" in their opposition to anti-socialist forces.[2]

---

[1] The proposed 1962 constitution envisaged a constitutional court also with power to invalidate legislative acts.

[2] Ranković, *op. cit.*, p. 33.

On the other hand, during a later period, when the trend away from totalitarianism seemed to have been sidetracked, Branko Jevremović, the federal public prosecutor, declared that "violation of legality cannot be justified by the interests of socialism." Even when the laws seem inadequate to deal with a specific situation, he said, "their violation [by enforcement agencies] means a greater potential danger for socialism than their unjustified application."[1]

Even if socialist legality was not a refuge for overt opponents of the regime, at least the individual rights of those willing to forgo active opposition were better protected than before. By 1954, arbitrary arrests were practically non-existent. UDBA had abandoned its system of informers and provocateurs as well as the practice of periodically questioning citizens on its blacklist. In any court on any day, ordinary people could be seen standing up for their rights. This was especially marked in the more advanced areas. In Serbia, officials noted "a passion for suing." In Croatia, a police official complained publicly that the courts discriminated against security officers. In Slovenia, court dockets were perennially jammed with cases brought under the Administrative Disputes Act. It was clear that there was redress against illegal action of both police and other officials.

Yet this was by no means the whole story. For the situation from the beginning has been different in the more backward areas of Yugoslavia, and for the nation as a whole the emphasis on legality has proved to be somewhat adjustable, reflecting to some extent the political climate of the moment, although never returning to pre-1951 conditions. Generally speaking, the more backward the area, the greater the abuses. Many people in the less developed sections remained ignorant of their legal rights, and others feared to take advantage of them or were unable to find defense lawyers. Whereas in Slovenia unjustified arrests in 1952 were 11.2 per cent of the total, in Montenegro they amounted to more than 50 per cent. With wry understatement, the late Moše Pijade commented: "This is a very bad sign for legality in Montenegro."[2] There has been improvement in the intervening years, but in 1958 the authors found even certain officials in Macedonia and Montenegro little acquainted with some of the reforms concerning legality, and in Bosnia there were thirty court districts without a single attorney.[3]

Evidence of the emphasis on legality appeared immediately after the passage of the criminal codes, not only in a decline in total arrests from

---

[1] *Politika*, April 7, 1959.

[2] Moše Pijade, "The Law on Criminal Procedure and the Work of the Organs of the Judiciary," *New Yugoslav Law*, July–December 1953, p. 9.

[3] One of the authors witnessed a court proceeding in Bosnia in 1958 in which a peasant was represented by a mullah who confessed that he knew "the laws of Mohammed and of God but not of Yugoslavia."

36,196 in 1950 to 22,259 in 1951 and to 15,484 in 1952, but also in a decline in unjustified arrests. In 1952 Pijade, one of the most stalwart Communist advocates of due process, complained that every fifth person arrested still had been "unwarrantedly deprived of liberty,"[1] though he did not define the phrase. If it is taken to mean persons against whom accusations were dropped without trial, the percentage in the first half of 1954 had fallen to 5.4.[2]

The number of reported arrests continued to drop. For the whole of 1957, only 5,000 persons were sentenced to prison terms of more than six months. Of these, 407 were listed as political offenders of one type or another, but only about 50 were involved in "anti-regime activity." More than half of the 407 were convicted of spreading "religious hatred," and 70 others were accused of promoting dissension among the nationalities.[3] The number of persons arrested for purposes of investigation decreased also; it dropped, for example, from 3,681 in the first half of 1956 to 2,692 in the first half of 1957, while the percentage of those released after investigation rose from 29 per cent to 36 per cent.[4] Belgrade officials were quick to point to these figures as evidence of the growing independence of the courts and the respect for legality.

The status of those Yugoslavs who have opposed the regime not out of opposition to Communism but out of support for the Cominform and the Soviet Union deserves a special note of comment. In 1952 Ranković revealed that "since 1948, 11,128 persons have been penalized by summary administrative procedure for pro-Cominform activities," in addition to 2,572 sentenced by regular civilian and military courts.[5] Arrests for Cominform activities continued through 1955, and during much of this period the attitude of the Tito regime toward supporters of the Soviet Union approached that of the late Senator McCarthy.[6] However, as early as 1953, an amnesty freed many of those taken into custody in the initial crackdown on Soviet sympathizers and reduced the sentences of most of the others. One of the most important of them, former Minister Sretan Žujović, having repented while in prison, was freed and given a responsible administrative post on *Borba*.

---

[1] *Op. cit.*, p. 9.

[2] Saveza Narodna Skupština, *Izveštaj Zaveznog Izvršnog Veča za 1954 Godinu* (*Report of the Federal Executive Council for 1954*), Kultura, Belgrade, 1955, p. 18.

[3] *New York Times*, November 1, 1959, p. 9.

[4] *Izveštaj Saveznog Izvršnog Veča za 1957 Godinu*, p. 45.

[5] Report of Aleksandar Ranković, *Sixth Congress of the Communist Party of Yugoslavia*, Belgrade, 1953, p. 67.

[6] Professor Alex Dragnich, a former cultural attaché in the U. S. Embassy in Belgrade, has asserted that charges of pro-Cominform activity were sometimes used as a pretext for arresting persons well known for their opposition to Communism of any type. See his *Tito's Promised Land — Yugoslavia*, Rutgers University Press, New Brunswick, N. J., 1954, p. 298.

During the height of the rapprochement with the Soviet Union in 1956 and 1957, no arrests of Cominformists were made as far as is known. Once the feud with Moscow flared again in 1958, however, several hundred persons known earlier to have been Cominform supporters were rounded up, and apparently dealt with by summary administrative procedure.[1]

Loopholes in Legality

The legal guarantees which evolved during the 1951-1955 period, as much of an advance as they were, themselves contained large loopholes which put Yugoslav legal practice in a different category from that of the West. Although public trial is provided in principle, and the great majority of trials are in fact public, the law is so worded that there is no absolute guarantee of this. At any time between the opening of a trial and the final rendering of a verdict, the public may be excluded "when the interests of preserving secrecy or the interests of public order or morals so require." Thus important political trials, such as those to which Milovan Djilas was subjected, have been for the most part non-public, although not strictly secret, either.

In addition a whole range of misconduct classified under the headings of ill-defined "petty offenses" and "more serious petty offenses" may be punished directly by republic administrative authorities, in some cases by prison sentences up to two years, with the right to counsel questionable. Search and seizure of property, which in criminal cases must be authorized by the court, is left to the discretion of administrative authorities in petty offenses. Although a person convicted of such offenses may bring action under the Administrative Disputes Act, and the courts may on their own initiative intervene, technically this type of conviction is appealable only to higher administrative authority and not to the courts.[2] In 1957, 347,857 persons were accused of petty offenses.[3]

Moreover, in a strict sense the judiciary has no real independence. The law authorizes republic assemblies and even people's committees to remove judges remiss in their duty or "injuring the reputation of the judicial service," and such removals sometimes occur. On one occasion, federal authorities virtually instructed people's assemblies to fire certain judges, although in this particular case nonpolitical considerations appear to have been involved.[4]

[1] Including, in some cases, exile on an Adriatic island. See p. 409. Several persons thus accused escaped across the border into Albania.

[2] Cf. Milorad Vučković and Negoslav Očokoljić, *Osnovni Zakon o Prekršajima* (*Basic Law on Petty Offenses*), fourth edition, Arhiva za Pravne i Društvene Nauke, Belgrade, 1956.

[3] *Report of the Federal Executive Council for 1957*, p. 41.

[4] See *Borba*, June 27, 1957. During 1959 there was discussion of provisions for strengthening judicial tenure.

The presidents of courts are without exception members of the League of Communists. A large percentage of other professional judges are also Communists. The proportion of the lay judges who are in the Party is smaller, although they are invariably affiliated with the Socialist Alliance and thus considered politically acceptable. The Communist influence on the bench, however, does not necessarily mean that the judges will connive at violations of legality nor does it always work against judicial independence. On occasion Communist judges have administered sharp scoldings to UDBA representatives, and the professional judges sometimes take a more objective attitude toward the law than the citizen judge-jurors.[1]

Still another factor is the position of lawyers. So-called "people's attorneys," paid by the government, are available to accused persons, but there are also a large number of private lawyers. In fact, the number doubled between 1950 and 1957. In the days of the police state, the area in which the legal profession could play its traditional role was small indeed. Defense of an accused person was itself regarded as more or less a hostile act. Denied any professional status, private lawyers were suspect as a group. Many who had been associated with political opposition to the regime were prohibited from practicing. After 1951 this situation changed. The new respect for legality combined with the entrance into the profession of younger, more adaptable men and a growing acceptance of the regime on the part of the older ones served to enhance the status of the lawyer. In addition, of course, the legal framework within which lawyers operate acquired a socialist base.[2] As a result, vigorous defense by private lawyers, even in political cases, has become the normal practice.

At the same time, the inviolable nature of the lawyer-client relationship characteristic of Western legal practice has never quite been recognized. While the legal profession is the only private one still existing on a large scale in Yugoslavia, membership in republic jurists' associations — united in a federal Union of Jurists' Associations — is compulsory for practicing attorneys. That this is considerably less than an independent bar is due chiefly to the fact that it is governed under the concepts of social management, its governing board including persons (not necessarily lawyers) named by the republic assemblies. The strong Communist influence thus brought to the jurists' associations has circumscribed efforts to work out a code of ethics comparable to those of most non-Communist countries, and meetings

[1] See Fred Warner Neal, *Titoism in Action: The Reforms in Yugoslavia after 1948*, University of California Press, Berkeley, 1958, p. 218.

[2] A reorganization of the curriculum of the law schools was designed to give legal education a definite Marxist coloration, although many non-Communist professors continue to teach in the universities.

of the associations are frequently the scene of impassioned demands for still further independence of the legal profession.

Financially, some lawyers are doing exceedingly well, although, for the most part, these are attorneys specializing in economic cases. A 1959 decree making it obligatory for lawyers to keep detailed accounts of fees seemed to presage tax moves to make private practice of the law less lucrative.

Nature of the Laws

Most basic of all the legal factors pointing to definite limits in the trend away from totalitarianism in Yugoslavia is the nature of many of the laws themselves. In particular, the laws aimed at political opposition are so broad and so general that, with the strictest legality, the government has virtually unrestricted authority when it wants to use it. That is to say, it is possible for the government quite legally to condemn almost any act of opposition to the regime. An émigré Yugoslav jurist, Dr. Alexander Adamovitch of the Library of Congress, points out, with some reason, that laws of this nature are themselves contrary to the *concept* of the rule of law as understood in the West.[1]

Perhaps the most flagrant example is the section of the 1951 criminal code on "hostile propaganda," under which Milovan Djilas, along with Vladimir Dedijer, was originally convicted in 1955. This section (116) reads as follows:

(1) Whoever, with intent to undermine the authority of the working people, defensive power of the country, or economic bases of socialist construction; or with intent to destroy the brotherhood and unity of the peoples of the Federal People's Republic of Yugoslavia by means of cartoons, writings, or speeches before gatherings, *or in any other way* carries out propaganda against the state and social organizations or against political, economic, military or other important measures of the people's authority, shall be punished by imprisonment.

(2) The same punishment shall be inflicted on an individual propagating fascist *or other ideas hostile to the people and the government.*[2]

Officially, Djilas and Dedijer were convicted not for their ideas but for the way they advanced them, i.e., stating them in interviews to foreign correspondents, and *Borba* insisted that they were free to hold "and fight for" their convictions.[3] If so, it would only be because the authorities decided to

---

[1] Cf. "Notes on a Belgrade Trial," *Highlights of Current Legislation and Activities in Mid-Europe,* Library of Congress Mid-European Law Project, April 1959, pp. 175–182.

[2] *Službeni List,* No. 13, March 9, 1951. (Italics added.)

[3] January 25, 1955. It must be remembered that no legal action was brought against Djilas for his original criticisms of the regime in 1953, which appeared in Yugoslav publications. See Chapter 12.

permit it. In fact, Djilas was denied any opportunity to publish his views in Yugoslavia once the Party had disciplined him, and, of course, publication of *The New Class* abroad brought down on him a second conviction under the same statute.

In 1952, the Supreme Court of Bosnia and Herzegovina went so far in interpreting the hostile propaganda statute as to hold that it covered a conversation between two individuals.[1] In later years, such a ruling would have been unlikely, and, if made, almost certainly would have been reversed by the Federal Supreme Court, but it illustrates the possible applications of ambiguous laws.

In 1959, a revised criminal code narrowed a little the definition of hostile propaganda,[2] with the intent, according to Belgrade experts, of making specific acts the test of a violation. Whether it accomplishes this is questionable. The new statute is more precise in specifying as a criminal act the calling for or inciting "with writings, speech or otherwise violent or unconstitutional change." But it is at least equally ambiguous when it extends to anyone representing "the social-political conditions in the country maliciously or untruthfully." The Djilas-Dedijer convictions and the 1952 ruling in Bosnia and Herzegovina indicate that although the regime may in fact exercise considerable latitude in permitting expression of opposition, the limits of such freedom depend not so much on the law as on the discretion of the government in invoking the law. It is difficult to see how the new hostile propaganda law changes the situation substantially.

Even if the 1959 code is more definite in making specific acts a test of violation, however, the problem remains. In 1958 three elderly Yugoslavs, including two leaders of the prewar Yugoslav Socialist Party, received sentences of from four to eight and a half years in prison for plotting the "forcible" overthrow of the regime. That is, they were convicted not of "hostile propaganda" but of having committed definite acts. The actual charges amounted to little more than that one of them had written a book critical of Tito which they tried to get published in the West and that they had met together from time to time to exchange anti-regime sentiments. Although the prosecution alleged that they tried to establish contact with Yugoslav exiles who had been associated with the wartime Četnik forces, there was no evidence that they tried to enlist support inside Yugoslavia or had any organizational plans whatsoever. One of the defense attorneys, a woman, after failing to have the prosecutor disqualified on grounds of bias,·

---

[1] Cited by Fran Gjupanovich, "The Djilas Case," *Highlights of Current Legislation and Activities in Mid-Europe*," V, September–October 1957, p. 414, from *Zbirka Odluka Vrhovnih Sudova (Collection of Decisions of Supreme Courts)*, 1954 edition.

[2] Article 118 of the 1959 code. See *Službeni List*, No. 30, July 29, 1959.

told the court: "Freedom of thought and an exchange of views cannot constitute a criminal offense."[1] She was, as it turned out, wrong.

One reason why the government decided to punish these particular men, despite their obvious political impotence, may have been the involvement of an anti-Tito manuscript. Since their experience with Djilas, the Yugoslav authorities have been especially touchy on this point and may have seized the opportunity to discourage potential authors of similar tracts.

Another factor may have been the connection with the Četnik movement, on any manifestation of which the regime is always ready to crack down. One of the defendants, 73-year-old Aleksandar Pavlević, had been the Socialist delegate to the Četnik political committee, and for this he had already served seven and a half years in prison right after the war. Another, Bogdan Krekić, 72, had been an official of the trade union movement in the period right after the war. A third was Milan Žujović, former dean of the University of Belgrade law faculty and the brother of a prominent Četnik exile in Paris. Sentenced with them was Bragoslav Stranjaković, a theological professor. All four were released on parole in February 1960.

Although these defendants were charged with actually plotting, the "hostile propaganda" law was in the past, at least, the usual statute for getting at former Četnici and Ustaše. There have been frequent newspaper accounts pertaining to the trials of those who fought with Mihailović and with the Croat forces. One such in 1958, for example, involved a certain Živko Popović, who had earlier served six years of a twelve-year sentence for his Četnik activity. "However," *Borba* reported, "he could not keep quiet and made use of every occasion to slander the social system. Because of that he again found himself before the court and was sentenced to two years of strict confinement."[2]

Yet if the nature of the laws gives dangerously wide latitude for interpretation, it should be noted also that the Yugoslav government has increasingly demonstrated a humane attitude toward those it taps as offenders. The treatment of Djilas and Dedijer as well as of the socialists — as unfair as it may have been — was considerably more lenient than the serious nature of the charges might have led one to anticipate. Similarly, while death sentences were often imposed on those convicted of embezzlement and theft of state property, all such sentences were commuted to prison terms, at least since the early 1950's, as far as the authors know. In 1950, the death penalty was made inapplicable to "economic crimes."

Although legal justification might, conceivably, still be found for arresting any Yugoslav who makes untoward remarks about the regime, in fact this

---

[1] *Christian Science Monitor*, February 5, 1958.
[2] *Borba*, March 14, 1958.

does not now happen. Both Communists and anti-Communists freely indulge in criticism and acid humor at the expense of the regime, without fear that such comments will get them in trouble.[1] Especially where there is no direct political intent involved, the authorities invariably turn a deaf ear. In the summer of 1958 one of the authors heard a peasant, arguing with a policeman in downtown Belgrade about a traffic violation, condemn Tito to the wrath of God and the Serbian saints. The militiaman waved him on without as much as a ticket. On the other hand, in the fall of 1959 a Yugoslav near the Italian border was given a year's jail sentence "for blaspheming the President of the Republic." The sentence was suspended, since the man was drunk and it was his first offense.[2] In the same way, while the laws against stirring up religious and national feelings are strictly enforced as far as political mani-festations are concerned, chance derogatory remarks by Serbs about Croats, or vice versa, are ordinarily safely made. Let the same remarks be dropped publicly by a priest or a former anti-Communist politician, however, and charges are apt to be brought in no time.

Those Yugoslav government experts who press for "more legality" are far from happy about the indefinite nature of many Yugoslav laws. They hope in time that the nature of these laws may be altered, but, they argue, given the present state of political and social life in Yugoslavia, wide discretion on the part of the authorities is necessary. In the meantime, these legal experts are influential in the more humane administration of the laws which char-acterizes Yugoslavia.[3] Also, they are under no illusions that all the legal prescriptions for which they secure enactment are always observed. They feel, however, that the more democratic legal institutions that are adopted, the more rapidly Yugoslavia will move toward political democracy — within, of course, the confines of a socialist system. Whether they are overly opti-mistic, time alone will tell.

Areas of Free Expression

One can distinguish between the Tito regime's attitude toward *general* political opposition and its attitude toward *specific* opposition to particular policies. The regime is inclined to be very hard on any manifestations of

---

[1] One such tidbit making the rounds of Belgrade concerns the little boy who asked his father what was the difference between capitalism and socialism. The answer was: "Capitalism is shiny automobiles, champagne and beautiful women. Socialism is Belgrade street cars, Serbian wine and your mother." Another answer one hears to the same question is: "In capitalism there are social errors. In socialism there are capital errors."

[2] *New York Times*, November 1, 1959, p. 9.

[3] Interestingly enough, in official Yugoslav government circles Aleksandar Ranković, of all people, is noted for his insistence on commutation of death sentences passed for non-capital offenses.

meaningful general opposition aimed at the system or the power of the top leadership. Opposition to specific policies, however, is treated with increasing tolerance. Much of this opposition, of course, reflects primarily differences over methods, but it can extend even to important issues.

One reason for this tolerance is that such opposition is almost never successful except on minor matters. Sharp and articulate opposition to many Federal Executive Council proposals is commonplace in the Skupština, for example, but after it is over the Council invariably has its way. Similarly, a few recalcitrant souls often stand up at voters' meetings to denounce government plans and then are usually voted down. One of the authors was present at a voters' meeting in Skoplje in 1958, however, when several locally important changes were made in the commune's social plan as a result of proposals from the floor which clearly surprised and annoyed those in charge. The 1958 educational reform, the 1959 decision to increase rents and, earlier, proposals for organizing the legal profession incurred widespread opposition in various government assemblies and Socialist Alliance meetings, and this was reported in the press. But the outcome was not affected.

Elections. Yugoslav elections illustrate two characteristics of the kind of opposition tolerated: it is not widespread in its public manifestations, and it is more prevalent and more successful at the local level than elsewhere. As far as can be seen from relatively detailed observations, Yugoslav elections are free both in form and in substance, itself an observation that could be made only after 1952. As indicated in an earlier chapter, there has been more often than not only one candidate for a seat in federal elections, while in local elections there have usually been two or more candidates. Real contests have not been uncommon in republic elections, and in local elections a number of candidates frowned on by Party officials have always been successful. Probably 99 per cent of the candidates put forward for the Federal Assembly have Party acceptance if not approval, although they run under a Socialist Alliance (not a Party) endorsement. In the 1957 election, in cases where there were two federal candidates they seldom if ever differed on major issues. When "opposition" candidates stand for election, there are often pressures on them to withdraw, and rarely have the few "oppositionists" reaching the election stage been successful at the Skupština level.

What would be the impact of electoral changes envisaged in the 1962 constitution was not clear. These changes — making election of members of all legislative bodies except commune people's committees indirect — would make the local elections, that is, the "most free" elections, more important. Removal of the Federal Council candidates from direct election probably would have less significance than might appear, since contests for these seats have been less vigorous. The most undemocratic aspect of the proposed changes in practice seemed to be the making of elections to the republic assemblies indirect — that is, election by commune people's committees rather than by the population as a whole. Given the ability of the Party directly and indirectly to control voters' meetings, the over-all impact of the proposed changes seemed likely to be to narrow the limits of effective electoral opposition.[1]

Strikes. That the regime's tolerance of specific opposition extends into areas usually considered way beyond the pale in Communist countries is borne out by the Slovenia coal mine strike of 1958. Technically, the right to strike exists in Yugoslavia. Ivan Božićević, secretary-general of the trade union Sindikat, has gone so far as to cite the "possibility" that the unions might lead a strike, although he added, quite correctly, that if the worker-management system works as it is supposed to strikes are unnecessary.[2]

There were, in fact, no strikes until 1958, and it was tacitly understood that if they were not officially prohibited, neither were they allowed. The trade unions' task, as Božićević told one of the authors in 1954, was to "make sure that there aren't any strikes by making sure that there aren't any reasons for strikes." This task, however, sometimes conflicts with the trade unions' other task of carrying out the Party's will in economic enterprises.

When a sitdown strike broke out in the Trbovlje coal mine in January 1958, with miners demanding a wage increase which their workers' council would not give and their trade union would not support, there was talk in Ljubljana of mobilizing troops. Miha Marinko, president of Slovenia and a member of the Party's Executive Committee — himself a former coal miner — rushed to the spot and alternately threatened and pleaded with the strikers. The matter was placed before Tito himself. The Yugoslav Communist leaders were confronted with an unprecedented situation and did not know how to cope with it.

What happened was that, after an investigation, the authorities concluded that the strike was no more than a spontaneous outburst against wage conditions recognized as unfair. No action was taken against the strikers, but there was a wholesale housecleaning in the Slovenian Sindikat organization. The Party took disciplinary action against the members of the Party unit in the Trbovlje mines, and the 250 Communists in Trbovlje received a dressing down. The district committee was dissolved. Marinko, who in 1919 himself had led a Communist-organized strike at the same mine, also scolded the

---

[1] For earlier reference to the proposed electoral changes, see Chapter 13, pp. 231–232.

[2] Ivan Božićević, "Necessity or Superfluity of Strikes as a Method and Means of Trade Union Activities under Our Conditions," *Sozijalizam*, No. 1, 1959 (*Joint Translation Service Bulletin*, Supplement, March 6, 1959).

workers and talked darkly about "elements of reaction or anarchism." He hinted that the workers' council of the mine itself might have had a hand in organizing the strike. But in the end the strikers got a raise.[1]

At least three smaller strikes occurred in Yugoslavia early in 1958. In each case, the results were much the same.

The press. There is no free press in Yugoslavia in the sense that newspapers ever formally oppose the regime.[2] Most publications operate under the aegis of the Socialist Alliance, managed by their own workers' councils. There is no formal censorship, but both the Socialist Alliance and the Party have watchdog committees to keep an eye on the press. If there are any editors who are not members of the League of Communists, they have escaped notice. Party membership is by no means required for all journalists, although most of them belong. An official news agency, Tanjug, and special correspondents of political reliability handle government news. An unofficial news service, Yugopres, organized in 1951 to compete with Tanjug, was dissolved in 1958.

As a result, on important domestic issues, like the Trbovlje strike, for instance, the newspapers print only official points of view. On matters of special interest to Party leaders, the newspapers serve the function of propaganda better than truth. For example, during the 1955–1958 period, when the Yugoslavs were hopeful of wooing the Chinese Communists to stand with them for "independent paths to socialism," reports from Peking seldom if ever probed beneath the surface of events in China. After the new break with Moscow in 1958, in which the Chinese attacks were more bitter than the Soviet, *Borba* openly admitted that its Peking dispatches had been "overly optimistic and misleading."[3]

On the other hand, the Yugoslav press prints a much wider variety of "straight news" than do newspapers in other Communist countries. It also is much more free to take sides on even controversial administrative questions and to express an independent position on matters where official attitudes are not definitive. The leading newspapers subscribe to and often use material from the Associated Press, United Press International and the *New York Times*. International news is well covered, by and large. Competing as they do for circulation, the newspapers go in for interesting feature stories, pictures and a variety of type make-up. Certain papers publish crime news and non-

---

[1] One element in the Trbovlje grievances was that miners in neighboring establishments were receiving higher wages. The Trbovlje mine is old and a high-cost operation.

[2] Djilas' articles in 1953 were in a way an exception; he was a top leader at the time, and it was not clear what the official line was. Following the episode, steps were taken to see that there was no recurrence.

[3] *Borba*, June 7, 1958.

political gossip. They all take advertisements from economic enterprises, and some of them print American comics.

The ambivalent position of the Yugoslav press is illustrated by the Hungarian revolution of 1956. The revolution was quite objectively reported, with all its bloody overtones, by Yugoslav correspondents in Budapest.[1] Once Tito indicated the narrow line he was taking on the revolution, however, individuality on the subject virtually ceased.

Some government policies have been the object of searching inquiry from *Ekonomska Politika,* itself more or less a Party organ. Other publications have carried "debates" between Yugoslav officials and foreign socialists in the course of which the one-party system was both defended and criticized. The Belgrade weekly *NIN* on several occasions has called attention to the impact on individuals of low wages and high prices; in December 1958 it published the results of a public opinion survey that could only have been embarrassing to the regime. Of those polled, *NIN* reported, 72 per cent were unable to make ends meet on their present wages, 44 per cent were dissatisfied with their living quarters and 31 per cent testified to being "unhappy."[2] The Yugoslav newspapers were not hesitant in criticizing proposals for the 1962 constitution. With the problems of Tito's succession in the air and proposals advocated for limiting tenure, *NIN* engaged in a sharp exchange with high Party officials over what it termed a "conflict of the generations."

Western publications are imported freely, and are sold at bookstores and newsstands in major cities. A notable exception, as might be expected, was Djilas' *The New Class.* The ban on *The New Class* also extended to "any kind of newspaper, magazines and other printed matter which, either in full or in excerpts, carry the text of the book." In 1957 a *Newsweek* correspondent visiting Yugoslavia was expelled for distributing copies of *The New Class.* Only one other Western correspondent, a Swiss, has gotten into trouble with the regime authorities in recent years. There is no censorship; correspondents do not always get cooperation from the authorities, but they are free to ferret out what they can and publish it without fear of the consequences.

The arts. The limited impact of "socialist realism" in the arts testifies to the comparative freedom of this sector of Yugoslav life from ideological and political controls. Although Party influence is sometimes exerted in favor of this traditional Communist view, artists generally complain more of favoritism than of direct pressure. As early as 1950, socialist realism virtually

---

[1] See *Borba* during the period between October 25 and November 5, 1956.

[2] *NIN,* December 16, 1958. Although few of its findings have been published, the Croatian Institute for Social Management has also been delving deeply into public attitudes, particularly as regards local government, voters' meetings and councils of producers. A new Institute for Social Sciences in Belgrade also planned to utilize public opinion poll techniques in its research.

disappeared from exhibits of paintings, and since that time the trend has been markedly toward abstraction. In 1959 an exhibition of Yugoslav modern art came to the United States under the auspices of the American Federation of Artists. The paintings were all abstract, so much so as to be less than representative of Yugoslav art as a whole. "Abstract art," wrote Zoran Kržišnik, director of the Modern Gallery in Ljubljana, "can give perhaps the best illustration of the present trend in Yugoslavia."[1] Yugoslav artists have won high awards in France and elsewhere in the West.

The trend in literature is less *avant-garde* but is also more in the modern, Western than in the Eastern European Communist tradition. There is no possibility of publishing anti-regime literature as such, but neither is there direct Party interference with what writers do. Both poetry and the novel in the past ten years in Yugoslavia have been much more concerned with non-ideological and non-political themes than otherwise.[2] During the heyday of the Soviet-Yugoslav rapprochement, a new literary publication appeared carrying articles denouncing "socialist realism."[3] In the theatre, too, non-Marxist themes predominate, with repertoires including many American offerings. One of the most popular was Gian-Carlo Menotti's opera *The Consul*, the plot of which centers around secret police persecution of the family of a political opponent in an unnamed Iron Curtain country.

However, as is so often the case in Yugoslav life, there are also instances — however infrequent — of clear-cut political interference, usually involving persons already marked for their anti-regime feelings. One such case is that of Dr. Anton Slodnjak and his book *History of Slovenian Literature*. The book was part of a series edited by Max Vasmer, a German Slavic expert, and was published in Berlin in 1958. Dr. Slodnjak was chairman of the department of Slovenian literature at the University of Ljubljana. The book was reviewed favorably by the Ljubljana newspaper *Slovenski Poročevalec* on January 5, 1959. But on January 31, the more official newspaper *Ljudska Pravica* denounced it in a review of two full pages. The reviewer, Jože Kastelić, director of the Slovenian National Museum, attacked the book for criticizing socialist authors while dealing too uncritically with Slovenian writers in exile. He complained that Dr. Slodnjak did not understand social and literary developments in Slovenian history because he did not understand the dialectical method of historical analysis and relied too much on religious method-

---

[1] *New Painting from Yugoslavia*, Commission for Foreign Cultural Relations, Belgrade, 1959, p. 1.

[2] An example is *The Bridge on the Drina*, by Ivo Andric, which was published in 1945 and won the Nobel Prize in 1961.

[3] See Ante Kadić, "Contemporary Yugoslav Literature," *Books Abroad*, 1959, pp. 139–143, for a good, brief discussion of this.

ology. Then, on April 12, *Slovenski Poročevalec* reported that, following criticism by a special faculty commission of the book's errors and "the deep moral damage" resulting from publication in a foreign country, Professor Slodnjak had requested to be retired from the University.[1]

Foreign Travel

Both for Yugoslavs and for foreigners, travel to and out of Yugoslavia is freer than is the case with any other Communist country. The policy on issuing passports has gradually eased since 1952. Currency restrictions are severe, but most Yugoslavs who can afford foreign travel can now obtain short-term passports simply by applying to the district people's committee internal affairs secretariat, and Yugoslav tourists in Italy, Austria, West Germany and elsewhere are, if not commonplace, not unusual. This liberal policy does not always extend to persons on whom the shadow of political opposition has fallen. Vladimir Dedijer, for example, although he traveled in Scandinavia after he was placed on probation in 1955, was later denied a passport for two years. He obtained one in 1959. The Yugoslavs are cautious about visas to citizens of Soviet bloc countries, but Westerners ordinarily can get a thirty-day visa with only a few minutes' wait, simply by applying at any Yugoslav diplomatic or consular mission, or at any border crossing, and then may have it extended for sixty days by district authorities. Visas or extensions for longer stays require the approval of the Federal Secretariat for Internal Affairs,[2] but Western scholars generally have no trouble gaining admittance for periods of extensive study.

The incessant following and police questioning of foreigners that so plagued Westerners, including diplomats, prior to 1950, is now a thing of the past. The authors know of only one case since 1952 where an American traveling in Yugoslavia was questioned by police, and that involved peculiar circumstances. In prior years, Yugoslav police, Soviet-fashion, often stopped foreigners from taking photographs. This happened to the authors only once in 1954, in Titograd, and an admonition to the policeman that it was not his concern sufficed to end the interference. In 1958 a policeman stopped an American from taking a snapshot of Party headquarters in Belgrade. Asked from what law his authority stemmed, the policeman blushed and stammered and said all he knew was that "they" didn't like photographs to be taken of the Party building. But the policeman added that if the American persisted,

---

[1] "Laibacher Universität verurteilt führenden Philologen" ("Ljubljana University Censures Leading Philologist"), *Der Donauraum* (Vienna), 1959, p. 113. It is an interesting although probably unrelated fact that the following year *Slovenski Poročevalec* ceased publication.

[2] Cf. *Službeni List*, No. 9, March 4, 1959.

he guessed there was nothing he could do about it. The American persisted. The policeman walked away, muttering under his breath.

Religion

In Yugoslavia, the regime does not so much oppose religion as attempt to limit its influence and, where possible, utilize it. There is complete freedom of religion in the sense that public worship is permitted without interference but not in the sense that the religious organizations or clergymen as such may take stands on important public issues at variance with the state. The Titoist leaders frankly look forward to a time when religion will have died out, but they recognize that this time may be several generations hence, and meanwhile they are pledged not to force the issue. According to Kardelj, "social development itself, i.e., the development of material forces, will be the factor which will bring the final decision . . . , and not political or ideological forms, regardless of their character."[1]

A law designed to "normalize relations between church and state" was passed in 1953. It provided for government assistance to the religious communities, the operation of theological seminaries and a religious press. Internal autonomy was guaranteed, interference with religious services prohibited and church rites following civil marriages permitted. Generally speaking, under this law an informal *modus vivendi* exists between the regime and Serbian Orthodox Church and the Moslem community, while there is an uneasy mutual toleration between the government and the Roman Catholic Church. Relations with the latter are complicated not only by its ties with Rome and the strongly anti-Communist tone of Roman Catholicism generally but also by its traditional association with Croat nationalism.

To help the churches keep in mind lessons taught by strong-arm methods during the police state period, the authorities do not hesitate to crack down on any priest who gets out of line or on individual confessants who use religious ideas for political propaganda. No high church official has been jailed since 1954,[2] when the Orthodox Metropolitan of Montenegro was convicted of "anti-state activities" for busying himself with local election matters. Occasionally priests, particularly Roman Catholics, are imprisoned.

Until his death early in 1960, Monsignor Stepinac, the Yugoslav primate, was a focal point of the hostility existing between the regime and the Roman Catholic Church. When the Archbishop was released from prison at the end of 1951, church-state relations appeared to be on the mend. But when the

---

[1] Address to the Fourth Congress of the People's Front, *Yugoslav Review*, March–April 1953, p. 18.

[2] The Roman Catholic Bishop of Skoplje, a target of press attacks in earlier years, was charged in March 1960 with smuggling and illegal dealings in foreign currency. He was allowed to go free pending trial.

Vatican followed this move by presenting him with a cardinal's hat, Yugoslavia angrily broke off relations and closed the Papal nunciature. Cardinal Stepinac had been restricted by government decree to his native Croatian village. Both he and the Holy See steadfastly ignored a standing Belgrade offer to allow him to leave the country provided he did not return. The cardinal shunned the regime. Although a number of Yugoslav bishops visited Rome in 1958, Monsignor Stepinac did not ask to be present at the Papal election later that year. Unlike many other Roman Catholic prelates, he refused to vote in either local or national Yugoslav elections.

Church and state tolerate each other but little more. High Roman Catholic churchmen in Zagreb complained to the authors in 1958 that threats by local Party officials against village priests "frequently occur as a result of our struggle with Communism." Indicative of the problem of national particularism involved, these Croat prelates tended to blame "Serbian influences" for at least part of their troubles.

The government has usually avoided formal hostility because of the strong position of Roman Catholicism in Croatia. Although the Zagreb Church officials cited above said they saw "no end" to their struggle with Communism, they also agreed that outward manifestations of regime hostility were less than at any time since the end of the war. In the fall of 1959, Vladimir Bakarić, the leading government and Party official in Croatia, indicated that Cardinal Stepinac would be permitted to resume his duties as primate when the sentence passed on him in 1946 had expired. On February 9, 1960, the Roman Catholic Archbishop of Belgrade, Josip Ujčić, received the Tito government's highest civilian decoration, the People's Order of Merit, First Class, on his eightieth birthday. The next day Cardinal Stepinac died, and Archbishop Ujčić became the acting head of the Roman Catholic Church in Yugoslavia. Later that year Archbishop Franjo Seper of Zagreb was named as the new Primate.

A persistent issue plaguing relations between the Roman Catholic Church and the regime has been the refusal of the hierarchy to authorize its priests to join government-approved clerical associations. There are five of these for Roman Catholic priests, and, despite episcopal opposition, about 40 per cent of the Catholic prelates in Yugoslavia are members. Importance is attached to the clerical associations because they enable the government to get its ideas across to the clergy and indicate a degree of acceptance of the regime on the part of the churches. Priests benefit through social insurance only if they are members of the clerical associations. The Orthodox Church and the Supreme Vakuf Assembly, ruling body of the Moslem community, permit their clergy to join similar associations.

While many hoped that events following Cardinal Stepinac's death would permit an easing of tensions between Belgrade and the Roman Catholic Church, the regime indicated it would give no quarter where political issues might be involved. Early in 1960, twenty-three Roman Catholic functionaries were brought to trial on charges of anti-state activity involving Croat separatism. One of the defendants, a thirty-seven-year-old Franciscan monk, was sentenced to fifteen years in prison.[1]

Nevertheless, chances for improvement in official relations appeared better than they had been since the end of the war. In presenting the Order of Merit to Archbishop Ujčić, Dobrivoje Radosavljević, in charge of church relations for the Federal Executive Council, predicted "normalization of relations" between the state and the Roman Catholic Church. The Archbishop replied: ". . . whenever it was possible I have worked gladly and will continue to work for the normalization of relations. . . . I am a convinced theologian, loyal to the Head of the Church, His Holiness the Pope, and as a citizen of this country I am also loyal to its chief, the President of the Republic."[2]

In the fall of 1960, the Yugoslav bench of Roman Catholic bishops submitted to the government a proposal for improving church-state relations. The bishops urged government restoration of some Church property, safeguards against local interference with religious education and dealing with the Council of Bishops instead of the priests' associations. In return, the Church would formally recognize the authority of the national constitution and refrain from opposition to the regime.[3]

While the regime does not directly interfere with internal administration in any of the churches, it does not hesitate to do so indirectly when political considerations are involved. A good example is the manner in which the Holy Synod of the Serbian Orthodox Church was pressured into accepting Macedonian demands for an autocephalous church in that republic in 1958.[4] The government was anxious to accommodate the Macedonian clergy in order not only to limit the power of the Serbian Church but also to mend its fences in Macedonia and minimize the impact of Bulgarian irridentist claims to that area.

[1] *New York Times*, February 7, 1960, p. 37.

[2] *Yugoslav Life*, February 1960, p. 6. Whether Monsignor Ujčić represents the views of many prelates in Croatia, however, is questionable.

[3] There was little indication that Belgrade considered this an adequate *quid pro quo*, or that the Church felt it could raise the ante. Future developments, of course, depended not only on politics in Yugoslavia but also on politics in the Vatican, in particular the stance taken by the Holy See toward the Communist countries generally.

[4] Macedonian bishops were elected, along with a Metropolitan of their choosing, although nominally the church continued as a part of the Serbian Church under the Serbian Patriarch. The ancient see of Ohrid was reactivated as the archbishopric of Skoplje and Ohrid. Cf. *Borba*, October 7, 1958.

In return for its toleration and material aid, the Tito regime receives formal tokens of support in a number of ways, at least from the Orthodox and Moslem organizations. One form consists of admonitions to the faithful to be loyal to the government. Usually the basis of this is along the line of giving "unto Caesar that which is Caesar's" but sometimes it goes further. The supreme Moslem Assembly, for instance, in 1957 declared its "greatest gratitude to our state leadership, with you at its head, Comrade Tito," for the fact that the Moslems were enabled to have "a completely free religious life, and, with the material aid of the state, to achieve their aims."[1] The annual conference of Moslem priests of Serbia went even further, pledging "to continue fighting tirelessly for the development of Socialist democracy and for the future development of Socialist Yugoslavia."[2]

Another area of support which the regime receives from the religious organizations is in foreign policy. The Serbian Moslem priests mentioned above, for example, denounced Albanian claims about the Albanian minority in Yugoslavia. Hadji Sulejman effendi Kemura, as the press deferentially refers to the Reis Ul Ulema, or chief, of the Moslem community, has toured the Middle East amid great fanfare both there and in Yugoslavia. Both Russian and Rumanian Orthodox Church leaders have exchanged visits with their opposite numbers in Yugoslavia, each time issuing joint statements calling for peace and international cooperation. The Serbian Orthodox clergy also maintains traditional ties with the Church of England and usually plays host to visiting churchmen from the West. These are not unimportant services for a small, isolated country steering a perilous course between Moscow and the West.

While there is no continuing campaign against religion in any formal sense, there are from time to time anti-religious articles in the press. The newspapers are quick to attack such things as time utilized for religious holidays and to cast a scandalized eye at such bacchanalian revels as sometimes occur on feast days in the villages. Overzealous priests are likely to find their faults magnified and their efforts publicly derided.

Religion is still a force in the lives of a majority of the people. Women remain the backbone of both Christian and Moslem congregations.[3] There are some evidences of a falling off of young people at services, particularly at the mosques, and older people invariably predominate among those active in all the faiths. However, there seems to have been no sharp change in the

---

[1] *Oslobodjenje*, Sarajevo, September 16, 1957.

[2] *Borba*, May 21, 1957.

[3] In 1950 the regime prohibited the wearing of veils in public, but many Moslem women circumvent the ban by shielding their faces in other ways. The fez, proscribed in Turkey, is still the headgear of many male Moslems.

age composition of either Orthodox or Roman Catholic confessants during the past decade.

The Right to Privacy

One usual aspect of totalitarianism is a demand by the leadership that citizens not only not oppose the regime, but actively support it. In Yugoslavia, the regime is less frenetic than formerly in trying to produce manifestations of positive support. There tends to be recognition of the average person's right not to participate and to lead his private life as he sees fit, within the bosom of his family or other groups, as long as this does not involve overt activity against the regime. It is significant that when the laws on apartment house councils and housing neighborhoods were being considered, there were specific assurances that these were not to provide house or block political organization.[1]

Although the Socialist Alliance is usually successful in producing large crowds for public events that the Party considers important, there are few of these compared with, say, the Soviet Union. May Day, which in the earlier years was the occasion for frenzied propaganda, speeches, parades and massed demonstrations, is still a holiday in Yugoslavia, but more restrained and with less publicly organized activity.

A "Tito cult" exists in the sense that when the Marshal speaks all listen and applaud. At the great Partisan rally in Bosnia in 1958, for example, the chant of "*Mi smo Titovo, Tito je naš!*" ("We are Tito's, Tito is ours!") echoed across the mountains with a rhythm and regularity seldom produced by complete spontaneity (but observers saw no evidence of a claque). Yet the more ostentatious aspects of the "cult of the individual" are by and large confined to strictly Party functions. The great, ikon-like pictures of Tito that one saw everywhere prior to 1950 have vanished — although some are put up in prominent places on special holidays — and no longer do school children sing songs comparing the Marshal to beautiful flowers. One cannot say that the Titoists do not take themselves seriously, but their new psychology gives them some sense of the ridiculous which so many totalitarians do not seem to possess.

Off-Again On-Again Liberalization

The trend away from totalitarianism in Yugoslavia has been neither constant nor certain. If one were to chart it on a graph, the line would undulate up and down, but certain general movements would be observable.

[1] Despite such assurances, the house and neighborhood councils provide the possibility of such organization, and it is yet too early to say for certain that they may not be used for this purpose.

The line would commence to rise in 1950, move up rapidly in 1951 and 1952, continue upward but much more slowly in 1953 and 1954 and then straighten out. In 1956 and 1957, it would zigzag sharply but with a marked downward trend and would level out again in 1958. Whether it would remain level, and if not, which way it would go, was uncertain.

What seems to have happened is that the leadership is enmeshed in the contradiction apparently inherent in its own ideology and system. On the one hand, it is impelled to liberalize. But each time it does so, the liberalizations show an "un-socialist" tendency to get out of hand, so there is a tightening up. The tightening up, in turn, runs counter to Titoism's basic philosophy, so it produces a reaction. And so it goes.

There are a number of specific reasons why a reverse trend was apparent in the 1956–1958 period. One was the reaction to Djilas' extremism and its disconcerting popularity in the country. A second was fear resulting from the Hungarian revolution. A third was the rapprochement with Moscow. In addition, an important but mainly non-political factor was the economic necessity to pull back somewhat from the perhaps excessive decentralization of controls in the preceding four years.

Like so many things in Communist Eastern Europe, the sharp trend away from totalitarianism in Yugoslavia originally was not a direct response to popular pressure but was decreed from the top after the Cominform-expelled leadership had re-thought its strategy and tactics. Although the liberalizations struck a warmly responsive chord among the Yugoslav people as a whole, including, probably, most Communists, the trend was less than completely popular among those hard-bitten Balkan bureaucrats comprising the secondary and tertiary levels of Party bosses. These included some who had never ceased to think it was a mistake to have stood up to Moscow and some who simply cared more for their personal power than for ideological innovation. These officials now began to reassert themselves, in part as a result of encouragement from the top leadership, in part on their own initiative.

The disciplining of Djilas by the Party in 1953 and his conviction in 1955 indicated the extent and limits of the relaxation of totalitarianism but not necessarily any reversal of the trend. Djilas had clearly violated the Party's precepts of democratic centralism. That legal action was not brought against him until 1955 and that then he was placed on probation under a comparatively light sentence testified, if anything, to the distance Yugoslavia had come from the high point of its totalitarianism. Even when in 1956 he was made to begin serving his prison term, it could be argued that he unquestionably violated the terms of his probation and was, in effect, "asking for it." The same could not be said, however, for the regime's continued harassment of Dedijer and others associated with Djilas, of the added sentence Djilas received as a result of *The New Class*, of the trial of the elderly socialists in 1958 or of several other actions smacking of totalitarianism. It is easy to exaggerate the situation. There was no open reappearance of the police state, and there were few if any arbitrary arrests. But the abandoned practice of UDBA interrogations of persons unaccused of crime but politically suspect was revived. Those who had indicated sympathy for Djilas or who objected to Tito's policy of making up to Moscow were suddenly denied passports. These included Dedijer and Edward Kočbek, a Roman Catholic Partisan leader and a postwar vice president of Slovenia. Stevan Dedijer, a Princeton graduate and an atomic physicist, was expelled from the League of Communists, apparently just for defending his elder brother, Vladimir. When he wrote a comparatively mild article for the *Bulletin of the Atomic Scientists* urging greater freedom in Communist countries,[1] he lost his fellowship at the Rudijer Bošković Institute, where he was completing his doctoral dissertation. Dedijer continued to work as a scientist, however, and in November 1959 contributed another article on the same subject, although less pointed politically, to the *Bulletin*.

The reverse trend could also be detected in the tenor of legal and ideological formulations. Laws providing for stricter governmental control of economic affairs were enacted, although, in this case, political considerations were often not primary. A move was launched to socialize completely the practice of medicine and discriminate against private physicians. In this period controls on lawyers were tightened up. Legal exile for political offenses, eliminated in 1951, was quietly re-enacted, and in such a way that sentence could be passed by police courts, without regular trial.[2] Party discipline was tightened, and Party interference in government and economic affairs, once frowned upon, was now discreetly encouraged. Emphasis in theoretical pronouncements was now on the centralism part of democratic centralism, less on democracy and more on the concept of proletarian dictatorship. The earlier practice of public condemnation of official abuses virtually ceased. Party activities, the public nature of which was once so emphatically asserted, seemed to be more and more cloaked with secrecy. Official criticism of the Soviet Union was abandoned, and private criticism was condemned.[3]

[1] "Research and Freedom in Underdeveloped Countries," *Bulletin of the Atomic Scientists*, September 1957, pp. 238–242.

[2] This measure was, apparently, aimed chiefly at Communists accused of supporting Moscow instead of Belgrade when the Soviet-Yugoslav feud was rekindled in 1958. Such exile, to remote villages or a barren island in the Adriatic, was imposed on 166 persons between June 1958 and June 1959. See *New York Times*, November 1, 1959, p. 9.

[3] One of Vladimir Dedijer's sins was that, on a lecture tour in Scandinavia in the spring of 1957, he criticized not the Tito regime but the USSR.

The real manifestations of the shift in emphasis of the new trend were most apparent, however, in areas removed from Belgrade, particularly the more backward ones. Here the Party militants subjected known opponents of the regime to harassment in many ways. Questionable errors were sometimes uncovered in tax reports, requiring sudden payment of burdensome sums. Owners of small private businesses were confronted with new, inexplicable inspections. Minor infractions of law were harshly dealt with. There were cases of intimidation. In at least one case, a Yugoslav who hears frequently from relatives in America was ordered to show the authorities letters he had received. An anti-Communist professor of engineering was tried and convicted by a lower court of violating a republic law requiring that films be obtained only from a central office. The law clearly concerned ordinary movies shown in motion picture houses, whereas the professor was showing his class films obtained from the U. S. consulate. In some of these instances, as in the case of the professor, these strong-arm methods were successfully challenged by legal action or appeals. But on the whole they did produce a tighter political climate generally than obtained during the period 1952–1955.

The reversal of the trend away from totalitarianism was, of course, of a limited nature. Most basic Titoist concepts were retained in both theory and practice. A good deal of tightening up was, in the first instance, inside the Party. Much of it involved economic affairs and reflected in large part clear-cut abuses permitted by a decentralization that was imprudently fast and sweeping. There were, also, certain extensions rather than restrictions in local autonomy during this period. Liberalized measures authorized government payments to former owners of nationalized property who were incapable of working and had no other means of livelihood. Although youth work brigades, which Tito had condemned in 1952, were reintroduced to cope with widespread apathy among young people, these appeared to be really voluntary this time instead of, as formerly, voluntary only in name. The strike in Slovenia was treated with considerably more understanding than might have been expected.

Some saw in the reverse trend a contradiction between the Tito regime's aspirations for democracy and its socialist goals. To these observers, it appeared as if the earlier, rapid trend toward democratization had resulted in a slackening of socialist development, and that, in order to spur the latter, the Yugoslav Communists were forced to jettison some of the former. The official Party line in Yugoslavia denies that such a contradiction exists. According to this view, the more socialism the more democracy, the less socialism the less democracy. Others in the Yugoslav League of Communists, however, perhaps thinking in more Western terms, freely grant that the

1956–1958 period resulted in stricter political controls, although they would agree that, generally speaking, political democracy in Yugoslavia must go hand in hand with socialism.

Regardless of such theorizing, the reverse trend produced a popular reaction that in itself indicated much about Yugoslavia. There were grumblings — among ordinary people, among non-Communist intellectuals and experts, who were playing a growing role in Titoist society, and among many Communists themselves. Party discipline may have been stiffened, but there was a marked falling off of the general public enthusiasm present earlier. That many feared rapprochement with Moscow and felt that the regime's efforts to demonstrate international Communist solidarity jeopardized independence did not help matters. Not only was the whole trend unpopular in itself, but the reassertion of Party bureaucratism accentuated individual economic difficulties. Everyone knew production was expanding, but few seemed to be benefiting correspondingly.

Even before the strikes in Slovenia and elsewhere shocked the top leadership into a reconsideration of the situation generally, many in high places in Belgrade were worried. Whether the Executive Committee's denunciation of abuses by lower Party officials would alone have brought about the new relaxation that was noticeable by the summer of 1958 is open to question. More than in other Communist countries, public opinion *is* a factor in Yugoslavia; but its impact is limited. In this case, the Party's apparent realization that things were going too far was followed by the failure of Tito's Soviet policy and a renewal of conflict with the USSR. If the earlier rapprochement had emboldened Party diehards, their public chastisement plus the new turn of international events had the opposite effect. Again, practical needs, combined with ideological interest, produced a change of climate.

The new tone was indicated, among other things, by a noticeable reticence on the part of the League of Communists and its members. Whereas in 1958 one still heard charges of Party favoritism in enterprises, in 1959 *Borba* complained rather plaintively that Communists were being discriminated against in jobs and salaries and that some enterprises refused to hire Party members as managers. *Borba* appealed to workers' councils to be "fair" and not to abuse their authority.[1]

Illustrative also was the official reaction to large-scale student riots in Zagreb and Skoplje in the spring of 1959, described by Tito as "very unpleasant demonstrations." Although disorderly conduct arrests were made at the time and Tito blamed both occurrences on unnamed "class enemies from abroad," the authorities convinced themselves that the riots were not

[1] September 19, 1959.

basically anti-regime manifestations, and apparently no political reprisals were taken.[1]

In the fall of 1959, the criminal code was liberalized, eliminating the death penalty for economic crimes and making it more difficult for the regime to act against opponents who did not commit specific acts of violence. And before the end of the year, Vladimir Dedijer received his passport and, accompanied by his family, headed for the United States to give a series of lectures. In February 1960, the elderly socialists, whose "plot" was held to be such a danger to the regime two years before, were quietly released from prison. In the economic sphere, new laws granted renewed autonomy to enterprises. And finally, in January 1961 Milovan Djilas was freed and placed on probation for the remaining five years of his sentence.[2]

If the trend away from totalitarianism was not actually being resumed, the reversal of the trend clearly had been halted.

Some Question Marks

At least it seemed that way. But there were some question marks. In November 1959 Tito had ominously denounced "uncontrolled talk and criticism," particularly by responsible Party officials. Communists, he told a Central Committee Plenum — the first since March 1958 — had to keep their disagreements within the Party and not "talk about it in the streets." A "liberal attitude" on such a question, the Yugoslav leader declared, would inflict "enormous harm on the community," and he threatened Party sanctions, and even legal action, against those who failed to realize "what can be said and what cannot be known." Tito also demanded a more circumspect attitude on the part of officials in dealing with foreigners, by which, apparently, he meant Westerners. Particularly he referred to "betrayal of various economic secrets."[3]

This blast of Tito's was clearly aimed at Party discipline and was concerned primarily with the very real problem of the growing conflict among the republics on economic matters.[4] It had not produced, a year later, any shift toward more totalitarian practices generally, nor were there indications that it would. Considered abstractly, of course, all Communists could be under rigid Party discipline without interfering legally with freedom of expression. But what would this amount to in practice? Indeed, it might be argued that

[1] See *Los Angeles Times*, May 22, 1959, p. 16, and *New York Times*, August 19, 1959, p. 7.

[2] Djilas promptly announced to reporters that "in essence" his views had not changed, although he added that he now had "hopes" that the trend in Yugoslavia was toward more democracy. *New York Times*, January 21, 1961, p. 2.

[3] *New York Times*, November 21, 1959, p. 3.

[4] See Chapter 23.

free expression *within* the Party, in a country like Yugoslavia, is more meaningful than free expression outside the Party. It is difficult to see how, under present conditions, any important developments can occur unless they are initiated by the League of Communists. While significant political innovations are sometimes successfully advocated by persons outside the Party, this is rare. And opposition by non-Communists to major regime policies tends either to be discouraged one way or another or to be tolerated because it is ineffective. Furthermore, in the past tightening up in general has been presaged by a tightening up of Party discipline. Djilas equated insistence on "ideological unity" in the Party with totalitarianism. The future of Titoism may show whether he was right or wrong.

PART V

THE IMPACT
OF TITOISM

FOREIGN POLICY—

EAST? WEST? OR BOTH?

TITO has described Yugoslavia's foreign policy as one of "active coexistence." To many both in the West and in the East who have watched Belgrade defy the laws of political gravity by balancing between them, the coexistence has sometimes seemed so active as to be precarious. Yet the balance has been maintained. In the gyrations of Yugoslavia's foreign policy since the Cominform dispute, the continued independence of the country stands out as the most persistent factor.

To the Yugoslavs, "active coexistence" — or "active peaceful coexistence," a term they also often use — means that while they will become a member of no bloc they will work positively in all ways possible, particularly in collaboration with other "neutrals," to further peace and Yugoslavia's national interest. The difficulties they have encountered — and sometimes erected — trying to practice this policy dramatically illustrate Yugoslavia's unique position as an independent socialist country.

The first decade of Yugoslav post-Cominform foreign policy falls into four periods. The first, 1948–1950, was the period when Yugoslavia was outside the Soviet bloc but, because of mutual suspicions, little cooperation with the West had yet developed. The second period, 1950–1955, was one of such close cooperation, politically and militarily, with the West that many Westerners mistakenly felt that Yugoslavia was about to become one of them; Yugoslavia was neutral, but neutral against the Soviet Union and for the West. The third period, 1955–1958, was marked by a rapprochement with the Soviet Union, begun on Moscow's initiative and characterized by constant ideological differences; Yugoslav neutrality was more inclined toward the Soviet Union, although not necessarily against the West. The fourth period began when

417

the USSR resumed its ideological offensive against Yugoslavia in the spring of 1958; Belgrade sought to be more impartial. Developments in international politics in 1960 and after, however, tended to bring Yugoslavia closer to Soviet than to Western positions on many important issues.

Cooperation with the West: U. S. Aid

Probably more important than any other single factor in reorienting Yugoslavia's foreign policy toward cooperation with the West in 1950 was the prompt and generous — if at first cautious — American response to Tito's request for economic aid in 1950. This is true not in the sense that Yugoslavia was thus "bought" by American dollars — as Moscow immediately charged — but in the sense that U. S. policy facilitated Yugoslav theoretical reorientation by helping to take the curse off capitalist nations.

The reluctance with which both Yugoslavia and the West more or less backed into rapprochement has been recounted earlier. Each side was undertaking it solely in its own interests and with continuing suspicions of the other. Once the collaboration began, however, it developed rapidly. Undoubtedly the fact that aid was given with no strings attached had a tremendous impact on the Yugoslavs, while the West, for its part, became more convinced of Tito's independence and was impressed by the nature of the reforms that were making over the Yugoslav system. Meanwhile, the increasing ferocity of Soviet hostility toward Belgrade acted as an important catalyst. From reluctant donors and reluctant recipients, both sides, by 1951, became willing participants in the aid bargain.

Even more important in terms of the new Western orientation of Yugoslav foreign policy was a military aid agreement with the United States and the arrival in Belgrade, in November 1951, of a U. S. military mission. In 1952 both economic and military aid were regularized. Yugoslav forces, President Truman told Congress, now constituted "a significant obstacle to aggression in Southeastern Europe," and military assistance to Tito was required in "the security interests of the United States and also of the free world."[1] The change of administration in the United States produced little change in over-all foreign policy and none at all in Washington's policy toward Belgrade.[2] The Yugoslavs, meanwhile, gave at least qualified verbal support to the American position in Korea.[3]

---

[1] *Department of State Bulletin*, Vol. XXV, No. 647, p. 826.

[2] Republican campaign talk about "liberation" proved to be only campaign talk. The ambivalent position of Yugoslavia was something of an embarrassment for American anti-Communist propaganda, particularly in the case of the theoretically unofficial "Radio Free Europe." The Voice of America simply ceased to criticize Yugoslavia.

[3] See, for example, discussions in *Borba*, September 15, 1950, and *Republika*, September 28, 1950.

The Balkan Treaty

The close military relationship between Yugoslavia and the United States which began in 1951 was, of course, short of an alliance. This was the period in which U. S. foreign policy was characterized by "pactomania." NATO, which blanketed Western Europe and anomalously included the two non-Atlantic states of Turkey and Greece, was soon to be extended in the Baghdad Pact and SEATO. Under the circumstances, it was perhaps not unnatural that Western policy makers, and especially the Americans, wanted to bind Yugoslavia formally into this arrangement. On their own initiative, the Yugoslavs had been quietly repairing their relations with their two Balkan NATO neighbors, Greece and Turkey. Viewing this development, the Western military pact makers hit on the idea of a Balkan Pact which would include Yugoslavia and create for it, in Admiral Carney's words, "an association with NATO." Tito had given some basis for Western hopes that he might affiliate in some way with NATO. Although in 1950 NATO was still regarded in Belgrade as a "provocative force,"[1] when the American military mission arrived in Belgrade in the fall of 1951, Tito spoke of the Atlantic Pact as "the logical consequence of Soviet policy." Where there was no conflict with Yugoslav principles, he pledged that he would collaborate with the NATO countries "on all questions of an international character."[2] Later Yugoslavia welcomed the prospect of West Germany as a NATO member. But, when it came to an actual treaty, Tito shied off. "We do not wish to create any pacts," he added, "not even a regional pact with Greece and Turkey."

Nevertheless, the course of events — fear of Soviet and satellite hostility, evidences of Western friendship and dependence on American aid — brought more and more Yugoslav collaboration with the West. One result was a Treaty of Friendship and Cooperation with Greece and Turkey, signed at Ankara on February 28, 1953.

Although the treaty, in addition to providing for cooperation in economic, technical and cultural fields, called for informal consultation among the three general staffs, it was still not the sort of Balkan Pact the West would have liked. In fact, one article specifically excluded any relationship with NATO. The West now pushed for a military alliance.[3]

One section of the Treaty looked toward addition to the signatories of "any other state whose cooperation all parties . . . shall consider useful." While this was primarily propaganda aimed at Bulgaria and Albania, the

[1] *Politika*, February 2, 1950.

[2] *Borba*, November 1, 1951.

[3] The 1953 Treaty of Friendship and Cooperation is sometimes mistakenly referred to as *the* Balkan Pact. It was *a* Balkan pact; the instrument formally given that name was not created until August 1954.

ambitious NATO planners were also thinking of the possibility that Italy might join the treaty. This would further cement Yugoslavia to NATO and, in addition, plug the so-called Ljubljana Gap, so often in the past a military highway connecting East and West.

The Trieste Issue

To the Yugoslavs, however, Greece and Turkey were one thing, Italy something else. There was still much bad feeling in Yugoslavia about Italy resulting from the war. More important was the unresolved issue of Trieste, still a "Free Territory" divided into Zone A under Anglo-American occupation and Zone B under Yugoslav occupation. In the spring of 1948, the unsuspecting American and British foreign offices had declared in favor of returning both zones to Italy. In 1952, despite the new alignment of Yugoslavia, the United States and Great Britain ignored a Yugoslav offer for possible compromise and proceeded to turn over civil administration of Zone A to the Italians without consulting Belgrade. Tito sharply protested this agreement as anti-Yugoslav in character and declared he would not consider Yugoslavia bound by it. His reaction was strong, but he centered his fire on the Italians — and on the Russians, whom he accused, somewhat illogically, of stirring up trouble — and avoided any break with the West.

If this move reflected ineptitude on the part of the West, what followed was a fiasco.[1] In October 1953 Britain and the United States, again without consulting Yugoslavia, announced they were withdrawing their troops from the city of Trieste and turning Zone A over to Italy altogether. Again nothing was said about Zone B, but the announcement expressed the hope that the move would "provide the basis for friendly and fruitful cooperation between Italy and Yugoslavia."[2] Promptly the Italians declared that they had not renounced their claim to Zone B.

Although Tito had previously indicated informally that he might consider a compromise which would give Zone A to Italy and Zone B to Yugoslavia, the fact that the West had acted without consulting him brought a violent and infuriated reaction. He now denounced the Americans and British in no uncertain terms. He requested that the Trieste issue be taken up by the UN Security Council and threatened to send troops into Zone A if the Italians should occupy it. Although Tito emphasized he would not fight the Americans

---

[1] The original agreement was announced just before important Italian elections. Both it and what came afterwards seem to have been inspired by advice from the U. S. Embassy in Rome that it was necessary to influence Italian public opinion. Whereas the Rome embassy might be excused for neglecting to consider Yugoslav reactions, which were not its primary responsibility, no such excuse can be made for the State Department.

[2] *Department of State Bulletin*, Vol. XXXIX, No. 747, p. 529.

or British, it seemed clear that he meant business as far as the Italians were concerned. Yugoslav troops in Zone B rushed to the frontier, and reinforcements were dispatched from Slovenia. In Belgrade there were obviously inspired anti-American and anti-British demonstrations. The U. S. Information Office was smashed and its director, William King, beaten up. The West backed down, the more hastily as the Soviet Union now indicated support for appointing a governor for the Free Territory rather than dividing it.[1] American and British troops remained in occupation of Zone A and called for direct negotiations between Italy and Yugoslavia.

It is not difficult to understand the Yugoslav reaction. The Yugoslavs had suffered severely at the hands of the Italians, and in the war they had been aligned with the West against them. Yugoslav troops had arrived first in the Trieste area, and there was substance to Yugoslav claims, particularly to Zone B. Furthermore, the Yugoslavs thought of themselves — not wholly without reason — as making a contribution to Western defense at least as important as the Italians. Regardless of the counter-arguments that might be made to these views, that the intensity of Yugoslav feelings was apparently not realized in Washington is inexplicable. Such cavalier treatment at the hands of the West rekindled Yugoslav suspicions and increased doubts that Belgrade would get fair treatment in a Western coalition.

Actually, despite the violence of the Yugoslav reaction, the Trieste issue did not provoke any profound anti-American feelings. Tito had, however, demonstrated that when he said Yugoslavia's foreign policy was independent, he meant independent. It is not certain that the lesson took in Washington, even then. For American policy still urged a military pact with Greece and Turkey and now — almost as though nothing had happened involving Italy — pressed to have the Italians taken in as the fourth member. And a Balkan Pact was seen as presaging Yugoslav affiliation with NATO.

Normalization

It was at this juncture that a new factor entered the picture — overtures from Moscow to Belgrade. In the summer of 1953, Moscow suddenly proposed that the two countries exchange ambassadors. Yugoslavia agreed, with the tart official comment that this proved the failure of Soviet anti-Yugoslav policies. At the same time, Soviet tactics in the Danube Commission, which had been to ostracize and discriminate against Yugoslavia, shifted. At the suggestion of Bucharest, Budapest and Sofia, commissions were established to deal with border matters. Early 1954 saw a proliferation of economic agreements with the Soviet satellites, and a Kremlin proposal for a

---

[1] Tito denounced this Soviet stand as "hypocritical."

Soviet-Yugoslav trade agreement. Belgrade termed the trend "normalization" of relations with the Soviet bloc and initially approached it with more suspicion than hope.

It was against this background that in the spring of 1954 Tito expressed his willingness to enter into a military pact with Greece and Turkey, two NATO states with a strong anti-Soviet orientation. Negotiations promptly got under way. Although Belgrade did not at first flatly say "no" to Italian membership, it was made clear that any consideration of this depended on a satisfactory settlement of the Trieste questions, on which negotiations were proceeding simultaneously. The Balkan Pact was signed amid diplomatic pomp and circumstance at Bled on August 9, 1954. Under its terms, an act of aggression against one was an act of aggression against all. A permanent secretariat for collaboration was established, and there were to be continuing military staff discussions and regular meetings of the three foreign ministers.

The West hailed the Balkan Pact, even without Italy, as a great victory. A British diplomat at Bled for the signing remarked: "We have extended NATO right up to the Kremlin walls." One of the authors heard a Western journalist predict to Foreign Secretary Popović that Yugoslavia would be a member of NATO within six months. He also heard Popović's reply: "You're either mad or drunk." Actually the journalist was neither mad nor drunk. He was simply reflecting the overly rosy glow with which some western diplomats naïvely saw Yugoslavia. This Western misconception of Yugoslavia's position worried Tito. There were limits beyond which he would not go in cooperation, and false hopes that he might go further could only cause trouble. The course of the Trieste negotiations, now about to result in an agreement dividing the two zones, had not made the Yugoslavs happy, nor had the continued Western urging to take Italy into the Balkan Pact. Progress in talks with the Russians, then going on, suggested the possibility of new vistas.

"Do not make of us what we are not," Tito warned the West on September 19, 1954, "We are Communists."

As Communists, but isolated from the rest of the Communist community, the Yugoslavs were in an ambivalent position. They were never happy about being forced by fate to collaborate with capitalism. The scorn of the rest of the Communist world was hard to take. As suspicious as they were of the Soviet Union, they had never altogether lost their suspicions of the anti-Communist West.

Now, possibly spurred on by the Balkan Pact, Soviet efforts at reconciliation stepped up. The economic blockade was lifted. Not only was the propaganda campaign against Yugoslavia halted, but Soviet publications began to speak favorably of Yugoslavia. Soviet trade negotiators went out of their way to impress the Yugoslavs with their conciliatory attitude. A trade agreement was concluded in the early fall. Furthermore, although the Yugoslav economy was still beset by problems, it was no longer as dependent on outside aid as in the dark days of 1950–1953. Diplomatically, the Balkan Pact strengthened Yugoslavia's hand in dealing with both East and West. In the light of these circumstances, Tito, if he ever had any intention of affiliating with NATO — as is doubtful — now definitely abandoned it. "The Atlantic Pact," he declared on September 20, "is increasingly becoming painted with a political, that is, an ideological color — its fight against Communism. They say it is just against Soviet Communism, but it is more than that. . . . We are painted with a socialist complexion, and there is no room for us in a bloc which has an anti-socialist tendency."

Belgrade's Reactions

The Soviet overtures toward normalization excited several different kinds of emotion in Belgrade. Having tended to blame much of their trouble with the USSR on Stalin, the Yugoslavs were not completely unprepared for a new approach by his successors. Moreover, in the hearts of many Yugoslav Communist leaders there had never died the hope of future solidarity with the Soviet Union and the rest of the Communist world. "This beginning of normalization [with the USSR] fills us with hope that the process will continue to develop," Tito declared in October 1954. The first hope, however, was more that normalization might free Yugoslavia from untoward dependence on the West than that it would result in Communist solidarity. The desire for independence was genuine. Thus, even while he hailed normalization, Tito also flaunted the Balkan Pact. He had regarded it, he said, "from the beginning as an absolute, vital necessity for the Balkan countries." Although he now deprecated the military importance of it, he warned against underestimating the Pact's "significance for the prevention of aggression." While he would not join NATO, he wanted to make it clear that he was "cooperating to some extent . . . on questions pertaining to the preservation of our country and that of other countries."

Tito did not, at first, discount the possibility that normalization concealed a trap. He was certain, however, that he could not be fooled and waved aside Western fears on this score. "If anybody is called upon to judge about this," he declared, "then it is we, with our experience, who . . . know how to distinguish between a maneuver and a positive step."

Tito soon became convinced that the new Soviet policy was genuine. The days when the USSR could be considered a "highly menacing, aggressive power," Tito announced, "are now over." The Yugoslavs would meet the Russians half way, he said, adding: "We are not a people who brood. . . . We have said, let bygones be bygones." On the other hand he was still cautious: Yugoslav relations with the Soviet bloc, would "never again be 100 per cent of what they once were."

The West expressed unhappiness, anxiety and annoyance at this new turn of affairs but generally reserved formal judgment. For one thing, Tito took pains to reassure the West step by step of the way. At the time of the Soviet-Yugoslav trade talks, on his own initiative he promised that no export of strategic materials to Russia would be involved. Over and over again he emphasized that normalization of relations with the Soviet bloc did not mean he was giving up his friendship with the West.

Tito was worried about both Western and Soviet misunderstanding of the snowballing normalization process. This process, he warned Moscow, "could not be by words alone. . . . We cannot merely embrace one another and say we love each other as though everything is now over." The Soviet bloc would have to prove its new intentions by "deeds as well." Tito wanted

to make it clear to the other side, namely the Soviet Union and the Eastern countries, that we cannot improve our relationships with them at the expense and to the detriment of our relations with the Western countries, that they must realize once and for all that we are conducting our own policy, that we cannot quarrel or break off relations with the Western countries . . . for the sole purpose of improving our relations with the East. We cannot now retract all that we have said and done so far. Western countries like the United States, Great Britain and France have not shown themselves to be our enemies; they have proved to be friends in need. Therefore we consider them as such.[1]

The Khrushchev-Bulganin Visit

In May 1955 it was announced that Nikita Khrushchev, first secretary of the Soviet Communist Party, and Nikolai Bulganin, chairman of the Council of Ministers, would visit Belgrade later that month. Taking cognizance of Western fears, which now broke out anew, Tito pledged that the talks with the Soviet leaders would be open "before the whole world." There was no intention, he said, of "maneuvering behind the scenes at the expense of someone else," and Western observers who imagined that "we will no longer be what we are will be mistaken." There should be no misunderstanding, Tito added, that Yugoslavia did not remain "grateful to the Western allies, particularly America, which extended and continues to extend us aid."[2] Leo Mates, Yugoslav ambassador to the United States, hurried to the State

[1] *Politika*, November 22, 1954.
[2] *Politika*, May 16, 1955.

Department to echo Tito's words and allay fears that the impending visit presaged a change in Belgrade's foreign policy.

As important as Tito considered normalization, he was not willing to mince words with the Russians about it, especially on the question of the steadfastness of his foreign policy. When Foreign Minister Molotov implied that the rapprochement reflected changes in Yugoslav as well as Soviet policy, Tito snapped back that this was "not in keeping with the facts" and half threatened to halt the normalization process where it was.

There was no doubt about the ardor of the Soviet wooing, however. Blandly turning the other cheek, *Pravda* (May 21, 1955) replied to Tito that certain differences between the two countries did exist but that there were more areas of agreement than disagreement and there existed "a solid basis for a broad and manifold cooperation between the Soviet and Yugoslav peoples." When Khrushchev and Bulganin came to Belgrade six days later, the offending Molotov was left behind.

The arrival of Khrushchev and Bulganin in Yugoslavia on May 27, 1955, was one of the most dramatic events of the postwar period. Humbly confessing error — although they blamed the 1948 rift with Yugoslavia on Beria — the two Soviet leaders, who themselves had earlier engaged in heaping abuse on Tito, asked forgiveness and a resumption of the traditional friendly ties at both state and Party levels.[1]

Tito showed no signs of being taken in.[2] He stood at attention, stiff and unsmiling, while Khrushchev radiated his well-known rumpled charm in a prepared address. When Khrushchev finished and turned expectantly to Tito, clearly anticipating public words of welcome, Tito merely motioned the two visitors into his waiting Rolls Royce. Throughout his stay in Yugoslavia, Khrushchev ebulliently called Tito *tovarishch* (comrade). Tito gravely responded each time with *gospodin* (mister). He insisted on keeping the ensuing discussions to the level of governments, excluding Party relationships.

Nevertheless, the Khrushchev-Bulganin visit signalized a shift in Soviet policy of enormous importance. This was acceptance — at least on the surface — of the Yugoslav position that each socialist nation had a right to its own "independent path to socialism." While the Belgrade Agreement, which resulted from the talks, referred to this idea only with regard to Yugo-

---

[1] Owing, possibly, to some reporter with an uncertain classical education, the journalists called the Khrushchev-Bulganin visit a "journey to Canossa." They referred to the humbling pilgrimage made by Henry IV in 1077 to ask forgiveness of Pope Gregory VII. There were certain elements in common between the two journeys, but the emphasis was reversed. Henry asked forgiveness after having been excommunicated. The Yugoslav case would have been analogous only if Tito had journeyed to Moscow to ask forgiveness.

[2] The view that the whole affair was an elaborate façade to conceal an agreement previously made and going beyond what appeared on the surface is advanced by Ernst Halperin, *The Triumphant Heretic*, Heinemann, London, 1958.

slavia, a *Pravda* editorial published during the visit, and, strangely enough, generally overlooked at the time in the West, expressed approval of the concept generally.[1] The Agreement itself committed both parties to non-interference in the affairs of other countries and "peaceful coexistence." It condemned aggression and all efforts at political and economic domination.[2]

These were, of course, the Yugoslav positions. Understandably, Tito now saw the Soviet leaders as "men who wish to follow a new path . . . who want peace no less than the Americans." The Russians, Tito said,

convinced themselves that Yugoslavia was independent and that she wanted to remain independent, both of West and East, that she had her own road of development, that she could not permit any interference in her internal affairs, etc. They agreed with this position, and we were consequently able to find a common language. It then became easier to take up the question of our future cooperation, economic and otherwise.[3]

Troubles with the West

The accord not only marked the end of the Soviet-Yugoslav quarrel; it signalized a new orientation in Yugoslav foreign policy as well. Also, opposition to the USSR began to be replaced by accommodation in limited areas. The Belgrade Agreement itself recorded Yugoslav support for the Soviet position on the prohibition of atomic weapons, the seating of Communist China in the United Nations[4] and the "legitimate rights" of Peking to Formosa. It was true, as the Yugoslavs pointed out, that there were valid arguments for holding these positions, irrespective of the Soviet views, but before the Belgrade Agreement the Yugoslavs did not espouse them publicly.

The anticipated cooperation came quickly, and in a form that boded no good for Yugoslavia's close cooperation with the West. The USSR canceled a pre-1948 Yugoslav debt of $90 million and in return Belgrade waived claims for damages resulting from the economic blockade. To the criticisms that were at once voiced in the West, Tito responded sharply. A dispute broke out in Belgrade between the American military mission and Yugoslav military authorities over the extent of the U. S. right of continued inspection of military aid. Reports followed of Soviet-Yugoslav negotiations on the construction of a MIG jet plant in Yugoslavia. The United States ambassador in Belgrade responded with a warning that this might adversely affect the course of American aid to Yugoslavia. In late July 1955, Tito complained of excessive interest rates on Western loans and assailed West Germany for failure to fulfill Yugoslav reparations claims. In August Anastas Mikoyan,

[1] *Pravda*, June 3, 1955.
[2] For text of the Belgrade Agreement, see *Borba* and *New York Times*, June 3, 1955, p. 3.
[3] *Borba*, July 28, 1955.
[4] Yugoslavia had voted for this in the United Nations during 1954.

the Soviet foreign trade chief, came to Yugoslavia for his "vacation." In September a new Soviet-Yugoslav trade agreement was announced.

Although the State Department commented at the time of the Belgrade Agreement that it was "gratified at the apparent acceptance by the USSR of Yugoslavia's independence," Washington was seriously concerned about it. Admiral Radford, chairman of the Joint Chiefs of Staff, talked about military implications, and Congressional criticism was rife, with charges that Tito was "lining up against us and the United Nations."[1] The United States had earlier issued to Tito, who had journeyed to London in 1953, an invitation to come to Washington on a state visit. The invitation was criticized from all sides. As developments following the Belgrade Agreement seemed to confirm American fears about Yugoslav policy, the State Department nervously withdrew the invitation, to the obvious annoyance of Belgrade and Tito personally. American-Yugoslav relations took a turn for the worse. Ambassador Riddleberger was summoned from Belgrade to report.

While there was no doubt that the antennae of Yugoslav foreign policy were feeling in other directions, those who concluded, after the dramatic summer of 1955, that there had been a complete about-face were in error. The error had its roots in misconceptions about Yugoslav foreign policy. Two misconceptions were widespread. One was that the break with Moscow in 1948 did not produce any real change in the nature of Yugoslav Communism and that Tito was simply waiting for a chance to doublecross the West. The other was that the change was so great that the Yugoslav leaders had departed from the basic tenets of Marxism-Leninism and, if they would not become Western-type democrats, at least would see their future as a part of the anti-Communist West. Those who suffered such misconceptions were unable to believe that independence was really the keystone of Yugoslav policy, albeit an independence of which the West might not approve. In the summer of 1955, there was no doubt that Tito hoped to have the best of both worlds. If to many this meant playing both ends against the middle, still it did not mean, as some Western critics of Yugoslavia thought, that Tito was "returning to the Cominform."

The United States was unusually fortunate in its ambassadors to Yugoslavia in this period and earlier. George V. Allen was in large part responsible for helping the State Department understand the reorientation in Yugoslavia after the Cominform break. And his successor, James W. Riddleberger, not only saw correctly but was able to persuade Secretary Dulles that Belgrade's rapprochement with the USSR did not necessarily mean hostility to the United States. At a time when the Secretary felt strongly that "neutralism"

[1] *New York Times*, June 5, 1955, p. 8.

was immoral and Washington generally viewed those not actively with us as against us, this took not only courage but sagacity as well.

Tito himself helped ease U. S. fears, and at the same time demonstrated to Moscow that he meant what he said about independence. When Moscow turned down President Eisenhower's 1955 summit conference proposal for interchange of military information, Tito praised Eisenhower for his efforts. Then, again assuring the United States that neither a return to the pre-1948 status nor a lessening of Western ties was involved in the new line, he invited Secretary Dulles to Brioni.

Neither Tito nor Dulles convinced each other of very much, apparently. But the Secretary of State, in a speech broadcast by Radio Belgrade, told the Yugoslavs: "More than once your people have made it plain that they will not be anyone's satellite. We applaud this stand."[1] Belgrade saw the talks as "a step toward closer friendship between the two countries," an American recognition of Yugoslavia's "independent and non-bloc position" and "another proof of the realism of American foreign policy."[2]

"Active Coexistence": Yugoslavia as a "Bridge"

As a result of the rapprochement with Moscow, the Yugoslavs saw themselves in a new and more important role in world affairs. Having become convinced that the Soviet Union presented no threat of aggression and still believing in the peaceful intentions of the West, they now envisaged possibilities for "peaceful coexistence" which before had been obscured. But this coexistence was something that would have to be worked out actively. Thus the Yugoslav foreign policy came to be called "active coexistence." Having ties with both sides in the cold war, the Yugoslavs considered themselves uniquely fitted to promote "active coexistence." Tito now termed Yugoslavia "the bridge between East and West."[3]

To some extent, the Yugoslavs had attempted to play this role before. In this connection, and also because they were really in neither the Soviet nor the Western bloc and felt the need of friends, they had assiduously cultivated uncommitted nations like India, Burma, Indonesia and Egypt. At the end of 1954, Tito went on an Asian tour in which he visited Nehru and other "neutralist" leaders. Now, with "active coexistence" the core of Yugoslav policy, relations with countries not taking sides in the cold war became a major concern. There were trade agreements. Nehru and U Nu of Burma paid state visits to Belgrade in the summer of 1955. A stream of cultural exchanges began.

---

[1] *Borba*, November 5, 1955.

[2] J. Arnejc, "After the Brioni Talks," *Review of International Affairs*, November 16, 1955, pp. 9–10.

[3] *Borba*, August 3, 1955.

This new emphasis also involved increased criticism of military pacts. In fact, the main ingredients of "active coexistence" appeared to be collaboration with uncommitted nations and an outspoken "anti-pactomania."

The Yugoslavs had, of course, previously condemned the Soviet Union's Warsaw Pact in strong terms. Now, although the earlier view was toned down, Belgrade still saw the Warsaw Pact as the "product of bloc mentality" and as contributing to international tension. Freed of much of their former reliance on the West, the Yugoslavs indulged in more outspoken criticism of the Atlantic Pact. NATO was, in fact, equated with the Warsaw Pact, the first brought on by aggressive Soviet policies, the second brought on by the first,

All military pacts were considered bad, but, possibly reflecting relations with India and Egypt particularly, especially strong criticism was aimed at the new Baghdad Pact, to which Yugoslavia's fellow member in the Balkan Pact, Turkey, became a signatory. It was at this time that the Balkan Pact — a year before hailed as "an absolute, vital necessity" — began to be downgraded in Belgrade's thinking. The military aspects of it were allowed to die. For a while thereafter, the Yugoslavs justified the Balkan Pact on the grounds that it emphasized "political, economic, and cultural" cooperation. Soon, however — further encumbered by the Greco-Turkish conflict over Cyprus — even the nonmilitary part of the Balkan Pact remained only on paper.[1]

Considering the American devotion to military pacts, the constant Yugoslav carping placed an added burden on U. S.-Yugoslav relations. It was also. of course, a clear manifestation of Yugoslav independence, because Moscow did not like it either, and — as events were to show — criticism of the Warsaw Pact was to be one of the most significant factors in future Soviet-Yugoslav relations. The Yugoslavs insisted, however, that their stand against pacts was in the interest of peace and should not mar their friendship with the pact nations of either bloc. The Yugoslav position, they insisted, was not "neutralism," which implied having no policy and "would only aid an aggressor." While "active coexistence" emphasized collaboration of independent non-bloc nations, it might also involve cooperation with members of one bloc or the other, depending on the specific situation. It meant "playing politics for peace."[2]

---

[1] However, bilateral relations with Greece remained friendly, and certain economic and cultural — and even some military — cooperation continued.

[2] For the Yugoslav attitude on military pacts, see L. Erven, "The Warsaw Treaty," *Review of International Affairs*, June 1, 1955, pp. 1–10; various articles in *Yugoslav Review*, January 1956; Aleš Bebler, "Jugoslavija i Evropa" ("Yugoslavia and Europe"), *Medjunarodna Politika*, September 16, 1956, pp. 5–6; "Joint Declaration: Tito-Nehru," *Review of International Affairs*, January 1, 1955, p. 7; and statements of Tito in *Politika*, May 16, 1955, and *Review of International Affairs*, March 15, 1955, pp. 3–4.

On the other hand, Tito constantly emphasized that collaboration with uncommitted states was to be informal and did not mean a "third force." This, he said, would be "nonsense . . . when neither we nor they have the necessary armaments." Rather there was to be a "moral force consisting of all those who love peace and freedom."[1]

Soviet Politics at Home and Abroad

Moscow's new policy toward Yugoslavia grew out of major changes — both tactical and fundamental — that were occurring in the Soviet Union. Certain totalitarian features were relaxed. In the inner world of the satellites, there was evidence that the Kremlin sought to persuade rather than order. In the outer world, Soviet foreign policy was characterized more by smiles and friendly words than by the earlier harsh intransigence. One objective, as set forth by Stalin before his death, was to win support for breaking up the anti-Soviet military pacts ringing the USSR and to influence the uncommitted nations. In this gambit, Stalin's attitude toward Belgrade was clearly an impediment.

In making up to Yugoslavia, Khrushchev had begun to overcome the adverse effects of the earlier rigid hostility toward Tito's form of Communism. But it was clear he had to go still further. Tito was not unfriendly, but Yugoslavia still remained outside the bloc and persisted in its independent foreign policy. The heritage of Stalinism, with its reputation for ruthlessness and arbitrariness, also stood in the way of the cooperation Moscow needed, not only from Yugoslavs but also from the socialist parties of Europe and Asia. There was, however, far from unanimity in the Kremlin about what should be done.

At the Twentieth Congress of the Communist Party of the Soviet Union, in February 1956, the spectre of Stalinism was exorcised when Khrushchev delivered a violent attack on the late Soviet dictator.[2] Many of his charges were precisely those heard earlier in Belgrade. The quarrel with Yugoslavia was now blamed altogether onto Stalin, where the Yugoslavs themselves had been placing it more and more of late. In addition, the Congress put its stamp of approval explicitly on the cornerstones of Titoism: independence, no interference and "independent paths to socialism."

The effect of the Twentieth Congress was to dispel any doubts lingering in official Yugoslav minds that the changes in Soviet attitude were sincere

[1] *Politika*, May 16, 1955. See also Tito-Nehru declaration in *Review of International Affairs*, January 1, 1955, p. 7. A more detailed analysis of Yugoslav relations with Asia and Africa is given in Chapter 21.

[2] It may be that Khrushchev did not at first intend to go as far as he did with his explicit anti-Stalinism and that he was spurred on as a result of maneuvering for position among his colleagues on the Presidium.

and profound. It is quite likely, in fact, that Tito was advised in advance of what was coming, for he sent his "comradely greetings" to the gathering and was represented by an official observer. Tito himself was silent, but Moše Pijade surely reflected his views when he declared: "Such a decisive and daring breach with Stalinism can be taken as firm proof of the deep and significant changes in the Soviet Union. We Yugoslavs have many reasons to be satisfied."[1]

Two months after the Twentieth Party Congress, as if to back words with deeds, Moscow announced the dissolution of the Cominform and called on other Communist parties to cooperate "at their own discretion and taking into account specific conditions of their work."[2] The Yugoslav victory, it seemed, was complete. Belgrade thus saw no reason why "normalization" could not be replaced with real intimacy. When, two months later, Milovan Djilas warned that the new Soviet policies were only tactics and that the Soviet system remained "aggressive in content," the Yugoslav press accused him of "base slanders and dirty insinuations" and said his articles — distributed abroad by the International News Service — were "wicked, malicious and reactionary."[3]

The trend from normalization to rapprochement to collaboration now developed an even more rapid tempo. The climax was reached June 2 when Tito arrived in Moscow on a state visit. The day before, Vyacheslav Molotov, who along with Stalin had read Yugoslavia out of the Cominform and with whom Tito had crossed swords the preceding year, was relieved of his post as foreign minister. The Kremlin appeared ready to go to any lengths to appease Tito.

Tito's Triumphal Visit to Moscow

All stops were pulled out in Moscow's welcome to the erstwhile heretic, who proceeded to travel about the Soviet Union like a conquering hero. It was, of course, a great moment for the one-time Comintern agent, guerrilla fighter, harried outcast and now head of a small country. In 1948 Tito was frightened, confused, defiantly at bay. Few if any had then anticipated that the time would come when Russian multitudes would chant "Ti-to, Ti-to" — just like home only louder. Such a reception would have turned the head of a more modest man than Josip Broz Tito.[4]

---

[1] *Borba*, March 28, 1956.

[2] *Pravda*, April 18, 1956.

[3] *Borba*, June 13, and *Politika*, June 14, 1956. Djilas' articles appeared in the United States in the Hearst newspapers, including the *San Francisco Examiner* on June 10, 11, 12 and 13, 1956.

[4] In Red Square, Tito reverently laid a wreath on Lenin's tomb; the remains of Stalin, a few feet away, he did not dignify with as much as a glance.

It was not surprising that Tito responded with unrestrained enthusiasm. Definite Party ties were now established. The Russians were *gospodin* no longer; now they were "dear comrades." Hailing "the Leninist policy of the government and . . . Communist Party of the Soviet Union," Tito said Yugoslavia and the USSR were together "marching shoulder to shoulder along the path of Marx, Engels and Lenin."[1] And he told Khrushchev: "We have easily found a common language and mutual understanding. We are part of the same family — the family of socialism. Our ways differ from your ways, but that does not mean that our aim is not the same. There are no longer any serious and difficult problems between us. Never again will anything come between us."[2]

As extreme as these statements were, Tito did not go all the way. He and other Yugoslav spokesmen were careful, even as they enjoyed the Kremlin's lavish hospitality, to stress their country's continuing independence. The communiqué issued at the end of his visit emphasized that cooperation between the two countries would be voluntary.[3] When Western correspondents erroneously quoted Tito as having said Yugoslavia was "part of the Soviet family," Yugoslav officials hastened into print with a correction. When Marshal Zhukov publicly hailed Yugoslavia as a military ally, Foreign Minister Popović quickly and just as publicly asserted that no military alliance was contemplated.[4] In Moscow, Tito protested again his friendship for the United States.[5]

What had happened, it seemed, was that Yugoslav policy was still independent, that no major departures from Titoist ideology or practice were intended. In the future, however, such independence was to be more in harmony with the rest of the Communist world. Inevitably, this meant less harmony with the West. The joint communiqué on Tito's visit endorsed the Soviet position on German unity, calling for negotiations between East and West Germany. Yet Belgrade insisted that as far as principles were concerned it was the Soviet Union, not Yugoslavia, that had changed. If this was true, it followed logically from Belgrade's viewpoint that the new relationship with the East did not pose the same threat to Western interests that it might have during Stalin's time.

An Important Contradiction

Soviet policies had indeed changed. Nevertheless, there was in the new Yugoslav view of the USSR an important contradiction with Yugoslav

[1] *Pravda*, June 3, 1956.
[2] *New York Times*, June 20, 1956, pp. 1 and 4.
[3] For the text of the communiqué, see *New York Times*, June 21, 1956, p. 10.
[4] *New York Times*, June 21, 1956, pp. 1 and 11.
[5] *New York Times*, June 17, 1956, p. 8.

theory. Post-Cominform Yugoslav theory charged that the Soviet Union had deviated from Marxism-Leninism not alone because under Stalin it denied the right of other countries to choose their own paths to socialism. More basic to the charge was Belgrade's formal view of the very structure of Soviet society. A state is not socialist, according to this theory, unless it begins to "wither away." State ownership of the means of production, although it is the "first step" to socialism, is also the "lowest step," and unless the state transfers control to the workers, such a system "degenerates into state capitalism." That the USSR had "strayed onto the path of imperialism" was simply a manifestation of the fact that the Soviet state was not "withering away" but getting stronger and was not really socialist but "bureaucratic state capitalism."[1] This, rather than any specific Soviet actions, foreign or domestic, was at the heart of the matter, from the point of view of Soviet Marxist theory. The fact was that in this regard there had been no basic change in the nature of the Soviet system, nor was there evidence that any was contemplated. There was talk about decentralization, and some action, but even the decentralization of economic administration which was to occur in 1957 involved no relinquishing of formal state control in the sense to which Yugoslavs referred to it.[2]

Actually, of course, it was clear to Tito that the Soviet Union in 1956 did not live up to all the Yugoslav specifications for being on "the path of Marx, Engels and Lenin." But in publicly flouting his own theoretical formulations he was taking a conscious gamble and, at the same time, plunging headlong into the politics not only of the Soviet bloc but of the Kremlin itself.

No doubt Tito and other Yugoslav leaders devoutly hoped that the new approach begun by Khrushchev would lead to more fundamental reforms. Kardelj, for example, earlier had seen the significance of the Twentieth Congress not only in the "decisions it concretely formulated but also in the processes it initiated or stimulated by its decisions."[3]

More important, Tito became convinced during his visit to the USSR that there was a serious split in the Kremlin, that the Soviet ruling hierarchy was divided between a "Stalinist" faction, presumably led by Molotov, and an "anti-Stalinist" faction led by Khrushchev. The Khrushchev faction, Tito believed, favored sweeping reforms at home and implementation of the policy of "independent paths to socialism" in the satellites. Tito's assistance may have been solicited by Khrushchev. At any rate, Tito came to the con-

---

[1] See Chapter 11.

[2] Even the "approach to Communism" heralded at the 21st Congress of the Soviet Party in 1959 appeared to shy away from the classic concept of "withering away of the state." See Khrushchev address to Congress, *Pravda*, January 28, 1959.

[3] *Borba*, February 1956.

clusion that he could influence the outcome of the conflict in the Kremlin and thus play a role of pivotal importance in the satellites. With a characteristic Yugoslav disregard for the proportions involved, he saw himself influencing the entire Communist movement along Yugoslav lines, toward "true socialism," peace and "active coexistence."

Even before his Moscow visit, apparently, Tito inclined to such ideas. The need for Yugoslav influence in Communist affairs was given by *Borba* as an explanation for the visit. And this explained also the emphasis given in Belgrade to that part of the Moscow communiqué that called for the Soviet and Yugoslav Communist parties to make "a comprehensive mutual study of socialist development in the two countries." It was particularly and immediately in connection with the satellites, however, where, if Khrushchev did not actually ask Tito's intervention, Tito at any rate decided to intervene. Even before returning to Belgrade he went to work. En route, he stopped off in Bucharest for talks with Gheorghiu-Dej and other Rumanian Communist leaders. A new phase of Yugoslav foreign policy had begun, and it was to have far-reaching implications.

"Titoism" in Eastern Europe

Ever since the death of Stalin, there had been political ferment in the Soviet empire — at home in the USSR and abroad in the satellites. At the root of the difficulty in the satellites, especially in Hungary and Poland, was a main ingredient of the Titoist heresy: nationalist opposition in Communist ranks to Stalinist-type policies. The opposition was motivated in large part by fears of growing popular unrest produced by bad economic conditions and police measures. How to cope with this nationalist opposition was a major issue dividing the Kremlin.

While at first there was no direct connection between Yugoslavia and such developments elsewhere in Eastern Europe, it seemed clear that the existence of the independent Titoist model, along with changes in the USSR itself, acted as a spur to nationalist sentiment. The formal approval of Titoism by the Kremlin, together with the Twentieth Party Congress and the denunciation of Stalin, now enormously accelerated the tempo of events.

As early as the fall of 1955, after Khrushchev bestowed his blessing on Tito, the Central Committee of the Polish Communist Party met to consider "the specific nature of Poland's road to socialism." The following spring saw the "rehabilitation" in Hungary and Bulgaria of Laszlo Rajk and Traicho Kostov, who had been executed for "Titoism," and the Poles announced the release from prison of their leading nationalist Communist, Wladyslaw

Gomulka.[1] The Bulgarian Communist, Vulko Chervenkov, who was an ostentatious foe of Tito, was demoted. In the summer, the most Stalinist of all the satellite leaders, Mátyás Rákosi, was deposed in Budapest. The "Titoists" were having their inning in Eastern Europe. With a role somewhere between that of spectator and participant, the Yugoslavs egged them on and cheered their performance.

The pressures seemed to be strongest in Poland. The Stalinist leadership there sought to hold back the tide with half measures. That these were not enough was dramatically demonstrated by the outbreak of riots, sparked by dissatisfied workers, in Poznan on June 28, 1956, less than a week after Tito ended his Soviet tour.

The Poznan riots appeared to strengthen the hand of the Kremlin's "Stalinist" faction, which held that endorsement of Titoism would result in just that kind of dangerous spontaneity. A decided change of tone appeared in Soviet pronouncements on Eastern Europe. On June 30, the Soviet Central Committee called for tighter discipline in foreign Communist parties. *Pravda*, on July 16, criticized nationalist tendencies in Communist parties. A week later, Bulganin, in Warsaw, declared: "We cannot idly bypass . . . weakening the international ties of the socialist camp under the slogan of so-called national peculiarities." Then, on September 3, the Soviet Central Committee dispatched a secret letter to the satellite Communist parties calling for solidarity under Soviet rule, warning against Tito's influence and raising questions about the nature of Yugoslav socialism.[2] In the meantime, in both Poland and Hungary the revolt of the nationalist Communists gathered momentum.

Satellite Policy Debated

Whether Khrushchev himself was beginning to have second thoughts about his encouragement of Titoism or whether, in the seesaw struggle for power then going on in the Kremlin, he was forced to give in is not clear. At any rate, soon after the secret letter was issued there occurred a series of sensational and mysterious comings and goings indicating that a great debate on Soviet satellite policy was in progress. First, it was revealed on September 19 that Khrushchev had arrived in Yugoslavia in great secrecy and was closeted with Tito at Brioni. A few days later came the baffling announcement that Tito — who ordinarily goes to great lengths to avoid air travel — had flown back to the USSR with Khrushchev. There, at Yalta, they were joined by

---

[1] Gomulka had been freed quietly at the end of 1954, but no announcement was made until later.

[2] The existence of the CPSU circular letter was not officially confirmed until October 12, when *Borba* referred to it. *Borba* added, however, that "the case has been clarified and will never reoccur."

other top Soviet leaders and by Erno Gerö, who had replaced Rákosi as top man in Hungary.[1]

The main question at Yalta was essentially this: How could socialism in Eastern Europe be strengthened? Tito argued that the socialist forces in the satellites were strong enough to persist without Stalinist-type repression. Liberalization combined with nationalism, he argued, would not only make socialism stronger, but if such a course were not taken socialism would be endangered. This was also, as it seemed to Tito, the line taken by Khrushchev. Against this point of view, the "Stalinists" advanced the need for rigid controls, both Soviet and local, in the satellites, and opposition to nationalist tendencies. Citing the Poznan riots, they held that liberalization and nationalism would risk destruction of socialism in Eastern Europe. Gerö, already worried by developments in Budapest, tended to side with the "Stalinists."

There was no final resolution of the issue at this time, but Khrushchev urged Tito to indicate support for Gerö, who, he promised, would carry on liberalizations, but more slowly. A slower pace was needed for stability in Eastern Europe, Khrushchev said, and if there were not stability there, he and his supporters in the Kremlin would lose strength to the "Stalinists." Although Tito considered that Gerö "differed in no way from Rákosi," almost against his better judgment he agreed to back him on the theory that in this way he could strengthen Khrushchev, help preserve the Soviet commitment to "independent paths," and thus further the cause of socialism as he saw it. He also "hoped that by not isolating the Hungarian Party he could more easily influence that country's development," and he urged on Khrushchev and Gerö the readmission of Imre Nagy to the Communist ranks in Hungary.

It is clear in retrospect that both Tito and Khrushchev, as well as the "Stalinists," miscalculated. Tito's misgivings about Gerö proved valid, and, furthermore, Communism in Eastern Europe had far less popular support than he thought. This was not so clear, however, when Tito, on returning to Belgrade, showed his support of Gerö by inviting him to come to Yugoslavia. Even as he did so, the macabre ritual of the reinterment of Laszlo Rajk in Budapest took on the aspects of a popular anti-Communist demonstration. While the Hungarian delegation was in Yugoslavia, Wladyslaw Gomulka resumed leadership of the Polish Communist Party on a platform calling for

---

[1] The authors were able to construct a picture of these conferences from conversations with Yugoslav officials, from Tito's speech at Pula on November 11, 1956, from Soviet and Yugoslav published reports and other sources. See, for example, U. S. Department of State, *Soviet Affairs Notes*, No. 224, July 28, 1958. For an interesting account, which, however, makes several statements the present authors were unable to verify, see Richard Lowenthal, "Tito's Gamble," *Encounter*, October 1958, pp. 56–65.

internal liberalization and national independence. As a delegation from the Soviet Presidium, headed by Khrushchev himself, stormed into Warsaw to see what was up, the Yugoslav press hailed Gomulka's advent to power as "a great victory for socialism."[1]

In Poland, Gomulka — with the cooperation of the Roman Catholic Church — was able to play something of the role of a Tito. He had enough ability and enough popularity to rally support behind a nationalist Communist regime. But in Hungary, the nationalist Communists had no Gomulka, no cooperative Catholic church, no wide popular support. Even if the Stalinist Gerö had given in to the nationalist opposition within his own party, one cannot say that things could have been kept in hand. On October 23, the day Gerö returned from Belgrade after his seven-day visit, the demonstrators were already defying the police in the streets of Budapest. Gerö's broadcast of a Yugoslav-Hungarian communiqué stressing party cooperation had no effect whatsoever in the electric atmosphere. His subsequent "hard-line" message to the nation only served as provocation. Frightened and impotent, Gerö called for Soviet troops. The tragic and bloody Hungarian revolution had begun.

Tito, the Russians and the Hungarian Revolution

It is necessary to distinguish between the two phases of the Hungarian revolution. There really were, as Tito said later, two uprisings and two Soviet interventions. The first uprising was still controlled, at least ostensibly, by nationalist Communists like Nagy and Janos Kadar, who became first secretary of the Hungarian Communist Party; and the first Soviet intervention appeared to have ceased, or to be ceasing, when the new Nagy-Kadar regime took over from Gerö. At this time, the Soviet government issued what was perhaps its "most Titoist" statement. The USSR had in the past wrongly "infringed the principle of equality in relations among socialist states," the declaration said, but in the future it promised to observe "full equality, respect of territorial integrity, state independence and sovereignty and non-interference in domestic affairs." The statement pledged to review the need for further Soviet advisers in the satellites. It recognized that "further presence of Soviet military units in Hungary could serve as an excuse for further aggravation" and said they would be withdrawn when the Hungarian government wanted. And the Soviet government, further, promised a mutual re-examination of the question of Soviet troops in Poland, Bulgaria and Rumania.[2]

[1] *Borba*, October 23, 1956.
[2] *Pravda*, October 31, 1956.

It is, of course, impossible to say whether this statement represented the real Soviet attitude. To the extent that it did, it indicated a triumph for Tito's concepts, supported presumably by Khrushchev. If so, the triumph was short-lived. For no sooner had the new Soviet policy been declared than the Hungarian revolution passed into its second phase. The nationalist Communists' control of the situation had been tenuous from the start; now they lost control altogether. The anti-Communists were in the saddle, and Nagy, a courageous and sincere man but never a dynamic leader, was forced to ride along. For the Kremlin, at any rate, the crucial factor was not so much the new coalition government that resulted as it was the renunciation of the Warsaw Pact and the request for protection from the United Nations and the great powers. With Soviet power threatened, differences in the Kremlin gave way to unity. Back into Budapest poured the Soviet troops. The Hungarian people now rose to the valiant but vain defense of their homeland.

Like Pandora, the Yugoslavs were appalled and frightened by the turn of events in Hungary. What appeared to be a triumph for Tito-type socialism had become an anti-Communist revolution at their very border. There was no assurance that either the revolution or the Soviet troops summoned by Gerö would stop at the Hungarian frontier, and there was the added danger that the West would become involved and a third world war would result.

While the Yugoslav leaders worried and debated what, if anything, to do,[1] they were suddenly informed by Soviet representatives during the night of November 3 that Soviet forces would re-enter Budapest the following day to crush the revolution and install Kadar in power. The only aim of the Soviet intervention, the Yugoslavs were advised, was to save socialism and prevent a civil war; as soon as this was accomplished, the Soviet troops would again withdraw.

Tito and his aides were both shocked and relieved by this dramatic Soviet announcement, but there is no doubt that they were persuaded by the Soviet arguments. The first Soviet intervention, Tito told the Soviet representatives, was completely unjustified, and, along with Rákosi and Gerö, was the cause of all the trouble. Another Soviet intervention would also be bad, he said, but if it would preserve socialism in Hungary — and he made it clear he meant *his* type of socialism — if it would preserve the peace and if the Soviet troops would withdraw as soon as things were in order, then he could see how it could be justified.[2]

---

[1] A British journalist, Richard Lowenthal, has reported that "some of them considered the idea of marching in [to Hungary] before the Soviets did, to insure both the survival of Communism and 'real' neutrality." *Op. cit.*, p. 60. The present authors' information indicates that although such a step may have been mentioned informally by some Yugoslav Communists below the top leadership, it was never seriously considered.

[2] This information comes from authoritative Yugoslav sources, and Tito implicitly confirmed it in his subsequent speech at Pula. Cf. *Borba*, November 16, 1956.

Tito later insisted that he "never advised them [the Russians] to go ahead and use the army." *Pravda* (November 23, 1956) was quick to challenge Tito's disclaimer, and it seems clear that in any event he more or less "agreed" to the Soviet intervention.[1]

That Tito was thus, in effect, committed to the second Soviet intervention helps explain the subsequent ambivalence of the Yugoslav position. The Hungarian revolution created an enormous impact in Yugoslavia, and Yugoslav newspaper reports of it were accurate and sometimes even vivid.[2] The extremely cautious and euphemistic statement of the Tanjug foreign editor on November 4 clearly testified to the widespread sympathy for the Hungarian revolutionists that existed among both Communists and non-Communists in Yugoslavia. The statement twice repeated the sentence: "Of course we look in a negative way on the fact that the new Hungarian government had to turn to the Soviet army for aid," and added that it was "obvious that neither the socialist and other progressive forces nor those in the rest of the world have looked with approval on such methods of struggle." The statement carefully avoided expressions of either approval or condemnation but implied, without quite saying so, that Soviet intervention — never referred to as such — was necessary even if unfortunate.

Impact of the Revolution

This attempt to ride both horses at once compromised the Yugoslav regime less in the West than in Moscow. Three days later, on November 8, *Pravda* printed an article by Enver Hoxha of Albania, an always thoroughly unreconstructed anti-Titoist, which denounced the Yugoslavs without mentioning them by name. Hoxha referred to the danger of being "ensnared" by "slogans of some brand of 'special socialism' or some sort of 'democracy' which savors of anything but a proletarian spirit." There were those, declared Hoxha, "who, making use of the just struggle against the cult of the personality carried out by the 20th Congress of the CPSU, are striving to revile Lenin's glorious Party in order to cultivate their own personality." And he added: "Such — if I may call them so — 'comrades' are trying with the aid of so-called socialist slogans to see a mote in another person's eye but do not notice the beam in their own!"

Angered by Moscow's publication of this article and feeling the need to give guidance to his own followers, now thoroughly confused about develop-

---

[1] Lowenthal in his *Encounter* article, cited above, asserts that Tito "gave his advance consent to the crushing of the Hungarian revolution." "Advance consent" is hardly the right phrase, since the Russians had already decided to intervene and, in fact, were doing so even as Tito was consulted.

[2] See various issues of *Borba* during the period October 25–November 5, 1956.

ments in Hungary, Tito on November 11, 1956, sought to clarify his position in a speech at Pula, on the Istrian peninsula. That the leadership was not certain how much clarification was accomplished is indicated by the fact that *Borba* delayed publication of the speech until November 16.

Although, as indicated above, Tito justified the second Soviet intervention, he outspokenly criticized the Soviet Union on three scores: for keeping Rákosi in power so long; for forcing Gerö as Rákosi's successor; and for responding to Gerö's request for armed assistance and sending in their forces in the first place. Apparently he had had second thoughts about the enthusiasm that previously led him to ignore Yugoslav theoretical analysis of the Soviet system. Whereas Khrushchev blamed earlier policies wholly on Stalin, Tito told his Pula comrades, the real trouble lay in the Soviet system itself, "in the bureaucratic apparatus, in the method of leadership and so-called one-man rule, in the ignoring of the role and aspirations of the working masses. . . . They [the Khrushchev faction] did not start to fight against that system."

Tito scoffed at Soviet charges that the Hungarian revolution was initiated by reactionaries and outside influences. It was begun, he said, by "progressive forces" understandably fighting against Stalinism. The first Soviet intervention "still further enraged the people" and, according to Tito, thus permitted "reactionaries to turn a justified revolt against a clique into an uprising of the whole nation against socialism and the Soviet Union." At this point, Tito felt, the choice was between the evil of Soviet intervention and the evil of "chaos, civil war, counter-revolution and a new world war." Since Soviet intervention was clearly the lesser evil, Tito was "deeply convinced" that it was not "a purely interventionist action."

A month later, however, Kardelj, in a more coherent theoretical explanation of the Yugoslav stand, indicated that if the leadership had not been beset with doubts about Soviet intervention from the first, it was now beginning to develop them. It was "probable," he told the Federal Assembly on December 6, that socialism would have survived in Hungary even without Soviet intervention, although the possibility of its defeat had to be considered. Soviet intervention would prove to be justified, he said, only if there resulted for "the working class, through workers' councils and other similar working class organs, influence in state politics which it lacked in the past."

In his Pula speech, Tito made no attempt to conceal the seriousness with which he regarded the Hungarian affair. "Socialism," he mourned, "has been dealt such a terrible blow. It has been compromised." Although he had often said that Stalinist methods "would only compromise socialism," he did not now "want us to beat our breasts and say gleefully, 'We told you so.' "

Of course, that was exactly what he was saying, albeit not very gleefully, and Moscow promptly took up the gauntlet. On November 19 and again on the 23rd, *Pravda* angrily accused Tito of "sowing disunity" in the Communist camp by claiming that "the Yugoslav road to socialism is the most correct and only possible road." This attitude reminded the *Pravda* writers of an old saying: "Without us even the sun does not rise." The fact was, the Soviet Communist newspaper insisted, that there were not only serious flaws in the Yugoslav system but that this system was made possible "only by aid from the imperialists." Somewhat ominously, *Pravda* inquired if Tito were not repeating "previous attacks on the Soviet Union [like those that were] fashionable . . . when relations were getting worse and worse?" For its part, the Soviet Communist Party felt that what was needed now was a "further consolidation of all forces of socialism on the basis of Marxist Leninist principles of socialist internationalism."

"Proletarian Internationalism"

"Socialist internationalism," or, as it is also called, "proletarian internationalism," now became the dominant issue in Yugoslav-Soviet relations and, indeed, in one way or another the dominant issue in relations among all the Communist countries. Moscow's new emphasis on it reflected one clear lesson of the Hungarian revolution that had been ignored in Belgrade. This was that maintenance of hegemony in Eastern Europe, in some form, remained the cardinal principle of Soviet foreign policy.

Since Stalin had signaled a shift at the Nineteenth Party Congress in 1952, Soviet foreign policy generally had been aimed at presenting a new, peace-loving and cooperative face to the world. Seeking to establish a "popular front" against United States influence, it had tried to demonstrate to the Western European socialists, and also to those of Asia and Africa, that they could trust the USSR and collaborate with the various Communist parties for peace and liberal nationalism. The brutal intervention in Hungary risked whatever gains Moscow might have made in this direction and also ran the risk of war itself. Yet, since the maintenance of Soviet hegemony in Eastern Europe was vital, there was little hesitation in the Kremlin.

It is likely that the Soviet acceptance of "individual paths to socialism" at the Twentieth Party Congress did not involve any concrete Soviet thinking about what this would entail. But if Khrushchev and company considered it anything more than an empty phrase, it seems clear they did not envisage any real change in the orientation of the Eastern European countries toward Moscow. Once it became apparent, as a result of the events in Poland and Hungary, that this was too sanguine a view, limits were promptly imposed.

Even before the Hungarian revolution had been completely crushed, these limits were set forth by Mikhail Suslov, the Kremlin's leading technical theoretician.[1]

As defined by Suslov, "individual paths to socialism" would be permitted if, and only if, they entailed:

(1) Acceptance of the principle of "proletarian internationalism," which means support of Soviet foreign policy and recognition of the Soviet Communist Party as the leader of the Communist world; and

(2) The "leading role of a Leninist party" in internal affairs, which means some form of Communist dictatorship.

In the case of Hungary at the time of the second Soviet intervention, it was clear that neither of these prerequisites obtained. The Poles barely stayed within the confines of "the leading role of a Leninist party," and Moscow was able to see to it that they quickly accepted "proletarian internationalism." The Yugoslav "path to socialism" might satisfy the Communist dictatorship part of the requirements, even though the Kremlin was not happy about its form, but it was obvious that Yugoslavia did not adhere to "proletarian internationalism" as it was understood in the Soviet Union.

At first, neither Khrushchev nor Tito seemed to comprehend that Titoism could not somehow qualify within the limits of acceptable "individual paths to socialism." Khrushchev apparently believed that he could either entice or bludgeon the Yugoslavs into line on "proletarian internationalism." Tito apparently thought the Russians did not really mean what they said. In any event, he failed to realize the all-embracing importance to the Kremlin of Soviet hegemony in Eastern Europe.

At first, relations went from bad to worse, and in the spring of 1957 Tito compared the state of things to that right after the Cominform Resolution. The Yugoslavs charged that the Soviet Union was demanding "ideological capitulation." When Foreign Secretary Popović said "the deliberate campaign to discredit Yugoslavia" was an example of Stalinism, *Pravda* snapped back that this was "monstrous and revolting blasphemy." On the heels of a Yugoslav-Soviet credit arrangement, Khrushchev warned there would be no aid if the Yugoslavs did not treat the USSR "fraternally." The satellites quickly joined the attack. "National Communism," said Kadar, with a finger pointed toward Belgrade, was the "twin brother of Nazism." The Albanians, as usual the most ferocious, justified the Cominform Resolution and aimed thinly veiled threats at Kosovo-Metohija, with its large Shiptar population.[2]

[1] In a speech delivered during the celebration of the 39th anniversary of the Bolshevik Revolution (*Pravda*, November 7, 1956), translated in *Current Digest of the Soviet Press*, December 12, 1956, pp. 3–8.

[2] *Borba*, February 12, 14, March 2, 10, 1957.

Yet it was at the Albanian Embassy in Moscow that Khrushchev declared on April 15 that he wanted to improve both state and Party relations with Yugoslavia. Promptly Tito responded: "The shift in Soviet attitude raises the question, Can we ever trust them again? It would be a mistake to say no, because one day, we hope not in the too distant future, this improper, insincere and uncomradely behavior toward us will gradually subside."[1] To make sure it did subside, he dispatched a personal note to Moscow, suggesting a truce. Khrushchev agreed.

Tito's hopes of achieving "socialist solidarity" while maintaining Yugoslav independence were buoyed in no small degree by the active interest the Chinese Communists were showing in international Communist matters. Although the Chinese had also taken issue with Tito's Pula speech, their criticism was milder than the Russians'. Moreover, soon thereafter they appeared to be throwing their influence toward an interpretation of "independent paths to socialism" more pleasing to Belgrade than to Moscow. Premier Chou En-lai, visiting Warsaw in January 1957, seemed to be encouraging the Poles to stand up to the USSR, and Peking had several times referred critically to the "great power chauvinism" displayed by Stalin. Although Mao Tse-tung's promise of February 27 to "let a hundred flowers bloom, let a hundred schools of thought contend" was short-lived, it too helped convince the Titoists that they might not be alone in their efforts to influence the Kremlin.[2]

Events in the Soviet Union in the summer of 1957 bolstered the Yugoslav view that the Kremlin was influenceable. In July Khrushchev announced a purge of Molotov and other high Soviet leaders considered to be "Stalinists." He followed this with a sweeping decentralization of the USSR's economic administrative machinery. This last was in the direction of the Yugoslav reforms, although it fell far short of altering the basic nature of the Soviet system.

Despite the fact that shortly before this Khrushchev publicly showed little inclination to compromise with Belgrade,[3] Aleksandar Ranković immediately hailed the changes as proving "the vital force of Soviet society." He predicted that they would have "far-reaching positive consequences" for the USSR's

---

[1] *Borba*, April 18, 1957.

[2] For discussion of these points, see Allen S. Whiting, "Contradictions in the Moscow-Peking Axis," in John H. Hallowell (ed.), *Soviet Satellite Nations*, Kallman Publishing Co., Gainesville, Florida, 1958, pp. 127–161; and Benjamin Schwartz, "China and the Communist Bloc: A Speculative Reconstruction," *Current History*, December 1958, pp. 321–326. It is likely that the Poles read more into Chou's attitude than he intended. The Chinese Premier apparently also urged them to maintain the unity of the socialist bloc. Cf. Zbigniew K. Brzezinski, *The Soviet Bloc*, Harvard University Press, Cambridge, 1960, p. 279.

[3] See particularly his speeches in Prague, *Rude Pravo* and *Le Monde*, July 12, 1957.

internal development and foreign policy, world peace and socialism in general.[1] It was felt in Belgrade that since the two countries were now following "at least roughly similar roads of development," Yugoslav-Soviet relations were bound to improve.[2]

Another Rapprochement

Both Tito and Khrushchev now considered the time ripe for another rapprochement, each, apparently, thinking he could win the other over to his views. Accordingly, in August they met at a "secret" conference in Bucharest.[3] At the meeting, both of the Communist leaders exchanged views on "socialist solidarity." Khrushchev seems to have made it clear that he thought of this in terms of Yugoslav affiliation with the Soviet bloc. He told Tito he agreed with him that the time had come for far-reaching liberalizations in both Soviet and satellite systems and that he was ready to support strongly the idea of "independent paths to socialism." But for this to be accomplished, Khrushchev reasoned, there had to be assurances of "socialist solidarity." Such assurances involved a definite Yugoslav choice of support for Soviet foreign policy as against Western foreign policy and, therefore, affiliation with the bloc. Earlier, Moscow had indicated that assistance for construction of a giant aluminum plant in Montenegro was predicated on Yugoslav recognition of East Germany.[4] Now Khrushchev pressed for such recognition as a demonstration of bloc solidarity.

Tito demurred at the idea of formally affiliating with the Soviet bloc, and it seems clear that this idea, as such, did not occur to him for a moment. In effect, however — certainly, at least, as the Russians seem to have interpreted it — he more or less agreed to be a "non-member," arguing that by remaining outside he could better serve the cause of both socialism and peace, to which, he was assured, Soviet policy was dedicated. Tito agreed, further, to attend a big meeting in Moscow in November at which all the Communist parties in the Soviet bloc countries would sign a declaration of "socialist solidarity." The question of "proletarian internationalism" came up at the meeting but, it seems, without any specific discussion about what it meant.

---

[1] *Borba*, July 4, 1957.

[2] See two articles reviewing Soviet economic reorganization by I. Dobravec, *Review of International Affairs*, June 1, 1957, pp. 7–8 and June 16, 1957, pp. 6–8.

[3] It is not clear whether the meeting was on Yugoslav or Soviet initiative. Khrushchev has stated that Tito requested it. (*Pravda*, June 4, 1958.) Although this has not been publicly denied by Belgrade, several Yugoslavs who accompanied Tito to Bucharest insist that Khrushchev proposed the conference. This report of what occurred is based mainly on conversations of one of the authors with these participants.

[4] *Borba*, February 26, 1957.

Again, as at Moscow in 1956, Tito seems to have been carried away by his dream of influencing the Kremlin and the Communist movement. Some of his aides insisted later that from the time of the Bucharest meeting they realized there was no hope of real agreement with the Kremlin, but it is clear that Tito, at least, thought otherwise. If he was not actually again taking a stand counter to Yugoslav theory — which plainly held there was no valid basis for division of the world into blocs — he was at least giving it an interpretation different from that formerly placed on it.

Manifestations of the new interpretation came quickly. In September when Gomulka visited Belgrade, Tito, for the first time since the Cominform dispute, accepted the Soviet Union as "the first country of socialism," albeit with the qualification that the USSR should play its role in relations between large and small Communist states so as "to stimulate powerfully the establishment of confidence." Tito emphasized that neither he nor the Polish leader were "national Communists." Rather, he said, "we think it is wrong to isolate ourselves from the great possibilities of strengthening socialist forces throughout the world." Gomulka added that Poland and Yugoslavia had "deep ideological conviction and common ideas of socialism and proletarian internationalism."[1]

Before Gomulka returned home, Yugoslavia joined the USSR and its satellites in the United Nations General Assembly in opposition to a resolution condemning Soviet intervention in Hungary.[2] The same day Tito accepted a Rumanian proposal for a Balkan conference that would include Albania, Bulgaria, Greece, Rumania, Turkey and Yugoslavia. On October 15, Belgrade recognized East Germany.

This last act was regarded as especially significant because it was taken to mean that Tito considered demonstrations of "socialist solidarity" more important than good relations with the West. No other nation outside the Soviet bloc had recognized East Germany, and Bonn quickly retaliated by severing relations with Yugoslavia. It might be true, as the Yugoslavs argued, that one could make a good case for such recognition on the merits of the issue. However, that case had not been made in Belgrade up to this time, and, in fact, Yugoslav relations with East Germany had been bad.

There were other indications that Tito was going all out for "socialist solidarity." Whether or not the new sentence imposed on Milovan Djilas at this time (as a result of publication abroad of *The New Class*) and other

---

[1] *Borba*, September 10, and *New York Times*, September 16, 1957, p. 1.

[2] During the Second Emergency Special Session of the General Assembly the previous November, Yugoslavia's mixed record of voting on resolutions condemning Soviet intervention reflected the ambivalent views of Belgrade on this matter generally.

internal "hard line" measures were taken to help persuade the Russians,[1] they were so interpreted in the West and quite possibly also in the Soviet Union. So was the Yugoslav silent acceptance, following a mild protest, of the insult administered by the Russians when they violated the safe conduct pledge given Imre Nagy and spirited him off to Rumania.

Further, this was a period of increasing Yugoslav criticism of Western, and especially American, foreign policy. In the fall issue of *Foreign Affairs*, Tito called for the dissolution of NATO and criticized the West for its "negative attitude" toward Moscow. In New Delhi, the Yugoslav delegates stomped out of the International Red Cross Conference, denouncing American insistence on admission of Nationalist China as "selfish and political."[2]

From the United States came a stiff reaction. The State Department notified Belgrade that, in view of the political uncertainties, the U. S. aid program was undergoing review. The Yugoslavs responded that if constant and "humiliating" review of U. S. aid was necessary it might be better to cease it altogether. Ambassador Riddleberger hurried home to consult with the American policy makers.[3] To many, it looked as if the Western links of the "Yugoslav bridge" were being severed, one by one.

At this point, Tito received a draft of the resolution of Communist unity which he was expected to sign in Moscow at a meeting commemorating the fortieth anniversary of the Soviet party. Whether Khrushchev decided the moment had arrived to turn the screws or whether — as is more probable — he never had other intentions, the draft resolution was couched in terms wholly unacceptable to Tito. It was based altogether on Soviet cold war positions and collided with Yugoslav principles at half a dozen points. Its analysis saw the world divided into two uncompromising blocs, with the United States the "center of world reaction" and the socialist bloc defined in terms of the Warsaw Pact. National differences were important, the draft resolution said, but their exaggeration and "departure, under the pretext of national peculiarities, from the universal Marxist-Leninist truth on socialist revolution and socialist construction" were just as harmful. "Dogmatism" was condemned but, the draft resolution declared, "in condemning dogmatism the Communist parties believe that the main danger at present is re-

---

[1] At the highest Yugoslav levels, it is flatly denied that any actions were taken to "appease" the Russians. However, some lesser Yugoslav officials say privately: "Maybe the sentence was imposed on Djilas because of the Russians, but not East German recognition"; while others say: "Maybe East Germany was recognized because of the Russians, but this had nothing to do with the treatment of Djilas."

[2] *Intelligence Information Brief*, U. S. Department of State, November 18, 1958, p. 12.

[3] See *New York Times*, October 24, 1957, p. 5, October 31, p. 1 and December 23, pp. 1 and 2.

visionism." There was repeated reference to "proletarian internationalism" and the important role of the Soviet Union.[1]

Tito must have read the draft resolution with an increasing feeling of dismay and bafflement. This was not at all what he had banked on. Although it is doubtful that he saw even then the total collapse of his hopes for influencing the Soviet Union toward Titoist directions, it was clear that Yugoslavia could not sign this document. Kardelj and Ranković took Tito's decision to the Moscow meeting, while Tito himself, pleading ill health, stayed home to brood and ponder.

In Moscow, Khrushchev reacted angrily to the Yugoslav refusal to sign. Yugoslavia could not continue to sit "in two chairs," he is reported to have told Kardelj and Ranković. Tito would have to choose between East and West. And he warned them, as he later said, that if Yugoslavia continued its critical stance it was in for trouble.[2] Kardelj and Ranković did join in signing another resolution, one calling for peace and endorsing many Soviet stands on foreign policy.[3] But it did not help. None of the Communist leaders indicated any support for the Yugoslav position, not even the Poles. And the Chinese, to whom Belgrade had once looked so hopefully, successfully proposed inclusion in the resolution of language explicitly placing on the Soviet Union the mantle of leadership in the international Communist movement.

The Yugoslav stand at the Fortieth Anniversary meeting clearly indicated that regardless of how much Tito would compromise in the interest of "socialist solidarity," there was a point beyond which he would not go, no matter what. Yet even now, Tito's hopes of participating in a "socialist solidarity" he could accept were not completely crushed. Nor, apparently, were Khrushchev's. With other Soviet leaders, he jovially participated in the National Day celebration at the Yugoslav Embassy in Moscow on November 29. Klimenty Voroshilov hailed Yugoslavia's "brotherly cooperation" with the USSR, and *Izvestia* commented that "increasingly more favorable results are being brought about by comprehensive developments of friendly ties." Belgrade responded by applauding Khrushchev's call for a summit conference, and a foreign office spokesman said Yugoslav-Soviet relations continued "to be based on principles of the Belgrade and Moscow declarations, are developing favorably and have proved mutually beneficial."[4]

---

[1] The draft followed very closely the final text, which was published in *Pravda*, December 22, 1957. For an English translation, see *Current Digest*, January 1, 1958, pp. 3–7.

[2] See *New York Times*, July 15, 1958, and Khrushchev's speech at the Fifth Congress of the German Socialist Unity Party, *Pravda*, July 12, 1958, cited from *Current Digest*, August 20, 1958, pp. 5–8.

[3] *Borba*, November 22, 1957.

[4] *Borba*, December 27, 1957.

The Yugoslav Communists' Program

For some time, chiefly because of uncertainty about relations with the Soviet Union, the Yugoslavs had postponed — quite against the Party statute — the Seventh Congress of the League of Communists, originally scheduled for 1956. Back in Belgrade, Kardelj, Ranković and others now went to work with Tito on fixing up the Draft Program that had been so long debated back and forth. As it finally emerged, the Draft Program repeated most of the essentials of Titoist theory as enunciated off and on since 1949, including the very points ignored during the search for "socialist solidarity." Military blocs were condemned as aggressive in content, the Warsaw Pact no less than NATO, and the basis for a division of the world into socialist and capitalist camps was denied. Some sharp words about Stalinism in the USSR were included, although new tendencies in Soviet administration were praised.

With either naïveté or bravado, the Yugoslavs then circulated their Draft Program to Communist parties of the socialist camp, the basis for the existence of which the document challenged. Promptly came back from Moscow detailed and extensive criticism, short of denunciation but its tones of anger thinly veiled. The Soviet criticism objected especially to the Draft Program's equal condemnation of both blocs. "Proletarian internationalism," the Russians said, meant support of other Communist countries, not criticism. They also took exception to Yugoslav ideas on the evolutionary nature of socialism and the withering away of the state. And they felt the Draft Program exaggerated the errors of Stalinism, which after all, it was said, were not fundamental, and wrongly talked about Soviet "hegemonism" in Eastern Europe.

At this point, Tito took an extreme step for a man whose reputation was built on objection to outside interference in Yugoslav affairs. Apparently still nursing hopes and ambitions of influencing Soviet views by convincing Moscow he sincerely wanted "socialist solidarity," he amended the Draft Program to alter some portions offensive to the Kremlin. It was his final gesture to please the Russians. And it accomplished nothing.

Three days before the Seventh Congress opened in Ljubljana, *Kommunist*, the chief Soviet theoretical journal, published the gist of the earlier criticisms in a long article,[1] calling for changes in the Draft Program which the Titoists could not make and still remain Titoists. Indicating that Moscow rightly anticipated these changes would not be made, it was announced on the same day that the entire Soviet bloc would turn down Yugoslav invitations to send official observers and would boycott the Ljubljana meeting.

[1] For an English translation, see *Current Digest of the Soviet Press*, Vol. X, No. 18 (June 11, 1958), pp. 3–11.

The fact was that the changes made by Tito in the Draft Program were not substantial. Certain criticisms of past Soviet policies were toned down; the Warsaw Pact was differentiated from NATO on the grounds that it was defensive and resulted from NATO. But the essence remained the same. Indeed, the Program, even in draft form, contained little the Yugoslavs had not been saying all along. It appeared either that Khrushchev expected, prior to receipt of the Draft Program, that Belgrade was really going to change its tune, or, as some have insisted, that even before that he had decided on an all-out ideological attack on Yugoslavia, and the Party Program merely furnished him with an excuse for it.[1] In any event, the chips at long last seemed to be down.

The Yugoslavs reacted characteristically. Tito himself, opening the Congress, was moderate enough. Although he called on Moscow to give up its "absurd" attempts to change Yugoslav ideas and charged that the USSR distorted the idea of "proletarian internationalism," he endorsed much of Soviet foreign policy as a force for peace. But, following Tito, Ranković and Kardelj aimed strong words at the Russians, although not mentioning them specifically. The Soviet ambassador ostentatiously stalked from the hall during Ranković's speech, obediently followed by all the satellite envoys except the Polish ambassador.[2]

While privately the Yugoslav leaders seethed with indignation, publicly the general tenor of the Congress indicated that Belgrade still hoped to avoid a knock-down, drag-out fight. For a time, it looked as though Moscow did too. While the Congress was still in session, Yekaterina Furtseva, the female member of the Soviet Party Presidium and no mean political figure, commented in Warsaw that she was sure there would be no break between Yugoslavia and the USSR like that of 1948.

The Attack from Peking

Yet a knock-down, drag-out fight was exactly what materialized, and soon. The first blow was landed by an unexpected source — Peking. On May 5 the Chinese Communist newspaper *Jen Min Jih Pao* charged that Titoism aimed at "splitting the international Communist movement and undermining the solidarity of the socialist countries." The Program of the Yugoslav League of Communists, the Chinese statement asserted, was "an anti-Marxist, anti-Leninist, out-and-out revisionist program." What's more, it added, the Cominform Resolution of 1948 was "basically correct." Peking compared

[1] Not long before the Draft Program was distributed, Tito had talks with Kadar in Yugoslavia, immediately following which Khrushchev visited Budapest. Some feel that Khrushchev's decision to "go after" Yugoslavia resulted from Kadar's report of Tito's thinking. See, for example, Lowenthal, *op. cit.*, p. 63.

[2] He was said to be asleep, but whether he was actually dozing or only "asleep" politically is not clear. Bloc country ambassadors were not present as official Party representatives.

the Yugoslavs to "reactionaries of all countries" and called for "open and uncompromising criticism" of their views.[1]

Although it is still somewhat unclear whether the Chinese were initiating the fight on their own or undertaking it at Soviet behest, there was no doubt, when *Pravda* reprinted the text of the Chinese editorial in full on its front page the next day, that the Kremlin approved.

The Yugoslavs were expecting bloc criticism but neither they nor anybody else — unless it was the Russians — were prepared for the violence of the Peking attack. Nor were they prepared for Moscow's follow-up on May 9, which took the form of a threat to end aid to Yugoslavia. Voroshilov's scheduled visit to Belgrade was called off. Day after day, *Pravda* printed biting criticisms of Yugoslavia — Soviet, satellite and Chinese. In a gesture interpreted in Belgrade as applying pressure, Khrushchev sent Tito birthday greetings and expressed hope that the differences would be overcome.

Having had the gauntlet flung in their faces, the Yugoslavs this time picked it up and prepared to hit back. *Borba* now hurled defiance at the Russians. "It is necessary to give a clear warning," *Borba* said, "that if anybody thinks the Communists of Yugoslavia and the people of Yugoslavia can be shaken in their beliefs through unprincipled attacks, these are sheer illusions."[2]

The Soviet attack developed momentum. On May 30, Belgrade announced that the Soviet Union had "postponed" for five years its $285 million credit commitment to Yugoslavia. On June 3, Khrushchev, addressing the Seventh Congress of the Bulgarian Communist Party in Sofia, excoriated Tito as a "Trojan Horse" and denied that Yugoslavia was truly socialist. "Some theoreticians," he said, "exist only because of the alms they receive from imperialist countries in the form of leftover goods."[3]

If Tito still had hopes that compromise with Khrushchev was possible, they were dashed by the Soviet leader's speech in Sofia. Tito's reply, in a speech at Labin on June 15, accused Khrushchev personally of having plotted the attack on Yugoslavia "over a long period of time" and said that various conciliatory statements uttered from time to time were only tactics "to isolate us and compromise us as much as possible." The Yugoslav Communist Program, Tito said, was only an excuse, and, moreover, quotations from it used in the Soviet bloc attacks were "incorrect and sometimes faked or taken out of context in such a way that they give a false picture."

Alluding to Khrushchev's criticism that "socialism cannot be built on U. S. wheat," Tito declared: "Those who know how can do it, while those

---

[1] See the English text of the Chinese statement in the *New York Times*, May 11, 1958, p. 34.

[2] *Borba*, May 15, 1958.

[3] *Pravda*, June 4, 1958.

who do not know how will not even be able to build socialism on their own wheat." As for the Chinese, Tito dismissed them as "warmongers," who criticized Yugoslavia because they were opposed to its "policy of peace" and wanted to focus attention away from their internal problems. Despite all this, Tito maintained, the Yugoslavs would "know how to preserve unstained the banner of Marx, Engels, and Lenin, which we have honorably carried through all past storms and attacks from all sides."[1]

The isolation of Yugoslavia from the rest of the Communist world was completed when even the Poles took up the cudgels. At the end of June 1958, Gomulka hit at "incorrect revisionist theories" and the "negative attitude of the League of Communists which separates Yugoslavia from the community of Socialist countries."[2] Titoism was again wholly beyond the pale. And despite Belgrade's support of Khrushchev's theories of coexistence, it seemed more rather than less likely to remain there. The statement adopted by the leaders of 81 Communist parties in Moscow in November 1960 harshly attacked Yugoslavia for both its foreign and domestic policies.[3] Replying for the Executive Committee of the League of Communists, Veljko Vlahović charged that the statement "inflicts damage on Socialism in general and extends direct support to anti-socialist forces." It proved, Vlahović asserted, that "bureaucratic dogmatic forces are still so strong they can impose their attitudes."[4]

The New Yugoslav Position

Meanwhile, the Yugoslavs set about to repair their battered relations with the West. Soon after the Seventh Party Congress, Leo Mates, Yugoslav ambassador in Washington, had declared his country's friendship for the United States in terms not heard for several months. Such friendship, Mates said, was not dependent on aid, although, he hastened to add, U. S. loans and credits were needed to help Yugoslavia's economic development. The same day, Dobrivoje Vidić, Belgrade's ambassador to the United Nations, asserted that Yugoslavia was determined to maintain "the best of relations with the rest of the world," despite Soviet threats.[5] That summer the Yugoslavs talked of re-establishing diplomatic ties with West Germany.

Reparation of relations with the West was not too difficult. Even during the period of his greatest pro-Soviet alignment, Tito had never completely destroyed the Western end of his "bridge." If there were doubts at one point

[1] *Borba*, June 15, 1958.
[2] Cited in *Borba*, November 14, 1958.
[3] For text of the statement, see *New York Times*, December 7, 1960, pp. 14–17.
[4] *Komunist*, February 24, 1961.
[5] *New York Times*, May 15, 1958, p. 11.

whether his yen for "socialist solidarity" would be carried so far as to jeopardize Yugoslav independence, these were removed when he refused to sign the Communist unity resolution. Now in October 1958, the Yugoslavs asked for loans of $100 million from the United States and Great Britain. By December, the United States decided on a new program of loans and aid in excess of that amount. The following year, American funds permitted the Yugoslavs to proceed with construction of the fertilizer plant that was jeopardized when Moscow reneged on its loan agreement. Yugoslavia's persistently strong support of revolutionary movements in underdeveloped countries — including Castro's regime in Cuba — annoyed Washington because, among other things, it often meant support of Soviet positions.[1] But this in itself seemed unlikely to cause a real breach.

Attention was also given to closer relations with the smaller, neighboring countries friendly to the West in one way or another. Although the Balkan Pact was unlikely to be revived, close amity with Greece continued, and Belgrade began to pay more attention to its erstwhile Turkish ally. Relations with Italy after 1958 were probably better than at any prior time in Yugoslav history. Of the non-Communist border countries, there was a sharp controversy only with Austria, where Yugoslav minorities, especially the Slovenes in South Carinthia, looked to Belgrade for help against various kinds of discrimination.

The new Soviet-Yugoslav dispute, as serious as it was, did not have the ominous overtones present after the Cominform resolution, for both the world view and the Soviet and Yugoslav views of it had changed somewhat. By the same token, the renewed friendship with the West did not become quite as intimate as formerly. For one thing, Belgrade continued to be convinced that the USSR had not gone "all the way back" to Stalinism and that its foreign policy was essentially peaceful. The United States was more responsible than the Soviet Union, according to official but private Yugoslav thinking, for the failure to achieve an East-West *détente* in the 1955–1958 period. And, indeed, some of the Yugoslav Communists were disposed to blame Washington, at least in part, for their new troubles with Moscow. This thinking, based on the old concept of Khrushchev as the leader of an anti-Stalinist faction in the Kremlin, held that Khrushchev sincerely wanted to compromise with the West and that when his offers were spurned, he himself had to become more uncompromising in order to maintain his position. Despite sharp ideological differences, producing strong criticism of Moscow, on specific foreign policy issues Yugoslavia sided with the USSR more often than with the West. But this attitude — stemming at least in part from the

---

[1] Support of Lumumba in the Congo was carried to the point of violent riots in Belgrade at the time the African leader's death was revealed.

Yugoslav leaders' inability to see errors in their own foreign policy — was accompanied by an increasingly critical view of China.[1] Inclined earlier to excoriate U. S. hostility toward Communist China, the Yugoslavs, as a result of Peking's hostility toward them, now had some second thoughts on the matter, although they still favored both recognition and admission to the United Nations.

Nor had Tito altogether lost his yen for "socialist solidarity." His illusions of being able to deal on an equal plane with the Soviet Union were badly battered, but the remnants of them still remained. If Moscow should again tender an olive branch, the gesture would be subject to more scrutiny in Belgrade than before, but it is quite likely that it would be accepted.[2] At the same time, the Yugoslav will to independence seemed stronger than ever. After the new break with the Soviet bloc, Belgrade was trying to focus its independence more in the center, as far as East and West were concerned, even if it did not always appear that way in either Washington or Moscow.

On the other hand, the Yugoslavs were anxious not to fall in between and be overlooked. Toward the end of 1958, Tito voiced fears that this might happen. Both Washington and Moscow were "big-power-centered," he said, and although he was all for a summit meeting, he saw dangers that an accord might be at the expense of small nations. He was worried about what would happen "to those countries that are not inside blocs," and he declared that "coexistence should be between countries and states, not blocs."[3]

One result of these fears appeared to be that Yugoslavia was redoubling its efforts to work closely with other "non-aligned" countries, particularly those in Asia and Africa. At the 1960 session of the United Nations General Assembly, Tito dramatically took the lead in bringing together the leaders of these countries to formulate independent "third force" proposals. Later he was the chief organizer of the Conference of Non-Aligned States that met in Belgrade in the summer of 1961.

Tito's role in connection with the neutralist countries led him along a precarious path in his relations with the West. While the neutralists' vociferous

[1] Kardelj devoted a whole book to an attack on the Chinese Communists for their hostility toward Yugoslavia and their negative stand on the Khrushchev thesis that war is not inevitable despite the existence of capitalism. Defending Khrushchev's position, the book is also an able exposition of the Yugoslav policy of "active coexistence." Edvard Kardelj, *War and Socialism*, Jugoslavija, Belgrade, 1960.

[2] One factor likely to make for closer relations with the Soviet Union was Moscow's clash with Albania — and with Peking — that broke out in 1961 after Khrushchev's new attack on Stalinism at the Twenty-Second Congress of the Soviet Communist Party. Since Albania and China had spearheaded anti-Yugoslav attacks earlier, the more they were estranged from Moscow the friendlier Moscow appeared in Belgrade. Furthermore, that the USSR would permit such a development to occur in Albania indicated to the Yugoslavs that Khrushchev was avoiding strong-arm intervention in Eastern Europe.

[3] *New York Times*, November 23, 1958.

opposition to "blocs" was as displeasing to Moscow as to Washington, on a number of important diplomatic issues — among them recognition of East Germany and the seating of Communist China in the United Nations — the neutralists stood much closer to Soviet than to American positions. And at the Belgrade Conference of 1961, the failure of the non-bloc states collectively and of Tito personally to criticize the Soviet resumption of nuclear testing raised a storm of protest in the United States.[1]

Actually, Tito in his remarks to the Conference not only said little new but was in some ways less critical of the West than he had been on certain previous occasions. There might be reasons for a re-evaluation of relations with Belgrade, but, unless the Kennedy Administration was to revert to an extreme form of the Dulles Doctrine — that neutralism was immoral — it was difficult to see why the 1961 Conference was among them. While on the broader issue of recurring Yugoslav support of Moscow's positions it was easier to understand U. S. sensitivity, even here Belgrade by no means went down the line with the USSR in all cases.[2] One had to remember, however, that — as Tito had reminded the West several times — Yugoslavia is a Communist state, even if outside the Communist bloc. And this meant that Washington, if it wanted to utilize Titoism's independent position to best advantage, would sooner or later have to realize that the choice was not between existing Yugoslav policies and Yugoslav policies more favorable to the West but between existing Yugoslav policies and Yugoslav policies still more favorable to Moscow.

In any event, it seemed certain that the little Balkan country of independent Communism would continue to raise its voice for its principles and interests in a volume not restricted by its size or even by its lack of success. Typical was the reaction of Foreign Secretary Koča Popović, handsome poet-scion of a wealthy family in prewar Yugoslavia and formerly Tito's chief of staff, to the 1958 fiasco in Yugoslav-Soviet policy. Grandly dismissing the world of *realpolitik*, Popović told one of the authors: "We are building up spiritual ammunition."

There was no sign that "active coexistence" was going to be any less active.

---

[1] The U. S. Embassy in Belgrade, of which George F. Kennan had become the chief a few months previously, apparently anticipated, on the basis of unofficial Yugoslav comments, that Tito's speech to the Conference would be pleasing to the United States.

[2] Indicative of this was the high degree of selectivity that marked Yugoslav voting behavior in the United Nations. During the 1959 session of the General Assembly, for instance, the Yugoslavs voted with the United States and against the Soviet Union on important resolutions concerning the U. N. Emergency Force and international development institutions. They abstained on such "East-West" issues as Tibet and Korea. They voted with the USSR and against the United States on questions involving Chinese representation, Hungary and some colonial issues. But in 1960, although they sided with Lumumba in the Congo, they did not support Khrushchev's attack on Secretary-General Hammarskjöld.

THE INFLUENCE OF

TITOISM ABROAD

THE impact of the Titoist development in Yugoslavia has been significant and widespread, both inside and outside the Soviet bloc. It is most clearly discernible in connection with the Soviet satellite countries in Eastern Europe. It is also evident in certain policies of the USSR itself. And outside Europe, it is apparent in the attraction Yugoslav developments have for the new, emerging and underdeveloped countries which are, as the Yugoslavs used to say of themselves, still searching for their way.

The Yugoslavs have consciously sought to enhance the influence of their independent brand of Communism. That they may have overestimated their success does not mean that the impact has been unimportant. Of course, certain new developments in the Communist movement would probably have emerged even if the Titoist heresy had not occurred. The fact is, however, that these did come about only after the Yugoslavs had demonstrated that a Communist system could be different in important aspects from that in the Soviet Union and could operate outside the aegis of the Kremlin. There is, therefore, some reason to search for the nature of Belgrade's influence in such matters as the relation of Moscow to its satellites, the decentralizing tendency in Eastern European governments and the increased emphasis on worker participation in many of these countries.

As pointed out in the previous chapter, elements of "Titoism" existed in all of the smaller Communist nations of Eastern Europe. They existed not only in the form of latent nationalism and anti-Soviet feeling but also in the very nature of the position in which the Communist politicians found themselves. For the Communists had two tasks. One was to serve the Soviet Union. The other was to stay in power and do as good a job as possible of creating socialism and Communism in their own countries. The two were not infrequently in conflict. Where Moscow decreed adoption of economic policies in the interest of the USSR but against the interest of the individual satellites, and where Moscow insisted on rigid conformity to Soviet practice, whether it fit or not, the satellite Communist leaders were compromised. But whereas Tito was not dependent for his power on the Soviet Union, his erstwhile comrades elsewhere in Eastern Europe were. They had no choice, therefore, but to knuckle under to the Kremlin's demands and make the best of it.

Segments of the satellite Communist parties never accepted this position gracefully. That Tito successfully went his own way made the pill they had to swallow all the more bitter. But any hopes that they might, like Tito, follow an independent path were dashed when Stalin cracked down on satellite nationalist opposition, actual and potential, following Yugoslavia's expulsion from the Cominform in 1948. In each of the other Communist countries, there was a major shake-up in leadership. Except for Yugoslavia, Eastern European Communism existed under the tight umbrella of the Cominform, held firmly in Stalin's iron grip.

At first, it appeared as though this negative impact of Titoism would be its only contribution. Not only had the remaining leaders no desire to be purged on Moscow's orders, but, to many devout Eastern European Communists, Stalin was able to make out a pretty good case against Tito. Tito *was* consorting with Western imperialists. He *was* favoring peasants against workers. He *was* abandoning central planning. And, in the early years of Titoism, the wages of all these anti-Communist sins seemed to be dire economic and political difficulties (exacerbated, to be sure, by the Kremlin's propaganda and economic blockade).

But Tito's persistence, encouraged and to some extent made possible by Western aid, plus difficulties in the satellite countries resulting from the very Soviet policies Tito opposed, were not to be gainsaid. Tito was a thorn in the Kremlin's side, particularly in connection with the pursuit of new foreign policies, and he had to be dealt with. There can be no question that the existence of Titoism as a going concern forced Khrushchev to espouse publicly the Yugoslav position on "independent paths to socialism." This amounted to repudiation of the Stalin theory of Communism primarily in the interest of the Soviet Union and a declaration of approval of Communism in the interest of each individual nation. There resulted a surge of Titoism from the Baltic to the Black Sea — not so much in the formal, theoretical sense but in the sense of manifestation of a desire for more independence from Soviet tutelage, for attending to the national rather than the Soviet interest and for liberalizing the harsh, rigid nature of the totalitarian pattern.

How meaningfully the Kremlin intended its new position on relations among Communist states it is difficult to say. Certainly it was never intended to abandon Soviet hegemony in Eastern Europe. But it is clear that from the time of the Twentieth Congress of the Communist Party of the Soviet Union relations among Communist states entered a new phase, characterized by acceptance of the symbols of Titoism if nothing else. The dissolution of the Cominform, for example, may have been largely tactical, but the very act of dissolving it showed the great impact of Titoism.

The most dramatic manifestations of the new phase were the revolution in Hungary and the near-revolution in Poland, and they resulted in Moscow's hasty imposition of limits on the leeway allowed. But before it was clear that the revolution in Hungary had assumed a definitely anti-Communist orientation, the Russians indicated a willingness to go a long way toward establishing the kind of relationship with the Eastern European countries that Tito had been demanding.[1] This, too, may have been tactical, but it was clearly a reflection of the Yugoslav position. Later, Soviet insistence on "proletarian internationalism" restored bloc solidarity to its pre-Hungary position, at least on the surface. Yet the satellites still have more leeway for maneuver than formerly, if only because Moscow now feels obliged to pay more attention to their sensibilities.

Poland

Only in the case of Poland has this new situation been noticeable in the realm of East-West relations generally. There is no doubt that in the months immediately following the Polish flare-up, Gomulka sought to emulate in part — although by no means completely — the Yugoslav foreign policy position at the time, that is, a sort of "independent member" of the Soviet bloc having relations with both East and West. He appears to have been motivated by a combination of conviction and tactics involving his own domestic position, to say nothing of his position vis-à-vis Moscow. But mounting Soviet pressures for bloc conformity forced the Poles to abandon hopes of a foreign policy independent of the Kremlin. It is true that Poland maintains a relationship with the USSR somewhat different from that of the other bloc countries. Indicative of its comparative independence are its closer relations with the United States, from which it has received credits. Also, there are in Poland latent factors which could, conceivably, again spark a move away from strict adherence to "proletarian internationalism." But Soviet troops remain stationed in Poland, and the fact is that Poland is a Soviet

---

[1] In the declaration "on the principles of development and further strengthening of friendship and cooperation between the Soviet Union and other Socialist states," *Pravda*, October 31, 1956. See pp. 437–438 above.

satellite — however unreliable from Moscow's point of view — while Yugoslavia is not in any way.

The impact of Titoism on Soviet-satellite relations is inextricably tied up with its impact on the internal political developments in the satellite countries. In one way or another, every country in Eastern Europe was affected, including — although in an entirely negative way — even "darkest Albania." It should be emphasized that in no country has there been introduced anything like the Titoist system as a whole. Poland and Hungary came the closest, but while the Poles, under Gomulka, stopped considerably short of "full Titoism," the Hungarians, under Nagy, attempted to go far beyond it and, in so doing, brought on Soviet invasion.

Many of the reforms springing from the Polish crisis of 1956 bear the strong imprint of the Yugoslav system, which had been studied in detail by the Poles.[1] Stefan Jedrychowski, a member of the Politburo, complained in 1957 that "some comrades . . . are inclined to copy slavishly Yugoslav patterns." Not everything Yugoslav, he warned, is "fit for copying and transplanting"; particularly he ruled out Belgrade's decentralized price and wage system. But he added that "what is good in the Yugoslav system and what should be applied in our country are workers' councils." He also recommended Titoist ideas on profit-sharing, competition and relating local government finance to enterprise profits. These things, he said, "could find application and should therefore be considered and discussed. This is the system used in Yugoslavia."[2]

In certain liberalizations — particularly those in the realm of freedom of expression — Poland at first went faster and further than Yugoslavia. The Poles themselves were quick to claim it. In regard to "public expression of opinion, socialist parliamentarianism and the democratic division of power," boasted the Warsaw daily, *Zycie Warszawy*, on November 19, 1956, "we have moved farther away from Stalinist practice than our Yugoslav friends."

While this may have overstated the case somewhat, there was much truth in it. For the first two years after the Polish "revolution," there was constant public criticism of the regime, some of it on basic issues. The official line of the Party was that there had to be "room for discussion and for differences of views even on fundamental matters" which would manifest themselves in "various political groupings."[3] Thus, the January 1957 election in Poland

[1] For example, Czeslaw Bobrowski, deputy chairman of the Polish Economic Council, wrote one of the most thorough analyses of the Yugoslav economic system yet to be published, *La Yougoslavie Socialiste*, A. Colin, Paris, 1956.

[2] Stefan Jedrychowski, *The Fundamental Principles of Economic Policy in Industry*, Polonia, Warsaw, 1957, pp. 11–12.

[3] *Trybuna Ludu*, December 1, 1956.

was freer than either the 1955 or 1958 elections in Yugoslavia, for despite the single ticket, several parties ran candidates and a number of mild anti-Communists — particularly the Roman Catholic bloc — were elected.[1] In this period also, debate in the Polish Sejm was freer and more spirited than in the Yugoslav Skupština. Party discipline was lax to the point of non-existence, and democratic centralism was not strictly enforced. While Djilas was sentenced and re-sentenced in Belgrade, some of the same heresies he preached were being practiced in Warsaw. Gomulka, it seemed, was "out-Titoing" Tito.

Western Enthusiasm for Poland

The dramatic appearance and the comparatively wide limits of free political expression in Poland was one factor which led many in the West, and especially in the United States, who had virtually ignored the reforms in Yugoslavia, to acclaim the Polish changes with enthusiasm. There were other factors in the Poles' "good press" too. The Polish liberalization resulted to a considerable extent from popular pressure, not only in the Party but also outside it. Whereas in Yugoslavia the Titoist Communists have also shared participation in government with non-Communists, their position is firm and without serious challenge. In Poland the regime is in part dependent on a certain cooperation from the Roman Catholic Church. At the time Gomulka came to power, he appeared to strike a more anti-Soviet pose than Tito, who was then still involved in the intricate ramifications of "normalization." Thus many saw in Poland the hope for abandonment of Communism altogether or, if not that, at least they saw Poland as more of a trouble maker for Moscow than Yugoslavia seemed to be. In addition, Tito was a vivid personality whose erstwhile violent hostility to the West early made him a focus of anti-Communist sentiment, while Gomulka was a less flamboyant figure not well known in the West.

Still another factor explaining the infatuation for the Polish reforms of many who overlooked Yugoslav developments or refused to take them at their face value is that the Poles traditionally have a "more Western" orientation than the Yugoslavs and were thus better able to attract attention in the West. Moreover, Polish-Americans far outnumber Yugoslav-Americans, and while the latter are split among themselves, with the majority strongly anti-Tito, Polish groups in the United States, if they have not all supported

[1] In 1961 the election laws were tightened by reducing the number of "non-approved" candidates and arranging in advance the party composition of the Sejm and peoples' councils, regardless of the election outcome. At the same time, however, the Polish Communist Party permitted nomination of Party candidates from the floor at special electoral meetings. *New York Times,* February 6, 1961, p. 4.

Gomulka as a practical necessity, have tended to refrain from strongly criticizing him.

Regardless of the explanation, the fact is that many Western observers have appeared to exaggerate the nature of the Polish changes. In particular, they have ignored the almost complete absence in Poland of any ideological departures from the general Soviet views of Marxism, at least in the formal position of the regime.[1] Indeed, the Poles carefully emphasize that their reforms are based only on practical necessity and requirements of efficiency. Thus, lacking the theoretical underpinning of Titoism, there was from the start much more of an "NEP" tactical coloration to the reforms in Poland than to those in Yugoslavia.

Gomulka's Position

Furthermore, many Western observers have paid inadequate attention to the basic personal attitudes of Wladyslaw Gomulka himself. Not only is Gomulka not a theoretical innovator but he is opposed to theoretical innovation. Even his "nationalism" has always been couched in terms of the necessity for solidarity — ideological as well as otherwise — with the Soviet Union. Although there are Polish Communists who go along with many of the precepts of Titoism as a system, and some who go further, Gomulka is not one of them, and he has seen to it that such Polish Communists have had little real power.

Thus the comparative freedom and experimentation of the 1956–1958 period in Poland reflected Gomulka's appreciation of the political realities more than anything else. Poland, after all, had only narrowly avoided a real revolution which would likely have incurred, as it did in Hungary, Soviet armed intervention. The Party maintained its rule only by virtue of non-Communist and even anti-Communist collaboration. Within the Party, Gomulka had not consolidated his position against the Stalinists, and, meanwhile, he was dependent on the most "liberal" wing.[2] Thus the Party, badly shaken by the October events, lacked the strength to enforce con-

---

[1] See, for example, discussions by Leonid Hurwicz and Peter Wiles in Gregory Grossman (ed.), *Value and Plan: Economic Calculation and Organization in Eastern Europe*, University of California Press, Berkeley and Los Angeles, 1960. Professor Hurwicz, ignoring the Yugoslav example in his treatment of decentralized economies, sees in Poland "some form of market mechanism . . . at least ideologically, if not actually." Professor Wiles, on the other hand, pointing out that decentralized and competitive price-making was "in essence the Yugoslav model," adds that "it is not clear to what extent the Yugoslav Communists accept the ideology of it."

[2] The terms "liberal" and "conservative" and "left" and "right" in this connection can become somewhat confusing. In traditional Soviet parlance, "left" communism always meant an extremely hard-boiled type. Earlier, Gomulka was accused of "right deviation." In Poland today, "left" identifies those who favor the maximum relaxation of controls, while "right" is a term applied to the more hard-boiled Stalinists. The Yugoslavs refer to Stalinists as "conservative" Communists, a terminology apparently adopted by Khrushchev, who so identified Molotov. Yet "reactionary" means anti-Communist.

formity in the country, and Gomulka, forced to balance opposing extremists, lacked the strength to enforce conformity in the Party.

Gomulka not only kept the new freedom of political expression from producing any fundamental changes in the Polish system but by 1958 felt strong enough to curb it and draw back from some of the cautious steps toward Titoism taken in 1956. Thus, although there may be more parliamentary "debate" in Poland than in Yugoslavia, the result is the same: what the Communist Party proposes is enacted. The earlier newspaper critics of Party policy have been silenced one way or another, and by 1958 attacks on either the Polish Communist Party or the Soviet Union were beyond the pale.

Western non-Communist publications are available in a few places in Poland, but there are fewer of them and they are much harder to obtain than in Yugoslavia. By the summer of 1958, the Poles were exercising caution in issuing visas to Westerners, especially newspaper correspondents. There is no censorship of foreign newsmen's dispatches, but in the fall of 1959 the Warsaw correspondent of the *New York Times* was expelled from Poland on the charge that he was "probing too deeply" into Polish political affairs.[1]

Having defeated his Stalinist opposition, Gomulka now echoed Moscow in centering his fire on "revisionists," meaning those who favor more liberalizations or, at least, insist on maintaining the "gains of October." In 1959 some members of the Stalinist group in the Party who had fought Gomulka were brought back into the government.

Curbs on the secret police and reforms connected with arrests and trials in Poland compare favorably with those in Yugoslavia, and the Poles have yet to have an incident like that involving Milovan Djilas. Most of the liberalizations, however, stopped short of their Titoist models even in 1956 and since then have been still further curtailed. A good example is the institution of workers' councils.

Workers' Councils in Poland

One of the first demands of workers and those Communist spokesmen who supported them at the time of the 1956 crisis was for workers' councils, and many of them had already sprung up in Polish factories with no legal basis. The first Polish law on workers' councils, of November 19, 1956,[2] was primarily a recognition of an existing situation. The Polish workers' councils, even at the beginning, however, did not have the competence of those in Yugoslavia. On the vital question of wages they shared authority with the shop committee, a trade union organization and thus strongly under Party

---

[1] *New York Times*, November 13, 1959, p. 3.
[2] *Dziennik Ustaw*, No. 51, 1958, Law No. 238.

control. In certain other areas, such as social welfare, social insurance and working conditions, the shop committee had predominant influence.

The Polish law of November 19, 1956, did resemble the original Yugoslav statute setting up workers' councils. The councils were to participate in management to a considerable degree and a hierarchical arrangement was provided under which they were subordinated to higher bodies representing the government. But while the Yugoslavs quickly expanded the autonomy and powers of their workers' councils, the trend in Poland was just the opposite.

Here the lack of an independent Polish ideological approach is significant. To the Yugoslavs, workers' councils represented a step in the decentralization of authority and the "withering away of the state." Thus they were prepared for a decentralization of the whole economy, from planning to prices and wages, without which workers' councils would have meant very little. In Poland there has been some decentralization of administrative *machinery* but virtually no decentralization of *authority*. Thus from the start of the Gomulka regime there was a built-in contradiction which resulted in constant conflict between workers' councils and state power.

In the free discussion that still flourished in 1957, one Polish critic put it this way:

> If in the very near future the system of economic administration is not radically changed, workers' councils may become one more of the Stalinists' fictions, which make a pretense of the government of the masses. . . . the law on workers' councils as we read it in the *Law Gazette* impresses the reader not as an act of victory of the working masses, but as an act of self-defense of bureaucracy.[1]

Workers' councils were not established in all factories under the 1956 law. By the end of 1957, 6,647 of them were functioning throughout Poland.[2] But while the workers' councils were demanding more autonomy, Gomulka had already decided they should have less. The fact is that Gomulka never accepted the principle of worker-management. Early in 1957 he declared:

> If every factory became a kind of cooperative enterprise of the workers, all the laws governing capitalist enterprise would immediately come into effect and produce all the usual results. Central planning and administration . . . would have to disappear. . . . Prices of goods would be determined by the market . . . Every factory would determine its production independent of other factories. Investments should be dictated by the market. . . . only with a worse result than under capitalism, because a capitalist is himself the owner of the factory and can thus devote an

---

[1] "Samorzad Robotniczy w Niebezpieczenstwie" ("Worker Self-Management in Safety"). *Prosto z Mostu*, January 20, 1957.

[2] J. Kofman, "Worker Self-Government," *Polish Perspectives*, July–August 1958, p. 16.

overwhelming part of the profits to investment . . . but workers as collective owners of a factory . . . would always have a tendency to raise their earnings as much as possible, without giving thought to investment.[1]

This, of course, is by and large just what developed in Yugoslavia, but whereas the Yugoslav Communists were prepared to put up with difficulties as "the price we must pay for beginners' school,"[2] the Polish Communists were not. Poland's leading economist, Oscar Lange, chairman of the Economic Council, put it this way: "If we are to compare ours to the Yugoslav economy, there is no doubt that the model which is crystallizing in our country will be based more on centralized planning than in Yugoslavia."[3]

The first step toward curbing the power of workers' councils in Poland was the instruction to the trade union organization to fight them. Numerous recall actions were launched by shop committees. In one case, reported by the chief Party newspaper, a meeting of 70 workers voted for recall of a workers' council in a factory employing nearly 1,000 workers.[4] By the spring of 1958, Gomulka had announced plans for legislation to reduce the status of workers' councils, and the plans were enacted into law on December 20 of that year.[5] The law created a new body known as a workers' conference, consisting of the workers' council, the trade union shop committee and the executive committee of the factory Party organization, and also, in certain instances, representatives of youth, technical and scientific organizations. Thus Party control of worker-management was assured.

The workers' council was supposed to keep its own identity by electing a chairman and a presidium or executive committee, charged with preparing the agenda for conference meetings. However, such election was subject to confirmation by the whole workers' conference, which, instead of the workers' council, was given jurisdiction over organization of work, distribution of surplus income and determination of bonuses. The workers' council itself was to concentrate on methods of raising productivity, strengthening labor discipline and other supervisory activities.

Although the workers' council presidium was given a voice in the hiring and firing of factory managers, the power and authority of the managers was substantially increased. Only the manager was authorized to issue orders to workers, even in areas under the jurisdiction of the workers' conference, and, apparently, he thus has the right of veto. Where a workers' conference

[1] *Przeglad Kulturalny*, January 23, 1957.

[2] Edvard Kardelj, in *Borba*, August 14, 1954.

[3] *Some Problems Relating to the Polish Road to Socialism*, Polonia, Warsaw, 1957, p. 20.

[4] *Trybuna Ludu*, September 27, 1957.

[5] *Dziennik Ustaw*, No. 77, 1958, Law No. 397.

persisted in its opinion, the matter went to an arbitration commission to be set up by the Council of Ministers in agreement with the Central Committee of the trade union organization.

Prices and Wages

Even without this virtual abandonment of worker-managment, the centralized determination of prices, wages and investment in Poland would have prevented the workers' councils from exercising anything like the authority they have in Yugoslavia. Administration was decentralized below the level of the ministeries. Various enterprises in each type of industry were organized into "unions," which operate much in the manner of the early Soviet "trusts." Theoretically the "unions" were considered to be independent of the government, with a board consisting of managers of the affiliated enterprises, but the ministry concerned names the general manager and administers the unions' decisions. For small businesses, especially in retail trade, there was encouragement of cooperatives under the administration of local governments, which may themselves organize new enterprises. And there was some revival of privately operated craft and retail shops.

Some 80 per cent of prices and investment funds in Poland in 1959 were centrally determined — just about the reverse of the situation in Yugoslavia. There was some decentralization of planning. Unlike Yugoslavia, however, production quotas were assigned by the state to the various branches of industry and from there ultimately to individual factories. Enterprises initially prepared their own plans, reporting how much additional capital they needed. Although most investment was centrally determined through 1959, Professor Bobrowski, Lange's chief aide on the Economic Council, was hopeful that the part coming out of enterprise funds would increase in the future. Such enterprise investment was created out of profits, at central direction. The enterprise could increase its funds by borrowing at the bank,[1] but use of these investments was subject to state approval.

A major change from the pre-1956 system was that enterprise-planned profits and "over-plan" profits were no longer all siphoned off by the government. The enterprise was now allowed to keep a portion of the profits for its own uses, which might include payment of bonuses to workers. The Poles sought to get at the problem of incentive by tying disbursable profits to increases in production in each factory over the preceding year's output, not to plan fulfillment as such.

---

[1] Professor Bobrowski wrote in 1958 that "the rate of interest provides at present the check to the incurrence of excessive debts by an enterprise" ("In Search of a New Economic Blueprint," *Polish Perspectives*, May 1958, p. 7).

Local Autonomy

An integral factor of Yugoslav decentralization has been increased authority and autonomy for local government, the separation of Communist Party officials from local governing bodies and the emergence of the commune as a major economic instrumentality. In Poland numerous changes have been made in local government also, particularly under the legislation of March 25, 1958.[1] The changes did not, however, give the people's councils the power or independence of the Yugoslav people's committees. Most of the increased powers were given to the *wojewodstwo*, or province, and the *powiat*, or district, rather than to truly local units, although village representation was provided.[2] A strict hierarchical system is in effect. Each people's council is subordinate to the people's council above it. Supervising the whole system is the Council of State in Warsaw, which may dissolve any people's council found wanting. Moreover, chairmen of both provincial and district people's councils as well as their presidia, or executive apparatus, must be approved by the office of the Council of Ministers, which may issue orders directly to local government administrative officials.

The economic independence of local governments in Poland is also severely restricted. They have no authority to determine investment or wages, and a tight checkrein is kept on their activity even in fields like local construction and transportation.[3] At the same time, the area of local economic activity has been substantially expanded. In 1958, people's councils were responsible for supervising expenditures involving about 25 per cent of total industrial production. In 1959, local responsibility in these areas was expected to cover 32 per cent of investment and 25 per cent of production in the socialized sector.[4]

People's council budgets are prepared locally, but are subject to revision from above. The proportion of revenues raised locally increased from about 18 per cent in 1954 to some 30 per cent in 1959. These funds came chiefly from taxes and profits of enterprises under local jurisdiction. The persistent tendency of many of these to operate at a loss has hampered local revenue-raising operations.[5]

Another important area of comparison between Poland and Yugoslavia is agriculture. In making collective farms entirely voluntary, the Poles went as

[1] *Dziennik Ustaw*, No. 15, 1958, Law No. 67.

[2] There also exist "block committees" at the neighborhood level. While these are elected, they are in the nature of "citizen aktivs" and perform a variety of functions without government authority. Cf. Stefan Rozmaryn, *The Seym and People's Councils in Poland*, Polonia, Warsaw, 1958, pp. 81–82.

[3] These are the so-called "limits" established by the State Commission for Economic Planning. Cf. *Rada Narodowa*, No. 20, 1958, p. 6.

[4] *Ibid.* See also *Trybuna Ludu*, January 7, 1958.

[5] Cf. *Rada Narodowa*, No. 31, 1958, p. 5.

far as the Yugoslavs did, with much the same result, namely, a general exodus of peasants from the collectives. But whereas in Yugoslavia decollectivization was accompanied by a complete freeing of agriculture and a recognition of the status of the private peasant, this was not the case in Poland. Particularly important is the fact that compulsory deliveries of crops to the state at fixed prices were only reduced rather than eliminated as in Yugoslavia. The reduction of compulsory deliveries by a third in Poland meant that about 50 per cent of all farm products were sold to the state at fixed prices, with state agencies buying the other half at "market prices." The principal items under compulsory delivery at fixed prices were grain, meat and potatoes.

The Yugoslavs are confident that they can build socialism without collectivization and that socialism in the rest of the country will eventually produce socialism in agriculture. The more orthodox Gomulka has never ceased to insist that decollectivization is only a temporary expedient and that a return to collectivization is essential to the development of socialism in Poland. However, despite the fact that Gomulka's minister of agriculture is Edward Ochab, who headed the Communist Party prior to the 1956 upheaval, the regime appeared firmly resolved not to employ force.[1]

Hungary

To the extent that it contributed to the 1956 revolution, Titoism has had its most dramatic impact in Hungary. However, even before that, Titoist manifestations were evident there in the short-lived "new course" introduced by Imre Nagy when he first became premier in 1953. Nagy stressed national independence and "different roads" to socialism as well as broader participation of "the working masses in theory and government."[2] And he made moderate efforts aimed at easing collectivization, limiting Party control, curbing police abuses and widening the area of free expression.[3]

Nagy, however, never held real power, because the Communist Party remained in the hands of Rákosi and his Stalinist henchmen. It is, of course, impossible to test the Yugoslav thesis that had Nagy not been ousted in 1955 and his reforms curtailed, the 1956 revolution would not have occurred. The reasoning is not unpersuasive, however, and the replacement of Rákosi by Gerö indicates an attempt to find a "Titoist solution" to Hungarian unrest,

---

[1] This resolve was not popular with all Polish Communists. See, for example, report on the Congress of the Polish United Workers (Communist) Party in the *New York Times*, March 15, 1959, p. 21.

[2] See Imre Nagy, *Imre Nagy on Communism: In Defense of the New Course*, Praeger, New York, 1957.

[3] Cf. F. Fejto, *Behind the Rape of Hungary*, David McKay Co., New York, 1957, pp. 97–101.

despite Tito's opinion that "Gerö differed in no way from Rákosi." When Gerö visited Yugoslavia just before the revolution, the Hungarian Communist newspaper *Szabad Nep* stressed the opportunity to study at first hand "the working of democracy in Yugoslav enterprises, the workers' councils and the problems of independence for enterprises, which interests us very much."[1]

In the Hungarian revolution itself, especially the first part, Yugoslav influence was clear. The whole rationale of the nationalist Communists was indisputably Titoist, that is, to strengthen the system by stressing independence and instituting reforms under the guiding hand of a liberalized Communist Party. And Janos Kadar, whom Soviet forces installed in power after their second intervention, was reported to have told an Italian journalist that his regime was "Hungarian national Communism," meaning "Marxism-Leninism applied to the particular requirements of our country."[2]

One of the first moves of the Hungarian revolutionists, even before the initial Soviet intervention, was the creation of workers' councils in many Hungarian factories by the workers themselves. This move proved so popular that, after the revolution had been crushed, the Kadar government not only legalized workers' councils but, in numerous official government and Party statements toward the end of 1956, appeared to be emphasizing them. For example, Kadar spoke of workers' councils as "fundamental institutions of people's democracy" and placed on their shoulders the task of solving problems of management.[3] These Hungarian workers' councils of 1956 had broad powers, not unlike those in Yugoslavia.

The post-revolutionary government in Hungary, however, made even less of a gesture than the Gomulka regime toward undertaking the economic and political decentralization that is essential for meaningful workers' councils. The result was that by June of 1957, Kadar was stressing the importance of central direction and talking of supervision of workers' councils by trade unions. Soon thereafter, it was officially denied that workers' councils were fundamental to a people's democracy.[4] And on November 17, 1957, workers' councils were ordered abolished.[5] Their place was taken by a new body known as a shop council. Only one-third of the members of the shop council was elected by the workers; the other two-thirds was named by the factory

[1] Quoted in *East Europe*, March 1959, p. 20.

[2] Report of interview with Kadar by Bruno Tedeschi, *Il Giornale d'Italia*, November 2, 1956, For English translation, see M. J. Lasky (ed.), *The Hungarian Revolution*, Praeger, New York, 1957, pp. 177–178.

[3] *Nepakarat*, December 12, 1956.

[4] Cf. *Nepszabadsag*, June 28, 1957, and *Nepakarat*, June 30, 1957.

[5] By a two-line Edict (No. 63) of the Republic Presidium.

trade union organization, known as the shop committee, whose president also headed the shop council. Ex-officio members included the secretaries of Party and Party youth organizations as well as the chief management officials. The shop council had wide jurisdiction but very little power, and it met only four times a year.

Another spontaneous action growing out of the Hungarian revolt was the dissolution of nearly two-thirds of the collective farms, as a result of which some 110,000 families repossessed more than 1,250,000 acres. Although the Kadar regime soon attacked this problem, it did so at first by using persuasion and financial incentives and permitting establishment of agricultural co-operatives with a less stringent form of organization than the *kolkhoz*. In less than a year, almost half of the collective farms that had been dissolved during the revolution were reorganized. In the fall of 1958, the Communist hierarchy ordered a new collectivization drive. By the spring of 1959, the government, calling for total collectivization of agriculture, declared that more than 49 per cent of Hungary's arable land had been socialized since the drive began.[1] Although the Hungarian press itself reported instances of coercion of peasants,[2] Hungarian officials insisted that there was no forced collectivization and that they were "not fools enough to repeat the mistakes made before 1956."[3]

Despite these departures from Titoist patterns, the impact of the revolution was not totally erased as far as relaxations were concerned. The easing of police controls could be in no way compared to that in Poland, for example, but at the same time there was more respect for legality than in the earlier period. Furthermore, the Kadar regime did decentralize its administration, abolishing nearly a third of the central ministries in Budapest and scaling down the top-heavy bureaucracy by some 25 per cent.[4] The economic lot of the average citizen was eased by a reduced emphasis on heavy industry and — as a deliberate effort to calm political passions — an increase in the supply of consumer goods, in part through large imports from the Soviet Union.

The Other Eastern European Satellites

Except for Poland and Hungary, the influence of Titoism in the other Eastern European satellites was more psychological than institutional. There was no evidence anywhere else of agitation for "independent paths to social-ism" or of "nationalist" strength in the other Communist parties. The

---

[1] *New York Times*, April 17, 1959, p. 4, and September 28, p. 4.

[2] See, for example, *Elet es Irodalom*, March 6, 1959, p. 5 and March 13, p. 3.

[3] *New York Times*, April 17, 1959, p. 4. By February 1960, however, it was claimed that 70 per cent of arable land had been collectivized. *Ibid.*, February 15, 1960, p. 4.

[4] *East Europe*, August 1958, p. 31.

Bulgarians and the Rumanians slavishly followed the Moscow line in the new campaign against Yugoslavia, and the Czechs, spearheading the attack, were critical even of incomplete conformity in Poland.

Except in Albania, a "thaw" of sorts did occur. Instances of unrest among intellectuals and student groups in Czechoslovakia and — to a much lesser extent — in Bulgaria produced some slight increases in the area of permitted expression rather than a crackdown. Prior to the new anti-Yugoslav campaign in 1958, in these countries, as well as in Rumania and East Germany, there was public discussion of workers' councils, although only the East German regime actually adopted them — giving them an entirely advisory capacity, divorced from management. Other evidences of change in Czechoslovakia, Rumania and Bulgaria were mild reforms in criminal codes and varying degrees of decentralization in economic administration. But collectivization efforts in these countries as well as in East Germany were stepped up, with the process nearly 100 per cent complete in Bulgaria and more than 90 per cent complete in Czechoslovakia by the end of 1959.

Three conclusions suggest themselves as a result of a comparative view of Eastern European Communism. One is that national differences do manifest themselves. A second is that, save for Poland in limited degree, post-Stalin reforms in none of these countries approached even the direction of those in Yugoslavia. The dictatorship is probably tightest in Czechoslovakia although most obvious in Bulgaria, where — at least in Sofia — police armed with tommy guns guarded the streets as late as 1958. But if one compares Czechoslovakia and Bulgaria with Rumania and Hungary, the extent of totalitarianism does not seem to differ essentially. The third conclusion is that apparently the "Western-ness" and cultural development of a country do not have much to do with the severity of the dictatorship that comes with Communism. Czechoslovakia, which has the most hard-boiled regime in many ways, is the most "Western" and most advanced. And while Yugoslavia may be more advanced and in certain aspects even more "Western" than Bulgaria and Rumania, Western influences and cultural development are certainly less pronounced in Yugoslavia than in Poland, considering the nation as a whole, or even in Hungary, as far as some aspects of Hungarian society are concerned. It is an interesting and perplexing paradox.

The USSR

Except for Poland, the "thaw" in the satellites seems to have produced even less melting than in the Soviet Union. And without denying the influence of Titoism as such, it is likely that many of the changes in the satellites reflect instead the Soviet "thaw" rather than a direct impact from Yugoslavia.

What caused the Soviet "thaw"? Clearly the pressure for it had been building up for some time, and the death of Stalin permitted a new orientation in which changes could come rather rapidly. In Belgrade, however, it is fashionable to consider that there has been a direct Titoist impact also on Soviet domestic policies. Yugoslav Communists point not only to the general relaxation of totalitarianism in the USSR but more specifically to the sweeping curbs on the MVD, the decentralization of economic administration, the elimination of machine tractor stations and the institution of the permanent production council, a Party-union-management *troika* in the factory to advise on problems of planning and operation.

There is some evidence to bear them out. Soviet economists made more than a passing study of the Yugoslav system between 1956 and 1958. The chief of a Soviet trade union delegation in Belgrade in April 1958 declared: "We have seriously studied the system of workers' self-management and the system of workers' wages in Yugoslav enterprises. We received the impression that workers' self-management had absolutely justified its existence."[1] And in September 1958 an article in the Soviet journal *Problems of Economics* treated the Yugoslav economic system rather objectively, in some detail and not without understanding.[2]

However, many if not most similarities between the Soviet innovations and Titoism are more apparent than real. The Soviet administrative decentralization has resulted in virtually no decentralization of government authority, and the central planning apparatus is, if anything, strengthened. The economy is still rigidly directed from the center, even if administered regionally. There have been no inroads on the principle of one-man rule in the factories. Moscow continues to insist that collectivization of agriculture is essential to socialism. Above all, there have been no ideological concessions whatever to Titoism — if one excepts the limited agreement to "independent paths to socialism" — and Yugoslav ideas on "withering away of the state" are derided by the Kremlin. Curbs on the police and emphasis on legality clearly reflect Soviet requirements almost entirely rather than Titoist influence.

And yet, if the Yugoslavs tend to exaggerate their influence, the Russians tend to underestimate it. *Izvestia* scoffed at *Ekonomska Politika* when this sprightly Yugoslav journal suggested that Moscow was guided by Titoist concepts in connection with decentralization.[3] Asked about the relationship between Soviet and Yugoslav developments, an official of the Soviet Academy

[1] V. S. Retivoi, quoted in *Borba*, April 6, 1958.

[2] V. Zolotarev and V. Pekshev, *Problems of Economics*, September 1958, pp. 62–68. This journal, consisting of English translations from Moscow's *Voprosy Ekonomiki*, is published in New York City.

[3] *Izvestia*, August 10, 1958.

of Sciences referred one of the present authors to "the Russian proverb which says, 'The tail does not wag the dog.' " But Yugoslavia is not a tail, and it has for some years now demonstrated its ability to move quite independently, often to the discomfiture of the Kremlin. The question is not whether the USSR copies Yugoslavia but whether, in moving toward new directions on its own, the Yugoslav departures — and the Yugoslav criticism — may not have had some effect. The evidence that they did is circumstantial, but there is a lot of it.

Marxists in Other Countries

Among Western Marxists outside the Soviet bloc, Titoism has attracted attention but thus far has exerted little discernible influence. While it has stimulated the sympathetic interest of numerous uncommitted intellectuals, generally speaking it is "too Communist" for the doctrinaire socialists and "too socialist" for the doctrinaire Communists. The Yugoslavs have established good relations with the mildly socialist Scandinavians, but little seems to have come out of it except an exchange of views. Certain persons in the left wing of the British Labor Party were earlier attracted to the Yugoslav experiments, but Belgrade's hard-boiled handling of such matters as the Djilas case was too much for most of them. The Yugoslavs themselves hardly recognize the French Socialists as such, and the French Communists have been among the most strident in their condemnation of Titoism. The League of Communists perhaps has better relations with Togliatti and the Italian Communists than with any other Communist Party. As badly split as is the American Communist Party, Yugoslav ideas as such do not seem to have made headway there either. The Norman Thomas-type socialists find too little political freedom in Yugoslavia, and, while that does not seem to bother a Marxist like Paul Sweezy, oriented toward the Third International but strictly independent of Party, Sweezy objects to Titoism on practical and technical economic grounds, much like the Pole Bobrowski.[1]

Underdeveloped Areas

Titoism may be having a significant impact on the new, underdeveloped nations of Asia and Africa. For both political and economic reasons, the Yugoslavs have sought to extend their influence to these areas, and also, more recently, to Latin America.[2] They have succeeded in establishing par-

[1] See Paul Sweezy's article, "The Yugoslav Experiment," *Monthly Review*, March 1958, pp. 362–374.

[2] The meeting in Belgrade in the late summer of 1961 of representatives of twenty-seven nations for a "Conference of Non-Aligned Countries," called largely on Yugoslav initiative, was an impressive example of Titoist activity of this sort.

ticularly close relations with India, Egypt, Indonesia and Burma. Since these countries had begun to follow a foreign policy of nonalignment on their own initiative, they had a natural affinity with Yugoslavia, which encouráges them by example and advice.

Furthermore, these and other underdeveloped countries have demonstrated socialist tendencies in varying degrees, while showing opposition to Soviet-type Communism. The Yugoslavs, again by advice and example, have helped strengthen these tendencies. Tito has made two extensive tours of the under-developed countries of Asia and Africa, and the leaders of many of them have come to Yugoslavia.[1] Hardly a week goes by without at least a Yugoslav mission of some sort in some of the underdeveloped nations and without a delegation from one or more of them in Yugoslavia. Vice President Kardelj was invited to Egypt in 1960 to advise the Nasser government on its economic and social problems. At the same time, the Federal Executive Council loaned Leon Geršković, one of its top administrative experts, as an adviser to the government of Ethiopia. In Ghana on a trade union mission, Vukmanović-Tempo signed a declaration stating that "the road toward social progress and happiness that leads to lasting peace can be secured only by means of a Marxist, Socialist policy adapted to the concrete needs of a country."[2]

Probably the strongest Yugoslav influence is noticeable in India and Egypt. Despite their different personalities and backgrounds, Tito and Nehru get along well, and the latter has displayed great interest in Yugoslav political and economic developments. Tito regularly gives Nehru informal advice on Soviet and Eastern European affairs, and some observers credit Tito and Kardelj with having persuaded Nehru to commit his Congress party formally to socialism. At the same time, Yugoslavs believe that Titiosm has also had an influence on the confused Indian Communist Party, which, traditionally, has contained some "moderate" and "nationalist" elements.

Associations with Egypt have been furthered not only by similarity in foreign policies and a close personal relationship between Tito and Nasser but also by the efforts of the Yugoslav Moslem community. The Yugoslavs feel that they have had a moderating effect on Nasser's tendency to extreme action and have helped him avoid getting too ensnared in his dealings with Moscow.[3] Nasser visited Yugoslavia four times, three times to meet with Tito and Nehru

---

[1] Tito's propensity for travel is the target of some amusement among the Yugoslav people. A story often told concerns one Yugoslav who asked another if he thought the moon were inhabited. "Positively not," said the second Yugoslav. Asked how he could be so sure, he said: "If there were people on the moon, certainly President Tito would have traveled there."

[2] *New York Times*, November 27, 1960, p. 25.

[3] The Yugoslavs repeatedly advised the United States informally that Nasser would be a bulwark against Soviet penetration of the Arab world if only he were not forced into the Kremlin's arms by Western policies.

and once, in 1958, alone on a state visit; and Tito made three trips to Egypt. Each apparently tried to outdo the other in extending a warm welcome. When Tito was in Cairo in 1959, the foreign editor of *Borba* reported that the spectacle of hundreds of thousands of people chanting "Ti-to, Ti-to" gave him the feeling of being at a mass meeting at home. Present at another occasion, when Nasser initiated a land reform in Damascus, Tito declared that "this great and significant act . . . leads to social democracy."[1] Thousands of copies of the Program of the League of Communists in Arabic were distributed in the United Arab Republic, and in honor of Tito's 1959 visit Nasser's information office published a book entitled *Yugoslavia and Positive Neutrality*.

Sukarno of Indonesia and U Nu of Burma have also been intrigued by Yugoslav ideas. Although the Yugoslavs have claimed no special credit, it was after his visit to Yugoslavia that Sukarno embarked on a program of "guided democracy," a term not altogether inapplicable to Titoism.

It should be noted that not all the Yugoslavs' interest in courting the underdeveloped countries is political. They also see them as customers for their increasing production of industrial goods. Although such trade is limited by the fact that new nations often do not have what Belgrade needs most, Yugoslavia is in the market for things like cotton and other fibers, coffee, sugar, cocoa and tropical fruits. Yugoslav trade interest in Asia and Africa is stimulated by fears that economic integration in Western Europe increases the difficulties of breaking into that market.

At the same time, like good materialists, the Yugoslavs feel that close economic relations bring close political relations. In Latin America, for example, only Mexico, Brazil, Argentina, Uruguay and Chile had official diplomatic ties with Yugoslavia in 1959. New trade relations were expected to bring a further exchange of ambassadors. Interestingly enough, Foreign Minister Popović, and also a Yugoslav trade group, visited Castro's Cuba in 1960, several months ahead of Anastas Mikoyan, and discussed long-term economic and technical cooperation. Earlier, a Cuban goodwill mission came to Belgrade, issuing a statement praising Yugoslavia's "deep sympathy" for the Cuban revolution.[2]

The Yugoslavs, like the Russians, are convinced that all roads lead to socialism in some form or other. They are hopeful that their independent and more moderate brand of Communism will show the new nations that nationalism and Marxism can mix. To the extent that they are right, some in the West profess to see in Tito's influence more of a menace than in the

---

[1] *Borba*, February 25, 1959.

[2] *New York Times*, August 22, 1959, p. 3.

Soviet influence. Others, however, who see the great underdeveloped parts of the world gripped by revolutionary nationalism with socialist overtones regardless of anybody's influence, hope that Tito's impact will be greater than Moscow's[1] and should, even, be encouraged rather than discouraged.

[1] Whether it will be or not, Tito's interest in the underdeveloped countries has not made the Kremlin happy, and on at least one occasion it has been sharply attacked by a member of the Presidium of the Central Committee of the Soviet Communist Party. (See *Borba*, February 6, 1959.) Even before this, Yugoslavia had been attacked by the Communist Party of Syria and Lebanon. Pinning the responsibility on Moscow, the Yugoslavs retorted that "such immoral acts . . . cannot compromise anyone but their perpetrators." Cf. Dragon Stojiljković, "A Fore-doomed Venture," *Review of International Affairs*, October 15, 1958, pp. 5–7.

PART VI

PROBLEMS OF

TITOISM

PROBLEMS OF A

CHANGING

PEASANT SOCIETY

THE Yugoslav "road to socialism" is producing a social and economic revolution in the country that appears to have a momentum all its own. It is reflected particularly in the changing structure of the population, in the spectacle of a peasant society in flux.

The most visible aspect of the change is the dramatic decrease in the agrarian population. Between 1921 and 1938, it dropped from 78.9 per cent of the total to 74.9 per cent. By 1960, it was down to 50 per cent. This steep decline in the number of people deriving their major income from agriculture brought about rapid changes in the peasant society. With increasing industrialization and greater use of modern agricultural techniques, the old way of life was disappearing. Relations between the peasants and the socialist state created new problems for both — the break-up of the once close-knit family structure; the large number of new industrial workers with little or no education or training; the peasant-worker who has abandoned agriculture but not the village; the utilization of increased mechanization, modernization and cooperative methods by independent landowners unaccustomed to modern farming practices.

The shift to nonagricultural employment is gradually solving the old Yugoslav problem of surplus agrarian labor. In the early 1950's, three and a half million persons or 35 per cent of the total population employed in agriculture were considered surplus. In 1958 there were four million more people in nonagricultural occupations than in 1938, but during the same period the agricultural population declined by nearly two million. This shift to nonagricultural employment is reflected in a rapidly increasing demand for foodstuffs and consumer goods and a slow but steady urbanization of the population.

Changing Structure of the Economy

The institutions characteristic of a peasant society are the family household and the village community. The whole concept of a peasant society meant "that the family should have control of sufficient land to supply its daily needs, and that the land should be cultivated by the members of the family with the minimum of outside help."[1]

By these standards, the Yugoslav peasant society had already lost some of its essential features by the outbreak of World War II. Generally speaking, the change was greatest in the northwestern parts of the country, and least in the south and in the less accessible parts of the interior Dinaric mountain core. Whereas in the past the peasant family tended to be economically self-contained and consumed all that was raised on its land, by 1939 an average of one-third of the personal income of peasant households was being spent in the market economy; and one-fifth of the food, something over one-third of the fuel and lighting, and two-thirds of the clothing and footwear had to be supplied by the market.

Changes were accelerated during and after World War II. The most important developments were the nationalization of all manufacturing, transportation, banking, and domestic and foreign trade enterprises; the confiscation of considerable private property; a reduction in the size of landholdings, and the distribution of the relatively small surplus among landless peasants and peasants moving to the fertile plains from the mountainous regions.

Top priority was at first given to industrialization of the country, and production increased 3.4 times between 1938 and 1958, and was 2.9 times higher in 1958 than in 1947 (Table 16-4). The one-sided emphasis on capital goods production changed gradually after 1954, the new Five Year Plan of 1957–1961 bringing a shift in policy. Major emphasis in economic planning was now placed on a more balanced economic growth, with investments in agriculture assuming a much more important role and consumer goods receiving a higher priority in over-all industrial production.

The results of this program since about 1956–1957 have been visible in the whole economic growth and structure of the country. The relative prosperity was greatly enhanced by the surprising success in agricultural production in 1957, 1959 and again in 1960. The rapid development of the country was accompanied by inflationary tendencies which remained a danger. But instead of restricting the already low level of personal consumption, the regime met it by emphasizing increased production, increased imports (even

[1] Ruth Trouton, *Peasant Renaissance in Yugoslavia, 1900–1950*, Routledge & Kegan Paul, Ltd., London, 1952, p. 3.

where this meant a greater balance of payments deficit), and higher labor productivity. Real wages have risen, and with them the standard of living, first among the urban population and then among the peasantry.

The problem of increased productivity is of special importance. While the average rate of production rose 8.8 per cent between 1952 and 1960, data available show that output per man-hour in individual enterprises was responsible for an average increase of 4.8 per cent, with structural changes in the economy and the influx of surplus workers accounting for an increase of 4 per cent. A more rapid change from the hourly wage basis to a productive bonus and piecework system was intended to provide greater incentives. The raising of labor productivity is basic to an improvement in the general standard of living and has become more urgent with the increasingly close integration of the Yugoslav economy with those of foreign countries.

The whole economy, meanwhile, has undergone remarkable structural changes. These are indicated by the contributions of various industries to the national income (in per cent):

	1939	1956	1959
Manufacturing and mining	26.8	43.5	42.0
Agriculture	44.3	29.3	29.2
Others (forestry, transport, construction, commerce, etc.)	28.9	27.2	28.8

National per capita income greatly increased, from $115 in 1939 to $278 in 1958, while net investments increased from 4 per cent of the national income in 1939 to an average of 23 per cent during 1957–1959. Table 22–1 summarizes the major economic changes since the low of 1952.

Table 22–1

SELECTED INDICATORS OF ECONOMIC CHANGES, 1957, 1959 AND 1960 ESTIMATES
(Index Numbers of Volume: 1952 = 100)

	1957	1959	1960 Plan[a]
Gross national product	176	210	227
Industrial output	189	237	270
Capital goods	193	250	295
Intermediate goods	187	234	269
Consumer goods	196	241	269
Output per worker in manufacturing	123	131	140
Agricultural output	185	219	212
Gross fixed investment	160	197	215
Personal consumption	158	202	216
Exports	164	211	252
Imports	165	184	206

Source: United Nations, *Economic Survey of Europe in 1959*, Geneva, 1960, Chapter 1, p. 21.
[a] *Službeni List*, No. 52, December 30, 1959, "The 1960 Federal Social Plan."

While Yugoslavia is still engaged in creating some of the essential pre-conditions for a modern industrial development — transportation, irrigation and soil improvements, agricultural storage and processing facilities, to mention only a few — the increasing economic activity has left its imprint on most parts of the country. It must be remembered that many of the economic activities which were carried on in most Western European countries during the nineteenth century or even earlier have been undertaken in Yugoslavia only since the war. The divergent historical backgrounds of the various regions of the country help explain this lag. For instance, large-scale irrigation and land improvements were started but a few years ago. Similarly, a unified approach to the building of roads and railways did not occur in Yugoslavia until after 1938.

Problems of the Underdeveloped Regions

The Yugoslav's struggle for economic development has faced special problems connected with the marked differences between the developed and underdeveloped regions of the country. The problems are not only economic; they are political as well, and this aspect is dealt with in the following chapter.

Per capita income in the underdeveloped regions is far below the Yugoslav average. Macedonia and Bosnia and Herzegovina fall below the average by 30 per cent; Montenegro and the autonomous region of Kosovo-Metohija, by 50 per cent. Differences between districts are even greater: the per capita income in the most advanced district is ten times that in the least developed. Differences of this order are not uncommon between individual communes within republics.

Vice President Mijalko Todorović in 1959 called "the gradual correction of this imbalance one of the nation's most important problems." The regime has been attempting to achieve gradual correction by allocating from the general investment fund and other federal sources funds for key industrial projects, irrigation and drainage development, and public services in Macedonia, Montenegro, Kosovo-Metohija and, before 1957, Bosnia and Herzegovina. Industrial investment in the underdeveloped republics was 21 per cent of the total in 1949, 38.5 per cent in 1953, 19.3 per cent in 1957, 21.2 per cent in 1958 and 25 per cent in 1960. (See Table 16–13).[1] Todorović declared that the 1960 figure was "probably near the limit of allocations for these purposes."[2]

[1] Jugoslovenska Investiciona Banka, *Investicije 1947–1958*, Belgrade, 1959 and communication from Bank, April 5, 1960.

[2] Mijalko Todorović, *Current Problems of Economic Policy: Report to Second Plenary Meeting of the Central Committee of the League of Communists*, November 18–19, 1959, Jugoslavija, Belgrade, 1959, p. 30.

The trouble has been that the more advanced republics consider the limit too high while the less advanced ones do not consider it high enough. The dispute has been a long-continuing one, to which there appears to be no easy solution. The government's decision that it must build up the backward areas, not only in human terms but also in political and economic terms, was understandable. The problem lies in the fact that the burden for such development has to be borne by the more advanced regions, while they, in turn, are more advanced only in a comparative sense and have a strong and natural desire for progress of their own. If to the people of Macedonia, for example, economic betterment means advancement to the level of Croatia and Slovenia, for the people of these republics economic betterment means advancement to the level of Western Europe. In a country as comparatively poor as Yugoslavia, both goals cannot be achieved simultaneously.

From an economic point of view, there has been the problem whether the country as a whole, including the backward areas, could be built up faster by permitting the more advanced republics to surge ahead first and then aid the poorer republics, or whether economic development in the advanced republics should be restricted in the immediate interest of the backward ones. The Slovenes and Croats have argued that if the regime would permit them to surge forward unchecked for a time, they soon could give even more aid to the backward republics. They contend that the drain on their resources is affecting the initiative of their peoples and that a large portion of the funds they provide — through the federal treasury — are being dissipated by mismanagement, waste, inefficiency and economically questionable projects. Many Croats and Slovenes have feared that instead of the backward republics being brought up to their level, they would be brought down to the level of the backward republics.

Regardless of the merit of these economic arguments, other factors are involved. The whole country has been a victim of the psychology of rising expectations. It is not only the Slovenes and Croats who have differences with the leadership on investment matters, but also the Macedonians, the Montenegrins and others. Whereas the former want to contribute less, the latter want to receive more.

That the underdeveloped regions have great economic potentialities is clear. They are rich, in varying degrees, in natural resources such as minerals, water power, forests and good agricultural land. Bosnia and Herzegovina, for example, contains 90 per cent of Yugoslavia's iron ore, 50 per cent of the lignite, 33 per cent of the timber and 28 per cent of the potential water power. The possibilities of expanding tobacco and cotton production in Macedonia, once adequate draining and irrigation have been provided, are great. Bauxite, coal and lead mining can be developed in Montenegro, where possibilities for land reclamation also exist. Kosovo-Metohija has coal reserves, and its Trepča mines, Europe's largest lead-zinc deposits, can be enlarged. The density of population in Kosmet makes possible numerous small-sized industries and handicrafts which, with modernization of agriculture, could bring new hope to this most backward of Yugoslav regions.

At the same time, representatives of the underdeveloped republics often have eyes bigger than their economic stomach. A 1959 study, for example, declared that if Yugoslavia were to invest about 500 billion dinars in manufacturing, agriculture and roads in Macedonia, such capital formation would result in a per capita national income in that republic equal to the 1953 level of Slovenia.[1] Total gross investment in 1959 amounted to 701 billion dinars, of which Macedonia had 40 billion (App. Table 16–1). Available investment funds would have to be completely committed for several years to this one republic for such an undertaking.

However, considerable economic progress has already been achieved in the backward areas as a result of federal investment funds. In Macedonia, for example, the Mavrovo hydroelectric power development has been completed; in Skoplje, a big engineering plant, several large textile mills and a chrome plate and alloy factory, to mention only the most important projects. In Montenegro, the Nikšić iron and steel plant has been put up, the port of Bar has been developed and a railroad constructed between Bar and Titograd (the first step toward a rail linking Belgrade to the Mediterranean). The impact of these developments can be seen in the industrial production indices: with 1939 as 100, the 1958 figures were 879 for Montenegro, 686 for Macedonia and 345 for Yugoslavia as a whole. Though it constitutes only a small beginning, this progress has enabled the backward republics to contribute more to their own development.

Not all the underdeveloped regions in Yugoslavia, it should be remembered, are in the underdeveloped republics. Each of the more advanced republics has one or more economically depressed area which it must develop in the main without federal aid. Among them are areas which suffered the heaviest fighting during the war, such as Lika in Croatia. While the federal government assisted these republics at various times, no long-term plan has been worked out, and on the whole the responsibility has remained with the individual republics and districts. Federal officials have severely criticized local authorities in the more advanced republics for their neglect and "insufficient under-

---

[1] Ivo Vinski, "National Product and Fixed Assets in the Territory of Yugoslavia, 1909–1958," *Sixth Conference, International Association for Research in Income and Wealth*, August 1959, p. 31 (mimeographed paper).

standing and use of their own resources" in assisting underdeveloped areas within their respective territories.[1]

Given all these factors, as well as the critical political issue of national particularism, Tito has counseled a middle-of-the-road policy "bearing in mind the interests of the whole community" and at the same time not letting the standard of living stagnate in the more advanced republics while raising it in the underdeveloped ones.[2] A part of this policy involves increased federal assistance to encourage greater local initiative, including financial contributions. The emphasis has been on the building of new industrial centers and more small and medium-sized enterprises employing fewer than 250 people and based on local resources.

Changes in the Social Structure

Industrialization, with its sharp decline in the agricultural population and resulting changes in the internal structure of the family, has raised some important social problems. The size of the Yugoslav family decreased from an average of 5.1 members in 1921 to 4.25 in 1953. In Croatia, where the family averaged 8.4 members in 1857, it declined to 3.8 in 1953, and in Serbia and Slovenia from 7.0 and 8.5 respectively in 1910 to 3.0 and 3.6 in 1953. The large rural family has been giving way to the small urban family, a trend accelerated by further fragmentation of land holdings and the decline of the self-sufficient farm unit. Also, as two-horse traction replaced the use of several pairs of oxen and the use of cows for plowing gave way to tractors with multi-purpose attachments, there was less need for large families in order to farm a given piece of land.[3]

The exodus from the farm is likely to increase. Already it exceeds the needs of the economy, with resulting unemployment, averaging 151,633 persons in 1959. Part of the reason for the unemployment is that a high percentage of those from the village lack industrial skills and training.

A good example of how an economic revolution produces a social revolution is seen in the changed role of women. As is usual in peasant societies, the position of women in Yugoslavia was an inferior one, particularly in areas under Moslem culture. The demands of industrialization, the changing structure of the family, and increased education have done more to "liberate" women than Communist propaganda and laws. Wives and single women

---

[1] Todorović, *op. cit.*, p. 31.

[2] Josip Broz Tito, *Concluding Speech at the Second (Special) Plenum of the Central Committee of the League of Communists*, November 18–19, 1959, Jugoslovija, Belgrade, 1959, pp. 13–14.

[3] Rudolf Bićanić, "Occupational Heterogeneity of Peasant Families in the Period of Accelerated Industrialization," *Third World Congress of Sociology*, Vol. IV, 1956, 2d book, p. 81.

working on a basis of equality with men became the rule rather than the exception in towns and cities, and if in the villages the life of women was difficult compared with Western standards, it had still improved distinctly. Women furnished 23.5 per cent of the total labor force in 1952 and 27 per cent in 1958. Of those seeking employment in 1959 women comprised from 50 to 55 per cent, with the percentage higher in the developed than in the underdeveloped regions.

The opening up of job opportunities in newly built industries and the extreme shortage of houses in the cities have produced the phenomenon of the peasant-worker, who works in a factory but lives on the farm.[1] Preliminary 1960 data showed that 19.3 per cent of the total labor force living on private farms are permanently employed outside their households and an additional 9.3 per cent have occasional outside employment. The largest percentage with permanent outside employment was in Slovenia (28) and the smallest in Bosnia and Herzegovina (13.7). Of those with occasional outside employment, the range was from 12 per cent in Bosnia and Herzegovina to 5.3 per cent in Montenegro. The peasant-worker arrangement permits families with small holdings to maintain their standard of living and those with larger holdings to improve their property with non-farm income. The large number of peasant-workers creates problems, however. Many workers in some areas had to spend considerable time and effort commuting to their place of employment; for example, in Zagreb in 1957 10 per cent of those employed lived outside the city and traveled distances up to 50 km, and 62 per cent of the commuters traveled between 10 and 30 km.[2] In Belgrade 9 per cent of the total number of employed commuted daily, with 20 per cent of the commuters covering a distance of over 50 km and 52 per cent between 10 and 30 km. Railways, buses and bicycles are the principal means of transport. The largest number of commuters is to be found in Bosnia and Herzegovina, with 30 per cent of the employed traveling several hours daily. Commuting such distances has a deleterious effect on productivity, especially where transportation facilities are crowded or a substantial amount of time must be spent in walking to reach rail or bus transportation or in bicycling all the way to work.

Another problem created by the peasant-worker is absenteeism. During the harvest season a worker will often prefer to help the family rather than work in the factory. If he feels that he has earned enough extra income, he

---

[1] For a discussion of the peasant-worker problem, see Cvetko Kostić, *Seljači Industriski Radnici* (*Peasant Industrial Workers*), Rad, Belgrade, 1955.

[2] For a discussion of the commuting problem in Zagreb see Stanko Žuljić, "O Dnevnim Kretanjima Radne Snage u Zagrebu" ("About the Daily Movement of the Labor Force in Zagreb"), *Geografski Glasnik*, 1957, pp. 135–147; see also *Statistički Bilten*, No. 101.

will discontinue outside work entirely. Moreover, the fact that the peasant-worker spends so much time in commuting leaves him no free time for professional self-advancement, for attending evening school and participating in commune activities.

Both local authorities and enterprises are making efforts to improve transportation — for example, by providing factory buses and constructing connecting roads between the main highways and the rural communities — and to provide housing close to industrial concentrations or on the outskirts of cities. Both long-term and short-term solutions are urgent as a greater number of farm people are continually being attracted to factory work.

As industries spread and adequate housing becomes available in the cities, more and more family members who are employed in nonagricultural pursuits will move to towns, further breaking the strong family ties. On the other hand, if Slovenia and certain parts of Croatia are taken as examples, many workers ultimately will want to own small family plots even though they move closer to their place of employment.

Urbanization of the Population

Industrialization brings about urbanization, but the two phenomena are by no means coextensive. Urbanization has developed slowly in Yugoslavia; it is still one of the least urbanized countries of Europe, even though the urban population has increased considerably during the postwar years. Between 1947 and 1949 there was a net movement from rural to urban settlements of 380,000 annually, and between 1953 and 1957, 170,000 annually; but between 1950 and 1952, at the height of the post-Cominform economic recession, roughly 240,000 people returned to the villages. Urbanization increased rapidly between 1945 and 1953, a period of heavy internal migrations; there were 1.3 million internal migrants between the two census years 1948 and 1953, about 25 per cent of whom settled in towns.[1]

In 1953, 28.2 per cent of Yugoslavia's population was considered urbanized, but great differences existed between the different regions. In Slovenia it was 39.5 per cent, in Croatia 23.3 per cent and in Kosmet 18.7 per cent. According to 1960 estimates, 36 per cent of the total population was urbanized.[2]

Urbanization has brought its own social problems. Perhaps the most pressing of these has been housing. Crowded living conditions have often made for low morale and in some cases even posed a hazard to health. It has

[1] Miloš Macura, *Stanovništvo i Radna Snaga kao Činioci Privrednog Razvoja Jugoslavije* (*Population and Labour-Force as Factors of Economic Development of Yugoslavia*), Ekonomska Biblioteka 7, Belgrade, 1958, pp. 53–76.

[2] *Ibid.*, pp. 90–92.

not been unusual for more than one family to live in a single apartment. This has produced some bizarre social relationships. One of the oddest, brought to light in a Belgrade court case in 1955, concerned a man who remarried after a divorce. A part of the apartment was allocated to his mother, and the divorced wife moved in with her mother while the man and his wife lived in the other part. The real difficulty arose in connection with the seven children involved.

The housing problem is being tackled, but slowly. Each year new apartments are added, but at the same time more and more people come to the cities. In the meantime a large backlog of demand for housing has built up and the condition of existing living quarters is deteriorating rapidly. Only in 1959 was the goal of the Five Year Plan met — an increase of 69,000 housing units annually.

International Cooperation

The closer economic relations between Yugoslavia and other countries, the steady growth in foreign tourists and the exchanges of official and semi-official missions are having an important effect both on the individual Yugoslav citizen and on the official planner. Not only does increased foreign trade tie Yugoslavia's productive efforts to the world economy, but the many foreign visitors and, for that matter, the Yugoslavs traveling in foreign countries (180,000 in 1958) bring a personal picture of the outside world even to the smallest village and the most remote peasant home. Among the foreign visitors to Yugoslavia are many former emigrants returning to their place of birth and reporting on conditions in their new homelands. The nation as a whole and the individual inhabitants are increasingly aware of international happenings and more closely tied to the Western world.

The breakdown of Yugoslavia's isolation was encouraged by the fact that Titoist economic policy has not been based on autarchy. On the contrary, the main aim has been a gradual integration of the nation's productive potential with the world economy, particularly after the break with the Soviet bloc forced a major shift in foreign trade. Economic assistance, in large part from the United States, played an important role. It not only helped the serious balance of payments problem but also permitted the Yugoslav government to undertake domestic projects which in turn either became dollar earners or reduced the necessity to import.

Yugoslavia has continued its efforts to expand exports and thus diminish the balance of payments deficit. Exports have increased steadily since 1954, in both quantity and value. Imports too have increased and efforts at slowing down the deficit have been successful only in part. The need for expansion into new markets, while holding on to present markets, presents serious long-term problems in Yugoslavia's foreign economic relations. Increasing ties with the world markets still further augment the need for modern, up-to-date industrial facilities and greater productivity of its labor force if Yugoslavia is to produce high-quality goods to meet growing foreign competition. Only in this way can it become an integral part of the world trade community, and only by becoming an integral part of the world trade community can it become economically viable.

SOME QUESTIONS

FOR THE FUTURE

AFTER they were expelled from the Cominform, in the period when the basic institutions and policies of Titoism were still emerging, the Yugoslav Communists used to be fond of saying: "We are searching for our way." One seldom hears this phrase any more, and the implication is that the way has been found. The successes achieved by the regime, material and otherwise, in the years since the Cominform Resolution, go a long way to justify this confidence. There are nevertheless some vital questions facing Yugoslav Communism, and how they are answered will have much to do in determining its future.

The first of these questions concerns the basic nature of the regime, especially the future of the democratic part of socialist democracy. The second major question is that of ethnic conflicts — the extent to which the economic aspects of national particularism may become a serious political problem. Third, and interrelated with the others, is the question of what is likely to happen after Tito.

How Deep Are the Roots?

Yugoslav Communism has moved away from its pre-1950 totalitarian pattern on an uneven, on-again, off-again course. How deep-rooted is this trend? Since it was the Party leadership that introduced the liberalizations in the regime, cannot the Party leadership at any time wipe them out? And does it wish to?

The answers are neither easy nor clear-cut. The regime certainly has the will and the means to crush political opposition like the heresies of Djilas, such "plots," real or imagined, as that of the elderly socialists, and any

Četnik or Ustaši manifestations. In theory, the same might be true of any opposition to official viewpoints. In practice, however, there are restraints. One, undoubtedly, is the comparatively liberal and humanized psychology of the leaders themselves, reflected in their new theoretical structure, which itself acts as an inhibition. This, in turn, led them to create and develop a political climate in which it would be difficult if not impossible to attempt to prohibit all expressions of differences of opinion. The leaders may slow down the trend they thus set in motion. They may halt it. They may restrict its significance. But it does not follow that they could reverse its course, even if they wanted to. A "national Communist" system like Yugoslavia's, since it must operate outside, if not in opposition to, the international Communist system, cannot operate successfully without a greater degree of popular support, or at least acceptance, than the Soviet-type regimes demand. This requires tolerance not only of a fairly widespread lack of "positive loyalty" in the totalitarian sense, but also of what might be called "benevolent opposition." And, in circular fashion, the types of opposition that classify as benevolent — that are not considered dangerous — tend to broaden.

Pertinent here is the extent to which there exists a real possibility of Yugoslavia becoming again an integral member of the Soviet bloc. Indeed, some observers interpret the yen demonstrated by Tito and certain other Yugoslav Communists for "solidarity" with the Soviet Union as stemming from a desire to be relieved of the necessity for "liberal Communism" at home. The course of Yugoslav foreign and domestic policy, however, indicates almost the reverse. If there is a connection between the two, it would seem to be that certain less liberal policies were adopted — in 1956 and 1957, for example — in order to further solidarity with the USSR, rather than that efforts to further solidarity with the USSR were pushed in order to adopt less liberal policies at home. In any event, the limits to which Yugoslavia will go in pursuit of "socialist solidarity" seem fairly well established. On the other hand, the Yugoslavs have by no means yet solved all their economic problems, and these would doubtless be sorely aggravated if Belgrade were to be deprived of Western economic assistance in one form or another. It is not at all impossible that Yugoslav foreign policy would become more in harmony with Soviet foreign policy. How the West would react to such an eventuality is unclear. But one cannot rule out that serious economic difficulties — whatever was responsible for them — could have an adverse effect on political development.

Even in such a case, however, the likelihood is that such an effect would be limited. A virtually impassable barrier to absolute political conformity is the decentralization of governmental functions and authority. Try as it might, the Party could not effectively control in detail all the myriad government, economic and social management bodies and activities. There are too many of them, and many are institutions where Party members are in a minority. Through these institutions, too, authority — important if limited — has been given to relatively independent-minded, non-Communist citizens, who in some places are acquiring significant status of their own. Not only is this true of technicians and managers, but it is inherent in such concepts as worker-management, commune autonomy and social management. Such concepts cannot be eliminated without eliminating Titoism itself.

Another difficulty standing in the way of tight Party control is the attitude of young people, and it is on the youth of today that the system must rely in the future. As everywhere, young people in Yugoslavia tend to be disenchanted. Where the disenchantment does not produce disinterest in, or opposition to, Communism, it tends to produce a pragmatism inherently hostile to rigid conformity. The extent of disinterest among younger people is demonstrated by the fact that of the 1,300,000 members of the People's Youth, more than a third are members of neither the League of Communists nor the Socialist Alliance, indicating that their participation in the youth organization is perfunctory. As for the People's Youth itself, Tito said one of its "biggest shortcomings . . . is the fact that a large number of boys and girls are not members."[1]

The Party, furthermore, is far from monolithic in certain aspects. It embraces widely varying opinions, and to many of its members ideology is more of a hindrance to be overcome than an infallible guide to action. At the top, the differences amount mainly to shadings of emphasis, as appears to be the case, say, with Tito, Ranković, Kardelj and Bakarić, and even more with certain lesser leaders. But on down the line these differences become differences of opinion, not, to be sure, about whether to have socialism or not, but — and this is the important question in contemporary Yugoslavia — about what kind of socialism to have. Tito may be able to minimize the differences and keep them from public view most of the time, but he cannot eliminate them or ignore them. Tito himself is undoubtedly an influence for conformity, and he has the prestige and authority to achieve it, at least on the surface. There is no assurance that those who succeed him can do so, however.

All of the foregoing must be considered in the light of two additional factors. First, there can be no doubt that the Yugoslav Communist leaders

---

[1] *The Building of Socialism and the Role and Tasks of the Socialist Alliance of the Working People of Yugoslavia*, Belgrade, 1960, pp. 41 and 44. This is Tito's report to the Fifth Congress of the Socialist Alliance.

believe, in one way or another and in varying degrees, in permitting a *comparatively* wide area of free expression. This is true even of Tito, despite the narrow limits he sometimes draws. They believe in it both because they consider it utilitarian and because they consider it Marxist, as they interpret the term. The implications of this conviction are sometimes obscured by the readiness of the leaders to jettison philosophical considerations if the freedom they permit should become non-utilitarian — if, in other words, it would jeopardize their own power.

Secondly, Yugoslavia seethes with ideological confusion more than with political discontent. A combination of foreign and domestic factors have produced a quite workable degree of popular acceptance of the regime. In part, this acceptance results from the elimination of anti-Communist leaders and from fear inculcated by the strong-arm methods used earlier and still held in patent reserve. In part it reflects the lassitude of a large segment of the population that is more or less apolitical and of others who are weary of conflict. In part it is due to the continual, if slow, improvement in living standards. But in part also it involves active support.

An element in the willingness of the people to go along is that a meaningful alternative to the Tito regime is far from clear. It is likely that a majority of Yugoslavs would not — in the abstract — declare themselves in favor of the present government if some means of accurately determining their views existed. But it also seems likely that the number that would declare some measure of support for the Tito regime would be greater than the number that could agree on any one probable alternative. Yugoslav politics up to Tito's time was based mostly on national, religious and social passions, and these passions still smoulder beneath the surface and divide the people. Whatever one thinks about Yugoslav Communism, it has been a unifying force, and many anti-Communists grant the regime credit on this score.

The most dramatic denunciation of the Tito regime has come from Milovan Djilas in *The New Class*. In another book, *Land Without Justice*,[1] Djilas has described with great vividness the Montenegrin milieu in which he was raised. It was a milieu of blood, brutality and betrayal in which human dignity fought an unending battle with poverty, ignorance and exaggerated individualism. Political democracy did not exist, nor did the concept of political democracy, among the masses of the people. Montenegro was, of course, atypical. In the years preceding World War I, for example, Serbia enjoyed a type of peasant democracy with parliamentary forms and a certain participation of

---

[1] Harcourt, Brace, New York, 1958. This book was also written between the time of Djilas' downfall and his incarceration and was smuggled out of Yugoslavia. It is essentially nonpolitical, as far as the current scene is concerned.

citizens. And the cultural level in the north, notably in Slovenia, was notice-ably higher than in Orthodox areas. Yet the absence of meaningful political democracy — in the Western sense, at least — in interwar Yugoslavia and the fratricidal conflicts that occurred throughout the country during World War II indicate that Montenegro was not wholly atypical. There is, therefore, reason to question just how favorable a climate such a background would provide for Western-type political institutions, to say nothing of the idealistic, almost utopian system Djilas seems to favor in *The New Class*. Djilas himself seems to have had such a question in mind when, in the days before he became a heretic among heretics, he expressed the fear that a trend toward "bourgeois democracy" in Yugoslavia would be "but a mask for turning back" to the "semi-feudal" conditions which existed before World War II.

In *The New Class* such fears are ignored. The book is largely polemical rather than descriptive, dwelling on the way in which Communism "by its very nature results in a stifling of thought." It is, especially from the stand of Western democrats, an heroic commentary on Communism generally. Its central theme is that ruling Communist groups are simply a new class of owners, historically no different from previous owning classes except that, since they can subject others to their will completely, their monopoly of ownership is complete.

Djilas is understandably bitter. "When the new class leaves the historical scene," he predicts, "there will be less sorrow over its passing than there was for any other class before it. Smothering everything except what suited its ego, it has condemned itself to failure and shameful ruin."

The New Class is not primarily an analysis of the Yugoslav system as such, although it makes acid and telling comments on facets of it. Rather, it treats all Communism, Yugoslav as well as Soviet, as a single system. Such an analysis obviously has something to recommend it. Yet in some ways, the views of Djilas the extreme anti-Communist suffer from the same lack of re-straint as did the earlier views of Djilas the extreme Communist. This does not alter the validity of much of the criticism made in *The New Class*, but it some-times impairs the logic of the conclusions Djilas draws from it.

"Obligatory ideological unity of the Party," Djilas asserts in one place, "is the inescapable road of every Communist system. The methods of estab-lishing totalitarian control, or ideological unity, may be less severe than Stalin's, but the essence is always the same." But in another place he states that "the essential thing in every policy is first of all the means."

Again, Djilas records his opinion that, "viewed from the standpoint of freedom, a military dictatorship in a Communist system would denote great progress." Yet further along he seems to imply that decentralization of the economy itself is a step forward. Whereas having two or more candidates for each office might be "the beginning of a turning toward democracy by the Communist system," he writes, "it seems to me . . . that development in Eastern Europe will *first* turn in the direction of the Yugoslav system of 'workers' management.'"[1] However, elsewhere he defines national Communism as "only Communism on the decline" and contends that workers' councils lack substance because in the absence of "universal freedom, only crumbs from the tables and illusions have been left to the workers."

The uncritical enthusiasm with which *The New Class* was received in the West, and in particular in the United States, has tended to obscure the progress Titoism has made away from totalitarian practices. But the violence with which the Yugoslav press unanimously denounced *The New Class* — as part of a "foreign-inspired campaign against Yugoslavia" — the ban on the book in the country and the harsh treatment accorded its defiant author show how far Titoism still has to go.

Unity versus National Differences

One of the outstanding achievements of the Tito regime has been to assuage the ethnic-religious hatreds that characterized Yugoslavia between the wars. Nevertheless, the problem of national differences and rivalries remains. In fact, during the latter half of the 1950's it became noticeably more acute. How to cope with it is one of the regime's major headaches.

The nationality question in contemporary Yugoslavia is vastly different from what it was in the past. Today the Orthodox Serbs and the Roman Catholic Croats are no longer locked in a deadly struggle for hegemony or autonomy. As pointed out in the preceding chapter, the question of nationality arises mainly in connection with economic development. Yet political questions are present, and beneath them lurk, in greater or lesser degree, some of the same old ethnic-religious passions which flared to such heat under the monarchy. The government is confident that these passions can be kept under control, and its confidence has some basis. The major immediate cause of the interwar conflict — the attempt of the Serbs to exercise hegemony over the whole country — has almost certainly disappeared forever, and with it political discrimination based on nationality. Political parties reflecting national origins have been eliminated. The Serbian Orthodox and Roman Catholic churches, which were so important in encouraging and abetting particularism, have been denuded of their formal political power and no longer play their earlier role. The spread of education and improved com-

---

[1] Italics added.

munications have helped break down the cultural isolation of the ethnic-religious groups which was such a breeder of conflict. The social ferment of industrialization has resulted in much more intermingling of the populations. In addition, Soviet pressure and attempts to exploit national differences have produced, if anything, more solidarity.

Consequently, there has been created a certain feeling of Yugoslav nationalism that did not exist before, although the time is not yet in sight when one can speak of a unified Yugoslav people. The Yugoslav peoples are still definitely plural. Despite growing exceptions, by and large they still tend to think of themselves as Serbs, Croats and Slovenes. In fact, by the conscious stimulation of Macedonian nationality and the extension of real autonomy to Montenegro, the dimensions of particularism have even widened. Recognizing this situation, the regime stresses its federal structure, gives repeated assurances that ethnic individuality will be preserved and goes to great lengths to arrange equitable representation from all republics on all major federal government and Party agencies.

Were it not for the great disparity in economic development among the republics, it is likely that the residuum of national feelings would be a cause of much less serious concern than it is. In order to overcome the disparity, the regime has in effect slowed down the economic development in Slovenia and Croatia in order to speed it up in Macedonia, Montenegro, Bosnia and Herzegovina, and parts of Serbia. The Slovenes and Croats have increasingly demurred. As the demands on them continue, with no end in sight, demurrers become complaints, complaints protests and protests opposition.

It is at this point that economic particularism tends to become political particularism, and it is at this point that the old bitter passions crop up, especially in Serb-Croat relations. In Zagreb, one can hear talk about a "Serbian clique." Among many Croats even the most innocent government plans are suspected of "Serbian influence" and an "anti-Croat orientation." In Belgrade, one hears charges of "Croat separatism" and "narrow-minded Croat selfishness."

Although Serbs outnumbered Croats on the Federal Executive Council, as far as the composition of the top Party organs are concerned the division is fair enough, on a basis of population. There were on the Central Committee, as named at the Seventh Party Congress, 46 Serbs, 29 Croats, 21 Slovenes, 16 Macedonians and 15 Montenegrins. In addition eight members were from Bosnian Moslem stock or the Slavic and non-Slavic minorities. On the Executive Committee there were four Serbs, four Croats, three Slovenes, three Montenegrins and one Macedonian. Talk of "Serbian domination" stems from the fact that the Montenegrins are of Serbian origin and usually tend to agree with the Serbs, and that members of minority groups represent the Vojvodina and Kosovo-Metohija, both attached to Serbia. The Macedonians, too, are psychologically closer to the Serbs than to the Croats and Slovenes. Furthermore, the Croat representation includes Tito, who clearly does not favor his native republic in initiating or approving policies. The Croat strength is further dissipated since some of those leaders included as Croat come in fact from Bosnia and Herzegovina (the same being true, of course, of some of the Serbs). Since the Serbs more often than not side with representatives from the underdeveloped republics, it is clear that in any question involving the developed regions versus the underdeveloped ones, the Slovenes and Croats would be in a minority.

The real decisions in this delicate area are taken in these two Party bodies, but their ethnic composition means less than it might seem. For one thing, decisions by vote on a formal parliamentary basis are hardly the rule in either the Central Committee or the Executive Committee. And the top leaders can by no stretch of the imagination be justly considered "pro-Serb" or "anti-Croat." They are pro-Communist and pro-Yugoslav, and their view of these positions makes them pro-underdeveloped area.

Nevertheless, the impression is widely prevalent in Slovenia and Croatia, among even some important leaders, that the federal authorities are not sufficiently cognizant of their interests. Especially where Croatian interests seem to suffer as against Serbian interests, the rub is acute. The major complaint concerns the extent of central investment in the backward republics. All taxes go into a common kitty, so that it is difficult if not impossible to see which republic contributes what.

There are also other complaints. In 1958, a portion of Zagreb city funds intended for housing — a serious need in the Croatian capital — was sequestered by the federal government as an anti-inflation measure. Some city officials with whom the authors discussed the matter plainly indicated their belief that this was not the real reason. Several important Croatian suggestions for improvements in rail and port facilities were disregarded in the 1957 Five Year Plan. This was especially true of those involving Split and, to a lesser extent, Rijeka, while emphasis in the Plan was put on improving the small and comparatively unused Montenegrin port of Bar. To a man Croat officials opposed the organization of an international fair in Belgrade. They protested that Zagreb was already well known for its fair and that a country like Yugoslavia needed no more than one. It was also pointed out that construction associated with the Belgrade fair was an elaborate and costly undertaking. But the Belgrade fair was held, and earlier than the previously announced date of the Zagreb fair.

At the higher Party levels, these Croat officials were understanding about the need for building up underdeveloped areas, and none of them talked about "pro-Serb" and "anti-Croat" policies. The lower down the ladder, the more noticeable were the particularist influences. But they all seemed to feel that there was not enough appreciation in Belgrade of Croatia's problems.

Apparently, at least as far as the top leadership is concerned, it is this emphasis on building up the backward areas, rather than any bias for or against certain republic or ethnic groups, that produces decisions unpalatable to the Croats and Slovenes. That there are many instances where criticism is justified is impossible to doubt. The decision for all-out support for the underdeveloped republics tends to create a psychology which makes it easy to underestimate the needs of the more advanced areas. This, in turn, provides a situation favorable to those Serbs, for example, with particularist attitudes.

The political implications of this situation are important, but they can easily be exaggerated. It is true that anti-Communist groups and individuals try to exacerbate the particularist attitudes growing out of differences on economic policy, and the Orthodox and Roman Catholic Churches often feed these sentiments where they can. There is no doubt that the ever-touchy problem of Serb-Croat relations is involved. But there is no indication that it will get out of hand. There is, for example, virtually no likelihood of a flare-up of ethnic passions that would endanger the federal republic or the regime. Nevertheless, the increasing evidences of nationalist feeling are a source of official concern. There is annoyance that doubt may be cast on the national unity which the Titoists regard as one of their most solid achievements. There is fear that the national cooperation considered vital for success may be jeopardized. Even more, there is worry about the impact on unity inside the League of Communists.

Indeed, it was nationalist opposition to the regime's economic program among the Communists that finally stirred the leaders to recognize something they preferred to ignore. The seriousness of the situation was revealed when Tito, who goes far to minimize Party differences, read the riot act to the Central Committee at a special plenary meeting in November 1959. Although he insisted that what was involved was "localism" rather than "chauvinism," he left no doubt that what he was talking about included "localism" at the republic level. Tito said flatly that he was "not satisfied with the resistance of the Communists to localist tendencies." He virtually accused unnamed members of the Central Committee of being "themselves the initiators" of these tendencies and of bucking the Party leadership on questions of economic development. They were guilty, he charged, of "petty-bourgeois" sentiments, which, in this case, meant ethnic particularism. In no uncertain terms, he demanded an end to all this.[1]

Tito's blast appeared to submerge the tensions existing among the republics at the top Party levels. Tito hoped it would also persuade the leaders of the various republics to be more reasonable in their demands. But the tensions were real, and they could not be ended merely by talking about them. Although it was not clear how deeply the leadership was convinced of this, certain positive steps were undertaken. The drive to build up the backward republics went forward, but now somewhat more slowly. Plans were worked out in Belgrade for earmarking republic contributions to federal investment funds, as the Croats and Slovenes had persistently demanded. A compromise on the issue of the fair was worked out, Zagreb keeping the Yugoslav international fair, while the Belgrade fair would specialize in certain types of products only. Plans for a railroad from Bar to Belgrade were postponed.[2]

The regime hoped that meanwhile successes already achieved in economic development would permit the poorer republics to contribute greater amounts to their own improvement, while the general economic development of the country would lessen the necessity for curbing development plans of the more advanced areas. On the political level, it was anticipated that a new constitutional court would help keep republic laws in line without constantly raising the issue of unconstitutionality, as now, in the Federal Assembly, where strong particularist feelings are to be found even though not usually voiced. Yugoslav federalism appeared to be becoming more federal.

Whether these measures, if they all materialized, would be enough was difficult to say. For one thing, the problem of ethnic tensions was intimately related to another hurdle facing the regime, in some ways maybe the highest hurdle of all. This is the problem of succession to Tito.

Titoism without Tito

After the death of Stalin, no Communist regime was as much personified by one man as that in Yugoslavia. In fact, Titoism depended on Tito to an even greater extent than Stalinism did on Stalin. Soviet Communism had other saints and symbols, and Stalinism as a system had outlived its usefulness by the time Stalin died. Yugoslav Communism, on the other hand, has virtually no personal symbol other than Tito; for most Yugoslavs, as well as for people of other countries, Yugoslav Communism means Tito and vice versa. And Titoism as a system is still evolving.

[1] Cf. *New York Times*, November 21, 1959, p. 3, and Josip Broz Tito, *Concluding Speech at the Second (Special) Plenum of the Central Committee of the League of Communists*, November 18–19, 1959, Jugoslavija, Belgrade, 1959, especially pp. 13–14.

[2] See Tito, *op. cit.*, p. 80.

In a very real sense, Tito himself built the Party of which he is senior member. Having masterminded its crucial wartime role, by the end of the war he was already a national figure, more popular than his Party, with a personal following that extended well beyond the confines of the Communists or even their conscious fellow-travelers. And it was Tito who then directed the unification and reconstruction of the country, defended its independence, and provided the political leadership for the new system of socialism which, in the vernacular, bears his name. As head of the Party, head of the government, head of the Socialist Alliance, and, despite his Croat birth, the closest thing Yugoslavia has ever had to a national leader, Tito is "Mr. Yugoslavia."

Inevitably under such circumstances, an aura of charisma has grown up about Tito. Before the Cominform Resolution, there was nearly as much of a "cult of the individual" in Yugoslavia as in the Soviet Union. When, after the break with the Soviet Union, the Yugoslav Communists began to deride the extremes of Stalin-worship in the USSR, it was not long before the more ridiculous forms of Tito-worship quietly disappeared. But a certain amount of charisma remains. In December 1957, on the 20th anniversary of Tito's assumption of the post of secretary general of the Yugoslav Communist Party, Aleksandar Ranković hailed his leader as having "undoubtedly preserved himself and the Party against growing old." "Comrade Tito," Ranković told a plenum of the Central Committee, "although judging by his age one of the most aged revolutionaries, has remained always fresh looking, of current interest, clear, intelligible, even for the youngest generations, the interpreter of the needs of contemporary revolutionary developments and successes."[1] Some months later, on his 66th birthday, Tito received a letter from the "Youth of Socialist Yugoslavia," declaring that "your life, our beloved Comrade Tito, will serve us, the young, as a shining example of self-sacrifices, revolutionary heroism and humanism."[2]

Whenever Tito appears in public, he is invariably greeted by mass acclaim of the kind that in America is reserved for football teams. The crowds roar "Ti-to! Ti-to! Ti-to!" and then chant: *"Tito je naš, mi smo Titovo!"* (Tito is ours, we are Tito's!). His comings and goings, as his public utterances, are chronicled in detail in the Yugoslav press. His trivial official acts are often made to seem significant. Typical was the reporting of the foreign reaction to Tito's New Year's message in 1958. In its January 4th issue, *Borba* quoted in detail from the Associated Press, Reuters, Agence France Press, and newspapers in the United States, the USSR, England, Germany, France, Italy, Greece, Poland, Czechoslovakia, Hungary and China, adding: "President

---

[1] *Borba*, December 8, 1957.
[2] *Borba*, May 24, 1958.

Tito's message produced a great reaction in the press of a number of other countries as well."

Tito appears to the Yugoslav public in many guises — as a benevolent father of his peoples, a stern, scolding uncle, a simple man of the soil, a world traveler, a comrade-at-arms of Partisan days, a dignified head of state in his Rolls Royce, a resplendent military leader on his white charger. In Yugoslavia today, few institutions are free from criticism, even the League of Communists. But no finger is ever pointed publicly at Tito who, indeed, takes credit for overcoming the mistakes of others. What? There are shortages amidst plenty? Tito says the people have every right to complain and excoriates the distributing agencies. What? A tightening of Party control results in a wave of popular bitterness? Tito sternly denounces the very Party bureaucrats he himself had spurred to exercise greater authority.

Naturally, this position of Tito's works both ways. Many of those who hate the regime focus their hatred on Tito. But there is no question that his popularity extends far outside Party ranks. When the streets are lined for a parade, it is not unusual to see a father who only a moment before has cursed the police holding back the crowd lift his son to his shoulders as Tito passes by and say: "See the Marshal? Wave to the Marshal." In 1958 Tito, clad in a brilliant blue uniform, addressed a great Partisan rally in the Bosnian mountains. After the speech, one of the authors hitched a ride back to town in a mail truck. The driver and his assistant, neither of them Communists, were dressed in patched and threadbare clothes. Yet one of their first remarks to their passenger concerned how fine the Marshal looked in his new uniform.

Despite this Yugoslav version of the "cult of the individual," it has never involved the exclusive one-man rule of the Stalin type. While there was never any question who was boss, there did exist almost from the first a sort of collective leadership. The only really top Communists who ever seriously· challenged Tito — Djilas and the Cominformist Hebrang — went to prison. Between Tito and his top lieutenants — Kardelj, Ranković, Vukmanović-Tempo, Bakarić and Pucar[1] — there has existed a loyalty that transcended issues. Between them and "Stari" — as Tito is known in the inner circle — there is the special friendship and trust of comrades-at-arms, which has permitted real sharing of power and authority.

Thus Tito's position as a symbol has long been more important than his position as a policy maker and administrator. This has become increasingly the case, as, after the reorganization of the Party and government in 1952–1953, Tito began to leave to others, especially Kardelj and Ranković, not

[1] And, until their death, Boris Kidrič and Moše Pijade.

only the day-to-day running of affairs but even the formulation and carrying out of major policies. Only on rare occasions does Tito attend a meeting of the Federal Executive Council, and Kardelj has become the real working head of the government. While Tito invariably presides over formal meetings of the Party's Executive and Central Committees, Party administration is left almost exclusively to Ranković. Tito now probably pays closer attention to foreign policy than anything else, but after the collapse of his efforts to achieve "socialist solidarity" he tended to leave the direction even of this area to others. He makes frequent speeches. He visits this part of the country and that. He travels about the world as a sort of salesman of Yugoslav socialism. With his attractive and Junoesque third wife, an ex-Partisan and former major in the Yugoslav army, he entertains visiting dignitaries. There is no question that Tito can have the last word, or the first one, if he desires it, but he does so less and less. He remains in close touch with major problems, but the real job of building Titoism is left almost entirely to Kardelj, Ranković and others.

One reason for Tito's increasing retirement from active affairs is that he is getting old. On May 25, 1961, he was 69. Although in fairly good health despite a number of minor ailments, he has behind him a life of deprivation, hardship and strain. Despite Ranković's fustian metaphor that Tito had preserved himself against growing old, the question of succession has had more and more to be phrased, not what happens *if* Tito dies but what happens *when* Tito dies.

In unchallenged second place to Tito are Kardelj and Ranković — or, possibly, Ranković and Kardelj. Both are secretaries of the League of Communists. Both are vice presidents of the government. Both have Tito's complete confidence. Kardelj was 51 years old in 1961, Ranković 52.

By most objective standards, Kardelj, a former schoolteacher and possessed of an absolutely first-rate mind, would probably be rated the more able of the two and, if one of them is to succeed Tito, the more felicitous choice. As a Slovene, he would be much less likely to precipitate a controversy over succession based on Serb-Croat rivalry. As former foreign minister and now the functioning head of the Federal Executive Council, he undoubtedly has a better grasp of governmental problems at home and abroad than any likely candidate. As chief ideologist of the regime and one of the most brilliant theoreticians in the Communist movement, he is more at home than anyone else in the intricacies of Marxist theory on which Titoism rests. His reputation is that of a more moderate Communist than Ranković, more willing to continue on the road to further liberalizations and less likely to become enmeshed in the lure of "socialist solidarity."

On the other hand, Ranković also is a man of no mean ability. While he has given little indication of being an original political thinker, he has handled the difficult task of running the League of Communists with considerable skill. Ranković's most serious handicaps are his ethnic origin and his reputation in the country. Because he is a Serb, his choice would raise a storm of hard feeling, suspicion and doubt in Croatia and, perhaps to a lesser extent, in Slovenia. Although since the emphasis on "legality" in 1951 he has, in fact, sometimes been a force for police moderation, he is firmly associated in the popular mind with the political police and the days of OZNA and UDBA terror. A belief persists, too, that he is inclined to be less than enthusiastic about the political liberalizations while maintaining a strong interest in closer relations with the Soviet Union.[1]

This man-in-the-street opinion was strengthened by the fact that during the years of closest rapprochement with the USSR, Ranković appeared to be edging ahead of Kardelj in power, especially in the Party, where the administrative apparatus operates under his personal direction. Interest in their respective positions was renewed in 1960 when Ranković replaced Kardelj as secretary general of the Socialist Alliance. Kardelj's going out of office may only have indicated that his governmental duties left him no time for anything else. On the other hand, since the Socialist Alliance is supposed to play an increasingly important role, the move also certainly enhances Ranković's power.[2]

The fact is, however, that although the popular view of differences between Kardelj and Ranković may reflect differences in emphasis, there seem to be no serious issues between them, nor are there any indications of personal rivalry. They work harmoniously together, and if they do not always see eye to eye on the future direction of Yugoslav Communism, both manage to conceal it, not only from the public but from their colleagues as well. If anything, Ranković tends to defer to Kardelj, even in Party matters, in apparent recognition of the Slovene's brilliance in both theory and administration.

However, political ambition is a strange thing, and it has unpredictable effects on people. What works well under Tito may not work at all without Tito. The chances are that those Yugoslavs who scoff at the idea of a power struggle between Kardelj and Ranković are correct. Yet, after Tito, it is quite likely that one of them is going to become more powerful, the other less. In

---

[1] For this very reason, apparently, Ranković was selected to make the major anti-Soviet speech at the Seventh Congress of the League of Communists in 1958.

[2] When Kardelj quietly went to England in 1961 and extended his stay over a period of several weeks, Belgrade buzzed with speculation that the reasons given — health and a desire to study English — were not the real ones. On his return to Yugoslavia, however, Kardelj appeared to occupy the same place in the hierarchy as before.

a regime that has not yet faced the problem of succession and where, more-over, instrumentalities of democratic choice lack both strength and tradition, one cannot know for sure how the contenders for position will react.

Within the Executive Committee, there is no sign — at least none perceiv-able to an outsider — of any conscious alignment with either Kardelj or Ranković. But if a choice between the two should ever have to be made, the attitude of other top Yugoslav Communist leaders would be important. Crucial would doubtless be the position of Vladimir Bakarić, the Croat chieftain; Ivan Gošnjak, also a Croat, who heads the armed forces; and Vukmanović-Tempo, the vigorous and ambitious Montenegrin who in 1958 moved from the post of economic "tsar" to take over leadership of the trade unions. By all odds, the most important of these is Bakarić, who, despite ill-health, is one of the regime's ablest men and the leading Party expert on agriculture. It appears likely that, faced with a clear choice between Kardelj and Ranković, Bakarić would prefer the former, not so much on ethnic grounds as because he is, if anything, more of a "liberal" even than the Slovene. Neither these men nor the other members of the Executive Com-mittee are in a position to challenge Kardelj or Ranković, and if appearances are any indication, their first concern would be to go along with any collective decision and strive to maintain unity.

In the question of succession to Tito, however, another problem is likely to be more fundamental than the ethnic origins or respective views and abilities of Kardelj or Ranković or even the possibilities of a power struggle between them. This problem is that Tito is irreplaceable. Neither Kardelj nor Ranković — nor anybody else in Yugoslavia — has anything like Tito's national popularity and renown or his dramatic qualities of leadership. Compared with Tito, both Kardelj, the former schoolteacher, and Ranković, the former policeman, are politically colorless. It is difficult to imagine, for example, masses of Yugoslavs hoarsely chanting "Kar-delj! Kar-delj!" or "Rank-o-vić! Rank-o-vić!" Neither of the two have enough political "it." The question arises, therefore, as to how well a country of such diversity as Yugoslavia can maintain a dictatorship that tries to base itself on popular approval if it lacks the symbol of a dynamic leader.

For a long time the problem of succession was not faced up to inside the Party, and it has not been yet, really. But in recent years there has been unofficial talk in certain Party circles about what to do. The various proposals have involved some kind of collective leadership and division of responsi-bility between Kardelj and Ranković. One was that Kardelj would take over the presidency and run the government, while Ranković would assume leadership of the Party. As things are now, Party power is undoubtedly more important than government power, so this solution would clearly mean elevating Ranković above Kardelj in fact if not in theory.

It is entirely likely that Kardelj, confident of his own position and possibly seeing the future of Titoism more in terms of government than Party relations, would not object to such a scheme. It would still, however, raise questions of Serb-Croat relations, both in and out of the Party. Whether for this or other reasons, the most recent plan bruited about Belgrade was different. According to this plan, the President would cease to be chairman of the Federal Executive Council and would occupy a position with more power than, say, the President of the Fourth Republic in France but less power than the President of the Fifth Republic. Ranković would then become President, while Kardelj would assume a new title, President of the Federal Executive Council, doing virtually his present job but with more status and power. As for the League of Communists, according to this suggestion Tito's post of secretary general would be eliminated, and the Party would be run by collective leadership in the Executive Committee, with Kardelj and Ranković, as now, sharing secretaryships and the latter personally directing administration of Party affairs. The plan envisaged in the 1962 constitution for separating the two top government posts appeared to herald some such development, although it was not certain who — after Tito — would fill which job. Nor was it clear how the proposed one-term limitation would affect the ensuing transfer of political power. There was discussion of applying the one-term limitation to top Party posts also — again after Tito — but as of 1961, at least, there had been no decision. If the limitation on tenure were really applied across the board and made to stick, it would be likely to mitigate the problem of succession.

Separation of the presidency and chairmanship of the Federal Executive Council in itself would go far toward laying the groundwork for a real compromise. How workable it would be depends primarily on how Ranković would react. About this, it is impossible to say. The best possible way of insuring its success seems not to be a likely eventuality. This would be for Tito formally to give up both his Party and government posts now and place his stamp of approval on the new arrangement. As *the* elder statesman of Yugoslav Communism, Tito would still have all the power and authority he has now. If need be, a new emeritus title could be created for him — for example, Marshal of the Republic. But regardless of titles, as long as he lived Tito could have his say about whatever he wanted to, and nobody would oppose him. At the same time, he could thus see to it that the succession proceeded in an orderly manner. In this way, the Yugoslavs could have their symbol and prepare to do without it at the same time.

Many Yugoslav Communists, despite their veneration of Tito, feel that other problems than succession might be solved if "Stari" would step aside. For Tito, while he must be credited with many if not most of the liberalizations, is more conservative than many Yugoslav Communists, especially some younger ones, would like. These Communists do not at all agree with Milovan Djilas that Tito is "a block to progress" and "has outlived his time."[1] But they do feel that he is inclined to be overly cautious, and overprotective of certain old Partisan comrades who constitute conservative influences in the Party, that is, those inclined to favor less rather than more political liberalization. Particularly, Tito's sortie into the international politics of "socialist solidarity" in 1956–1958 worried some of these Communists, who fear new overtures in this regard. All such talk is indignantly dismissed in the higher Party echelons, but there is much truth to it. So far as Titoism is a new and dynamic system of democratized socialism, Tito has become something less than a wholehearted Titoist.

Possibly because he fears just such attitudes, Tito himself has never even remotely hinted that he would consider retiring, and it seems extremely unlikely that he will, despite the obvious advantages his retirement would have. Like many another autocrat, Tito is unable, apparently, to come to grips with the problem of his own succession. The question is almost never discussed in his presence. Many of those around him, on the contrary, go out of their way to emphasize the importance of his remaining in harness. Any mention of the succession problem among members of the Executive Committee, at least by outsiders, tends to produce acute embarrassment.

Titoism has achieved remarkable successes in its short life. However, half totalitarian, half democratic, half in the East and half in the West, with internal and external forces pulling both ways, it has yet to prove its long-run stability. How smoothly it meets the hurdle of succession may be the crucial test. The Yugoslav Communists are confident they can meet it without difficulty. Most students of contemporary Yugoslavia would be inclined to agree. Regardless of what they may think of Titoism, those who wish well for the Yugoslavs can only hope they are right.

[1] Cf. Fred Warner Neal, "Yugoslav Communist Theory," *American Universities Field Staff Reports*, FWN–5–'54, p. 9.

APPENDIX

Appendix Table 3-1

DISTRIBUTION, DENSITY AND LITERACY RATE OF YUGOSLAV POPULATION, BY AREA, 1953

	Total Population		Number of Males (Thousands)	Number of Females (Thousands)	Number of Households (Thousands)	Average Number of People		Literacy Rate (Population 10 Years of Age and Over)	Agricultural Population as Per Cent of Total Population
	Number (Thousands)	Percentage Distribution				Per Household	Per Square Mile		
FNRJ	16,937	100.0	8,205	8,732	3,945	4.3	170	74.5	60.9
Serbia	6,979	41.2	3,412	3,568	1,617	4.3	204	72.1	66.6
Serbia proper	4,471	26.4	2,182	2,290	1,006	4.5	207	70.5	67.1
Vojvodina	1,700	10.0	817	882	485	3.5	204	87.1	62.4
AKM (Kosmet)	808	4.8	413	396	126	6.4	196	45.2	72.2
Croatia	3,919	23.1	1,852	2,682	1,027	3.8	181	83.7	56.4
Slovenia	1,466	8.7	693	773	389	3.7	189	97.3	41.1
Bosnia and Herzegovina	2,848	16.8	1,386	1,462	565	5.0	145	59.7	62.2
Macedonia	1,305	7.7	660	645	246	5.3	132	64.2	62.7
Montenegro	420	2.5	202	218	92	4.6	78	69.8	61.5

Source: Statistički Godišnjak, 1957, p. 442.

Appendix Table 16-1

GROSS INVESTMENTS,* BY REPUBLIC, 1947–1959

| | FNRJ | | | | ALL SERBIA | | | | SERBIA | | | | | | | | | | | |
| | | | | | | | | | VOJVODINA | | | | SERBIA PROPER | | | | KOSMET | | | |
	1947a	1952	1956	1959	1947a	1952	1956	1959	1947a	1952	1956	1959	1947a	1952	1956	1959	1947a	1952	1956	1959
Amount (Billions of Dinars at Current Prices)																				
Total	42.6	245.3	402.9	701.3	13.9	70.5	151.4	308.6	2.6	6.5	31.9	90.2	10.3	60.5	113.1	195.8	1.0	3.5	6.4	22.6
Manufacturing and mining	15.1	173.0	167.4	223.9	5.3	51.3	60.0	91.3	0.9	3.4	9.4	20.1	4.2	45.0	46.9	59.9	0.2	2.9	3.7	11.3
Agriculture	2.0	10.0	34.1	111.8	0.8	4.0	19.2	65.8	0.4	2.6	11.5	44.7	0.4	1.2	7.0	14.9	—	0.2	0.7	6.2
Forestry	0.8	2.0	8.6	9.6	0.2	0.1	0.6	1.2	—	—	0.2	0.1	0.2	0.1	0.4	1.0	—	—	—	0.1
Construction	0.8	5.6	8.2	15.4	0.3	1.6	3.4	6.7	0.1	—	0.2	2.4	0.2	1.6	3.1	4.0	—	—	0.1	0.3
Transport	10.5	24.3	79.4	131.2	1.8	5.0	26.7	54.7	0.4	0.2	4.1	2.9	1.0	4.6	22.3	50.6	0.4	0.2	0.3	1.2
Commerce and catering trade	2.8	2.2	18.2	37.0	2.0	0.6	6.5	16.8	0.4	0.1	1.7	6.4	1.5	0.5	4.6	9.5	0.1	—	0.2	0.9
Handicrafts	0.2	0.2	3.5	8.8	0.1	0.1	1.3	3.3	—	—	0.5	1.1	0.1	0.1	0.7	2.0	—	—	0.1	0.2
Total economic activities	32.2	217.3	319.4	537.7	10.5	62.7	117.7	239.8	2.2	6.3	27.6	77.7	7.6	53.1	85.0	141.9	0.7	3.3	5.1	20.2
Housing and communal services	5.4	21.3	55.0	96.3	1.7	5.5	21.3	39.3	0.3	0.2	2.5	8.4	1.3	5.1	18.2	29.4	0.1	0.2	0.6	1.5
Cultural and social activity	2.5	4.2	15.9	34.3	0.9	1.2	5.9	14.1	0.1	—	1.2	2.3	0.7	1.2	4.3	11.3	0.1	—	0.4	0.5
State administration	2.5	2.5	12.6	33.0	0.8	1.1	6.5	15.4	—	—	0.6	1.8	0.7	1.1	5.6	13.2	0.1	—	0.3	0.4
Total social	10.4	28.0	83.5	163.6	3.4	7.8	33.7	68.8	0.4	0.2	4.3	12.5	2.7	7.4	28.1	53.9	0.3	0.2	1.3	2.4
Per Cent																				
Total	100.0	100.0	100.0	100.0	100.0	100.0	100.0	100.0	100.0	100.0	100.0	100.0	100.0	100.0	100.0	100.0	100.0	100.0	100.0	100.0
Manufacturing and mining	35.4	70.5	41.5	31.9	38.1	72.8	39.6	29.6	34.6	52.3	29.5	22.3	40.8	74.4	41.5	30.6	20.0	82.9	57.8	50.0
Agriculture	4.7	4.1	8.5	15.9	5.8	5.7	12.7	21.3	15.4	40.0	36.1	49.6	3.9	2.0	6.2	7.6	—	5.7	10.9	27.4
Forestry	1.9	0.8	2.1	1.4	1.4	0.1	0.4	0.4	—	—	0.6	0.1	1.9	0.1	0.4	0.5	—	—	—	0.4
Construction	1.9	2.3	2.0	2.2	2.2	2.3	2.2	2.2	3.8	—	0.6	2.7	1.9	2.6	2.7	2.0	—	—	1.6	1.3
Transport	24.6	9.9	19.7	18.7	12.9	7.1	17.6	17.7	15.4	3.1	12.6	3.2	9.7	7.6	19.7	25.8	40.0	5.7	4.7	5.3
Commerce and catering trade	6.6	0.9	4.5	5.3	14.4	0.8	4.3	5.4	15.4	1.5	5.3	7.1	14.6	0.8	4.1	4.9	10.0	—	3.1	4.0
Handicrafts	0.5	0.1	1.0	1.3	0.7	0.1	0.9	1.1	—	—	1.8	1.1	1.0	0.2	0.6	1.1	—	—	1.6	1.0
Total economic activities	75.6	88.6	79.3	76.7	75.5	88.9	77.7	77.7	84.6	96.9	86.5	86.1	73.8	87.8	75.2	72.5	70.0	94.3	79.7	89.4
Housing and communal services	12.6	8.7	13.7	13.7	12.2	7.8	14.1	12.7	11.5	3.1	7.8	9.3	12.6	8.4	16.1	15.0	10.0	5.7	9.4	6.6
Cultural and social activity	5.9	1.7	3.9	4.9	6.5	1.7	3.9	4.6	3.9	—	3.8	2.5	6.8	2.0	3.8	5.8	10.0	—	6.2	2.2
State administration	5.9	1.0	3.1	4.7	5.8	1.6	4.3	5.0	—	—	1.9	2.1	6.8	1.8	4.9	6.7	10.0	—	4.7	1.8
Total social	24.4	11.4	20.7	23.3	24.5	11.1	22.3	22.3	15.4	3.1	13.5	13.9	26.2	12.2	24.8	27.5	30.0	5.7	20.3	10.6

	CROATIA				SLOVENIA				BOSNIA & HERZEGOVINA				MACEDONIA				MONTENEGRO			
	1947a	1952	1956	1959	1947a	1952	1956	1959	1947a	1952	1956	1959	1947a	1952	1956	1959	1947a	1952	1956	1959
Amount (Billions of Dinars at Current Prices)																				
Total	10.7	53.2	97.4	158.9	5.3	27.0	51.5	86.9	8.1	71.6	58.4	83.6	1.7	13.3	23.8	40.3	1.3	9.1	20.4	23.0
Manufacturing and mining	3.7	37.4	32.5	47.0	2.8	19.8	19.4	30.1	2.1	51.1	32.3	34.1	0.7	7.9	11.9	11.8	0.1	5.5	11.3	9.6
Agriculture	0.5	1.7	6.3	20.2	0.1	1.4	2.5	7.5	0.3	0.9	1.7	7.2	0.1	1.9	4.0	10.2	0.1	0.1	0.4	0.9
Forestry	—	—	3.1	2.2	0.1	—	1.5	1.5	0.4	1.8	2.6	3.8	0.1	0.1	0.5	0.6	—	—	0.3	0.3
Construction	0.1	1.1	2.4	3.0	0.1	0.6	0.5	2.1	0.2	1.0	1.2	2.0	—	0.5	0.5	0.9	—	0.4	0.2	0.7
Transport	3.0	6.8	27.6	38.5	0.6	0.8	9.1	12.3	3.5	10.0	8.8	12.5	0.3	0.5	1.8	5.8	0.4	1.2	5.4	7.4
Commerce and catering trade	0.4	0.3	5.8	8.9	0.1	0.2	3.1	4.8	0.1	0.4	1.8	3.5	0.1	0.4	0.6	2.0	0.1	0.3	0.4	1.0
Handicrafts	—	—	0.8	1.9	0.1	—	0.8	2.1	—	0.1	0.3	1.0	—	—	0.2	0.5	—	—	0.1	—
Total economic activities	7.7	47.3	78.5	121.7	3.9	22.8	36.9	60.4	6.6	65.3	48.7	64.1	1.3	11.3	19.5	31.8	0.7	7.5	18.1	19.9
Housing and communal services	1.9	4.8	13.7	22.5	0.5	2.4	8.4	16.7	0.8	5.9	7.2	10.9	0.1	1.4	3.0	5.0	0.4	1.3	1.4	1.9
Cultural and social activity	0.4	0.9	3.5	6.8	0.4	1.0	3.8	5.9	0.4	0.3	1.5	5.5	0.2	0.5	0.8	1.4	0.2	0.2	0.5	0.6
State administration	0.7	0.2	1.7	7.9	0.5	0.8	2.4	3.9	0.3	0.1	1.0	3.1	0.1	0.1	0.5	2.1	—	0.1	0.5	0.6
Total social	3.0	5.9	18.9	37.2	1.4	4.2	14.6	26.5	1.5	6.3	9.7	19.5	0.4	2.0	4.3	8.5	0.6	1.6	2.3	3.1
Per Cent																				
Total	100.0	100.0	100.0	100.0	100.0	100.0	100.0	100.0	100.0	100.0	100.0	100.0	100.0	100.0	100.0	100.0	100.0	100.0	100.0	100.0
Manufacturing and mining	34.6	70.3	33.4	29.6	52.8	73.3	37.7	34.6	25.9	71.4	55.3	40.8	41.2	59.4	50.0	29.3	7.7	60.4	55.4	41.7
Agriculture	4.7	3.2	6.5	12.7	1.9	5.2	4.9	8.6	3.7	1.2	2.9	8.6	5.9	14.3	16.8	25.3	7.7	1.1	2.0	3.9
Forestry	—	—	3.2	1.4	1.9	—	2.9	1.7	4.9	2.5	4.5	4.5	5.9	0.8	2.1	1.5	—	—	1.5	1.3
Construction	0.9	2.1	2.5	1.9	1.9	2.2	1.0	2.4	2.5	1.4	2.0	2.4	—	3.8	2.1	2.2	—	4.4	1.0	3.0
Transport	28.0	12.8	28.3	24.2	11.3	3.0	17.7	14.2	43.2	14.0	15.1	15.0	17.6	3.8	7.6	14.4	30.7	13.2	26.5	32.2
Commerce and catering trade	3.8	0.5	6.0	5.6	1.9	0.7	6.0	5.5	1.3	0.6	3.1	4.2	5.9	2.9	2.5	5.0	7.7	3.3	2.0	4.4
Handicrafts	—	—	0.7	1.2	1.9	—	1.5	2.5	—	0.1	0.5	1.2	—	—	0.8	1.2	—	—	0.5	—
Total economic activities	72.0	88.9	80.6	76.6	73.6	84.4	71.7	69.5	81.5	91.2	83.4	76.7	76.5	85.0	81.9	78.9	53.8	82.4	88.9	86.5
Housing and communal services	17.8	9.0	14.1	14.2	9.4	8.9	16.3	19.2	9.9	8.3	12.3	13.0	5.9	10.5	12.6	12.4	30.7	14.3	6.9	8.3
Cultural and social activity	3.7	1.7	3.6	4.3	7.6	3.7	7.4	6.8	4.9	0.4	2.6	6.6	11.7	3.8	3.4	3.5	15.5	2.2	2.0	2.6
State administration	6.5	0.4	1.7	4.9	9.4	3.0	4.6	4.5	3.7	0.1	1.7	3.7	5.9	0.7	2.1	5.2	—	1.1	2.2	2.6
Total social	28.0	11.1	19.4	23.4	26.4	15.6	28.3	30.5	18.5	8.8	16.6	23.3	23.5	15.0	18.1	21.1	46.2	17.6	11.1	13.5

Sources: Jugoslovenska Investiciona Banka, *Investicije, 1947–1958,* Belgrade, 1959, and data supplied by the Economic Research Department of Jugoslovenska Investiciona Banka.

* Excluding private investments.

a Dinar data before 1952 are not comparable to those recorded after that date. Following the introduction of the new economic system, there was an increase in the level of prices. For some categories of goods this increase amounted to more than 4.5 times the pre-1952 level.

SELECTED BIBLIOGRAPHY

I. GENERAL BACKGROUND BOOKS

II. YUGOSLAV BOOKS AND PAMPHLETS

III. OTHER BOOKS AND PAMPHLETS

IV. ARTICLES

V. STATISTICAL REFERENCE MATERIALS

I. GENERAL BACKGROUND BOOKS

Adamic, Louis. *The Eagle and the Roots*. Doubleday, Garden City, N. Y., 1952.

A sympathetic account of developments and attitudes in Yugoslavia at the time of the break with the Cominform, based on the author's revisit to his native land and his conversations with Tito and other officials.

Armstrong, Hamilton Fish. *Tito and Goliath*. Macmillan, New York, 1951.

A discussion of factors involved in the Soviet-Yugoslav dispute in the context of Soviet policy toward Eastern Europe generally.

Byrnes, Robert F. (ed.). *Yugoslavia*. Mid-European Studies Center, Frederick A. Praeger, New York, 1957.

A collection of studies of selected aspects of Yugoslavia published as a part of the Free Europe Committee's series entitled "East-Central Europe under the Communists." The volume contains useful analyses and compendia of data, but generally reflects the political biases of the sponsor.

Cvijić, Jovan. *La Péninsule Balkanique*. Armand Colin, Paris, 1918.

A standard work on Balkan geography by a famous Yugoslav geographer.

Dedijer, Vladimir. *With Tito through the War*. Alexander Hamilton, London, 1951.

The English translation of the diary kept in the field during World War II in Yugoslavia by the author, the Partisans' leading journalist-soldier.

———. *Tito*. Simon & Schuster, New York, 1953.

The official biography of the Yugoslav Communist leader, presenting an intimate picture of the conflict with the Soviet Union from the Yugoslav point of view. The author has since fallen from favor as a result of his support of Milovan Djilas.

511

Djilas, Milovan. *Land without Justice.* Harcourt, Brace, New York, 1958.

A fascinating, non-political account of life in the author's native Montenegro in the period between the wars.

Dragnich, Alex N. *Tito's Promised Land—Yugoslavia.* Rutgers University Press, New Brunswick, N. J., 1954.

A critical survey of Communism in Yugoslavia, with emphasis on the period preceding the post-Cominform reforms.

Kerner, Robert J. (ed.). *Yugoslavia.* University of California Press, Berkeley, 1949.

A good reference work, covering many aspects of Yugoslav life and culture, by leading scholars.

Korbel, Josef. *Tito's Communism.* University of Denver Press, Denver, 1951.

The first years of Communism in Yugoslavia, as seen by the then ambassador of Czechoslovakia.

Maclean, Fitzroy. *The Heretic: The Life and Times of Josip Broz-Tito.* Harper, New York, 1957.

A generally sympathetic account of Tito, in many places based on first-hand knowledge and experience, by the head of the British mission to the Partisans during the war.

Markert, Werner (ed.). *Jugoslawien.* Osteuropa-Handbuch, Böhlau-Verlag, Köln-Graz, 1954.

A general compendium of economic, geographic and political information about postwar Yugoslavia.

McVicker, Charles P. *Titoism, Pattern for International Communism.* St. Martin's Press, New York, 1957.

An analysis of the Yugoslav system as it emerged after the dispute with the Soviet Union, by a former American diplomat.

Melik, Anton. *Jugoslavija.* Državna Založba Slovenije, Ljubljana, 1958.

A general geography of Yugoslavia with considerable detailed regional information.

Neal, Fred Warner. *Titoism in Action: The Reforms in Yugoslavia after 1948.* University of California Press, Berkeley, 1958.

A critical study of the institutions and policies of Titoism and the theories on which they are based.

Ostović, P. D. *The Truth about Yugoslavia.* Roy Publishers, New York, 1952.

In part a defense of the Tito regime for its handling of the nationalities problem. Especially interesting because the author is an eminent non-Communist Croatian *émigré* who played a leading role in the founding of Yugoslavia after World War I.

Spulber, Nicholas. *The Economics of Communist Eastern Europe.* Wiley and Technology Press, New York, 1957.

Contains detailed statistical material on the economic development of Yugoslavia and other Eastern European countries.

Tomasevich, Jozo. *Peasants, Politics and Economic Change in Yugoslavia.* Stanford University Press, Stanford, 1955.

A thorough, scholarly and well-documented economic history of the Yugoslavs, from before the Turkish conquest to World War II.

Trouton, Ruth. *Peasant Renaissance in Yugoslavia, 1900–1950*. Routledge & Kegan Paul, Ltd., London, 1952.
A study of Yugoslav peasant culture as it has developed in the twentieth century.

Ulam, Adam B. *Titoism and the Cominform*. Harvard University Press, Cambridge, 1952.
A study of the factors involved in the Soviet-Yugoslav dispute and the impact of Titoism elsewhere in Eastern Europe.

West, Rebecca. *Black Lamb and Grey Falcon*. The Viking Press, New York, 1940.
A well-told travelogue of Yugoslavia on the eve of World War II, with interesting historical essays. Presented generally from the point of view of the Serbs.

Wolff, Robert Lee. *The Balkans in Our Time*. Harvard University Press, Cambridge, 1956.
A thorough, scholarly history of the Balkans, with excellent chapters on Yugoslavia.

II. YUGOSLAV BOOKS AND PAMPHLETS

Agricultural Cooperatives in Yugoslavia. Information Service Yugoslavia, Jugoslavija, Belgrade, 1960.

Babić, I., and Filipović, M. *Scientific Institutions in Yugoslavia*. Jugoslavija, Belgrade, 1958.

Bićanić, Rudolf. *Agrarna Prenapučenost (Agricultural Overpopulation)*. Zavod Za Proučavanje Seljačkog i Narodnog Gospodarstva 'Gospodarska sloga,' Zagreb, 1941.

Brelith, Milos. *Yugoslav Water Resources as a Power Reserve*. Jugoslavija, Belgrade, 1958.

Capital Expenditures in Agriculture and Results in Yugoslavia. Information Service Yugoslavia, Jugoslavija, Belgrade, 1960.

The Church in the Federal People's Republic of Yugoslavia. Information Service Yugoslavia, Belgrade, 1959.

Čobeljić, Nikola. *Politika i Metodi, Privrednog Pazvoja Jugoslavije (1947–1956)* (*Policies and Methods, The Economic Development of Yugoslavia 1947–1956*). Ekonomska Biblioteka, 10, Belgrade, 1959.

Condensed Report of the Central Committee on the Work of the League of Communists of Yugoslavia Between the Sixth and Seventh Congress. Service d'information Yugoslavie, Belgrade, 1948.

Congress of Workers' Councils of Yugoslavia. Central Council of the Confederation of Trade Unions of Yugoslavia, Belgrade, 1957.

Čulinović, Ferdo. *Nacionalno Pitanje u Jugoslavenskim Zemljama*. (*The National Question in Yugoslav Lands*). Biblioteka Instituta, Zagreb, 1955.

Davičo, J., and Bogosavljević, M. *The Economy of Yugoslavia.* Jugoslavija, Belgrade, 1960.

Development of Agriculture in Yugoslavia. Information Service Yugoslavia, Jugoslavija, Belgrade, 1960.

Djaković, Bogdan. *Yugoslavia's Non-Ferrous Metals.* Jugoslavija, Belgrade, 1958.

Djordjević, Jovan. *Le Problème de L'Opinion Publique dans la Democratie Socialiste.* P. U. F., Paris, 1957.

————. *Novi Ustav Federativne Narodne Republike Jugoslavije (New Constitution of the Federal People's Republic of Yugoslavia).* Službenog Lista FNRJ, 1953.

————. *Ustavno Pravo Federatione Narodne Republike Jugoslavije (Constitutional Law of the Federal People's Republic of Yugoslavia).* Arhiva za Pravne i Društvene Nauke, Belgrade, 1953.

Federal Social Security Institute: Belgrade
1. Law on Health Insurance of Workers and Employees, 1955.
2. Decree on the Organization of Social Insurance Institutes, 1956.
3. Decree on Children's Allowances, 1956.
4. Social Insurance of Liberal Professions, 1956.
5. Law on Pension Insurance, 1958.

Investicije 1947–1958. Dokumentacioni Materijali No. 2, Jugoslovenska Investiciona Banka, Belgrade, 1959.

Jončić, Koča. *The National Minorities in Yugoslavia.* Information Service Yugoslavia, Jugoslavija, Belgrade, 1960.

Kardelj, Edvard. *Medjunarodna Scena i Jugoslovenski Položaj (The International Scene and the Yugoslav Position).* Belgrade, 1951.

————. *Les Problèmes de la Politique Socialiste dans les Campagnes.* La Nef de Paris Editions, Paris, 1960.

————. *Socialist Democracy in Yugoslav Practice.* Yugoslav Embassy, New Delhi, 1956.

————. *Socijalistička Demokratija (Socialist Democracy).* Belgrade, 1952.

————. *War and Socialism.* Jugoslavija, Belgrade, 1960.

Kidrić, Boris. *On the Construction of Socialist Economy in the FPRY.* Speech delivered at the Fifth Congress of the CPY, Office of Information Yugoslav Government, Belgrade, 1948.

Kolak, Rudi, Vujović, Vlado, and others. *Yugoslavia, Economic Guide.* Privredni Pregled, Belgrade, 1958.

Koliševski, Lazar. *Macedonian National Question.* Jugoslavija, Belgrade, 1959.

Kostić, Cvetko. *Seljači Industriski Radnici (Peasant Industrial Workers).* Rad, Belgrade, 1955.

Kubović, Branko, Širotković, Jakov, and Šefer, Berislav. *Economic Planning in Yugoslavia*. Jugoslavija, Belgrade, 1959.

Law on the Five Year Plan. Jugoslovenska Knjiga, Belgrade, 1947.

Macura, Miloš. *Stanovništvo i Radna Snaga kao Činioci Privrednog Razvoja Jugoslavije* (*Population and Labour-Force as Factors of Economic Development of Yugoslavia*). Ekonomska Biblioteka 7, Belgrade, 1958.

Milojević, Borivoje Ž. *Yugoslavia, Geographical Survey*. Committee for Cultural Relations with Foreign Countries, Belgrade, 1958.

Narodna Banka. *Annual Report 1958*. Belgrade, 1959.

New Fundamental Law of Yugoslavia. Union of Jurists' Association of Yugoslavia, Belgrade, 1953.

Opšti Zakon o Narodnim Odborima. Službenog Lista FNRJ, Belgrade, 1952.

Osolnik, Bogdan. *The Development of the School System in Yugoslavia*. Information Service Yugoslavia, Jugoslavija, Belgrade, 1960.

Pertot, Vladimir. *Yugoslav Foreign Trade*. Jugoslavija, Belgrade, 1958.

Privreda F.N.R.J. u Periodu Od 1947–1956 Godine (*The Economy of the Federal People's Republic of Yugoslavia in the Period 1947–1956*). Ekonomski Institut FNRJ, Belgrade, 1957.

Rašić, Petko. *Agricultural Development in Yugoslavia*. Jugoslavija, Belgrade, 1955.

Rubić, Ivo. *Naši Otoci na Jadranu* (*Our Islands in the Adriatic*). Slobodna Dalmacija, Split, 1952.

Savezna Narodna Skupština. *Društveni Plan Privrednog Razvoja Jugoslavije 1957–1961* (*The Social Plan of Economic Development of Yugoslavia 1957–1961*). Kultura, Belgrade, 1957.

———. *Industriski Razvitak Jugoslavije* (*Industrial Development of Yugoslavia*). Kultura, Belgrade, 1957.

———. *Izveštaj Saveznog Izvršnog Veča za 1954 Godinu* (*Report of the Federal Executive Council for 1954*). Kultura, Belgrade, 1955.

———. *Stanje Poljoprivrede i Zadrugarstva i Perspektive Njihovog Razvoja* (*The Condition of Agriculture and Cooperation and the Perspectives of Their Development*). Kultura, Belgrade, 1957.

VII Kongres Saveza Komunista Jugoslavije (*VII Congress of the League of Communists of Yugoslavia*). Kultura, Belgrade, 1958.

Sixth Congress of the Communist Party of Yugoslavia. Belgrade, 1953.

Stoiković, Ljubiša, and Martić, Miloš. *National Minorities in Yugoslavia*. Jugoslavija, Belgrade, 1952.

Tito, Josip Broz. *The Building of Socialism and the Role and Tasks of the Socialist Alliance of the Working People of Yugoslavia.* Report to the Fifth Congress of the Socialist Alliance of the Working People of Yugoslavia, Belgrade, April 18, 1960.

———. *Concluding Speech at the Second (Special) Plenum of the Central Committee of the League of Communists,* November 18–19, 1959. Jugoslavija, Belgrade, 1959.

———. *Third Congress of the People's Front of Yugoslavia: Political Report Delivered by Marshal Tito.* Jugoslavenska Knjiga, Belgrade, 1949.

———. *Workers Manage Factories in Yugoslavia.* Jugoštampa, Belgrade, 1950.

Todorović, Mijalko. *Current Problems of Economic Policy: Report to Second Plenary Meeting of the Central Committee of the League of Communists,* November 18–19, 1959. Jugoslavija, Belgrade, 1959.

The Trial of Dragoljub-Draža Mihailović. Belgrade, 1946.

Ugrinova, Radmila, Koneski, Blaže, and others. *The Macedonian Literary Language.* Jugoslavija, Belgrade, 1959.

Vinski, Ivo. *Procjena Nacionalnog Bogatstva po Područjima Jugoslavije (Regional Wealth Estimates for National Regions of Yugoslavia).* Ekonomski Institut, NRH, Zagreb, 1959.

Vogelnik, Dolfe. *Urbanizacija kao Odraz Privrednog Razvoja FNRJ (Urbanization in Yugoslavia as Expression of Its Economic Development).* Ekonomska Biblioteka, 13, Belgrade, 1961.

Vučković, Milorad, and Očokoljić, Negoslav. *Osnovni Zakon o Prekršajima (Basic Law on Petty Offenses),* fourth edition. Arhiva za Pravne i Društvene Nauke, Belgrade, 1956.

Vujošević, Todor. *Social Insurance in Yugoslavia,* Jugoslavija, Belgrade, 1957.

White Book on Aggressive Activities by the Governments of the USSR, Poland, Czechoslovakia, Hungary, Rumania, Bulgaria and Albania toward Yugoslavia. Ministry of Foreign Affairs of the Federal People's Republic of Yugoslavia, Belgrade, 1951.

Yugoslav National Committee of the World Power Conference. *Energetski Izvori Jugoslavije (Power Resources of Yugoslavia).* Vol. 1, Belgrade, 1956. (In Serbo-Croatian and English.)

III. OTHER BOOKS AND PAMPHLETS

Andriotes, Nic. P. *The Confederate State of Skopje and Its Language.* Athens, 1957.

Avsenek, Ivan. *The Iron and Steel Industry in Yugoslavia, 1939–1953.* Mid-European Studies Center, Mimeographed Series No. 25. New York, April 1956.

Bass, Robert, and Marbury, Elizabeth (eds.). *The Soviet-Yugoslav Controversy, 1948-1958: A Documentary Record.* Prospect Books, New York, 1959.

Black, C. E. (ed.). *Readings on Contemporary Eastern Europe.* Mid-European Studies Center of the National Committee for a Free Europe, New York, 1953.

Blanc, André. *La Croatie Occidentale.* Etude de Géographie Humaine, Paris, 1957.

Bobrowski, Czeslaw. *La Yougoslavie Socialiste.* A. Colin, Paris, 1956.

Brailsford, Henry N. *Macedonia: Its Races and Their Future.* Methuen & Co., London, 1906.

Brashich, Ranko M. *Land Reform and Ownership in Yugoslavia, 1919-1953.* Mid-European Studies Center, Free Europe Committee, New York, 1954.

Brzezinski, Zbigniew K. *The Soviet Bloc.* Harvard University Press, Cambridge, 1960.

Churchill, Winston. *The Second World War,* Vol. VI, *Triumph and Tragedy.* Houghton Mifflin, Boston, 1953.

Clissold, Stephen. *Whirlwind.* Cresset Press, London, 1949.

Conrad, G. J. *Die Wirtschaft Jugoslawiens (The Economy of Yugoslavia).* Deutsches Institut für Wirtschaftsforschung, Sonderheft, Neue Folge No. 17, Reihe A: Forschung, Duncker & Humbolt, Berlin, 1953.

Crossman, Richard (ed.). *The God That Failed.* Harper, New York, 1949.

Cvijić, Jovan. *Rèmarques sur l'Ethographie de la Macédoine.* Rouston, Paris, 1907.

Djilas, Milovan. *Is Stalin Turning in a Circle?* National Committee for a Free Europe, New York, 1952.

———. *The New Class,* Frederick A. Praeger, New York, 1957.

European Refugee Problems 1959. A Special Report by the Zellerbach Commission on the European Refugee Situation, New York, March 1959.

Fejto, F. *Behind the Rape of Hungary.* David McKay Co., New York, 1957.

Hallowell, John H. (ed.). *Soviet Satellite Nations.* Kallman Publishing Co., Gainesville, Florida, 1958.

Halperin, Ernst. *The Triumphant Heretic.* Heinemann, London, 1958.

Halpern, Joel Martin. *Social and Cultural Change in a Serbian Village.* Columbia University Press, New York, 1958.

Heppell, Muriel, and Singleton, Frank B. *Yugoslavia.* Frederick A. Praeger, 1961.

International Cooperation Administration:
Counterpart Funds and ICA Foreign Currency Accounts, 1955-1960.
Operations Reports, 1954-1960.
Projects, By Country and Field of Activity, 1954 to 1960.

Jedrychowski, Stefan. *The Fundamental Principles of Economic Policy in Industry*. Polonia, Warsaw, 1957.

Kommunisticheskii International v Dokumentakh (*Communist International in Documents*). Gosizdat, Moscow, 1953.

Lange, Oscar. *Some Problems Relating to the Polish Road to Socialism*. Polonia, Warsaw, 1957.

Maclean, Fitzroy. *Escape to Adventure*. Little, Brown, Boston, 1950.

Meier, Paul J. *Der Sozialistische Wohlfahrtsnationalstaat als Spaetform der Industriellen Produktions-gesellschaft* (*The Socialistic Welfare National State as a Late Development of the Industrial Production Society*). Keller Verlag, Aarau, 1956.

Meier, Viktor. *Das Neue Jugoslawische Wirtschaftsystem* (*The New Yugoslav Economic System*). Verlag P. G. Keller, Winterthur, 1956.

Mellon, Melrad, and Winston, Victor H. *The Coal Resources of Yugoslavia*. Mid-European Studies Center, New York, 1956.

Myers, Paul F., and Campbell, Arthur A. *The Population of Yugoslavia*. International Population Statistics Reports, Series P-90, No. 5, Bureau of the Census, U. S. Government Printing Office, Washington, 1954.

Nagy, Imre. *Imre Nagy on Communism: In Defense of the New Course*. Frederick A. Praeger, New York, 1957.

Pridonoff, Eric. *Tito's Yugoslavia*. Public Affairs Press, Washington, 1955.

Proudfoot, Malcolm J. *European Refugees: 1939–1952, A Study in Forced Population Movement*. Faber & Faber Ltd., London, 1957.

Report of the Special Study Mission to Germany and Certain Other Countries: Supplemental Report on Austria, Yugoslavia, Italy and Spain. U. S. Government Printing Office, Washington, April 7, 1952.

Royal Institute of International Affairs. *Central and South East Europe, 1945–1948*. Oxford University Press, London, 1950.

———. *The Soviet-Yugoslav Dispute*. Oxford University Press, London, 1948.

Rozmaryn, Stefan. *The Seym and People's Councils in Poland*. Polonia, Warsaw, 1958.

Sanders, Irwin T. (ed.). *Collectivization of Agriculture in Eastern Europe*. University of Kentucky Press, Lexington, 1958.

Seton-Watson, Hugh. *Eastern Europe Between the Wars, 1918–1941*. Cambridge University Press, Cambridge, 1946.

———. *The Eastern European Revolution*. Methuen & Co., London, 1950.

Stalin, J. V. *Voprosy Leninizma* (*Problems of Leninism*). Gosizdat, Moscow, 1934.

Syrop, Konrad. *Spring in October*. Frederick A. Praeger, New York, 1957.

Tomasic, Dinko. *National Communism and Soviet Strategy.* Public Affairs Press, Washington, 1957.

————. *Personality and Culture in Eastern European Politics.* George W. Stewart, New York, 1948.

United Nations:
Economic Survey of Europe in 1953: "Yugoslavia." Chapter 8, pp. 106–122. Geneva, 1954.

Economic Survey of Europe in 1955: "Notes on Investments and Investment Policies in Yugoslavia." Appendix A. pp. A1–A6. Geneva, 1956.

Economic Survey of Europe in 1959: "Notes on Developments During 1959 in Yugoslavia." Chapter I, pp. 21–22. "Recent Experience in Raising Output in Yugoslavia." Appendix A. pp. 46–50. Geneva, 1960.

Economic Commission for Europe. "Economic Planning and Management in Yugoslavia." *Economic Bulletin for Europe* (Geneva). Vol. 10, No. 3, 1958, pp. 43–62.

————. "Policies and Prospects in Western Europe: Note on Yugoslavia." *Economic Bulletin for Europe* (Geneva). Vol. 12, No. 3, 1960, p. 25.

————. *Possibilities of Electric Power Exchanges between the Countries of Central and South Eastern Europe.* E/ECE/304. Geneva, 1958.

————. *Prospects of Exporting Electric Power from Yugoslavia.* 2 vols. Geneva, April 1955.

Economic and Social Council. *Report of the Expert Group on the Economic Development of Southern Europe.* E/ECE/233, Add. 1., March 12, 1956.

Food and Agriculture Organization. *Mediterranean Development Project: The Integrated Development of Mediterranean Agriculture and Forestry in Relation to Economic Growth.* Rome, 1959, pp. 181–191.

————. *Yougoslavie, rapport national. Project FAO de Développement Méditerranean.* Rome, 1959.

Wanklyn, H. G. *The Eastern Marchlands of Europe.* George Philip & Son, London, 1941.

Warriner, Doreen. *Revolution in Eastern Europe.* Turnstile Press, London, 1950.

Wilkinson, H. R. *Maps and Politics: A Review of the Ethnographic Cartography of Macedonia.* University of Liverpool Press, Liverpool, 1951.

Woodbridge, George. *UNRRA, The History of the United Nations Relief and Rehabilitation Administration.* 3 vols., Columbia University Press, New York, 1950.

Yugoslavia's Way: The Program of the League of Communists of Yugoslavia. Translated by Stoyan Pribichevich, All Nations Press, New York, 1958.

Zinner, Paul (ed.). *National Communism and Popular Revolt in Eastern Europe.* Columbia University Press, New York, 1956.

IV. ARTICLES

Adamovitch, Alexander. "Yugoslavia: Industrial Management." *Highlights of Current Activities in Mid-Europe*, Library of Congress Mid-European Law Project, Vol. V, Nos. 3–4, March–April 1957, pp. 165–178.

Arnejc, J. "After the Brioni Talks." *Review of International Affairs*, November 16, 1955, pp. 9–10.

Babić, Milan. "Problemi Statističkog Ispitivanja Narodnosne Pripadnosti Stanovništva" ("Problems of Statistical Assessment of Nationality Groups"). *Statistička Revija*, Vol. IV, Nos. 3–4, December 1954, pp. 385–388.

Bače, Maks. "O Kritike i Samo-Kritike u USSR" ("On Criticism and Self-Criticism in the USSR"). *Komunist*, No. 6, November 1949, pp. 61–143.

Bebler, Aleš. "Jugoslavija i Evropa" ("Yugoslavia and Europe"). *Medjunarodna Politika*, September 16, 1956, pp. 5–6.

Bićanić, Rudolf. "Distribucija Osobnih Dohodaka Seljačkih Obitelji u FNRJ 1955, g." ("Personal Income Distribution of Peasant Families in the FPRY, 1955"). *Statistička Revija*, Vol. VII, No. 3, October 1957, pp. 249–269.

―――. "Economic Growth under Centralized and Decentralized Planning in Yugoslavia — A Case Study." *Economic Development and Cultural Change*, Vol. VI, No. 1, October 1957, pp. 63–74.

―――. "The Effects of War on Rural Yugoslavia." *Geographical Journal*, Vol. CIII, Nos. 1–2, January–February 1944, pp. 30–49.

―――. "Neopoljoprivredna Zanimanja u Seljačkom Gospodarstvu" ("Non-agricultural Occupations in Peasant Family Households"). *Statistička Revija*, Vol. VI, No. 2, August 1956, pp. 97–119.

―――. "Occupational Heterogeneity of Peasant Families in the Period of Accelerated Industrialisation." *Third World Congress of Sociology*, Vol. IV, 1956, 2d book, pp. 80–96.

Blanc, André. "L'Habitat Rural en Croatie Occidentale." ("Rural Habitat in Western Croatia"). *Annales Géographie*, Vol. LXII, 1953, pp. 107–117.

Bobrowski, Czeslaw. "In Search of a New Economic Blueprint." *Polish Perspectives*, May 1958, p. 7.

Božičević, Ivan. "Necessity or Superfluity of Strikes as a Method and Means of Trade Union Activities under Our Conditions." *Sozijalizam*, No. 1, 1959, Supplement to *Joint Translation Service Bulletin*, No. 2702, March 6, 1959.

Bukurov, Branislav. "Poreklo Stanovništva Vojvodina" ("Origin of the Population of the Vojvodina"). *Matica Srpska* (Posebna Izdanja), Novi Sad, 1957.

Cornish, Vaughan. "Bosnia, the Borderland of Serb and Croat." *Geography*, Vol. XX, No. 4, December 1935, pp. 260–270.

Crkvenčić, I. "Hrvatsko Zagorje kao Emigraciono Žarište" ("The Croatian Zagorje as a Center for Emigration"). *Geografski Glasnik*, Vol. XVIII, 1956, pp. 33–45.

D. C. "Foreign Trade in the Postwar Period." *Yugoslav Survey*, Vol. I, No. 2, September 1960, pp. 227–236.

Darling, Malcolm. "Collective Farming in Yugoslavia." *Manchester Guardian Weekly*, April 24, 1952, p. 7.

Davidović, Radivoje. "Die Industrialisierung Jugoslawiens" ("The Industrialization of Yugoslavia"). *Südosteuropa-Jahrbuch* (Munich), Vol. I, 1956, pp. 167–177.

Dedijer, Stevan. "Research and Freedom in Underdeveloped Countries." *Bulletin of the Atomic Scientists*, Vol. XIII, No. 7, September 1957, pp. 238–242.

Djilas, Milovan. "Lenjin o Odnosima Medju Socialističkim Državama" ("Lenin on Relations between Socialist States"). *Komunist*, No. 3, September 1949, pp. 1–53.

Djordjević, Jovan. "From Local Self-Government to Communes." *Review of International Affairs*, November 1, 1954, p. 13.

———. "Local Self-Government in Yugoslavia." *American Slavic and East European Review*, Vol. XII, April 1953, pp. 188–200.

———. "The New Code of Criminal Procedure." *Yugoslav Review*, Vol. III, Nos. 1–2, January–February 1954, pp. 10–12.

———. "Regulations Governing Real Estate in Yugoslavia." *Review of International Affairs*, February 16, 1956, p. 4.

———. "Some Principles of Socialist Democracy in Yugoslavia," *New Yugoslav Law*, Nos. 3–4, July–December 1952, pp. 18–22.

———. "Status and Role of the Executive Organs during the First Stage of Yugoslavia's Political and Constitutional Development." *International Social Science Bulletin*, Vol. X, No. 2, 1958, pp. 259–269.

Dragičević, Nikola. "Perspektiva Razvoja Potencijalnih Izvora FNRJ" ("Prospective Development of Yugoslav Resources"). *Ekonomski Pregled* (Zagreb), April 1957, pp. 203–225.

Erven, L. "The Warsaw Treaty." *Review of International Affairs*, June 1, 1955, pp. 1–10.

"The Forms of Co-operation in the Village." *Bulletin of Information and Documentation* (Glavni Zadružni Savez FNRJ), Vol. VI, No. 2, 1957, pp. 8–11.

Govorchin, Gerald G. "Reconstruction in New Yugoslavia." *Social Science*, Vol. 23, April 1948, pp. 112–116.

Hoffman, George W. "Changes in the Agricultural Geography of Yugoslavia," in Norman J. G. Pounds (ed.), *Geographical Essays on Eastern Europe*. Russian and East European Series, Vol. 24, Indiana University Publications, Bloomington, 1961, pp. 101–140.

————. "Eastern Europe," in George W. Hoffman (ed.), *A Geography of Europe*, 2d edition. The Ronald Press, New York, 1961, pp. 539–637.

————. "The Geography of U. S. Foreign Aid: Yugoslavia, A Case Study." *Annals, Association of American Geographers*, Vol. 50, No. 3, September 1960, p. 326.

————. "The Vojvodina (Yugoslavia), A Study in Agricultural Evolution." *Bulletin of the Geological Society of America*, Vol. 71, No. 12, Part 2, December 1960, pp. 2098–2099.

————. "Yugoslavia: Changing Character of Rural Life and Rural Economy." *American Slavic and East European Review*, Vol. XVIII, No. 4, December 1959, pp. 555–578.

————. "Yugoslavia in Transition: Industrial Expansion and Resource Bases." *Economic Geography*, Vol. XXXII, No. 4, October 1956, pp. 294–315.

Horvat, Bronko, and Rascović, Vlado. "Worker Management in Yugoslavia, A Comment." *Journal of Political Economy*, Vol. LXVII, April 1959, pp. 194–198.

Humo, Avdo. "Basic Characteristics of Yugoslavia's Plan of Economic Development for 1961–1965." *Review of International Affairs*, Vol. XII, No. 260, February 5, 1961, pp. 1–5.

"The Investment Policy in Agriculture." *Vesnik*, Jugoslovenske Investicione Banke, February 1958, English edition.

Johnson, W. B. and Crkvenčić, I. "Changing Peasant Agriculture in North-Western Hrvatsko Primorje Yugoslavia." *Geographical Review*, Vol. XLIV, No. 3, July 1954, pp. 352–372.

————. "Examples of Changing Peasant Agriculture in Croatia, Yugoslavia." *Economic Geography*, Vol. XXXIII, No. 1, January 1957, pp. 51–71.

"Joint Declaration: Tito-Nehru." *Review of International Affairs*, January 1, 1955, p. 7.

Kardelj, Edvard. "Svaki Napredak u Poljoprivredi Značice Spontano Jačanje Socialističkih Snaga na Selu" ("Every Advance in Agriculture Means Strengthening of Socialist Power in the Village"). *Komunist*, Nos. 5–6, June 1953, pp. 330–340.

Kayser, Kurt. "Jugoslavien, ein Beitrag zur Laenderkundlichen Analyse Eines Staatsgebietes" ("Yugoslavia, A Contribution to the Regional Geographic Analysis of a Territory"), in Kurt Kayser (ed.), *Landschaft und Land der Forschungsgegenstand der Geographie*, Festzeitschrift Erich Obst, Verlag des Amtes für Landeskunde, Remagen, 1951, pp. 73–88.

Kidrić, Boris. "From State Socialism to Economic Democracy." *Yugoslav Review*, Vol. I, No. 2, February 1952, pp. 5–6.

Koeller, Harold L. "Yugoslavia Experiences an Agricultural Explosion." *Foreign Agriculture*, Vol. XXIV, June 1960, pp. 15–16.

Kofman, J. "Worker Self-Government." *Polish Perspectives*, July–August 1958, p. 16.

Komar, Slavko. "Agricultural Production Today and Prospects for Its Further Increase." *Review of International Affairs*, June 1, 1959, pp. 16–18.

Krebs, Norbert. "Die Geographische Struktur der Südslawischen Länder" ("The Geographic Structure of the South Slavic Countries"). *Geographische Zeitschrift*, No. 47, 1941, pp. 241–256.

Lichtenberger, Elisabeth, and Bobek, Hans. "Zur Kulturgeographischen Gliederung Jugoslawiens" ("Contribution to the Cultural-Geographic Structure of Yugoslavia"). *Geographischer Jahresbericht aus Osterreich*, Vol. XXVI, 1955–56, pp. 78–154.

Lodge, Olive. "Villages and Houses in Yugoslavia." *Geography*, Vol. XXI, No. 2, June 1936, pp. 94–106.

Lopandić, Dušan. "Die Agrarpolitik Jugoslawiens" ("Yugoslav Agrarian Politics"). *Südosteuropa-Jahrbuch* (Munich), Vol. I, 1956, pp. 179–196.

———. "System of Co-operation in Yugoslav Agriculture." *Review of International Affairs*, February 16, 1960, pp. 17–20.

Lowenthal, Richard. "Tito's Gamble." *Encounter*, October 1958, pp. 56–65.

Lukić, Radomir D. "Načelo Jedinstva Vlasti u Saveznom Ustavnom Zakonu" ("The Principle of Unity of Powers in the Federal Constitutional Law"). *Arhiv za Pravne i Društvene Nauke*, Nos. 1–2, 1953, pp. 40–51.

M. F. "Reform of Higher Education." *Yugoslav Survey*, Vol. 1, No. 2, September 1960, pp. 251–255.

Macura, Miloš. "Osvrt na Demografski i Sociološki Faktor u Poljoprivredi Jugoslavije" ("A Glance at Demographic and Sociological Factors in Yugoslav Agriculture"). *Ekonomist*, Vol. VIII, No. 2, 1955, pp. 309–348.

———. "Projekcija Ekonomskog Sastva Radne Snage i Stanovništva Jugoslavije 1953–1959" ("Economic Structure Projection of Yugoslav Labor Force and Population 1953–1959"). *Ekonomist*, Vol. VIII, No. 1, 1955, pp. 16–44.

Mandich, Oleg. "Yugoslavia," in Arnold M. Rose (ed.), *The Institutions of Advanced Societies*. University of Minnesota Press, Minneapolis, 1958, pp. 275–389.

Matter, Otto. "On Yugoslavia's Industrialization." *Swiss Review of World Affairs*, Vol. I, February 1952, pp. 11–13.

Milhaud, Edgard (ed.). "Collective Economy of Yugoslavia." *Annals of Collective Economy*, Vol. XXX, Nos. 2–3, April–November 1959, p. 363.

Milojević, Borivoje Ž. "The Geographical Regions of Yugoslavia." *Proceedings, XVIIth Congress International Geographic Union*, Washington, D. C., 1952, pp. 591–595.

————. "Die Geographischen Gebiete Serbiens" ("The Geographic Regions of Serbia"). *Mitteilungen der Geographischen Gesellschaft Wien*, Vol. 99, No. 1, 1957, pp. 45–51.

————. "Les Vallées Principales de la Yougoslavie" ("Principal Valleys of Yugoslavia"). *Mémoires de la Société Serbe de Géographie*, Vol. IX (Belgrade), 1958.

"Minorities in Eastern Europe." *East Europe*, Vol. VIII, No. 4, April 1959, pp. 3–6 and 11.

Mladek, J. V., Sturc, E., and Wyczalkowski, M. R. "The Change in the Yugoslav Economic System." *Staff Papers*, International Monetary Fund, Vol. II, No. 3, November 1952, pp. 407–438.

Montias, John Michael. "Economic Reform and Retreat in Yugoslavia." *Foreign Affairs*, January 1959, pp. 293–305.

Mosely, Philip E. "Adaptation for Survival: The Varžić Zadruga." *Slavonic and East European Review* (New York), Vol. XXI, 1943, pp. 147–173.

————. "The Peasant Family: the Zadruga, or Communal Joint-Family in the Balkans and Its Recent Evolution," in Caroline F. Ware (ed.), *The Cultural Approach to History*. Columbia University Press, New York, 1940, pp. 95–108.

Neal, Fred Warner. "Certain Aspects of the New Reforms in Yugoslavia." *University of Colorado Studies*, Series in Political Science, No. 1, June 1953, pp. 51–64.

————. "The Communist Party of Yugoslavia." *American Political Science Review*, Vol. LI, No. 1, March 1957, pp. 88–111.

————. "The Reforms in Yugoslavia." *American Slavic and East European Review*, Vol. XIII, April 1954, pp. 227–244.

————. "Tito's Communism: Independent and Moderate." *Foreign Policy Bulletin*, Vol. XXXIX, No. 6, December 1, 1959, pp. 45–47.

————. "Yugoslav Communist Theory." *American Slavic and East European Review*, Vol. XIX, February 1960, pp. 42–62.

Neuberger, Egon. "The Yugoslav Investment Auctions." *Quarterly Journal of Economics*, Vol. LXXIII, No. 1, February 1959, pp. 88–115.

"Notes on a Belgrade Trial." *Highlights of Current Legislation and Activities in Mid-Europe*, Library of Congress Mid-European Law Project, Vol. VII, No. 4, April 1959, pp. 175–182.

"People Leaving Agriculture — How and Why?" *Ekonomska Politika*, No. 362, March 7, 1959 (*Joint Translation Service*, No. 2738, April 17, 1959, pp. 5–10).

Petrovich, Michael Boro. "The Central Government of Yugoslavia." *Political. Science Quarterly*, Vol. LXII, No. 4, December 1947, pp. 504–530.

Pijade, Moše. "The Law on Criminal Procedure and the Work of the Organs of the Judiciary." *New Yugoslav Law*, Nos. 3–4, July–December 1953, pp. 3–18.

Pusić, Eugen. "Citizens' Management of the Social Services in Yugoslavia." *Saertryk of Nordisk Administrativt Tidsskrift* (Reykjavik), Spring 1957, pp. 132–145.

———. "The Family in the Process of Social Change in Yugoslavia." *Sociological Review*, Vol. V, No. 2, New Series, December 1957, pp. 207–224.

Ranković, Aleksandar. "Za Dalje Jačanje Pravosudja i Zakonitosti" ("For Further Strengthening of the Judiciary and Legality"). *Komunist*, No. 2, March–May 1951, pp. 6–42.

Richter, E. "Beiträge zur Landeskunde Bosniens und der Herzegowina" ("Contributions to the Geography of Bosnia and Herzegovina"). *Wissenschaftliche Mitteilungen aus Bosnien und der Herzegowina*, Vol. X, 1907, pp. 383–545.

Rogic, Veljko. "Beograd, Polažaj, Funkcije i Razvoj" ("Belgrade, Situation, Function and Development"). *Geografski Horizont*, Vol. IV, No. 3, 1959, pp. 1–20.

Roglić, Josip. "O Geografskom Položaju i Ekonomskom Razvoju Jugoslavije" ("About the Geographical Position and Economic Development of Yugoslavia"). *Geografski Glasnik*, Vol. XI–XII, 1950, pp. 11–26.

———. "Prilog Regionalnoj Podjeli Jugoslavije" ("Contribution to the Understanding of the Regional Division of Yugoslavia"). *Geografski Glasnik*, Vol. XVI–XVII, 1954–1955, pp. 9–22.

———. "The Geographical Setting of Medieval Dubrovnik" in Norman J. G. Pounds (ed.), *Geographical Essays on Eastern Europe*. Russian and East European Series, Vol. 24, Indiana University Publications, Bloomington, 1961, pp. 141–159.

Saičič, Vladimir. "Yugoslav-Soviet Economic Relations." *Review of International Affairs*, October 1, 1955, pp. 10–12.

Schwartz, Benjamin. "China and the Communist Bloc: A Speculative Reconstruction." *Current History*, December 1958, pp. 321–326.

Smilevski, Vidoje. "Federation and the Less Developed Areas." *Review of International Affairs*, January 16, 1958, pp. 28–31.

"Social Security in Yugoslavia." *Bulletin of the International Social Security Association*, Vol. IX, Nos. 5–6, May–June 1956, pp. 179–237.

"Soviet Yugoslav Economic Relations 1945–1955." *The World Today*, Vol. XII, January 1956, pp. 38–46.

Stipetić, Vladimir. "Agrarna Reforma I Kolonizacija u FRNJ Godine 1945–1948" ("Agrarian Reform and Colonization in Yugoslavia between 1945–1948"). *Jugoslovenska Akademija Znanosti I Umjetnosti* (Zagreb), 1954, pp. 431–472.

———. "Poljoprivredna Proižodna na Današnjem Području FNR Jugoslavije 1929–1955" ("Agricultural Output on the Present Territory of the Federal People's Republic of Yugoslavia 1929–1955"). *Ekonomski Problemi* (Zbornik Radova, Belgrade), 1957, pp. 89–138.

Stojiljković, Dragon. "A Foredoomed Venture." *Review of International Affairs*, October 15, 1958, pp. 5–7.

Stroehm, Carl G. "Der Ostblock und das Jugoslawische Nationalitätenproblem" ("The East Bloc and the Yugoslav Nationality Problem"). *Osteuropa*, Vol. VIII, Nos. 10–11, 1958, pp. 714–720.

Sweezy, Paul. "The Yugoslav Experiment." *Monthly Review*, Vol. IX, No. 11, March 1958, pp. 362–374.

Valnišanin, M. "West European Integration and Yugoslav Exports." *Review of International Affairs*, Vol. 10, No. 211, January 18, 1959, pp. 7–9.

Vasić, Filip. "The Yugoslav System of Investment Financing and the Application of Criteria in the Selection of Investment Projects." *Engineering Economist*, Vol. 6, No. 1, Fall 1960, pp. 1–8.

Vinski, Ivo. "National Product and Fixed Assets in the Territory of Yugoslavia, 1909–1958." *Sixth Conference, International Association for Research in Income and Wealth*, August 1959.

Vogelnik, Dolfe. "Demografski Gubici Jugoslavije u Drugom Svetskom Ratu" ("Demographic Losses of Yugoslavia in Second World War"). *Statistički Revija*, Vol. I, No. 2, May 1952, pp. 15–36.

Vučković, M. "Recent Trends in Yugoslav Co-operative Movement." *International Labor Review*, Vol. LXXVI, No. 5, November 1957, pp. 467–478.

———. "Uredjenje Saveznog Isvršnog Veća" ("Organization of the Federal Executive Council"). *Nova Administracija*, No. 4, July–August 1954, pp. 1–18.

Ward, Benjamin. "Workers' Management in Yugoslavia." *Journal of Political Economy*, Vol. LXV, October 1957, pp. 373–386.

Warriner, Doreen. "Changes in European Peasant Farming." *International Labor Review*, Vol. LXXVI, No. 5, November 1957, pp. 446–466.

———. "Urban Thinkers and Peasant Policy in Yugoslavia, 1918–1959." *Slavonic and East European Review*, Vol. XXXVIII, 1959, pp. 59–81.

Wilkinson, H. R. "Jugoslav Kosmet: The Evolution of a Frontier Province and Its Landscape." *Transactions and Papers, The Institute of British Geographers*, No. 21, 1955, pp. 171–193.

———. "Jugoslav Macedonia in Transition." *Geographical Journal*, Vol. CXVIII, No. 4, December 1952, pp. 389–405.

Žuljić, Stanko. "O Dnevnim Kretanjima Radne Snage u Zagrebu" ("About the Daily Movement of the Labor Force in Zagreb"). *Geografski Glasnik*, Vol. XIX, 1957, pp. 135–147.

V. STATISTICAL REFERENCE MATERIALS (SELECTED)

Savezni Zavod Za Statistiku (Federal Statistical Institute):
  Statistički Bilten, irregular with English, French or German translation
  Statistički Godišnjak FNRJ, annually with English translation
  Statistička Spoljne Trgovine FNR Jugoslavije, annually
  Indeks, monthly with English translation
  Statistical Pocketbook of Yugoslavia, annually

Narodna Banka FNRJ (National Bank of Yugoslavia):
  Statistički Bilten, monthly
  Annual Report

Jugoslovenska Investiciona Banka (Yugoslav Investment Bank):
  Annual Report
  Vesnik, monthly
  Vesnik, Quarterly Supplements, in English

Yugoslav Federal Chamber of Foreign Trade
  Almanac, annual

LIST OF TABLES

L I S T   O F   M A P S   A N D   G R A P H S

INDEX

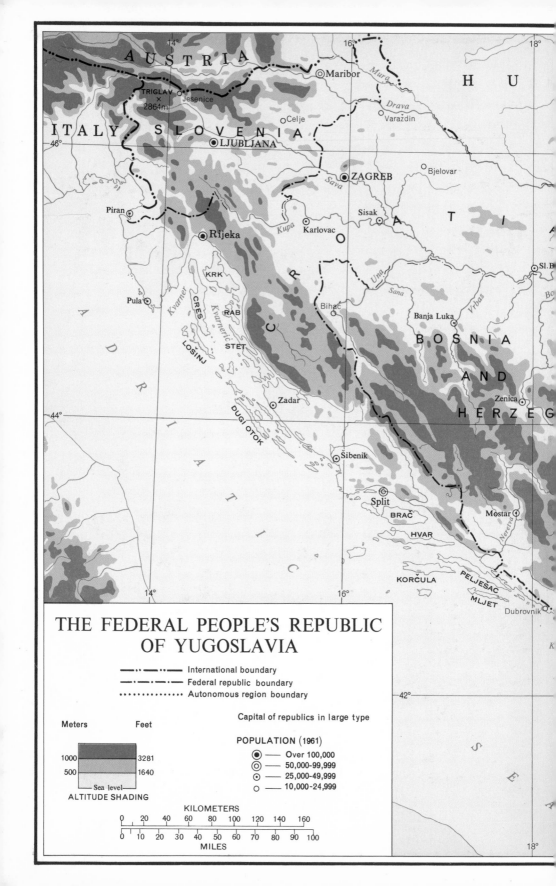

AUSTRIA

H U

14°

16°

18°

Maribor

Mura

Drava

TRIGLAV
×
2864m

Jesenice

Celje

Varaždin

ITALY

S L O V E N I A

46°

LJUBLJANA

ZAGREB

Bjelovar

Sava

Piran

Rijeka

Sisak

Kupa

Karlovac

C R O A T I A

Sl. B

KRK

Una

Sana

Bihać

Vrbas

Bo

Pula

CRES

RAB

Banja Luka

Kvarnerić

LOŠINJ

STET

B O S N I A

Kvarner

44°

Zadar

DUGI OTOK

A N D

Zenica

H E R Z E G

A D R I A T I C

Šibenik

Split

BRAČ

Mostar

Neretva

HVAR

S E A

KORČULA

PELJEŠAC

42°

MLJET

Dubrovnik

K

THE FEDERAL PEOPLE'S REPUBLIC
OF YUGOSLAVIA

—··—···— International boundary
—·—·—·— Federal republic boundary
·············· Autonomous region boundary

Capital of republics in large type

Meters   Feet

1000   3281

500   1640

Sea level
ALTITUDE SHADING

POPULATION (1961)

⊚ — Over 100,000
◉ — 50,000-99,999
⊙ — 25,000-49,999
○ — 10,000-24,999

KILOMETERS
0 20 40 60 80 100 120 140 160

0 10 20 30 40 50 60 70 80 90 100
MILES

14°

16°

18°